STRUCTURED
COMPUTER ORGANIZATION

STRUCTURED
COMPUTER ORGANIZATION

FIFTH EDITION

ANDREW S. TANENBAUM

Vrije Universiteit

Amsterdam, The Netherlands

PHI Learning Private Limited

New Delhi-110001

2012

This Indian Reprint—Rs. 425.00
(Original U.S. Edition—Rs. 5119.00)

STRUCTURED COMPUTER ORGANIZATION, 5th ed., (with CD-ROM)
by Andrew S. Tanenbaum

Original edition, entitled *Structured Computer Organization*, *5th ed.*, (with CD-ROM), by Andrew S. Tanenbaum, published by Pearson Education, Inc., publishing as Pearson Prentice Hall.

ISBN-978-81-203-2913-3

Published by Asoke K. Ghosh, PHI Learning Private Limited, M-97, Connaught Circus, New Delhi-110001 and Printed by Mudrak, 30-A, Patparganj, Delhi-110091.

To Suzanne, Barbara, Marvin, and the memory of Sweetie π and Bram

CONTENTS

PREFACE   xviii

1 INTRODUCTION   1

2   COMPUTER SYSTEMS ORGANIZATION   51

3 THE DIGITAL LOGIC LEVEL   135

4   THE MICROARCHITECTURE LEVEL   231

5 THE INSTRUCTION SET ARCHITECTURE LEVEL 331

6 THE OPERATING SYSTEM MACHINE LEVEL 427

7   THE ASSEMBLY LANGUAGE LEVEL   507

8 PARALLEL COMPUTER ARCHITECTURES   547

9 READING LIST AND BIBLIOGRAPHY   655

A BINARY NUMBERS   679

B FLOATING-POINT NUMBERS   691

C ASSEMBLY LANGUAGE PROGRAMMING   701

PREFACE

The first four editions of this book were based on the idea that a computer can be regarded as a hierarchy of levels, each one performing some well-defined function. This fundamental concept is as valid today as it was when the first edition came out, so it has been retained as the basis for the fifth edition. As in the first four editions, the digital logic level, the microarchitecture level, the instruction set architecture level, the operating system machine level, and the assembly language level are all discussed in detail.

Although the basic structure has been maintained, this fifth edition does contain many changes, both small and large, that bring it up to date in the rapidly changing computer industry. For example, the example machines used have been brought up to date. The current examples are the Intel Pentium 4, the Sun Ultra-SPARC III, and the Intel 8051. The Pentium 4 is an example of a popular CPU used on desktop machines. The UltraSPARC III is an example of a popular server, widely used in medium and large mutiprocessors.

However, the 8051 may come as a surprise to some people. It is a venerable chip that has been around for decades. However, with the enormous growth of embedded systems, it has finally come into its own. With computers running everything from clock radios to microwave ovens, interest in embedded systems is surging, and the 8051 is a widely-used choice due to its extremely low cost (pennies), the wealth of software and peripherals for it, and the large number of 8051 programmers available.

Over the years, many professors teaching from the course have repeatedly asked for material on assembly language programming. With the fifth edition, that material is now available in Appendix C and on the accompanying CD-ROM.

The assembly language chosen is the 8088 since it is a stripped down version of the enormously popular Pentium. I could have used the UltraSPARC or the MIPS or some other CPU almost no one has ever heard of, but as a motivational tool, the 8088 is a better choice since large numbers of students have a Pentium at home and the Pentium is capable of running 8088 programs. However, since debugging assembly code is very difficult, I have provided a set of tools for learning assembly language programming, including an 8088 assembler, a simulator, and a tracer. These tools are provided for Windows UNIX, and Linux. The tools are on the CD-ROM and also on the book's Website (see below).

The book has become longer over the years. Such an expansion is inevitable as a subject develops and there is more known about it. As a result, when the book is used for a course, it may not always be possible to finish the book in a single course (e.g., in a trimester system). A possible approach would be to do all of Chaps. 1, 2, and 3, the first part of Chap. 4 (up through and including Sec. 4.4), and Chap. 5 as a bare minimum. The remaining time could be filled with the rest of Chap. 4, and parts of Chaps. 6, 7, and 8, depending on the interest of the instructor.

A chapter-by-chapter rundown of the major changes since the fourth edition follows. Chapter 1 still contains an historical overview of computer architecture, pointing out how we got where we are now and what the milestones were along the way. The enlarged spectrum of computers that exist is now discussed, and our three major examples (Pentium 4, UltraSPARC III, and 8051) are introduced.

In Chapter 2, the material on input/output devices has been updated, emphasizing the technology of modern devices, including digital cameras, DSL, and Internet over cable.

Chapter 3 has undergone some revision and now treats computer buses and modern I/O chips. The three new examples are described here at the chip level. New material has been added about the PCI Express bus, which is expected to replace the PCI bus shortly.

Chapter 4 has always been a popular chapter for explaining how a computer really works, so most of it is unchanged since the fourth edition. However, there are new sections discussing the microarchitecture level of Pentium 4, the UltraSPARC III, and the 8051.

Chapters 5, 6, and 7 have been updated using the new examples, but are otherwise relatively unchanged. Chapter 6 uses Windows XP rather than Windows NT as an example, but at the level of discussion here, the changes are minimal.

In contrast, Chapter 8 has been heavily modified to reflect all the new activity in parallel computers of all forms. It covers five different classes of parallel systems, from on-chip parallelism (instruction-level parallelism, on-chip multithreading, and single-chip multiprocessors), through coprocessors, shared-memory systems, and clusters, and ends up with a brief discussion of grids. Numerous new examples are discussed here, from the TriMedia CPU, to the BlueGene/L, Red Storm and Google clusters.

The references in Chap. 9 have been updated heavily. Computer organization is a dynamic field. Over half the references in this 5th edition are to books and papers written after the 4th edition of this book was published.

Appendices A and B are unchanged since last time, but Appendix C on assembly language programming is completely new. It is a hands-on, how-to guide to assembly language programming using the tools provided on the CD-ROM and the Website. Appendix C was written by Dr. Evert Wattel of the Vrije Universiteit, Amsterdam. Dr. Wattel has had many years of experience teaching students using these tools. My thanks to him for writing this appendix.

In addition to the assembly language tools, the Website also contains a graphical simulator to be used in conjunction with Chap. 4. This simulator was written by Prof. Richard Salter of Oberlin College. It can be used by students to help grasp the principles discussed in this chapter. My thanks to him for providing this software.

In addition, the figures used in the book and PowerPoint sheets for instructors are also available on the Website. The URL is

http:/www.prenhall.com/tanenbaum

From there, click on the Companion Website for this book and select the page you are looking for from the menu.

A number of people have read (parts of) the manuscript and provided useful suggestions or have been helpful in other ways. In particular, I would like to thank Nikitas Alexandridis, Shekar Borkar, Herbert Bos, Scott Cannon, Doug Carmean, Alan Charlesworth, Eric Cota-Robles, Michael Fetterman, Quinn Jacobson, Thilo Kielmann, Iffat Kazi, Saul Levy, Ahmed Louri, Abhijit Pandya, Krist Petersen, Mark Russinovich, Ronald Schroeder, and Saim Ural for their help, for which I am most grateful. Thank you.

I would also like to thank Jim Goodman for his contributions to this book, especially to Chaps, 4 and 5. The idea of using the Java Virtual Machine was his and the book is better for it.

Finally, I would like to thank Suzanne once more for her love and patience. It never ends, not even after 15 books. Barbara and Marvin are always a joy and now know what professors do for a living. The Royal Netherlands Academy of Arts and Sciences granted me a much-coveted Academy Professorship in 2004, freeing me from some of the less attractive aspects of academia (such as endless boring committee meetings), for which I am eternally grateful.

                                                        Andrew S. Tanenbaum

1

INTRODUCTION

A digital computer is a machine that can solve problems for people by carrying out instructions given to it. A sequence of instructions describing how to perform a certain task is called a **program**. The electronic circuits of each computer can recognize and directly execute a limited set of simple instructions into which all its programs must be converted before they can be executed. These basic instructions are rarely much more complicated than

Add two numbers.

Check a number to see if it is zero.

Copy a piece of data from one part of the computer's memory to another.

Together, a computer's primitive instructions form a language in which people can communicate with the computer. Such a language is called a **machine language**. The people designing a new computer must decide what instructions to include in its machine language. Usually, they try to make the primitive instructions as simple as possible, consistent with the computer's intended use and performance requirements, in order to reduce the complexity and cost of the electronics needed. Because most machine languages are so simple, it is difficult and tedious for people to use them.

This simple observation has, over the course of time, led to a way of structuring computers as a series of abstractions, each abstraction building on the one below it. In this way, the complexity can be mastered and computer systems can be designed in a systematic, organized way. We call this approach **structured computer organization** and have named the book after it. In the next section we will describe what we mean by this term. After that we will look at some historical developments, the state-of-the-art, and some important examples.

1.1 STRUCTURED COMPUTER ORGANIZATION

As mentioned above, there is a large gap between what is convenient for people and what is convenient for computers. People want to do X, but computers can only do Y. This leads to a problem. The goal of this book is to explain how this problem can be solved.

1.1.1 Languages, Levels, and Virtual Machines

The problem can be attacked in two ways: both involve designing a new set of instructions that is more convenient for people to use than the set of built-in machine instructions. Taken together, these new instructions also form a language, which we will call L1, just as the built-in machine instructions form a language, which we will call L0. The two approaches differ in the way programs written in L1 are executed by the computer, which, after all, can only execute programs written in its machine language, L0.

One method of executing a program written in L1 is first to replace each instruction in it by an equivalent sequence of instructions in L0. The resulting program consists entirely of L0 instructions. The computer then executes the new L0 program instead of the old L1 program. This technique is called **translation**.

The other technique is to write a program in L0 that takes programs in L1 as input data and carries them out by examining each instruction in turn and executing the equivalent sequence of L0 instructions directly. This technique does not require first generating a new program in L0. It is called **interpretation** and the program that carries it out is called an **interpreter**.

Translation and interpretation are similar. In both methods, the computer carries out instructions in L1 by executing equivalent sequences of instructions in L0. The difference is that, in translation, the entire L1 program is first converted to an L0 program, the L1 program is thrown away, and then the new L0 program is loaded into the computer's memory and executed. During execution, the newly generated L0 program is running and in control of the computer.

In interpretation, after each L1 instruction is examined and decoded, it is carried out immediately. No translated program is generated. Here, the interpreter is in control of the computer. To it, the L1 program is just data. Both methods, and increasingly, a combination of the two, are widely used.

Rather than thinking in terms of translation or interpretation, it is often simpler to imagine the existence of a hypothetical computer or **virtual machine** whose machine language is L1. Let us call this virtual machine M1 (and let us call the virtual machine corresponding to L0, M0). If such a machine could be constructed cheaply enough, there would be no need for having language L0 or a machine that executed programs in L0 at all. People could simply write their programs in L1 and have the computer execute them directly. Even if the virtual machine whose language is L1 is too expensive or complicated to construct out of electronic circuits, people can still write programs for it. These programs can either be interpreted or translated by a program written in L0 that itself can be directly executed by the existing computer. In other words, people can write programs for virtual machines, just as though they really existed.

To make translation or interpretation practical, the languages L0 and L1 must not be "too" different. This constraint often means that L1, although better than L0, will still be far from ideal for most applications. This result is perhaps discouraging in light of the original purpose for creating L1— relieving the programmer of the burden of having to express algorithms in a language more suited to machines than people. However, the situation is not hopeless.

The obvious approach is to invent still another set of instructions that is more people-oriented and less machine-oriented than L1. This third set also forms a language, which we will call L2 (and with virtual machine M2). People can write programs in L2 just as though a virtual machine with L2 as its machine language really existed. Such programs can either be translated to L1 or executed by an interpreter written in L1.

The invention of a whole series of languages, each one more convenient than its predecessors, can go on indefinitely until a suitable one is finally achieved. Each language uses its predecessor as a basis, so we may view a computer using this technique as a series of **layers** or **levels**, one on top of another, as shown in Fig. 1-1. The bottommost language or level is the simplest and the topmost language or level is the most sophisticated.

There is an important relation between a language and a virtual machine. Each machine has a machine language, consisting of all the instructions that the machine can execute. In effect, a machine defines a language. Similarly, a language defines a machine—namely, the machine that can execute all programs written in the language. Of course, the machine defined by a certain language may be enormously complicated and expensive to construct directly out of electronic circuits but we can imagine it nevertheless. A machine with C or C++ or Java as its machine language would be complex indeed but could easily be built using today's technology. There is a good reason, however, for not building such a computer: it would not be cost effective compared to other techniques. Merely being doable is not good enough: a practical design must be cost effective as well.

In a certain sense, a computer with n levels can be regarded as n different virtual machines, each with a different machine language. We will use the terms

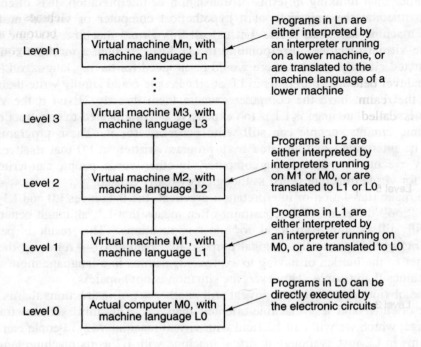

Figure 1-1. A multilevel machine.

"level" and "virtual machine" interchangeably. Only programs written in language L0 can be directly carried out by the electronic circuits, without the need for intervening translation or interpretation. Programs written in L1, L2, ..., Ln must either be interpreted by an interpreter running on a lower level or translated to another language corresponding to a lower level.

A person who writes programs for the level n virtual machine need not be aware of the underlying interpreters and translators. The machine structure ensures that these programs will somehow be executed. It is of no real interest whether they are carried out step by step by an interpreter which, in turn, is also carried out by another interpreter, or whether they are carried out by the electronic circuits directly. The same result appears in both cases: the programs are executed.

Most programmers using an n-level machine are interested only in the top level, the one least resembling the machine language at the very bottom. However, people interested in understanding how a computer really works must study all the levels. People who design new computers or new levels (i.e., new virtual machines) must also be familiar with levels other than the top one. The concepts and techniques of constructing machines as a series of levels and the details of the levels themselves form the main subject of this book.

1.1.2 Contemporary Multilevel Machines

Most modern computers consist of two or more levels. Machines with as many as six levels exist, as shown in Fig. 1-2. Level 0, at the bottom, is the machine's true hardware. Its circuits carry out the machine-language programs of level 1. For the sake of completeness, we should mention the existence of yet another level below our level 0. This level, not shown in Fig. 1-2 because it falls within the realm of electrical engineering (and is thus outside the scope of this book), is called the **device level**. At this level, the designer sees individual transistors, which are the lowest-level primitives for computer designers. If one asks how transistors work inside, that gets us into solid-state physics.

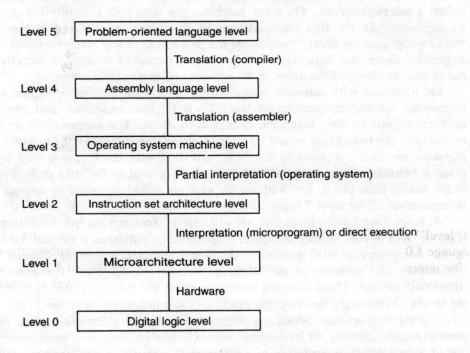

Figure 1-2. A six-level computer. The support method for each level is indicated below it (along with the name of the supporting program).

At the lowest level that we will study, the **digital logic level**, the interesting objects are called **gates**. Although built from analog components, such as transistors, gates can be accurately modeled as digital devices. Each gate has one or more digital inputs (signals representing 0 or 1) and computes as output some simple function of these inputs, such as AND or OR. Each gate is built up of at most a handful of transistors. A small number of gates can be combined to form a 1-bit memory, which can store a 0 or a 1. The 1-bit memories can be combined in groups of (for example) 16, 32, or 64 to form registers. Each **register** can hold a single binary number up to some maximum. Gates can also be combined to form the main computing engine itself. We will examine gates and the digital logic level in detail in Chap. 3.

The next level up is the **microarchitecture level**. At this level we see a collection of (typically) 8 to 32 registers that form a local memory and a circuit called an **ALU** (**Arithmetic Logic Unit**), which is capable of performing simple arithmetic operations. The registers are connected to the ALU to form a **data path**, over which the data flow. The basic operation of the data path consists of selecting one or two registers, having the ALU operate on them (for example, adding them together), and storing the result stored back in some register.

On some machines the operation of the data path is controlled by a program called a **microprogram**. On other machines the data path is controlled directly by hardware. In the first three editions of this book, we called this level the "microprogramming level," because in the past it was nearly always a sofware interpreter. Since the data path is now often (partially) controlled directly by hardware, we changed the name in the previous edition to reflect this.

On machines with software control of the data path, the microprogram is an interpreter for the instructions at level 2. It fetches, examines, and executes instructions one by one, using the data path to do so. For example, for an ADD instruction, the instruction would be fetched, its operands located and brought into registers, the sum computed by the ALU, and finally the result routed back to the place it belongs. On a machine with hardwired control of the data path, similar steps would take place, but without an explicit stored program to control the interpretation of the level 2 instructions.

At level 2 we have a level that we will call the **Instruction Set Architecture level** or (**ISA level**). Every computer manufacturer publishes a manual for each of the computers it sells, entitled "Machine Language Reference Manual" or "Principles of Operation of the Western Wombat Model 100X Computer" or something similar. These manuals are really about the ISA level, not the underlying levels. When they describe the machine's instruction set, they are in fact describing the instructions carried out interpretively by the microprogram or hardware execution circuits. If a computer manufacturer provides two interpreters for one of its machines, interpreting two different ISA levels, it will need to provide two "machine language" reference manuals, one for each interpreter.

The next level is usually a hybrid level. Most of the instructions in its language are also in the ISA level. (There is no reason why an instruction appearing at one level cannot be present at other levels as well.) In addition, there is a set of new instructions, a different memory organization, the ability to run two or more programs concurrently, and various other features. More variation exists between level 3 designs than between those at either level 1 or level 2.

The new facilities added at level 3 are carried out by an interpreter running at level 2, which, historically, has been called an operating system. Those level 3 instructions that are identical to level 2's are carried out directly by the microprogram (or hardwired control), not by the operating system. In other words, some of the level 3 instructions are interpreted by the operating system and some are interpreted directly by the microprogram. This is what we mean by "hybrid" level. Throughout this book we will call this level the **operating system machine level**.

There is a fundamental break between levels 3 and 4. The lowest three levels are not designed for use by the average garden-variety programmer. Instead they are intended primarily for running the interpreters and translators needed to support the higher levels. These interpreters and translators are written by people called **systems programmers** who specialize in designing and implementing new virtual machines. Levels 4 and above are intended for the applications programmer with a problem to solve.

Another change occurring at level 4 is the method by which the higher levels are supported. Levels 2 and 3 are always interpreted. Levels 4, 5, and above are usually, although not always, supported by translation.

Yet another difference between levels 1, 2, and 3, on the one hand, and levels 4, 5, and higher, on the other, is the nature of the language provided. The machine languages of levels 1, 2, and 3 are numeric. Programs in them consist of long series of numbers, which are fine for machines but bad for people. Starting at level 4, the languages contain words and abbreviations meaningful to people.

Level 4, the assembly language level, is really a symbolic form for one of the underlying languages. This level provides a method for people to write programs for levels 1, 2, and 3 in a form that is not as unpleasant as the virtual machine languages themselves. Programs in assembly language are first translated to level 1, 2, or 3 language and then interpreted by the appropriate virtual or actual machine. The program that performs the translation is called an **assembler**.

Level 5 usually consists of languages designed to be used by applications programmers with problems to solve. Such languages are often called **high-level languages**. Literally hundreds exist. A few of the better known ones are C, C++, Java, LISP, and Prolog. Programs written in these languages are generally translated to level 3 or level 4 by translators known as **compilers**, although occasionally they are interpreted instead. Programs in Java, for example, are usually first translated to a an ISA-like language called Java byte code, which is then interpreted.

In some cases, level 5 consists of an interpreter for a specific application domain, such as symbolic mathematics. It provides data and operations for solving problems in this domain in terms that people knowledgeable in that domain can understand easily.

In summary, the key thing to remember is that computers are designed as a series of levels, each one built on its predecessors. Each level represents a distinct abstraction, with different objects and operations present. By designing and analyzing computers in this fashion, we are temporarily able to suppress irrelevant detail and thus reduce a complex subject to something easier to understand.

The set of data types, operations, and features of each level is called its **architecture**. The architecture deals with those aspects that are visible to the user of that level. Features that the programmer sees, such as how much memory is available, are part of the architecture. Implementation aspects, such as what kind of technology is used to implement the memory, are not part of the architecture. The study of how to design those parts of a computer system that are visible to the programmers is called **computer architecture**. In common practice, however, computer architecture and computer organization mean essentially the same thing.

1.1.3 Evolution of Multilevel Machines

To provide some perspective on multilevel machines, we will briefly examine their historical development, showing how the number and nature of the levels has evolved over the years. Programs written in a computer's true machine language (level 1) can be directly executed by the computer's electronic circuits (level 0), without any intervening interpreters or translators. These electronic circuits, along with the memory and input/output devices, form the computer's **hardware**. Hardware consists of tangible objects—integrated circuits, printed circuit boards, cables, power supplies, memories, and printers—rather than abstract ideas, algorithms, or instructions.

Software, in contrast, consists of **algorithms** (detailed instructions telling how to do something) and their computer representations—namely, programs. Programs can be stored on hard disk, floppy disk, CD-ROM, or other media, but the essence of software is the set of instructions that makes up the programs, not the physical media on which they are recorded.

In the very first computers, the boundary between hardware and software was crystal clear. Over time, however, it has blurred considerably, primarily due to the addition, removal, and merging of levels as computers have evolved. Nowadays, it is often hard to tell them apart (Vahid, 2003). In fact, a central theme of this book is

Hardware and software are logically equivalent.

Any operation performed by software can also be built directly into the hardware, preferably after it is sufficiently well understood. As Karen Panetta Lentz put it: "Hardware is just petrified software." Of course, the reverse is also true: any instruction executed by the hardware can also be simulated in software. The decision to put certain functions in hardware and others in software is based on such factors as cost, speed, reliability, and frequency of expected changes. There are few hard-and-fast rules to the effect that X must go into the hardware and Y must be programmed explicitly. These decisions change with trends in technology economics, demand, and computer usage.

The Invention of Microprogramming

The first digital computers, back in the 1940s, had only two levels: the ISA level, in which all the programming was done, and the digital logic level, which executed these programs. The digital logic level's circuits were complicated, difficult to understand and build, and unreliable.

In 1951, Maurice Wilkes, a researcher at the University of Cambridge, suggested designing a three-level computer in order to drastically simplify the hardware (Wilkes, 1951). This machine was to have a built-in, unchangeable interpreter (the microprogram), whose function was to execute ISA-level programs by interpretation. Because the hardware would now only have to execute microprograms, which have a limited instruction set, instead of ISA-level programs, which have a much larger instruction set, fewer electronic circuits would be needed. Because electronic circuits were then made from vacuum tubes, such a simplification promised to reduce tube count and hence enhance reliability (i.e., the number of crashes per day).

A few of these three-level machines were constructed during the 1950s. More were constructed during the 1960s. By 1970 the idea of having the ISA level be interpreted by a microprogram, instead of directly by the electronics, was dominant. All the major machines of the day used it.

The Invention of the Operating System

In these early years, most computers were "open shop," which meant that the programmer had to operate the machine personally. Next to each machine was a sign-up sheet. A programmer wanting to run a program signed up for a block of time, say Wednesday morning 3 to 5 A.M. (many programmers liked to work when it was quiet in the machine room). When the time arrived, the programmer headed for the machine room with a deck of 80-column punched cards (an early input medium) in one hand and a sharpened pencil in the other. Upon arriving in the computer room, he or she gently nudged the previous programmer toward the door and took over the computer.

If the programmer wanted to run a FORTRAN program, the following steps were necessary:

1. He† went over to the cabinet where the program library was kept, took out the big green deck labeled FORTRAN compiler, put it in the card reader, and pushed the START button.

2. He put his FORTRAN program in the card reader and pushed the CONTINUE button. The program was read in.

---

† "He" should be read as "he or she" throughout this book.

3. When the computer stopped, he read his FORTRAN program in a second time. Although some compilers required only one pass over the input, many required two or more. For each pass, a large card deck had to be read in.

4. Finally, the translation neared completion. The programmer often became nervous near the end because if the compiler found an error in the program, he had to correct it and start the entire process all over again. If there were no errors, the compiler punched out the translated machine language program on cards.

5. The programmer then put the machine language program in the card reader along with the subroutine library deck and read them both in.

6. The program began executing. More often than not it did not work and unexpectedly stopped in the middle. Generally, the programmer fiddled with the console switches and looked at the console lights for a little while. If lucky, he figured out the problem, corrected the error, and went back to the cabinet containing the big green FORTRAN compiler to start all over again. If less fortunate, he made a printout of the contents of memory, called a **core dump**, and took it home to study.

This procedure, with minor variations, was normal at many computer centers for years. It forced the programmers to learn how to operate the machine and to know what to do when it broke down, which was often. The machine was frequently idle while people were carrying cards around the room or scratching their heads trying to find out why their programs were not working properly.

Around 1960 people tried to reduce the amount of wasted time by automating the operator's job. A program called an **operating system** was kept in the computer at all times. The programmer provided certain control cards along with the program that were read and carried out by the operating system. Figure 1-3 shows a sample job for one of the first widespread operating systems, FMS (FORTRAN Monitor System), on the IBM 709.

The operating system read the *JOB card and used the information on it for accounting purposes. (The asterisk was used to identify control cards, so they would not be confused with program and data cards.) Later, it read the *FORTRAN card, which was an instruction to load the FORTRAN compiler from a magnetic tape. The compiler then read in and compiled the FORTRAN program. When the compiler finished, it returned control back to the operating system, which then read the *DATA card. This was an instruction to execute the translated program, using the cards following the *DATA card as the data.

Although the operating system was designed to automate the operator's job (hence the name), it was also the first step in the development of a new virtual machine. The *FORTRAN card could be viewed as a virtual "compile program"

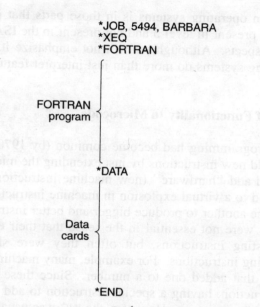

Figure 1-3. A sample job for the FMS operating system.

instruction. Similarly, the *DATA card could be regarded as a virtual "execute program" instruction. A level with only two instructions was not much of a level but it was a start in that direction.

In subsequent years, operating systems became more and more sophisticated. New instructions, facilities, and features were added to the ISA level until it began to take on the appearance of a new level. Some of this new level's instructions were identical to the ISA-level instructions, but others, particularly input/output instructions, were completely different. The new instructions were often known as **operating system macros** or **supervisor calls**. The usual term now is **system call**.

Operating systems developed in other ways as well. The early ones read card decks and printed output on the line printer. This organization was known as a **batch system**. Usually, there was a wait of several hours between the time a program was submitted and the time the results were ready. Developing software was difficult under those circumstances.

In the early 1960s researchers at Dartmouth College, M.I.T., and elsewhere developed operating systems that allowed (multiple) programmers to communicate directly with the computer. In these systems, remote terminals were connected to the central computer via telephone lines. The computer was shared among many users. A programmer could type in a program and get the results typed back almost immediately, in the office, in a garage at home, or wherever the terminal was located. These systems were called **timesharing systems**.

Our interest in operating systems is in those parts that interpret the instructions and features present in level 3 and not present in the ISA level rather than in the timesharing aspects. Although we will not emphasize it, you should keep in mind that operating systems do more than just interpret features added to the ISA level.

The Migration of Functionality to Microcode

Once microprogramming had become common (by 1970), designers realized that they could add new instructions by just extending the microprogram. In other words, they could add "hardware" (new machine instructions) by programming. This revelation led to a virtual explosion in machine instruction sets, as designers competed with one another to produce bigger and better instruction sets. Many of these instructions were not essential in the sense that their effect could be easily achieved by existing instructions, but often they were slightly faster than a sequence of existing instructions. For example, many machines had an instruction INC (INCrement) that added one to a number. Since these machines also had a general ADD instruction, having a special instruction to add 1 (or to add 720, for that matter) was not necessary. However, the INC was usually a little faster than the ADD, so it got thrown in.

For the same reason, many other instructions were added to the microprogram. These often included

1. Instructions for integer multiplication and division.

2. Floating-point arithmetic instructions.

3. Instructions for calling and returning from procedures.

4. Instructions for speeding up looping.

5. Instructions for handling character strings.

Furthermore, once machine designers saw how easy it was to add new instructions, they began looking around for other features to add to their microprograms. A few examples of these additions include

1. Features to speed up computations involving arrays (indexing and indirect addressing).

2. Features to permit programs to be moved in memory after they have started running (relocation facilities).

3. Interrupt systems that signal the computer as soon as an input or output operation is completed.

4. The ability to suspend one program and start another in a small number of instructions (process switching).

5. Special instructions for processing audio, image, and multimedia files.

Numerous other features and facilities have been added over the years as well, usually for speeding up some particular activity.

The Elimination of Microprogramming

Microprograms grew fat during the golden years of microprogramming (1960s and 1970s). They also tended to get slower and slower as they acquired more bulk. Finally, some researchers realized that by eliminating the microprogram, vastly reducing the instruction set, and having the remaining instructions be directly executed (i.e., hardware control of the data path), machines could be speeded up. In a certain sense, computer design had come full circle, back to the way it was before Wilkes invented microprogramming in the first place.

But the wheel is still turning. Java programs are generally executed by compiling them to an intermediate language (Java byte code), and then interpreting the Java byte code.

The point of this discussion is to show that the boundary between hardware and software is arbitrary and constantly changing. Today's software may be tomorrow's hardware, and vice versa. Furthermore, the boundaries between the various levels are also fluid. From the programmer's point of view, how an instruction is actually implemented is unimportant (except perhaps for its speed). A person programming at the ISA level can use its multiply instruction as though it were a hardware instruction without having to worry about it, or even be aware of whether it really is a hardware instruction. One person's hardware is another person's software. We will come back to all these topics later in this book.

1.2 MILESTONES IN COMPUTER ARCHITECTURE

Hundreds of different kinds of computers have been designed and built during the evolution of the modern digital computer. Most have been long forgotten, but a few have had a significant impact on modern ideas. In this section we will give a brief sketch of some of the key historical developments in order to get a better understanding of how we got where we are now. Needless to say, this section only touches on the highlights and leaves many stones unturned. Figure 1-4 lists some of the milestone machines to be discussed in this section. Slater (1987) is a good place to look for additional historical material on the people who founded the computer age. For short biographies and beautiful color photographs by Louis Fabian Bachrach of some of the key people who founded the computer age, see Morgan's coffee-table book (1997).

Year	Name	Made by	Comments
1834	Analytical Engine	Babbage	First attempt to build a digital computer
1936	Z1	Zuse	First working relay calculating machine
1943	COLOSSUS	British gov't	First electronic computer
1944	Mark I	Aiken	First American general-purpose computer
1946	ENIAC I	Eckert/Mauchley	Modern computer history starts here
1949	EDSAC	Wilkes	First stored-program computer
1951	Whirlwind I	M.I.T.	First real-time computer
1952	IAS	Von Neumann	Most current machines use this design
1960	PDP-1	DEC	First minicomputer (50 sold)
1961	1401	IBM	Enormously popular small business machine
1962	7094	IBM	Dominated scientific computing in the early 1960s
1963	B5000	Burroughs	First machine designed for a high-level language
1964	360	IBM	First product line designed as a family
1964	6600	CDC	First scientific supercomputer
1965	PDP-8	DEC	First mass-market minicomputer (50,000 sold)
1970	PDP-11	DEC	Dominated minicomputers in the 1970s
1974	8080	Intel	First general-purpose 8-bit computer on a chip
1974	CRAY-1	Cray	First vector supercomputer
1978	VAX	DEC	First 32-bit superminicomputer
1981	IBM PC	IBM	Started the modern personal computer era
1981	Osborne-1	Osborne	First portable computer
1983	Lisa	Apple	First personal computer with a GUI
1985	386	Intel	First 32-bit ancestor of the Pentium line
1985	MIPS	MIPS	First commercial RISC machine
1987	SPARC	Sun	First SPARC-based RISC workstation
1990	RS6000	IBM	First superscalar machine
1992	Alpha	DEC	First 64-bit personal computer
1993	Newton	Apple	First palmtop computer

Figure 1-4. Some milestones in the development of the modern digital computer.

1.2.1 The Zeroth Generation—Mechanical Computers (1642–1945)

The first person to build a working calculating machine was the French scientist Blaise Pascal (1623–1662), in whose honor the programming language Pascal is named. This device, built in 1642, when Pascal was only 19, was designed to help his father, a tax collector for the French government. It was entirely mechanical, using gears, and powered by a hand-operated crank.

Pascal's machine could only do addition and subtraction operations, but thirty years later the great German mathematician Baron Gottfried Wilhelm von Leibniz (1646–1716) built another mechanical machine that could multiply and divide as well. In effect, Leibniz had built the equivalent of a four-function pocket calculator three centuries ago.

Nothing much happened for 150 years until a professor of mathematics at the University of Cambridge, Charles Babbage (1792–1871), the inventor of the speedometer, designed and built his **difference engine**. This mechanical device, which like Pascal's could only add and subtract, was designed to compute tables of numbers useful for naval navigation. The entire construction of the machine was designed to run a single algorithm, the method of finite differences using polynomials. The most interesting feature of the difference engine was its output method: it punched its results into a copper engraver's plate with a steel die, thus foreshadowing later write-once media such as punched cards and CD-ROMs.

Although the difference engine worked reasonably well, Babbage quickly got bored with a machine that could run only one algorithm. He began to spend increasingly large amounts of his time and family fortune (not to mention 17,000 pounds of the government's money) on the design and construction of a successor called the **analytical engine**. The analytical engine had four components: the store (memory), the mill (computation unit), the input section (punched card reader), and the output section (punched and printed output). The store consisted of 1000 words of 50 decimal digits, each used to hold variables and results. The mill could accept operands from the store, then add, subtract, multiply, or divide them, and finally return the result to the store. Like the difference engine, it was entirely mechanical.

The great advance of the analytical engine was that it was general purpose. It read instructions from punched cards and carried them out. Some instructions commanded the machine to fetch two numbers from the store, bring them to the mill, be operated on (e.g., added), and have the result sent back to the store. Other instructions could test a number and conditionally branch depending on whether it was positive or negative. By punching a different program on the input cards, it was possible to have the analytical engine perform different computations, something not true of the difference engine.

Since the analytical engine was programmable in a simple assembly language, it needed software. To produce this software, Babbage hired a young woman named Ada Augusta Lovelace, who was the daughter of the famed British poet, Lord Byron. Ada Lovelace was thus the world's first computer programmer. The programming language Ada® is named in her honor.

Unfortunately, like many modern designers, Babbage never quite got the hardware debugged. The problem was that he needed thousands upon thousands of cogs and wheels and gears produced to a degree of precision that nineteenth-century technology was unable to provide. Nevertheless, his ideas were far ahead of his time, and even today most modern computers have a structure very similar to the analytical engine, so it is certainly fair to say that Babbage was the (grand)father of the modern digital computer.

The next major development occurred in the late 1930s, when a German engineering student named Konrad Zuse built a series of automatic calculating machines using electromagnetic relays. He was unable to get government funding after the war began because government bureaucrats expected to win the war so quickly that the new machine would not be ready until after it was over. Zuse was unaware of Babbage's work, and his machines were destroyed by the Allied bombing of Berlin in 1944, so his work did not have any influence on subsequent machines. Still, he was one of the pioneers of the field.

Slightly later, in the United States, two people also designed calculators, John Atanasoff at Iowa State College and George Stibbitz at Bell Labs. Atanasoff's machine was amazingly advanced for its time. It used binary arithmetic and had capacitors for memory, which were periodically refreshed to keep the charge from leaking out, a process he called "jogging the memory." Modern dynamic memory (DRAM) chips work the same way. Unfortunately the machine never really became operational. In a way, Atanasoff was like Babbage: a visionary who was ultimately defeated by the inadequate hardware technology of his time.

Stibbitz' computer, although more primitive than Atanasoff's, actually worked. Stibbitz gave a public demonstration of it at a conference at Dartmouth College in 1940. One of the people in the audience was John Mauchley, an unknown professor of physics at the University of Pennsylvania. The computing world would hear more about Prof. Mauchley later.

While Zuse, Stibbitz, and Atanasoff were designing automatic calculators, a young man named Howard Aiken was grinding out tedious numerical calculations by hand as part of his Ph.D. research at Harvard. After graduating, Aiken recognized the importance of being able to do calculations by machine. He went to the library, discovered Babbage's work, and decided to build out of relays the general-purpose computer that Babbage had failed to build out of toothed wheels.

Aiken's first machine, the Mark I, was completed at Harvard in 1944. It had 72 words of 23 decimal digits each, and had an instruction time of 6 sec. Input and output used punched paper tape. By the time Aiken had completed its successor, the Mark II, relay computers were obsolete. The electronic era had begun.

1.2.2 The First Generation—Vacuum Tubes (1945–1955)

The stimulus for the electronic computer was World War II. During the early part of the war, German submarines were wreaking havoc on British ships. Commands were sent from the German admirals in Berlin to the submarines by radio, which the British could, and did, intercept. The problem was that these messages were encoded using a device called the **ENIGMA**, whose forerunner was designed by amateur inventor and former U.S. president, Thomas Jefferson.

Early in the war, British intelligence managed to acquire an ENIGMA machine from Polish Intelligence, which had stolen it from the Germans. However, to break a coded message, a huge amount of computation was needed, and it was needed very soon after the message was intercepted to be of any use. To decode these messages, the British government set up a top secret laboratory that built an electronic computer called the COLOSSUS. The famous British mathematician Alan Turing helped design this machine. The COLOSSUS was operational in 1943, but since the British government kept virtually every aspect of the project classified as a military secret for 30 years, the COLOSSUS line was basically a dead end. It is only worth noting because it was the world's first electronic digital computer.

In addition to destroying Zuse's machines and stimulating the construction of the COLOSSUS, the war also affected computing in the United States. The army needed range tables for aiming its heavy artillery. It produced these tables by hiring hundreds of women to crank them out using hand calculators (women were thought to be more accurate than men). Nevertheless, the process was time consuming and errors often crept in.

John Mauchley, who knew of Atanasoff's work as well as Stibbitz', was aware that the army was interested in mechanical calculators. Like many computer scientists after him, he put together a grant proposal asking the army for funding to build an electronic computer. The proposal was accepted in 1943, and Mauchley and his graduate student, J. Presper Eckert, proceeded to build an electronic computer, which they called the **ENIAC (Electronic Numerical Integrator And Computer)**. It consisted of 18,000 vacuum tubes and 1500 relays. The ENIAC weighed 30 tons and consumed 140 kilowatts of power. Architecturally, the machine had 20 registers, each capable of holding a 10-digit decimal number. (A decimal register is very small memory that can hold one number up to some maximum number of decimal digits, somewhat like the odometer that keeps track of how far a car has traveled in its lifetime.) The ENIAC was programmed by setting up 6000 multiposition switches and connecting a multitude of sockets with a veritable forest of jumper cables.

The machine was not finished until 1946, when it was too late to be of any use for its original purpose. However, since the war was over, Mauchley and Eckert were allowed to organize a summer school to describe their work to their scientific colleagues. That summer school was the beginning of an explosion of interest in building large digital computers.

After that historic summer school, many other researchers set out to build electronic computers. The first one operational was the EDSAC (1949), built at the University of Cambridge by Maurice Wilkes. Others included the JOHNIAC at the Rand Corporation, the ILLIAC at the University of Illinois, the MANIAC at Los Alamos Laboratory, and the WEIZAC at the Weizmann Institute in Israel.

Eckert and Mauchley soon began working on a successor, the **EDVAC (Electronic Discrete Variable Automatic Computer)**. However, that project was fatally wounded when they left the University of Pennsylvania to form a startup company, the Eckert-Mauchley Computer Corporation, in Philadelphia (Silicon Valley had not yet been invented). After a series of mergers, this company became the modern Unisys Corporation.

As a legal aside, Eckert and Mauchley filed for a patent claiming they invented the digital computer. In retrospect, this would not be a bad patent to own. After years of litigation, the courts decided that the Eckert-Mauchley patent was invalid and that John Atanasoff invented the digital computer, even though he never patented it.

While Eckert and Mauchley were working on the EDVAC, one of the people involved in the ENIAC project, John von Neumann, went to Princeton's Institute of Advanced Studies to build his own version of the EDVAC, the **IAS machine**. Von Neumann was a genius in the same league as Leonardo Da Vinci. He spoke many languages, was an expert in the physical sciences and mathematics, and had total recall of everything he ever heard, saw, or read. He was able to quote from memory the verbatim text of books he had read years earlier. At the time he became interested in computers, he was already the most eminent mathematician in the world.

One of the things that was soon apparent to him was that programming computers with huge numbers of switches and cables was slow, tedious, and inflexible. He came to realize that the program could be represented in digital form in the computer's memory, along with the data. He also saw that the clumsy serial decimal arithmetic used by the ENIAC, with each digit represented by 10 vacuum tubes (1 on and 9 off) could be replaced by using parallel binary arithmetic, something Atanasoff had realized years earlier.

The basic design, which he first described, is now known as a **von Neumann machine**. It was used in the EDSAC, the first stored program computer, and is still the basis for nearly all digital computers, even now, more than half a century later. This design, and the IAS machine, built in collaboration with Herman Goldstine, has had such an enormous influence that it is worth describing briefly. Although Von Neumann's name is always attached to this design, Goldstine and others made substantial contributions to it as well. A sketch of the architecture is given in Fig. 1-5.

The von Neumann machine had five basic parts: the memory, the arithmetic logic unit, the control unit, and the input and output equipment. The memory consisted of 4096 words, a word holding 40 bits, each a 0 or a 1. Each word held either two 20-bit instructions or a 40-bit signed integer. The instructions had 8 bits devoted to telling the instruction type, and 12 bits for specifying one of the 4096 memory words. Together, the arithmetic logic unit and the control unit formed the "brain" of the computer. In modern computers they are combined onto a single chip called the **CPU** (**Central Processing Unit**).

Inside the arithmetic logic unit was a special internal 40-bit register called the **accumulator.** A typical instruction added a word of memory to the accumulator

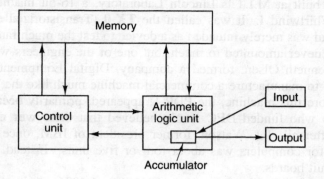

Figure 1-5. The original von Neumann machine.

or stored the contents of the accumulator in memory. The machine did not have floating-point arithmetic because von Neumann felt that any competent mathematician ought to be able to keep track of the decimal point (actually the binary point) in his or her head.

At about the same time von Neumann was building the IAS machine, researchers at M.I.T. were also building a computer. Unlike IAS, ENIAC and other machines of its type, which had long word lengths and which were intended for heavy number crunching, the M.I.T. machine, the Whirlwind I, had a 16-bit word and was designed for real-time control. This project led to the invention of the magnetic core memory by Jay Forrester, and then eventually to the first commercial minicomputer.

While all this was going on, IBM was a small company engaged in the business of producing card punches and mechanical card sorting machines. Although IBM had provided some of Aiken's financing, it was not terribly interested in computers until it produced the 701 in 1953, long after Eckert and Mauchley's company was number one in the commercial market with its UNIVAC computer. The 701 had 2048 36-bit words, with two instructions per word. It was the first in a series of scientific machines that came to dominate the industry within a decade. Three years later came the 704, which initially had 4096 words of core memory, 36-bit instructions, and a new innovation, floating-point hardware. In 1958, IBM began production of its last vacuum tube machine, the 709, which was basically a beefed-up 704.

1.2.3 The Second Generation—Transistors (1955–1965)

The transistor was invented at Bell Labs in 1948 by John Bardeen, Walter Brattain, and William Shockley, for which they were awarded the 1956 Nobel Prize in physics. Within 10 years the transistor revolutionized computers, and by the late 1950s, vacuum tube computers were obsolete. The first transistorized computer was built at M.I.T.'s Lincoln Laboratory, a 16-bit machine along the lines of the Whirlwind I. It was called the **TX-0** (Transistorized eXperimental computer 0) and was merely intended as a device to test the much fancier TX-2.

The TX-2 never amounted to much, but one of the engineers working at the Laboratory, Kenneth Olsen, formed a company, Digital Equipment Corporation (DEC) in 1957 to manufacture a commercial machine much like the TX-0. It was four years before this machine, the PDP-1, appeared, primarily because the venture capitalists who funded DEC firmly believed that there was no market for computers. After all, T.J. Watson, former president of IBM, once said that the world market for computers was about four or five units. Instead, DEC mostly sold small circuit boards.

When the PDP-1 finally appeared in 1961, it had 4096 words of 18-bit words and could execute 200,000 instructions/sec. This performance was half that of the IBM 7090, the transistorized successor to the 709, and fastest computer in the world at the time. The PDP-1 cost $120,000; the 7090 cost millions. DEC sold dozens of PDP-1s, and the minicomputer industry was born.

One of the first PDP-1s was given to M.I.T., where it quickly attracted the attention of some of the budding young geniuses so common at M.I.T. One of the PDP-1's many innovations was a visual display and the ability to plot points anywhere on its 512 by 512 screen. Before long, the students had programmed the PDP-1 to play spacewar, and the world had its first video game.

A few years later DEC introduced the PDP-8, which was a 12-bit machine, but much cheaper than the PDP-1 ($16,000). The PDP-8 had a major innovation: a single bus, the omnibus, as shown in Fig. 1-6. A **bus** is a collection of parallel wires used to connect the components of a computer. This architecture was a major departure from the memory-centered IAS machine and has been adopted by nearly all small computers since. DEC eventually sold 50,000 PDP-8s, which established it as the leader in the minicomputer business.

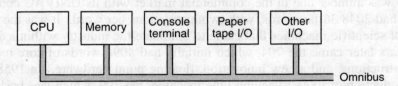

Figure 1-6. The PDP-8 omnibus.

Meanwhile, IBM's reaction to the transistor was to build a transistorized version of the 709, the 7090, as mentioned above, and later the 7094. The 7094 had a cycle time of 2 microsec and 32,536 words of 36-bit words of core memory. The 7090 and 7094 marked the end of the ENIAC-type machines, but they dominated scientific computing for years in the 1960s.

At the same time IBM had become a major force in scientific computing with the 7094, it was making a huge amount of money selling a little business-oriented machine called the 1401. This machine could read and write magnetic tapes, read and punch cards, and print output almost as fast as the 7094, and at a fraction of the price. It was terrible at scientific computing, but for business record keeping it was perfect.

The 1401 was unusual in that it did not have any registers, or even a fixed word length. Its memory was 4000 8-bit bytes, although later models supported up to a then-astounding 16,000 bytes. Each byte contained a 6-bit character, an administrative bit, and a bit used to indicate end-of-word. A MOVE instruction, for example, had a source and a destination address and began moving bytes from the source to the destination until it hit one with the end-of-word bit set to 1.

In 1964 a tiny unknown company, Control Data Corporation (CDC), introduced the 6600, a machine that was nearly an order of magnitude faster than the mighty 7094 and every other machine in existence at the time. It was love at first sight among the number crunchers, and CDC was launched on its way to success. The secret to its speed, and the reason it was so much faster than the 7094, was that inside the CPU was a highly parallel machine. It had several functional units for doing addition, others for doing multiplication, and still another for division, and all of them could run in parallel. Although getting the most out of it required careful programming, with some work it was possible to have 10 instructions being executed at once.

As if this was not enough, the 6600 had a number of little computers inside to help it, sort of like Snow White and the Seven Vertically Challenged People. This meant that the CPU could spend all its time crunching numbers, leaving all the details of job management and input/output to the smaller computers. In retrospect, the 6600 was decades ahead of its time. Many of the key ideas found in modern computers can be traced directly back to the 6600.

The designer of the 6600, Seymour Cray, was a legendary figure, in the same league as Von Neumann. He devoted his entire life to building faster and faster machines, now called **supercomputers**, including the 6600, 7600, and Cray-1. He also invented a now-famous algorithm for buying cars: you go to the dealer closest to your house, point to the car closest to the door and say: "I'll take that one." This algorithm wastes the least time on unimportant things (like buying cars) to leave you the maximum time for doing important things (like designing supercomputers).

There were many other computers in this era, but one stands out for quite a different reason and is worth mentioning: the Burroughs B5000. The designers of machines like the PDP-1, 7094, and 6600 were all totally preoccupied with the hardware, either making it cheap (DEC) or fast (IBM and CDC). Software was almost completely irrelevant. The B5000 designers took a different tack. They built a machine specifically with the intention of having it programmed in Algol 60, a forerunner of C and Java, and included many features in the hardware to ease the compiler's task. The idea that software also counted was born. Unfortunately it was forgotten almost immediately.

1.2.4 The Third Generation—Integrated Circuits (1965–1980)

The invention of the silicon integrated circuit by Robert Noyce in 1958 allowed dozens of transistors to be put on a single chip. This packaging made it possible to build computers that were smaller, faster, and cheaper than their transistorized predecessors. Some of the more significant computers from this generation are described below.

By 1964 IBM was the leading computer company and had a big problem with its two highly successful machines, the 7094 and the 1401: they were as incompatible as two machines could be. One was a high-speed number cruncher using parallel binary arithmetic on 36-bit registers, and the other was a glorified input/output processor using serial decimal arithmetic on variable-length words in memory. Many of its corporate customers had both and did not like the idea of having two separate programming departments with nothing in common.

When the time came to replace these two series, IBM took a radical step. It introduced a single product line, the System/360, based on integrated circuits, that was designed for both scientific and commercial computing. The System/360 contained many innovations, the most important of which was that it was a family of about a half-dozen machines with the same assembly language, and increasing size and power. A company could replace its 1401 with a 360 Model 30 and its 7094 with a 360 Model 75. The Model 75 was bigger and faster (and more expensive), but software written for one of them could, in principle, run on the other. In practice, software written for a small model would run on a large model without problems, but when moving to a smaller machine, the program might not fit in memory. Still, this was a major improvement over the situation with the 7094 and 1401. The idea of machine families caught on instantly, and within a few years most computer manufacturers had a family of common machines spanning a wide range of price and performance. Some characteristics of the initial 360 family are shown in Fig. 1-7. Other models were introduced later.

Property	Model 30	Model 40	Model 50	Model 65
Relative performance	1	3.5	10	21
Cycle time (in billionths of a sec)	1000	625	500	250
Maximum memory (bytes)	65,536	262,144	262,144	524,288
Bytes fetched per cycle	1	2	4	16
Maximum number of data channels	3	3	4	6

Figure 1-7. The initial offering of the IBM 360 product line.

Another major innovation in the 360 was **multiprogramming**, having several programs in memory at once, so that when one was waiting for input/output to complete, another could compute. This resulted in a higher CPU utilization.

The 360 also was the first machine that could emulate (simulate) other computers. The smaller models could emulate the 1401, and the larger ones could emulate the 7094, so that customers could continue to run their old unmodified binary programs while converting to the 360. Some models ran 1401 programs so much faster than the 1401 itself that many customers never converted their programs.

Emulation was easy on the 360 because all the initial models and most of the later models were microprogrammed. All IBM had to do was write three microprograms, for the native 360 instruction set, the 1401 instruction set, and the 7094 instruction set. This flexibility was one of the main reasons microprogramming was introduced.

The 360 solved the dilemma of binary-parallel versus serial decimal with a compromise: the machine had 16 32-bit registers for binary arithmetic, but its memory was byte-oriented, like that of the 1401. It also had 1401 style serial instructions for moving variable-sized records around memory.

Another major feature of the 360 was a (for that time) huge address space of 2^{24} (16,777,216) bytes. With memory costing several dollars per byte in those days, this much memory looked very much like infinity. Unfortunately, the 360 series was later followed by the 370 series, 4300 series, 3080 series, and 3090 series, all using the same architecture. By the mid 1980s, the memory limit became a real problem, and IBM had to partially abandon compatibility when it went to 32-bit addresses needed to address the new 2^{32} byte memory.

With hindsight, it can be argued that since they had 32-bit words and registers anyway, they probably should have had 32-bit addresses as well, but at the time no one could imagine a machine with 16 million bytes of memory. Faulting IBM for this lack of vision is like faulting a modern personal computer vendor for having only 32-bit addresses. In a few years personal computers may need far more than 4 billion bytes of memory, at which time 32-bit addresses will become intolerably small.

The minicomputer world also took a big step forward in the third generation with DEC's introduction of the PDP-11 series, a 16-bit successor to the PDP-8. In many ways, the PDP-11 series was like a little brother to the 360 series just as the PDP-1 was like a little brother to the 7094. Both the 360 and PDP-11 had word-oriented registers and a byte-oriented memory and both came in a range spanning a considerable price/performance ratio. The PDP-11 was enormously successful, especially at universities, and continued DEC's lead over the other minicomputer manufacturers.

1.2.5 The Fourth Generation—Very Large Scale Integration (1980-?)

By the 1980s, **VLSI (Very Large Scale Integration)** had made it possible to put first tens of thousands, then hundreds of thousands, and finally millions of transistors on a single chip. This development soon led to smaller and faster computers. Before the PDP-1, computers were so big and expensive that companies and universities had to have special departments called **computer centers** to run them. With the advent of the minicomputer, a department could buy its own computer. By 1980, prices had dropped so low that it was feasible for a single individual to have his or her own computer. The personal computer era had begun.

Personal computers were used in a very different way than large computers. They were used for word processing, spreadsheets, and numerous highly interactive applications (such as games) that the larger computers could not handle well.

The first personal computers were usually sold as kits. Each kit contained a printed circuit board, a bunch of chips, typically including an Intel 8080, some cables, a power supply, and perhaps an 8-inch floppy disk. Putting the parts together to make a computer was up to the purchaser. Software was not supplied. If you wanted any, you wrote your own. Later, the CP/M operating system, written by Gary Kildall, became popular on 8080s. It was a true (floppy) disk operating system, with a file system, and user commands typed in from the keyboard to a command processor (shell).

Another early personal computer was the Apple and later the Apple II, designed by Steve Jobs and Steve Wozniak in the proverbial garage. This machine was enormously popular with home users and at schools and made Apple a serious player almost overnight.

After much deliberating and observing what other companies were doing, IBM, then the dominant force in the computer industry, finally decided it wanted to get into the personal computer business. Rather than design the entire machine from scratch, using only IBM parts, which would have taken far too long, IBM did something quite uncharacteristic. It gave an IBM executive, Philip Estridge, a large bag of money and told him to go somewhere far from the meddling bureaucrats at corporate headquarters in Armonk, NY, and not come back until he had a working personal computer. Estridge set up shop far from headquarters, in Boca Raton, FL, chose the Intel 8088 as his CPU, and built the IBM Personal Computer from commercial components. It was introduced in 1981 and instantly became the best-selling computer in history.

IBM also did something uncharacteristic that it would later come to regret. Rather than keeping the design of the machine totally secret (or at least, guarded by a wall of patents), as it normally did, it published the complete plans, including all the circuit diagrams, in a book that it sold for $49. The idea was to make it possible for other companies to make plug-in boards for the IBM PC, to increase its flexibility and popularity. Unfortunately for IBM, since the design was now completely public and all the parts were easily available from commercial vendors, numerous other companies began making **clones** of the PC, often for far less money than IBM was charging. Thus an entire industry started.

Although other companies made personal computers using non-Intel CPUs, including Commodore, Apple, and Atari, the momentum of the IBM PC industry was so large that the others were steamrollered. Only a few survived, and these were in niche markets.

One that did survive, although barely, was the Apple Macintosh. The Macintosh was introduced in 1984 as the successor to the ill-fated Apple Lisa, which was the first computer to come with a **GUI (Graphical User Interface)**, similar to the now-popular Windows interface. The Lisa failed because it was too expensive, but the lower-priced Macintosh introduced a year later was a huge success and inspired love and passion among its many admirers.

The early personal computer market also led to the then-unheard of desire for portable computers. At that time, a portable computer made as much sense as a portable refrigerator does now. The first true portable personal computer was the Osborne-1, which at 11 kg was more of a luggable computer than a portable computer. Still, it proved that portables were possible. The Osborne-1 was a modest commercial success, but a year later Compaq brought out its first portable IBM PC clone and was quickly established as the leader in the market for portable computers.

The initial version of the IBM PC came equipped with the MS-DOS operating system supplied by the then-tiny Microsoft Corporation. As Intel was able to produce increasingly powerful CPUs, IBM and Microsoft were able to develop a successor to MS-DOS called OS/2, which featured a graphical user interface, similar to that of the Apple Macintosh. Meanwhile, Microsoft also developed its own operating system, Windows, which ran on top of MS-DOS, just in case OS/2 did not catch on. To make a long story short, OS/2 did not catch on, IBM and Microsoft had a big and extremely public falling out, and Microsoft went on to make Windows a huge success. How tiny Intel and even tinier Microsoft managed to dethrone IBM, one of the biggest, richest, and most powerful corporations in the history of the world, is a parable no doubt related in great detail in business schools around the world.

With the success of the 8088 in hand, Intel went on to make bigger and better versions of it. Particularly noteworthy was the 386, released in 1985, which was essentially the first Pentium. Although modern Pentiums are much faster than the 386, in terms of architecture, the modern Pentium is basically a souped-up 386.

By the mid-1980s, a new development called RISC began to take over, replacing complicated (CISC) architectures with much simpler (but faster) ones. In the 1990s, superscalar CPUs began to appear. These machines could execute multiple instructions at the same time, often in a different order than they appeared in the program. We will introduce the concepts of CISC, RISC, and superscalar in Chap. 2 and discuss them at length throughout this book.

Up until 1992, personal computers were either 8-bit, 16-bit, or 32-bit. Then DEC came out with the revolutionary 64-bit Alpha, a true 64-bit RISC machine that outperformed all other personal computers by a wide margin. It had a modest success, but it was almost a decade later before 64-bit machines began to catch on in a big way, and then mostly as high-end servers.

1.2.6 The Fifth Generation—Invisible Computers

In 1981, the Japanese government announced that they were planning to spend $500 million to help Japanese companies develop fifth-generation computers, which would be based on artificial intelligence and represent a quantum leap over "dumb" fourth-generation computers. Having seen Japanese companies take over the market in many industries, from cameras to stereos to televisions, American and European computer makers went from 0 to full panic in a millisecond, demanding government subsidies and more. Despite lots of fanfare, the Japanese fifth-generation project basically failed and was quietly abandoned. In a sense, it was like Babbage's analytical engine—a visionary idea but so far ahead of its time that the technology for actually building it was nowhere in sight.

Nevertheless, what might be called the fifth generation did happen, but in an unexpected way: computers shrunk. The Apple Newton, released in 1993, showed that a computer could be built in a package no bigger than a portable audio cassette player. The Newton used handwriting for user input, which proved to be a big stumbling block, but later machines of this class, now called **PDAs** (**Personal Digital Assistants**), had improved user interfaces and became very popular. Many of these now have almost as much computing power as personal computers from a few years earlier.

But even the PDAs are not really revolutionary. Even more important are the "invisible" computers, which are embedded into appliances, watches, bank cards, and numerous other devices (Bechini et al., 2004). These processors allow increased functionality and lower cost in a wide variety of applications. Whether these chips form a true generation is debatable (they have been around since the 1970s), but they are revolutionizing how thousands of appliances and other devices work. They are already starting to have a major impact on the world and their influence will increase rapidly in the coming years. One unusual aspects of these embedded computers is that the hardware and software are often **codesigned** (Henkel et al., 2003). We will come back to them later in this book.

If we see the first generation as vacuum tube machines (e.g. ENIAC), the second generation as transistor machines (e.g., the IBM 7094), the third generation as early integrated circuit machines (e.g., the IBM 360), and the fourth generation as personal computers (e.g., the Intel CPUs), the real fifth generation is more a paradigm shift than a specific new architecture. In the future, computers will be everywhere and embedded in everything—indeed, invisible. They will be part of the framework of daily life, opening doors, turning on lights, dispensing money, and thousands of other things. This model, devised by the late Mark Weiser was originally called **ubiquitous computing** but the term **pervasive computing** is also used frequently now (Weiser, 2002). It will change the world as profoundly as the industrial revolution did. We will not discuss it further in this book, but for more information about it, see (Lyytinen and Yoo, 2002; Saha and Mukherjee, 2003; and Sakamura, 2002).

1.3 THE COMPUTER ZOO

In the previous section, we gave a very brief history of computer systems. In this one we will look at the present and gaze toward the future. Although personal computers are the best known computers, there are other kinds of machines around these days, so it is worth taking a brief look at what else is out there.

1.3.1 Technological and Economic Forces

The computer industry is moving ahead like no other. The primary driving force is the ability of chip manufacturers to pack more and more transistors per chip every year. More transistors, which are tiny electronic switches, means larger memories and more powerful processors. Gordon Moore, co-founder and former chairman of Intel, once joked that if aviation technology had moved ahead as fast as computer technology, an airplane would cost $500 and circle the earth in 20 minutes on 5 gallons of fuel. However, it would be the size of a shoebox.

Specifically, while preparing a speech for an industry group, Moore noticed that each new generation of memory chips was being introduced 3 years after the previous one. Since each new generation had four times as much memory as its predecessor, he realized that the number of transistors on a chip was increasing at a constant rate and predicted this growth would continue for decades to come. This observation has become known as **Moore's law**. Today, Moore's law is often expressed as the number of transistors doubling every 18 months. Note that this is equivalent to about a 60 percent increase in transistor count per year. The sizes of the memory chips and their dates of introduction shown in Fig. 1-8 confirm that Moore's law has held for over three decades.

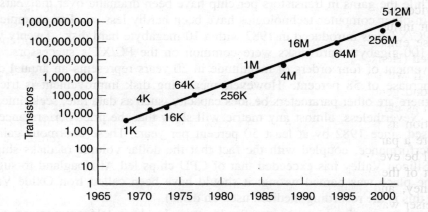

Figure 1-8. Moore's law predicts a 60-percent annual increase in the number of transistors that can be put on a chip. The data points given in this figure are memory sizes, in bits.

Of course, Moore's law is not a law at all, but simply an empirical observation about how fast solid state physicists and process engineers are advancing the state-of-the-art, and a prediction that they will continue at the same rate in the future. Some industry observers expect Moore's law to continue for at least another decade, maybe longer. At that point transistors will consist of too few atoms to be reliable, although advances in quantum computing may conceivable change that (Oskin et al., 2002). However, other observers expect energy dissipation, current leakage, and other effects to kick in earlier and cause serious problems that need to be solved (Bose, 2004; Kim et al., 2003).

Moore's law has created what economist's call a **virtuous circle**. Advances in technology (transistors/chip) lead to better products and lower prices. Lower prices lead to new applications (nobody was making video games for computers when computers cost $10 million each). New applications lead to new markets and new companies springing up to take advantage of them. The existence of all these companies leads to competition, which in turn, creates economic demand for better technologies with which to beat the others. The circle is then round.

Another factor driving technological improvement is Nathan's first law of software (due to Nathan Myhrvold, a former top Microsoft executive). It states: "Software is a gas. It expands to fill the container holding it." Back in the 1980s, word processing was done with programs like troff (still used for this book). Troff occupies kilobytes of memory. Modern word processors occupy megabytes of memory. Future ones will no doubt require gigabytes of memory. (To a first approximation, the prefixes kilo, mega, and giga mean thousand, million, and billion, respectively, but see Sec. 1.5 for details.) Software that continues to acquire features (not unlike boats that continue to acquire barnacles) creates a constant demand for faster processors, bigger memories, and more I/O capacity.

While the gains in transistors per chip have been dramatic over the years, the gains in other computer technologies have been hardly less so. For example, the IBM PC/XT was introduced in 1982 with a 10-megabyte hard disk. Twenty years later, 100-gigabyte hard disks were common on the PC/XT's successors. This improvement of four orders of magnitude in 20 years represents an annual capacity increase of 58 percent. However, measuring disk improvement is trickier, since there are other parameters besides capacity, such as data rate, seek time, and price. Nevertheless, almost any metric will show that the price/performance has increased since 1982 by at least 50 percent per year. These enormous gains in disk performance, coupled with the fact that the dollar volume of disks shipped from Silicon Valley has exceeded that of CPU chips led Al Hoagland to suggest that the place was named wrong: it should have been called Iron Oxide Valley (since this is the recording medium used on disks).

Another area that has seen spectacular gains has been telecommunication and networking. In less than two decades, we have gone from 300 bit/sec modems, to analog modems at 56,000 bits/sec to fiber-optic networks at 10^{12} bits/sec. Fiber-optic transatlantic telephone cables, such as TAT-12/13, cost about $700 million, last for 10 years, and can carry 300,000 simultaneous calls, which comes to under one cent for a 10-minute intercontinental call. Optical communication systems running at 10^{12} bits/sec) over distances exceeding 100 km without amplifiers have been proven feasible. The exponential growth of the Internet hardly needs comment here.

1.3.2 The Computer Spectrum

Richard Hamming, a former researcher at Bell Labs, once observed that a change of an order of magnitude in quantity causes a change in quality. Thus a racing car that can go 1000 km/hour in the Nevada desert is a fundamentally different kind of machine than a normal car that goes 100 km/hour on a highway. Similarly, a 100-story skyscraper is not just a scaled up 10-story apartment building. And with computers, we are not talking about factors of 10, but over the course of three decades, factors of a million.

The gains afforded by Moore's law can be used in several different ways. One way is to build increasingly powerful computers at constant price. Another approach is to build the same computer for less and less money every year. The computer industry has done both of these and more, resulting in a wide variety of computers available now. A very rough categorization of current computers is given in Fig. 1-9.

Type	Price ($)	Example application
Disposable computer	0.5	Greeting cards
Microcontroller	5	Watches, cars, appliances
Game computer	50	Home video games
Personal computer	500	Desktop or notebook computer
Server	5K	Network server
Collection of Workstations	50–500K	Departmental minisupercomputer
Mainframe	5M	Batch data processing in a bank

Figure 1-9. The current spectrum of computers available. The prices should be taken with a grain (or better yet, a metric ton) of salt.

In the following sections we will examine each of these categories and discuss their properties briefly.

1.3.3 Disposable Computers

At the bottom end, we find single chips glued to the inside of greeting cards for playing "Happy Birthday," "Here Comes the Bride," or some equally appalling ditty. The author has not yet spotted a condolence card that plays a funeral dirge, but having now released this idea into the public domain, he expects it shortly. To anyone who grew up with multimillion-dollar mainframes, the idea of disposable computers makes about as much sense as disposable aircraft.

However, disposable computers are here to stay. Probably the most important development in the area of throwaway computers is the **RFID** (**Radio Frequency IDentification**) chip. It is now possible to manufacture, for a few cents, battery-less RFID chips smaller than 0.5 mm on edge that contain a tiny radio transponder and a built-in unique 128-bit number. When pulsed from an external antenna, they are powered by the incoming radio signal long enough to transmit their number back to the antenna. While the chips are tiny, their implications are certainly not.

Let us start with a mundane application: removing bar codes from products. Experimental trials have already been held in which products in stores have RFID chips (instead of bar codes) attached by the manufacturer. The customer selects her products, puts them in a shopping cart, and just wheels them out of the store, bypassing the checkout counter. At the store's exit, a reader with an antenna sends out a signal asking each product to identify itself, which it does by a short wireless transmission. The customer is also identified by a chip on her bank card or credit card. At the end of the month, the store sends the customer an itemized bill for this month's purchases. If the customer does not have a valid RFID bank or credit card, an alarm is sounded. Not only does this system eliminate the need for cashiers and the corresponding wait in line, but it also serves as an antitheft system because hiding a product in a pocket or bag has no effect.

An interesting property of this system is that while bar codes identify the product type, they do not identify the specific item. With 128 bits available, RFID chips do. As a consequence, every package of, say, aspirins, on a supermarket shelf will have a different RFID code. This means that if a drug manufacturer discovers a manufacturing defect in a batch of aspirins after they have been shipped, supermarkets all over the world can be told to sound the alarm when a customer buys any package whose RFID number lies in the affected range, even if the purchase happens in a distant country months later. Aspirins not in the defective batch will not sound the alarm.

But labeling packages of aspirins, cookies, and dog biscuits is only the start. Why stop at labeling the dog biscuits when you can label the dog? Pet owners are already asking veterinarians to implant RFID chips in their animals, to allow them to be traced if they are stolen or lost. Farmers want their livestock tagged as well. The obvious next step is for nervous parents to ask their pediatrician to implant RFID chips in their children in case they get stolen or lost. While we are at it, why not have hospitals put them in all newborns to avoid mixups at the hospital. Governments and the police can no doubt think of many good reasons for tracking all citizens all the time. By now, the "implications" of RFID chips alluded to above may be getting a bit clearer.

Another (slightly less controversial) application of RFID chips is vehicle tracking. When a string of railroad cars with embedded RFID chips passes by a reader, the computer attached to the reader then has a list of which cars passed by. This system makes it easy to keep track of the location of all railroad cars, which helps suppliers, their customers, and the railroads. A similar scheme can be applied to trucks. For cars, the idea can be used for collecting tolls electronically.

Airline baggage systems and many other package transport systems can also use RFID chips. An experimental system tested at Heathrow airport in London allowed arriving passengers to remove the lugging from their luggage. Bags carried by passengers purchasing this service were tagged with RFID chips, routed separately within the airport, and delivered directly to the passengers' hotels. Other uses of RFID chips include having cars arriving at the painting station of the assembly line specify what color they are supposed to be, studying animal migrations, having clothes tell the washing machine what temperature to use, and many more. Some chips may be integrated with sensors so that the low-order bits may contain the current temperature, pressure, humidity or other environmental variable.

Advanced RFID chips also contain permanent storage. This capability led the European Central Bank to make a decision to put RFID chips in euro banknotes in the coming years. The chips would record where they have been. Not only would this make counterfeiting euro notes virtually impossible, but it would make tracing kidnapping ransoms, the loot taken from robberies, and laundered money much easier to track and possibly remotely invalidated. When cash is no longer anonymous, standard police procedure in the future may be to check out where the suspect's money has been recently. Who needs to implant chips in people when their wallets are full of them? Again, when the public learns about what RFID chips can do, there is likely to be some public discussion about the matter.

The technology used in RFID chips is developing rapidly. The smallest ones are passive (not internally powered) and only capable of transmitting their unique numbers when queried. However, larger ones are active, can contain a small battery and a primitive computer, and are capable of doing some calculations. Smart cards used in financial transactions fall into this category.

RFID chips differ not only in being active or passive, but also in the range of radio frequencies they respond to. Those operating at low frequences have a limited data rate but can be sensed at great distances from the antenna. Those operating at high frequencies have a higher data rate and a shorter range. The chips also differ in other ways and are being improved all the time. The Internet is full of information about RFID chips, with *www.rfid.org* being one good starting point.

1.3.4 Microcontrollers

Next up the ladder we have computers that are embedded inside devices that are not sold as computers. The embedded computers, sometimes called **microcontrollers**, manage the devices and handle the user interface. Microcontrollers are found in a large variety of different devices, including the following. Some examples of each category are given in parentheses.

1. Appliances (clock radio, washer, dryer, microwave, burglar alarm).

2. Communications gear (cordless phone, cell phone, fax, pager).

3. Computer peripherals (printer, scanner, modem, CD ROM drive).

4. Entertainment devices(VCR, DVD, stereo, MP3 player, set top box).

5. Imaging devices (TV, digital camera, camcorder, lens, photocopier).

6. Medical devices (X-ray, MRI, heart monitor, digital thermometer).

7. Military weapon systems (cruise missile, ICBM, torpedo).

8. Shopping devices (vending machine, ATM, cash register).

9. Toys (talking doll, game console, radio-controlled car or boat).

A high-end car could easily contain 50 microcontrollers, running subsystems including the antilock brakes, fuel injection, radio, and GPS. A jet plane could easily have 200 or more of them. A family might easily own several hundred computers without knowing it. Within a few years, practically everything that runs on electricity or batteries will contain a microcontroller. The numbers of microcontrollers sold every year dwarfs all other kinds of computers except disposable computers by orders of magnitude.

While RFID chips are minimal systems, microcontrollers are small, but complete, computers. Each microcontroller has a processor, memory, and I/O capability. The I/O capability usually includes sensing the device's buttons and switches and controlling the device's lights, display, sound. motors In most cases, the software is hardwired into the chip in the form of a read-only memory created when the microcontroller is manufactured. Microcontrollers come in two general types: general purpose and special purpose. The former are just small, but ordinary computers; the latter have an architecture and instruction set tuned to some specific application, for example, multimedia. Microcontrollers come in 4-bit, 8-bit, 16-bit, and 32-bit versions.

However, even the general-purpose microcontrollers differ from standard PCs in important ways. First, they are extremely cost sensitive. A company buying millions of units may make the choice based on a 1 cent price difference per unit. This constraint makes microcontroller manufacturers make architectural choices based on manufacturing costs much more than on chips costing hundreds of dollars. Although microcontroller prices vary greatly depending on how many bits wide they are, how much and what kind of memory they have, and other factors; to get an idea, an 8-bit microcontroller purchased in large enough volume can probably be had for as little as 10 cents per unit. This price is what makes it possible to put a computer inside a $9.95 clock radio.

Second, virtually all microcontrollers operate in real time. They get a stimulus and are expected to give an instantaneous response. For example, when the user presses a button, often a light goes on, and there should not be any delay between the button being pressed and the light going on. The need to operate in real time often has impact on the architecture.

Third, embedded systems often have physical constraints in terms of size, weight, battery consumption, and other electrical and mechanical limits. The microcontrollers used in them have to be designed with these restrictions in mind.

1.3.5 Game Computers

A step up are the video game machines. They are normal computers, with special graphics and sound capability, but limited software and little extensibility. They started out as low-end CPUs for playing simple action games like ping pong on TV sets. Over the years they have evolved into far more powerful systems, rivaling or even outperforming personal computers in certain dimensions.

To get an idea of what is inside a game computer, consider the specifications of three popular products. First, the Sony PlayStation 2. It contains a 295-MHz 128-bit proprietary CPU (called the Emotion Engine), which is based on the MIPS IV RISC CPU. The PlayStation 2 also contains 32 MB of RAM, a 160-MHz custom graphics chip, a 48-channel custom audio chip, and a DVD player. Second, the Microsoft XBOX. It contains a 733-MHz Intel Pentium III with 64 MB of RAM, a 300-MHz custom graphics chip, a 256-channel custom audio chip, a DVD player and an 8-GB hard disk. Third, the Nintendo GameCube. It contains a 485-MHz 32-bit custom CPU (called the Gekko) derived from the IBM PowerPC RISC CPU, 24 MB of RAM, a 200-MHz custom graphics chip, a 64-channel audio chip, and a proprietary 1.5 gigabyte optical disk.

While these machines are not quite as powerful as personal computers produced in the same time period, they are not that far behind, and in some ways are ahead (e.g., the 128-bit CPU in the PlayStation 2 is wider than the CPU in any PC, although the clock speed is much lower). The main difference between a game machine and a PC is not so much the CPU as it is the fact that game machines are closed systems. Users may not expand them with plug-in cards, although USB or FireWire interfaces are sometimes provided. Also, and perhaps most important, game machines are carefully optimized for a single application area: highly interactive 3D games with high quality stereo audio. Everything else is secondary. These hardware and software restrictions, slow clock speeds, small memories, absence of a high-resolution monitor, and (usually) absence of a hard disk make it possible to build and sell these machines more cheaply than personal computers. Despite these restrictions, millions of game machines have been sold.

The same companies that make the main game machines also make portable game machines that are handheld and run on batteries. These are closer to the embedded systems we discussed above than to personal computers though.

1.3.6 Personal Computers

Next, we come to the personal computers that most people think of when they hear the term "computer." These include desktop and notebook models. They usually come with hundreds of megabytes of memory, a hard disk holding around 100 gigabytes of data, a CD-ROM/DVD drive, modem, sound card, network interface, high-resolution monitor, and other peripherals. They have elaborate operating systems, many expansion options, and a huge range of available software. Some people reserve the term "PC" for those machines that have an Intel CPU and use "workstation" for those powered by a high-end RISC chip, such as the Sun UltraSPARC. Conceptually, however, there is little difference between them.

The heart of every personal computer is a printed circuit board at the bottom of the case. It usually contains the CPU. memory, various I/O devices (such as a sound chip and possibly a modem), as well as interfaces to the keyboard, mouse, disk, network, etc., and some expansion slots. A picture of one of these circuit boards is given in Fig. 1-10.

Notebook computers are basically PCs in a smaller package. The use the same hardware components, but manufactured in smaller sizes. They also run the same software as desktop PCs.

Yet another closely related machine type is the PDA. While these are even smaller than notebook computers, each one has a CPU, memory, keyboard, display, and most of the other features of a personal computer in miniature. Since most readers are probably quite familiar with personal computers, additional introductory material is hardly needed.

1.3.7 Servers

Beefed-up personal computers or workstations are often used as network servers, both for local area networks (typically within a single company), and for the Internet. These come in single-processor and multiple-processor configurations, have gigabytes of memory, hundreds of gigabytes of hard disk space, and high-speed networking capability. Some of them can handle thousands of transactions per second.

Architecturally, however, a single-processor server is not really very different from a single-processor personal computer. It is just faster, bigger, has more disk space and possibly a faster network connection. Servers run the same operating systems as personal computers, typically some flavor of UNIX or Windows.

1.3.8 Collections of Workstations

Due to almost continuous improvements in the price/performance ratio of workstations and personal computers, in recent years system designers have begun connecting large numbers of them together to form **COWs** (**Clusters of**

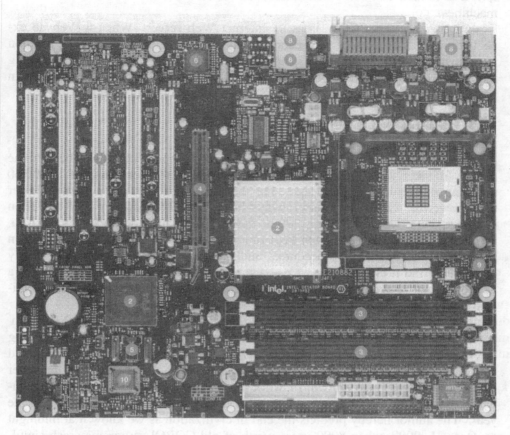

Figure 1-10. A printed circuit board is at the heart of every personal computer. This figure is a photograph of the Intel D875PBZ board. The photograph is copyrighted by the Intel Corporation, 2003 and used by permission.

1. Pentium 4 socket	5. Disk interface	8. USB 2.0 ports
2. 875P Support chip	6. Gigabit Ethernet	9. Cooling technology
3. Memory sockets	7. Five PCI slots	10. BIOS
4. AGP connector		

Workstations), or sometimes just **clusters**. They consist of standard personal computers or workstations connected by gigabit/sec networks, and running special software that allow all the machines to work together on a single problem, often in science or engineering. Normally they are what are called **COTS** (**Commodity Off The Shelf**) computers that anyone can just buy from a normal PC vendor. The main addition is high-speed networking, but sometimes that is also a standard commercial network card too. Clusters scale easily, from a handful of machines to thousands of them. Usually, the amount of money available is the limiting factor. Due to their low component price, individual departments can now own such machines.

Another use for a COW is as an Internet Web server. When a Website expects thousands of requests per second for its pages, the most economical solution is often a cluster with hundreds, or even thousands, of servers. The incoming requests are then sprayed among the servers to allow them to be processed in parallel. When used this way, a COW is often called a **server farm**.

1.3.9 Mainframes

Now we come to the mainframes: room-sized computers that hark back to the 1960s. In many cases, these machines are the direct descendants of IBM 360 mainframes acquired decades ago. For the most part, they are not much faster than powerful servers, but they always have more I/O capacity and are often equipped with vast disk farms, often holding thousands of gigabytes of data. While expensive, they are often kept running due to the immense investment in software, data, operating procedures, and personnel that they represent. Many companies find it cheaper to just pay a few million dollars once in a while for a new one, than to even contemplate the effort required to reprogram all their applications for smaller machines.

It is this class of computer that led to the now-infamous Year 2000 problem, which was caused by COBOL programmers in the 1960s and 1970s representing the year as two decimal digits (in order to save memory). They never envisioned their software lasting three or four decades. While the predicted disaster never occurred due to a huge amount of work put into fixing the problem, many companies have repeated the same mistake by simply adding two more digits to the year. The author hereby predicts the end of civilization as we know it at midnight on Dec. 31, 9999, when 8000 years worth of old COBOL programs crash simultaneously.

In addition to their use for running 30-year-old legacy software, the Internet has breathed new life into mainframes in recent years. They have found a new niche as powerful Internet servers, for example, by handling massive numbers of e-commerce transactions per second, particularly in businesses where huge data bases are required. Although the focus of this book is on PCs, servers, and microcontrollers, we will look at mainframes a bit more in Chap. 5.

Up until recently, there was another category of computers even more powerful than mainframes: **supercomputers.** They had enormously fast CPUs, many gigabytes of main memory, and very fast disks and networks. They were used for massive scientific and engineering calculations such as simulating colliding galaxies, synthesizing new medicines, or modeling the flow of air around an airplane wing. However, in recent years, COWs have come to offer as much computing power at much lower prices, and the true supercomputers are now a dying breed.

1.4 EXAMPLE COMPUTER FAMILIES

In this book we will focus on three kinds of computers: personal computers. servers, and embedded computers. Personal computers are of interest because every reader has undoubtedly used one. Servers are of interest because they run all the services on the Internet. Finally, embedded computers are invisible to their users but control cars, televisions, microwave ovens, washing machines, and practically every other electrical device costing more than $50.

In this section we will give a brief introduction to the three computers that will be used as examples in the rest of the book, one in each of these three categories. They are the Pentium 4, the UltraSPARC III, and the 8051.

1.4.1 Introduction to the Pentium 4

In 1968, Robert Noyce, inventor of the silicon integrated circuit, Gordon Moore, of Moore's law fame, and Arthur Rock, a San Francisco venture capitalist, formed the Intel Corporation to make memory chips. In its first year of operation, Intel sold only $3000 worth of chips, but business has picked up since then.

In the late 1960s, calculators were large electromechanical machines the size of a modern laser printer and weighing 20 kg. In Sept. 1969, a Japanese company, Busicom, approached Intel with a request for it to manufacture 12 custom chips for a proposed electronic calculator. The Intel engineer assigned to this project, Ted Hoff, looked at the plan and realized that he could put a 4-bit general-purpose CPU on a single chip that would do the same thing and be simpler and cheaper as well. Thus in 1970, the first single-chip CPU, the 2300-transistor 4004 was born (Faggin et al., 1996).

It is worth noting that neither Intel nor Busicom had any idea what they had just done. When Intel decided that it might be worth a try to use the 4004 in other projects, it offered to buy back all the rights to the new chip from Busicom by returning the $60,000 Busicom had paid Intel to develop it. Intel's offer was quickly accepted, at which point it began working on an 8-bit version of the chip, the 8008, introduced in 1972. The Intel family, starting with the 4004 and 8008 is shown in Fig. 1-11.

Intel did not expect much demand for the 8008, so it set up a low-volume production line. Much to everyone's amazement, there was an enormous amount of interest, so Intel set about designing a new CPU chip that got around the 8008's limit of 16 kilobytes of memory (imposed by the number of pins on the chip). This design resulted in the 8080, a small, general-purpose CPU, introduced in 1974. Much like the PDP-8, this product took the industry by storm and instantly became a mass market item. Only instead of selling thousands, as DEC had, Intel sold millions.

In 1978 came the 8086, a genuine 16-bit CPU on a single chip. The 8086 was designed to be similar to the 8080, but it was not completely compatible with the

Chip	Date	MHz	Transistors	Memory	Notes
4004	4/1971	0.108	2300	640	First microprocessor on a chip
8008	4/1972	0.108	3500	16 KB	First 8-bit microprocessor
8080	4/1974	2	6000	64 KB	First general-purpose CPU on a chip
8086	6/1978	5–10	29,000	1 MB	First 16-bit CPU on a chip
8088	6/1979	5–8	29,000	1 MB	Used in IBM PC
80286	2/1982	8–12	134,000	16 MB	Memory protection present
80386	10/1985	16–33	275,000	4 GB	First 32-bit CPU
80486	4/1989	25–100	1.2M	4 GB	Built-in 8-KB cache memory
Pentium	3/1993	60–233	3.1M	4 GB	Two pipelines; later models had MMX
Pentium Pro	3/1995	150–200	5.5M	4 GB	Two levels of cache built in
Pentium II	5/1997	233–450	7.5M	4 GB	Pentium Pro plus MMX instructions
Pentium III	2/1999	650–1400	9.5M	4 GB	SSE Instructions for 3D graphics
Pentium 4	11/2000	1300–3800	42M	4 GB	Hyperthreading; more SSE instructions

Figure 1-11. The Intel CPU family. Clock speeds are measured in MHz (megahertz) where 1 MHz is 1 million cycles/sec.

8080. The 8086 was followed by the 8088, which had the same architecture as the 8086, and ran the same programs but had an 8-bit bus instead of a 16-bit bus, making it both slower and cheaper than the 8086. When IBM chose the 8088 as the CPU for the original IBM PC, this chip quickly became the personal computer industry standard.

Neither the 8088 nor the 8086 could address more than 1 megabyte of memory. By the early 1980s this became more and more of a serious problem, so Intel designed the 80286, an upward compatible version of the 8086. The basic instruction set was essentially the same as that of the 8086 and 8088, but the memory organization was quite different, and rather awkward, due to the requirement of compatibility with the older chips. The 80286 was used in the IBM PC/AT and in the midrange PS/2 models. Like the 8088, it was a huge success, mostly because people viewed it as a faster 8088.

The next logical step was a true 32-bit CPU on a chip, the 80386, brought out in 1985. Like the 80286, this one was more-or-less compatible with everything back to the 8080. Being backward compatible was a boon to people for whom running old software was important, but a nuisance to people who would have preferred a simple, clean, modern architecture unencumbered by the mistakes and technology of the past.

Four years later the 80486 came out. It was essentially a faster version of the 80386 that also had a floating-point unit and 8 kilobytes of cache memory on chip. **Cache memory** is used to hold the most commonly used memory words inside or close to the CPU, to avoid (slow) accesses to main memory. The 80486 also had built-in multiprocessor support, to allow manufacturers to build systems containing multiple CPUs sharing a common memory.

At this point, Intel found out the hard way (by losing a trademark infringement lawsuit) that numbers (like 80486) cannot be trademarked, so the next generation got a name: **Pentium** (from the Greek word for five, πεντε). Unlike the 80486, which had one internal pipeline, the Pentium had two of them, which helped make it twice as fast (we will discuss pipelines in detail in Chap. 2).

Later in the production run, Intel added special **MMX** (**MultiMedia eXtension**) instructions. These instructions were intended to speed up computations required to process audio and video, making the addition of special multimedia coprocessors unnecessary.

When the next generation appeared, people who were hoping for the Sexium (*sex* is Latin for six) were disappointed. The name Pentium was now so well known that the marketing people wanted to keep it, and the new chip was called the Pentium Pro. Despite the small name change from its predecessor, this processor represented a major break with the past. Instead of having two or more pipelines, the Pentium Pro had a very different internal organization and could execute up to five instructions at a time.

Another innovation found in the Pentium Pro was a two-level cache memory. The processor chip itself had 8 kilobytes of fast memory to hold commonly-used instructions and another 8 kilobytes of fast memory to hold commonly-used data. In the same cavity within the Pentium Pro package (but not on the chip itself) was a second cache memory of 256 kilobytes.

Although the Pentium Pro had a big cache, it lacked the MMX instructions (because Intel was unable to manufacture such a large chip with acceptable yields). When the technology improved enough to get both the MMX instructions and the cache on one chip, the combined product was released as the Pentium II. Next, yet more multimedia instructions, called **SSE** (**Streaming SIMD Extensions**), were added for enhanced 3D graphics (Raman et al., 2000). The new chip was dubbed the Pentium III, but internally it was essentially a Pentium II.

The next Pentium was based on a different internal architecture. To celebrate this event, Intel switched from Roman numerals to Arabic numbers and called it the Pentium 4. As usual, the Pentium 4 was faster than all its predecessors. The 3.06 GHz version also introduced an intriguing new feature—hyperthreading. This feature allowed programs to split their work into two threads of control which the Pentium 4 could run in parallel, speeding up execution. In addition, another batch of SSE instructions was added to speed up audio and video processing even more. A photograph of the Pentium 4 chip is given in Fig. 1-12. In reality, it is about 16.0 mm × 13.5 mm, an extremely large chip.

In addition to the mainline desktop CPUs discussed above, Intel has manufactured variants of some of the Pentium chips for special markets. In early 1998, Intel introduced a new product line called the **Celeron**, which was basically a low-price, low-performance version of the Pentium 2 intended for low-end PCs.

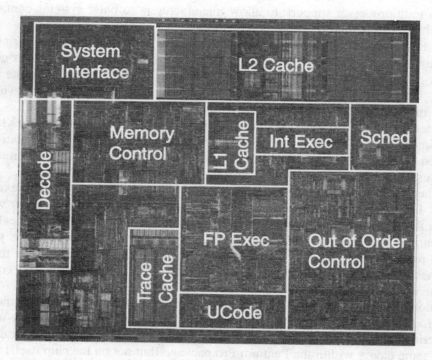

Figure 1-12. The Pentium 4 chip. The photograph is copyrighted by the Intel Corporation, 2003 and used by permission.

Since the Celeron has the same architecture as the Pentium 2, we will not discuss it further in this book. In June 1998, Intel introduced a special version of the Pentium 2 for the upper end of the market. This processor, called the **Xeon**, had a larger cache, a faster bus, and better multiprocessor support, but was otherwise a normal Pentium 2, so we will not discuss it separately either. The Pentium III also had a Xeon version.

In Nov. 2000, Intel released the Pentium 4, which ran the same programs as the Pentium III and Xeon, but internally was a completely new design. The 3.06 GHz version of the Pentium 4 introduced hyperthreading, a subject we will discuss in Chap. 8.

In 2003, Intel introduced the Pentium M (as in Mobile), a chip designed for notebook computers. This chip was part of the Centrino architecture, whose goals were lower power consumption for longer battery lifetime; smaller, lighter, computers; and built-in wireless networking capability using the IEEE 802.11 (WiFi) standard. Intel intends to introduce chip sets for other specific applications in the future, for example, home entertainment devices and IEEE 802.16 (WiMax) notebooks.

All the Intel chips are backward compatible with their predecessors back as far as the 8086. In other words, a Pentium 4 can run old 8086 programs without modification. This compatibility has always been a design requirement for Intel, to allow users to maintain their existing investment in software. Of course, the Pentium 4 is three orders of magnitude more complex than the 8086, so it can do quite a few things that the 8086 could not do. These piecemeal extensions have resulted in an architecture that is not as elegant as it might have been had someone given the Pentium 4 architects 42 million transistors and instructions to start all over again.

It is interesting to note that although Moore's law has long been associated with the number of bits in a memory, it applies equally well to CPU chips. By plotting the transistor counts given in Fig. 1-12 against the date of introduction of each chip on a semilog scale, we see that Moore's law holds here too. This graph is given in Fig. 1-13.

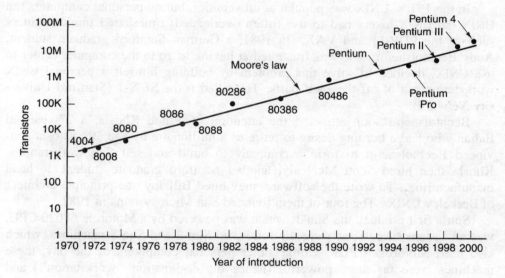

Figure 1-13. Moore's law for (Intel) CPU chips.

While Moore's law will probably continue to hold for some years to come, another problem is starting to overshadow it: heat dissipation. Smaller transistors make it possible to run at higher clock frequencies, which requires higher using a higher voltage. Power consumed and heat dissipated is proportional to the square of the voltage, so going faster means having more heat to get rid of. At 3.6 GHz, the Pentium 4 consumes 115 watts of power. That means it gets about as hot as a 100-watt light bulb. Speeding up the clock makes the problem worse.

In November 2004, Intel canceled the 4-GHz Pentium 4 due to problems dissipating the heat. Large fans can help but the noise they make is not popular with users and water cooling, while used on large mainframes, is not an option for desktop machines (and even less so for notebook computers). As a consequence, the once-relentless march of the clock may be temporarily stymied, at least until

Intel's engineers figure out how to get rid of all the heat generated in an efficient way. Instead, Intel's future plans call for putting two CPUs on a single chip, along with large shared cache. Because of the way power consumption is related to voltage and clock speed, two CPUs on a chip consumes far less power than one CPU at the twice the speed. As a consequence, the gain offered by Moore's law may be increasingly exploited in the future to include larger and larger on-chip caches, rather than higher and higher clock speeds (because memory does not consume much power).

1.4.2 Introduction to the UltraSPARC III

In the 1970s, UNIX was popular at universities, but no personal computers ran UNIX, so UNIX-lovers had to use (often overloaded) timeshared minicomputers such as the PDP-11 and VAX. In 1981, a German Stanford graduate student, Andy Bechtolsheim, who was frustrated at having to go to the computer center to use UNIX, decided to solve this problem by building himself a personal UNIX workstation out of off-the-shelf parts. He called it the SUN-1 (Stanford University Network).

Bechtolsheim soon attracted the attention of Vinod Khosla, a 27-year-old Indian who had a burning desire to retire as a millionaire by age 30. Khosla convinced Bechtolsheim to form a company to build and sell Sun workstations. Khosla then hired Scott McNealy, another Stanford graduate student, to head manufacturing. To write the software, they hired Bill Joy, the principle architect of Berkeley UNIX. The four of them founded Sun Microsystems in 1982.

Sun's first product, the Sun-1, which was powered by a Motorola 68020 CPU, was an instant success, as were the follow-up Sun-2 and Sun-3 machines, which also used Motorola CPUs. Unlike other personal computers of the day, these machines were far more powerful (hence the designation "workstation") and were designed from the start to be run on a network. Each Sun workstation came equipped with an Ethernet connection and with TCP/IP software for connecting to the ARPANET, the forerunner of the Internet.

By 1987, Sun, now selling half a billion dollars a year worth of systems, decided to design its own CPU, basing it upon a revolutionary new design from the University of California at Berkeley (the RISC II). This CPU, called the **SPARC** (**Scalable Processor ARChitecture**), formed the basis of the Sun-4 workstation. Within a short time, all of Sun's products used the SPARC CPU.

Unlike many other computer companies, Sun decided not to manufacture the SPARC CPU chip itself. Instead, it licensed several different semiconductor manufacturers to produce them, hoping that competition among them would drive performance up and prices down. These vendors produced a number of different chips, based on different technologies, running at different clock speeds, and with various prices. These chips included the MicroSPARC, HyperSPARC, Super-

SPARC, and TurboSPARC. Although these CPUs differed in minor ways, all were binary compatible and ran the same user programs without modification.

Sun always wanted SPARC to be an open architecture, with many suppliers of parts and systems, in order to build an industry that could compete in a personal computer world already dominated by Intel-based CPUs. To gain the trust of companies that were interested in the SPARC but did not want to invest in a product controlled by a competitor, Sun created an industry consortium, SPARC International, to manage the development of future versions of the SPARC architecture. Thus it is important to distinguish between the SPARC architecture, which is a specification of the instruction set and other programmer-visible features, and a particular implementation of it. In this book we will study both the generic SPARC architecture, and, when discussing CPU chips in Chaps. 3 and 4, a specific SPARC chip used in Sun workstations.

The initial SPARC was a full 32-bit machine, running at 36 MHz. The CPU, called the **IU (Integer Unit)** was lean and mean, with only three major instruction formats and only 55 instructions in all. In addition, a floating-point unit added another 14 instructions. This history can be contrasted to the Intel line, which started out with 8- and 16-bit chips (8088, 8086, 80286) and finally became a 32-bit chip with the 80386.

The SPARC's first break with the past occurred in 1995, with the development of Version 9 of the SPARC architecture, a full 64-bit architecture, with 64-bit addresses and 64-bit registers. The first Sun workstation to implement the V9 (Version 9) architecture was the **UltraSPARC I**, introduced in 1995 (Tremblay and O'Connor, 1996). Despite its being a 64-bit machine, it was also fully binary compatible with the existing 32-bit SPARCs.

The UltraSPARC was intended to break new ground. Whereas previous machines were designed for handling alphanumeric data and running programs like word processors and spreadsheets, the UltraSPARC was designed from the beginning to handle images, audio, video, and multimedia in general. Among other innovations besides the 64-bit architecture were 23 new instructions, including some for packing and unpacking pixels from 64-bit words, scaling and rotating images, block moves, and performing real-time video compression and decompression. These instructions, called **VIS (Visual Instruction Set)** were aimed at providing general multimedia capability, analogous to Intel's MMX instructions.

The UltraSPARC was aimed at high-end applications, such as large multiprocessor Web servers with dozens of CPUs and physical memories of up to 8 TB [1 TB (terabyte) = 10^{12} bytes]. However, smaller versions can be used in notebook computers as well.

The successors to the UltraSPARC I were the UltraSPARC II, UltraSPARC III, and UltraSPARC IV. These models differ primarily in clock speed, but some new features were added in each iteration as well. In most of this book, when we discuss the SPARC architecture, we will primarily use the 64-bit V9 UltraSPARC III Cu as our example. The UltraSPARC IV is essentially a dual processor in which two UltraSPARC IIIs are colocated on the same CPU chip and share the same memory. We will cover it when we come to multiprocessors in Chap. 8.

1.4.3 Introduction to the 8051

Our third example is very different from our first (the Pentium 4, used in personal computers) and the second (the UltraSPARC III, used in servers). It is the 8051, which is used in embedded systems. The 8051 story starts in 1976, when the 8-bit 8080 had been on the market for about two years. Appliance makers were starting to incorporate the 8080 into their devices, but to build a complete system they needed the 8080 CPU chip, one or more memory chips, and one or more I/O chips. The cost of at least three chips and their interconnection was substantial, and restricted the use of computers in embedded systems to fairly large and expensive items. Many manufacturers asked Intel to put the whole computer (CPU, memory, and I/O) on a single chip to reduce costs.

Intel responded to its customers by producing the 8748 chip, a 17,000-transistor microcontroller containing an 8080-like CPU, 1 KB of read-only memory for the program, 64 bytes of read/write memory for the variables, an 8-bit timer, and 27 I/O lines for controlling switches, buttons, and lights. While primitive, the chip was a commercial success, which led Intel to release the 8051 in 1980. This new chip contained 60,000 transistors, a much faster CPU, 4 KB of read-only memory, 128 bytes of read-write memory, 32 I/O lines, a serial port, and two 16-bit timers. It was soon followed by other members of what Intel called the **MCS-51 family**, shown in Fig. 1-14.

Chip	Program memory	Mem. type	RAM	Timers	Interrupts
8031	0 KB		128	2	5
8051	4 KB	ROM	128	2	5
8751	8 KB	EPROM	128	2	5
8032	0 KB		256	3	6
8052	8 KB	ROM	256	3	6
8752	8 KB	EPROM	256	3	6

Figure 1-14. Members of the MCS-51 family.

All of these chips use read-only memories for the program plus a small amount of read-write memory, called **RAM** (**Random Access Memory**) for data storage. With the 8031 and 8032, the program memory is external, allowing more than 8 KB to be used if needed. We will study **ROM** (**Read Only Memory**) and **EPROM** (**Erasable Programmable ROM**) in Chap. 3. For the moment, it is sufficient to know that the 8051 and 8052 are single chip microcontrollers used in actual products. Each batch is custom manufactured for the customer (e.g., an appliance manufacturer) and contains the program supplied by the customer.

In order to develop the software, however, the customer needs a development system. That is where the 8751 and 8752 come in. They are much more expensive than the 8051 and 8052, but can be programmed by the customer for the purpose of software testing. If a bug is found in the code, the program in the 8751 or 8752 can be erased by exposing the chip to an ultraviolet light. A new program can then be burned into it. When the software is finished, it can be delivered to the chip manufacturer, which then produces custom 8051s or 8052s containing the code.

In terms of architecture, interfacing, and programming, all the MCS-51 family members are very similar. For simplicity, we will mostly refer to the 8051, pointing out differences with the other chips where that is needed.

To some people, using an 8-bit chip that is more than 20 years old as an example may seem like a strange idea, but there are good reasons for doing so. The number of microcontrollers sold each year is around 8 billion, and climbing rapidly. This number is orders of magnitude more than the number of Pentiums sold annually. It was not until 2001 until the number of 8-bit microcontrollers sold per year exceeded the volume of the 4-bit microcontrollers. Currently 8-bit microcontrollers outsell all the others combined, and the MCS-51 family is the most popular 8-bit family. Given the growing importance of embedded systems, anyone studying computer architecture should be familiar with the chips used in them, and the 8051 is one of the most popular ones.

There are a variety of reasons for the success of the 8051. First, and foremost, is the price. Depending on the number of units ordered, an 8051 can be had for around 10 to 15 cents per chip, maybe less in large volume. In contrast, a 32-bit microcontroller typically costs 30 times as much, with a 16-bit one somewhere in between. For products that sell for under $50 in competitive markets, knocking a couple of dollars off the manufacturing cost can make a significant difference in retail price and in sales. This is the main reason the 8051 is so popular—it is very cheap.

Second, over half a dozen companies manufacture 8051s under license from Intel. Their products cover a wide range of speeds, from the original 12 MHz to 100 MHz, and use many different manufacturing and packaging technologies. Not only does this competition keep prices low, but large customers are much happier when they are not dependent on a single supplier.

Third, because the 8051 has been around for so long, there is a vast amount of software for it, including assemblers, compilers for C and other languages, libraries of all kinds, debuggers, simulators, test software, and much more. There are also many complete development systems on the market, which speed up developing the embedded hardware and software. Finally, large numbers of programmers and hardware engineers are familiar with the 8051, making it easy to find skilled personnel.

This popularity feeds on itself. Researchers interested in embedded systems often choose the 8051 as their main object of study due to its widespread use, for example, for testing out new energy-efficient technologies (Martin et al., 2003) or fault tolerance (Lima et al., 2002).

There is a great deal of information about the 8051 on the Internet. One good starting place is *www.8051.com*. In addition, people are still writing new books about it (Ayala, 2004; Calcutt et al., 2004; MacKenzie et al., 2005; and Mazidi et al., 2005).

1.5 METRIC UNITS

To avoid any confusion, it is worth stating explicitly that in this book, as in computer science in general, metric units are used instead of traditional English units (the furlong-stone-fortnight system). The principal metric prefixes are listed in Fig. 1-15. The prefixes are typically abbreviated by their first letters, with the units greater than 1 capitalized (KB, MB, etc.). One exception (for historical reasons) is kbps for kilobits/sec. Thus, a 1-Mbps communication line transmits 10^6 bits/sec and a 100 psec (or 100 ps) clock ticks every 10^{-10} seconds. Since milli and micro both begin with the letter "m," a choice had to be made. Normally, "m" is for milli and "μ" (the Greek letter mu) is for micro.

Exp.	Explicit	Prefix	Exp.	Explicit	Prefix
10^{-3}	0.001	milli	10^3	1,000	Kilo
10^{-6}	0.000001	micro	10^6	1,000,000	Mega
10^{-9}	0.000000001	nano	10^9	1,000,000,000	Giga
10^{-12}	0.000000000001	pico	10^{12}	1,000,000,000,000	Tera
10^{-15}	0.000000000000001	femto	10^{15}	1,000,000,000,000,000	Peta
10^{-18}	0.000000000000000001	atto	10^{18}	1,000,000,000,000,000,000	Exa
10^{-21}	0.000000000000000000001	zepto	10^{21}	1,000,000,000,000,000,000,000	Zetta
10^{-24}	0.000000000000000000000001	yocto	10^{24}	1,000,000,000,000,000,000,000,000	Yotta

Figure 1-15. The principal metric prefixes.

It is also worth pointing out that for measuring memory, disk, file, and database sizes, in common industry practice, the units have slightly different meanings. There, kilo means 2^{10} (1024) rather than 10^3 (1000) because memories are always a power of two. Thus, a 1-KB memory contains 1024 bytes, not 1000 bytes. Similarly, a 1-MB memory contains 2^{20} (1,048,576) bytes, a 1-GB memory contains 2^{30} (1,073,741,824) bytes, and a 1-TB database contains 2^{40} (1,099,511,627,776) bytes. However, a 1-kbps communication line can transmit 1000 bits per second and a 10-Mbps LAN runs at 10,000,000 bits/sec because these speeds are not powers of two. Unfortunately, many people tend to mix up these two systems, especially for disk sizes. To avoid ambiguity, in this book, we will use the symbols KB, MB, GB, and TB for 2^{10}, 2^{20}, 2^{30}, and 2^{40} bytes, respectively, and the symbols kbps, Mbps, Gbps, and Tbps for 10^3, 10^6, 10^9, and 10^{12} bits/sec, respectively.

1.6 OUTLINE OF THIS BOOK

This book is about multilevel computers (which includes nearly all modern computers) and how they are organized. We will examine four levels in considerable detail—namely, the digital logic level, the microarchitecture level, the ISA level, and the operating system machine level. Some of the basic issues to be examined include the overall design of the level (and why it was designed that way), the kinds of instructions and data available, the memory organization and addressing, and the method by which the level is implemented. The study of these topics, and similar ones, is called computer organization or computer architecture.

We are primarily concerned with concepts rather than details or formal mathematics. For that reason, some of the examples given will be highly simplified, in order to emphasize the central ideas and not the details.

To provide some insight into how the principles presented in this book can be, and are, applied in practice, we will use the Pentium 4, the UltraSPARC III, and the 8051 as running examples throughout the book. These three have been chosen for several reasons. First, all are widely used and the reader is likely to have access to at least one of them. Second, each one has its own unique architecture, which provides a basis for comparison and encourages a "what are the alternatives?" attitude. Books dealing with only one machine often leave the reader with a "true machine design revealed" feeling, which is absurd in light of the many compromises and arbitrary decisions that designers are forced to make. The reader is encouraged to study these and all other computers with a critical eye and to try to understand why things are the way they are, as well as how they could have been done differently rather than simply accepting them as given.

It should be made clear from the beginning that this is not a book about how to program the Pentium 4, UltraSPARC III, or 8051. These machines will be used for illustrative purposes where appropriate, but we make no pretense of being complete. Readers wishing a thorough introduction to one of them should consult the manufacturer's publications.

Chapter 2 is an introduction to the basic components of a computer—processors, memories, and input/output equipment. It is intended to provide an overview of the system architecture and an introduction to the following chapters.

Chapters 3, 4, 5, and 6 each deal with one specific level shown in Figure 1-2. Our treatment is bottom-up, because machines have traditionally been designed that way. The design of level k is largely determined by the properties of level $k - 1$, so it is hard to understand any level unless you already have a good grasp of the underlying level that motivated it. Also, it is educationally sound to proceed from the simpler lower levels to the more complex higher levels rather than vice versa.

Chapter 3 is about the digital logic level, the machine's true hardware. It discusses what gates are and how they can be combined into useful circuits. Boolean algebra, a tool for analyzing digital circuits, is also introduced. Computer buses are explained, especially the popular PCI bus. Numerous examples from industry are discussed in this chapter, including the three running examples mentioned above.

Chapter 4 introduces the architecture of the microarchitecture level and its control. Since the function of this level is to interpret the level 2 instructions in the layer above it, we will concentrate on this topic and illustrate it by means of examples. The chapter also contains discussions of the microarchitecture level of some real machines.

Chapter 5 discusses the ISA level, the one most computer vendors advertise as the machine language. We will look at our example machines here in detail.

Chapter 6 covers some of the instructions, memory organization, and control mechanisms present at the operating system machine level. The examples used here are Windows XP (popular on high-end Pentium 4 server systems) and UNIX, used on the UltraSPARC III.

Chapter 7 is about the assembly language level. It covers both assembly language and the assembly process. The subject of linking also comes up here.

Chapter 8 discusses parallel computers, an increasingly important topic nowadays. Some of these parallel computers have multiple CPUs that share a common memory. Others have multiple CPUs without common memory. Some are supercomputers; some are systems on a chip; others are COWs.

Chapter 9 contains an annotated list of suggested readings, arranged by subject, and an alphabetical list of literature citations. It is the most important chapter in the book. Use it.

PROBLEMS

1. Explain each of the following terms in your own words:

   a. Translator.
   b. Interpreter.
   c. Virtual machine.

2. What is the difference between interpretation and translation?

3. Is it conceivable for a compiler to generate output for the microarchitecture level instead of for the ISA level? Discuss the pros and cons of this proposal.

4. Can you imagine any multilevel computer in which the device level and digital logic levels were not the lowest levels? Explain.

5. Consider a multilevel computer in which all the levels are different. Each level has instructions that are m times as powerful as those of the level below it; that is, one level r instruction can do the work of m level $r - 1$ instructions. If a level 1 program requires k seconds to run, how long would equivalent programs take at levels 2, 3, and 4, assuming n level r instructions are required to interpret a single $r + 1$ instruction?

6. Some instructions at the operating system machine level are identical to ISA language instructions. These instructions are carried out directly by the microprogram rather than by the operating system. In light of your answer to the preceding problem, why do you think this is the case?

7. Consider a computer with identical interpreters at levels 1, 2, and 3. It takes an interpreter n instructions to fetch, examine, and execute one instruction. A level 1 instruction takes k nanoseconds to execute. How long does it take for an instruction at levels 2, 3, and 4?

8. In what sense are hardware and software equivalent? Not equivalent?

9. Babbage's difference engine had a fixed program that could not be changed. Is this essentially the same thing as a modern CD-ROM that cannot be changed? Explain your answer.

10. One of the consequences of von Neumann's idea to store the program in memory is that programs can be modified, just like data. Can you think of an example where this facility might have been useful? (Hint: Think about doing arithmetic on arrays.)

11. The performance ratio of the 360 model 75 was 50 times that of the 360 model 30, yet the cycle time was only five times as fast. How do you account for this discrepancy?

12. Two basic system designs are shown in Figure 1-5 and Figure 1-6. Describe how input/output might occur in each system. Which one has the potential for better overall system performance?

13. Suppose that each of the 300 million people in the United States fully consumes two packages of goods a day bearing RFID tags. How many RFID tags have to be produced annually to meet that demand? At a penny a tag, what is the total cost of the tags? Given the size of GDP, is this amount of money going to be an obstacle to their use on every package offered for sale?

14. Name three appliances that are candidates for being run by an embedded CPU.

15. At a certain point in time, a transistor on a microprocessor was 0.1 micron in diameter. According to Moore's law, how big would a transistor be on next year's model?

16. The legal issue of who invented the computer was settled in April 1973 by Judge Earl Larson, who handled a patent infringement lawsuit filed by the Sperry Rand Corporation, which had acquired the ENIAC patents. Sperry Rand's position was that everybody making a computer owed them royalties because it owned the key patents. The case went to trial in June 1971 and over 30,000 exhibits were entered. The court transcript ran to over 20,000 pages. Study this case more carefully using the extensive information available on the Internet and write a report discussing the technical aspects of the case. What exactly did Eckert and Mauchley patent and why did the judge feel their system was based on Atanasoff's earlier work?

17. Pick the three people you think were most influential in creating modern computer hardware and write a short report describing their contributions and why you picked them.

18. Repeat the previous question for computer software.

2

COMPUTER SYSTEMS

ORGANIZATION

A digital computer consists of an interconnected system of processors, memories, and input/output devices. This chapter is an introduction to these three components and to their interconnection, as background for the detailed examination of specific levels in the five succeeding chapters. Processors, memories, and input/output are key concepts and will be present at every level, so we will start our study of computer architecture by looking at all three in turn.

2.1 PROCESSORS

The organization of a simple bus-oriented computer is shown in Fig. 2-1. The **CPU (Central Processing Unit)** is the "brain" of the computer. Its function is to execute programs stored in the main memory by fetching their instructions, examining them, and then executing them one after another. The components are connected by a **bus**, which is a collection of parallel wires for transmitting address, data, and control signals. Buses can be external to the CPU, connecting it to memory and I/O devices, but also internal to the CPU, as we will see shortly.

The CPU is composed of several distinct parts. The control unit is responsible for fetching instructions from main memory and determining their type. The arithmetic logic unit performs operations such as addition and Boolean AND needed to carry out the instructions.

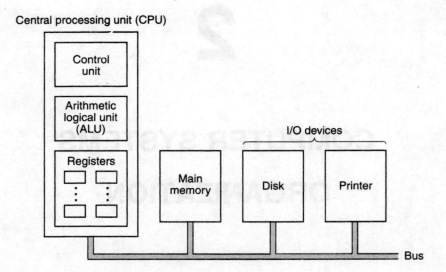

Figure 2-1. The organization of a simple computer with one CPU and two I/O devices.

The CPU also contains a small, high-speed memory used to store temporary results and certain control information. This memory is made up of a number of registers, each of which has a certain size and function. Usually, all the registers have the same size. Each register can hold one number, up to some maximum determined by the size of the register. Registers can be read and written at high speed since they are internal to the CPU.

The most important register is the **Program Counter** (**PC**), which points to the next instruction to be fetched for execution. (The name "program counter" is somewhat misleading because it has nothing to do with *counting* anything, but the term is universally used. Also important is the **Instruction Register** (**IR**), which holds the instruction currently being executed. (Most computers have numerous other registers as well, some of them general purpose as well as some for specific purposes.

2.1.1 CPU Organization

The internal organization of part of a typical von Neumann CPU is shown in Fig. 2-2 in more detail. This part is called the **data path** and consists of the registers (typically 1 to 32), the **ALU** (**Arithmetic Logic Unit**), and several buses connecting the pieces. The registers feed into two ALU input registers, labeled *A* and *B* in the figure. These registers hold the ALU input while the ALU is performing some computation. The data path is very important in all machines and we will discuss it at great length throughout this book.

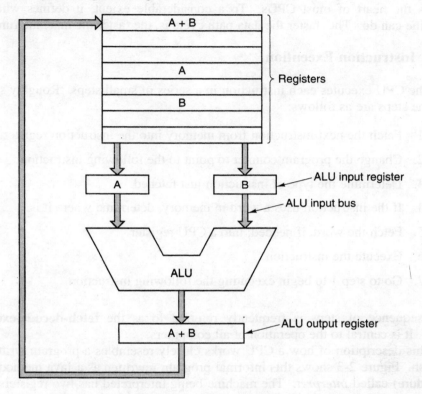

Figure 2-2. The data path of a typical von Neumann machine.

The ALU itself performs addition, subtraction, and other simple operations on its inputs, thus yielding a result in the output register. This output register can be stored back into a register. Later on, the register can be written (i.e., stored) into memory, if desired. Not all designs have the *A*, *B*, and output registers. In the example, addition is illustrated.

Most instructions can be divided into one of two categories: register-memory or register-register. Register-memory instructions allow memory words to be fetched into registers, where they can be used as ALU inputs in subsequent instructions, for example. ("Words" are the units of data moved between memory and registers. A word might be an integer. We will discuss memory organization later in this chapter.) Other register-memory instructions allow registers to be stored back into memory.

The other kind of instruction is register-register. A typical register-register instruction fetches two operands from the registers, brings them to the ALU input registers, performs some operation on them, for example, addition or Boolean

AND, and stores the result back in one of the registers. The process of running two operands through the ALU and storing the result is called the **data path cycle** and is the heart of most CPUs. To a considerable extent, it defines what the machine can do. The faster the data path cycle is, the faster the machine runs.

2.1.2 Instruction Execution

The CPU executes each instruction in a series of small steps. Roughly speaking, the steps are as follows:

1. Fetch the next instruction from memory into the instruction register.

2. Change the program counter to point to the following instruction.

3. Determine the type of instruction just fetched.

4. If the instruction uses a word in memory, determine where it is.

5. Fetch the word, if needed, into a CPU register.

6. Execute the instruction.

7. Go to step 1 to begin executing the following instruction.

This sequence of steps is frequently referred to as the **fetch-decode-execute** cycle. It is central to the operation of all computers.

This description of how a CPU works closely resembles a program written in English. Figure 2-3 shows this informal program rewritten as a Java method (i.e., procedure) called *interpret*. The machine being interpreted has two registers visible to user programs: the program counter (PC), for keeping track of the address of the next instruction to be fetched, and the accumulator (AC), for accumulating arithmetic results. It also has internal registers for holding the current instruction during its execution (instr), the type of the current instruction (instr_type), the address of the instruction's operand (data_loc), and the current operand itself (data). Instructions are assumed to contain a single memory address. The memory location addressed contains the operand, for example, the data item to add to the accumulator.

The very fact that it is possible to write a program that can imitate the function of a CPU shows that a program need not be executed by a "hardware" CPU consisting of a box full of electronics. Instead, a program can be carried out by having another program fetch, examine, and execute its instructions. A program (such as the one in Fig. 2-3) that fetches, examines, and executes the instructions of another program is called an **interpreter**, as mentioned in Chap. 1.

This equivalence between hardware processors and interpreters has important implications for computer organization and the design of computer systems. After having specified the machine language, L, for a new computer, the design team

```
public class Interp {
    static int PC;                    // program counter holds address of next instr
    static int AC;                    // the accumulator, a register for doing arithmetic
    static int instr;                 // a holding register for the current instruction
    static int instr_type;            // the instruction type (opcode)
    static int data_loc;              // the address of the data, or -1 if none
    static int data;                  // holds the current operand
    static boolean run_bit = true;    // a bit that can be turned off to halt the machine

    public static void interpret(int memory[ ], int starting_address) {
        // This procedure interprets programs for a simple machine with instructions having
        // one memory operand. The machine has a register AC (accumulator), used for
        // arithmetic. The ADD instruction adds an integer in memory to the AC, for example.
        // The interpreter keeps running until the run bit is turned off by the HALT instruction.
        // The state of a process running on this machine consists of the memory, the
        // program counter, the run bit, and the AC. The input parameters consist of
        // of the memory image and the starting address.

        PC = starting_address;
        while (run_bit) {
            instr = memory[PC];                   // fetch next instruction into instr
            PC = PC + 1;                          // increment program counter
            instr_type = get_instr_type(instr);   // determine instruction type
            data_loc = find_data(instr, instr_type);  // locate data (-1 if none)
            if (data_loc >= 0)                    // if data_loc is -1, there is no operand
                data = memory[data_loc];          // fetch the data
            execute(instr_type, data);            // execute instruction
        }

    }

    private static int get_instr_type(int addr) { ... }
    private static int find_data(int instr, int type) { ... }
    private static void execute(int type, int data) { ... }
}
```

Figure 2-3. An interpreter for a simple computer (written in Java).

can decide whether they want to build a hardware processor to execute programs in *L* directly or whether they want to write an interpreter to interpret programs in *L* instead. If they choose to write an interpreter, they must also provide some hardware machine to run the interpreter. Certain hybrid constructions are also possible, with some hardware execution as well as some software interpretation.

An interpreter breaks the instructions of its target machine into small steps. As a consequence, the machine on which the interpreter runs can be much simpler and less expensive than a hardware processor for the target machine would be. This saving is especially significant if the target machine has a large number of instructions and the instructions are fairly complicated, with many options. The saving comes essentially from the fact that hardware is being replaced by software (the interpreter) and it costs more to replicate hardware than software.

Early computers had small, simple sets of instructions. But the quest for more powerful computers led, among other things, to more powerful individual instructions. Very early on, it was discovered that more complex instructions often led to faster program execution even though individual instructions might take longer to execute. A floating-point instruction is an example of a more complex instruction. Direct support for accessing array elements is another. Sometimes it was as simple as observing that the same two instructions often occurred consecutively, so a single instruction could accomplish the work of both.

The more complex instructions were better because the execution of individual operations could sometimes be overlapped or otherwise executed in parallel using different hardware. For expensive, high-performance computers, the cost of this extra hardware could be readily justified. Thus expensive, high-performance computers came to have many more instructions than lower-cost ones. However, the rising cost of software development and instruction compatibility requirements created the need to implement complex instructions even on low-cost computers where cost was more important than speed.

By the late 1950s, IBM (then the dominant computer company) had recognized that supporting a single family of machines, all of which executed the same instructions, had many advantages, both for IBM and for its customers. IBM introduced the term **architecture** to describe this level of compatibility. A new family of computers would have one architecture but many different implementations that could all execute the same program, differing only in price and speed. But how to build a low-cost computer that could execute all the complicated instructions of high-performance, expensive machines?

The answer lay in interpretation. This technique, first suggested by Wilkes (1951), permitted the design of simple, lower-cost computers that could nevertheless execute a large number of instructions. The result was the IBM System/360 architecture, a compatible family of computers, spanning nearly two orders of magnitude, both in price and capability. A direct hardware (i.e., not interpreted) implementation was used only on the most expensive models.

Simple computers with interpreted instructions also had other benefits. Among the most important were

1. The ability to fix incorrectly implemented instructions in the field, or even make up for design deficiencies in the basic hardware.

2. The opportunity to add new instructions at minimal cost, even after delivery of the machine.

3. Structured design that permitted efficient development, testing, and documenting of complex instructions.

As the market for computers exploded dramatically in the 1970s and computing capabilities grew rapidly, the demand for low-cost computers favored designs of computers using interpreters. The ability to tailor the hardware and the interpreter for a particular set of instructions emerged as a highly cost-effective design for processors. As the underlying semiconductor technology advanced rapidly, the advantages of the cost outweighed the opportunities for higher performance, and interpreter-based architectures became the conventional way to design computers. Nearly all new computers designed in the 1970s, from minicomputers to mainframes, were based on interpretation.

By the late 70s, the use of simple processors running interpreters had become very widespread except among the most expensive, highest-performance models, such as the Cray-1 and the Control Data Cyber series. The use of an interpreter eliminated the inherent cost limitations of complex instructions, and architectures began to explore much more complex instructions, particularly the ways to specify the operands to be used.

This trend reached its zenith with Digital Equipment Corporation's VAX computer, which had several hundred instructions, and more than 200 different ways of specifying the operands to be used in each instruction. Unfortunately, the VAX architecture was conceived from the beginning to be implemented with an interpreter, with little thought given to the implementation of a high-performance model. This mind set resulted in the inclusion of a very large number of instructions of marginal value and which were difficult to execute directly. This omission proved to be fatal to the VAX, and ultimately to DEC as well (Compaq bought DEC in 1998 and Hewlett-Packard bought Compaq in 2001).

Though the earliest 8-bit microprocessors were very simple machines with very simple instruction sets, by the late 70s, even microprocessors had switched to interpreter-based designs. During this period, one of the major challenges facing microprocessor designers was dealing with the growing complexity possible through integrated circuits. A major advantage of the interpreter-based approach was the ability to design a simple processor, with the complexity largely confined to the memory holding the interpreter. Thus a complex hardware design could be turned into a complex software design.

The success of the Motorola 68000, which had a large interpreted instruction set, and the concurrent failure of the Zilog Z8000 (which had an equally large instruction set, but without an interpreter) demonstrated the advantages of an interpreter for bringing a new microprocessor to market quickly. This success was all the more surprising given Zilog's head start (the Z8000's predecessor, the Z80, was far more popular than the 68000's predecessor, the 6800). Of course, other factors were instrumental here too, not the least of which was Motorola's long history as a chip manufacturer and Exxon's (Zilog's owner) long history of being an oil company, not a chip manufacturer.

Another factor working in favor of interpretation during that era was the existence of fast read-only memories, called **control stores**, to hold the interpreters. Suppose that a typical interpreted instruction took the interpreter 10 instructions, called **microinstructions**, at 100 nsec each, and two references to main memory, at 500 nsec each. Total execution time was then 2000 nsec, only a factor of two worse than the best that direct execution could achieve. Had the control store not been available, the instruction would have taken 6000 nsec. A factor of six penalty is a lot harder to swallow than a factor of two penalty.

2.1.3 RISC versus CISC

During the late 70s there was experimentation with very complex instructions, made possible by the interpreter. Designers tried to close the "semantic gap" between what machines could do and what high-level programming languages required. Hardly anyone thought about designing simpler machines, just as now not a lot of research goes into designing less powerful operating systems, networks, word processors, etc. (perhaps unfortunately).

One group that bucked the trend and tried to incorporate some of Seymour Cray's ideas in a high-performance minicomputer was led by John Cocke at IBM. This work led to an experimental minicomputer, named the **801**, Although IBM never marketed this machine and the results were not published until years later (Radin, 1982), word got out and other people began investigating similar architectures.

In 1980, a group at Berkeley led by David Patterson and Carlo Séquin began designing VLSI CPU chips that did not use interpretation (Patterson, 1985; Patterson and Séquin, 1982). They coined the term **RISC** for this concept and named their CPU chip the RISC I CPU followed shortly by the RISC II. Slightly later, in 1981, across the San Francisco Bay at Stanford, John Hennessy designed and fabricated a somewhat different chip he called the **MIPS** (Hennessy, 1984). These chips evolved into commercially important products, the SPARC and the MIPS, respectively.

These new processors were significantly different than commercial processors of the day. Since these new CPUs did not have to be backward compatible with existing products, their designers were free to choose new instruction sets that would maximize total system performance. While the initial emphasis was on simple instructions that could be executed quickly, it was soon realized that designing instructions that could be **issued** (started) quickly was the key to good performance. How long an instruction actually took mattered less than how many could be started per second.

At the time these simple processors were being first designed, the characteristic that caught everyone's attention was the relatively small number of instructions available, typically around 50. This number was far smaller than the 200 to 300 on established computers such as the DEC VAX and the large IBM mainframes. In fact, the acronym RISC stands for **Reduced Instruction Set Computer**, which was contrasted with CISC, which stands for **Complex Instruction Set Computer** (a thinly-veiled reference to the VAX, which dominated university

Computer Science Departments at the time). Nowadays, few people think that the size of the instruction set is a major issue, but the name stuck.

To make a long story short, a great religious war ensued, with the RISC supporters attacking the established order (VAX, Intel, large IBM mainframes). They claimed that the best way to design a computer was to have a small number of simple instructions that execute in one cycle of the data path of Figure 2-2, namely, fetching two registers, combining them somehow (e.g., adding or ANDing them), and storing the result back in a register. Their argument was that even if a RISC machine takes four or five instructions to do what a CISC machine does in one instruction, if the RISC instructions are 10 times as fast (because they are not interpreted), RISC wins. It is also worth pointing out that by this time the speed of main memories had caught up to the speed of read-only control stores, so the interpretation penalty had greatly increased, strongly favoring RISC machines.

One might think that given the performance advantages of RISC technology, RISC machines (such as the Sun UltraSPARC) would have mowed over CISC machines (such as the Intel Pentium) in the marketplace. Nothing like this has happened. Why not?

First of all, there is the issue of backward compatibility and the billions of dollars companies have invested in software for the Intel line. Second, surprisingly, Intel has been able to employ the same ideas even in a CISC architecture. Starting with the 486, the Intel CPUs contain a RISC core that executes the simplest (and typically most common) instructions in a single data path cycle, while interpreting the more complicated instructions in the usual CISC way. The net result is that common instructions are fast and less common instructions are slow. While this hybrid approach is not as fast as a pure RISC design, it gives competitive overall performance while still allowing old software to run unmodified.

2.1.4 Design Principles for Modern Computers

Now that more than two decades have passed since the first RISC machines were introduced, certain design principles have come to be accepted as a good way to design computers given the current state of the hardware technology. If a major change in technology occurs (e.g., a new manufacturing process suddenly makes memory cycle time 10 times faster than CPU cycle time), all bets are off. Thus machine designers should always keep an eye out for technological changes that may affect the balance among the components.

That said, there is a set of design principles, sometimes called the **RISC design principles**, that architects of general-purpose CPUs do their best to follow. External constraints, such as the requirement of being backward compatible with some existing architecture, often require compromises from time to time, but these principles are goals that most designers strive to meet. Below we will discuss the major ones.

All Instructions Are Directly Executed by Hardware

All common instructions are directly executed by the hardware. They are not interpreted by microinstructions. Eliminating a level of interpretation provides high speed for most instructions. For computers that implement CISC instruction sets, the more complex instructions may be broken into separate parts, which can then be executed as a sequence of microinstructions. This extra step slows the machine down, but for less frequently occurring instructions it may be acceptable.

Maximize the Rate at Which Instructions Are Issued

Modern computers resort to many tricks to maximize their performance, chief among which is trying to start as many instructions per second as possible. After all, if you can issue 500 million instructions/sec, you have built a 500-MIPS processor, no matter how long the instructions actually take to complete. (**MIPS** stands for Millions of Instructions Per Second; the MIPS processor was so-named as to be a pun on this acronym.) This principle suggests that parallelism can play a major role in improving performance, since issuing large numbers of slow instructions in a short time interval is only possible if multiple instructions can execute at once.

Although instructions are always encountered in program order, they are not always issued in program order (because some needed resource might be busy) and they need not finish in program order. Of course, if instruction 1 sets a register and instruction 2 uses that register, great care must be taken to make sure that instruction 2 does not read the register until it contains the correct value. Getting this right requires a lot of bookkeeping but has the potential for performance gains by executing multiple instructions at once.

Instructions Should be Easy to Decode

A critical limit on the rate of issue of instructions is decoding individual instructions to determine what resources they need. Anything that can aid this process is useful. That includes making instructions regular, fixed length, with a small number of fields. The fewer different formats for instructions, the better.

Only Loads and Stores Should Reference Memory

One of the simplest ways to break operations into separate steps is to require that operands for most instructions come from—and return to—CPU registers. The operation of moving operands from memory into registers can be performed in separate instructions. Since access to memory can take a long time, and the delay is unpredictable, these instructions can best be overlapped with other instructions if they do nothing but move operands between registers and memory. This observation means that only LOAD and STORE instructions should reference memory. All other instructions should operate only on registers.

Provide Plenty of Registers

Since accessing memory is relatively slow, many registers (at least 32) need to be provided, so that once a word is fetched, it can be kept in a register until it is no longer needed. Running out of registers and having to flush them back to memory only to later reload them is undesirable and should be avoided as much as possible. The best way to accomplish this is to have enough registers.

2.1.5 Instruction-Level Parallelism

Computer architects are constantly striving to improve performance of the machines they design. Making the chips run faster by increasing their clock speed is one way, but for every new design, there is a limit to what is possible by brute force at that moment in history. Consequently, most computer architects look to parallelism (doing two or more things at once) as a way to get even more performance for a given clock speed.

Parallelism comes in two general forms, namely, instruction-level parallelism and processor-level parallelism. In the former, parallelism is exploited within individual instructions to get more instructions/sec out of the machine. In the latter, multiple CPUs work together on the same problem. Each approach has its own merits. In this section we will look at instruction-level parallelism; in the one after it, we will look at processor-level parallelism.

Pipelining

It has been known for years that the actual fetching of instructions from memory is a major bottleneck in instruction execution speed. To alleviate this problem, computers going back at least as far as the IBM Stretch (1959) have had the ability to fetch instructions from memory in advance, so they would be there when they were needed. These instructions were stored in a set of registers called the **prefetch buffer**. This way, when an instruction was needed, it could usually be taken from the prefetch buffer rather than waiting for a memory read to complete.

In effect, prefetching divides instruction execution up into two parts: fetching and actual execution. The concept of a **pipeline** carries this strategy much further. Instead of dividing instruction execution into only two parts, it is often divided into many (often a dozen or more) parts, each one handled by a dedicated piece of hardware, all of which can run in parallel.

Figure 2-4(a) illustrates a pipeline with five units, also called **stages**. Stage 1 fetches the instruction from memory and places it in a buffer until it is needed. Stage 2 decodes the instruction, determining its type and what operands it needs. Stage 3 locates and fetches the operands, either from registers or from memory. Stage 4 actually does the work of carrying out the instruction, typically by running the operands through the data path of Figure 2-2. Finally, stage 5 writes the result back to the proper register.

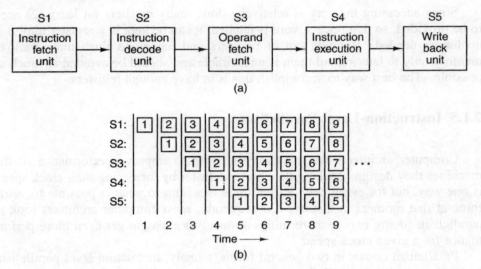

Figure 2-4. (a) A five-stage pipeline. (b) The state of each stage as a function of time. Nine clock cycles are illustrated.

In Fig. 2-4(b) we see how the pipeline operates as a function of time. During clock cycle 1, stage S1 is working on instruction 1, fetching it from memory. During cycle 2, stage S2 decodes instruction 1, while stage S1 fetches instruction 2. During cycle 3, stage S3 fetches the operands for instruction 1, stage S2 decodes instruction 2, and stage S1 fetches the third instruction. During cycle 4, stage S4 executes instruction 1, S3 fetches the operands for instruction 2, S2 decodes instruction 3, and S1 fetches instruction 4. Finally, during cycle 5, S5 writes the result of instruction 1 back, while the other stages work on the following instructions.

Let us consider an analogy to make the concept of pipelining clearer. Imagine a cake factory in which the baking of the cakes and the packaging of the cakes for shipment are separated. Suppose that the shipping department has a long conveyor belt with five workers (processing units) lined up along it. Every 10 sec (the clock cycle), worker 1 places an empty cake box on the belt. The box is carried down to worker 2, who places a cake in it. A little later, the box arrives at worker 3's station, where it is closed and sealed. Then it continues to worker 4, who puts a label on the box. Finally, worker 5 removes the box from the belt and puts it in a large container for later shipment to a supermarket. Basically, this is the way computer pipelining works too: each instruction (cake) goes through several processing steps before emerging completed at the far end.

Getting back to our pipeline of Fig. 2-4, suppose that the cycle time of this machine is 2 nsec. Then it takes 10 nsec for an instruction to progress all the way through the five-stage pipeline. At first glance, with an instruction taking 10 nsec, it might appear that the machine can run at 100 MIPS, but in fact it does much better than this. At every clock cycle (2 nsec), one new instruction is completed, so the actual rate of processing is 500 MIPS, not 100 MIPS.

Pipelining allows a trade-off between **latency** (how long it takes to execute an instruction), and **processor bandwidth** (how many MIPS the CPU has). With a cycle time of T nsec, and n stages in the pipeline, the latency is nT nsec because each instruction passes through n stages, each of which takes T nsec.

Since one instruction completes every clock cycle and there are $10^9/T$ clock cycles/second, the number of instructions executed per second is $10^9/T$. For example, if $T = 2$ nsec, 500 million instructions are executed each seconds. To get the number of MIPS, we have to divide the instruction execution rate by 1 million to get $(10^9/T)/10^6 = 1000/T$ MIPS. Theoretically, we could measure instruction execution rate in BIPS instead of MIPS, but nobody does that so we will not either.

Superscalar Architectures

If one pipeline is good, then surely two pipelines are better. One possible design for a dual pipeline CPU, based on Figure 2-4, is shown in Fig. 2-5. Here a single instruction fetch unit fetches pairs of instructions together and puts each one into its own pipeline, complete with its own ALU for parallel operation. To be able to run in parallel, the two instructions must not conflict over resource usage (e.g., registers), and neither must depend on the result of the other. As with a single pipeline, either the compiler must guarantee this situation to hold (i.e., the hardware does not check and gives incorrect results if the instructions are not compatible), or conflicts are detected and eliminated during execution using extra hardware.

Although pipelines, single or double, are mostly used on RISC machines (the 386 and its predecessors did not have any), starting with the 486 Intel began introducing data pipelines into its CPUs. The 486 had one pipeline and the original Pentium had two five-stage pipelines roughly as in Fig. 2-5, although the exact division of work between stages 2 and 3 (called decode-1 and decode-2) was slightly different than in our example. The main pipeline, called the **u pipeline**, could execute an arbitrary Pentium instruction. The second pipeline, called the **v pipeline**, could execute only simple integer instructions (and also one simple floating-point instruction—FXCH).

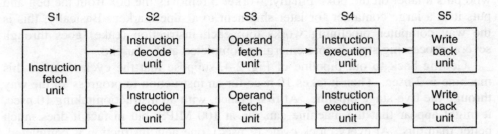

Figure 2-5. Dual five-stage pipelines with a common instruction fetch unit.

Fixed rules determined whether a pair of instructions were compatible so they could be executed in parallel. If the instructions in a pair were not simple enough or incompatible, only the first one was executed (in the u pipeline). The second one was then held and paired with the instruction following it. Instructions were always executed in order. Thus Pentium-specific compilers that produced compatible pairs could produce faster-running programs than older compilers. Measurements showed that a Pentium running code optimized for it was exactly twice as fast on integer programs as a 486 running at the same clock rate (Pountain, 1993). This gain could be attributed entirely to the second pipeline.

Going to four pipelines is conceivable, but doing so duplicates too much hardware (computer scientists, unlike folklore specialists, do not believe in the number three). Instead, a different approach is used on high-end CPUs. The basic idea is to have just a single pipeline but give it multiple functional units, as shown in Fig. 2-6. For example, the Pentium II has a structure similar to this figure. It will be discussed in Chap. 4. The term **superscalar architecture** was coined for this approach in 1987 (Agerwala and Cocke, 1987). Its roots, however, go back more than 40 years to the CDC 6600 computer. The 6600 fetched an instruction every 100 nsec and passed it off to one of 10 functional units for parallel execution while the CPU went off to get the next instruction.

The definition of "superscalar" has evolved somewhat over time. It is now used to describe processors that issue multiple instructions—often four or six—in a single clock cycle. Of course, a superscalar CPU must have multiple functional units to hand all these instructions to. Since superscalar processors generally have one pipeline, they tend to look like Fig. 2-6.

Using this definition, the 6600 was technically not superscalar because it issued only one instruction per cycle. However, the effect was almost the same: instructions were issued at a much higher rate than they could be executed. The difference between a CPU with a 100 nsec clock that issues one instruction every cycle to a group of functional units and a CPU with a 400 nsec clock that issues four instructions per cycle to the same group of functional units is very small. In both cases, the key idea is that the issue rate is much higher than the execution rate, with the workload being spread across a collection of functional units.

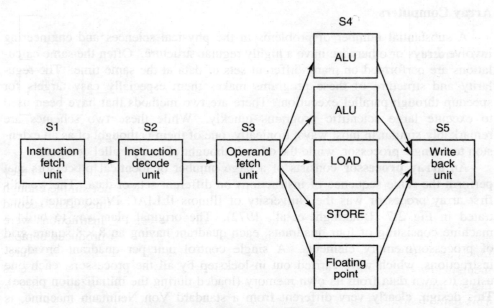

Figure 2-6. A superscalar processor with five functional units.

Implicit in the idea of a superscalar processor is that the S3 stage can issue instructions considerably faster than the S4 stage is able to execute them. If the S3 stage issued an instruction every 10 nsec and all the functional units could do their work in 10 nsec, no more than one would ever be busy at once, negating the whole idea. In reality, most of the functional units in stage 4 take appreciably longer than one clock cycle to execute, certainly the ones that access memory or do floating-point arithmetic. As can be seen from the figure, it is possible to have multiple ALUs in stage S4.

2.1.6 Processor-Level Parallelism

The demand for ever faster computers seems to be insatiable. Astronomers want to simulate what happened in the first microsecond after the big bang, economists want to model the world economy, and teenagers want to play 3D interactive multimedia games over the Internet with their virtual friends. While CPUs keep getting faster, eventually they are going to run into the problems with the speed of light, which is likely to stay at 20 cm/nanosecond in copper wire or optical fiber, no matter how clever Intel's engineers are. Faster chips also produce more heat, whose dissipation is a problem.

Instruction-level parallelism helps a little, but pipelining and superscalar operation rarely win more than a factor of five or ten. To get gains of 50, 100, or more, the only way is to design computers with multiple CPUs, so we will now take a look at how some of these are organized.

Array Computers

A substantial number of problems in the physical sciences and engineering involve arrays or otherwise have a highly regular structure. Often the same calculations are performed on many different sets of data at the same time. The regularity and structure of these programs makes them especially easy targets for speedup through parallel execution. There are two methods that have been used to execute large scientific programs quickly. While these two schemes are remarkably similar in most ways, ironically, one of them is thought of as an extension to a single processor, while the other is thought of as a parallel computer.

An **array processor** consists of a large number of identical processors that perform the same sequence of instructions on different sets of data. The world's first array processor was the University of Illinois ILLIAC IV computer, illustrated in Fig. 2-7 (Bouknight et al., 1972). The original plan was to build a machine consisting of four quadrants, each quadrant having an 8×8 square grid of processor/memory elements. A single control unit per quadrant broadcast instructions, which were carried out in lockstep by all the processors, each one using its own data from its own memory (loaded during the initialization phase). This design, clearly very different from a standard Von Neumann machine, is sometimes referred to as a **SIMD (Single Instruction-stream Multiple Data-stream)** processor. Due to a cost overrun by a factor of four, only one quadrant was ever built, but it did achieve a performance of 50 megaflops (million floating-point operations per second). It is said that had the entire machine been completed and had it achieved its original performance goal (1 gigaflop), it would have doubled the computing power of the entire world.

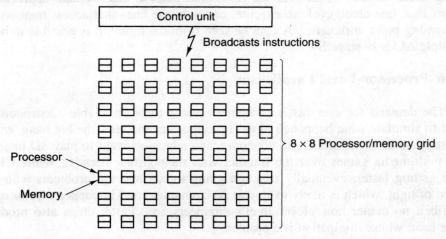

Figure 2-7. An array processor of the ILLIAC IV type.

A **vector processor** appears to the programmer very much like an array processor. Like an array processor, it is very efficient at executing a sequence of operations on pairs of data elements. But unlike an array processor, all of the addition operations are performed in a single, heavily-pipelined adder. The company Seymour Cray founded, Cray Research, produced many vector processors, starting with the Cray-1 back in 1974 and continuing through current models (Cray Research is now part of SGI).

Both array processors and vector processors work on arrays of data. Both execute single instructions that, for example, add the elements together pairwise for two vectors. But while the array processor does it by having as many adders as elements in the vector, the vector processor has the concept of a **vector register**, which consists of a set of conventional registers that can be loaded from memory in a single instruction, which actually loads them from memory serially. Then a vector addition instruction performs the pairwise addition of the elements of two such vectors by feeding them to a pipelined adder from the two vector registers. The result from the adder is another vector, which can either be stored into a vector register, or used directly as an operand for another vector operation.

While no array processors are currently in production, the idea is far from dead. The MMX and SSE instructions available on the Pentium 4 use this execution model to speed up multimedia software. In this respect, the Pentium 4 has the ILLIAC IV as one of its ancestors.

Multiprocessors

The processing elements in an array processor are not independent CPUs, since there is only one control unit shared among all of them. Our first parallel system with multiple full-blown CPUs is the **multiprocessor**, a system with more than one CPU sharing a common memory, like a group of people in a room sharing a common blackboard. Since each CPU can read or write any part of memory, they must co-ordinate (in software) to avoid getting in each other's way. When two or more CPUs have the ability to interact closely, as is the case with multiprocessors, they are said to be tightly coupled.

Various implementation schemes are possible. The simplest one is to have single bus with multiple CPUs and one memory all plugged into it. A diagram such a bus-based multiprocessor is shown in Fig. 2-8(a).

It does not take much imagination to realize that with a large number processors constantly trying to access memory over the same bus, contention result. Multiprocessor designers have come up with various schemes this contention and improve performance. One design, shown in gives each processor some local memory of its own, not accessible to This memory can be used for program code and those data items that shared. Access to this private memory does not use the main bus ing bus traffic. Other schemes (e.g., caching) are also possible.

Multiprocessors have the advantage over other kinds of parallel that the programming model of a single shared memory is an

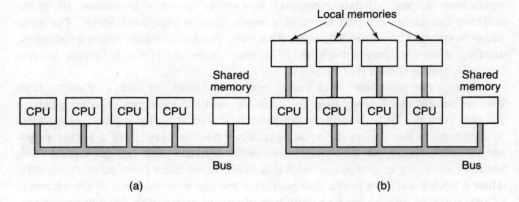

Figure 2-8. (a) A single-bus multiprocessor. (b) A multicomputer with local memories.

with. For example, imagine a program looking for cancer cells in a photograph of some tissue taken through a microscope. The digitized photograph could be kept in the common memory, with each processor assigned some region of the photograph to hunt in. Since each processor has access to the entire memory, studying a cell that starts in its assigned region but straddles the boundary into the next region is no problem.

Multicomputers

Although multiprocessors with a modest number of processors (≤ 256) are relatively easy to build, large ones are surprisingly difficult to construct. The difficulty is in connecting all the processors to the memory. To get around these problems, many designers have simply abandoned the idea of having a shared memory and just build systems consisting of large numbers of interconnected computers, each having its own private memory, but no common memory. These systems are called **multicomputers**. The CPUs in a multicomputer are sometimes said to be loosely coupled, to contrast them with the tightly-coupled CPUs in a multiprocessor.

The CPUs in a multicomputer communicate by sending each other messages, something like e-mail, but much faster. For large systems, having every computer connected to every other computer is impractical, so topologies such as 2D and 3D grids, trees, and rings are used. As a result, messages from one computer to another often must pass through one or more intermediate computers or switches to get from the source to the destination. Nevertheless, message-passing times on the order of a few microseconds can be achieved without much difficulty. Multicomputers with nearly 10,000 CPUs have been built and put into operation.

Since multiprocessors are easier to program and multicomputers are easier to build, there is much research on designing hybrid systems that combine the good properties of each. Such computers try to present the illusion of shared memory, without going to the expense of actually constructing it. We will go into multiprocessors and multicomputers in detail in Chap. 8.

2.2 PRIMARY MEMORY

The **memory** is that part of the computer where programs and data are stored. Some computer scientists (especially British ones) use the term **store** or **storage** rather than memory, although more and more, the term "storage" is used to refer to disk storage. Without a memory from which the processors can read and write information, there would be no stored-program digital computers.

2.2.1 Bits

The basic unit of memory is the binary digit, called a **bit**. A bit may contain a 0 or a 1. It is the simplest possible unit. (A device capable of storing only zeros could hardly form the basis of a memory system; at least two values are needed.)

People often say that computers use binary arithmetic because it is "efficient." What they mean (although they rarely realize it) is that digital information can be stored by distinguishing between different values of some continuous physical quantity, such as voltage or current. The more values that must be distinguished, the less separation between adjacent values, and the less reliable the memory. The binary number system requires only two values to be distinguished. Consequently, it is the most reliable method for encoding digital information. If you are not familiar with binary numbers, see Appendix A.

Some computers, such as the large IBM mainframes, are advertised as having decimal as well as binary arithmetic. This trick is accomplished by using 4 bits to store one decimal digit using a code called **BCD** (**Binary Coded Decimal**). Four bits provide 16 combinations, used for the 10 digits 0 through 9, with six combinations not used. The number 1944 is shown below encoded in decimal and in pure binary, using 16 bits in each example:

decimal: 0001 1001 0100 0100   binary: 0000011110011000

Sixteen bits in the decimal format can store the numbers from 0 to 9999, giving only 10,000 combinations, whereas a 16-bit pure binary number can store 65,536 different combinations. For this reason, people say that binary is more efficient.

However, consider what would happen if some brilliant young electrical engineer invented a highly reliable electronic device that could directly store the digits 0 to 9 by dividing the region from 0 to 10 volts into 10 intervals. Four of these devices could store any decimal number from 0 to 9999. Four such devices would provide 10,000 combinations. They could also be used to store binary numbers, by only using 0 and 1, in which case, four of them could only store 16 combinations. With such devices, the decimal system is obviously more efficient.

2.2.2 Memory Addresses

Memories consist of a number of **cells** (or **locations**) each of which can store a piece of information. Each cell has a number, called its **address**, by which programs can refer to it. If a memory has n cells, they will have addresses 0 to $n - 1$. All cells in a memory contain the same number of bits. If a cell consists of k bits, it can hold any one of 2^k different bit combinations. Figure 2-9 shows three different organizations for a 96-bit memory. Note that adjacent cells have consecutive addresses (by definition).

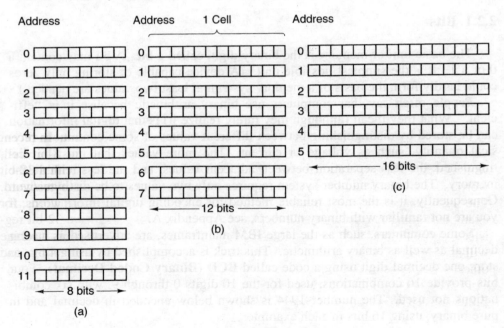

Figure 2-9. Three ways of organizing a 96-bit memory.

Computers that use the binary number system (including octal and hexadecimal notation for binary numbers) express memory addresses as binary numbers. If an address has m bits, the maximum number of cells addressable is 2^m. For example, an address used to reference the memory of Fig. 2-9(a) needs at least 4 bits in order to express all the numbers from 0 to 11. A 3-bit address is sufficient for Fig. 2-9(b) and (c), however. The number of bits in the address determines the maximum number of directly addressable cells in the memory and is independent of the number of bits per cell. A memory with 2^{12} cells of 8 bits each and a memory with 2^{12} cells of 64 bits each need 12-bit addresses.

The number of bits per cell for some computers that have been sold commercially is listed in Fig. 2-10.

Computer	Bits/cell
Burroughs B1700	1
IBM PC	8
DEC PDP-8	12
IBM 1130	16
DEC PDP-15	18
XDS 940	24
Electrologica X8	27
XDS Sigma 9	32
Honeywell 6180	36
CDC 3600	48
CDC Cyber	60

Figure 2-10. Number of bits per cell for some historically interesting commercial computers.

The significance of the cell is that it is the smallest addressable unit. In recent years, nearly all computer manufacturers have standardized on an 8-bit cell, which is called a **byte**. Bytes are grouped into **words**. A computer with a 32-bit word has 4 bytes/word, whereas a computer with a 64-bit word has 8 bytes/word. The significance of a word is that most instructions operate on entire words, for example, adding two words together. Thus a 32-bit machine will have 32-bit registers and instructions for manipulating 32-bit words, whereas a 64-bit machine will have 64-bit registers and instructions for moving, adding, subtracting, and otherwise manipulating 64-bit words.

2.2.3 Byte Ordering

The bytes in a word can be numbered from left-to-right or right-to-left. At first it might seem that this choice is unimportant, but as we shall see shortly, it has major implications. Figure 2-11(a) depicts part of the memory of a 32-bit computer whose bytes are numbered from left-to-right, such as the SPARC or the big IBM mainframes. Figure 2-11(b) gives the analogous representation of a 32-bit computer using right-to-left numbering, such as the Intel family. The former system, where the numbering begins at the "big" (i.e., high-order) end is called a **big endian** computer, in contrast to the **little endian** of Fig. 2-11(b). These terms are due to Jonathan Swift, whose *Gulliver's Travels* satirized politicians who made war over their dispute about whether eggs should be broken at the big end or the little end. The term was first used in computer architecture in a delightful article by Cohen (1981).

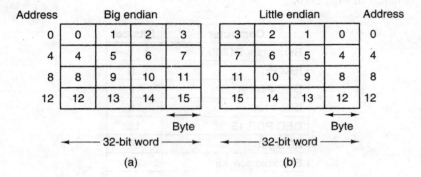

Figure 2-11. (a) Big endian memory. (b) Little endian memory.

It is important to understand that in both the big endian and little endian systems, a 32-bit integer with the numerical value of, say, 6, is represented by the bits 110 in the rightmost (low-order) 3 bits of a word and zeros in the leftmost 29 bits. In the big endian scheme, the 110 bits are in byte 3 (or 7, or 11, etc.), whereas in the little endian scheme they are in byte 0 (or 4, or 8, etc.). In both cases, the word containing this integer has address 0.

If computers only stored integers, there would not be any problem. However, many applications require a mixture of integers, character strings, and other data types. Consider, for example, a simple personnel record consisting of a string (employee name), and two integers (age and department number). The string is terminated with 1 or more 0 bytes to fill out a word. The big endian representation is shown in Fig. 2-12(a); the little endian representation is shown in Fig. 2-12(b) for Jim Smith, age 21, department 260 ($1 \times 256 + 4 = 260$).

Both of these representations are fine and internally consistent. The problems begin when one of the machines tries to send the record to the other one over a network. Let us assume that the big endian sends the record to the little endian one byte at a time, starting with byte 0 and ending with byte 19. (We will be optimistic and assume the bits of the bytes are not reversed by the transmission, as we have enough problems as is.) Thus the big endian's byte 0 goes into the little endian's memory at byte 0, and so on, as shown in Fig. 2-12(c).

When the little endian tries to print the name, it works fine, but the age comes out as 21×2^{24} and the department is just as garbled. This situation arises because the transmission has reversed the order of the characters in a word, as it should, but it has also reversed the bytes in an integer, which it should not.

An obvious solution is to have the software reverse the bytes within a word after the copy has been made. Doing this leads to Fig. 2-12(d) which makes the

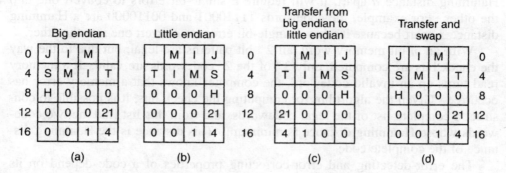

Figure 2-12. (a) A personnel record for a big endian machine. (b) The same record for a little endian machine. (c) The result of transferring the record from a big endian to a little endian. (d) The result of byte-swapping (c).

two integers fine but turns the string into "MIJTIMS" with the "H" hanging in the middle of nowhere. This reversal of the string occurs because when reading it, the computer first reads byte 0 (a space), then byte 1 (M), and so on.

There is no simple solution. One way that works, but is inefficient, is to include a header in front of each data item telling what kind of data follows (string, integer, or other) and how long it is. This allows the receiver to perform the necessary conversions only. In any event, it should be clear that the lack of a standard for byte ordering is a major nuisance when exchanging data between different machines.

2.2.4 Error-Correcting Codes

Computer memories can make errors occasionally due to voltage spikes on the power line or other causes. To guard against such errors, some memories use error-detecting or error-correcting codes. When these codes are used, extra bits are added to each memory word in a special way. When a word is read out of memory, the extra bits are checked to see if an error has occurred.

To understand how errors can be handled, it is necessary to look closely at what an error really is. Suppose that a memory word consists of m data bits to which we will add r redundant, or check bits. Let the total length be n (i.e., $n = m + r$). An n-bit unit containing m data and r check bits is often referred to as an n-bit **codeword**.

Given any two codewords, say, 10001001 and 10110001, it is possible to determine how many corresponding bits differ. In this case, 3 bits differ. To determine how many bits differ, just compute the bitwise Boolean EXCLUSIVE OR of the two codewords, and count the number of 1 bits in the result. The number of bit positions in which two codewords differ is called the **Hamming distance** (Hamming, 1950). Its main significance is that if two codewords are a

Hamming distance d apart, it will require d single-bit errors to convert one into the other. For example, the codewords 11110001 and 00110000 are a Hamming distance 3 apart because it takes 3 single-bit errors to convert one into the other.

With an m-bit memory word, all 2^m bit patterns are legal, but due to the way the check bits are computed, only 2^m of the 2^n codewords are valid. If a memory read turns up an invalid codeword, the computer knows that a memory error has occurred. Given the algorithm for computing the check bits, it is possible to construct a complete list of the legal codewords, and from this list find the two codewords whose Hamming distance is minimum. This distance is the Hamming distance of the complete code.

The error-detecting and error-correcting properties of a code depend on its Hamming distance. To detect d single-bit errors, you need a distance $d + 1$ code because with such a code there is no way that d single-bit errors can change a valid codeword into another valid codeword. Similarly, to correct d single-bit errors, you need a distance $2d + 1$ code because that way the legal codewords are so far apart that even with d changes, the original codeword is still closer than any other codeword, so it can be uniquely determined.

As a simple example of an error-detecting code, consider a code in which a single **parity bit** is appended to the data. The parity bit is chosen so that the number of 1 bits in the codeword is even (or odd). Such a code has a distance 2, since any single-bit error produces a codeword with the wrong parity. In other words, it takes two single-bit errors to go from a valid codeword to another valid codeword. It can be used to detect single errors. Whenever a word containing the wrong parity is read from memory, an error condition is signaled. The program cannot continue, but at least no incorrect results are computed.

As a simple example of an error-correcting code, consider a code with only four valid codewords:

> 0000000000, 0000011111, 1111100000, and 1111111111

This code has a distance 5, which means that it can correct double errors. If the codeword 0000000111 arrives, the receiver knows that the original must have been 0000011111 (if there was no more than a double error). If, however, a triple error changes 0000000000 into 0000000111, the error cannot be corrected.

Imagine that we want to design a code with m data bits and r check bits that will allow all single-bit errors to be corrected. Each of the 2^m legal memory words has n illegal codewords at a distance 1 from it. These are formed by systematically inverting each of the n bits in the n-bit codeword formed from it. Thus each of the 2^m legal memory words requires $n + 1$ bit patterns dedicated to it (for the n possible errors and correct pattern). Since the total number of bit patterns is 2^n we must have $(n + 1)2^m \leq 2^n$. Using $n = m + r$ this requirement becomes $(m + r + 1) \leq 2^r$. Given m, this puts a lower limit on the number of check bits needed to correct single errors. Figure 2-13 shows the number of check bits required for various memory word sizes.

Word size	Check bits	Total size	Percent overhead
8	4	12	50
16	5	21	31
32	6	38	19
64	7	71	11
128	8	136	6
256	9	265	4
512	10	522	2

Figure 2-13. Number of check bits for a code that can correct a single error.

This theoretical lower limit can be achieved using a method due to Richard Hamming (1950). Before taking a look at Hamming's algorithm, let us look at a simple graphical representation that clearly illustrates the idea of an error-correcting code for 4-bit words. The Venn diagram of Fig. 2-14(a) contains three circles, A, B, and C, which together form seven regions. As an example, let us encode the 4-bit memory word 1100 in the regions AB, ABC, AC, and BC, 1 bit per region (in alphabetical order). This encoding is shown in Fig. 2-14(a).

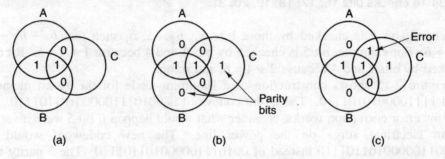

Figure 2-14. (a) Encoding of 1100. (b) Even parity added. (c) Error in AC.

Next we add a parity bit to each of the three empty regions to produce even parity, as illustrated in Fig. 2-14(b). By definition, the sum of the bits in each of the three circles, A, B, and C, is now an even number. In circle A, we have the four numbers 0, 0, 1, and 1, which add up to 2, an even number. In circle B, the numbers are 1, 1, 0, and 0, which also add up to 2, an even number. Finally, in circle C, we have the same thing. In this example all the circles happen to be the same, but sums of 0 and 4 are also possible in other examples. This figure corresponds to a codeword with 4 data bits and 3 parity bits.

Now suppose that the bit in the AC region goes bad, changing from a 0 to a 1, as shown in Fig. 2-14(c). The computer can now see that circles A and C have the wrong (odd) parity. The only single-bit change that corrects them is to restore AC

back to 0, thus correcting the error. In this way, the computer can repair single-bit memory errors automatically.

Now let us see how Hamming's algorithm can be used to construct error-correcting codes for any size memory word. In a Hamming code, r parity bits are added to an m-bit word, forming a new word of length $m + r$ bits. The bits are numbered starting at 1, not 0, with bit 1 the leftmost (high-order) bit. All bits whose bit number is a power of 2 are parity bits; the rest are used for data. For example, with a 16-bit word, 5 parity bits are added. Bits 1, 2, 4, 8, and 16 are parity bits, and all the rest are data bits. In all, the memory word has 21 bits (16 data, 5 parity). We will (arbitrarily) use even parity in this example.

Each parity bit checks specific bit positions; the parity bit is set so that the total number of 1s in the checked positions is even. The bit positions checked by the parity bits are

Bit   1 checks bits 1, 3, 5, 7, 9, 11, 13, 15, 17, 19, 21.

Bit   2 checks bits 2, 3, 6, 7, 10, 11, 14, 15, 18, 19.

Bit   4 checks bits 4, 5, 6, 7, 12, 13, 14, 15, 20, 21.

Bit   8 checks bits 8, 9, 10, 11, 12, 13, 14, 15.

Bit 16 checks bits 16, 17, 18, 19, 20, 21.

In general, bit b is checked by those bits $b_1, b_2, ..., b_j$ such that $b_1 + b_2 + ... + b_j = b$. For example, bit 5 is checked by bits 1 and 4 because $1 + 4 = 5$. Bit 6 is checked by bits 2 and 4 because $2 + 4 = 6$, and so on.

Figure 2-15 shows construction of a Hamming code for the 16-bit memory word 1111000010101110. The 21-bit codeword is 001011100000101101110. To see how error correction works, consider what would happen if bit 5 were inverted by an electrical surge on the power line. The new codeword would be 001001100000101101110 instead of 001011100000101101110. The 5 parity bits will be checked, with the following results:

Parity bit   1 incorrect (1, 3, 5, 7, 9, 11, 13, 15, 17, 19, 21 contain five 1s).

Parity bit   2 correct (2, 3, 6, 7, 10, 11, 14, 15, 18, 19 contain six 1s).

Parity bit   4 incorrect (4, 5, 6, 7, 12, 13, 14, 15, 20, 21 contain five 1s).

Parity bit   8 correct (8, 9, 10, 11, 12, 13, 14, 15 contain two 1s).

Parity bit 16 correct (16, 17, 18, 19, 20, 21 contain four 1s).

The total number of 1s in bits 1, 3, 5, 7, 9, 11, 13, 15, 17, 19, and 21 should be an even number because even parity is being used. The incorrect bit must be one of the bits checked by parity bit 1—namely, bit 1, 3, 5, 7, 9, 11, 13, 15, 17, 19, or 21. Parity bit 4 is incorrect, meaning that one of bits 4, 5, 6, 7, 12, 13, 14, 15, 20, or

21 is incorrect. The error must be one of the bits in both lists, namely, 5, 7, 13, 15, or 21. However, bit 2 is correct, eliminating 7 and 15. Similarly, bit 8 is correct, eliminating 13. Finally, bit 16 is correct, eliminating 21. The only bit left is bit 5, which is the one in error. Since it was read as a 1, it should be a 0. In this manner, errors can be corrected.

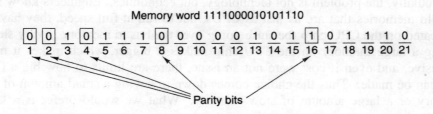

Figure 2-15. Construction of the Hamming code for the memory word 1111000010101110 by adding 5 check bits to the 16 data bits.

A simple method for finding the incorrect bit is first to compute all the parity bits. If all are correct, there was no error (or more than one). Then add up all the incorrect parity bits, counting 1 for bit 1, 2 for bit 2, 4 for bit 4, and so on. The resulting sum is the position of the incorrect bit. For example, if parity bits 1 and 4 are incorrect but 2, 8, and 16 are correct, bit 5 (1 + 4) has been inverted.

2.2.5 Cache Memory

Historically, CPUs have always been faster than memories. As memories have improved, so have CPUs, preserving the imbalance. In fact, as it becomes possible to put more and more circuits on a chip, CPU designers are using these new facilities for pipelining and superscalar operation, making CPUs go even faster. Memory designers have usually used new technology to increase the capacity of their chips, not the speed, so the problem appears to be getting worse in time. What this imbalance means in practice is that after the CPU issues a memory request, it will not get the word it needs for many CPU cycles. The slower the memory, the more cycles the CPU will have to wait.

As we pointed out above, there are two ways to deal with this problem. The simplest way is to just start memory READs when they are encountered but continue executing and stall the CPU if an instruction tries to use the memory word before it has arrived. The slower the memory, the more often this problem will occur and the greater the penalty when it does occur. For example, if the memory delay is 10 cycles, it is very likely that one of the next 10 instructions will try to use the word read.

The other solution is to have machines that do not stall but instead require the compilers not to generate code to use words before they have arrived. The trouble is that this approach is far easier said than done. Often after a LOAD there is nothing else to do, so the compiler is forced to insert NOP (no operation) instructions, which do nothing but occupy a slot and waste time. In effect, this approach is a software stall instead of a hardware stall, but the performance degradation is the same.

Actually, the problem is not technology, but economics. Engineers know how to build memories that are as fast as CPUs, but to run at full speed, they have to be located on the CPU chip (because going over the bus to memory is very slow). Putting a large memory on the CPU chip makes it bigger, which makes it more expensive, and even if cost were not an issue, there are limits to how big a CPU chip can be made. Thus the choice comes down to having a small amount of fast memory or a large amount of slow memory. What we would prefer is a large amount of fast memory at a low price.

Interestingly enough, techniques are known for combining a small amount of fast memory with a large amount of slow memory to get the speed of the fast memory (almost) and the capacity of the large memory at a moderate price. The small, fast memory is called a **cache** (from the French *cacher*, meaning to hide, and pronounced "cash"). Below we will briefly describe how caches are used and how they work. A more detailed description will be in Chap. 4.

The basic idea behind a cache is simple: the most heavily used memory words are kept in the cache. When the CPU needs a word, it first looks in the cache. Only if the word is not there does it go to main memory. If a substantial fraction of the words are in the cache, the average access time can be greatly reduced.

Success or failure thus depends on what fraction of the words are in the cache. For years, people have known that programs do not access their memories completely at random. If a given memory reference is to address A, it is likely that the next memory reference will be in the general vicinity of A. A simple example is the program itself. Except for branches and procedure calls, instructions are fetched from consecutive locations in memory. Furthermore, most program execution time is spent in loops, in which a limited number of instructions are executed over and over. Similarly, a matrix manipulation program is likely to make many references to the same matrix before moving on to something else.

The observation that the memory references made in any short time interval tend to use only a small fraction of the total memory is called the **locality principle** and forms the basis for all caching systems. The general idea is that when a word is referenced, it and some of its neighbors are brought from the large slow memory into the cache, so that the next time it is used, it can be accessed quickly. A common arrangement of the CPU, cache, and main memory is illustrated in Fig. 2-16. If a word is read or written k times in a short interval, the computer will need 1 reference to slow memory and $k - 1$ references to fast memory. The larger k is, the better the overall performance.

We can formalize this calculation by introducing c, the cache access time, m, the main memory access time, and h, the **hit ratio**, which is the fraction of all

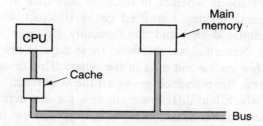

Figure 2-16. The cache is logically between the CPU and main memory. Physically, there are several possible places it could be located.

references that can be satisfied out of the cache. In our little example of the previous paragraph, $h = (k - 1)/k$. Some authors also define the **miss ratio**, which is $1 - h$.

With these definitions, we can calculate the mean access time as follows:

$$\text{mean access time} = c + (1 - h)\, m$$

As $h \to 1$, all references can be satisfied out of the cache, and the access time approaches c. On the other hand, as $h \to 0$, a memory reference is needed every time, so the access time approaches $c + m$, first a time c to check the cache (unsuccessfully), and then a time m to do the memory reference. On some systems, the memory reference can be started in parallel with the cache search, so that if a cache miss occurs, the memory cycle has already been started. However, this strategy requires that the memory can be stopped in its tracks on a cache hit, making the implementation more complicated.

Using the locality principle as a guide, main memories and caches are divided up into fixed-size blocks. When talking about these blocks inside the cache, they are commonly referred to as **cache lines**. When a cache miss occurs, the entire cache line is loaded from the main memory into the cache, not just the word needed. For example, with a 64-byte line size, a reference to memory address 260 will pull the line consisting of bytes 256 to 319 into one cache line. With a little bit of luck, some of the other words in the cache line will be needed shortly. Operating this way is more efficient than fetching individual words because it is faster to fetch k words all at once than one word k times. Also, having cache entries be more than one word means there are fewer of them, hence a smaller overhead is required.

Cache design is an increasingly important subject for high-performance CPUs. One issue is cache size. The bigger the cache, the better it performs, but also the more it costs. A second issue is the size of the cache line. A 16-KB cache can be divided up into 1024 lines of 16 bytes, 2048 lines of 8 bytes, and other combinations. A third issue is how the cache is organized, that is, how does the cache keep track of which memory words are currently being held? We will examine caches in detail in Chap. 4.

A fourth design issue is whether instructions and data are kept in the same cache or different ones. Having a **unified cache** (instructions and data use the same cache) is a simpler design and automatically balances instruction fetches against data fetches. Nevertheless, the trend these days is toward a **split cache**, with instructions in one cache and data in the other. This design is also called a **Harvard architecture**, the reference going all the way back to Howard Aiken's Mark III computer, which had different memories for instructions and data. The force driving designers in this direction is the widespread use of pipelined CPUs. The instruction fetch unit needs to access instructions at the same time the oper- and fetch unit needs access to data. A split cache allows parallel accesses; a unified one does not. Also, since instructions are not modified during execution, the contents of the instruction cache never has to be written back into memory.

Finally, a fifth issue is the number of caches. It is not uncommon these days to have chips with a primary cache on chip, a secondary cache off chip but in the same package as the CPU chip, and a third cache still further away.

2.2.6 Memory Packaging and Types

From the early days of semiconductor memory until the early 1990s, memory was manufactured, bought, and installed as single chips. Chip densities went from 1K bits to 1M bits and beyond, but each chip was sold as a separate unit. Early PCs often had empty sockets into which additional memory chips could be plugged, if and when the purchaser needed them.

At present, a different arrangement is used. A group of chips, typically 8 or 16, is mounted on a tiny printed circuit board and sold as a unit. This unit is called a **SIMM (Single Inline Memory Module)** or a **DIMM (Dual Inline Memory Module)**, depending on whether it has a row of connectors on one side or both sides of the board. SIMMs have one edge connector with 72 contacts and transfer 32 bits per clock cycle. DIMMs usually have edge connectors with 84 contacts on each side of the board, for a total of 168 contacts and transfer 64 bits per clock cycle. An example SIMM is illustrated in Fig. 2-17.

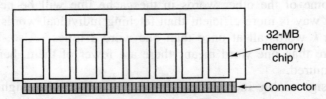

Figure 2-17. A single inline memory module (SIMM) holding 256 MB. Two of the chips control the SIMM.

A typical SIMM or DIMM configuration might have eight data chips with 256 megabits (32 MB) each. The entire module would then hold 256 MB. Many computers have room for four modules, giving a total capacity of 1 GB when using 256-MB modules and more when using larger ones.

A physically smaller DIMM, called an **SO-DIMM (Small Outline DIMM)** is used in notebook computers. SIMMs and DIMMS can have a parity bit or error correction added, but since the average error rate of a module is one error every 10 years, for most garden-variety computers, error detection and correction are omitted.

2.3 SECONDARY MEMORY

No matter how big the main memory is, it is always way too small. People always want to store more information than it can hold, primarily because as technology improves, people begin thinking about storing things that were previously entirely in the realm of science fiction. For example, as the U.S. government's budget discipline forces government agencies to generate their own revenue, one can imagine the Library of Congress deciding to digitize and sell its full contents as a consumer article ("All of human knowledge for only $99.95"). Roughly 50 million books, each with 1 MB of text and 1 MB of compressed pictures, requires storing 10^{14} bytes or 100 terabytes. Storing all 50,000 movies ever made is also in this general ballpark. This amount of information is not going to fit in main memory, at least not for a few decades.

2.3.1 Memory Hierarchies

The traditional solution to storing a great deal of data is a memory hierarchy, as illustrated in Fig. 2-18. At the top are the CPU registers, which can be accessed at full CPU speed. Next comes the cache memory, which is currently on the order of 32 KB to a few megabytes. Main memory is next, with sizes currently ranging from 16 MB for entry-level systems to tens of gigabytes at the high end. After that come magnetic disks, the current work horse for permanent storage. Finally, we have magnetic tape and optical disks for archival storage.

As we move down the hierarchy, three key parameters increase. First, the access time gets bigger. CPU registers can be accessed in a few nanoseconds. Cache memories take a small multiple of CPU registers. Main memory accesses are typically a few tens of nanoseconds. Now comes a big gap, as disk access times are at least 10 msec, and tape or optical disk access can be measured in seconds if the media have to be fetched and inserted into a drive.

Second, the storage capacity increases as we go downward. CPU registers are good for perhaps 128 bytes, caches for a few megabytes, main memories for tens to thousands of megabytes, magnetic disks for a few gigabytes to tens of gigabytes. Tapes and optical disks are usually kept off-line, so their capacity is limited only by the owner's budget.

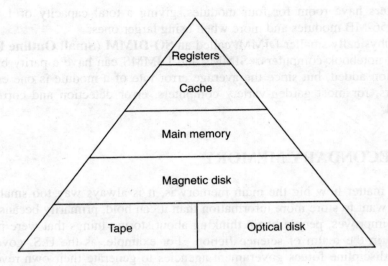

Figure 2-18. A five-level memory hierarchy.

Third, the number of bits you get per dollar spent increases down the hierarchy. Although the actual prices change rapidly, main memory is measured in dollars/megabyte, magnetic disk storage in pennies/megabyte, and magnetic tape in dollars/gigabyte or less.

We have already looked at registers, cache, and main memory. In the following sections we will look at magnetic disks; after that, we will study optical ones. We will not study tapes because they are rarely used except for backup, and there is not a lot to say about them anyway.

2.3.2 Magnetic Disks

A magnetic disk consists of one or more aluminum platters with a magnetizable coating. Originally these platters were as much as 50 cm in diameter, but at present they are typically 3 to 12 cm, with disks for notebook computers already under 3 cm and still shrinking. A disk head containing an induction coil floats just over the surface, resting on a cushion of air (except for floppy disks, where it touches the surface). When a positive or negative current passes through the head, it magnetizes the surface just beneath the head, aligning the magnetic particles facing left or facing right, depending on the polarity of the drive current. When the head passes over a magnetized area, a positive or negative current is induced in the head, making it possible to read back the previously stored bits. Thus as the platter rotates under the head, a stream of bits can be written and later read back. The geometry of a disk track is shown in Fig. 2-19.

The circular sequence of bits written as the disk makes a complete rotation is called a **track**. Each of the tracks is divided up into some number of fixed-length

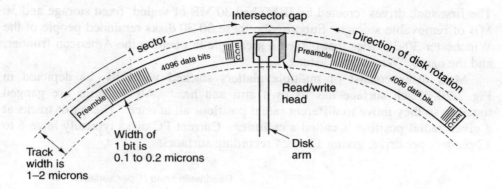

Figure 2-19. A portion of a disk track. Two sectors are illustrated.

sectors, typically containing 512 data bytes, preceded by a **preamble** that allows the head to be synchronized before reading or writing. Following the data is an Error-Correcting Code (ECC), either a Hamming code, or more commonly, a code that can correct multiple errors called a **Reed-Solomon code**. Between consecutive sectors is a small **intersector gap**. Some manufacturers quote their disks' capacities in unformatted state (as if each track contained only data), but a more honest measurement is the formatted capacity, which does not count the preambles, ECCs and gaps as data. The formatted capacity is typically about 15 percent lower than the unformatted capacity.

All disks have movable arms that are capable of moving in and out to different radial distances from the spindle about which the platter rotates. At each radial distance, a different track can be written. The tracks are thus a series of concentric circles about the spindle. The width of a track depends on how large the head is and how accurately the head can be positioned radially. With current technology, disks have between 5000 and 10,000 tracks per centimeter, giving track widths in the 1- to 2-micron range (1 micron = 1/1000 mm). It should be noted that a track is not a physical groove in the surface, but simply an annulus (ring) of magnetized material, with small guard areas separating it from the tracks inside and outside it.

The linear bit density around the circumference of the track is different from the radial one. It is determined largely by the purity of the surface and air quality. Current disks achieve densities of 50,000 to 100,000 bits/cm. Thus a bit is about 50 times as big in the radial direction as along the circumference.

To go to even higher densities, disk manufacturers are developing technologies in which the "long" dimension of the bits are not along the circumference of the disk, but vertically, down into the iron oxide. This technique is called **perpendicular recording** and will be commercialized soon.

In order to achieve high surface and air quality, most disks are sealed at the factory to prevent dust from getting in. Such drives are called **Winchester disks**.

The first such drives (created by IBM) had 30 MB of sealed, fixed storage and 30 MB of removable storage. Supposedly, these 30-30 disks reminded people of the Winchester 30-30 rifles that played a great role in opening the American frontier, and the name "Winchester" stuck.

Most disks consist of multiple platters stacked vertically, as depicted in Fig. 2-20. Each surface has its own arm and head. All the arms are ganged together so they move to different radial positions all at once. The set of tracks at a given radial position is called a **cylinder**. Current PC disks typically have 6 to 12 platters per drive, giving 12 to 24 recording surfaces.

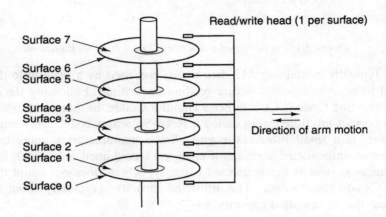

Figure 2-20. A disk with four platters.

Disk performance depends on a variety of factors. To read or write a sector, first the arm must be moved to the right radial position. This action is called a **seek**. Average seek times (between random tracks) range in the 5- to 10-msec range, although seeks between consecutive tracks are now down below 1 msec. Once the head is positioned radially, there is a delay, called the **rotational latency**, until the desired sector rotates under the head. Most disks rotate at 5400 RPM, 7200 RPM, or 10,800 RPM, so the average delay (half a rotation) is 3 to 6 msec. Transfer time depends on the linear density and rotation speed. With typical transfer rates of 20 to 40 MB/sec, a 512-byte sector takes between 13 and 26 μsec. Consequently, the seek time and rotational latency dominate the transfer time. Reading random sectors all over the disk is clearly an inefficient way to operate.

It is worth mentioning that on account of the preambles, the ECCs, the inter-sector gaps, the seek times, and the rotational latencies, there is a big difference between a drive's maximum burst rate and its maximum sustained rate. The maximum burst rate is the data rate once the head is over the first data bit. The computer must be able to handle data coming in this fast. However, the drive can only keep up that rate for one sector. For some applications, such as multimedia, what matters is the average sustained rate over a period of seconds, which has to take into account the necessary seeks and rotational delays as well.

A little thought and the use of that old high-school math formula for the circumference of a circle, $c = 2\pi r$, will reveal that the outer tracks have more linear distance around them than the inner ones do. Since all magnetic disks rotate at a constant angular velocity, no matter where the heads are, this observation creates a problem. In older drives, manufacturers used the maximum possible linear density on the innermost track, and successively lower linear bit densities on tracks further out. If a disk had 18 sectors per track, for example, each one occupied 20 degrees of arc, no matter which cylinder it was in.

Nowadays, a different strategy is used. Cylinders are divided into zones (typically 10 to 30 per drive), and the number of sectors per track is increased in each zone moving outward from the innermost track. This change makes keeping track of information harder but increases the drive capacity, which is viewed as more important. All sectors are the same size. A disk with five zones is shown in Fig. 2-21.

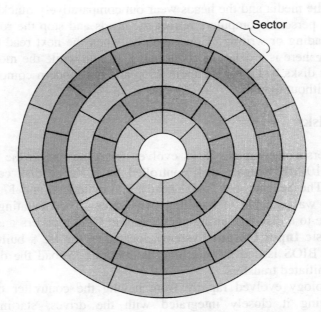

Figure 2-21. A disk with five zones. Each zone has many tracks.

Associated with each drive is a **disk controller**, a chip that controls the drive. Some controllers contain a full CPU. The controller's tasks include accepting commands from the software, such as READ, WRITE, and FORMAT (writing all the preambles), controlling the arm motion, detecting and correcting errors, and converting 8-bit bytes read from memory into a serial bit stream and vice versa. Some controllers also handle buffering of multiple sectors, caching sectors read for potential future use, and remapping bad sectors. This latter function is caused by the existence of sectors with a bad (permanently magnetized) spot. When the controller discovers a bad sector, it replaces it by one of the spare sectors reserved for this purpose within each cylinder or zone.

2.3.3 Floppy Disks

With the advent of the personal computer, a way was needed to distribute software. The solution was found in the **diskette** or **floppy disk**, a small, removable medium so called because the early ones were physically flexible. The floppy disk was actually invented by IBM for recording maintenance information about its mainframes for the service staff but was quickly seized on by personal computer manufacturers as a convenient way to distribute software for sale.

The general characteristics are the same as the disks we have just described, except that unlike hard disks, where the heads float just above the surface on a cushion of rapidly-moving air, floppy disk heads actually touch the diskettes. As a result, both the media and the heads wear out comparatively quickly. To reduce wear and tear, personal computers retract the heads and stop the rotation when a drive is not reading or writing. Consequently, when the next read or write command is given, there is a delay of about half a second while the motor gets up to speed. Floppy disks had a run of about 20 years, but modern computers are usually shipped without them.

2.3.4 IDE Disks

Modern personal computer disks evolved from the one in the IBM PC XT, which was a 10-MB Seagate disk controlled by a Xebec disk controller on a plug-in card. The Seagate disk had 4 heads, 306 cylinders, and 17 sectors/track. The controller was capable of handling two drives. The operating system read from and wrote to a disk by putting parameters in CPU registers and then calling the **BIOS** (**Basic Input Output System**), located in the PC's built-in read-only memory. The BIOS issued the machine instructions to load the disk controller registers that initiated transfers.

The technology evolved rapidly from having the controller on a separate board, to having it closely integrated with the drives, starting with **IDE** (**Integrated Drive Electronics**) drives in the mid 1980s. However, the BIOS calling conventions were not changed for reasons of backward compatibility. These calling conventions addressed sectors by giving their head, cylinder, and sector numbers, with the heads and cylinders numbered starting at 0 and the sectors starting at 1. This choice was probably due to a mistake on the part of the original BIOS programmer, who wrote his masterpiece in 8088 assembler. With 4 bits for the head, 6 bits for the sector, and 10 bits for the cylinder, the maximum drive could have 16 heads, 63 sectors, and 1024 cylinders, for a total of 1,032,192 sectors. Such a maximum drive has a capacity of 504 MB, which probably seemed like infinity at the time but certainly does not today. (Would you fault a new machine today that could not handle drives bigger than a petabyte?)

Before too long, drives above 504 MB appeared, but with the wrong geometry (e.g., 4 heads, 32 sectors, 2000 cylinders). There was no way for the operating system to address them due to the long-frozen BIOS calling conventions. As a result, disk controllers began to lie, pretending that the geometry was within the BIOS limits but actually remapping the virtual geometry onto the real geometry. Although this approach worked, it wreaked havoc with operating systems that carefully placed data to minimize seek times.

Eventually, IDE drives evolved into **EIDE** drives (**Extended IDE**), which also support a second addressing scheme called **LBA** (**Logical Block Addressing**), which just numbers the sectors starting at 0 up until a maximum of $2^{28} - 1$. This scheme requires the controller to convert LBA addresses to head, sector, and cylinder addresses, but it does get beyond the 504-MB limit. Unfortunately, it created a new bottleneck at $2^{28} \times 2^9$ bytes (128 GB). In 1994, when the EIDE standard was adopted, nobody could imagine 128 GB disks. Standards committees, like politicians, have a tendency to push problems forward in time so the next committee has to solve them.

EIDE drives and controllers also had other improvements as well. For example, EIDE controllers could have two channels, each with a primary and a secondary drive. This arrangement allowed a maximum of four drives per controller. CD-ROM and DVD drives were also supported, and the transfer rate was increased from 4 MB/sec to 16.67 MB/sec.

As disk technology continued to improved, the EIDE standard, continued to evolve, but for some reason the successor to EIDE was called **ATA-3** (**AT Attachment**), a reference to the IBM PC/AT (where AT referred to the then-Advanced Technology of a 16-bit CPU running at 8 MHz). In the next edition, the standard was called **ATAPI-4 (ATA Packet Interface)** and the speed was increased to 33 MB/sec. In ATAPI-5 it went to 66 MB/sec.

By this time, the 128-GB limit imposed by the 28-bit LBA addresses was looming larger and larger, so ATAPI-6 changed the LBA size to 48 bits. The new standard will run into trouble when disks reach $2^{48} \times 2^9$ bytes (128 PB). With a 50% annual increase in capacity, the 48-bit limit will probably last until about 2035. To find out how the problem was solved, please consult the 11th edition of this book. The smart money is betting on increasing the LBA size to 64 bits. The ATAPI-6 standard also increased the transfer rate to 100 MB/sec and addressed the issue of disk noise for the first time.

The ATAPI-7 standard is a radical break with the past. Instead of increasing the size of the drive connector (to increase the data rate), this standard uses what is called **serial ATA** to transfer 1 bit at a time over a 7-pin connector at speeds starting at 150 MB/sec and expected to rise over time to 1.5 GB/sec. Replacing the current 80-wire flat cable with a round cable only a few mm thick improves airflow within the computer. Also, serial ATA uses 0.5 volts for signaling (compared to 5 volts on ATAPI-6 drives), which reduces power consumption. It is likely that within a few years; all computers will use serial ATA. The issue of power consumption by disks is an increasingly important one, both at the high end, where data centers have vast disk farms as at the low end, where notebooks are power limited (Gurumurthi et al., 2003).

2.3.5 SCSI Disks

SCSI disks are not different from IDE disks in terms of how their cylinders, tracks, and sectors are organized, but they have a different interface and much higher transfer rates. SCSI traces its history back to Howard Shugart, the inventor of the floppy disk, whose company introduced the SASI (Shugart Associates System Interface) disk in 1979. After some modification and much discussion, ANSI standardized it in 1986 and changed the name to **SCSI (Small Computer System Interface)**. SCSI is pronounced "scuzzy." Since then, increasingly faster versions have been standardized under the names Fast SCSI (10 Mhz), Ultra SCSI (20 MHz), Ultra2 SCSI (40 MHz), Ultra3 SCSI (80 MHz), and Ultra4 SCSI (160 MHz). Each of these has a wide (16-bit) version as well. The main combinations are shown in Fig. 2-22.

Name	Data bits	Bus MHz	MB/sec
SCSI-1	8	5	5
Fast SCSI	8	10	10
Wide Fast SCSI	16	10	20
Ultra SCSI	8	20	20
Wide Ultra SCSI	16	20	40
Ultra2 SCSI	8	40	40
Wide Ultra2 SCSI	16	40	80
Ultra3 SCSI	8	80	80
Wide Ultra3 SCSI	16	80	160
Ultra4 SCSI	8	160	160
Wide Ultra4 SCSI	16	160	320

Figure 2-22. Some of the possible SCSI parameters.

Because SCSI disks have high transfer rates, they are the standard disk in most UNIX workstations from Sun, HP, SGI, and other vendors. They are also the standard disk in Macintoshes and high-end Intel PCs, especially network servers.

SCSI is more than just a hard disk interface. It is a bus to which a SCSI controller and up to seven devices can be attached. These can include one or more SCSI hard disks, CD-ROMs, CD recorders, scanners, tape units, and other SCSI peripherals. Each SCSI device has a unique ID, from 0 to 7 (15 for wide SCSI). Each device has two connectors: one for input and one for output. Cables connect the output of one device to the input of the next one, in series, like a string of cheap Christmas tree lamps. The last device in the string must be terminated to prevent reflections from the ends of the SCSI bus from interfering with other data on the bus. Typically, the controller is on a plug-in card and the start of the cable chain, although this configuration is not strictly required by the standard.

The most common cable for 8-bit SCSI has 50 wires, 25 of which are grounds paired one-to-one with the other 25 wires to provide the excellent noise immunity needed for high-speed operation. Of the 25 wires, 8 are for data, 1 is for parity, 9 are for control, and the remainder are for power or are reserved for future use. The 16-bit (and 32-bit) devices need a second cable for the additional signals. The cables may be several meters long, allowing for external drives, scanners, etc.

SCSI controllers and peripherals can operate either as initiators or as targets. Usually, the controller, acting as initiator, issues commands to disks and other peripherals acting as targets. These commands are blocks of up to 16 bytes telling the target what to do. Commands and responses occur in phases, using various control signals to delineate the phases and arbitrate bus access when multiple devices are trying to use the bus at the same time. This arbitration is important because SCSI allows all the devices to run at once, potentially greatly improving performance in an environment with multiple processes active at once (e.g., UNIX or Windows XP). IDE and EIDE allow only one active device at a time.

2.3.6 RAID

CPU performance has been increasing exponentially over the past decade, roughly doubling every 18 months. Not so with disk performance. In the 1970s, average seek times on minicomputer disks were 50 to 100 msec. Now seek times are 10 msec. In most technical industries (say, automobiles or aviation), a factor of 5 to 10 performance improvement in two decades would be major news, but in the computer industry it is an embarrassment. Thus the gap between CPU performance and disk performance has become much larger over time.

As we have seen, parallel processing is often used to speed up CPU performance. It has occurred to various people over the years that parallel I/O might be a good idea too. In their 1988 paper, Patterson et al. suggested six specific disk organizations that could be used to improve disk performance, reliability, or both (Patterson et al., 1988). These ideas were quickly adopted by industry and have led to a new class of I/O device called a **RAID**. Patterson et al. defined **RAID** as **Redundant Array of Inexpensive Disks**, but industry redefined the I to be "Independent" rather than "Inexpensive" (maybe so they could use expensive disks?). Since a villain was also needed (as in RISC versus CISC, also due to Patterson), the bad guy here was the **SLED** (**Single Large Expensive Disk**).

The idea behind a RAID is to install a box full of disks next to the computer, typically a large server, replace the disk controller card with a RAID controller, copy the data over to the RAID, and then continue normal operation. In other words, a RAID should look like a SLED to the operating system but have better performance and better reliability. Since SCSI disks have good performance, low price, and the ability to have up to 7 drives on a single controller (15 for wide SCSI), it is natural that most RAIDs consist of a RAID SCSI controller plus a box of SCSI disks that appear to the operating system as a single large disk. In this way, no software changes are required to use the RAID, a big selling point for many system administrators.

In addition to appearing like a single disk to the software, all RAIDs have the property that the data are distributed over the drives, to allow parallel operation. Several different schemes for doing this were defined by Patterson et al., and they are now known as RAID level 0 through RAID level 5. In addition, there are a few other minor levels that we will not discuss. The term "level" is something of a misnomer since there is no hierarchy involved; there are simply six different organizations possible.

RAID level 0 is illustrated in Fig. 2-23(a). It consists of viewing the virtual disk simulated by the RAID as being divided up into strips of k sectors each, with sectors 0 to $k - 1$ being strip 0, sectors k to $2k - 1$ as strip 1, and so on. For $k = 1$, each strip is a sector; for $k = 2$ a strip is two sectors, etc. The RAID level 0 organization writes consecutive strips over the drives in round robin fashion, as depicted in Fig. 2-23(a) for a RAID with four disk drives. Distributing data over multiple drives like this is called **striping**. For example, if the software issues a command to read a data block consisting of four consecutive strips starting at a strip boundary, the RAID controller will break this command up into four separate commands, one for each of the four disks, and have them operate in parallel. Thus we have parallel I/O without the software knowing about it.

RAID level 0 works best with large requests, the bigger the better. If a request is larger than the number of drives times the strip size, some drives will get multiple requests, so that when they finish the first request they start the second one. It is up to the controller to split the request up and feed the proper commands to the proper disks in the right sequence and then assemble the results in memory correctly. Performance is excellent and the implementation is straightforward.

RAID level 0 works worst with operating systems that habitually ask for data one sector at a time. The results will be correct, but there is no parallelism and hence no performance gain. Another disadvantage of this organization is that the reliability is potentially worse than having a SLED. If a RAID consists of four disks, each with a mean time to failure of 20,000 hours, about once every 5000 hours a drive will fail and all the data will be completely lost. A SLED with a mean time to failure of 20,000 hours would be four times more reliable. Because no redundancy is present in this design, it is not really a true RAID.

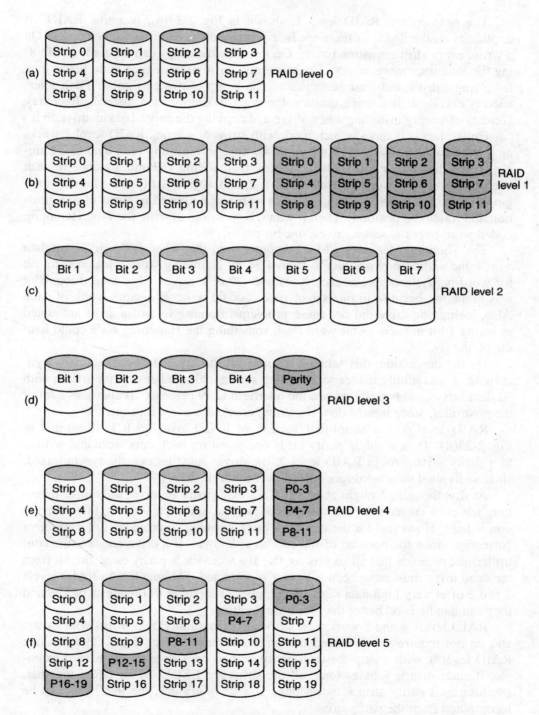

Figure 2-23. RAID levels 0 through 5. Backup and parity drives are shown shaded.

The next option, RAID level 1, shown in Fig. 2-23(b), is a true RAID. It duplicates all the disks, so there are four primary disks and four backup disks. On a write, every strip is written twice. On a read, either copy can be used, distributing the load over more drives. Consequently, write performance is no better than for a single drive, but read performance can be up to twice as good. Fault tolerance is excellent: if a drive crashes, the copy is simply used instead. Recovery consists of simply installing a new drive and copying the entire backup drive to it.

Unlike levels 0 and 1, which work with strips of sectors, RAID level 2 works on a word basis, possibly even a byte basis. Imagine splitting each byte of the single virtual disk into a pair of 4-bit nibbles, then adding a Hamming code to each one to form a 7-bit word, of which bits 1, 2, and 4 were parity bits. Further imagine that the seven drives of Fig. 2-23(c) were synchronized in terms of arm position and rotational position. Then it would be possible to write the 7-bit Hamming coded word over the seven drives, one bit per drive.

The Thinking Machines CM-2 computer used this scheme, taking 32-bit data words and adding 6 parity bits to form a 38-bit Hamming word, plus an extra bit for word parity, and spread each word over 39 disk drives. The total throughput was immense, because in one sector time it could write 32 sectors worth of data. Also, losing one drive did not cause problems, because loss of a drive amounted to losing 1 bit in each 39-bit word read, something the Hamming code could handle on the fly.

On the down side, this scheme requires all the drives to be rotationally synchronized, and it only makes sense with a substantial number of drives (even with 32 data drives and 6 parity drives, the overhead is 19 percent). It also asks a lot of the controller, since it must do a Hamming checksum every bit time.

RAID level 3 is a simplified version of RAID level 2. It is illustrated in Fig. 2-23(d). Here a single parity bit is computed for each data word and written to a parity drive. As in RAID level 2, the drives must be exactly synchronized, since individual data words are spread over multiple drives.

At first thought, it might appear that a single parity bit gives only error detection, not error correction. For the case of random undetected errors, this observation is true. However, for the case of a drive crashing, it provides full 1-bit error correction since the position of the bad bit is known. If a drive crashes, the controller just pretends that all its bits are 0s. If a word has a parity error, the bit from the dead drive must have been a 1, so it is corrected. Although both RAID levels 2 and 3 offer very high data rates, the number of separate I/O requests per second they can handle is no better than for a single drive.

RAID levels 4 and 5 work with strips again, not individual words with parity, and do not require synchronized drives. RAID level 4 [see Fig. 2-23(e)] is like RAID level 0, with a strip-for-strip parity written onto an extra drive. For example, if each strip is k bytes long, all the strips are EXCLUSIVE ORed together, resulting in a parity strip k bytes long. If a drive crashes, the lost bytes can be recomputed from the parity drive.

This design protects against the loss of a drive but performs poorly for small updates. If one sector is changed, it is necessary to read all the drives in order to recalculate the parity, which then must be rewritten. Alternatively, it can read the old user data and the old parity data and recompute the new parity from them. Even with this optimization, a small update requires two reads and two writes, clearly a bad arrangement.

As a consequence of the heavy load on the parity drive, it may become a bottleneck. This bottleneck is eliminated in RAID level 5 by distributing the parity bits uniformly over all the drives, round robin fashion, as shown in Fig. 2-23(f). However, in the event of a drive crash, reconstructing the contents of the failed drive is a complex process.

2.3.7 CD-ROMs

Optical disks were originally developed for recording television programs, but they can be put to more esthetic use as computer storage devices. Due to their large capacity and low price optical disks are widely used for distributing software, books, movies, and data of all kinds, as well as making backups of hard disks.

First-generation optical disks were invented by the Dutch electronics conglomerate Philips for holding movies. They were 30 cm across and marketed under the name LaserVision, but they did not catch on, except in Japan.

In 1980, Philips, together with Sony, developed the CD (Compact Disc), which rapidly replaced the 33 1/3 RPM vinyl record for music. The precise technical details for the CD were published in an official International Standard (IS 10149), popularly called the **Red Book**, due to the color of its cover. (International Standards are issued by the International Organization for Standardization, which is the international counterpart of national standards groups like ANSI, DIN, etc. Each one has an IS number.) The point of publishing the disk and drive specifications as an International Standard is to allow CDs from different music publishers and players from different electronics manufacturers to work together. All CDs are 120 mm across and 1.2 mm thick, with a 15-mm hole in the middle. The audio CD was the first successful mass market digital storage medium. They are supposed to last 100 years. Please check back in 2080 for an update on how well the first batch did.

A CD is prepared by using a high-power infrared laser to burn 0.8-micron diameter holes in a coated glass master disk. From this master, a mold is made, with bumps where the laser holes were. Into this mold, molten polycarbonate is injected to form a CD with the same pattern of holes as the glass master. Then a thin layer of reflective aluminum is deposited on the polycarbonate, topped by a protective lacquer and finally a label. The depressions in the polycarbonate substrate are called **pits**; the unburned areas between the pits are called **lands**.

When played back, a low-power laser diode shines infrared light with a wavelength of 0.78 micron on the pits and lands as they stream by. The laser is on the polycarbonate side, so the pits stick out in the direction of the laser as bumps in the otherwise flat surface. Because the pits have a height of one-quarter the wavelength of the laser light, light reflecting off a pit is half a wavelength out of phase with light reflecting off the surrounding surface. As a result, the two parts interfere destructively and return less light to the player's photodetector than light bouncing off a land. This is how the player tells a pit from a land. Although it might seem simplest to use a pit to record a 0 and a land to record a 1, it is more reliable to use a pit/land or land/pit transition for a 1 and its absence as a 0, so this scheme is used.

The pits and lands are written in a single continuous spiral starting near the hole and working out a distance of 32 mm toward the edge. The spiral makes 22,188 revolutions around the disk (about 600 per mm). If unwound, it would be 5.6 km long. The spiral is illustrated in Fig. 2-24.

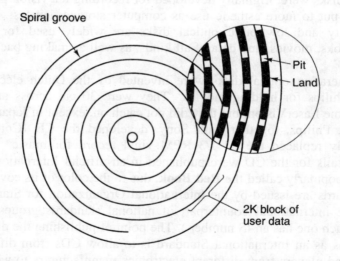

Figure 2-24. Recording structure of a Compact Disc or CD-ROM.

To make the music play at a uniform rate, it is necessary for the pits and lands to stream by at a constant linear velocity. Consequently, the rotation rate of the CD must be continuously reduced as the reading head moves from the inside of the CD to the outside. At the inside, the rotation rate is 530 RPM to achieve the desired streaming rate of 120 cm/sec; at the outside it has to drop to 200 RPM to give the same linear velocity at the head. A constant linear velocity drive is quite different than a magnetic disk drive, which operates at a constant angular velocity, independent of where the head is currently positioned. Also, 530 RPM is a far cry from the 3600 to 7200 RPM that most magnetic disks whirl at.

In 1984, Philips and Sony realized the potential for using CDs to store computer data, so they published the **Yellow Book** defining a precise standard for what are now called **CD-ROM**s (**Compact Disc-Read Only Memory**). To piggyback on the by-then already substantial audio CD market, CD-ROMs were to be the same physical size as audio CDs, mechanically and optically compatible with them, and produced using the same polycarbonate injection molding machines. The consequences of this decision were that slow variable-speed motors were required, but also that the manufacturing cost of a CD-ROM would be well under one dollar in moderate volume.

What the Yellow Book defined was the formatting of the computer data. It also improved the error-correcting abilities of the system, an essential step because although music lovers do not mind losing a bit here and there, computer lovers tend to be Very Picky about that. The basic format of a CD-ROM consists of encoding every byte in a 14-bit symbol. As we saw above, 14 bits is enough to Hamming encode an 8-bit byte with 2 bits left over. In fact, a more powerful encoding system is used. The 14-to-8 mapping for reading is done in hardware by table lookup.

At the next level up, a group of 42 consecutive symbols forms a 588-bit **frame**. Each frame holds 192 data bits (24 bytes). The remaining 396 bits are used for error correction and control. So far, this scheme is identical for audio CDs and CD-ROMs.

What the Yellow Book adds is the grouping of 98 frames into a **CD-ROM sector**, as shown in Fig. 2-25. Every CD-ROM sector begins with a 16-byte preamble, the first 12 of which are 00FFFFFFFFFFFFFFFFFFFF00 (hexadecimal), to allow the player to recognize the start of a CD-ROM sector. The next 3 bytes contain the sector number, needed because seeking on a CD-ROM with its single data spiral is much more difficult than on a magnetic disk with its uniform concentric tracks. To seek, the software in the drive calculates approximately where to go, moves the head there, and then starts hunting around for a preamble to see how good its guess was. The last byte of the preamble is the mode.

The Yellow Book defines two modes. Mode 1 uses the layout of Fig. 2-25, with a 16-byte preamble, 2048 data bytes, and a 288-byte error-correcting code (a cross-interleaved Reed-Solomon code). Mode 2 combines the data and ECC fields into a 2336-byte data field for those applications that do not need (or cannot afford the time to perform) error correction, such as audio and video. Note that to provide excellent reliability, three separate error-correcting schemes are used: within a symbol, within a frame, and within a CD-ROM sector. Single-bit errors are corrected at the lowest level, short burst errors are corrected at the frame level, and any residual errors are caught at the sector level. The price paid for this reliability is that it takes 98 frames of 588 bits (7203 bytes) to carry a single 2048-byte payload, an efficiency of only 28 percent.

Single-speed CD-ROM drives operate at 75 sectors/sec, which gives a data rate of 153,600 bytes/sec in mode 1 and 175,200 bytes/sec in mode 2. Double-

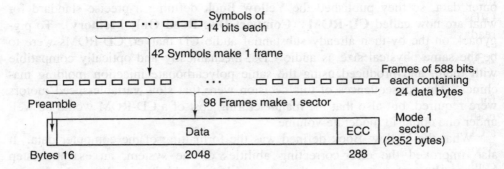

Figure 2-25. Logical data layout on a CD-ROM.

speed drives are twice as fast, and so on up to the highest speed. A standard audio CD has room for 74 minutes of music, which, if used for mode 1 data, gives a capacity of 681,984,000 bytes. This figure is usually reported as 650 MB because 1 MB is 2^{20} bytes (1,048,576 bytes), not 1,000,000 bytes.

Note that even a 32x CD-ROM drive (4,915,200 bytes/sec) is no match for a fast SCSI-2 magnetic disk drive at 10 MB/sec, even though many CD-ROM drives use the SCSI interface (IDE CD-ROM drives also exist). When you realize that the seek time is often several hundred milliseconds, it should be clear that CD-ROM drives are not at all in the same performance category as magnetic disk drives, despite their large capacity.

In 1986, Philips struck again with the **Green Book**, adding graphics and the ability to interleave audio, video and data in the same sector, a feature essential for multimedia CD-ROMs.

The last piece of the CD-ROM puzzle is the file system. To make it possible to use the same CD-ROM on different computers, agreement was needed on CD-ROM file systems. To get this agreement, representatives of many computer companies met at Lake Tahoe in the High Sierras on the California-Nevada boundary and devised a file system that they called **High Sierra**. It later evolved into an International Standard (IS 9660). It has three levels. Level 1 uses file names of up to 8 characters optionally followed by an extension of up to 3 characters (the MS-DOS file naming convention). File names may contain only uppercase letters, digits, and the underscore. Directories may be nested up to eight deep, but directory names may not contain extensions. Level 1 requires all files to be contiguous, which is not a problem on a medium written only once. Any CD-ROM conformant to IS 9660 level 1 can be read using MS-DOS, an Apple computer, a UNIX computer, or just about any other computer. CD-ROM publishers regard this property as being a big plus.

IS 9660 level 2 allows names up to 32 characters, and level 3 allows noncontiguous files. The Rock Ridge extensions (whimsically named after the town in the Mel Brooks film *Blazing Saddles*) allow very long names (for UNIX), UIDs, GIDs, and symbolic links, but CD-ROMs not conforming to level 1 will not be readable on all computers.

2.3.8 CD-Recordables

Initially, the equipment needed to produce a master CD-ROM (or audio CD, for that matter) was extremely expensive. But as usual in the computer industry, nothing stays expensive for long. By the mid 1990s, CD recorders no bigger than a CD player were a common peripheral available in most computer stores. These devices were still different from magnetic disks because once written, CD-ROMs could not be erased. Nevertheless, they quickly found a niche as a backup medium for large hard disks and also allowed individuals or startup companies to manufacture their own small-run CD-ROMs or make masters for delivery to high-volume commercial CD duplication plants. These drives are known as **CD-R**s (**CD-Recordables**).

Physically, CD-Rs start with 120-mm polycarbonate blanks that are like CD-ROMs, except that they contain a 0.6-mm wide groove to guide the laser for writing. The groove has a sinusoidal excursion of 0.3 mm at a frequency of exactly 22.05 kHz to provide continuous feedback so the rotation speed can be accurately monitored and adjusted if need be. The first CD-Rs looked like regular CD-ROMs, except that they were gold colored on top instead of silver colored. The gold color came from the use of real gold instead of aluminum for the reflective layer. Unlike silver CDs, which have physical depressions on them, on CD-Rs the differing reflectivity of pits and lands has to be simulated. This is done by adding a layer of dye between the polycarbonate and the reflective layer, as shown in Fig. 2-26. Two kinds of dye are used: cyanine, which is green, and pthalocyanine, which is a yellowish orange. Chemists can argue endlessly about which one is better. These dyes are similar to those used in photography, which explains why Kodak and Fuji are major manufacturers of CD-Rs. Eventually, an aluminum reflective layer replaced the gold one.

In its initial state, the dye layer is transparent and lets the laser light pass through and reflect off the reflective layer. To write, the CD-R laser is turned up to high power (8–16 mW). When the beam hits a spot of dye, it heats up, breaking a chemical bond. This change to the molecular structure creates a dark spot. When read back (at 0.5 mW), the photodetector sees a difference between the dark spots where the dye has been hit and transparent areas where it is intact. This difference is interpreted as the difference between pits and lands, even when read back on a regular CD-ROM reader or even on an audio CD player.

No new kind of CD could hold up its head with pride without a colored book, so CD-R has the **Orange Book**, published in 1989. This document defines CD-R and also a new format, **CD-ROM XA**, which allows CD-Rs to be written incrementally, a few sectors today, a few tomorrow, and a few next month. A group of consecutive sectors written at once is called a **CD-ROM track**.

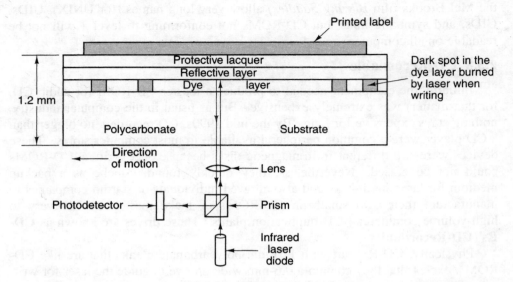

Figure 2-26. Cross section of a CD-R disk and laser (not to scale). A CD-ROM has a similar structure, except without the dye layer and with a pitted aluminum layer instead of a reflective layer.

One of the first uses of CD-R was for the Kodak PhotoCD. In this system the customer brings a roll of exposed film and his old PhotoCD to the photo processor and gets back the same PhotoCD with the new pictures added after the old ones. The new batch, which is created by scanning in the negatives, is written onto the PhotoCD as a separate CD-ROM track. Incremental writing is needed because the CD-R blanks are too expensive to provide a new one for every film roll.

However, incremental writing creates a new problem. Prior to the Orange Book, all CD-ROMs had a single **VTOC** (**Volume Table of Contents**) at the start. That scheme does not work with incremental (i.e., multitrack) writes. The Orange Book's solution is to give each CD-ROM track its own VTOC. The files listed in the VTOC can include some or all of the files from previous tracks. After the CD-R is inserted into the drive, the operating system searches through all the CD-ROM tracks to locate the most recent VTOC, which gives the current status of the disk. By including some, but not all, of the files from previous tracks in the current VTOC, it is possible to give the illusion that files have been deleted. Tracks can be grouped into **sessions**, leading to **multisession** CD-ROMs. Standard audio CD players cannot handle multisession CDs since they expect a single VTOC at the start.

Each track has to be written in a single continuous operation without stopping. As a consequence, the hard disk from which the data are coming has to be fast enough to deliver it on time. If the files to be copied are spread all over the hard disk, the seek times may cause the data stream to the CD-R to dry up and cause a dreaded buffer underrun. A buffer underrun results in producing a nice shiny (but somewhat expensive) coaster for your drinks, or a 120-mm gold- or silver-colored frisbee. CD-R software usually offers the option of collecting all the input files into a single contiguous 650-MB CD-ROM image prior to burning the CD-R, but this process typically doubles the effective writing time, requires 650 MB of free disk space, and still does not protect against hard disks that panic and decide to do a thermal recalibration when they get too hot.

CD-R makes it possible for individuals and companies to easily copy CD-ROMs (and audio CDs), generally in violation of the publisher's copyright. Several schemes have been devised to make such piracy harder and to make it difficult to read a CD-ROM using anything other than the publisher's software. One of them involves recording all the file lengths on the CD-ROM as multigigabyte, thwarting any attempts to copy the files to hard disk using standard copying software. The true lengths are embedded in the publisher's software or hidden (possibly encrypted) on the CD-ROM in an unexpected place. Another scheme uses intentionally incorrect ECCs in selected sectors, in the expectation that CD copying software will "fix" the errors. The application software checks the ECCs itself, refusing to work if they are correct. Using nonstandard gaps between the tracks and other physical "defects" are also possibilities.

2.3.9 CD-Rewritables

Although people are used to other write-once media such as paper and photographic film, there is a demand for a rewritable CD-ROM. One technology now available is **CD-RW** (**CD-ReWritable**), which uses the same size media as CD-R. However, instead of cyanine or pthalocyanine dye, CD-RW uses an alloy of silver, indium, antimony, and tellurium for the recording layer. This alloy has two stable states: crystalline and amorphous, with different reflectivities.

CD-RW drives use lasers with three different powers. At high power, the laser melts the alloy, converting it from the high-reflectivity crystalline state to the low-reflectivity amorphous state to represent a pit. At medium power, the alloy melts and reforms in its natural crystalline state to become a land again. At low power, the state of the material is sensed (for reading), but no phase transition occurs.

The reason CD-RW has not replaced CD-R completely is that the CD-RW blanks are more expensive than the CD-R blanks. Also, for applications consisting of backing up hard disks, the fact that once written, a CD-R cannot be accidentally erased is a big plus.

2.3.10 DVD

The basic CD/CD-ROM format has been around since 1980. The technology has improved since then, so higher-capacity optical disks are now economically feasible and there is great demand for them. Hollywood would dearly love to replace analog video tapes by digital disks, since disks have a higher quality, are cheaper to manufacture, last longer, take up less shelf space in video stores, and do not have to be rewound. The consumer electronics companies are looking for a new blockbuster product, and many computer companies want to add multi-media features to their software.

This combination of technology and demand by three immensely rich and powerful industries has led to **DVD**, originally an acronym for **Digital Video Disk**, but now officially **Digital Versatile Disk**. DVDs use the same general design as CDs, with 120-mm injection-molded polycarbonate disks containing pits and lands that are illuminated by a laser diode and read by a photodetector. What is new is the use of

1. Smaller pits (0.4 microns versus 0.8 microns for CDs).

2. A tighter spiral (0.74 microns between tracks versus 1.6 microns for CDs).

3. A red laser (at 0.65 microns versus 0.78 microns for CDs).

Together, these improvements raise the capacity sevenfold, to 4.7 GB. A 1x DVD drive operates at 1.4 MB/sec (versus 150 KB/sec for CDs). Unfortunately, the switch to the red lasers used in supermarkets means that DVD players will require a second laser or fancy conversion optics to be able to read existing CDs and CD-ROMs, something not all of them may provide. Also, reading CD-Rs and CD-RWs on a DVD drive may not be possible.

Is 4.7 GB enough? Maybe. Using MPEG-2 compression (standardized in IS 13346), a 4.7 GB DVD disk can hold 133 minutes of full-screen, full-motion video at high resolution (720×480), as well as soundtracks in up to eight languages and subtitles in 32 more. About 92 percent of all the movies Holly-wood has ever made are under 133 minutes. Nevertheless, some applications such as multimedia games or reference works may need more, and Hollywood would like to put multiple movies on the same disk, so four formats have been defined:

1. Single-sided, single-layer (4.7 GB).

2. Single-sided, dual-layer (8.5 GB).

3. Double-sided, single-layer (9.4 GB).

4. Double-sided, dual-layer (17 GB).

Why so many formats? In a word: politics. Philips and Sony wanted single-sided, dual-layer disks for the high capacity version, but Toshiba and Time Warner wanted double-sided, single-layer disks. Philips and Sony did not think people would be willing to turn the disks over, and Time Warner did not believe putting two layers on one side could be made to work. The compromise: all com-binations, but the market will determine which ones survive.

The dual layering technology has a reflective layer at the bottom, topped with a semireflective layer. Depending on where the laser is focused, it bounces off one layer or the other. The lower layer needs slightly larger pits and lands to be read reliably, so its capacity is slightly smaller than the upper layer's.

Double-sided disks are made by taking two 0.6-mm single-sided disks and gluing them together back to back. To make the thicknesses of all versions the same, a single-sided disk consists of a 0.6-mm disk bonded to a blank substrate (or perhaps in the future, one consisting of 133 minutes of advertising, in the hope that people will be curious as to what is down there). The structure of the double-sided, dual-layer disk is illustrated in Fig. 2-27.

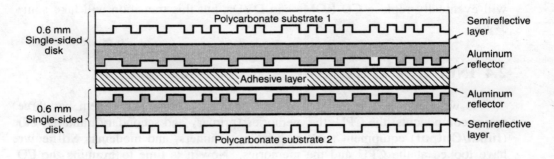

Figure 2-27. A double-sided, dual layer DVD disk.

DVD was devised by a consortium of 10 consumer electronics companies, seven of them Japanese, in close cooperation with the major Hollywood studios (some of which are owned by the Japanese electronics companies in the consortium). The computer and telecommunications industries were not invited to the picnic, and the resulting focus was on using DVD for movie rental and sales shows. For example, standard features include real-time skipping of dirty scenes (to allow parents to turn a film rated NC17 into one safe for toddlers), six-channel sound, and support for Pan-and-Scan. The latter feature allows the DVD player to dynamically decide how to crop the left and right edges off movies (whose width:height ratio is 3:2) to fit on current television sets (whose aspect ratio is 4:3).

Another item the computer industry probably would not have thought of is an intentional incompatibility between disks intended for the United States and disks intended for Europe and yet other standards for other continents. Hollywood demanded this "feature" because new films are always released first in the United States and then shipped to Europe when the videos come out in the United States. The idea was to make sure European video stores could not buy videos in the U.S. too early, thereby reducing new movies' European theater sales. If Hollywood had been running the computer industry, we would have had 3.5-inch floppy disks in the United States and 9-cm floppy disks in Europe.

2.3.11 Blu-Ray

Nothing stands still in the computer business, certainly not storage technology. DVD was barely introduced before its successor threatened to make it obsolete. The successor to DVD is **Blu-Ray**, so called because it uses a blue laser instead of the red one used by DVDs. A blue laser has a shorter wavelength than a red one, which allows it to focus more accurately and thus support smaller pits and lands. Single-sided Blu-Ray disks hold about 25 GB of data; double-sided ones hold about 50 GB. The data rate is about 4.5 MB/sec, which is good for an optical disk, but still insignificant compared to magnetic disks (cf. ATAPI-6 at 100 MB/sec and wide Ultra4 SCSI at 320 MB/sec). It is expected that Blu-Ray will eventually replace CD-ROMs and DVDs, but this transition will take some years.

2.4 INPUT/OUTPUT

As we mentioned at the start of this chapter, a computer system has three major components: the CPU, the memories (primary and secondary), and the **I/O (Input/Output)** equipment such as printers, scanners, and modems. So far we have looked at the CPU and the memories. Now it is time to examine the I/O equipment and how it is connected to the rest of the system.

2.4.1 Buses

Physically, most personal computers and workstations have a structure similar to the one shown in Fig. 2-28. The usual arrangement is a metal box with a large printed circuit board at the bottom, called the **motherboard** (parentboard, for the politically correct). The motherboard contains the CPU chip, some slots into which DIMM modules can be clicked, and various support chips. It also contains a bus etched along its length, and sockets into which the edge connectors of I/O boards can be inserted (the PCI bus). Older PCs also have a second bus (the ISA bus), for legacy I/O boards, but modern computers usually lack it and it is rapidly dying off.

The logical structure of a simple low-end personal computer is shown in Fig. 2-29. This one has a single bus used to connect the CPU, memory, and I/O devices; most systems have two or more buses. Each I/O device consists of two parts: one containing most of the electronics, called the **controller**, and one containing the I/O device itself, such as a disk drive. The controller is usually contained on a board plugged into a free slot, except for those controllers that are not optional (such as the keyboard), which are sometimes located on the motherboard. Even though the display (monitor) is not an option, the video controller is sometimes located on a plug-in board to allow the user to choose between boards with

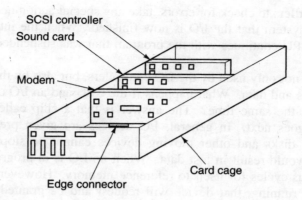

Figure 2-28. Physical structure of a personal computer.

or without graphics accelerators, extra memory, and so on. The controller connects to its device by a cable attached to a connector on the back of the box.

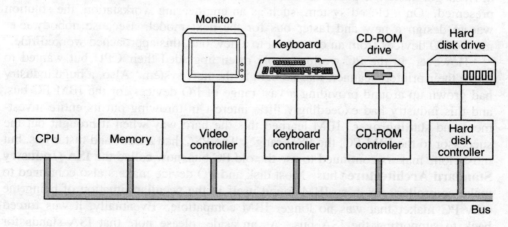

Figure 2-29. Logical structure of a simple personal computer.

The job of a controller is to control its I/O device and handle bus access for it. When a program wants data from the disk for example, it gives a command to the disk controller, which then issues seeks and other commands to the drive. When the proper track and sector have been located, the drive begins outputting the data as a serial bit stream to the controller. It is the job of the controller to break the bit stream up into units, and write each unit into memory, as it is assembled. A unit is typically one or more words. A controller that reads or writes data to or from memory without CPU intervention is said to be performing **Direct Memory Access**, better known by its acronym **DMA**. When the transfer is completed, the controller normally causes an **interrupt**, forcing the CPU to immediately suspend running its current program and start running a special procedure, called an

interrupt handler, to check for errors, take any special action needed, and inform the operating system that the I/O is now finished. When the interrupt handler is finished, the CPU continues with the program that was suspended when the interrupt occurred.

The bus is not only used by the I/O controllers, but also by the CPU for fetching instructions and data. What happens if the CPU and an I/O controller want to use the bus at the same time? The answer is that a chip called a **bus arbiter** decides who goes next. In general, I/O devices are given preference over the CPU, because disks and other moving devices cannot be stopped, and forcing them to wait would result in lost data. When no I/O is in progress, the CPU can have all the bus cycles for itself to reference memory. However, when some I/O device is also running, that device will request and be granted the bus when it needs it. This process is called **cycle stealing** and it slows down the computer.

This design worked fine for the first personal computers, since all the components were roughly in balance. However, as the CPUs, memories, and I/O devices got faster, a problem arose: the bus could no longer handle the load presented. On a closed system, such as an engineering workstation, the solution was to design a new and faster bus for the next model. Because nobody ever moved I/O devices from an old model to a new one, this approached worked fine.

However, in the PC world, people often upgraded their CPU but wanted to move their printer, scanner, and modem to the new system. Also, a huge industry had grown up around providing a vast range of I/O devices for the IBM PC bus, and this industry had exceedingly little interest in throwing out its entire investment and starting over. IBM learned this the hard way when it brought out the successor to the IBM PC, the PS/2 range. The PS/2 had a new, and faster bus, but most clone makers continued to use the old PC bus, now called the **ISA (Industry Standard Architecture)** bus. Most disk and I/O device makers also continued to make controllers for it, so IBM found itself in the peculiar situation of being the only PC maker that was no longer IBM compatible. Eventually, it was forced back to supporting the ISA bus. As an aside, please note that ISA stands for Instruction Set Architecture in the context of machine levels whereas it stands for Industry Standard Architecture in the context of buses.

Nevertheless, despite the market pressure not to change anything, the old bus really was too slow, so something had to be done. This situation led to other companies developing machines with multiple buses, one of which was the old ISA bus, or its backward-compatible successor, the **EISA (Extended ISA)** bus. The most popular of these now is the **PCI (Peripheral Component Interconnect)** bus. It was designed by Intel, but Intel decided to put all the patents in the public domain, to encourage the entire industry (including its competitors) to adopt it.

The PCI bus can be used in many configurations, but a typical one is illustrated in Fig. 2-30. Here the CPU talks to a memory controller over a dedicated high-speed connection. The controller talks to the memory and to the PCI bus directly, so CPU-memory traffic does not go over the PCI bus. However, high-bandwidth (i.e., high data rate) peripherals can connect to the PCI bus directly. In addition, here the PCI bus has a bridge to the ISA bus, so that ISA controllers and their devices can still be used, although as mentioned earlier, the ISA bus is being phased out. A machine of this design would typically contain three or four empty PCI slots and one or two ISA slots, to allow customers to plug in both old ISA I/O cards (usually for slow devices) and new PCI I/O cards (usually for fast devices).

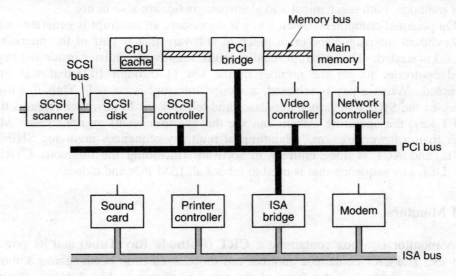

Figure 2-30. A typical modern PC with a PCI bus and an ISA bus. The modem and sound card are ISA devices; the SCSI controller is a PCI device.

Many kinds of I/O devices are available today. A few of the more common ones are discussed below.

2.4.2 Terminals

Computer terminals consist of two parts: a keyboard and a monitor. In the mainframe world, these parts are often integrated into a single device and attached to the main computer by a serial line or over a telephone line. In the airline reservation, banking, and other mainframe-oriented industries, these devices are still in widespread use. In the personal computer world, the keyboard and monitor are independent devices. Either way, the technology of the two parts is the same.

Keyboards

Keyboards come in several varieties. The original IBM PC came with a keyboard that had a snap-action switch under each key that gave tactile feedback and made a click when the key was depressed far enough. Nowadays, the cheaper keyboards have keys that just make mechanical contact when depressed. Better ones have a sheet of elastometric material (a kind of rubber) between the keys and the underlying printed circuit board. Under each key is a small dome that buckles when depressed far enough. A small spot of conductive material inside the dome closes the circuit. Some keyboards have a magnet under each key that passes through a coil when struck, thus inducing a current that can be detected. Various other methods, both mechanical and electromagnetic, are also in use.

On personal computers, when a key is depressed, an interrupt is generated and the keyboard interrupt handler (a piece of software that is part of the operating system) is started. The interrupt handler reads a hardware register inside the keyboard controller to get the number of the key (1 through 102) that was just depressed. When a key is released, a second interrupt is caused. Thus if a user depresses the SHIFT key, then depresses and releases the M key, then releases the SHIFT key, the operating system can see that the user wants an uppercase "M" rather than a lowercase "m." Handling of multikey sequences involving SHIFT, CTRL, and ALT is done entirely in software (including the infamous CTRL-ALT-DEL key sequence that is used to reboot all IBM PCs and clones).

CRT Monitors

A monitor is a box containing a **CRT** (**Cathode Ray Tube**) and its power supplies. The CRT contains a gun that can shoot an electron beam against a phosphorescent screen near the front of the tube, as shown in Fig. 2-31(a). (Color monitors have three electron guns, one each for red, green, and blue.) During the horizontal scan, the beam sweeps across the screen in about 50 usec, tracing out an almost horizontal line on the screen. Then it executes a horizontal retrace to get back to the left-hand edge in order to begin the next sweep. A device like this that produces an image line by line is called a **raster scan** device.

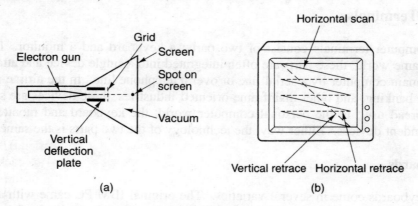

(a)   (b)

Figure 2-31. (a) Cross section of a CRT. (b) CRT scanning pattern.

Horizontal sweeping is controlled by a linearly increasing voltage applied to the horizontal deflection plates placed to the left and right of the electron gun. Vertical motion is controlled by a much more slowly linearly increasing voltage applied to the vertical deflection plates placed above and below the gun. After somewhere between 400 and 1000 sweeps, the voltages on the vertical and horizontal deflection plates are rapidly reversed together to put the beam back in the upper left-hand corner. A full-screen image is normally repainted between 30 and 60 times a second. The beam motions are shown in Fig. 2-31(b). Although we have described CRTs as using electric fields for sweeping the beam across the screen, many models use magnetic fields instead of electric ones, especially in high-end monitors.

To produce a pattern of dots on the screen, a grid is present inside the CRT. When a positive voltage is applied to the grid, the electrons are accelerated, causing the beam to hit the screen and make it glow briefly. When a negative voltage is used, the electrons are repelled, so they do not pass through the grid and the screen does not glow. Thus the voltage applied to the grid causes the corresponding bit pattern to appear on the screen. This mechanism allows a binary electrical signal to be converted into a visual display consisting of bright and dark spots.

Flat Panel Displays

CRTs are far too bulky and heavy to be used in notebook computers, so a completely different technology is needed for their screens. The most common one is **LCD** (**Liquid Crystal Display**) technology. It is highly complex, has many variations, and is changing rapidly, so this description will, of necessity, be brief and greatly simplified.

Liquid crystals are viscous organic molecules that flow like a liquid but also have spatial structure, like a crystal. They were discovered by an Austrian botanist (Rheinitzer) in 1888, and first applied to displays (e.g., calculators, watches) in the 1960s. When all the molecules are lined up in the same direction, the optical properties of the crystal depend on the direction and polarization of the incoming light. Using an applied electric field, the molecular alignment, hence the optical properties, can be changed. In particular, by shining a light through a liquid crystal, the intensity of the light exiting from it can be controlled electrically. This property can be exploited to construct flat panel displays.

An LCD display screen consists of two parallel glass plates between which is a sealed volume containing a liquid crystal. Transparent electrodes are attached to both plates. A light behind the rear plate (either natural or artificial) illuminates the screen from behind. The transparent electrodes attached to each plate are used to create electric fields in the liquid crystal. Different parts of the screen get different voltages, to control the image displayed. Glued to the front and rear of the screen are polaroids because the display technology requires the use of polarized light. The general setup is shown in Fig. 2-32(a).

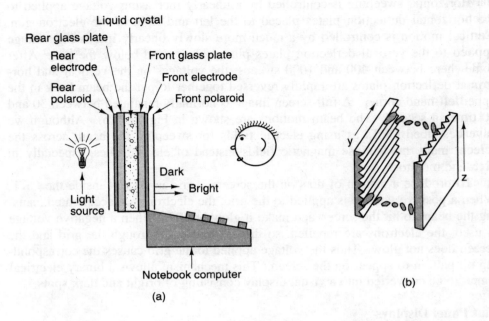

Figure 2-32. (a) The construction of an LCD screen. (b) The grooves on the rear and front plates are perpendicular to one another.

Although many kinds of LCD displays are in use, we will now consider one particular kind of display, the **TN** (**Twisted Nematic**) display as an example. In this display, the rear plate contains tiny horizontal grooves and the front plate contains tiny vertical grooves, as illustrated in Fig. 2-32(b). In the absence of an electric field, the LCD molecules tend to align with the grooves. Since the front and rear alignments differ by 90 degrees, the molecules (and thus the crystal structure) twist from rear to front.

At the rear of the display is a horizontal polaroid. It only allows in horizontally polarized light. At the front of the display is a vertical polaroid. It only allows vertically polarized light to pass through. If there were no liquid present between the plates, horizontally polarized light let in by the rear polaroid would be blocked by the front polaroid, making the screen uniformly black.

However the twisted crystal structure of the LCD molecules guides the light as it passes and rotates its polarization, making it come out vertically. Thus in the absence of an electric field, the LCD screen is uniformly bright. By applying a voltage to selected parts of the plate, the twisted structure can be destroyed, blocking the light in those parts.

Two schemes can be used for applying the voltage. In a (low-cost) **passive matrix display**, both electrodes contain parallel wires. In a 640 × 480 display, for example, the rear electrode might have 640 vertical wires and the front one might have 480 horizontal ones. By putting a voltage on one of the vertical wires and then pulsing one of the horizontal ones, the voltage at one selected pixel position can be changed, making it go dark briefly. By repeating this pulse with the next pixel and then the next one, a dark scan line can be painted, analogous to how a CRT works. Normally, the entire screen is painted 60 times a second to fool the eye into thinking there is a constant image there, again, the same way as a CRT.

The other scheme in widespread use is the **active matrix display**. It is more expensive but it gives a better image. Instead of just having two sets of perpendicular wires, it has a tiny switching element at each pixel position on one of the electrodes. By turning these on and off, an arbitrary voltage pattern can be created across the screen, allowing for an arbitrary bit pattern. The switching elements are called **thin film transistors** and the flat panel displays using them are often called **TFT displays**. Most notebook computers and stand-alone flat panel displays for desktop computers use TFT technology now.

So far we have described how a monochrome display works. Suffice it to say that color displays use the same general principles as monochrome displays, but that the details are a great deal more complicated. Optical filters are used to separate the white light into red, green, and blue components at each pixel position so these can be displayed independently. Every color can be built up from a linear superposition of these three primary colors.

Video RAM

Both CRTs and TFT displays are refreshed 60–100 times per second from a special memory, called a **video RAM**, on the display's controller card. This memory has one or more bit maps that represent the screen. On a screen with, say, 1600×1200 picture elements, called **pixels**, the video RAM would contain 1600×1200 values, one for each pixel. In fact, it might contain many such bit maps, to allow rapid switching from one screen image to another.

On a high-end display, each pixel would be represented as a 3-byte RGB value, one each for the intensity of the red, green, and blue components of the pixel's color. From the laws of physics, it is known that any color can be constructed from a linear superposition of red, green, and blue light.

A video RAM with 1600×1200 pixels at 3 bytes/pixels requires almost 5.5 MB to store the image and a fair amount of CPU time to do anything with it. For this reason, some computers compromise by using an 8-bit number to indicate the color desired. This number is then used as an index into a hardware table, called the **color palette** that contains 256 entries, each holding a 24-bit RGB value. Such a design, called **indexed color**, reduces the memory video RAM memory requirements by 2/3, but allows only 256 colors on the screen at once. Usually, each window on the screen has its own mapping, but with only one hardware color palette, often when multiple windows are present on the screen, only the current one has its colors rendered correctly.

Bit-mapped video displays require a lot of bandwidth. To display full-screen, full-color multimedia on a 1600×1200 display requires copying 5.5 MB of data to the video RAM for every frame. For full-motion video, a rate of at least 25 frame/sec is needed, for a total data rate of 137.5 MB/sec. This load is far more than the (E)ISA bus can handle, and even more than the original PCI bus could handle (127.2 MB/sec). Of course, smaller images require less bandwidth, but bandwidth is still a major issue.

To allow more bandwidth from the CPU to the video RAM, starting with the Pentium II, Intel added support for a new bus to the video RAM, the **AGP bus** (**Accelerated Graphics Port**), which can transfer 32 bits at a rate of 66 MHz for a data rate of 252 MB/sec. Subsequent versions ran at 2x, 4x, and even 8x to provide sufficient bandwidth for highly interactive graphics without overloading the main PCI bus.

2.4.3 Mice

As time goes on, computers are being used by people with less expertise in how computers work. Computers of the ENIAC generation were used only by the people who built them. In the 1950s, computers were only used by highly-skilled professional programmers. Now, computers are widely used by people who need to get some job done and do not know (or even want to know) much about how computers work or how they are programmed.

In the old days, most computers had command line interfaces, to which users typed commands. Since people who are not computer specialists often perceived command line interfaces as user-unfriendly, if not downright hostile, many computer vendors developed point-and-click interfaces, such as the Macintosh and Windows. Using this model requires having a way to point at the screen. The most common way of allowing users to point at the screen is with a mouse.

A **mouse** is a small plastic box that sits on the table next to the keyboard. When it is moved around on the table, a little pointer on the screen moves too, allowing users to point at screen items. The mouse has one, two, or three buttons on top, to allow users to select items from menus. Much blood has been spilled as a result of arguments about how many buttons a mouse ought to have. Naive users prefer one (it is hard to push the wrong button if there is only one), but sophisticated ones like the power of multiple buttons to do fancy things.

Three kinds of mice have been produced: mechanical mice, optical mice, and optomechanical mice. The first mice had two rubber wheels protruding through the bottom, with their axles perpendicular to one another. When the mouse was moved parallel to its main axis, one wheel turned. When it is moved perpendicular to its main axis, the other one turned. Each wheel drove a variable resistor or potentiometer. By measuring changes in the resistance, it was possible to see how much each wheel had rotated and thus calculate how far the mouse had moved in each direction. In recent years, this design has largely been replaced by one in which a ball that protrudes slightly from the bottom is used instead of wheels. It is shown in Fig. 2-33.

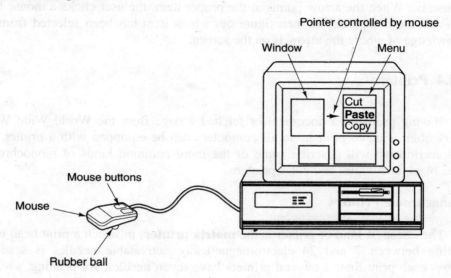

Figure 2-33. A mouse being used to point to menu items.

The second kind of mouse is the optical mouse. This kind has no wheels or ball. Instead, it has an **LED (Light Emitting Diode)** and a photodetector on the bottom. The optical mouse is used on top of a special plastic pad containing a rectangular grid of closely spaced lines. As the mouse moves over the grid, the photodetector senses line crossings by seeing the changes in the amount of light being reflected back from the LED. Electronics inside the mouse count the number of grid lines crossed in each direction.

The third kind of mouse is optomechanical. Like the newer mechanical mouse, it has a rolling ball that turns two shafts aligned at 90 degrees to each other. The shafts are connected to encoders that have slits through which light can pass. As the mouse moves, the shafts rotate, and light pulses strike the detectors whenever a slit comes between an LED and its detector. The number of pulses detected is proportional to the amount of motion.

Although mice can be set up in various ways, a common arrangement is to have the mouse send a sequence of 3 bytes to the computer every time the mouse moves a certain minimum distance (e.g., 0.01 inch), sometimes called a **mickey**. Usually, these characters come in on a serial line, one bit at time. The first byte contains a signed integer telling how many units the mouse has moved in the *x*-direction since the last time. The second byte gives the same information for *y* motion. The third byte contains the current state of the mouse buttons. Sometimes 2 bytes are used for each coordinate.

Low-level software in the computer accepts this information as it comes in and converts the relative movements sent by the mouse to an absolute position. It then displays an arrow on the screen at the position corresponding to where the mouse is. When the arrow points at the proper item, the user clicks a mouse button, and the computer can then figure out which item has been selected from its knowledge of where the arrow is on the screen.

2.4.4 Printers

Having prepared a document or fetched a page from the World Wide Web, users often want to print it, so all computers can be equipped with a printer. In this section we will describe some of the more common kinds of monochrome (i.e., black and white) and color printers.

Monochrome Printers

The cheapest kind of printer is the **matrix printer**, in which a print head containing between 7 and 24 electromagnetically activatable needles is scanned across each print line. Low-end printers have seven needles, for printing, say, 80 characters in a 5×7 matrix across the line. In effect, the print line then consists of 7 horizontal lines, each consisting of $5 \times 80 = 400$ dots. Each dot can be printed or not printed, depending on the characters to be printed. Figure 2-34(a) illustrates the letter "A" printed on a 5×7 matrix.

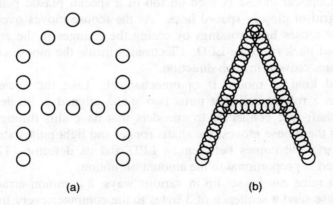

(a)   (b)

Figure 2-34. (a) The letter "A" on a 5×7 matrix. (b) The letter "A" printed with 24 overlapping needles.

The print quality can be increased by two techniques: using more needles and having the circles overlap. Figure 2-34(b) shows an "A" printed using 24 needles that produce overlapping dots. Usually, multiple passes over each scan line are required to produce overlapping dots, so increased quality goes hand in hand with slower printing rates. Most matrix printers can operate in several modes, offering different trade-offs between print quality and speed.

Matrix printers are cheap (especially in terms of consumables) and highly reliable, but slow, noisy, and poor at graphics. They have three main uses in current systems. First, they are popular for printing on large (> 30 cm) preprinted forms. Second, they are good at printing on small pieces of paper, such as cash register receipts, ATM machine or credit card transaction slips, or airline boarding passes. Third, for printing on multipart continuous forms with carbon paper embedded between the copies, they are usually the cheapest technology.

For low-cost home printing, **inkjet printers** are a favorite. The movable print head, which holds an ink cartridge, is swept horizontally across the paper by a belt while ink is sprayed from its tiny nozzles. The ink droplets have a volume of about 1 picoliter, which means that 100 million of them would fit nicely in a single drop of water.

Inkjet printers come in two varieties: piezoelectric (used by Epson) and thermal (used by Canon, HP, and Lexmark). The piezoelectric inkjet printers have a special kind of crystal next to the ink chamber. When a voltage is applied to the crystal, it deforms slightly, forcing a droplet of ink out of the nozzle. The higher the voltage, the larger the droplet, allowing the software to control the droplet size.

Thermal inkjet printers (also called **bubblejet** printers) contain a tiny resistor inside each nozzle. When a voltage is applied to the resistor, it heats up extremely fast, instantly raising the temperature of the ink touching it to the boiling point until the ink vaporizes to form a gas bubble. The gas bubble takes up more volume than the ink that created it, producing pressure in the nozzle. The only place the ink can go is out the front of the nozzle onto the paper. The nozzle is then cooled and the resulting vacuum sucks in another ink droplet from the ink tank. The speed of the printer is limited by how fast the boil/cool cycle can be repeated. The droplets are all the same size, but usually smaller than what the piezo-electric printers produce.

Inkjet printers typically have resolutions of at least 1200 **dpi** (**dots per inch**) and at the high end, 4800 dpi, They are cheap, quiet, and have good quality, although they are also slow, and use expensive ink cartridges. When the best of the high-end inkjet printers is used to print a high-resolution photograph on specially-coated photographic paper, the results are indistinguishable from conventional photography, even up to 8×10 prints.

Probably the most exciting development in printing since Johann Gutenberg invented movable type in the fifteenth century is the **laser printer**. This device combines a high quality image, excellent flexibility, great speed, and moderate cost into a single peripheral. Laser printers use almost the same technology as photocopy machines. In fact, many companies make devices that combine copying and printing (and sometimes fax as well).

   The basic technology is illustrated in Fig. 2-35. The heart of the printer is a
rotating precision drum (or in some high-end systems, a belt). At the start of each
page cycle, it is charged up to about 1000 volts and coated with a photosensitive
material. Then light from a laser is scanned along the length of the drum much
like the electron beam in a CRT, only instead of achieving the horizontal deflection using a voltage, a rotating octagonal mirror is used to scan the length of the
drum. The light beam is modulated to produce a pattern of light and dark spots.
The spots where the beam hits lose their electrical charge.

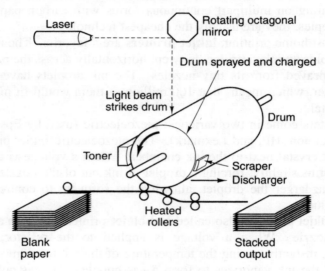

Figure 2-35. Operation of a laser printer.

   After a line of dots has been painted, the drum rotates a fraction of a degree to
allow the next line to be painted. Eventually, the first line of dots reaches the
toner, a reservoir of an electrostatically sensitive black powder. The toner is
attracted to those dots that are still charged, thus forming a visual image of that
line. A little later in the transport path, the toner-coated drum is pressed against
the paper, transferring the black powder to the paper. The paper is then passed
through heated rollers to fuse the toner to the paper permanently, fixing the image.
Later in its rotation, the drum is discharged and scraped clean of any residual
toner, preparing it for being charged and coated again for the next page.

   That this process is an exceedingly complex combination of physics, chemistry, mechanical engineering, and optical engineering hardly needs to be said.
Nevertheless, complete assemblies, called **print engines**, are available from
several vendors. Laser printer manufacturers combine the print engines with their
own electronics and software to make a complete printer. The electronics consists
of a fast embedded CPU along with megabytes of memory to hold a full-page bit
map and numerous fonts, some of them built in and some of them downloadable.

Most printers accept commands that describe the pages to be printed (as opposed to simply accepting bit maps prepared by the main CPU). These commands are given in languages such as HP's PCL and Adobe's PostScript.

Laser printers at 600-dpi and up can do a reasonable job of printing black and white photographs but the technology is trickier than it might at first appear. Consider a photograph scanned in at 600 dpi that is to be printed on a 600 dpi printer. The scanned image contains 600×600 pixels/inch, each one consisting of a gray value from 0 (white) to 255 (black). The printer can also print 600 dpi, but each printed pixel is either black (toner present) or white (no toner present). Gray values cannot be printed.

The usual solution to printing images with gray values is to use **halftoning**, the same as commercially printed posters. The image is broken up into halftone cells, each typically 6×6 pixels. Each cell can contain between 0 and 36 black pixels. The eye perceives a cell with many pixels as darker than one with fewer pixels. Gray values in the range 0 to 255 are represented by dividing this range into 37 zones. Values from 0 to 6 are in zone 0, values from 7 to 13 are in zone 1, and so on (zone 36 is slightly smaller than the others because 37 does not divide 256 exactly). Whenever a gray value in zone 0 is encountered, its halftone cell on the paper is left blank, as illustrated in Fig. 2-36(a). A zone 1 value is printed as 1 black pixel. A zone 2 value is printed as 2 black pixels, as shown in Fig. 2-36(b). Other zone values are shown in Fig. 2-36(c)-(f). Of course, taking a photograph scanned at 600 dpi and halftoning this way reduces the effective resolution to 100 cells/inch, called the **halftone screen frequency**, conventionally measured in **lpi** (**lines per inch**).

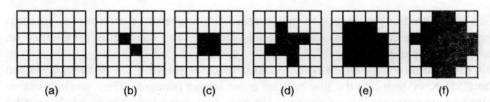

Figure 2-36. Halftone dots for various gray scale ranges. (a) 0–6. (b) 14–20. (c) 28–34. (d) 56–62. (e) 105–111. (f) 161–167.

Color Printers

Color images can be viewed in one of two ways: transmitted light and reflected light. Transmitted light images, such as those produced on CRT monitors, are built up from the linear superposition of the three additive primary colors, red, green, and blue. Reflected light images, such as color photographs and pictures in glossy magazines, absorb certain wavelengths of light and reflect the rest.

These are built up from a linear superposition of the three subtractive primary colors, cyan (all red absorbed), yellow (all blue absorbed), and magenta (all green absorbed). In theory, every color can be produced by mixing cyan, yellow, and magenta ink. In practice it is difficult to get the inks pure enough to absorb all light and produce a true black. For this reason, nearly all color printing systems use four inks: cyan, yellow, magenta, and black. These systems are called **CYMK printers** (K is for blacK, to avoid confusion with Blue). Monitors, in contrast, use transmitted light and the RGB system for producing colors.

The complete set of colors that a display or printer can produce is called its **gamut**. No device has a gamut that matches the real world, since at best each color comes in 256 intensities, giving only 16,777,216 discrete colors. Imperfections in the technology reduce the total more, and the remaining ones are not always uniformly spaced over the color spectrum. Furthermore, color perception has a lot to do with how the rods and cones in the human retina work, and not just the physics of light.

As a consequence of the above observations, converting a color image that looks fine on the screen to an identical printed one is far from trivial. Among the problems are

1. Color monitors use transmitted light; color printers use reflected light.

2. CRTs produce 256 intensities per color; color printers must halftone.

3. Monitors have a dark background; paper has a light background.

4. The RGB and CMYK gamuts are different.

Getting printed color images to match real life (or even to match screen images) requires device calibration, sophisticated software, and considerable expertise on the part of the user.

Five technologies are in common use for color printing, all of them based on the CMYK system. At the low end are color ink jet printers. They work the same way as monochrome ink jet printers, but with four cartridges (for C, M, Y, and K) instead of one. They give good results for color graphics and passable results for photographs at modest cost (the printers are cheap but the ink cartridges are not).

For best results, special ink and paper should be used. Two kinds of ink exist. **Dye-based inks** consist of colored dyes dissolved in a fluid carrier. They give bright colors and flow easily. Their main disadvantage is that they fade when exposed to ultraviolet light, such as that contained in sunlight. **Pigment-based ink** contains solid particles of pigment suspended in a fluid carrier that evaporates from the paper, leaving the pigment behind. They do not fade in time but are not as bright as dye-based inks and the pigment particles have a tendency to clog the nozzles, requiring periodic cleaning. Coated or glossy paper is required for printing photographs. These kinds of paper have been specially designed to hold the ink droplets and not let them spread out.

A step up from ink jet printers leads to the **solid ink printers**. These accept four solid blocks of a special waxy ink which are then melted into hot ink reservoirs. Startup times of these printers can be as much as 10 minutes, while the ink blocks are melting. The hot ink is sprayed onto the paper, where it solidifies and is fused with the paper by forcing it between two hard rollers

The third kind of color printer is the color laser printer. It works like its monochrome cousin, except that separate C, Y, M, and K images are laid down and transferred to a roller using four different toners. Since the full bit map is generally produced in advance, a 1200×1200 dpi image for a page containing 80 square inches needs 115 million pixels. With 4 bits/pixels, the printer needs 55 MB just for the bit map, exclusive of memory for the internal processors, fonts, etc. This requirement makes color laser printers expensive, but printing is fast, the quality is high, and the images are stable over time.

The fourth kind of color printer is the **wax printer**. It has a wide ribbon of four-color wax that is segmented into page-size bands. Thousands of heating elements melt the wax as the paper moves under it. The wax is fused to the paper in the form of pixels using the CMYK system. Wax printers used to be the main color printing technology, but they are being replaced by the other kinds, which have cheaper consumables.

The fifth kind of color printer is the **dye sublimation printer**. Although it has Freudian undertones, sublimation is the scientific name for a solid changing into a gas without passing through the liquid state. Dry ice (frozen carbon dioxide) is a well-known material that sublimates. In a dye sublimation printer, a carrier containing the CMYK dyes passes over a thermal print head containing thousands of programmable heating elements. The dyes are vaporized instantly and absorbed by a special paper close by. Each heating element can produce 256 different temperatures. The higher the temperature, the more dye that is deposited and the more intense the color. Unlike all the other color printers, nearly continuous colors are possible for each pixel, so no halftoning is needed. Small snapshot printers often use the dye sublimation process to produce highly realistic photographic images on special (and expensive) paper.

2.4.5 Telecommunications Equipment

Most computers nowadays are connected to a computer network, often the Internet. Achieving this access requires special equipment. In this section we will see how this equipment works.

Modems

With the growth of computer usage in the past years, it is common for one computer to need to communicate with another computer. For example, many people have personal computers at home that they use for communicating with their computer at work, with an Internet Service Provider, or with a home banking system. In many cases, the telephone line provides the physical communication.

However, a raw telephone line (or cable) is not suitable for transmitting computer signals, which generally represent a 0 as 0 volts and a 1 as 3 to 5 volts as shown in Fig. 2-37(a). Two-level signals suffer considerable distortion when transmitted over a voice-grade telephone line, thereby leading to transmission errors. A pure sine wave signal at a frequency of 1000 to 2000 Hz, called a **carrier**, can be transmitted with relatively little distortion, however, and this fact is exploited as the basis of most telecommunication systems.

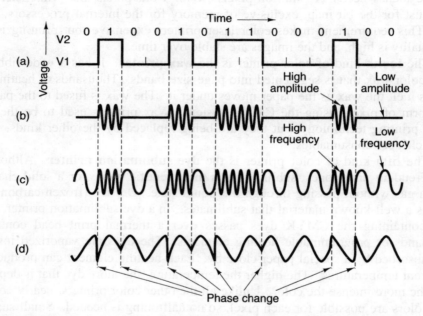

Figure 2-37. Transmission of the binary number 01001011000100 over a telephone line bit by bit. (a) Two-level signal. (b) Amplitude modulation. (c) Frequency modulation. (d) Phase modulation.

Because the pulsations of a sine wave are completely predictable, a pure sine wave transmits no information at all. However, by varying the amplitude, frequency, or phase, a sequence of 1s and 0s can be transmitted, as shown in Fig. 2-37. This process is called **modulation**. In **amplitude modulation** [see Fig. 2-37(b)], two different voltage levels are used, for 0 and 1, respectively. A person listening to digital data transmitted at a very low data rate would hear a loud noise for a 1 and no noise for a 0.

In **frequency modulation** [see Fig. 2-37(c)], the voltage level is constant but the carrier frequency is different for 1 and 0. A person listening to frequency modulated digital data would hear two tones, corresponding to 0 and 1. Frequency modulation is often referred to as **frequency shift keying**.

In simple **phase modulation** [see Fig. 2-37(d)], the amplitude and frequency do not change, but the phase of the carrier is reversed 180 degrees when the data switch from 0 to 1 or 1 to 0. In more sophisticated phase-modulated systems, at the start of each indivisible time interval, the phase of the carrier is abruptly shifted by 45, 135, 225, or 315 degrees, to allow 2 bits per time interval, called **dibit** phase encoding. For example, a phase shift of 45 degrees could represent 00, a phase shift of 135 degrees could represent 01, and so on. Other schemes, for transmitting 3 or more bits per time interval also exist. The number of time intervals (i.e., the number of potential signal changes per second) is **baud** rate. With 2 or more bits per interval, the bit rate will exceed the baud rate. Many people confuse these two terms.

If the data to be transmitted consist of a series of 8-bit characters, it would be desirable to have a connection capable of transmitting 8 bits simultaneously—that is, eight pairs of wires. Because voice-grade telephone lines provide only one channel, the bits must be sent serially, one after another (or in groups of two if dibit encoding is being used). The device that accepts characters from a computer in the form of two-level signals, one bit at a time, and transmits the bits in groups of one or two, in amplitude-, frequency-, or phase-modulated form, is the modem. To mark the start and end of each character, an 8-bit character is normally sent preceded by a start bit and followed by a stop bit, making 10 bits in all.

The transmitting modem sends the individual bits within one character at regularly-spaced time intervals. For example, 9600 baud implies one signal change every 104 μsec. A second modem at the receiving end is used to convert a modulated carrier to a binary number. Because the bits arrive at the receiver at regularly-spaced intervals, once the receiving modem has determined the start of the character, its clock tells it when to sample the line to read the incoming bits.

Modern modems operate at data rates ranging from 28,800 bits/sec to 57,600 bits/sec, usually at much lower baud rates. They use a combination of techniques to send multiple bits per baud, modulating the amplitude, frequency, and phase. Nearly all of them are **full-duplex**, meaning they can transmit in both directions at the same time (using different frequencies). Modems or transmission lines that can only transmit in one direction at a time (like a single-track railroad that can handle north-bound trains or south-bound trains but not at the same time) are called **half-duplex**. Lines that can only transmit in one direction are **simplex**.

Digital Subscriber Lines

When the telephone industry finally got to 56 kbps, it patted itself on the back for a job well done. Meanwhile, the cable TV industry was offering speeds up to 10 Mbps on shared cables, and satellite companies were planning to offer upward of 50 Mbps. As Internet access became an increasingly important part of their business, the **telcos** (**telephone companies**) began to realize they needed a more competitive product than dialup lines. Their answer was to start offering a new digital Internet access service. Services with more bandwidth than standard telephone service are sometimes called **broadband**, although the term really is more of a marketing concept than a specific technical concept.

Initially, there were many overlapping offerings, all under the general name of **xDSL (Digital Subscriber Line)**, for various x. Below we will discuss what is probably going to become the most popular of these services, **ADSL (Asymmetric DSL)**. Since ADSL is still being developed and not all the standards are fully in place, some of the details given below may change in time, but the basic picture should remain valid. For more information about ADSL, see (Summers, 1999; and Vetter et al., 2000).

The reason that modems are so slow is that telephones were invented for carrying the human voice and the entire system has been carefully optimized for this purpose. Data have always been stepchildren. The wire, called the **local loop**, from each subscriber to the telephone company's office has traditionally been limited to about 3000 Hz by a filter in the telco office. It is this filter that limits the data rate. The actual bandwidth of the local loop depends on its length, but for typical distances of a few kilometers, 1.1 MHz is feasible.

The most common approach to offering ADSL is illustrated in Fig. 2-38. In effect, what it does is remove the filter and divide the available 1.1 MHz spectrum on the local loop into 256 independent channels of 4312.5 Hz each. Channel 0 is used for **POTS (Plain Old Telephone Service)**. Channels 1–5 are not used, to keep the voice signal and data signals from interfering with each other. Of the remaining 250 channels, one is used for upstream control and one is used for downstream control. The rest are available for user data. ADSL is like having 250 modems.

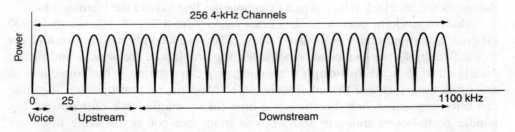

Figure 2-38. Operation of ADSL.

In principle, each of the remaining channels can be used for a full-duplex data stream, but harmonics, crosstalk, and other effects keep practical systems well below the theoretical limit. It is up to the provider to determine how many channels are used for upstream and how many for downstream. A 50–50 mix of upstream and downstream is technically possible, but most providers allocate something like 80%–90% of the bandwidth to the downstream channel since most users download more data than they upload. This choice gives rise to the "A" in ADSL. A common split is 32 channels for upstream and the rest downstream.

Within each channel the line quality is constantly monitored and the data rate adjusted continuously as needed, so different channels may have different data rates. The actual data are sent using a combination of amplitude and phase modulation with up to 15 bits per baud. With, for example, 224 downstream channels and 15 bits/baud at 4000 baud, the downstream bandwidth is 13.44 Mbps. In practice, the signal-to-noise ratio is never good enough to achieve this rate, but 4–8 Mbps is possible on short runs over high-quality loops.

A typical ADSL arrangement is shown in Fig. 2-39. In this scheme, the user or a telephone company technician must install a **NID** (**Network Interface Device**) on the customer's premises. This small plastic box marks the end of the telephone company's property and the start of the customer's property. Close to the NID (or sometimes combined with it) is a **splitter**, an analog filter that separates the 0-4000 Hz band used by POTS from the data. The POTS signal is routed to the existing telephone or fax machine, and the data signal is routed to an ADSL modem. The ADSL modem is actually a digital signal processor that has been set up to act as 250 modems operating in parallel at different frequencies. Since most current ADSL modems are external, the computer must be connected to it at high speed. Usually, this is done by putting an Ethernet card in the computer and operating a very short two-node Ethernet containing only the computer and ADSL modem. (Ethernet is a popular and inexpensive local area network standard.) Occasionally the USB port is used instead of Ethernet. In the future, internal ADSL modem cards will no doubt become available.

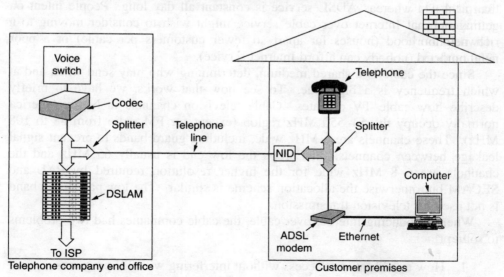

Figure 2-39. A typical ADSL equipment configuration.

At the other end of the wire, on the telco side, a corresponding splitter is installed. Here the voice portion of the signal is filtered out and sent to the normal voice switch. The signal above 26 kHz is routed to a new kind of device called a **DSLAM** (**Digital Subscriber Line Access Multiplexer**), which contains the same kind of digital signal processor as the ADSL modem. Once the digital signal has been recovered into a bit stream, packets are formed and sent off to the ISP.

Internet over Cable

Many cable TV companies are now offering Internet access over their cables. Since the technology is quite different from ADSL, it is worth looking at briefly. The cable operator in each city has a main office and a large number of boxes full of electronics, called **headends**, spread all over its territory. The headends are connected to the main office by high-bandwidth cables or fiber optics.

Each headend has one or more cables that run from it past hundreds of homes and offices. Each cable customer taps onto the cable as it passes the customer's premises. Thus hundreds of users share the same cable to the headend. Usually, the cable has a bandwidth of about 750 MHz. This system is radically different from ADSL because each telephone user has a private (i.e., not shared) wire to the telco office. However, in practice, having your own 1.1 MHz channel to a telco office is not that different than sharing a 200-MHz piece of cable spectrum to the headend with 400 users, half of whom are not using it at any one instant. It does mean, however, that a cable Internet user will get much better service at 4 A.M. than at 4 P.M whereas ADSL service is constant all day long. People intent on getting optimal Internet over cable service might wish to consider moving to a rich neighborhood (houses far apart so fewer customers per cable) or a poor neighborhood (nobody can afford Internet service).

Since the cable is a shared medium, determining who may send when and at which frequency is a big issue. To see how that works, we have to briefly describe how cable TV operates. Cable television channels in North America normally occupy the 54–550 MHz region (except for FM radio from 88 to 108 MHz). These channels are 6 MHz wide, including guard bands to prevent signal leakage between channels. In Europe the low end is usually 65 MHz and the channels are 6–8 MHz wide for the higher resolution required by PAL and SECAM but otherwise the allocation scheme is similar. The low part of the band is not used for television transmission.

When introducing Internet over cable, the cable companies had two problems to solve:

1. How to add Internet access without interfering with TV programs.

2. How to have two-way traffic when amplifiers are inherently one way.

The solutions chosen are as follows. Modern cables operate well above 550 MHz, often to 750 MHz or more. The upstream (i.e., user to headend) channels go in the 5–42 MHz band (slightly higher in Europe) and the downstream (i.e., headend to user) traffic uses the frequencies at the high end, as illustrated in Fig. 2-40.

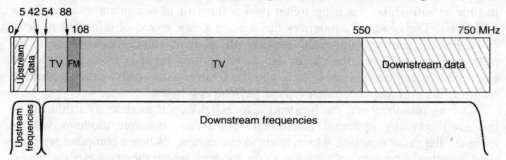

Figure 2-40. Frequency allocation in a typical cable TV system used for Internet access.

Note that since the television signals are all downstream, it is possible to use upstream amplifiers that work only in the 5–42 MHz region and downstream amplifiers that work only at 54 MHz and up, as shown in the figure. Thus, we get an asymmetry in the upstream and downstream bandwidths because more spectrum is available above television than below it. On the other hand, most of the traffic is likely to be downstream, so cable operators are not unhappy with this fact of life. As we saw earlier, telephone companies usually offer an asymmetric DSL service, even though they have no technical reason for doing so.

Internet access requires a cable modem, a device that has two interfaces on it: one to the computer and one to the cable network. The computer-to-cable-modem interface is straightforward. It is normally Ethernet, just as with ADSL. In the future, the entire modem might be a small card plugged into the computer, just as with V.9x internal modems.

The other end is more complicated. A large part of the cable standard deals with radio engineering, a subject far beyond the scope of this book. The only part worth mentioning here is that cable modems, like ADSL modems, are always on. They make a connection when turned on and maintain that connection as long as they are powered up because cable operators do not charge for connect time.

To better understand how they work, let us see what happens when a cable modem is plugged in and powered up. The modem scans the downstream channels looking for a special packet periodically put out by the headend to provide system parameters to modems that have just come on-line. Upon finding this packet, the new modem announces its presence on one of the upstream channels. The headend responds by assigning the modem to its upstream and downstream channels. These assignments can be changed later if the headend deems it necessary to balance the load.

The modem then determines its distance from the headend by sending it a special packet and seeing how long it takes to get the response. This process is called

ranging. It is important for the modem to know its distance to accommodate the way the upstream channels operate and to get the timing right. They are divided in time in **minislots**. Each upstream packet must fit in one or more consecutive minislots. The headend announces the start of a new round of minislots periodically, but the starting gun is not heard at all modems simultaneously due to the propagation time down the cable. By knowing how far it is from the headend, each modem can compute how long ago the first minislot really started. Minislot length is network dependent. A typical payload is 8 bytes.

During initialization, the headend also assigns each modem to a minislot to use for requesting upstream bandwidth. As a rule, multiple modems will be assigned the same minislot, which leads to contention. When a computer wants to send a packet, it transfers the packet to the modem, which then requests the necessary number of minislots for it. If the request is accepted, the headend puts an acknowledgement on the downstream channel telling the modem which minislots have been reserved for its packet. The packet is then sent, starting in the minislot allocated to it. Additional packets can be requested using a field in the header.

On the other hand, if there is contention for the request minislot, there will be no acknowledgement and the modem just waits a random time and tries again. After each successive failure, the randomization time is doubled to spread out the load when there is heavy traffic.

The downstream channels are managed differently from the upstream channels. For one thing, there is only one sender (the headend) so there is no contention and no need for minislots, which is actually just time division statistical multiplexing. For another, the traffic downstream is usually much larger than upstream, so a fixed packet size of 204 bytes is used. Part of that is a Reed-Solomon error-correcting code and some other overhead, leaving a user payload of 184 bytes. These numbers were chosen for compatibility with digital television using MPEG-2, so the TV and downstream data channels are formatted the same way. Logically, the connections are as depicted in Fig. 2-41.

Getting back to modem initialization, once the modem has completed ranging and gotten its upstream channel, downstream channel, and minislot assignments, it is free to start sending packets. These packets go to the headend, which relays them over a dedicated channel to the cable company's main office and then to the ISP (which may be the cable company itself). The first packet is one to the ISP requesting a network address (technically, an IP address), which is dynamically assigned. It also requests and gets an accurate time of day.

The next step involves security. Since cable is a shared medium, anybody who wants to go to the trouble to do so can read all the traffic going past him. To prevent everyone from snooping on their neighbors (literally), all traffic is encrypted in both directions. Part of the initialization procedure involves establishing encryption keys. At first one might think that having two strangers, the headend and the modem, establish a secret key in broad daylight with thousands of people watching would be impossible to accomplish. Turns out it is not, but

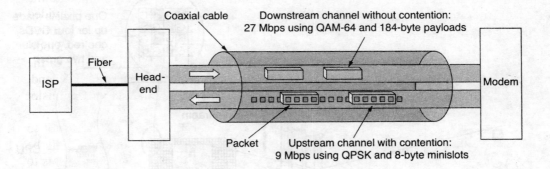

Figure 2-41. Typical details of the upstream and downstream channels in North America. QAM-64 (Quadrature Amplitude Modulation) allows 6 bits/Hz but only works at high frequencies. QPSK (Quadrature Phase Shift Keying) works at low frequencies but allows only 2 bits/Hz.

the technique used (the Diffie-Hellman algorithm) is beyond the scope of this book. See Kaufman et al. (2002) for a discussion of it.

Finally, the modem has to log in and provide its unique identifier over the secure channel. At this point the initialization is complete. The user can now log in to the ISP and get to work.

There is much more to be said about cable modems. Some relevant references are (Adams and Dulchinos, 2001; Donaldson and Jones, 2001; and Dutta-Roy, 2001).

2.4.6 Digital Cameras

An increasingly popular use of computers is for digital photography, making digital cameras a kind of computer peripheral. Let us briefly see how that works. All cameras have a lens that forms an image of the subject in the back of the camera. In a conventional camera, the back of the camera is lined with film, on which a latent image is formed when light strikes it. The latent image can be made visible by the action of certain chemicals in the film developer. A digital camera works the same way except that the film is replaced by a rectangular array of **CCDs** (**Charge-Coupled Devices**) that are sensitive to light. (Some digital cameras use CMOS, but we will concentrate on the more common CCDs here.)

When light strikes a CCD, it acquires an electrical charge. The more light, the more charge. The charge can be read off by an analog-to-digital converter as an integer from 0 to 255 (on low-end cameras) or 0 to 4095 (on digital single lens reflex cameras). The basic arrangement is shown in Fig. 2-42.

Each CCD produces a single value, independent of the color of light striking it. To form color images, the CCDs are organized in groups of four elements. A **Bayer filter** is placed on top of the CCD to allow only red light to strike one of

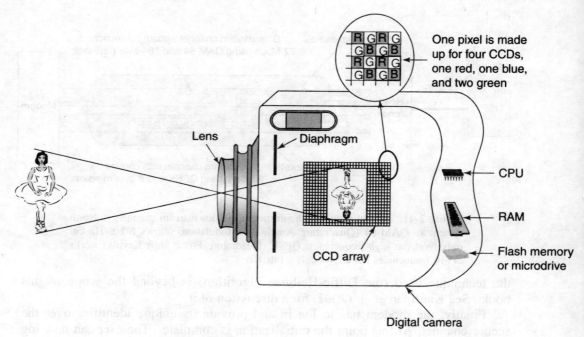

Figure 2-42. A digital camera.

the four CCDs in each group, blue light to strike another one, and green light to strike the other two. Two greens are used because using four CCDs to represent one pixel is much more convenient than using three, and the eye is more sensitive to green light than to red or blue light. When a digital camera manufacturer claims a camera has, say, 6 million pixels, it is lying. The camera has 6 million CCDs, which together form 1.5 million pixels. The image will be read out as an array of 2828×2121 pixels (on low-end cameras) or 3000 times 2000 pixels (on digital SLRs), but the extra pixels are produced by interpolation by software inside the camera.

When the camera's shutter button is depressed, software in the camera performs three tasks: setting the focus, determining the exposure, and performing the white balance. The autofocus works by analyzing the high frequency information in the image and then moving the lens until it is maximized, to give the most detail. The exposure is determined by measuring the light falling on the CCDs and then adjusting the lens diaphragm and exposure time to have the light intensity fall in the middle of the CCDs' range. Setting the white balance has to do with measuring the spectrum of the incident light to perform necessary color corrections later.

Then the image is read off the CCDs and stored as a pixel array in the camera's internal RAM. High-end digital SLRs used by photojournalists can shoot eight high-resolution frames per second for 5 seconds, and need around 1

GB of internal RAM to store the images before processing and storing them permanently. Low-end cameras have less RAM, but still quite a bit.

In the post-capture phase, the camera's software applies the white balance color correction to compensate for reddish or bluish light (e.g., from a subject in shadow or use of a flash). Then it applies an algorithm to do noise reduction and another one to compensate for defective CCDs. After that, it attempts to sharpen the image (unless this feature has been disabled) by looking for edges and increasing the intensity gradient around them.

Finally, the image may be compressed to reduce the amount of storage required. A common format is **JPEG** (**Joint Photographic Experts Group**), in which a two-dimensional spatial Fourier transform is applied and some of the high-frequency components omitted. The result of this transformation is that the image requires fewer bits to store but fine detail is lost.

When all the in-camera processing is completed, the image is written to the storage medium, usually a flash memory or a tiny removable hard disk called a **microdrive**. The postprocessing and writing can take several seconds per image.

When the user gets home, the camera can be connected to a computer, usually using, for example, a USB or FireWire cable. The images are then transferred from the camera to the computer's hard disk. Using special software, such as Adobe Photoshop, the user can then crop the image, adjust brightness, contrast, and color balance, sharpen, blur or remove portions of the image, and apply numerous filters. When the user is content with the result, the image files can be printed on a color printer, uploaded over the Internet to a photofinisher, or written to CD-ROM or DVD for archival storage or subsequent printing.

The amount of computing power, RAM, hard disk space, and software in a digital SLR camera is mind boggling. Not only does the computer have to do all the things mentioned above, but it also has to communicate with the CPU in the lens and the CPU in the flash, refresh the image on the LCD screen, and manage all the buttons, wheels, lights, displays, and gizmos on the camera in real time. This is an extremely powerful embedded system, often rivaling a desktop computer of only a few years earlier.

2.4.7 Character Codes

Each computer has a set of characters that it uses. As a bare minimum, this set includes the 26 uppercase letters, the 26 lowercase letters, the digits 0 through 9, and a set of special symbols, such as space, period, minus sign, comma, and carriage return.

In order to transfer these characters into the computer, each one is assigned a number: for example, a = 1, b = 2, ..., z = 26, + = 27, – = 28. The mapping of characters onto integers is called a **character code**. It is essential that communicating computers use the same code or they will not be able to understand one another. For this reason, standards have been developed. Below we will examine two of the most important ones.

ASCII

One widely used code is called **ASCII** (**American Standard Code for Information Interchange**). Each ASCII character has 7 bits, allowing for 128 characters in all. Figure 2-43 shows the ASCII code. Codes 0 to 1F (hexadecimal) are control characters and do not print.

Many of the ASCII control characters are intended for data transmission. For example, a message might consist of an SOH (Start of Header) character, a header, an STX (Start of Text) character, the text itself, an ETX (End of Text) character and then an EOT (End of Transmission) character. In practice, however, the messages sent over telephone lines and networks are formatted quite differently, so the ASCII transmission control characters are not used much any more.

The ASCII printing characters are straightforward. They include the upper and lowercase letters, digits, punctuation marks and a few math symbols.

UNICODE

The computer industry grew up mostly in the U.S., which led to the ASCII character set. ASCII is fine for English but less fine for other languages. French needs accents (e.g., système); German needs diacritical marks (e.g., für), and so on. Some European languages have a few letters not found in ASCII, such as the German β and the Danish ø. Some languages have entirely different alphabets (e.g., Russian and Arabic), and a few languages have no alphabet at all (e.g., Chinese). As computers spread to the four corners of the globe, and software vendors want to sell products in countries where most users do not speak English, a different character set is needed.

The first attempt at extending ASCII was IS 646, which added another 128 characters to ASCII, making it an 8-bit code called **Latin-1**. The additional characters were mostly Latin letters with accents and diacritical marks. The next attempt was IS 8859, which introduced the concept of a **code page**, a set of 256 characters for a particular language or group of languages. IS 8859-1 is Latin-1. IS 8859-2 handles the Latin-based Slavic languages (e.g., Czech, Polish, and Hungarian). IS 8859-3 contains the characters needed for Turkish, Maltese, Esperanto, and Galician, and so on. The trouble with the code page approach is that the software has to keep track of which page it is on, it is impossible to mix languages over pages, and the scheme does not cover Japanese and Chinese at all.

A group of computer companies decided to solve this problem by forming a consortium to create a new system, called **UNICODE**, and getting it proclaimed an International Standard (IS 10646). UNICODE is now supported by some

Hex	Name	Meaning	Hex	Name	Meaning
0	NUL	Null	10	DLE	Data Link Escape
1	SOH	Start Of Heading	11	DC1	Device Control 1
2	STX	Start Of Text	12	DC2	Device Control 2
3	ETX	End Of Text	13	DC3	Device Control 3
4	EOT	End Of Transmission	14	DC4	Device Control 4
5	ENQ	Enquiry	15	NAK	Negative AcKnowledgement
6	ACK	ACKnowledgement	16	SYN	SYNchronous idle
7	BEL	BELl	17	ETB	End of Transmission Block
8	BS	BackSpace	18	CAN	CANcel
9	HT	Horizontal Tab	19	EM	End of Medium
A	LF	Line Feed	1A	SUB	SUBstitute
B	VT	Vertical Tab	1B	ESC	ESCape
C	FF	Form Feed	1C	FS	File Separator
D	CR	Carriage Return	1D	GS	Group Separator
E	SO	Shift Out	1E	RS	Record Separator
F	SI	Shift In	1F	US	Unit Separator

Hex	Char	Hex	Char	Hex	Char	Hex	Char	Hex	Char	Hex	Char
20	(Space)	30	0	40	@	50	P	60	`	70	p
21	!	31	1	41	A	51	Q	61	a	71	q
22	"	32	2	42	B	52	R	62	b	72	r
23	#	33	3	43	C	53	S	63	c	73	s
24	$	34	4	44	D	54	T	64	d	74	t
25	%	35	5	45	E	55	U	65	e	75	u
26	&	36	6	46	F	56	V	66	f	76	v
27	'	37	7	47	G	57	W	67	g	77	w
28	(	38	8	48	H	58	X	68	h	78	x
29	)	39	9	49	I	59	Y	69	i	79	y
2A	*	3A	:	4A	J	5A	Z	6A	j	7A	z
2B	+	3B	;	4B	K	5B	[	6B	k	7B	{
2C	,	3C	<	4C	L	5C	\	6C	l	7C		
2D	-	3D	=	4D	M	5D	]	6D	m	7D	}
2E	.	3E	>	4E	N	5E	^	6E	n	7E	~
2F	/	3F	?	4F	O	5F	_	6F	o	7F	DEL

Figure 2-43. The ASCII character set.

programming languages (e.g., Java), some operating systems (e.g., Windows XP), and many applications. It is likely to become increasingly accepted as the computer industry goes global.

The idea behind UNICODE is to assign every character and symbol a unique 16-bit value, called a **code point**. No multibyte characters or escape sequences are used. Having every symbol be 16 bits makes writing software simpler.

With 16-bit symbols, UNICODE has 65,536 code points. Since the world's languages collectively use about 200,000 symbols, code points are a scarce resource that must be allocated with great care. About half the code points have already been allocated, and the UNICODE consortium is continually reviewing proposals to eat up the rest. To speed the acceptance of UNICODE, the consortium cleverly used Latin-1 as code points 0 to 255, making conversion between ASCII and UNICODE easy. To avoid wasting code points, each diacritical mark has its own code point. It is up to software to combine diacritical marks with their neighbors to form new characters.

The code point space is divided up into blocks, each one a multiple of 16 code points. Each major alphabet in UNICODE has a sequence of consecutive zones. Some examples (and the number of code points allocated) are Latin (336), Greek (144), Cyrillic (256), Armenian (96), Hebrew (112), Devanagari (128), Gurmukhi (128), Oriya (128), Telugu (128), and Kannada (128). Note that each of these languages has been allocated more code points than it has letters. This choice was made in part because many languages have multiple forms for each letter. For example, each letter in English has two forms—lowercase and UPPERCASE. Some languages have three or more forms, possibly depending on whether the letter is at the start, middle, or end of a word.

In addition to these alphabets, code points have been allocated for diacritical marks (112), punctuation marks (112), subscripts and superscripts (48), currency symbols (48), math symbols (256), geometric shapes (96), and dingbats (192).

After these come the symbols needed for Chinese, Japanese, and Korean. First are 1024 phonetic symbols (e.g., katakana and bopomofo) and then the unified Han ideographs (20,992) used in Chinese and Japanese, and the Korean Hangul syllables (11,156).

To allow users to invent special characters for special purposes, 6400 code points have been allocated for local use.

While UNICODE solves many problems associated with internationalization, it does not (attempt to) solve all the world's problems. For example, while the Latin alphabet is in order, the Han ideographs are not in dictionary order. As a consequence, an English program can examine "cat" and "dog" and sort them alphabetically by simply comparing the UNICODE value of their first character. A Japanese program needs external tables to figure out which of two symbols comes before the other in the dictionary.

Another issue is that new words are popping up all the time. Fifty years ago nobody talked about applets, cyberspace, gigabytes, lasers, modems, smileys, or videotapes. Adding new words in English does not require new code points. Adding them in Japanese does. In addition to new technical words, there is a demand for adding at least 20,000 new (mostly Chinese) personal and place names. Blind people think Braille should be in there, and special interest groups of all kinds want what they perceive as their rightful code points. The UNICODE consortium reviews and decides on all new proposals.

UNICODE uses the same code point for characters that look almost identical but have different meanings or are written slightly differently in Japanese and Chinese (as though English word processors always spelled "blue" as blew" because they sound the same). Some people view this as an optimization to save scarce code points; others see it as Anglo-Saxon cultural imperialism (and you thought assigning 16-bit values to characters was not highly political?). To make matters worse, a full Japanese dictionary has 50,000 kanji (excluding names), so with only 20,992 code points available for the Han ideographs, choices had to be made. Not all Japanese people think that a consortium of computer companies, even if a few of them are Japanese, is the ideal forum to make these choices.

2.5 SUMMARY

Computer systems are built up from three types of components: processors, memories, and I/O devices. The task of a processor is to fetch instructions one at a time from a memory, decode them, and execute them. The fetch-decode-execute cycle can always be described as an algorithm and, in fact, is sometimes carried out by a software interpreter running at a lower level. To gain speed, many computers now have one or more pipelines or have a superscalar design with multiple functional units that operate in parallel.

Systems with multiple processors are increasingly common. Parallel computers include array processors, on which the same operation is performed on multiple data sets at the same time, multiprocessors, in which multiple CPUs share a common memory, and multicomputers, in which multiple computers each have their own memories but communicate by message passing.

Memories can be categorized as primary or secondary. The primary memory is used to hold the program currently being executed. Its access time is short—a few tens of nanoseconds at most—and independent of the address being accessed. Caches reduce this access time even more. Some memories are equipped with error-correcting codes to enhance reliability.

Secondary memories, in contrast, have access times that are much longer (milliseconds or more) and dependent on the location of the data being read or written. Tapes, magnetic disks and optical disks are the most common secondary memories. Magnetic disks come in many varieties, including floppy disks, Winchester disks, IDE disks, SCSI disks, and RAIDs. Optical disks include CD-ROMs, CD-Rs, and DVDs.

I/O devices are used to transfer information into and out of the computer. They are connected to the processor and memory by one or more buses. Examples are terminals, mice, printers, and modems. Most I/O devices use the ASCII character code, although UNICODE is rapidly gaining acceptance as the computer industry goes global.

PROBLEMS

1. Consider the operation of a machine with the data path of Figure 2-2. Suppose that loading the ALU input registers takes 5 nsec, running the ALU takes 10 nsec, and storing the result back in the register scratchpad takes 5 nsec. What is the maximum number of MIPS this machine is capable of in the absence of pipelining?

2. What is the purpose of step 2 in the list of Sec. 2.1.2? What would happen if this step were omitted?

3. On computer 1, all instructions take 10 nsec to execute. On computer 2, they all take 5 nsec to execute. Can you say for certain that computer 2 is faster? Discuss.

4. Imagine you are designing a single-chip computer for an embedded system. The chip is going to have all its memory on chip and running at the same speed as the CPU with no access penalty. Examine each of the principles discussed in Sec. 2.1.4 and tell whether they are so important (assuming that high performance is still desired).

5. A certain computation is highly sequential—that is, each step depends on the one preceding it. Would an array processor or a pipeline processor be more appropriate for this computation? Explain.

6. To compete with the newly-invented printing press, a medieval monastery decided to mass-produce handwritten paperback books by assembling a vast number of scribes in a huge hall. The head monk would then call out the first word of the book to be produced and all the scribes would copy it down. Then the head monk would call out the second word and all the scribes would copy it down. This process was repeated until the entire book had been read aloud and copied. Which of the parallel processor systems discussed in Sec. 2.1.6 does this system resemble most closely?

7. As one goes down the five-level memory hierarchy discussed in the text, the access time increases. Make a reasonable guess about the ratio of the access time of optical disk to that of register memory. Assume that the disk is already on-line.

8. Sociologists can get three possible answers to a typical survey question such as "Do you believe in the tooth fairy?"—namely, yes, no, and no opinion. With this in mind, the Sociomagnetic Computer Company has decided to build a computer to process survey data. This computer has a trinary memory—that is, each byte (tryte?) consists of 8 trits, with a trit holding a 0, 1, or 2. How many trits are needed to hold a 6-bit number? Give an expression for the number of trits needed to hold n bits.

9. Compute the data rate of the human eye using the following information. The visual field consists of about 10^6 elements (pixels). Each pixel can be reduced to a superposition of the three primary colors, each of which has 64 intensities. The time resolution is 100 msec.

10. Compute the data rate of the human ear from the following information. People can hear frequencies up to 22 kHz. To capture all the information in a sound signal at 22 kHz, it is necessary to sample the sound at twice that frequency, that is, at 44 kHz. A 16-bit sample is probably enough to capture most of the auditory information (i.e., the ear cannot distinguish more than 65,535 intensity levels).

11. Genetic information in all living things is coded as DNA molecules. A DNA molecule is a linear sequence of the four basic nucleotides: A, C, G, and T. The human genome contains approximately 3×10^9 nucleotides in the form of about 30,000 genes. What is the total information capacity (in bits) of the human genome? What is the maximum information capacity (in bits) of the average gene?

12. A certain computer can be equipped with 268,435,456 bytes of memory. Why would a manufacturer choose such a peculiar number, instead of an easy-to-remember number like 250,000,000?

13. Devise a 7-bit even-parity Hamming code for the digits 0 to 9.

14. Devise a code for the digits 0 to 9 whose Hamming distance is 2.

15. In a Hamming code, some bits are "wasted" in the sense that they are used for checking and not information. What is the percentage of wasted bits for messages whose total length (data + check bits) is $2^n - 1$? Evaluate this expression numerically for values of n from 3 to 10.

16. The disk illustrated in Figure 2-19 has 1024 sectors/track and a rotation rate of 7200 RPM. What is the sustained transfer rate of the disk over one track?

17. A computer has a bus with a 5 nsec cycle time, during which it can read or write a 32-bit word from memory. The computer has an Ultra4-SCSI disk that uses the bus and runs at 160 Mbytes/sec. The CPU normally fetches and executes one 32-bit instruction every 1 nsec. How much does the disk slow down the CPU?

18. Imagine you are writing the disk management part of an operating system. Logically, you represent the disk as a sequence of blocks, from 0 on the inside to some maximum on the outside. As files are created, you have to allocate free sectors. You could do it from the outside in or the inside out. Does it matter which strategy you choose? Explain your answer.

19. How long does it take to read a disk with 10,000 cylinders, each containing four tracks of 2048 sectors? First, all the sectors of track 0 are to be read starting at sector 0, then all the sectors of track 1 starting at sector 0, and so on. The rotation time is 10 msec, and a seek takes 1 msec between adjacent cylinders and 20 msec for the worst case. Switching between tracks of a cylinder can be done instantaneously.

20. RAID level 3 is able to correct single-bit errors using only one parity drive. What is the point of RAID level 2? After all, it also can only correct one error and takes more drives to do so.

21. What is the exact data capacity (in bytes) of a mode 2 CD-ROM containing the now-standard 80-min media? What is the capacity for user data in mode 1?

22. To burn a CD-R, the laser must pulse on and off at a high speed. When running at 10x speed in mode 1, what is the pulse length, in nanoseconds?

23. To be able to fit 133 minutes worth of video on a single-sided single-layer DVD, a fair amount of compression is required. Calculate the compression factor required. Assume that 3.5 GB of space is available for the video track, that the image resolution is 720×480 pixels with 24-bit color, and images are displayed at 30 frames/sec.

24. Blu-Ray runs at 4.5 MB/sec and has a capacity of 25 GB. How long does it take to read the entire disk?

25. The transfer rate between a CPU and its associated memory is orders of magnitude higher than the mechanical I/O transfer rate. How can this imbalance cause inefficiencies? How can it be alleviated?

26. A manufacturer advertises that its color bit-map terminal can display 2^{24} different colors. Yet the hardware only has 1 byte for each pixel. How can this be done?

27. A bit-map terminal has a 1600×1200 display. The display is redrawn 75 times a second. How long is the pulse corresponding to one pixel?

28. In a certain font, a monochrome laser printer can print 50 lines of 80 characters per page. The average character occupies a box 2 mm $\times$ 2 mm, about 25% of which is toner. The rest is blank. The toner layer is 25 microns thick. The printer's toner cartridge measures $25 \times 8 \times 2$ cm. How many pages is one toner cartridge good for?

29. When odd-parity ASCII text is transmitted asynchronously at a rate of 5600 characters/sec over a 56,000 bps modem, what percent of the received bits actually contain data (as opposed to overhead)?

30. The Hi-Fi Modem Company has just designed a new frequency-modulation modem that uses 64 frequencies instead of just 2. Each second is divided into n equal time intervals, each of which contains one of the 64 possible tones. How many bits per second can this modem transmit, using synchronous transmission?

31. An Internet user has subscribed to a 2 Mbps ADSL service. Her neighbor has subscribed to a cable Internet service that has a shared bandwidth of 12 MHz. The modulation scheme in use is QAM-64. There are n houses on the cable, each with one computer. A fraction f of these computers are online at any one time. Under what conditions will the cable user get better service than the ADSL user?

32. A digital camera has a resolution of 3000×2000 pixels, with 3 bytes/pixel for RGB color. The manufacturer of the camera wants to be able to write a JPEG image at a 5x compression factor to the flash memory in 2 sec. What data rate is required?

33. A high-end digital camera has a sensor with 16 million pixels, each with 3 bytes/pixel. How many pictures can be stored on a 1-GB flash memory card if the compression factor is 5x? Assume that 1 GB means 2^{30} bytes.

34. Estimate how many characters, including spaces, a typical computer science textbook contains. How many bits are needed to encode a book in ASCII with parity? How many CD-ROMs are needed to store a computer science library of 10,000 books? How many double-side, dual-layer DVDs are needed for the same library?

35. Write a procedure *hamming*(*ascii*, *encoded*) that converts the low-order 7 bits of *ascii* into an 11-bit integer codeword stored in *encoded*.

36. Write a function *distance*(*code*, *n*, *k*) that takes an array *code* of *n* characters of *k* bits each as input, and returns the distance of the character set as output.

3

THE DIGITAL LOGIC LEVEL

At the bottom of the hierarchy of Fig. 1-2 we find the digital logic level, the computer's real hardware. In this chapter, we will examine many aspects of digital logic, as a building block for the study of higher levels in subsequent chapters. This subject is on the boundary of computer science and electrical engineering, but the material is self-contained, so no previous hardware or engineering experience is needed to follow it.

The basic elements from which all digital computers are constructed are amazingly simple. We will begin our study by looking at these basic elements and also at the special two-valued algebra (Boolean algebra) used to analyze them. Next we will examine some fundamental circuits that can be built using gates in simple combinations, including circuits for doing arithmetic. The following topic is how gates can be combined to store information, that is, how memories are organized. After that, we come to the subject of CPUs and especially how single-chip CPUs interface with memory and peripheral devices. Numerous examples from industry will be discussed later in this chapter.

3.1 GATES AND BOOLEAN ALGEBRA

Digital circuits can be constructed from a small number of primitive elements by combining them in innumerable ways. In the following sections we will describe these primitive elements, show how they can be combined, and introduce a powerful mathematical technique that can be used to analyze their behavior.

135

3.1.1 Gates

A digital circuit is one in which only two logical values are present. Typically, a signal between 0 and 1 volt represents one value (e.g., binary 0) and a signal between 2 and 5 volts represents the other value (e.g., binary 1). Voltages outside these two ranges are not permitted. Tiny electronic devices, called **gates**, can compute various functions of these two-valued signals. These gates form the hardware basis on which all digital computers are built.

The details of how gates work inside is beyond the scope of this book, belonging to the **device level**, which is below our level 0. Nevertheless, we will now digress ever so briefly to take a quick look at the basic idea, which is not difficult. All modern digital logic ultimately rests on the fact that a transistor can be made to operate as a very fast binary switch. In Fig. 3-1(a) we have shown a bipolar transistor (the circle) embedded in a simple circuit. This transistor has three connections to the outside world: the **collector**, the **base**, and the **emitter**. When the input voltage, V_{in}, is below a certain critical value, the transistor turns off and acts like an infinite resistance. This causes the output of the circuit, V_{out}, to take on a value close to V_{cc}, an externally regulated voltage, typically +5 volts for this type of transistor. When V_{in} exceeds the critical value, the transistor switches on and acts like a wire, causing V_{out} to be pulled down to ground (by convention, 0 volts).

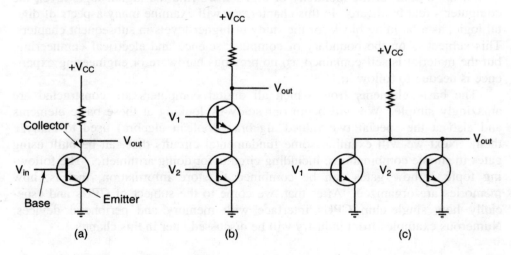

Figure 3-1. (a) A transistor inverter. (b) A NAND gate. (c) A NOR gate.

The important thing to notice is that when V_{in} is low, V_{out} is high, and vice versa. This circuit is thus an inverter, converting a logical 0 to a logical 1, and a logical 1 to a logical 0. The resistor (the jagged line) is needed to limit the amount of current drawn by the transistor so it does not burn out. The time required to switch from one state to the other is typically a few nanoseconds.

In Fig. 3-1(b) two transistors are cascaded in series. If both V_1 and V_2 are high, both transistors will conduct and V_{out} will be pulled low. If either input is low, the corresponding transistor will turn off, and the output will be high. In other words, V_{out} will be low if and only if both V_1 and V_2 are high.

In Fig. 3-1(c) the two transistors are wired in parallel instead of in series. In this configuration, if either input is high, the corresponding transistor will turn on and pull the output down to ground. If both inputs are low, the output will remain high.

These three circuits, or their equivalents, form the three simplest gates. They are called NOT, NAND, and NOR gates, respectively. NOT gates are often called **inverters**; we will use the two terms interchangeably. If we now adopt the convention that "high" (V_{cc} volts) is a logical 1, and that "low" (ground) is a logical 0, we can express the output value as a function of the input values. The symbols used to depict these three gates are shown in Fig. 3-2(a)–(c), along with the functional behavior for each circuit. In these figures, A and B are inputs and X is the output. Each row specifies the output for a different combination of the inputs.

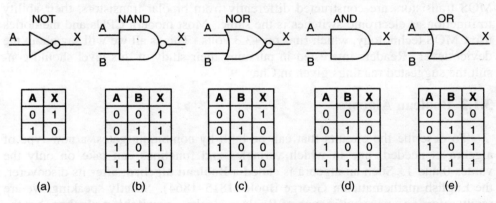

Figure 3-2. The symbols and functional behavior for the five basic gates.

If the output signal of Fig. 3-1(b) is fed into an inverter circuit, we get another circuit with precisely the inverse of the NAND gate—namely, a circuit whose output is 1 if and only if both inputs are 1. Such a circuit is called an AND gate; its symbol and functional description are given in Fig. 3-2(d). Similarly, the NOR gate can be connected to an inverter to yield a circuit whose output is 1 if either or both inputs is a 1 but 0 if both inputs are 0. The symbol and functional description of this circuit, called an OR gate, are given in Fig. 3-2(e). The small circles used as part of the symbols for the inverter, NAND gate, and NOR gate are called **inversion bubbles**. They are often used in other contexts as well to indicate an inverted signal.

The five gates of Fig. 3-2 are the principal building blocks of the digital logic level. From the foregoing discussion, it should be clear that the NAND and NOR gates require two transistors each, whereas the AND and OR gates require three each. For this reason, many computers are based on NAND and NOR gates rather than the more familiar AND and OR gates. (In practice, all the gates are implemented somewhat differently, but NAND and NOR are still simpler than AND and OR.) In passing it is worth noting that gates may well have more than two inputs. In principle, a NAND gate, for example, may have arbitrarily many inputs, but in practice more than eight inputs is unusual.

Although the subject of how gates are constructed belongs to the device level, we would like to mention the major families of manufacturing technology because they are referred to frequently. The two major technologies are **bipolar** and **MOS** (Metal Oxide Semiconductor). The major bipolar types are **TTL** (Transistor-Transistor Logic), which had been the workhorse of digital electronics for years, and **ECL** (Emitter-Coupled Logic), which was used when very high-speed operation is required. For computer circuits, MOS has now largely taken over.

MOS gates are slower than TTL and ECL but require much less power and take up much less space, so large numbers of them can be packed together tightly. MOS comes in many varieties, including PMOS, NMOS, and CMOS. While MOS transistors are constructed differently from bipolar transistors, their ability to function as electronic switches is the same. Most modern CPUs and memories use CMOS technology, which runs on +3.3 volts. This is all we will say about the device level. Readers interested in pursuing their study of this level should consult the suggested readings given in Chap. 9.

3.1.2 Boolean Algebra

To describe the circuits that can be built by combining gates, a new type of algebra is needed, one in which variables and functions can take on only the values 0 and 1. Such an algebra is called a **Boolean algebra**, after its discoverer, the English mathematician George Boole (1815–1864). Strictly speaking, we are really referring to a specific type of Boolean algebra, a **switching algebra**, but the term "Boolean algebra" is so widely used to mean "switching algebra" that we will not make the distinction.

Just as there are functions in "ordinary" (i.e., high school) algebra, so are there functions in Boolean algebra. A Boolean function has one or more input variables and yields a result that depends only on the values of these variables. A simple function, f, can be defined by saying that $f(A)$ is 1 if A is 0 and $f(A)$ is 0 if A is 1. This function is the NOT function of Fig. 3-2(a).

Because a Boolean function of n variables has only 2^n possible combinations of input values, the function can be completely described by giving a table with 2^n rows, each row telling the value of the function for a different combination of input values. Such a table is called a **truth table**. The tables of Fig. 3-2 are all examples of truth tables. If we agree to always list the rows of a truth table in numerical order (base 2), that is, for two variables in the order 00, 01, 10, and 11, the function can be completely described by the 2^n-bit binary number obtained by reading the result column of the truth table vertically. Thus NAND is 1110, NOR is 1000, AND is 0001, and OR is 0111. Obviously, only 16 Boolean functions of two variables exist, corresponding to the 16 possible 4-bit result strings. In contrast, ordinary algebra has an infinite number of functions of two variables, none of which can be described by giving a table of outputs for all possible inputs because each variable can take on any one of an infinite number of possible values.

Figure 3-3(a) shows the truth table for a Boolean function of three variables: $M = f(A, B, C)$. This function is the majority logic function, that is, it is 0 if a majority of its inputs are 0 and 1 if a majority of its inputs are 1. Although any Boolean function can be fully specified by giving its truth table, as the number of variables increases, this notation becomes increasingly cumbersome. Instead, another notation is frequently used.

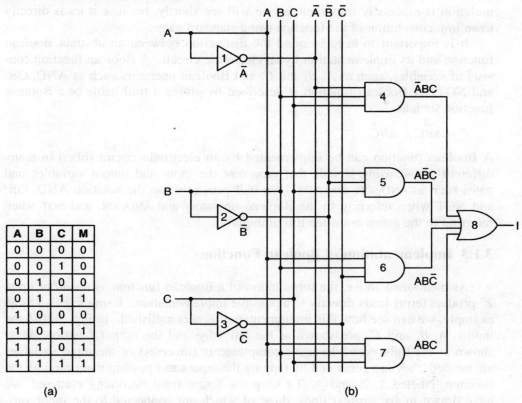

A	B	C	M
0	0	0	0
0	0	1	0
0	1	0	0
0	1	1	1
1	0	0	0
1	0	1	1
1	1	0	1
1	1	1	1

(a)   (b)

Figure 3-3. (a) The truth table for the majority function of three variables. (b) A circuit for (a).

To see how this other notation comes about, note that any Boolean function can be specified by telling which combinations of input variables give an output value of 1. For the function of Fig. 3-3(a) there are four combinations of input variables that make M 1. By convention, we will place a bar over an input variable to indicate that its value is inverted. The absence of a bar means that it is not inverted. Furthermore, we will use implied multiplication or a dot to mean the Boolean AND function and + to mean the Boolean OR function. Thus, for example, $A\bar{B}C$ takes the value 1 only when $A = 1$ and $B = 0$ and $C = 1$. Also, $A\bar{B} + \bar{B}C$ is 1 only when ($A = 1$ and $B = 0$) or ($B = 1$ and $C = 0$). The four rows of Fig. 3-3(a) producing 1 bits in the output are: $\bar{A}\bar{B}C$, $\bar{A}B\bar{C}$, $AB\bar{C}$, and ABC. The function, M, is true (i.e., 1) if any one of these four conditions is true; hence we can write

$$M = \bar{A}\bar{B}C + \bar{A}B\bar{C} + AB\bar{C} + ABC$$

as a compact way of giving the truth table. A function of n variables can thus be described by giving a "sum" of at most 2^n n-variable "product" terms. This formulation is especially important, as we will see shortly, because it leads directly to an implementation of the function using standard gates.

It is important to keep in mind the distinction between an abstract Boolean function and its implementation by an electronic circuit. A Boolean function consists of variables, such as A, B, and C, and Boolean operators such as AND, OR, and NOT. A Boolean function is described by giving a truth table or a Boolean function such as

$$F = A\bar{B}C + AB\bar{C}$$

A Boolean function can be implemented by an electronic circuit (often in many different ways) using signals that represent the input and output variables and gates such as AND, OR, and NOT. We will generally use the notation AND, OR, and NOT when referring to the Boolean operators and AND, OR, and NOT when referring to the gates, but often it is ambiguous.

3.1.3 Implementation of Boolean Functions

As mentioned above, the formulation of a Boolean function as a sum of up to 2^n product terms leads directly to a possible implementation. Using Fig. 3-3 as an example, we can see how this implementation is accomplished. In Fig. 3-3(b), the inputs, A, B, and C, are shown at the left edge and the output function, M, is shown at the right edge. Because complements (inverses) of the input variables are needed, they are generated by tapping the inputs and passing them through the inverters labeled 1, 2, and 3. To keep the figure from becoming cluttered, we have drawn in six vertical lines, three of which are connected to the input variables, and three of which are connected to their complements. These lines provide a convenient source for the inputs to subsequent gates. For example, gates 5, 6, and 7 all use A as an input. In an actual circuit these gates would probably be wired directly to A without using any intermediate "vertical" wires.

The circuit contains four AND gates, one for each term in the equation for M (i.e., one for each row in the truth table having a 1 bit in the result column). Each

AND gate computes one row of the truth table, as indicated. Finally, all the product terms are ORed together to get the final result.

The circuit of Fig. 3-3(b) uses a convention that we will use repeatedly throughout this book: when two lines cross, no connection is implied unless a heavy dot is present at the intersection. For example, the output of gate 3 crosses all six vertical lines but it is connected only to C. Be warned that some authors use other conventions.

From the example of Fig. 3-3 it should be clear how to implement a circuit for any Boolean function:

1. Write down the truth table for the function.

2. Provide inverters to generate the complement of each input.

3. Draw an AND gate for each term with a 1 in the result column.

4. Wire the AND gates to the appropriate inputs.

5. Feed the output of all the AND gates into an OR gate.

Although we have shown how any Boolean function can be implemented using NOT, AND, and OR gates, it is often convenient to implement circuits using only a single type of gate. Fortunately, it is straightforward to convert circuits generated by the preceding algorithm to pure NAND or pure NOR form. To make such a conversion, all we need is a way to implement NOT, AND, and OR using a single gate type. The top row of Fig. 3-4 shows how all three of these can be implemented using only NAND gates; the bottom row shows how it can be done using only NOR gates. (These are straightforward, but there are other ways, too.)

One way to implement a Boolean function using only NAND or only NOR gates is first follow the procedure given above for constructing it with NOT, AND, and OR. Then replace the multi-input gates with equivalent circuits using two-input gates. For example, $A + B + C + D$ can be computed as $(A + B) + (C + D)$, using three two-input OR gates. Finally, the NOT, AND, and OR gates are replaced by the circuits of Fig. 3-4.

Although this procedure does not lead to the optimal circuits, in the sense of the minimum number of gates, it does show that a solution is always feasible. Both NAND and NOR gates are said to be **complete**, because any Boolean function can be computed using either of them. No other gate has this property, which is another reason they are often preferred for the building blocks of circuits.

3.1.4 Circuit Equivalence

Circuit designers often try to reduce the number of gates in their products to reduce component cost, printed circuit board space, power consumption, and so on. To reduce the complexity of a circuit, the designer must find another circuit

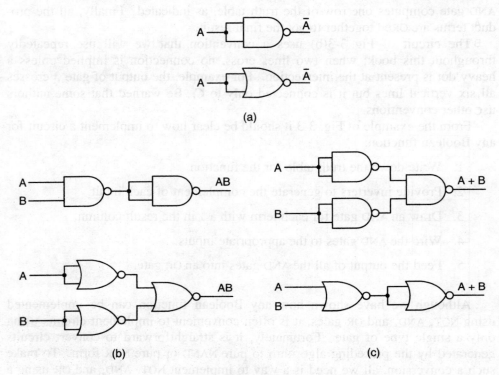

Figure 3-4. Construction of (a) NOT, (b) AND, and (c) OR gates using only NAND gates or only NOR gates.

that computes the same function as the original but does so with fewer gates (or perhaps with simpler gates, for example, two-input gates instead of four-input gates). In the search for equivalent circuits, Boolean algebra can be a valuable tool.

As an example of how Boolean algebra can be used, consider the circuit and truth table for $AB + AC$ shown in Fig. 3-5(a). Although we have not discussed them yet, many of the rules of ordinary algebra also hold for Boolean algebra. In particular, $AB + AC$ can be factored into $A(B + C)$ using the distributive law. Figure 3-5(b) shows the circuit and truth table for $A(B + C)$. Because two functions are equivalent if and only if they have the same output for all possible inputs, it is easy to see from the truth tables of Fig. 3-5 that $A(B + C)$ is equivalent to $AB + AC$. Despite this equivalence, the circuit of Fig. 3-5(b) is clearly better than that of Fig. 3-5(a) because it contains fewer gates.

In general, a circuit designer starts with a Boolean function and then applies the laws of Boolean algebra to it in an attempt to find a simpler but equivalent one. From the final function, a circuit can be constructed.

To use this approach, we need some identities from Boolean algebra. Figure 3-6 shows some of the major ones. It is interesting to note that each law has two

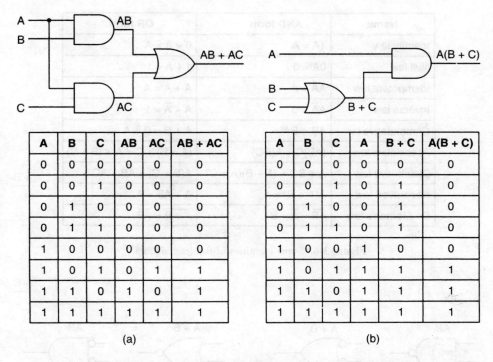

Figure 3-5. Two equivalent functions. (a) $AB + AC$. (b) $A(B + C)$.

forms that are **duals** of each other. By interchanging AND and OR and also 0 and 1, either form can be produced from the other one. All the laws can be easily proven by constructing their truth tables. Except for DeMorgan's law, the absorption law, and the AND form of the distributive law, the results are reasonably intuitive. DeMorgan's law can be extended to more than two variables, for example, $\overline{ABC} = \overline{A} + \overline{B} + \overline{C}$.

DeMorgan's law suggests an alternative notation. In Fig. 3-7(a) the AND form is shown with negation indicated by inversion bubbles, both for input and output. Thus an OR gate with inverted inputs is equivalent to a NAND gate. From Fig. 3-7(b), the dual form of DeMorgan's law, it should be clear that a NOR gate can be drawn as an AND gate with inverted inputs. By negating both forms of DeMorgan's law, we arrive at Fig. 3-7(c) and (d), which show equivalent representations of the AND and OR gates. Analogous symbols exist for the multiple variable forms of DeMorgan's law (e.g., an n input NAND gate becomes an OR gate with n inverted inputs).

Using the identities of Fig. 3-7 and the analogous ones for multi-input gates, it is easy to convert the sum-of-products representation of a truth table to pure NAND or pure NOR form. As an example, consider the EXCLUSIVE OR function of Fig. 3-8(a). The standard sum-of-products circuit is shown in Fig. 3-8(b). To

Name	AND form	OR form
Identity law	$1A = A$	$0 + A = A$
Null law	$0A = 0$	$1 + A = 1$
Idempotent law	$AA = A$	$A + A = A$
Inverse law	$A\overline{A} = 0$	$A + \overline{A} = 1$
Commutative law	$AB = BA$	$A + B = B + A$
Associative law	$(AB)C = A(BC)$	$(A + B) + C = A + (B + C)$
Distributive law	$A + BC = (A + B)(A + C)$	$A(B + C) = AB + AC$
Absorption law	$A(A + B) = A$	$A + AB = A$
De Morgan's law	$\overline{AB} = \overline{A} + \overline{B}$	$\overline{A + B} = \overline{A}\overline{B}$

Figure 3-6. Some identities of Boolean algebra.

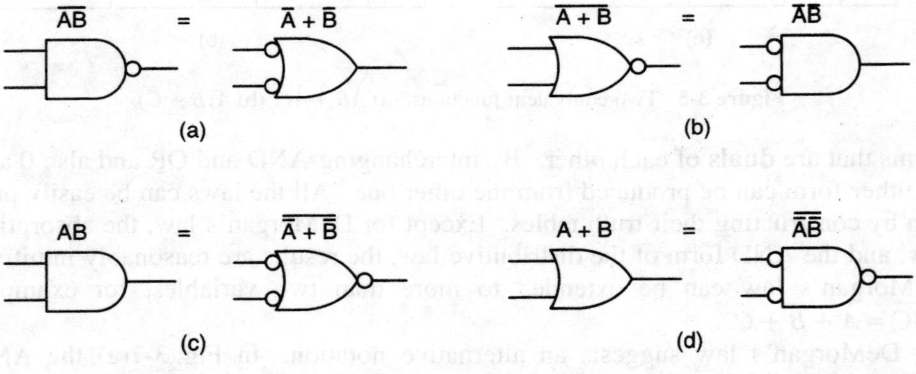

Figure 3-7. Alternative symbols for some gates: (a) NAND. (b) NOR. (c) AND. (d) OR.

convert to NAND form, the lines connecting the output of the AND gates to the input of the OR gate should be redrawn with two inversion bubbles, as shown in Fig. 3-8(c). Finally, using Fig. 3-7(a), we arrive at Fig. 3-8(d). The variables A and $\overline{B}$ can be generated from A and B using NAND or NOR gates with their inputs tied together. Note that inversion bubbles can be moved along a line at will, for example, from the outputs of the input gates in Fig. 3-8(d) to the inputs of the output gate.

As a final note on circuit equivalence, we will now demonstrate the surprising result that the same physical gate can compute different functions, depending on the conventions used. In Fig. 3-9(a) we show the output of a certain gate, F, for

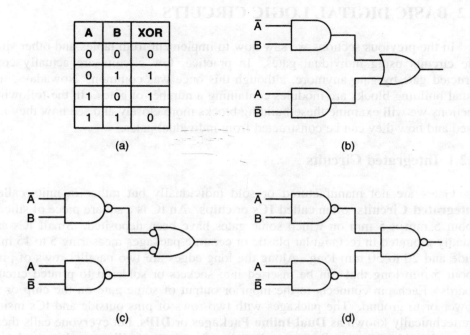

A	B	XOR
0	0	0
0	1	1
1	0	1
1	1	0

(a)

(b)

(c)

(d)

Figure 3-8. (a) The truth table for the XOR function. (b)-(d) Three circuits for computing it.

different input combinations. Both inputs and outputs are shown in volts. If we adopt the convention that 0 volts is logical 0 and 3.3 volts or 5 volts is logical 1, called **positive logic**, we get the truth table of Fig. 3-9(b), the AND function. If, however, we adopt **negative logic**, which has 0 volts as logical 1 and 3.3 volts or 5 volts as logical 0, we get the truth table of Fig. 3-9(c), the OR function.

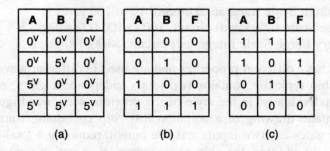

A	B	F
0^V	0^V	0^V
0^V	5^V	0^V
5^V	0^V	0^V
5^V	5^V	5^V

(a)

A	B	F
0	0	0
0	1	0
1	0	0
1	1	1

(b)

A	B	F
1	1	1
1	0	1
0	1	1
0	0	0

(c)

Figure 3-9. (a) Electrical characteristics of a device. (b) Positive logic. (c) Negative logic.

Thus the convention chosen to map voltages onto logical values is critical. Except where otherwise specified, we will henceforth use positive logic, so the terms logical 1, true, and high are synonyms, as are logical 0, false, and low.

3.2 BASIC DIGITAL LOGIC CIRCUITS

In the previous sections we saw how to implement truth tables and other simple circuits using individual gates. In practice, few circuits are actually constructed gate-by-gate anymore, although this once was common. Nowadays, the usual building blocks are modules containing a number of gates. In the following sections we will examine these building blocks more closely and see how they are used and how they can be constructed from individual gates.

3.2.1 Integrated Circuits

Gates are not manufactured or sold individually but rather in units called **Integrated Circuits**, often called **ICs** or **chips**. An IC is a square piece of silicon about 5 mm × 5 mm on which some gates have been deposited. Small ICs are usually mounted in rectangular plastic or ceramic packages measuring 5 to 15 mm wide and 20 to 50 mm long. Along the long edges are two parallel rows of pins about 5 mm long that can be inserted into sockets or soldered to printed circuit boards. Each pin connects to the input or output of some gate on the chip or to power or to ground. The packages with two rows of pins outside and ICs inside are technically known as **Dual Inline Packages** or **DIPs**, but everyone calls them chips, thus blurring the distinction between the piece of silicon and its package. The most common packages have 14, 16, 18, 20, 22, 24, 28, 40, 64, or 68 pins. For large chips, square packages with pins on all four sides or on the bottom are often used.

Chips can be divided into rough classes based on the number of gates they contain, as given below. This classification scheme is obviously extremely crude, but it is sometimes useful.

    SSI (Small Scale Integrated) circuit: 1 to 10 gates.
    MSI (Medium Scale Integrated) circuit: 10 to 100 gates.
    LSI (Large Scale Integrated) circuit: 100 to 100,000 gates.
    VLSI (Very Large Scale Integrated) circuit: >100,000 gates.

These classes have different properties and are used in different ways.

An SSI chip typically contains two to six independent gates, each of which can be used individually, in the style of the previous sections. Figure 3-10 illustrates a schematic drawing of a common SSI chip containing four NAND gates. Each of these gates has two inputs and one output, requiring a total of 12 pins for the four gates. In addition, the chip needs power (V_{cc}), and ground (GND), which are shared by all gates. The package generally has a notch near pin 1 to identify the orientation. To avoid clutter in circuit diagrams, neither power, nor ground, nor unused gates are conventionally shown.

Many other chips like this are available for a few cents each. Each SSI chip has a handful of gates and up to 20 or so pins. In the 1970s, computers were con-

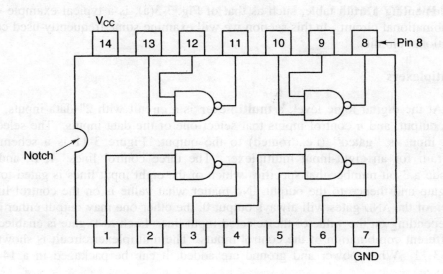

Figure 3-10. An SSI chip containing four gates.

structed out of large numbers of these chips, but nowadays an entire CPU and a substantial amount of (cache) memory is etched onto a single chip.

For our purposes, all gates are ideal in the sense that the output appears as soon as the input is applied. In reality, chips have a finite **gate delay**, which includes both the signal propagation time through the chip and the switching time. Typical delays are 1 to 10 nsec.

It is within the current state of the art to put almost 10 million transistors on a chip. Because any circuit can be built up from NAND gates, you might think that a manufacturer could make a very general chip containing 5 million NAND gates. Unfortunately, such a chip would need 15,000,002 pins. With the standard pin spacing of 0.1 inch, the chip would be over 19 km long, which might have a negative effect on sales. Clearly, the only way to take advantage of the technology is to design circuits with a high gate/pin ratio. In the following sections we will look at simple MSI circuits that combine a number of gates internally to provide a useful function requiring only a limited number of external connections (pins).

3.2.2 Combinational Circuits

Many applications of digital logic require a circuit with multiple inputs and multiple outputs in which the outputs are uniquely determined by the current inputs. Such a circuit is called a **combinational circuit**. Not all circuits have this property. For example, a circuit containing memory elements may well generate outputs that depend on the stored values as well as the input variables. A circuit implementing a truth table, such as that of Fig. 3-3(a), is a typical example of a combinational circuit. In this section we will examine some frequently-used combinational circuits.

Multiplexers

At the digital logic level, a **multiplexer** is a circuit with 2^n data inputs, one data output, and n control inputs that select one of the data inputs. The selected data input is "gated" (i.e., routed) to the output. Figure 3-11 is a schematic diagram for an eight-input multiplexer. The three control lines, A, B, and C, encode a 3-bit number that specifies which of the eight input lines is gated to the OR gate and thence to the output. No matter what value is on the control lines, seven of the AND gates will always output 0; the other one may output either 0 or 1, depending on the value of the selected input line. Each AND gate is enabled by a different combination of the control inputs. The multiplexer circuit is shown in Fig. 3-11. When power and ground are added, it can be packaged in a 14-pin package.

Using the multiplexer, we can implement the majority function of Fig. 3-3(a), as shown in Fig. 3-12(b). For each combination of A, B, and C, one of the data input lines is selected. Each input is wired to either V_{cc} (logical 1) or ground (logical 0). The algorithm for wiring the inputs is simple: input D_i is the same as the value in row i of the truth table. In Fig. 3-3(a), rows 0, 1, 2, and 4 are 0, so the corresponding inputs are grounded; the remaining rows are 1, so they are wired to logical 1. In this manner any truth table of three variables can be implemented using the chip of Fig. 3-12(a).

We just saw how a multiplexer chip can be used to select one of several inputs and how it can implement a truth table. Another of its applications is as a parallel-to-serial data converter. By putting 8 bits of data on the input lines and then stepping the control lines sequentially from 000 to 111 (binary), the 8 bits are put onto the output line in series. A typical use for parallel-to-serial conversion is in a keyboard, where each keystroke implicitly defines a 7- or 8-bit number that must be output serially over a telephone line.

The inverse of a multiplexer is a **demultiplexer**, which routes its single input signal to one of 2^n outputs, depending on the values of the n control lines. If the binary value on the control lines is k, output k is selected.

Decoders

As a second example, we will now look at a circuit that takes an n-bit number as input and uses it to select (i.e., set to 1) exactly one of the 2^n output lines. Such a circuit, illustrated for $n = 3$ in Fig. 3-13, is called a **decoder**.

To see where a decoder might be useful, imagine a small memory consisting of eight chips, each containing 1 MB. Chip 0 has addresses 0 to 1 MB, chip 1 has

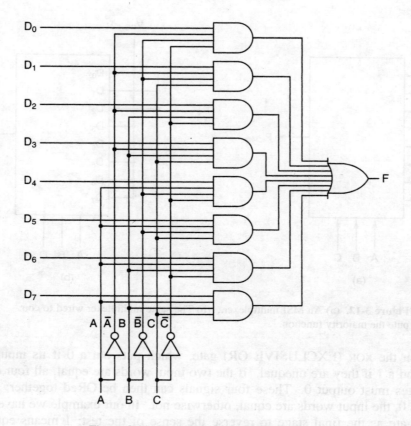

Figure 3-11. An eight-input multiplexer circuit.

addresses 1 MB to 2 MB, and so on. When an address is presented to the memory, the high-order 3 bits are used to select one of the eight chips. Using the circuit of Fig. 3-13, these 3 bits are the three inputs, A, B, and C. Depending on the inputs, exactly one of the eight output lines, D_0, ..., D_7, is 1; the rest are 0. Each output line enables one of the eight memory chips. Because only one output line is set to 1, only one chip is enabled.

The operation of the circuit of Fig. 3-13 is straightforward. Each AND gate has three inputs, of which the first is either A or $\overline{A}$, the second is either B or $\overline{B}$, and the third is either C or $\overline{C}$. Each gate is enabled by a different combination of inputs: D_0 by $\overline{A}\ \overline{B}\ \overline{C}$, D_1 by $\overline{A}\ \overline{B}\ C$, and so on.

Comparators

Another useful circuit is the **comparator**, which compares two input words. The simple comparator of Fig. 3-14 takes two inputs, A and B, each of length 4 bits, and produces a 1 if they are equal and a 0 if they are not equal. The circuit is

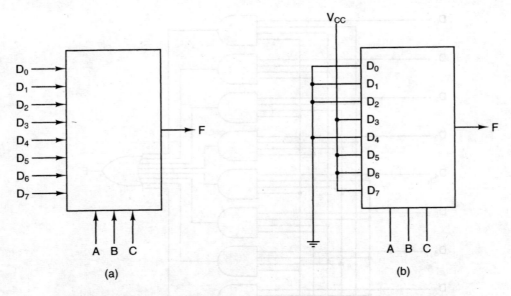

Figure 3-12. (a) An MSI multiplexer.. (b) The same multiplexer wired to compute the majority function.

based on the XOR (EXCLUSIVE OR) gate, which puts out a 0 if its inputs are equal and a 1 if they are unequal. If the two input words are equal, all four of the XOR gates must output 0. These four signals can then be ORed together; if the result is 0, the input words are equal, otherwise not. In our example we have used a NOR gate as the final stage to reverse the sense of the test: 1 means equal, 0 means unequal.

Programmable Logic Arrays

We saw earlier that arbitrary functions (truth tables) can be constructed by computing product terms with AND gates and then ORing the products together. A very general chip for forming sums of products is the **Programmable Logic Array** or **PLA**, a small example of which is shown in Fig. 3-15. This chip has input lines for 12 variables. The complement of each input is generated internally, making 24 input signals in all. The heart of the circuit is an array of 50 AND gates, each of which can potentially have any subset of the 24 input signals as an input. Which input signal goes to which AND gate is determined by a 24×50 bit matrix supplied by the user. Each input line to the 50 AND gates contains a fuse. When shipped from the factory, all 1200 fuses are intact. To program the matrix the user burns out selected fuses by applying a high voltage to the chip.

The output part of the circuit consists of six OR gates, each of which has up to 50 inputs, corresponding to the 50 outputs of the AND gates. Again here, a user-

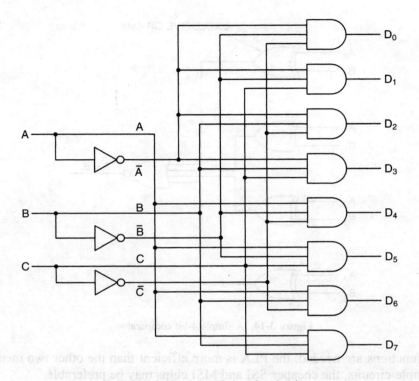

Figure 3-13. A 3-to-8 decoder circuit.

supplied (50×6) matrix tells which of the potential connections actually exist. The chip has 12 input pins, 6 output pins, power, and ground, for a total of 20.

As an example of how a PLA can be used, let us reconsider the circuit of Fig. 3-3(b) again. It has three inputs, four AND gates, one OR gate, and three inverters. With the appropriate internal connections made, our PLA can compute the same function using three of its 12 inputs, four of its 50 AND gates, and one of its six OR gates. (The four AND gates should compute $\overline{A}BC$, $A\overline{B}C$, $AB\overline{C}$, and ABC, respectively; the OR gate takes these four product terms as input.) In fact, the same PLA could be wired up to compute simultaneously a total of four functions of similar complexity. For these simple functions the number of input variables is the limiting factor; for more complicated ones it might be the AND or OR gates.

Although the field-programmable PLAs described above are still in use, for many applications custom-made PLAs are preferable. These are designed by the (large-volume) customer and fabricated by the manufacturer to the customer's specifications. Such PLAs are cheaper than field-programmable ones.

We can now compare the three different ways we have discussed for implementing the truth table of Fig. 3-3(a). Using SSI components, we need four chips. Alternatively, we could suffice with one MSI multiplexer chip, as shown in Fig. 3-12(b). Finally, we could use a quarter of one PLA chip. Obviously, if

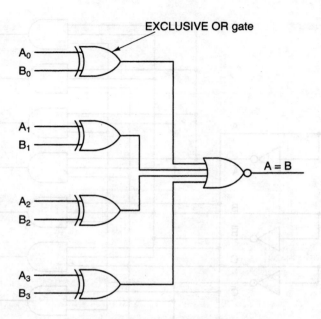

Figure 3-14. A simple 4-bit comparator.

many functions are needed, the PLA is more efficient than the other two methods. For simple circuits, the cheaper SSI and MSI chips may be preferable.

3.2.3 Arithmetic Circuits

It is now time to move on from the general-purpose MSI circuits discussed above to MSI combinational circuits used for doing arithmetic. We will begin with a simple 8-bit shifter, then look at how adders are constructed, and finally examine arithmetic logic units, which play a central role in any computer.

Shifters

Our first arithmetic MSI circuit is an eight-input, eight-output shifter (see Fig. 3-16). Eight bits of input are presented on lines $D_0, ..., D_7$. The output, which is just the input shifted 1 bit, is available on lines $S_0, ..., S_7$. The control line, C, determines the direction of the shift, 0 for left and 1 for right. On a left shift, a 0 is inserted into bit 7. Similarly, on a right shift, a 1 is inserted into bit 0.

To see how the circuit works, notice the pairs of AND gates for all the bits except the gates on the end. When $C = 1$, the right member of each pair is turned on, passing the corresponding input bit to output. Because the right AND gate is wired to the input of the OR gate to its right, a right shift is performed. When $C = 0$, it is the left member of the AND gate pair that turns on, doing a left shift.

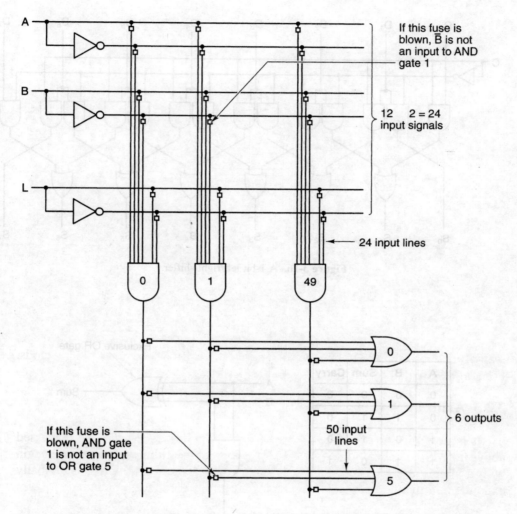

A
If this fuse is blown, $\bar{B}$ is not an input to AND gate 1

B
12 2 = 24 input signals

L

24 input lines

0   1   49

0

1

If this fuse is blown, AND gate 1 is not an input to OR gate 5

50 input lines

6 outputs

5

Figure 3-15. A 12-input, 6-output programmable logic array. The little squares represent fuses that can be burned out to determine the function to be computed. The fuses are arranged in two matrices: the upper one for the AND gates and the lower one for the OR gates.

Adders

A computer that cannot add integers is almost unthinkable. Consequently, a hardware circuit for performing addition is an essential part of every CPU. The truth table for addition on 1-bit integers is shown in Fig. 3-17(a). Two outputs are present: the sum of the inputs, A and B, and the carry to the next (leftward) position. A circuit for computing both the sum bit and the carry bit is illustrated in Fig. 3-17(b). This simple circuit is generally known as a **half adder**.

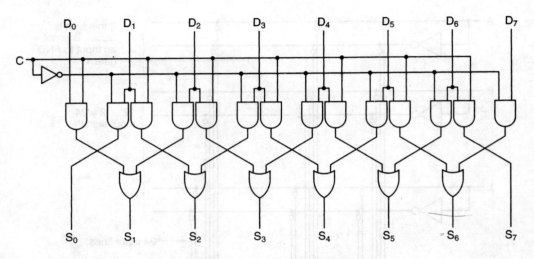

Figure 3-16. A 1-bit left/right shifter.

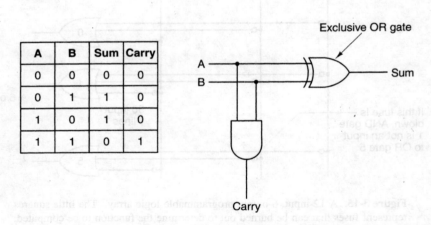

Figure 3-17. (a) Truth table for 1-bit addition. (b) A circuit for a half adder.

Although a half adder is adequate for summing the low-order bits of two multibit input words, it will not do for a bit position in the middle of the word because it does not handle the carry into the position from the right. Instead, the **full adder** of Fig. 3-18 is needed. From inspection of the circuit it should be clear that a full adder is built up from two half adders. The *Sum* output line is 1 if an odd number of A, B, and the *Carry in* are 1. The *Carry out* is 1 if either A and B are both 1 (left input to the OR gate) or exactly one of them is 1 and the *Carry in* bit is also 1. Together the two half adders generate both the sum and the carry bits.

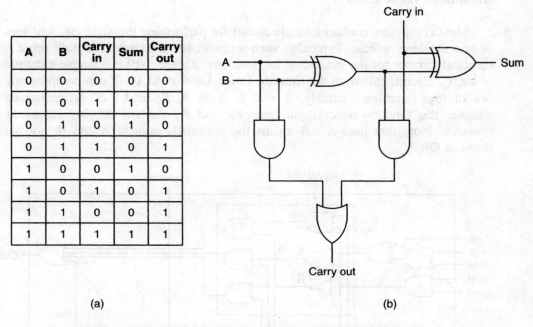

A	B	Carry in	Sum	Carry out
0	0	0	0	0
0	0	1	1	0
0	1	0	1	0
0	1	1	0	1
1	0	0	1	0
1	0	1	0	1
1	1	0	0	1
1	1	1	1	1

(a)   (b)

Figure 3-18. (a) Truth table for full adder. (b) Circuit for a full adder.

To build an adder for, say, two 16-bit words, one just replicates the circuit of Fig. 3-18(b) 16 times. The carry out of a bit is used as the carry into its left neighbor. The carry into the rightmost bit is wired to 0. This type of adder is called a **ripple carry adder**, because in the worst case, adding 1 to 111...111 (binary), the addition cannot complete until the carry has rippled all the way from the rightmost bit to the leftmost bit. Adders that do not have this delay, and hence are faster, also exist and are usually preferred.

As a simple example of a faster adder, consider breaking a 32-bit adder up into a 16-bit lower half and a 16-bit upper half. When the addition starts, the upper adder cannot yet get to work because it will not know the carry into it for 16 addition times.

However, consider this modification. Instead of having a single upper half, give the adder two upper halves in parallel by duplicating the upper half's hardware. Thus the circuit now consists of three 16-bit adders: a lower half and two upper halves, *U0* and *U1* that run in parallel. A 0 is fed into *U0* as a carry; a 1 is fed into *U1* as a carry. Now both of these can start at the same time the lower half starts, but only one will be correct. After 16 bit-addition times, it will be known what the carry into the upper half is, so the correct upper half can now be selected from the two available answers. This trick reduces the addition time by a factor of two. Such an adder is called a **carry select adder**. This trick can then be repeated to build each 16-bit adder out of replicated 8-bit adders, and so on.

Arithmetic Logic Units

Most computers contain a single circuit for performing the AND, OR, and sum of two machine words. Typically, such a circuit for n-bit words is built up of n identical circuits for the individual bit positions. Figure 3-19 is a simple example of such a circuit, called an **Arithmetic Logic Unit** or **ALU**. It can compute any one of four functions—namely, A AND B, A OR B, $\bar{B}$, or $A + B$, depending on whether the function-select input lines F_0 and F_1 contain 00, 01, 10, or 11 (binary). Note that here $A + B$ means the arithmetic sum of A and B, not the Boolean OR.

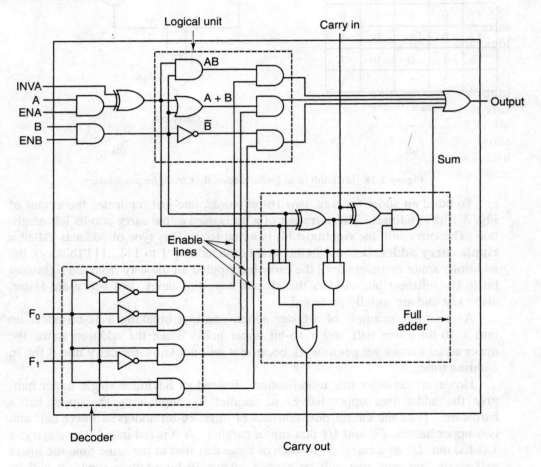

Figure 3-19. A 1-bit ALU.

The lower left-hand corner of our ALU contains a 2-bit decoder to generate enable signals for the four operations, based on the control signals F_0 and F_1. Depending on the values of F_0 and F_1 exactly one of the four enable lines is selected. Setting this line allows the output for the selected function to pass through to the final OR gate for output.

The upper left-hand corner has the logic to compute A AND B, A OR B, and $\overline{B}$, but at most one of these results is passed onto the final OR gate, depending on the enable lines coming out of the decoder. Because exactly one of the decoder outputs will be 1, exactly one of the four AND gates driving the OR gate will be enabled; the other three will output 0, independent of A and B.

In addition to being able to use A and B as inputs for logical or arithmetic operations, it is also possible to force either one to 0 by negating ENA or ENB, respectively. It is also possible to get $\overline{A}$, by setting INVA. We will see uses for INVA, ENA, and ENB in Chap. 4. Under normal conditions, ENA and ENB are both 1 to enable both inputs and INVA is 0. In this case, A and B are just fed into the logic unit unmodified.

The lower right-hand corner of the ALU contains a full adder for computing the sum of A and B, including handling the carries, because it is likely that several of these circuits will eventually be wired together to perform full-word operations. Circuits like Fig. 3-19 are actually available and are known as **bit slices**. They allow the computer designer to build an ALU of any desired width. Figure 3-20 shows an 8-bit ALU built up of eight 1-bit ALU slices. The INC signal is only useful for addition operations. When present, it increments (i.e., adds 1 to) the result, making it possible to compute sums like $A + 1$ and $A + B + 1$.

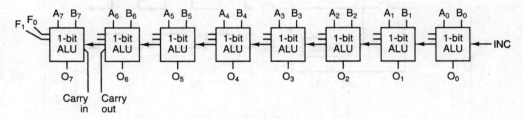

Figure 3-20. Eight 1-bit ALU slices connected to make an 8-bit ALU. The enables and invert signals are not shown for simplicity.

3.2.4 Clocks

In many digital circuits the order in which events happen is critical. Sometimes one event must precede another, sometimes two events must occur simultaneously. To allow designers to achieve the required timing relations, many digital circuits use clocks to provide synchronization. A **clock** in this context is a circuit that emits a series of pulses with a precise pulse width and precise interval between consecutive pulses. The time interval between the corresponding edges of two consecutive pulses is known as the **clock cycle time**. Pulse frequencies are commonly between 1 and 500 MHz, corresponding to clock cycles of 1000 nsec to 2 nsec. To achieve high accuracy, the clock frequency is usually controlled by a crystal oscillator.

In a computer, many events may happen during a single clock cycle. If these events must occur in a specific order, the clock cycle must be divided into subcycles. A common way of providing finer resolution than the basic clock is to tap the primary clock line and insert a circuit with a known delay in it, thus generating a secondary clock signal that is phase-shifted from the primary, as shown in Fig. 3-21(a). The timing diagram of Fig. 3-21(b) provides four time references for discrete events:

1. Rising edge of C1.

2. Falling edge of C1.

3. Rising edge of C2.

4. Falling edge of C2.

By tying different events to the various edges, the required sequencing can be achieved. If more than four time references are needed within a clock cycle, more secondary lines can be tapped from the primary, with different delays.

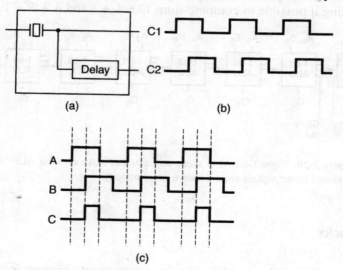

Figure 3-21. (a) A clock. (b) The timing diagram for the clock. (c) Generation of an asymmetric clock.

In some circuits, one is interested in time intervals rather than discrete instants of time. For example, some event may be allowed to happen any time C1 is high, rather than precisely at the rising edge. Another event may only happen when C2 is high. If more than two different intervals are needed, more clock lines can be provided or the high states of the two clocks can be made to overlap partially in time. In the latter case four distinct intervals can be distinguished: $\overline{C1}$ AND $\overline{C2}$, $\overline{C1}$ AND C2, C1 AND $\overline{C2}$, and C1 AND C2.

As an aside, clocks are symmetric, with time spent in the high state equal to the time spent in the low state, as shown in Fig. 3-21(b). To generate an asymmetric pulse train, the basic clock is shifted using a delay circuit and ANDed with the original signal, as shown in Fig. 3-21(c) as C.

3.3 MEMORY

An essential component of every computer is its memory. Without memory there could be no computers as we now know them. Memory is used for storing both instructions to be executed and data. In the following sections we will examine the basic components of a memory system starting at the gate level to see how they work and how they are combined to produce large memories.

3.3.1 Latches

To create a 1-bit memory, we need a circuit that somehow "remembers" previous input values. Such a circuit can be constructed from two NOR gates, as illustrated in Fig. 3-22(a). Analogous circuits can be built from NAND gates. We will not mention these further, however, because they are conceptually identical to the NOR versions.

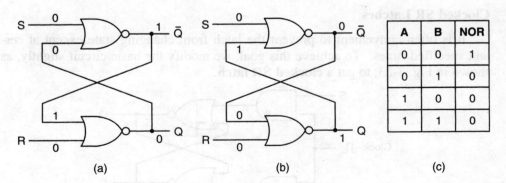

A	B	NOR
0	0	1
0	1	0
1	0	0
1	1	0

Figure 3-22. (a) NOR latch in state 0. (b) NOR latch in state 1. (c) Truth table for NOR.

The circuit of Fig. 3-22(a) is called an **SR latch**. It has two inputs, S, for Setting the latch, and R, for Resetting (i.e., clearing) it. It also has two outputs, Q and $\overline{Q}$, which are complementary, as we will see shortly. Unlike a combinational circuit, the outputs of the latch are not uniquely determined by the current inputs.

To see how this comes about, let us assume that both S and R are 0, which they are most of the time. For argument's sake, let us further assume that $Q = 0$. Because Q is fed back into the upper NOR gate, both of its inputs are 0, so its output, $\overline{Q}$, is 1. The 1 is fed back into the lower gate, which then has inputs 1 and 0, yielding $Q = 0$. This state is at least consistent and is depicted in Fig. 3-22(a).

Now let us imagine that Q is not 0 but 1, with R and S still 0. The upper gate has inputs of 0 and 1, and an output, $\overline{Q}$, of 0, which is fed back to the lower gate. This state, shown in Fig. 3-22(b), is also consistent. A state with both outputs equal to 0 is inconsistent, because it forces both gates to have two 0s as input, which, if true, would produce 1, not 0, as output. Similarly, it is impossible to have both outputs equal to 1, because that would force the inputs to 0 and 1, which yields 0, not 1. Our conclusion is simple: for $R = S = 0$, the latch has two stable states, which we will refer to as 0 and 1, depending on Q.

Now let us examine the effect of the inputs on the state of the latch. Suppose that S becomes 1 while $Q = 0$. The inputs to the upper gate are then 1 and 0, forcing the $\overline{Q}$ output to 0. This change makes both inputs to the lower gate 0, forcing the output to 1. Thus setting S (i.e., making it 1) switches the state from 0 to 1. Setting R to 1 when the latch is in state 0 has no effect because the output of the lower NOR gate is 0 for inputs of 10 and inputs of 11.

Using similar reasoning, it is easy to see that setting S to 1 when in state $Q = 1$ has no effect but that setting R drives the latch to state $Q = 0$. In summary, when S is set to 1 momentarily, the latch ends up in state $Q = 1$, regardless of what state it was previously in. Likewise, setting R to 1 momentarily forces the latch to state $Q = 0$. The circuit "remembers" whether S or R was last on. Using this property we can build computer memories.

Clocked SR Latches

It is often convenient to prevent the latch from changing state except at certain specified times. To achieve this goal, we modify the basic circuit slightly, as shown in Fig. 3-23, to get a **clocked SR latch**.

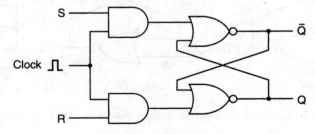

Figure 3-23. A clocked SR latch.

This circuit has an additional input, the clock, which is normally 0. With the clock 0, both AND gates output 0, independent of S and R, and the latch does not change state. When the clock is 1, the effect of the AND gates vanishes and the latch becomes sensitive to S and R. Despite its name, the clock signal need not be driven by a clock. The terms **enable** and **strobe** are also widely used to mean that the clock input is 1; that is, the circuit is sensitive to the state of S and R.

Up until now we have carefully swept the problem of what happens when both S and R are 1 under the rug. And for good reason: the circuit becomes non-deterministic when both R and S finally return to 0. The only consistent state for $S = R = 1$ is $Q = \overline{Q} = 0$, but as soon as both inputs return to 0, the latch must jump to one of its two stable states. If either input drops back to 0 before the other, the one remaining 1 longest wins, because when just one input is 1, it forces the state. If both inputs return to 0 simultaneously (which is very unlikely), the latch jumps to one of its stable states at random.

Clocked D Latches

A good way to resolve the SR latch's ambiguity (caused when $S = R = 1$) is to prevent it from occurring. Figure 3-24 gives a latch circuit with only one input, D. Because the input to the lower AND gate is always the complement of the input to the upper one, the problem of both inputs being 1 never arises. When $D = 1$ and the clock is 1, the latch is driven into state $Q = 1$. When $D = 0$ and the clock is 1, it is driven into state $Q = 0$. In other words, when the clock is 1, the current value of D is sampled and stored in the latch. This circuit, called a **clocked D latch**, is a true 1-bit memory. The value stored is always available at Q. To load the current value of D into the memory, a positive pulse is put on the clock line.

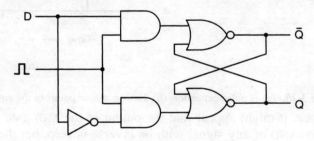

Figure 3-24. A clocked D latch.

This circuit requires 11 transistors. More sophisticated (but less obvious) circuits can store 1 bit with as few a six transistors. In practice, such designs are normally used.

3.3.2 Flip-Flops

In many circuits it is necessary to sample the value on a certain line at a particular instant in time and store it. In this variant, called a **flip-flop**, the state transition does not occur when the clock is 1 but during the clock transition from 0 to

1 (rising edge) or from 1 to 0 (falling edge) instead. Thus the length of the clock pulse is unimportant, as long as the transitions occur fast.

For emphasis, we will repeat the difference between a flip-flop and a latch. A flip-flop is **edge triggered**, whereas a latch is **level triggered**. Be warned, however, that in the literature these terms are often confused. Many authors use "flip-flop" when they are referring to a latch, and vice versa.

There are various approaches to designing a flip-flop. For example, if there were some way to generate a very short pulse on the rising edge of the clock signal, that pulse could be fed into a D latch. There is, in fact, such a way, and the circuit for it is shown in Fig. 3-25(a).

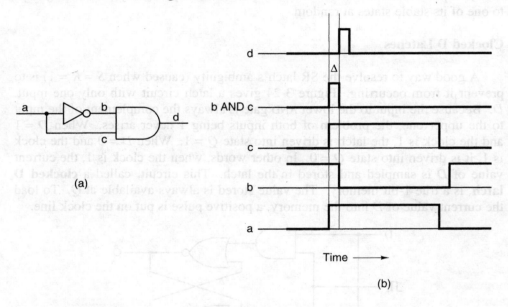

Figure 3-25. (a) A pulse generator. (b) Timing at four points in the circuit.

At first glance, it might appear that the output of the AND gate would always be zero, since the AND of any signal with its inverse is zero, but the situation is a bit more subtle than that. The inverter has a small, but nonzero propagation delay through it, and that delay is what makes the circuit work. Suppose that we measure the voltage at the four measuring points a, b, c, and d. The input signal, measured at a, is a long clock pulse, as shown in Fig. 3-25(b) on the bottom. The signal at b is shown above it. Notice that it is both inverted and delayed slightly, typically a few nanoseconds depending on the kind of inverter used.

The signal at c is delayed, too, but only by the signal propagation time (at the speed of light). If the physical distance between a and c is, for example, 20 microns, then the propagation delay is 0.0001 nsec, which is certainly negligible compared to the time for the signal to propagate through the inverter. Thus for all intents and purposes, the signal at c is as good as identical to the signal at a.

When the inputs to the AND gate, *b* and *c*, are ANDed together, the result is a short pulse, as shown in Fig. 3-25(b), where the width of the pulse, Δ, is equal to the gate delay of the inverter, typically 5 nsec or less. The output of the AND gate is just this pulse shifted by the delay of the AND gate, as shown at the top of Fig. 3-25(b). This time shifting just means that the D latch will be activated at a fixed delay after the rising edge of the clock, but it has no effect on the pulse width. In a memory with a 50-nsec cycle time, a 5-nsec pulse telling it when to sample the *D* line may be short enough, in which case the full circuit can be the one of Fig. 3-26. It is worth noting that this flip-flop design is nice because it is easy to understand, but in practice more sophisticated flip-flops are normally used.

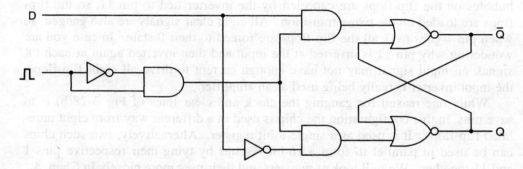

Figure 3-26. A D flip-flop.

The standard symbols for latches and flip-flops are shown in Fig. 3-27. Figure 3-27(a) is a latch whose state is loaded when the clock, *CK*, is 1, in contrast to Fig. 3-27(b) which is a latch whose clock is normally 1 but which drops to 0 momentarily to load the state from *D*. Figure 3-27(c) and (d) are flip-flops rather than latches, which is indicated by the pointy symbol on the clock inputs. Figure 3-27(c) changes state on the rising edge of the clock pulse (0 to 1 transition), whereas Fig. 3-27(d) changes state on the falling edge (1 to 0 transition). Many, but not all, latches and flip-flops also have $\overline{Q}$ as an output, and some have two additional inputs *Set* or *Preset* (force state to $Q = 1$) and *Reset* or *Clear* (force state to $Q = 0$).

3.3.3 Registers

Flip-flops are available in a variety of configurations. A simple one, containing two independent D flip-flops with clear and preset signals, is illustrated in Fig. 3-28(a). Although packaged together in the same 14-pin chip, the two flip-flops are unrelated. A quite different arrangement is the octal flip-flop of Fig. 3-28(b). Here the eight (hence the term "octal") D flip-flops are not only missing the $\overline{Q}$ and preset lines, but all the clock lines are ganged together and driven by

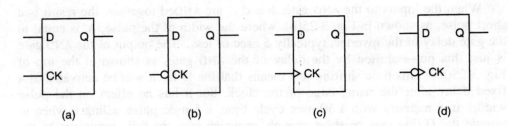

Figure 3-27. D latches and flip-flops.

pin 11. The flip-flops themselves are of the Fig. 3-27(d) type, but the inversion bubbles on the flip-flops are canceled by the inverter tied to pin 11, so the flip-flops are loaded on the rising transition. All eight clear signals are also ganged, so when pin 1 goes to 0, all the flip-flops are forced to their 0 state. In case you are wondering why pin 11 is inverted at the input and then inverted again at each CK signal, an input signal may not have enough current to drive all eight flip-flops; the input inverter is really being used as an amplifier.

While one reason for ganging the clock and clear lines of Fig. 3-28(b) is to save pins, in this configuration the chip is used in a different way from eight unrelated flip-flops. It is used as a single 8-bit register. Alternatively, two such chips can be used in parallel to form a 16-bit register by tying their respective pins 1 and 11 together. We will look at registers and their uses more closely in Chap. 4.

3.3.4 Memory Organization

Although we have now progressed from the simple 1-bit memory of Fig. 3-24 to the 8-bit memory of Fig. 3-28(b) to build large memories a different organization is required, one in which individual words can be addressed. A widely-used memory organization that meets this criterion is shown in Fig. 3-29. This example illustrates a memory with four 3-bit words. Each operation reads or writes a full 3-bit word. While the total memory capacity of 12 bits is hardly more than our octal flip-flop, it requires fewer pins and most important, the design extends easily to large memories.

While the memory of Fig. 3-29 may look complicated at first, it is really quite simple due to its regular structure. It has eight input lines and three output lines. Three inputs are data: I_0, I_1, and I_2; two are for the address: A_0 and A_1; and three are for control: CS for Chip Select, RD for distinguishing between read and write, and OE for Output Enable. The three outputs are for data: O_0, O_1, and O_2. In principle this memory could be put into a 14-pin package, including power and ground versus 20 pins for the octal flip-flop.

To select this memory chip, external logic must set CS high and also set RD high (logical 1) for read and low (logical 0) for write. The two address lines must be set to indicate which of the four 3-bit words is to be read or written. For a read

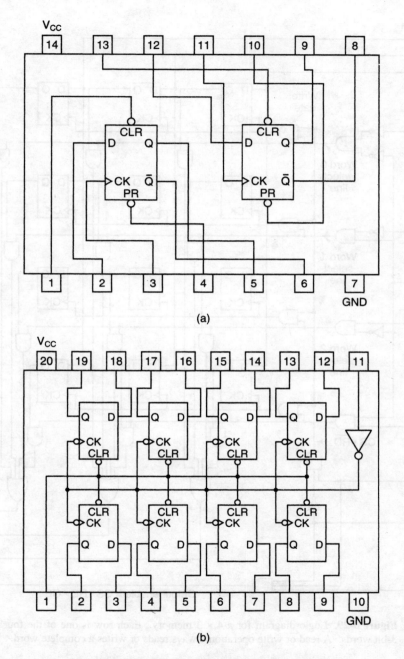

Figure 3-28. (a) Dual D flip-flop. (b) Octal flip-flop.

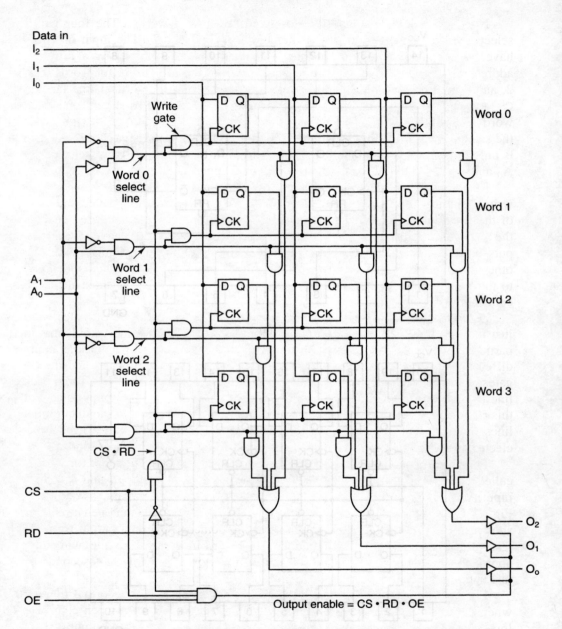

Figure 3-29. Logic diagram for a 4 × 3 memory. Each row is one of the four 3-bit words. A read or write operation always reads or writes a complete word.

operation, the data input lines are not used, but the word selected is placed on the data output lines. For a write operation, the bits present on the data input lines are loaded into the selected memory word; the data output lines are not used.

Now let us look at Fig. 3-29 closely to see how it works. The four word-select AND gates at the left of the memory form a decoder. The input inverters have been placed so that each gate is enabled (output is high) by a different address. Each gate drives a word select line, from top to bottom, for words 0, 1, 2, and 3. When the chip has been selected for a write, the vertical line labeled $CS \cdot \overline{RD}$ will be high, enabling one of the four write gates, depending on which word select line is high. The output of the write gate drives all the CK signals for the selected word, loading the input data into the flip-flops for that word. A write is only done if CS is high and RD is low, and even then only the word selected by A_0 and A_1 is written; the other words are not changed.

Read is similar to write. The address decoding is exactly the same as for write. But now the $CS \cdot \overline{RD}$ line is low, so all the write gates are disabled and none of the flip-flops is modified. Instead, the word select line that is chosen enables the AND gates tied to the Q bits of the selected word. Thus the selected word outputs its data into the four-input OR gates at the bottom of the figure, while the other three words output 0s. Consequently, the output of the OR gates is identical to the value stored in the word selected. The three words not selected make no contribution to the output.

Although we could have designed a circuit in which the three OR gates were just fed into the three output data lines, doing so sometimes causes problems. In particular, we have shown the data input lines and the data output lines as being different, but in actual memories the same lines are used. If we had tied the OR gates to the data output lines, the chip would try to output data, that is, force each line to a specific value, even on writes, thus interfering with the input data. For this reason, it is desirable to have a way to connect the OR gates to the data output lines on reads but disconnect them completely on writes. What we need is an electronic switch that can make or break a connection in a few nanoseconds.

Fortunately, such switches exist. Figure 3-30(a) shows the symbol for what is called a **noninverting buffer**. It has a data input, a data output, and a control input. When the control input is high, the buffer acts like a wire, as shown in Fig. 3-30(b). When the control input is low, the buffer acts like an open circuit, as shown in Fig. 3-30(c); it is as though someone detached the data output from the rest of the circuit with a wirecutter. However, in contrast to the wirecutter approach, the connection can be subsequently restored in a few nanoseconds by just making the control signal high again.

Figure 3-30(d) shows an **inverting buffer**, which acts like a normal inverter when control is high and disconnects the output from the circuit when control is low. Both kinds of buffers are **tri-state devices**, because they can output 0, 1, or none of the above (open circuit). Buffers also amplify signals, so they can drive many inputs simultaneously. They are sometimes used in circuits for this reason, even when their switching properties are not needed.

Getting back to the memory circuit, it should now be clear what the three noninverting buffers on the data output lines are for. When CS, RD, and OE are all

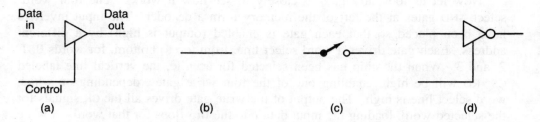

Figure 3-30. (a) A noninverting buffer. (b) Effect of (a) when control is high. (c) Effect of (a) when control is low. (d) An inverting buffer.

high, the output enable signal is also high, enabling the buffers and putting a word onto the output lines. When any one of CS, RD, or OE is low, the data outputs are disconnected from the rest of the circuit.

3.3.5 Memory Chips

The nice thing about the memory of Fig. 3-29 is that it extends easily to larger sizes. As we drew it, the memory is 4×3, that is, four words of 3 bits each. To extend it to 4×8 we need only add five more columns of four flip-flops each, as well as five more input lines and five more output lines. To go from 4×3 to 8×3 we must add four more rows of three flip-flops each, as well as an address line A_2. With this kind of structure, the number of words in the memory should be a power of 2 for maximum efficiency, but the number of bits in a word can be anything.

Because integrated circuit technology is well suited to making chips whose internal structure is a repetitive two-dimensional pattern, memory chips are an ideal application for it. As the technology improves, the number of bits that can be put on a chip keeps increasing, typically by a factor of two every 18 months (Moore's law). The larger chips do not always render the smaller ones obsolete due to different trade-offs in capacity, speed, power, price, and interfacing convenience. Commonly, the largest chips currently available sell at a premium and thus are more expensive per bit than older, smaller ones.

For any given memory size, there are various ways of organizing the chip. Figure 3-31 shows two possible organizations for an older memory chip of size 4-Mbit: $512K \times 8$ and $4096K \times 1$. (As an aside, memory chip sizes are usually quoted in bits, rather than in bytes, so we will stick to that convention here.) In Fig. 3-31(a), 19 address lines are needed to address one of the 2^{19} bytes, and eight data lines are needed for loading or storing the byte selected.

A note on terminology is in order here. On some pins, the high voltage causes an action to happen. On others, the low voltage causes the action. To avoid confusion, we will consistently say that a signal is **asserted** (rather than saying it goes **high or goes low**) to mean that it is set to **cause some** action. Thus for some pins,

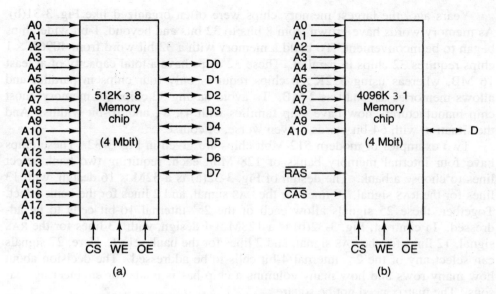

Figure 3-31. Two ways of organizing a 4-Mbit memory chip.

asserting it means setting it high. For others, it means setting the pin low. Pins that are asserted low are given signal names containing an overbar. Thus a signal named CS is asserted high, but one named $\overline{CS}$ is asserted low. The opposite of asserted is **negated**. When nothing special is happening, pins are negated.

Now let us get back to our memory chip. Since a computer normally has many memory chips, a signal is needed to select the chip that is currently needed so that it responds and all the others do not. The $\overline{CS}$ (Chip Select) signal is provided for this purpose. It is asserted to enable the chip. Also, a way is needed to distinguish reads from writes. The $\overline{WE}$ signal (Write Enable) is used to indicate that data are being written rather than being read. Finally, the $\overline{OE}$ (Output Enable) signal is asserted to drive the output signals. When it is not asserted, the chip output is disconnected from the circuit.

In Fig. 3-31(b), a different addressing scheme is used. Internally, this chip is organized as a 2048×2048 matrix of 1-bit cells, which gives 4 Mbits. To address the chip, first a row is selected by putting its 11-bit number on the address pins. Then the $\overline{RAS}$ (Row Address Strobe) is asserted. After that, a column number is put on the address pins and $\overline{CAS}$ (Column Address Strobe) is asserted. The chip responds by accepting or outputting one data bit.

Large memory chips are often constructed as $n \times n$ matrices that are addressed by row and column. This organization reduces the number of pins required but also makes addressing the chip slower, since two addressing cycles are needed, one for the row and one for the column. To win back some of the speed lost by this design, some memory chips can be given a row address followed by a sequence of column addresses to access consecutive bits in a row.

Years ago, the largest memory chips were often organized like Fig. 3-31(b). As memory words have grown from 8 bits to 32 bits and beyond, 1-bit wide chips began to be inconvenient. To build a memory with a 32-bit word from 4096K × 1 chips requires 32 chips in parallel. These 32 chips have a total capacity of at least 16 MB, whereas using 512K × 8 chips requires only four chips in parallel and allows memories as small as 2 MB. To avoid having 32 chips for memory, most chip manufacturers now have chip families with 4-, 8-, and 16-bit widths. And the situation with 64-bit words is even worse, of course.

Two examples of modern 512-Mbit chips are given in Fig. 3-32. These chips have four internal memory banks of 128 Mbit each, requiring two bank select lines to choose a bank. The design of Fig. 3-32(a) is a 32M × 16 design, with 13 lines for the $\overline{\text{RAS}}$ signal, 10 lines for the $\overline{\text{CAS}}$ signal, and 2 lines for the bank select. Together, these 25 signals allow each of the 2^{25} internal 16-bit cells to be addressed. In contrast, Fig. 3-32(b) is a 128M × 4 design, with 13 lines for the $\overline{\text{RAS}}$ signal, 12 lines for the $\overline{\text{CAS}}$ signal, and 2 lines for the bank select. Here, 27 signals can select any of the 2^{27} internal 4-bit cells to be addressed. The decision about how many rows and how many columns a chip has is made for engineering reasons. The matrix need not be square.

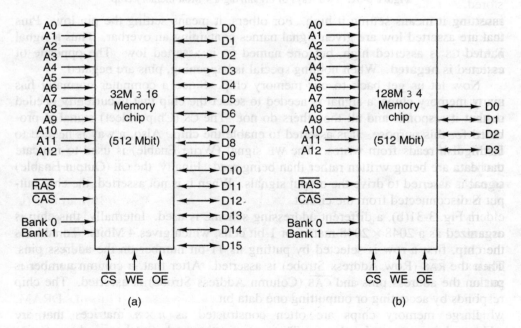

Figure 3-32. Two ways of organizing a 512-Mbit memory chip.

These examples demonstrate two separate and independent issues for memory chip design. First is the output width (in bits): does the chip deliver 1, 4, 8, 16, or some other number of bits at once? Second, are all the address bits presented on separate pins at once or are the row and columns presented sequentially as in the examples of Fig. 3-32? A memory chip designer has to answer both questions before starting the chip design.

3.3.6 RAMs and ROMs

The memories we have studied so far can all be read and written. Such memories are called **RAM**s (Random Access Memories), which is a misnomer because all memory chips are randomly accessible, but the term is too well established to get rid of now. RAMs come in two varieties, static and dynamic. **Static RAM**s (**SRAM**s), are constructed internally using circuits similar to our basic D flip-flop. These memories have the property that their contents are retained as long as the power is kept on: seconds, minutes, hours, even days. Static RAMs are very fast. A typical access times is a few nsec. For this reason, static RAMS are popular as level 2 cache memory.

Dynamic RAMs (**DRAM**s), in contrast, do not use flip-flops. Instead, a dynamic RAM is an array of cells, each cell containing one transistor and a tiny capacitor. The capacitors can be charged or discharged, allowing 0s and 1s to be stored. Because the electric charge tends to leak out, each bit in a dynamic RAM must be **refreshed** (reloaded) every few milliseconds to prevent the data from leaking away. Because external logic must take care of the refreshing, dynamic RAMs require more complex interfacing than static ones, although in many applications this disadvantage is compensated for by their larger capacities.

Since dynamic RAMs need only one transistor and one capacitor per bit (vs. six transistors per bit for the best static RAM), dynamic RAMs have a very high density (many bits per chip). For this reason, main memories are nearly always built out of dynamic RAMs. However, this large capacity has a price: dynamic RAMs are slow (tens of nanoseconds). Thus the combination of a static RAM cache and a dynamic RAM main memory attempts to combine the good properties of each.

Several types of dynamic RAM chips exist. The oldest type still around (in elderly computers) is **FPM** (**Fast Page Mode**) DRAM. Internally it is organized as a matrix of bits and it works by having the hardware present a row address and then step through the column addresses, as we described with $\overline{RAS}$ and $\overline{CAS}$ in the context of Fig. 3-31. Explicit signals tell the memory when it is time to respond, so the memory runs asynchronously from the main system clock.

FPM DRAM was replaced with **EDO** (**Extended Data Output**) DRAM, which allows a second memory reference to begin before the previous memory reference has been completed. This simple pipelining did not make a single memory reference go faster but did improve the memory bandwidth, giving more words per second.

FPM and EDO worked reasonably well when memory chips had cycle times of 12 nsec and slower. When processors got so fast that faster memories were really needed, FPM and EDO were replaced by **SDRAM (Synchronous DRAM)**, which is a hybrid of static and dynamic RAM and is driven by the main system clock. The big advantage of SDRAM is that the clock eliminates the need for control signals to tell the memory chip when to respond. Instead, the CPU tells the memory how many cycles it should run, then starts it. On each subsequent cycle, the memory outputs 4, 8, or 16 bits, depending on how many output lines it has. Eliminating the need for control signals increases the data rate between CPU and memory.

The next improvement over SDRAM was **DDR (Double Data Rate)** SDRAM. With this kind of memory, the memory chip produces output on both the rising edge of the clock and the falling edge, doubling the data rate. Thus an 8-bit wide DDR chip running at 200 MHz outputs two 8-bit values 200 million times a second (for a short interval, of course), giving a theoretical burst rate of 3.2 Gbps.

Nonvolatile Memory Chips

RAMs are not the only kind of memory chips. In many applications, such as toys, appliances, and cars, the program and some of the data must remain stored even when the power is turned off. Furthermore, once installed, neither the program nor the data are ever changed. These requirements have led to the development of **ROM**s (Read-Only Memories), which cannot be changed or erased, intentionally or otherwise. The data in a ROM are inserted during its manufacture, essentially by exposing a photosensitive material through a mask containing the desired bit pattern and then etching away the exposed (or unexposed) surface. The only way to change the program in a ROM is to replace the entire chip.

ROMs are much cheaper than RAMs when ordered in large enough volumes to defray the cost of making the mask. However, they are inflexible, because they cannot be changed after manufacture, and the turnaround time between placing an order and receiving the ROMs may be weeks. To make it easier for companies to develop new ROM-based products, the **PROM** (Programmable ROM) was invented. A PROM is like a ROM, except that it can be programmed (once) in the field, eliminating the turnaround time. Many PROMs contain an array of tiny fuses inside. A specific fuse can be blown out by selecting its row and column and then applying a high voltage to a special pin on the chip.

The next development in this line was the **EPROM** (Erasable PROM), which can be not only field-programmed but also field-erased. When the quartz window in an EPROM is exposed to a strong ultraviolet light for 15 minutes, all the bits are set to 1. If many changes are expected during the design cycle, EPROMs are far more economical than PROMs because they can be reused. EPROMs usually have the same organization as static RAMs. The 4-Mbit 27C040 EPROM, for example, uses the organization of Fig. 3-32(a), which is typical of a static RAM.

Even better than the EPROM is the **EEPROM** which can be erased by applying pulses to it instead of requiring it to be put in a special chamber for exposure to ultraviolet light. In addition, an EEPROM can be reprogrammed in place whereas an EPROM has to be inserted in a special EPROM programming device to be programmed. On the minus side, the biggest EEPROMs are typically only 1/64 as large as common EPROMs and they are only half as fast. EEPROMs cannot compete with DRAMs or SRAMs because they are 10 times slower, 100 times smaller in capacity, and much more expensive. They are only used in situations where their nonvolatility is crucial.

A more recent kind of EEPROM is **flash memory**. Unlike EPROM, which is erased by exposure to ultraviolet light, and EEPROM, which is byte erasable, flash memory is block erasable and rewritable. Like EEPROM, flash memory can be erased without removing it from the circuit. Various manufacturers produce small printed circuit cards with up to 1 GB of flash memory on them for use as "film" for storing pictures in digital cameras and many other purposes. Someday flash memories may be used to replace disks, which would be an enormous improvement, given their 50-nsec access times. The main engineering problem at present is that they wear out after about 100,000 erasures, whereas disks last for many years, no matter how often they are rewritten. A summary of the various kinds of memory is given in Fig. 3-33.

Type	Category	Erasure	Byte alterable	Volatile	Typical use
SRAM	Read/write	Electrical	Yes	Yes	Level 2 cache
DRAM	Read/write	Electrical	Yes	Yes	Main memory (old)
SDRAM	Read/write	Electrical	Yes	Yes	Main memory (new)
ROM	Read-only	Not possible	No	No	Large volume appliances
PROM	Read-only	Not possible	No	No	Small volume equipment
EPROM	Read-mostly	UV light	No	No	Device prototyping
EEPROM	Read-mostly	Electrical	Yes	No	Device prototyping
Flash	Read/write	Electrical	No	No	Film for digital camera

Figure 3-33. A comparison of various memory types.

3.4 CPU CHIPS AND BUSES

Armed with information about SSI chips, MSI chips, and memory chips, we can now start to put all the pieces together to look at complete systems. In this section, we will first look at some general aspects of CPUs as viewed from the digital logic level, including **pinout** (what the signals on the various pins mean).

Since CPUs are so closely intertwined with the design of the buses they use, we will also provide an introduction to bus design in this section. In succeeding sections we will give detailed examples of both CPUs and their buses and how they are interfaced.

3.4.1 CPU Chips

All modern CPUs are contained on a single chip. This makes their interaction with the rest of the system well defined. Each CPU chip has a set of pins, through which all its communication with the outside world must take place. Some pins output signals from the CPU to the outside world; others accept signals from the outside world; some can do both. By understanding the function of all the pins, we can learn how the CPU interacts with the memory and I/O devices at the digital logic level.

The pins on a CPU chip can be divided into three types: address, data, and control. These pins are connected to similar pins on the memory and I/O chips via a collection of parallel wires called a bus. To fetch an instruction, the CPU first puts the memory address of that instruction on its address pins. Then it asserts one or more control lines to inform the memory that it wants to read (for example) a word. The memory replies by putting the requested word on the CPU's data pins and asserting a signal saying that it is done. When the CPU sees this signal, it accepts the word and carries out the instruction.

The instruction may require reading or writing data words, in which case the whole process is repeated for each additional word. We will go into the detail of how reading and writing works below. For the time being, the important thing to understand is that the CPU communicates with the memory and I/O devices by presenting signals on its pins and accepting signals on its pins. No other communication is possible.

Two of the key parameters that determine the performance of a CPU are the number of address pins and the number of data pins. A chip with m address pins can address up to 2^m memory locations. Common values of m are 16, 20, 32 and 64. Similarly, a chip with n data pins can read or write an n-bit word in a single operation. Common values of n are 8, 16, 32, 36, and 64. A CPU with 8 data pins will take four operations to read a 32-bit word, whereas one with 32 data pins can do the same job in one operation. Thus the chip with 32 data pins is much faster, but is invariably more expensive as well.

In addition to address and data pins, each CPU has some control pins. The control pins regulate the flow and timing of data to and from the CPU and have other miscellaneou⌐ uses. All CPUs have pins for power (usually +3.3 volts or +5 volts), ground, and a clock signal (a square wave at some well-defined frequency), but the other pins vary greatly from chip to chip. Nevertheless, the control pins can be roughly grouped into the following major categories:

1. Bus control.

2. Interrupts.

3. Bus arbitration.

4. Coprocessor signaling.

5. Status.

6. Miscellaneous.

We will briefly describe each of these categories below. When we look at the Pentium 4, UltraSPARC III, and 8051 chips later, we will provide more detail. A generic CPU chip using these signal groups is shown in Fig. 3-34.

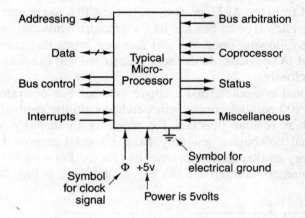

Figure 3-34. The logical pinout of a generic CPU. The arrows indicate input signals and output signals. The short diagonal lines indicate that multiple pins are used. For a specific CPU, a number will be given to tell how many.

The bus control pins are mostly outputs from the CPU to the bus (thus inputs to the memory and I/O chips) telling whether the CPU wants to read or write memory or do something else. The CPU uses these pins to control the rest of the system and tell it what it wants to do.

The interrupt pins are inputs from I/O devices to the CPU. In most systems, the CPU can tell an I/O device to start an operation and then go off and do something else while the I/O device is doing its work. When the I/O has been completed, the I/O controller chip asserts a signal on one of these pins to interrupt the CPU and have it service the I/O device, for example to check to see if I/O errors occurred. Some CPUs have an output pin to acknowledge the interrupt signal.

The bus arbitration pins are needed to regulate traffic on the bus, in order to prevent two devices from trying to use it at the same time. For arbitration purposes, the CPU counts as a device and has to request it like any other device.

Some CPU chips are designed to operate with coprocessors such as floating-point chips, but sometimes graphics or other chips as well. To facilitate communication between CPU and coprocessor, special pins are provided for making and granting various requests.

In addition to these signals, there are various miscellaneous pins that some CPUs have. Some of these provide or accept status information, others are useful for resetting the computer, and still others are present to assure compatibility with older I/O chips.

3.4.2 Computer Buses

A **bus** is a common electrical pathway between multiple devices. Buses can be categorized by their function. They can be used internal to the CPU to transport data to and from the ALU, or external to the CPU, to connect it to memory or to I/O devices. Each type of bus has its own requirements and properties. In this section and the following ones, we will focus on buses that connect the CPU to the memory and I/O devices. In the next chapter we will examine the buses inside the CPU more closely.

Early personal computers had a single external bus or **system bus**. It consisted of 50 to 100 parallel copper wires etched onto the motherboard, with connectors spaced at regular intervals for plugging in memory and I/O boards. Modern personal computers generally have a special-purpose bus between the CPU and memory and (at least) one other bus for the I/O devices. A minimal system, with one memory bus and one I/O bus, is illustrated in Fig. 3-35.

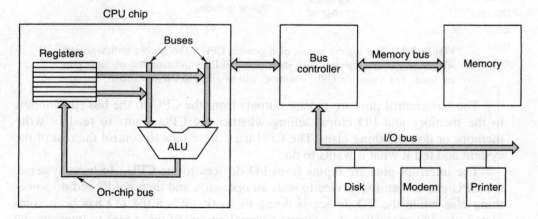

Figure 3-35. A computer system with multiple buses.

In the literature, buses are sometimes drawn as "fat" arrows, as in this figure. The distinction between a fat arrow and a single line with a diagonal line through it and a bit count next to it is subtle. When all the bits are the same type, say, all address bits or all data bits, then the short diagonal line approach is commonly used. When there are address, data, and control lines involved, a fat arrow is more common.

While the designers of the CPU are free to use any kind of bus they want inside the chip, in order to make it possible for boards designed by third parties to attach to the system bus, there must be well-defined rules about how the bus works, and which all devices attached to it must obey. These rules are called the **bus protocol**. In addition, there must be mechanical and electrical specifications, so that third-party boards will fit in the card cage and have connectors that match those on the motherboard mechanically and in terms of voltages, timing, etc.

A number of buses are in widespread use in the computer world. A few of the better known ones, historical and current, (with examples) are the Omnibus (PDP-8), Unibus (PDP-11), Multibus (8086), VME bus (physics lab equipment), IBM PC bus (PC/XT), ISA bus (PC/AT), EISA bus (80386), Microchannel (PS/2), Nubus (Macintosh), PCI bus (many PCs), SCSI bus (many PCs and workstations), Universal Serial Bus (modern PCs), and FireWire (consumer electronics). The world would probably be a better place if all but one would suddenly vanish from the face of the earth (well, all right, how about all but two?). Unfortunately, standardization in this area seems very unlikely as there is already too much invested in all these incompatible systems.

Let us now begin our study of how buses work. Some devices that attach to a bus are active and can initiate bus transfers, whereas others are passive and wait for requests. The active ones are called **masters**; the passive ones are called **slaves**. When the CPU orders a disk controller to read or write a block, the CPU is acting as a master and the disk controller is acting as a slave. However, later on, the disk controller may act as a master when it commands the memory to accept the words it is reading from the disk drive. Several typical combinations of master and slave are listed in Fig. 3-36. Under no circumstances can memory ever be a master.

Master	Slave	Example
CPU	Memory	Fetching instructions and data
CPU	I/O device	Initiating data transfer
CPU	Coprocessor	CPU handing instruction off to coprocessor
I/O	Memory	DMA (Direct Memory Access)
Coprocessor	CPU	Coprocessor fetching operands from CPU

Figure 3-36. Examples of bus masters and slaves.

The binary signals that computer devices output are frequently too weak to power a bus, especially if it is relatively long or has many devices on it. For this reason, most bus masters are connected to the bus by a chip called a **bus driver**, which is essentially a digital amplifier. Similarly, most slaves are connected to the bus by a **bus receiver**. For devices that can act as both master and slave, a combined chip called a **bus transceiver** is used. These bus interface chips are often tri-state devices, to allow them to float (disconnect) when they are not needed, or are hooked up in a somewhat different way, called **open collector**, that achieves a similar effect. When two or more devices on an open collector line assert the line at the same time, the result is the Boolean OR of all the signals. This arrangement is often called **wired-OR**. On most buses, some of the lines are tri-state and others, which need the wired-OR property, are open collector.

Like a CPU, a bus also has address, data, and control lines. However, there is not necessarily a one-to-one mapping between the CPU pins and the bus signals. For example, some CPUs have three pins that encode whether it is doing a memory read, memory write, I/O read, I/O write, or some other operation. A typical bus might have one line for memory read, a second for memory write, a third for I/O read, a fourth for I/O write, and so on. A decoder chip would then be needed between the CPU and such a bus to match the two sides up, that is, to convert the 3-bit encoded signal into separate signals that can drive the bus lines.

Bus design and operation are sufficiently complex subjects that a number of entire books have been written about them (Anderson et al., 2004; Solari and Willse, 2004). The principal bus design issues are bus width, bus clocking, bus arbitration, and bus operations. Each of these issues has a substantial impact on the speed and bandwidth of the bus. We will now examine each of these in the next four sections.

3.4.3 Bus Width

Bus width is the most obvious design parameter. The more address lines a bus has, the more memory the CPU can address directly. If a bus has n address lines, then a CPU can use it to address 2^n different memory locations. To allow large memories, buses need many address lines. That sounds simple enough.

The problem is that wide buses need more wires than narrow ones. They also take up more physical space (e.g., on the motherboard) and need bigger connectors. All of these factors make the bus more expensive. Thus there is a trade-off between maximum memory size and system cost. A system with a 64-line address bus and 2^{32} bytes of memory will cost more than one with 32 address lines and the same 2^{32} bytes of memory. The possibility of expansion later is not free.

The result of this observation is that many system designers tend to be short-sighted, with unfortunate consequences later. The original IBM PC contained an 8088 CPU and a 20-bit address bus, as shown in Fig. 3-37(a). Having 20 bits allowed the PC to address 1 MB of memory.

When the next CPU chip (the 80286) came out, Intel decided to increase the address space to 16 MB, so four more bus lines had to be added (without disturbing the original 20, for reasons of backward compatibility), as illustrated in Fig. 3-37(b). Unfortunately, more control lines had to be added to deal with the

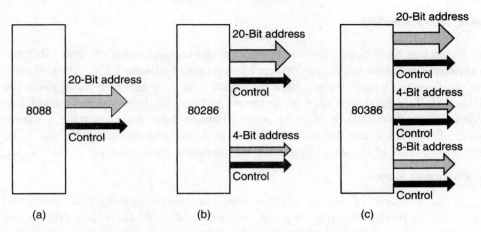

Figure 3-37. Growth of an address bus over time.

new address lines. When the 80386 came out, another eight address lines were added, along with still more control lines, as shown in Fig. 3-37(c). The resulting design (the EISA bus) is much messier than it would have been had the bus been given 32 lines at the start.

Not only does the number of address lines tend to grow over time, but so does the number of data lines, but for a somewhat different reason. There are two ways to increase the data bandwidth of a bus: decrease the bus cycle time (more transfers/sec) or increase the data bus width (more bits/transfer). Speeding the bus up is possible, but difficult because the signals on different lines travel at slightly different speeds, a problem known as **bus skew**. The faster the bus, the more serious bus skew becomes.

Another problem with speeding up the bus is that doing this will not be backward compatible. Old boards designed for the slower bus will not work with the new one. Invalidating old boards makes both the owners of the old boards and the manufacturers of the old boards unhappy. Therefore the usual approach to improving performance is to add more data lines, analogous to Fig. 3-37. As you might expect, however, this incremental growth does not lead to a clean design in the end. The IBM PC and its successors, for example, went from eight data lines to 16 and then 32 on essentially the same bus.

To get around the problem of very wide buses, sometimes designers opt for a **multiplexed bus**. In this design, instead of having the address and data lines be separate, there are, say, 32 lines for address and data together. At the start of a bus operation, the lines are used for the address. Later on, they are used for data. For a write to memory, for example, this means that the address lines must be set up and propagated to the memory before the data can be put on the bus. With separate lines, the address and data can be put on together. Multiplexing the lines reduces bus width (and cost), but results in a slower system. Bus designers have to carefully weigh all these options when making choices.

3.4.4 Bus Clocking

Buses can be divided into two distinct categories depending on their clocking. A **synchronous bus** has a line driven by a crystal oscillator. The signal on this line consists of a square wave with a frequency generally between 5 MHz and 100 MHz. All bus activities take an integral number of these cycles, called **bus cycles**. The other kind of bus, the **asynchronous bus**, does not have a master clock. Bus cycles can be of any length required and need not be the same between all pairs of devices. Below we will examine each bus type.

Synchronous Buses

As an example of how a synchronous bus works, consider the timing of Fig. 3-38(a). In this example, we will use a 100-MHz clock, which gives a bus cycle of 10 nsec. While this may seem a bit slow compared to CPU speeds of 3 GHz and more, few existing PC buses are much faster. For example, the popular PCI bus usually runs at either 33 MHz or 66 MHz. The reasons current buses are slow were given above: technical design problems such as bus skew and the need for backward compatibility.

In our example, we will further assume that reading from memory takes 15-nsec from the time the address is stable. As we will see shortly, with these parameters, it will take three bus cycles to read a word. The first cycle starts at the rising edge of T_1 and the third one ends at the rising edge of T_4, as shown in the figure. Note that none of the rising or falling edges has been drawn vertically, because no electrical signal can change its value in zero time. In this example we will assume that it takes 1 nsec for a signal to change. The clock, ADDRESS, DATA, $\overline{\text{MREQ}}$, $\overline{\text{RD}}$, and $\overline{\text{WAIT}}$ lines are all shown on the same time scale.

The start of T_1 is defined by the rising edge of the clock. Part way through T_1 the CPU puts the address of the word it wants on the address lines. Because the address is not a single value, like the clock, we cannot show it as a single line in the figure; instead, it is shown as two lines, with a crossing at the time that the address changes. Furthermore, the shading prior to the crossing indicates that the shaded value is not important. Using the same shading convention, we see that the contents of the data lines are not significant until well into T_3.

After the address lines have had a chance to settle down to their new values, $\overline{\text{MREQ}}$ and $\overline{\text{RD}}$ are asserted. The former indicates that memory (as opposed to an I/O device) is being accessed, and the latter is asserted for reads and negated for writes. Since the memory takes 15 nsec after the address is stable (part way into the first clock cycle), it cannot provide the requested data during T_2. To tell the CPU not to expect it, the memory asserts the $\overline{\text{WAIT}}$ line at the start of T_2. This action will insert **wait states** (extra bus cycles) until the memory is finished and negates $\overline{\text{WAIT}}$. In our example, one wait state (T_2) has been inserted because the memory is too slow. At the start of T_3, when it is sure it will have the data during the current cycle, the memory negates $\overline{\text{WAIT}}$.

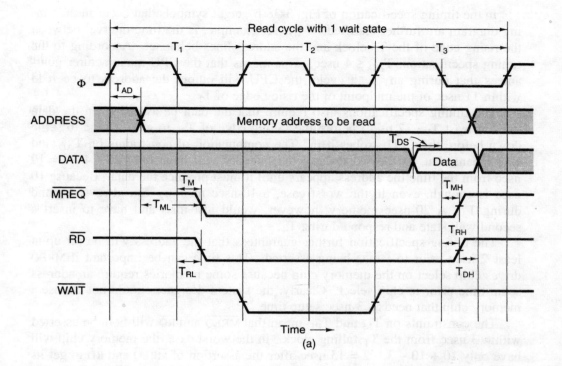

Figure 3-38. (a) Read timing on a synchronous bus. (b) Specification of some critical times.

During the first half of T_3, the memory puts the data onto the data lines. At the falling edge of T_3 the CPU strobes (i.e., reads) the data lines, latching (i.e., storing) the value in an internal register. Having read the data, the CPU negates $\overline{MREQ}$ and $\overline{RD}$. If need be, another memory cycle can begin at the next rising edge of the clock. This sequence can be repeatedly indefinitely.

In the timing specification of Fig. 3-38(b), eight symbols that occur in the timing diagram are further clarified. T_{AD}, for example, is the time interval between the rising edge of the T_1 clock and the address lines being set. According to the timing specification, $T_{AD} \leq 4$ nsec. This means that the CPU manufacturer guarantees that during any read cycle, the CPU will output the address to be read within 11 nsec of the midpoint of the rising edge of T_1.

The timing specifications also require that the data be available on the data lines at least T_{DS} (2 nsec) before the falling edge of T_3, to give it time to settle down before the CPU strobes it in. The combination of constraints on T_{AD} and T_{DS} means that, in the worst case, the memory will have only $25 - 4 - 2 = 19$ nsec from the time the address appears until it must produce the data. Because 10 nsec is enough, even in the worst case, a 10-nsec memory can always respond during T_3. A 20-nsec memory, however, would just miss and have to insert a second wait state and respond during T_4.

The timing specification further guarantees that the address will be set up at least 2 nsec prior to $\overline{MREQ}$ being asserted. This time can be important if $\overline{MREQ}$ drives chip select on the memory chip because some memories require an address setup time prior to chip select. Clearly, the system designer should not choose a memory chip that needs a 3-nsec setup time.

The constraints on T_M and T_{RL} mean that $\overline{MREQ}$ and $\overline{RD}$ will both be asserted within 3 nsec from the T_1 falling clock. In the worst case, the memory chip will have only $10 + 10 - 3 - 2 = 15$ nsec after the assertion of $\overline{MREQ}$ and $\overline{RD}$ to get its data onto the bus. This constraint is in addition to (and independent of) the 15-nsec interval needed after the address is stable.

T_{MH} and T_{RH} tell how long it takes $\overline{MREQ}$ and $\overline{RD}$ to be negated after the data have been strobed in. Finally, T_{DH} tells how long the memory must hold the data on the bus after $\overline{RD}$ has been negated. As far as our example CPU is concerned, the memory can remove the data from the bus as soon as $\overline{RD}$ has been negated; on some actual CPUs, however, the data must be kept stable a little longer.

We would like to point out that Fig. 3-38 is a highly simplified version of real timing constraints. In reality, many more critical times are always specified. Nevertheless, it gives a good flavor for how a synchronous bus works.

A last point worth making is that control signals can be asserted high or low. It is up to the bus designers to determine which is more convenient, but the choice is essentially arbitrary. One can regard it as the hardware equivalent of a programmer's choice to represent free disk blocks in a bit map as 0s versus 1s.

Asynchronous Buses

Although synchronous buses are easy to work with due to their discrete time intervals, they also have some problems. For example, everything works in multiples of the bus clock. If a CPU and memory are able to complete a transfer in 3.1 cycles, they have to stretch it to 4.0 because fractional cycles are forbidden.

Worse yet, once a bus cycle has been chosen, and memory and I/O cards have been built for it, it is difficult to take advantage of future improvements in technology. For example, suppose a few years after the system of Fig. 3-38 was built, new memories became available with access times of 8 nsec instead of 15 nsec. These would get rid of the wait state, speeding up the machine. Then suppose 4-nsec memories became available. There would be no further gain in performance because the minimum time for a read is two cycles with this design.

Putting this fact in slightly different terms, if a synchronous bus has a heterogeneous collection of devices, some fast and some slow, the bus has to be geared to the slowest one and the fast ones cannot use their full potential.

Mixed technology can be handled by going to an asynchronous bus, that is, one with no master clock, as shown in Fig. 3-39. Instead of tying everything to the clock, when the bus master has asserted the address, $\overline{\text{MREQ}}$, $\overline{\text{RD}}$, and anything else it needs to, it then asserts a special signal that we will call $\overline{\text{MSYN}}$ (Master SYNchronization). When the slave sees this, it performs the work as fast as it can. When it is done, it asserts $\overline{\text{SSYN}}$ (Slave SYNchronization).

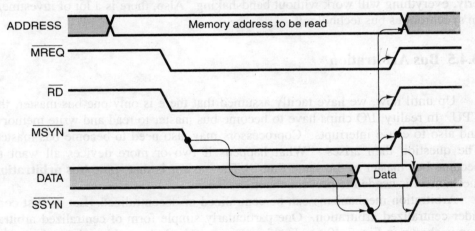

Figure 3-39. Operation of an asynchronous bus.

As soon as the master sees $\overline{\text{SSYN}}$ asserted, it knows that the data are available, so it latches them, and then negates the address lines, along with $\overline{\text{MREQ}}$, $\overline{\text{RD}}$, and $\overline{\text{MSYN}}$. When the slave sees the negation of $\overline{\text{MSYN}}$, it knows that the cycle has been completed, so it negates $\overline{\text{SSYN}}$, and we are back in the original situation, with all signals negated, waiting for the next master.

Timing diagrams of asynchronous buses (and sometimes synchronous buses as well) use arrows to show cause and effect, as in Fig. 3-39. The assertion of $\overline{\text{MSYN}}$ causes the data lines to be asserted and also causes the slave to assert $\overline{\text{SSYN}}$. The assertion of $\overline{\text{SSYN}}$, in turn, causes the negation of the address lines, $\overline{\text{MREQ}}$, $\overline{\text{RD}}$, and $\overline{\text{MSYN}}$. Finally, the negation of $\overline{\text{MSYN}}$ causes the negation of $\overline{\text{SSYN}}$, which ends the read and returns the system to its original state.

A set of signals that interlocks this way is called a **full handshake**. The essential part consists of four events:

1. $\overline{\text{MSYN}}$ is asserted.

2. $\overline{\text{SSYN}}$ is asserted in response to $\overline{\text{MSYN}}$.

3. $\overline{\text{MSYN}}$ is negated in response to $\overline{\text{SSYN}}$.

4. $\overline{\text{SSYN}}$ is negated in response to the negation of $\overline{\text{MSYN}}$.

It should be clear that full handshakes are timing independent. Each event is caused by a prior event, not by a clock pulse. If a particular master-slave pair is slow, that in no way affects a subsequent master-slave pair that is much faster.

The advantage of an asynchronous bus should now be clear, but the fact is that most buses are synchronous. The reason is that it is easier to build a synchronous system. The CPU just asserts its signals, and the memory just reacts. There is no feedback (cause and effect), but if the components have been chosen properly, everything will work without handshaking. Also, there is a lot of investment in synchronous bus technology.

3.4.5 Bus Arbitration

Up until now, we have tacitly assumed that there is only one bus master, the CPU. In reality, I/O chips have to become bus master to read and write memory, and also to cause interrupts. Coprocessors may also need to become bus master. The question then arises: "What happens if two or more devices all want to become bus master at the same time?" The answer is that some **bus arbitration** mechanism is needed to prevent chaos.

Arbitration mechanisms can be centralized or decentralized. Let us first consider centralized arbitration. One particularly simple form of centralized arbitration is shown in Fig. 3-40(a). In this scheme, a single bus arbiter determines who goes next. Many CPUs have the arbiter built into the CPU chip, but sometimes a separate chip is needed. The bus contains a single wired-OR request line that can be asserted by one or more devices at any time. There is no way for the arbiter to tell how many devices have requested the bus. The only categories it can distinguish are some requests and no requests.

When the arbiter sees a bus request, it issues a grant by asserting the bus grant line. This line is wired through all the I/O devices in series, like a cheap string of Christmas tree lamps. When the device physically closest to the arbiter sees the grant, it checks to see if it made a request. If so, it takes over the bus but does not propagate the grant further down the line. If it has not made a request, it propagates the grant to the next device in line, which behaves the same way, and so on until some device accepts the grant and takes the bus. This scheme is called

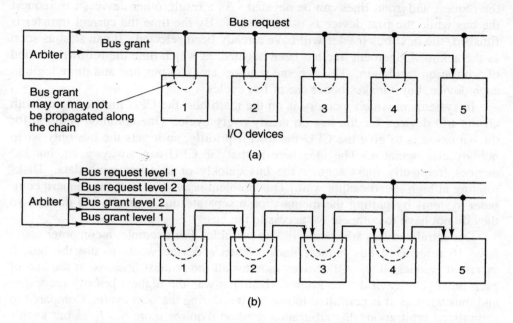

Figure 3-40. (a) A centralized one-level bus arbiter using daisy chaining.
(b) The same arbiter, but with two levels.

daisy chaining. It has the property that devices are effectively assigned priorities depending on how close to the arbiter they are. The closest device wins.

To get around the implicit priorities based on distance from the arbiter, many buses have multiple priority levels. For each priority level there is a bus request line and a bus grant line. The one of Fig. 3-40(b) has two levels, 1 and 2 (real buses often have 4, 8, or 16 levels). Each device attaches to one of the bus request levels, with more time-critical devices attaching to the higher priority ones. In Fig. 3-40(b) devices, 1, 2, and 4 use priority 1 while devices 3 and 5 use priority 2.

If multiple priority levels are requested at the same time, the arbiter issues a grant only on the highest priority one. Among devices of the same priority, daisy chaining is used. In Fig. 3-40(b), in the event of conflicts, device 2 beats device 4, which beats 3. Device 5 has the lowest priority because it is at the end of the lowest priority daisy chain.

As an aside, it is not technically necessary to wire the level 2 bus grant line serially through devices 1 and 2, since they cannot make requests on it. However, as an implementation convenience, it is easier to wire all the grant lines through all the devices, rather than making special wiring that depends on which device has which priority.

Some arbiters have a third line that a device asserts when it has accepted a grant and seized the bus. As soon as it has asserted this acknowledgement line, the request and grant lines can be negated. As a result, other devices can request the bus while the first device is using the bus. By the time the current transfer is finished, the next bus master will have already been selected. It can start as soon as the acknowledgement line has been negated, at which time the following round of arbitration can begin. This scheme requires an extra bus line and more logic in each device, but it makes better use of bus cycles.

In systems in which memory is on the main bus, the CPU must compete with all the I/O devices for the bus on nearly every cycle. One common solution for this situation is to give the CPU the lowest priority, so it gets the bus only when nobody else wants it. The idea here is that the CPU can always wait, but I/O devices frequently must acquire the bus quickly or lose incoming data. Disks rotating at high speed cannot wait. This problem is avoided in many modern computer systems by putting the memory on a separate bus from the I/O devices so they do not have to compete for access to the bus.

Decentralized bus arbitration is also possible. For example, a computer could have 16 prioritized bus request lines. When a device wants to use the bus, it asserts its request line. All devices monitor all the request lines, so at the end of each bus cycle, each device knows whether it was the highest priority requester, and thus whether it is permitted to use the bus during the next cycle. Compared to centralized arbitration, this arbitration method requires more bus lines but avoids the potential cost of the arbiter. It also limits the number of devices to the number of request lines.

Another kind of decentralized bus arbitration, shown in Fig. 3-41, only uses three lines, no matter how many devices are present. The first bus line is a wired-OR line for requesting the bus. The second bus line is called BUSY and is asserted by the current bus master. The third line is used to arbitrate the bus. It is daisy chained through all the devices. The head of this chain is held asserted by tying it to the 5-volt power supply.

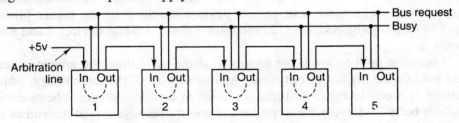

Figure 3-41. Decentralized bus arbitration.

When no device wants the bus, the asserted arbitration line is propagated through to all devices. To acquire the bus, a device first checks to see if the bus is idle and the arbitration signal it is receiving, IN, is asserted. If IN is negated, it may not become bus master, and it negates OUT. If IN is asserted, however, the device negates OUT, which causes its downstream neighbor to see IN negated and to negate its OUT. Hence, downstream devices all see IN negated and correspondingly negate OUT. When the dust settles, only one device will have IN asserted and OUT negated. This device becomes bus master, asserts BUSY and OUT, and begins its transfer.

Some thought will reveal that the leftmost device that wants the bus gets it. Thus this scheme is similar to the original daisy chain arbitration, except without having the arbiter, so it is cheaper, faster, and not subject to arbiter failure.

3.4.6 Bus Operations

Up until now, we have only discussed ordinary bus cycles, with a master (typically the CPU) reading from a slave (typically the memory) or writing to one. In fact, several other kinds of bus cycles exist. We will now look at some of these.

Normally, one word at a time is transferred. However, when caching is used, it is desirable to fetch an entire cache line (e.g., 16 consecutive 32-bit words) at once. Often block transfers can be made more efficient than successive individual transfers. When a block read is started, the bus master tells the slave how many words are to be transferred, for example, by putting the word count on the data lines during T_1. Instead of just returning one word, the slave outputs one word during each cycle until the count has been exhausted. Figure 3-42 shows a modified version of Fig. 3-38(a), but now with an extra signal $\overline{BLOCK}$ that is asserted to indicate that a block transfer is requested. In this example, a block read of 4 words takes 6 cycles instead of 12.

Other kinds of bus cycles also exist. For example, on a multiprocessor system with two or more CPUs on the same bus, it is often necessary to make sure that only one CPU at a time uses some critical data structure in memory. A typical way to arrange this is to have a variable in memory that is 0 when no CPU is using the data structure and 1 when it is in use. If a CPU wants to gain access to the data structure, it must read the variable, and if it is 0, set it to 1. The trouble is, with some bad luck, two CPUs might read it on consecutive bus cycles. If each one sees that the variable is 0 then each one sets it to 1 and thinks that it is the only CPU using the data structure. This sequence of events leads to chaos.

To prevent this situation, multiprocessor systems often have a special read-modify-write bus cycle that allows any CPU to read a word from memory, inspect and modify it, and write it back to memory, all without releasing the bus. This type of cycle prevents competing CPUs from being able to use the bus and thus interfere with the first CPU's operation.

Another important kind of bus cycle is for handling interrupts. When the CPU commands an I/O device to do something, it usually expects an interrupt when the work is done. The interrupt signaling requires the bus.

Since multiple devices may want to cause an interrupt simultaneously, the same kind of arbitration problems are present here that we had with ordinary bus cycles. The usual solution is to assign priorities to devices, and use a centralized

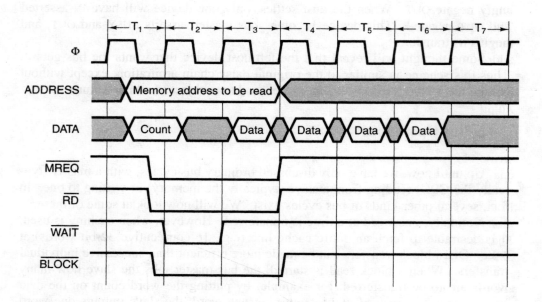

Figure 3-42. A block transfer.

arbiter to give priority to the most time-critical devices. Standard interrupt controller chips exist and are widely used. The IBM PC and all its successors use the Intel 8259A chip, illustrated in Fig. 3-43.

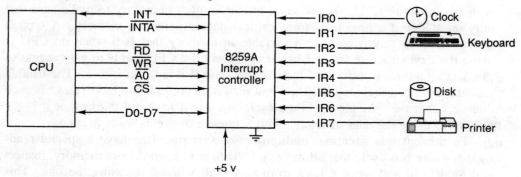

Figure 3-43. Use of the 8259A interrupt controller.

Up to eight I/O controller chips can be directly connected to the eight IRx (Interrupt Request) inputs to the 8259A. When any of these devices wants to cause an interrupt, it asserts its input line. When one or more inputs are asserted, the 8259A asserts INT (INTerrupt), which directly drives the interrupt pin on the CPU. When the CPU is able to handle the interrupt, it sends a pulse back to the 8259A on INTA (INTerrupt Acknowledge). At that point the 8259A must specify which input caused the interrupt by outputting that input's number on the data bus. This operation requires a special bus cycle. The CPU hardware then uses that number to index into a table of pointers, called **interrupt vectors**, to find the address of the procedure to run to service the interrupt.

The 8259A has several registers inside of it that the CPU can read and write using ordinary bus cycles and the $\overline{RD}$ (ReaD), $\overline{WR}$ (WRite), $\overline{CS}$ (Chip Select), and $\overline{A0}$ pins. When the software has handled the interrupt and is ready to take the next one, it writes a special code into one of the registers, which causes the 8259A to negate INT, unless it has another interrupt pending. These registers can also be written to put the 8259A in one of several modes, mask out a set of interrupts, and enable other features.

When more than eight I/O devices are present, the 8259As can be cascaded. In the most extreme case, all eight inputs can be connected to the outputs of eight more 8259As, allowing for up to 64 I/O devices in a two-stage interrupt network. The 8259A has a few pins devoted for handling this cascading, which we have omitted for the sake of simplicity.

While we have by no means exhausted the subject of bus design, the material above should give enough background to understand the essentials of how a bus works, and how CPUs and buses interact. Let us now move from the general to the specific and take a look at some examples of actual CPUs and their buses.

3.5 EXAMPLE CPU CHIPS

In this section we will examine the Pentium 4, the UltraSPARC III, and the 8051 chips in some detail at the hardware level.

3.5.1 The Pentium 4

The Pentium 4 is a direct descendant of the 8088 CPU used in the original IBM PC. The first Pentium 4 was introduced in Nov. 2000 as a 42-million transistor CPU running at 1.5 GHz with a line width of 0.18 micron. The line width is how wide the wires between transistors are (as well as being a measure of the size of the transistors themselves). The narrower the line width, the more transistors can fit on the chip. Moore's law is fundamentally about the ability of process engineers to keep reducing the line widths. Smaller line widths also allow higher clock speeds. For comparison purposes, human hairs range from 20 microns to 100 microns in diameter, with blonde hair being finer than black hair.

During the course of the next three years, as Intel gained experience with the manufacturing process, it evolved to having 55 million transistors running at speeds up to 3.2 GHz with line widths of 0.09 micron. Although the Pentium 4 is a far cry from the 29,000-transistor 8088, it is fully backward compatible with the

8088 and can run unmodified 8088 binary programs (not to mention programs for all the intermediate processors as well).

From a software point of view, the Pentium 4 is a full 32-bit machine. It has all the same user-level ISA features as the 80386, 80486, Pentium, Pentium II, Pentium Pro, and Pentium III, including the same registers, same instructions, and a full on-chip implementation of the IEEE 754 floating-point standard. In addition, though, it has some new instructions intended primarily for multimedia applications.

However, from a hardware perspective, Pentium 4 is partially a 64-bit machine since it can transfer data to and from memory in units of 64 bits. Although the programmer cannot observe these 64-bit transfers, they do make the machine faster than a pure 32-bit machine would be.

Internally, at the microarchitecture level, the Pentium 4 is radically different from all its predecessors. Its immediate predecessors— the Pentium II, the Pentium Pro, and the Pentium III—all used the same internal microarchitecture (called P6), differing only in speed and in a few minor ways. In contrast, the Pentium 4 uses a new microarchitecture (called NetBurst), which is significantly different from the P6. It has a deeper pipeline, two ALUs (each of which runs at twice the clock frequency to allow two operations per cycle), and supports hyperthreading. The latter feature provides two sets of registers and some other internal resources, allowing the Pentium 4 to switch between two programs very quickly, as though the computer contained two physical CPUs. We will examine the microarchitecture in Chap. 4. However, like its predecessors, the Pentium 4 can carry out multiple instructions at once, making it a superscalar machine.

Some models of the Pentium 4 have a two-level cache and some have a three-level cache. All models have an 8-KB on-chip SRAM level-one (L1) cache. Unlike Pentium III L1 cache, which just holds raw bytes from the memory, the Pentium 4 goes further. When instructions are fetched from memory, they are converted to micro-operations for actual execution in the Pentium 4 RISC core. The L1 cache on the Pentium 4 holds up to 12,000 decoded micro-operations, eliminating the need to decode them repeatedly. The second level cache holds up to 256 KB of memory in the older models and up to 1 MB of bytes in the newer ones. Nothing is decoded; pure bytes from memory are stored in the L2 cache. It can hold a mixture of code and data. The Pentium 4 Extreme Edition also has a 2-MB level 3 cache, to raise the performance even more.

Since all Pentium 4 chips have at least two levels of cache, a problem arises in a multiprocessor system when one CPU has modified a word in its cache. If another CPU tries to read that word from memory, it will get a stale value since modified cache words are not written back to memory immediately. To maintain memory consistency, each CPU in a multiprocessor system **snoops** on the memory bus looking for references to words it has cached. When it sees such a reference, it jumps in and supplies the required data before the memory gets a chance to do so. We will study snooping in Chap. 8.

Two primary external buses are used in Pentium 4 systems, both of them synchronous. The memory bus is used to access the main (S)DRAM; the PCI bus is used for talking to I/O devices. Sometimes a **legacy** (i.e., ancient) bus is attached to the PCI bus to allow old peripheral devices to be plugged in.

One substantial difference between the Pentium 4 and all of its predecessors is its packaging. A problem with all modern chips is the amount of power they consume and heat they produce. The Pentium 4 consumes between 63 watts and 82 watts, depending on the frequency. Consequently, Intel is constantly searching for ways to manage the heat produced by the CPU chips. The Pentium 4 comes in a square package 35 mm on edge. It contains 478 pins on the bottom, 85 of which are for power and 180 of which are grounded to reduce noise. The pins are arranged as a 26 × 26 square, with the middle 14 × 14 missing. Two pins in one corner are also missing, to prevent the chip from being inserted incorrectly in its socket. The physical pinout is shown in Fig. 3-44.

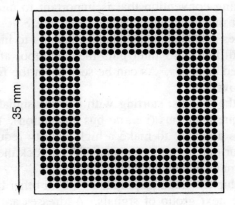

Figure 3-44. The Pentium 4 physical pinout.

The chip is outfitted with a mounting bracket for a heat sink to distribute the heat and a fan to cool it. To get some idea of what the problem is, turn on a 60-watt light bulb, let it warm up, and then put your hands around it (but do not touch it). This amount of heat must be dissipated continuously. Consequently, when a Pentium 4 has outlived its usefulness as a CPU, it can always be used as a camp stove.

According to the laws of physics, anything that puts out a lot of heat must suck in a lot of energy. In a portable computer with a limited battery charge, using a lot of energy is not desirable because it drains the battery quickly. To address this issue, Intel has provided a way to put the CPU to sleep when it is idle and to put it into a deep sleep when it is likely to be that way for a while. There are five states provided, ranging from fully active to deep sleep. In the intermediate states, some functionality (such as cache snooping and interrupt handling) is enabled, but other functions are disabled. When in deep sleep state, the cache and register values are preserved, but the clock and all the internal units are turned off. When in deep sleep, a hardware signal is required to wake it up. It is not known whether a Pentium 4 can dream when it is in deep sleep.

The Pentium 4's Logical Pinout

The 478 pins on the Pentium 4 are used for 198 signals, 85 power connections (at several different voltages), 180 grounds, and 15 spares for future use. Some of the logical signals use two or more pins (such as the memory address requested), so there are only 56 different signals. A somewhat simplified logical pinout is given in Fig. 3-45. On the left side of the figure are five major groups of memory bus signals; on the right side are various miscellaneous signals. The names given entirely in uppercase are the actual Intel signal names. The ones given in mixed case are collective names for multiple related signals.

Intel uses a naming convention that is important to understand. Because all chips are designed using computers these days, there is a need to be able to represent signal names as ASCII text. Using overbars to indicate signals that are asserted low is too difficult, so Intel puts the # symbol after the name instead. Thus $\overline{\text{BPRI}}$ is expressed as BPRI#. As can be seen from the figure, most Pentium 4 signals are asserted low.

Let us examine the signals, starting with the bus signals. The first group of signals is used to request the bus (i.e., do bus arbitration). BR0 is used to request the bus. BPRI# allows a device to make a high priority request, which takes precedence over a regular one. LOCK# allows a CPU to lock the bus, to prevent other devices from getting in until it is done.

Once bus ownership has been acquired, a CPU or other bus master can make a bus request using the next group of signals. Addresses are 36 bits, but the low-order 3 bits must always be 0 and therefore do not have pins assigned, so A# has only 33 pins. All transfers are 8 bytes, aligned on an 8-byte boundary. With 36 address bits, the maximum addressable memory is 2^{36}, which is 64 GB.

When an address is put onto the bus, the ADS# signal is asserted to tell the target (e.g., the memory) that the address lines are valid. The type of bus cycle (e.g., read one word or write a block) goes on the REQ# lines. The two parity lines protect A# and REQ#.

The five error lines are used to report floating-point errors, internal errors, machine check (i.e., hardware) errors, and certain other errors.

The Response group contains signals used by the slave to report back to the master. RS# contains the status code. TRDY# indicates that the slave (the target) is ready to accept data from the master. These signals are also parity checked. $\overline{\text{BNR}}$ is used to assert a wait state when the target addressed cannot respond on time.

The last bus group is for the actual data transfer. D# is used to put 8 data bytes onto the bus. When they are placed there, DRDY# is asserted to announce their presence. DBSY# is used to tell the world that the bus is currently busy. Parity is

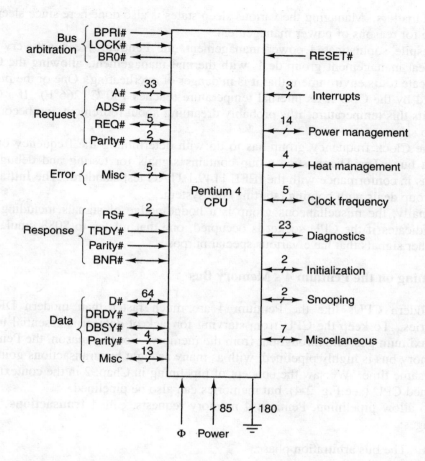

Figure 3-45. Logical pinout of the Pentium 4. Names in uppercase are the official Intel names for individual signals. Names in mixed case are groups of related signals or signal descriptions.

also used here to check the data. The miscellaneous data signals deal with latching values and similar things.

RESET# is used to reset the CPU in the event of a calamity or when the user presses the reset button on the front of the PC.

The Pentium 4 can be configured to use the interrupts the same way as on the 8088 (for purposes of backward compatibility) or it can also use a new interrupt system using a device called an **APIC (Advanced Programmable Interrupt Controller)**.

The Pentium 4 can run at any one of several predefined voltages, but it has to know which one. The power management signals are used for automatic power supply voltage selection, telling the CPU that power is stable, and other power-related matters. Managing the various sleep states is also done here since sleeping is done for reasons of power management.

Despite sophisticated power management, the Pentium 4 can get very hot. The Heat management group deals with thermal management, allowing the CPU to indicate to its environment that it is in danger of overheating. One of the pins is asserted by the CPU if its internal temperature reaches 130°C (266°F). If a CPU ever hits this temperature, it is probably dreaming about retirement and becoming a camp stove.

The Clock frequency group has to do with determining the frequency of the system bus. The Diagnostics group contains signals for testing and debugging systems in conformance with the IEEE 1149.1 JTAG test standard. The Initialization group deals with booting (starting) the system.

Finally, the miscellaneous group is a hodge-podge of signals including one that indicates if the CPU socket is occupied, one that relates to 8088 emulation, and other signals that have various special purposes.

Pipelining on the Pentium 4's Memory Bus

Modern CPUs like the Pentium 4 are much faster than modern DRAM memories. To keep the CPU from starving for lack of data, it is essential to get the maximum possible throughput from the memory. For this reason, the Pentium 4 memory bus is highly pipelined, with as many as eight bus transactions going on at the same time. We saw the concept of pipelining in Chap. 2 in the context of a pipelined CPU (see Fig. 2-4), but memories can also be pipelined.

To allow pipelining, Pentium 4 memory requests, called **transactions**, have six stages:

1. The bus arbitration phase.

2. The request phase.

3. The error-reporting phase.

4. The snoop phase.

5. The response phase.

6. The data phase.

Not all phases are needed on all transactions. The bus arbitration phase determines which of the potential bus masters goes next. The request phase allows the address to be put onto the bus and the request made. The error-reporting phase allows the slave to announce that the address had a parity error or that something else is wrong. The snoop phase allows one CPU to snoop on the other one, something only needed in a multiprocessor system. The response phase is where the master learns about whether it is about to get the data it wants. Finally, the data phase allows the data to be sent back to the CPU requesting it.

The secret to the Pentium 4's pipelined memory bus is that each phase uses different bus signals, so that each one is completely independent of the other ones. The six groups of signals needed are the ones shown in Fig. 3-45 on the left. For example, one CPU can try to get the bus using the arbitration signals. Once it has acquired the right to go next, it releases these bus lines and starts using the Request group's lines. Meanwhile, the other CPU or some I/O device can enter the bus arbitration phase, and so on. Figure 3-46 shows how multiple bus transactions can be outstanding at the same time.

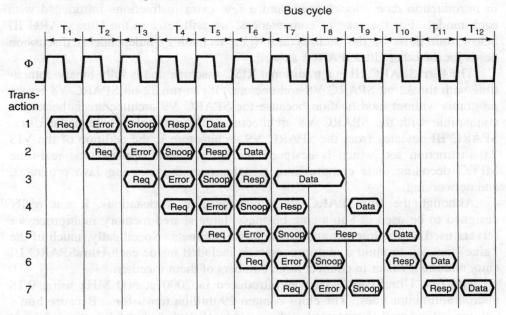

Figure 3-46. Pipelining requests on the Pentium 4's memory bus.

In Fig. 3-46 the bus arbitration phase is not shown because it is not always needed. For example, if the current bus owner (often the CPU) wants to run another transaction, it does not have to reacquire the bus. It only has to ask for the bus again after it passes bus ownership to another requesting device. Transactions 1 and 2 are straightforward: five phases in five bus cycles. Transaction 3 introduces a longer data phase, for example, because it is a block transfer or because the memory addressed inserted a wait state. As a consequence, transaction 4 cannot start its data phase when it would like to. It observes that the DBSY# signal is still asserted and just waits for it to be negated. In transaction 5 we see that the response phase can also take multiple bus cycles, thus delaying transaction 6. Finally, in transaction 7, we notice that once a bubble has been introduced into the pipeline it remains there if new transactions keep starting consecutively. In actual practice, however, it is unlikely that the CPU will attempt to start a new transaction on every single bus cycle, so bubbles do not last so long.

3.5.2 The UltraSPARC III

As our second example of a CPU chip, we will now examine the Sun UltraSPARC family. The UltraSPARC family is Sun's line of 64-bit SPARC CPUs. These CPUs fully conform to the Version 9 SPARC architecture, which is also for 64-bit CPUs. They are used in Sun workstations and servers, as well as various other applications. This family includes the UltraSPARC I, UltraSPARC II, and UltraSPARC III, which are architecturally very similar, differing primarily in introduction date, clock speed, and a few extra instructions introduced with each model. For the sake of concreteness, we will refer to the UltraSPARC III below, but most of the architectural (i.e., technology-independent) discussion holds for the other UltraSPARCs as well.

The UltraSPARC III is a traditional RISC machine and is fully binary compatible with the 32-bit SPARC V8 architecture. It can run 32-bit SPARC V8 binary programs without modification because the SPARC V9 architecture is backward compatible with the SPARC V8 architecture. The only place where the Ultra-SPARC III deviates from the SPARC V9 architecture is the addition of the VIS 2.0 instruction set, which is designed for 3D graphical applications, real-time MPEG decoding, data compression, signal processing, running Java programs, and networking.

Although the UltraSPARC III is also used in workstations, it was really designed to be used in Sun's core business, large shared-memory multiprocessor servers used on the Internet and on corporate intranets. Specifically, much of the "glue" needed to build a multiprocessor is included inside each UltraSPARC III chip, making it easier to connect large numbers of them together.

The first UltraSPARC III was introduced in 2000 at 600 MHz using 0.18 micron aluminum lines. The chips contain 29 million transistors. Because Sun's volume is too small to warrant building a state-of-the-art chip fabrication plant, it prefers to concentrate on chip design and software and contract CPU manufacturing out to chip vendors. In the case of the UltraSPARC III, the chips are manufactured by Texas Instruments. In 2001, TI improved its technology and began making 900 MHz 0.15 micron chips using copper instead of aluminum wires. In 2002, the line width dropped to 0.13 microns and the clock was raised to 1.2 GHz. These chips require 50 watts of power and thus have about the same heat dissipation problems as the Pentium 4.

It is difficult to compare a CISC chip (like the Pentium 4) and a RISC chip (like the UltraSPARC III) based on clock speed alone. For example, the UltraSPARC III can continuously issue four instructions per clock cycle, giving it almost the same execution rate as a single-issue CPU running at 4.8 GHz. The UltraSPARC also has six internal pipelines, including two 14-stage pipelines for integer operations, two for floating-point operations, one for load/store operations, and one for branches. It also has a different approach to caching, wider buses, and other factors that improve performance. The Pentium 4 also has its particular strengths. The point here is that just comparing two very different chips based on their relative clock speeds says very little about relative performance at some specific task.

The UltraSPARC III comes in a 1368-pin Land Grid Array, as shown in Fig. 3-47. This package consists of a square array of $37 \times 37 = 1369$ pins on the bottom of the chip, with the pin in the lower left-hand corner missing. The socket exactly matches the chip to prevent the chip from being inserted incorrectly in the socket.

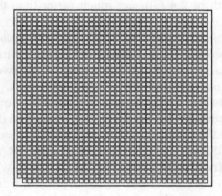

Figure 3-47. The UltraSPARC III CPU chip.

The UltraSPARC III has two main internal L1 caches: 32 KB for instructions and 64 KB for data. There is also a 2-KB prefetch cache and a 2-KB write cache used to collect writes to the level 2 cache so they can be done in large bursts to improve bandwidth usage. Like the Pentium 4, it also uses an off-chip level 2 cache, but unlike the Pentium 4, the UltraSPARC III is not packaged with the level 2 cache on chip. The cache controller and logic for locating cache blocks is on chip, but the actual SRAM memory is not. Instead, system designers are free to choose any commercially-available cache chips they want for the level 2 cache.

The decision to integrate the level 2 cache on the Pentium 4 and separate it on the UltraSPARC III is partly due to technical issues and partly due to different business models used by Intel and Sun. On the technical side, an external cache is larger and more flexible (UltraSPARC III L2 caches can range from 1 MB to 8 MB; Pentium 4 L2 caches are fixed at 512 KB). However, it may be slower due to its greater distance from the CPU. It also requires more visible signals to address the cache. In particular, the connection between the UltraSPARC III and its L2 caches is 256 bits wide, allowing for an entire 32-byte cache block to be transferred in one cycles.

On the business side, Intel is a semiconductor vendor and has the capability to design and manufacture its own level 2 cache chip and connect it to the CPU via a high-performance proprietary interface. Sun, in contrast, makes computers, not chips. It does design some of its own chips (like the UltraSPARCs), but farms out the manufacturing to semiconductor manufacturers. When it can, Sun prefers to use commercially available chips that have been keenly honed by the competitive marketplace. The SRAMs used for level 2 caches are available from numerous chip vendors, so there was no special need for Sun to design its own. This decision implies making the level 2 cache independent of the CPU chip.

The UltraSPARC III uses a 43-bit wide address bus, allowing it to have up to 8 TB of main memory. The data bus is 128 bits wide, allowing 16 bytes at a time to be transferred between the CPU and memory. The bus speed is 150 MHz, giving a memory bandwidth of 2.4 GB/sec, much faster than the 528 MB/sec of the PCI bus.

To connect (multiple) UltraSPARC CPUs to communicate with (multiple) memories, Sun developed the **UPA (Ultra Port Architecture**). The UPA can be implemented as a bus, a switch, or a combination of the two. Different workstation and server models use different UPA implementations. The UPA implementation does not matter to the CPU because the interface to the UPA is precisely defined, and it is this interface that the CPU chip must (and does) support.

In Fig. 3-48 we see the core of an UltraSPARC III system, showing the CPU chip, UPA interface, and level 2 cache (two commodity SRAMs). The figure also contains a **UDB II (UltraSPARC Data Buffer II**) chip, whose function will be discussed below. When the CPU needs a memory word, it first looks in one of its (internal) level 1 caches for it. If it finds the word, it continues execution at full speed. If it does not find the word in the level 1 cache, it tries the level 2 cache.

While we will discuss caching in detail in Chap. 4, a few words about it here will be useful. All of main memory is divided up into cache lines (blocks) of 64 bytes. The 256 most heavily used instruction lines and the 256 most heavily used data lines are in the level 1 cache. Cache lines that are heavily used but which do not fit in the level 1 cache are kept in the level 2 cache. This cache contains both data lines and instruction lines mixed at random. These are stored in the rectangle labeled "Level 2 cache data." The system has to keep track of which lines are in the level 2 cache. This information is kept in a second SRAM, labeled "Level 2 cache tags."

On a level 1 cache miss, the CPU sends the identifier of the line it is looking for (Tag address) to the level 2 cache. The reply (Tag data) provides the information for the CPU to tell whether the line is in the level 2 cache, and if so, what state it is in. If the line is cached there, the CPU goes and gets it. The data transfers are 16 bytes wide, so four cycles are needed to fetch an entire line into the level 1 cache.

If the cache line is not in the level 2 cache, it must be fetched from main memory via the UPA interface. The UltraSPARC III UPA is implemented with a centralized controller. The address and control signals from the CPU (all the CPUs if there are more than one of them) go there. To access memory, the CPU must first use the bus arbitration pins to acquire permission to go next. Once permission has been granted, the CPU outputs the memory address pins, specifies the

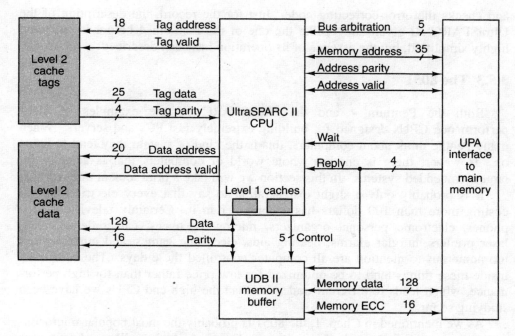

Figure 3-48. The main features of the core of an UltraSPARC III system.

request type, and asserts the address valid pin. (These pins are bidirectional since other CPUs in a UltraSPARC III multiprocessor need access to remote caches to keep all the caches consistent.) The address and bus cycle type are put out in two cycles on the Address pins, with the row going out in the first cycle and the column going out in the second cycle, as we saw in Fig. 3-31.

While waiting for the results, the CPU may well be able to continue with other work. For example, a cache miss while prefetching an instruction does not inhibit the execution of one or more instructions already fetched, each of which may refer to data not in any cache. Thus multiple transactions to the UPA may be outstanding at once. The UPA can handle two independent transaction streams (typically reads and writes), each with multiple transactions pending. It is up to the centralized controller to keep track of all this and to make actual memory requests in the most efficient order.

When data finally arrives from the memory, it can come in 8 bytes at a time, and with a 16-bit error-correcting code for greater reliability. A transaction may ask for an entire cache block, a quadword (8 bytes), or even fewer bytes. All incoming data go to the UDB, which buffers them. The purpose of the UDB is to further decouple the CPU from the memory system, so they can work asynchronously. For example, if the CPU has to write a word or cache line to memory, instead of waiting to access the UPA, it can write the data to the UDB immediately and let the UDB handle getting them to memory later. The UDB also generates and checks the error-correcting code. Just for the record, the description of the UltraSPARC III given above, like the one of the Pentium 4 before it, has been highly simplified, but the essence of its operation has been described.

3.5.3 The 8051

Both the Pentium 4 and the UltraSPARC III are examples of high-performance CPUs designed for building extremely fast PCs and servers. When many people think about computers, this is the kind of system they tend to focus on. However, there is another whole world of computers that is actually far larger: embedded systems. In this section we will take a brief look at that world.

It is probably only a slight exaggeration to say that every electrical device costing more than 100 dollars has a computer in it. Certainly televisions, cell phones, electronic personal organizers, microwave ovens, camcorders, VCRs, laser printers, burglar alarms, hearing aids, electronic games, and other devices too numerous to mention are all computer controlled these days. The computers inside these things tend to be optimized for low price rather than for high performance, which leads to different trade-offs than the high-end CPUs we have been studying so far.

As we mentioned in Chap. 1, the 8051 is probably the most popular microcontroller in current use, mostly due to its very low cost. As we will see shortly, it is also a simple chip, which makes interfacing to it simple and inexpensive. So let us now examine the 8051 chip, whose physical pinout is shown in Fig. 3-49.

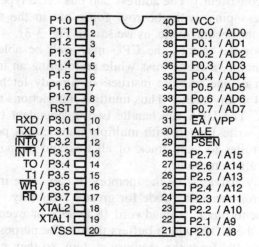

Figure 3-49. Physical pinout of the 8051.

As can be seen from the figure, the 8051 normally comes in a standard 40-pin package (although other packages are available for special uses). It has 16 address lines, so it can address up to 64 KB of memory. The data bus is 8 bits wide, so data transfers between the CPU and memory are done one byte at a time (versus 8 bytes at a time on the Pentium 4 and 16 bytes at a time on the UltraSPARC III). It has a variety of control lines, described below, but the greatest contrast with the Pentium 4 and UltraSPARC, which are pure CPUs, is the presence of 32 I/O lines, arranged in four groups of 8 bits each. Each of these I/O lines can be attached to a button, switch, LED (Light Emitting Diode), or other real-world device to provide input to the 8051 or output from the 8051. For example, in a clock radio, each of the buttons and switches could be wired to a different I/O line, with other I/O lines controlling the display. In this way, most, if not all, the functions of the clock radio could be controlled in software, eliminating the need for costly discrete logic.

The logical pinout of the 8051 is shown in Fig. 3-50. The 8051 comes with 4 KB of internal ROM (8 KB on the 8052). If that is insufficient for the application, up to 64 KB of external memory may be connected to the 8051 over a bus. The first seven signals on the left-hand side of Fig. 3-50 are used to interface to external memories, if present. The first signal, A, contains 16 address lines to address the byte of external memory to be read or written. The eight D lines are used for data transport. The low-order eight address lines are multiplexed onto the same pins as the data lines to reduce pin count. On a bus transaction, these pins output the address on the first clock cycle and carry the data on subsequent cycles.

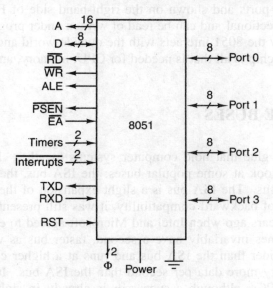

Figure 3-50. Logical pinout of the 8051.

When an external memory is used, the 8051 has to indicate whether it is reading or writing memory by asserting either $\overline{\text{RD}}$ or $\overline{\text{WR}}$, respectively. The ALE

(Address Latch Enable) signal is used when an external memory is present. The CPU asserts this signal to indicate that the address is valid. External memories typically use it to latch the address lines, since they will be released shortly thereafter so the pins can be reused for the data.

The $\overline{\text{PSEN}}$ and EA# signals also relate to external memory. The $\overline{\text{PSEN}}$ (Program Store ENable) signal is asserted to indicate that the 8051 wants to read from the program memory. Typically, it would be connected to the memory's OE signal, as illustrated in Fig. 3-29.

The $\overline{\text{EA#}}$ (External Access) signal is usually wired high or low so it always has the same value. If it is wired high, the internal 4 KB (8 KB on the 8052) memory is used for addresses within range and external memory is used for addresses above 4 KB (8 KB on the 8052). If it is wired low, the external memory is used for all addresses and the on-chip memory is effectively bypassed. On the 8031 and 8032, $\overline{\text{EA#}}$ must be wired low because there is no on-chip memory.

The two timer lines allow external timers to be input to the CPU. The two interrupt lines allow two different external devices to interrupt the CPU. The TXD and RXD lines are to allow serial I/O to a terminal or modem. Finally, the RST line allows the user or external hardware device to reset the 8051. This line is typically asserted when something has gone wrong and the system has to be rebooted.

So, far the 8051 is similar to most other 8-bit CPUs, except for the presence of the serial I/O lines. What sets the 8051 apart is the presence of 32 I/O lines, organized as four ports and shown on the right-hand side of Fig. 3-50. Each of these lines is bidirectional and can be read or written under program control. This is the primary way the 8051 interacts with the outside world and what makes it so valuable: a single chip is all that is needed for CPU, memory, and I/O capability.

3.6 EXAMPLE BUSES

Buses are the glue that hold computer systems together. In this section we will take a close look at some popular buses: the ISA bus, the PCI bus, and the Universal Serial Bus. The ISA bus is a slight expansion of the original IBM PC bus. For reasons of backward compatibility, it was still present in all Intel-based PCS until a few years ago when Intel and Microsoft agreed to eliminate it. However, these machines invariably have a second, faster bus as well: the PCI bus. The PCI bus is wider than the ISA bus and runs at a higher clock rate. Consequently it can carry more data per second than the ISA bus. It is the workhorse for most current PCs, although a successor is already in sight. The Universal Serial Bus is an increasingly popular I/O bus for low-speed peripherals such as mice and keyboards. A second version of the USB bus runs at much higher speeds. In the following sections, we will look at each of these buses in turn to see how they work.

3.6.1 The ISA Bus

The IBM PC bus was the de facto standard on 8088-based systems because nearly all PC clone vendors copied it in order to allow the many existing third-party I/O boards to be used with their systems. It had 62 signal lines, including 20 for a memory address, 8 for data, and one each for asserting memory read, memory write, I/O read, and I/O write. There were also signals for requesting and granting interrupts and using DMA, and that was about it. It was a very simple bus.

Physically, the bus was etched onto the PC's motherboard, with about half a dozen connectors spaced 2 cm apart into which cards could be inserted. Each card had a tab on it that fit in the connector. The tab had 31 gold-plated strips on each side that made electrical contact with the connector.

When IBM introduced the 80286-based PC/AT, it had a major problem on its hands. If it had started from scratch and designed an entirely new 16-bit bus, many potential customers would have hesitated to buy it because none of the vast number of PC plug-in boards available from third-party vendors would have worked using the new machine. On the other hand, sticking with the PC bus and its 20 address lines and 8 data lines would not have taken advantage of the 80286's ability to address 16 MB of memory and transfer 16-bit words.

The solution chosen was to extend the PC bus. PC plug-in cards have an edge connector with 62 contacts, but this edge connector does not run the full length of the board. The PC/AT solution was to put a second edge connector on the bottom of the board, adjacent to the main one, and design the AT circuitry to work with both types of boards. The general idea is illustrated in Fig. 3-51.

The second connector on the PC/AT bus contains 36 lines. Of these, 31 are provided for more address lines, more data lines, more interrupt lines, and more DMA channels, as well as power and ground. The rest deal with differences between 8-bit and 16-bit transfers.

When IBM brought out the PS/2 series as the successor to the PC and PC/AT, it decided that it was time to start again. Part of this decision may have been technical (the PC bus was by this time really obsolete), but part was, no doubt, caused by a desire to put an obstacle in the way of companies making PC clones, which had taken over an uncomfortably large part of the market. Thus the mid- and upper-range PS/2 machines were equipped with a bus, the Microchannel, that was completely new, and which was protected by a wall of patents backed by an army of lawyers.

The rest of the personal computer industry reacted to this development by adopting its own standard, the **ISA** (**Industry Standard Architecture**) bus, which was basically the PC/AT bus running at 8.33 MHz. The big advantage of this approach was that it retained compatibility with existing machines and cards. It also was based on a bus that IBM had liberally licensed to many companies in order to ensure that as many third parties as possible produced cards for the

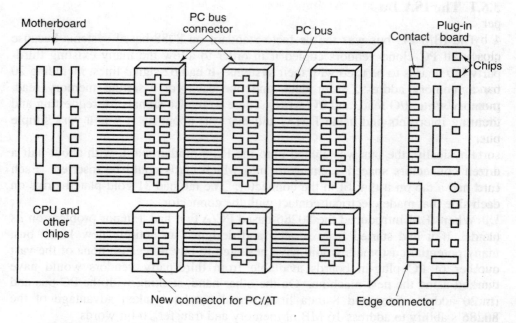

Figure 3-51. The PC/AT bus has two components, the original PC part and the new part.

original PC, something that came back to haunt IBM and ultimately drive it from the PC business. Until a few years ago, most Intel-based PCs still had this bus present, although with one or more other buses as well.

Later, the ISA bus was extended to 32 bits with some new features thrown in (e.g., for multiprocessing). The new bus was called the **EISA** (**Extended ISA**) bus.

3.6.2 The PCI Bus

On the original IBM PC, most applications were text based. Gradually, with the introduction of Windows, graphical user interfaces came into use. None of these applications put much of a strain on the ISA bus. However, as time went on and many applications, especially multimedia games, began to use computers to display full-screen, full-motion video, the situation changed radically.

Let us make a simple calculation. Consider a 1024×768 screen used for true color (3 bytes/pixel) moving images. One screen contains 2.25 MB of data. For smooth motion, at least 30 screens/sec are needed, for a data rate of 67.5 MB/sec. In fact, it is worse than this, since to display a video from a hard disk, CD-ROM, or DVD, the data must pass from the disk drive over the bus to the memory. Then for the display, the data must travel over the bus again to the graphics adapter. Thus we need a bus bandwidth of 135 MB/sec for the video alone, not counting the bandwidth the CPU and other devices need.

The ISA bus ran at a maximum rate of 8.33 MHz, and could transfer 2 bytes per cycle, for a maximum bandwidth of 16.7 MB/sec. The EISA bus could move 4 bytes per cycle, to achieve 33.3 MB/sec. Clearly, neither of these was even close to what is needed for full-screen video.

In 1990, Intel saw this coming and designed a new bus with a much higher bandwidth than even the EISA bus. It was called the **PCI bus** (**Peripheral Component Interconnect bus**). To encourage its use, Intel patented the PCI bus and then put all the patents into the public domain, so any company could build peripherals for it without having to pay royalties. Intel also formed an industry consortium, the PCI Special Interest Group, to manage the future of the PCI bus. As a result of these actions, the PCI bus became extremely popular. Virtually every Intel-based computer since the Pentium has a PCI bus, and many other computers do, too. Sun even has a version of the UltraSPARC that uses the PCI bus, the UltraSPARC IIIi. The PCI bus is covered in gory detail in Shanley and Anderson (1999) and Solari and Willse (2004).

The original PCI bus transferred 32 bits per cycle and ran at 33 MHz (30 nsec cycle time) for a total bandwidth of 133 MB/sec. In 1993, PCI 2.0 was introduced, and in 1995, PCI 2.1 came out. PCI 2.2 has features for mobile computers (mostly for saving battery power). The PCI bus runs at up to 66 MHz and can handle 64-bit transfers, for a total bandwidth of 528 MB/sec. With this kind of capacity, full-screen, full-motion video is doable (assuming the disk and the rest of the system are up to the job). In any event, the PCI bus will not be the bottleneck.

Even though 528 MB/sec sounds pretty fast, it still had two problems. First, it was not good enough for a memory bus. Second, it was not compatible with all those old ISA cards out there. The solution Intel thought of was to design computers with three or more buses, as shown in Fig. 3-52. Here we see that the CPU can talk to the main memory on a special memory bus, and that an ISA bus can be connected to the PCI bus. This arrangement met all requirements, and as a consequence was widely used in the 1990s.

Two key components in this architecture are the two bridge chips (which Intel manufactures—hence its interest in this whole project). The PCI bridge connects the CPU, memory and PCI bus. The ISA bridge connects the PCI bus to the ISA bus and also supports one or two IDE disks. Nearly all Pentium 4 systems come with one or more free PCI slots for adding new high-speed peripherals, and one or more ISA slots, for adding low-speed peripherals.

The big advantage of the design of Fig. 3-52 is that the CPU has an extremely high bandwidth to memory using a proprietary memory bus; the PCI bus offers high bandwidth for fast peripherals such as SCSI disks, graphics adaptors, etc.; and old ISA cards can still be used. The USB box in the figure refers to the Universal Serial Bus, which will be discussed later in this chapter.

It would have been nice had there been only one kind of PCI card. Unfortunately, such is not the case. Options are provided for voltage, width, and timing.

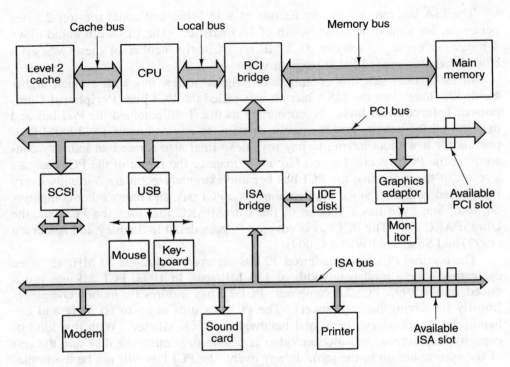

Figure 3-52. Architecture of an early Pentium system. The thicker buses have more bandwidth than the thinner ones but the figure is not to scale.

Older computers often use 5 volts and newer ones tend to use 3.3 volts, so the PCI bus supports both. The connectors are the same except for two bits of plastic that are there to prevent people from inserting a 5-volt card in a 3.3-volt PCI bus or vice versa. Fortunately, universal cards, which support both voltages and can plug into either kind of slot, exist. In addition to the voltage option, cards come in 32-bit and 64-bit versions. The 32-bit cards have 120 pins; the 64-bit cards have the same 120 pins plus an additional 64 pins, analogous to the way the IBM PC bus was extended to 16 bits (see Fig. 3-51). A PCI bus system that supports 64-bit cards can also take 32-bit cards, but the reverse is not true. Finally, PCI buses and cards can run at either 33 MHz or 66 MHz. The choice is made by having one pin wired either to the power supply or wired to ground. The connectors are identical for both speeds.

By the late 1990s, pretty much everyone agreed that the ISA bus was dead, so new designs excluded it. However, by then, monitor resolution had increased in some cases to 1600×1200 and the demand for full-screen full motion video had also increased, especially in the context of highly interactive games, so Intel added yet another bus just to drive the graphics card. This bus was called the **AGP bus (Accelerated Graphics Port bus)**. The initial version, AGP 1.0, ran at

264 MB/sec, which was defined as 1x. While slower than the PCI bus, it was dedicated to driving the graphics card. Over the years, new versions came out, with AGP 3.0 running at 2.1 GB/sec (8x). A modern Pentium 4 system is illustrated in Fig. 3-53.

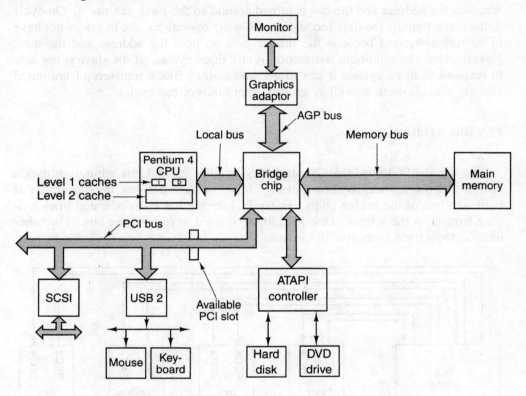

Figure 3-53. The bus structure of a modern Pentium 4.

In this design, the bridge chip is now central. It connects the five major pieces of the system: the CPU, memory, the graphics card, the ATAPI controller, and the PCI bus. In some variations, it also has support for Ethernet and other high-speed devices. The lower-speed devices are attached to the PCI bus.

Internally, the bridge chip is divided into two parts: the memory bridge and the I/O bridge. The memory bridge connects the CPU to the memory and to the graphics adaptor. The I/O bridge connects the ATAPI controller, PCI bus, and (optionally) other fast I/O devices with a direct bridge connection to each other. The two bridges are connected by a very high speed interconnect.

The PCI bus is synchronous, like all PC buses going back to the original IBM PC. All transactions on the PCI bus are between a master, officially called the **initiator**, and a slave, officially called the **target**. To keep the PCI pin count down, the address and data lines are multiplexed. In this way, only 64 pins are needed on PCI cards for address plus data signals, even though PCI supports 64-bit addresses and 64-bit data.

The multiplexed address and data pins work as follows. On a read operation, during cycle 1, the master puts the address onto the bus. On cycle 2, the master removes the address and the bus is turned around so the slave can use it. On cycle 3, the slave outputs the data requested. On write operations, the bus does not have to be turned around because the master puts on both the address and the data. Nevertheless, the minimum transaction is still three cycles. If the slave is not able to respond in three cycles, it can insert wait states. Block transfers of unlimited size are also allowed, as well as several other kinds of bus cycles.

PCI Bus Arbitration

To use the PCI bus, a device must first acquire it. PCI bus arbitration uses a centralized bus arbiter, as shown in Fig. 3-54. In most designs, the bus arbiter is built into one of the bridge chips. Every PCI device has two dedicated lines running from it to the arbiter. One line, REQ#, is used to request the bus. The other line, GNT#, is used to receive bus grants.

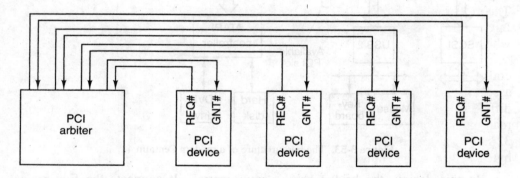

Figure 3-54. The PCI bus uses a centralized bus arbiter.

To request the bus, a PCI device (including the CPU), asserts REQ# and waits until it sees its GNT# line asserted by the arbiter. When that event happens, the device can use the bus on the next cycle. The algorithm used by the arbiter is not defined by the PCI specification. Round-robin arbitration, priority arbitration, and other schemes are all allowed. Clearly, a good arbiter will be fair, so as not to let some devices wait forever.

A bus grant is for only one transaction, although the length of this transaction is theoretically unbounded. If a device wants to run a second transaction and no other device is requesting the bus, it can go again, although often one idle cycle between transactions has to be inserted. However, under special circumstances, in the absence of competition for the bus, a device can make back-to-back transactions without having to insert an idle cycle. If a bus master is making a very long transfer and some other device has requested the bus, the arbiter can negate the GNT# line. The current bus master is expected to monitor the GNT# line, so when it sees the negation, it must release the bus on the next cycle. This scheme allows very long transfers (which are efficient) when there is only one candidate bus master but still gives fast response to competing devices.

PCI Bus Signals

The PCI bus has a number of mandatory signals, shown in Fig. 3-55(a), and a number of optional signals, shown in Fig. 3-55(b). The remainder of the 120 or 184 pins are used for power, ground, and related miscellaneous functions and are not listed here. The *Master* (initiator) and *Slave* (target) columns tell who asserts the signal on a normal transaction. If the signal is asserted by a different device (e.g., CLK), both columns are left blank.

Let us now look at each of the PCI bus signals briefly. We will start with the mandatory (32-bit) signals; then we will move on to the optional (64-bit) signals. The CLK signal drives the bus. Most of the other signals are synchronous with it. In contrast to the ISA bus, a PCI bus transaction begins at the falling edge of CLK, which is in the middle of the cycle, rather than at the start.

The 32 AD signals are for the address and data (for 32-bit transactions). Generally, during cycle 1 the address is asserted and during cycle 3 the data are asserted. The PAR signal is a parity bit for AD. The C/BE# signal is used for two different things. On cycle 1, it contains the bus command (read 1 word, block read, etc.). On cycle 2 it contains a bit map of 4 bits, telling which bytes of the 32-bit word are valid. Using C/BE# it is possible to read or write any 1, 2, or 3 bytes, as well as an entire word.

The FRAME# signal is asserted by the bus master to start a bus transaction. It tells the slave that the address and bus commands are now valid. On a read, usually IRDY# is asserted at the same time as FRAME#. It says the master is ready to accept incoming data. On a write, IRDY# is asserted later, when the data are on the bus.

The IDSEL signal relates to the fact that every PCI device must have a 256-byte configuration space that other devices can read (by asserting IDSEL). This configuration space contains properties of the device. The Plug-and-Play feature of some operating systems uses the configuration space to find out what devices are on the bus.

Now we come to signals asserted by the slave. The first of these, DEVSEL#, announces that the slave has detected its address on the AD lines and is prepared to engage in the transaction. If DEVSEL# is not asserted within a certain time limit, the master times out and assumes the device addressed is either absent or broken.

Signal	Lines	Master	Slave	Description
CLK	1			Clock (33 MHz or 66 MHz)
AD	32	×	×	Multiplexed address and data lines
PAR	1	×		Address or data parity bit
C/BE	4	×		Bus command/bit map for bytes enabled
FRAME#	1	×		Indicates that AD and C/BE are asserted
IRDY#	1	×		Read: master will accept; write: data present
IDSEL	1	×		Select configuration space instead of memory
DEVSEL#	1		×	Slave has decoded its address and is listening
TRDY#	1		×	Read: data present; write: slave will accept
STOP#	1		×	Slave wants to stop transaction immediately
PERR#	1			Data parity error detected by receiver
SERR#	1			Address parity error or system error detected
REQ#	1			Bus arbitration: request for bus ownership
GNT#	1			Bus arbitration: grant of bus ownership
RST#	1			Reset the system and all devices

(a)

Signal	Lines	Master	Slave	Description
REQ64#	1	×		Request to run a 64-bit transaction
ACK64#	1		×	Permission is granted for a 64-bit transaction
AD	32	×		Additional 32 bits of address or data
PAR64	1	×		Parity for the extra 32 address/data bits
C/BE#	4	×		Additional 4 bits for byte enables
LOCK	1	×		Lock the bus to allow multiple transactions
SBO#	1			Hit on a remote cache (for a multiprocessor)
SDONE	1			Snooping done (for a multiprocessor)
INTx	4			Request an interrupt
JTAG	5			IEEE 1149.1 JTAG test signals
M66EN	1			Wired to power or ground (66 MHz or 33 MHz)

(b)

Figure 3-55. (a) Mandatory PCI bus signals. (b) Optional PCI bus signals.

The second slave signal is TRDY#, which the slave asserts on reads to announce that the data are on the AD lines and on writes to announce that it is prepared to accept data.

The next three signals are for error reporting. The first of these is STOP#, which the slave asserts if something disastrous happens and it wants to abort the current transaction. The next one, PERR#, is used to report a data parity error on the previous cycle. For a read, it is asserted by the master; for a write it is asserted by the slave. It is up to the receiver to take the appropriate action. Finally, SERR# is for reporting address errors and system errors.

The REQ# and GNT# signals are for doing bus arbitration. These are not asserted by the current bus master, but rather by a device that wants to become bus master. The last mandatory signal is RST#, used for resetting the system, either due to the user pushing the RESET button or some system device noticing a fatal error. Asserting this signal resets all devices and reboots the computer.

Now we come to the optional signals, most of which relate to the expansion from 32 bits to 64 bits. The REQ64# and ACK64# signals allow the master to ask permission to conduct a 64-bit transaction and allow the slave to accept, respectively. The AD, PAR64, and C/BE# signals are just extensions of the corresponding 32-bit signals.

The next three signals are not related to 32 bits versus 64 bits, but to multiprocessor systems, something that PCI boards are not required to support. The LOCK signal allows the bus to be locked for multiple transactions. The next two relate to bus snooping to maintain cache coherence.

The INTx signals are for requesting interrupts. A PCI card can have up to four separate logical devices on it, and each one can have its own interrupt request line. The JTAG signals are for the IEEE 1149.1 JTAG testing procedure. Finally, the M66EN signal is either wired high or wired low, to set the clock speed. It must not change during system operation.

PCI Bus Transactions

The PCI bus is really very simple (as buses go). To get a better feel for it, consider the timing diagram of Fig. 3-56. Here we see a read transaction, followed by an idle cycle, followed by a write transaction by the same bus master.

When the falling edge of the clock happens during T_1, the master puts the memory address on AD and the bus command on C/BE#. It then asserts FRAME# to start the bus transaction.

During T_2, the master floats the address bus to let it turn around in preparation for the slave to drive it during T_3. The master also changes C/BE# to indicate which bytes in the word addressed it wants to enable (i.e., read in).

In T_3, the slave asserts DEVSEL# so the master knows it got the address and is planning to respond. It also puts the data on the AD lines and asserts TRDY# to tell the master that it has done so. If the slave was not able to respond so quickly, it would still assert DEVSEL# to announce its presence but keep TRDY# negated until it could get the data out there. This procedure would introduce one or more wait states.

In this example (and often in reality), the next cycle is idle. Starting in T_5 we see the same master initiating a write. It starts out by putting the address and

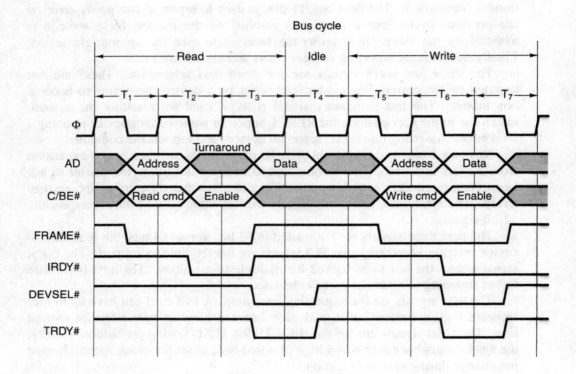

Figure 3-56. Examples of 32-bit PCI bus transactions. The first three cycles are used for a read operation, then an idle cycle, and then three cycles for a write operation.

command onto the bus, as usual. Only now, in the second cycle it asserts the data. Since the same device is driving the AD lines, there is no need for a turnaround cycle. In T_7, the memory accepts the data.

3.6.3 PCI Express

Although the PCI bus works adequately for most current applications, the need for greater I/O bandwidth is making a mess of the once-clean internal PC architecture. In Fig. 3-53, it is clear that the PCI bus is no longer the central element that holds the parts of the PC together. The bridge chip has taken over part of that role.

The essence of the problem is that there are increasingly many I/O devices that are too fast for the PCI bus. Cranking up the clock frequency on the bus is not a good solution because then problems with bus skew, crosstalk between the wires, and capacitance effects just get worse. Every time an I/O device gets too fast for the PCI bus (like the graphics card, hard disk, network, etc.), Intel adds a new special port to the bridge chip to allow that device to bypass the PCI bus. Clearly, this is not a long-term solution either.

Another problem with the PCI bus is that the cards are quite large. They do not fit in laptop computers and palmtop computers and manufacturers would like to produce even smaller devices. Also, some manufacturers would like to repartition the PC, with the CPU and memory in a tiny sealed box and the hard disk inside the monitor. With PCI cards, doing this is impossible.

Several solutions have been proposed, but the one most likely to win out (in no small part because Intel is behind it) is called **PCI Express**. It has little to do with the PCI bus, and in fact, is not a bus at all, but the marketing folks did not like letting go of the well-known PCI name. PCs containing it have been on the market for some time already. Let us now see how it works.

The PCI Express Architecture

The heart of the PCI Express solution is to get rid of the parallel bus with its many masters and slaves and go to a design based on high-speed point-to-point serial connections. This solution represents a radical break with the ISA/EISA/PCI bus tradition, and borrows many ideas from the world of local area networking, especially switched Ethernet. The basic idea comes down to this: deep inside, a PC is a collection of CPU, memory, and I/O controller chips that need to be interconnected. What PC Express does is provide a general-purpose switch for connecting chips using serial links. A typical configuration is illustrated in Fig. 3-57.

As shown in Fig. 3-57, the CPU, memory, and cache are connected to the bridge chip in the traditional way. What is new here is a switch connected to the bridge (possibly part of the bridge chip itself). Each of the I/O chips has a dedicated point-to-point connection to the switch. Each connection consists of a pair of unidirectional channels, one to the switch and one from it. Each channel is made up of two wires, one for the signal and one for ground, to provide high noise immunity during high-speed transmission. This architecture will replace the current one with a much more uniform model, in which all devices are treated equally.

The PCI Express architecture differs from the old PCI bus architecture in three key ways. We have already seen two of them: a centralized switch versus a multidrop bus and a the use of narrow serial point-to-point connections versus a wide parallel bus. The third one is more subtle. The conceptual model behind the PCI bus is that of a bus master issuing a command to a slave to read a word or a block of words. The PCI Express model is that of a device sending a data packet to another device. The concept of a **packet**, which consists of a header and a payload, is taken from the networking world. The **header** contains control information, thus eliminating the need for the many control signals present on the PCI

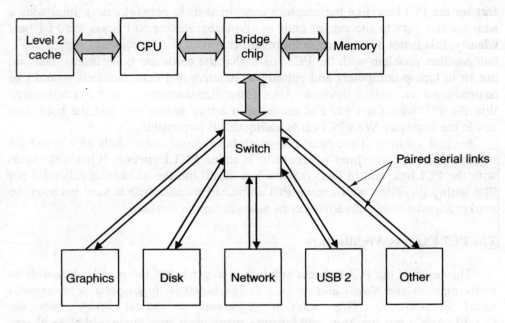

Figure 3-57. A typical PCI Express system.

bus. The **payload** contains the data to be transferred. In effect, a PC with PCI Express is a miniature packet-switching network.

In addition to these three major breaks with the past, there are also several minor differences as well. Fourth, an error-detecting code is used on the packets, providing a higher degree of reliability than on the PCI bus. Fifth, the connection between a chip and the switch is longer than it was, up to 50 cm, to allow system partitioning. Sixth, the system is expandable because a device may actually be another switch, allowing a tree of switches. Seventh, devices are hot pluggable, meaning that they can be added or removed from the system while it is running. Finally, since the serial connectors are much smaller than the old PCI connectors, devices and computers can be made much smaller. All in all, a major departure from the PCI bus.

The PCI Express Protocol Stack

In keeping with the model of a packet-switching network, the PCI Express system has a layered protocol stack. A **protocol** is a set of rules governing the conversation between two parties. A protocol stack is a hierarchy of protocols that deal with different issues at different layers. For example, consider a business letter. It has certain conventions about the placement and content of the letterhead, the recipient's address, the date, the salutation, the body, the signature, and so on. This might be thought of as the letter protocol. In addition, there is another set of conventions about the envelope, such as its size, where the sender's address goes and its format, where the receiver's address goes and its format, where the stamp goes, and so on. These two layers and their protocols are independent. For example, it is possible to completely reformat the letter but use the same envelope or vice versa. Layered protocols make for a modular flexible design, and have been widely used in the world of network software for decades. What is new here is building them into the "bus" hardware.

The PCI Express protocol stack is shown in Fig. 3-58(a).

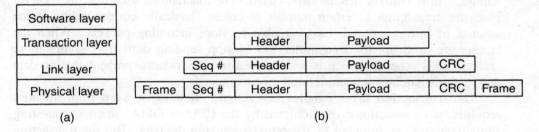

Figure 3-58. (a) The PCI Express protocol stack. (b) The format of a packet.

Let us examine the layers from the bottom up. The lowest layer is the **physical layer**. It deals with moving bits from a sender to a receiver over a point-to-point connection. Each point-to-point connection consists of one or more pairs of simplex (i.e., unidirectional) links. In the simplest case, there is one pair in each direction, but having 2, 4, 8, 16, or 32 pairs is also allowed. Each link is called a **lane**. The number of lanes in each direction must be the same. First-generation products must support a data rate each way of at least 2.5 Gbps, but the speed is expected to migrate to 10 Gbps each way fairly soon.

Unlike the ISA/EISA/PCI buses, PCI Express does not have a master clock. Devices are free to start transmitting as soon as they have data to send. This freedom makes the system faster, but also leads to a problem. Suppose that a 1 bit is encoded as +3 volts and a 0 bit is encoded as 0 volts. If the first few bytes are all 0s, how does the receiver know data is being transmitted? After all a run of 0 bits looks the same as an idle link. The problem is solved using what is called **8b/10b encoding**. In this scheme, 10 bits are used to encode 1 byte of actual data in a 10-bit symbol. Of the 1024 possible 10-bit symbols, the legal ones have been chosen to have enough clock transitions to keep the sender and receiver synchronized on the bit boundaries even without a master clock. A consequence of 8b/10b encoding is that a link with a gross capacity of 2.5 Gbps can carry only 2 Gbps of (net) user data.

Whereas the physical layer deals with bit transmission, the **link layer** deals with packet transmission. It takes the header and payload given to it by the transaction layer and adds to them a sequence number and a error-correcting code called a **CRC** (**Cyclic Redundancy Check**). The CRC is generated by running a certain algorithm on the header and payload data. When a packet is received, the receiver performs the same computation on the header and data and compares the result with the CRC attached to the packet. If they agree, it sends back a short **acknowledgment packet** affirming its correct arrival. If they disagree, the receiver asks for a retransmission. In this way, data integrity is greatly improved over the PCI bus system, which does not have any provision for verification and retransmission of data sent over the bus.

To prevent having a fast receiver bury a slow receiver in packets it cannot handle, a **flow control** mechanism is used. The mechanism used that the receiver gives the transmitter a certain number of credits, basically corresponding to the amount of buffer space it has available to store incoming packets. When the credits are used up, the transmitter has to stop sending until it is giving more credits. This scheme, which is widely used in all networks, prevents losing data due to a mismatch of transmitter and receiver speeds.

The **transaction layer** handles bus actions. Reading a word from memory requires two transactions: one initiated by the CPU or DMA channel requesting some data and one initiated by the target supplying the data. But the transaction layer does more than handle pure reads and writes. It adds value to the raw packet transmission offered by the link layer. To start with, it can divide each lane into up to eight **virtual circuits**, each handling a different class of traffic. The transaction layer can tag packets according to their traffic class, which may include attributes such as high priority, low priority, do not snoop, may be delivered out of order, and more. The switch may use these tags when deciding which packet to handle next.

Each transaction uses one of four address spaces:

1. Memory space (for ordinary reads and writes).

2. I/O space (for addressing device registers).

3. Configuration space (for system initialization, etc.).

4. Message space (for signaling, interrupts, etc.).

The memory and I/O spaces are similar to what current systems have. The configuration space can be used to implement features such as plug-and-play. The message space takes over the role of many of the existing control signals. Something like this space is needed because none of the PCI bus' control lines exist in PCI express.

The **software layer** interfaces the PCI Express system to the operating system. It can emulate the PCI bus, making it possible to run existing operating systems unmodified on PCI Express systems. Of course, operating like this will not exploit the full power of PCI Express, but backward compatibility is a necessary evil that is needed until operating systems have been modified to fully utilize PCI Express. Experience shows that can take a while.

The flow of information is illustrated in Fig. 3-58(b). When a command is given to the software layer, it hands it to the transaction layer, which formulates it in terms of a header and a payload. These two parts are then passed to the link layer, which attaches a sequence number to the front and a CRC to the back. This enlarged packet is then given to the physical layer, which adds framing information on each end to form the physical packet that is actually transmitted. At the receiving end, the reverse process takes place, with the link header and trailer being stripped and the result being given to the transaction layer.

The concept of each layer adding additional information to the data as it works its way down the protocol has been used for decades in the networking world with great success. The big difference between a network and PCI Express is that in the networking world the code in the various layers is nearly always software that is part of the operating system. With PCI Express it is all part of the device hardware.

PCI Express is a complicated subject. For more information see (Mayhew and Krishnan, 2003; and Solari and Congdon, 2005).

3.6.4 The Universal Serial Bus

The PCI bus and PCI Express are fine for attaching high-speed peripherals to a computer, but they are too expensive for low-speed I/O devices such as keyboards and mice. Historically, each standard I/O device was connected to the computer in a special way, with some free ISA and PCI slots for adding new devices. Unfortunately, this scheme has been fraught with problems from the beginning.

For example, each new I/O device often comes with its own ISA or PCI card. The user is often responsible for setting switches and jumpers on the card and making sure the settings do not conflict with other cards. Then the user must open up the case, carefully insert the card, close the case, and reboot the computer. For many users, this process is difficult and error prone. In addition, the number of ISA and PCI slots is very limited (two or three typically). Plug-and-play cards eliminate the jumper settings, but the user still has to open the computer to insert the card and bus slots are still limited.

To deal with this problem, in 1993, representatives from seven companies (Compaq, DEC, IBM, Intel, Microsoft, NEC, and Northern Telecom) got together to design a better way to attach low-speed I/O devices to a computer. Since then, hundreds of other companies have joined them. The resulting standard, officially released in 1998, is called **USB** (**Universal Serial Bus**) and it is being widely implemented in personal computers. It is described further in Anderson (1997) and Tan (1997).

Some of the goals of the companies that originally conceived of the USB and started the project were as follows:

1. Users must not have to set switches or jumpers on boards or devices.

2. Users must not have to open the case to install new I/O devices.

3. There should be only one kind of cable, good for connecting all devices.

4. I/O devices should get their power from the cable.

5. Up to 127 devices should be attachable to a single computer.

6. The system should support real-time devices (e.g., sound, telephone).

7. Devices should be installable while the computer is running.

8. No reboot should be needed after installing a new device.

9. The new bus and its I/O devices should be inexpensive to manufacture.

USB meets all these goals. It is designed for low-speed devices such as keyboards, mice, still cameras, snapshot scanners, digital telephones, and so on. Version 1.0 has a bandwidth of 1.5 Mbps, which is enough for keyboards and mice. Version 1.1 runs at 12 Mbps, which is enough for printers, digital cameras, and many other devices. These low limits were chosen to keep the cost down.

A USB system consists of a **root hub** that plugs into the main bus (see Fig. 3-52). This hub has sockets for cables that can connect to I/O devices or to expansion hubs, to provide more sockets, so the topology of a USB system is a tree with its root at the root hub, inside the computer. The cables have different connectors on the hub end and on the device end, to prevent people from accidentally connecting two hub sockets together.

The cable consists of four wires: two for data, one for power (+5 volts), and one for ground. The signaling system transmits a 0 as a voltage transition and a 1 as the absence of a voltage transition, so long runs of 0s generate a regular pulse stream.

When a new I/O device is plugged in, the root hub detects this event and interrupts the operating system. The operating system then queries the device to find out what it is and how much USB bandwidth it needs. If the operating system decides that there is enough bandwidth for the device, it assigns the new device a unique address (1 – 127) and downloads this address and other information to configuration registers inside the device. In this way, new devices can be added on-the-fly, without any user configuration required and without having to install new ISA or PCI cards. Uninitialized cards start out with address 0, so they can be addressed. To make the cabling simpler, many USB devices contain built-in hubs to accept additional USB devices. For example, a monitor might have two hub sockets to accommodate the left and right speakers.

Logically, the USB system can be viewed as a set of bit pipes from the root hub to the I/O devices. Each device can split its bit pipe up into at most 16 sub-pipes for different types of data (e.g., audio and video). Within each pipe or sub-pipe, data flows from the root hub to the device or the other way. There is no traffic between two I/O devices.

Precisely every 1.00 ± 0.05 msec, the root hub broadcasts a new frame to keep all the devices synchronized in time. A frame is associated with a bit pipe, and consists of packets, the first of which is from the root hub to the device. Subsequent packets in the frame may also be in this direction, or they may be back from the device to the root hub. A sequence of four frames is shown in Fig. 3-59.

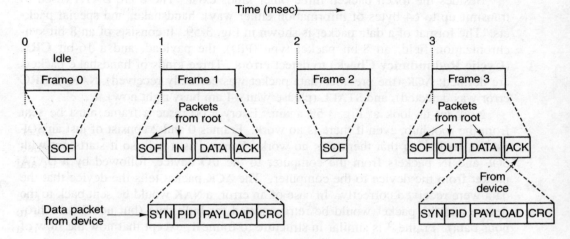

Figure 3-59. The USB root hub sends out frames every 1.00 msec.

In Fig. 3-59 there is no work to be done in frames 0 and 2, so all that is needed is one SOF (Start of Frame) packet. This packet is always broadcast to all devices. Frame 1 is a poll, for example, a request to a scanner to return the bits it has found on the image it is scanning. Frame 3 consists of delivering data to some device, for example to a printer.

USB supports four kinds of frames: control, isochronous, bulk, and interrupt. Control frames are used to configure devices, give them commands, and inquire about their status. Isochronous frames are for real-time devices such as microphones, loudspeakers, and telephones that need to send or accept data at precise time intervals. They have a highly-predictable delay but provide no retransmissions in the event of errors. Bulk frames are for large transfers to or from devices with no real-time requirements such as printers. Finally, interrupt frames are needed because USB does not support interrupts. For example, instead of having the keyboard cause an interrupt whenever a key is struck, the operating system can poll it every 50 msec to collect any pending keystrokes.

A frame consists of one or more packets, possibly some in each direction. Four kinds of packets exist: token, data, handshake, and special. Token packets are from the root to a device and are for system control. The SOF, IN, and OUT packets in Fig. 3-59 are token packets. The SOF (Start of Frame) packet is the first one in each frame and marks the beginning of the frame. If there is no work to do, the SOF packet is the only one in the frame. The IN token packet is a poll, asking the device to return certain data. Fields in the IN packet tell which bit pipe is being polled so the device knows which data to return (if it has multiple streams). The OUT token packet announces that data for the device will follow. A fourth type of token packet, SETUP (not shown in the figure), is used for configuration.

Besides the token packet, three other kinds exist. These are DATA (used to transmit up to 64 bytes of information either way), handshake, and special packets. The format of a data packet is shown in Fig. 3-59. It consists of an 8-bit synchronization field, an 8-bit packet type (PID), the payload, and a 16-bit **CRC** (**Cyclic Redundancy Check**) to detect errors. Three kinds of handshake packets are defined: ACK (the previous data packet was correctly received), NAK (a CRC error was detected), and STALL (please wait—I am busy right now).

Now let us look at Fig. 3-59 again. Every 1.00 msec a frame must be sent from the root hub, even if there is no work. Frames 0 and 2 consist of just an SOF packet, indicating that there was no work. Frame 1 is a poll, so it starts out with SOF and IN packets from the computer to the I/O device, followed by a DATA packet from the device to the computer. The ACK packet tells the device that the data were received correctly. In case of an error, a NAK would be sent back to the device and the packet would be retransmitted for bulk data (but not for isochronous data). Frame 3 is similar in structure to frame 1, except that now the flow of data are from the computer to the device.

After the USB standard was finalized in 1998, the people designing USB had nothing to do so they began working on a new high-speed version of USB, called **USB 2.0**. This standard is similar to the older USB 1.1 and backward compatible with it, except that it adds a third speed, 480 Mbps, to the two existing speeds. There are also some minor differences, such as the interface between the root hub and the controller. With USB 1.1 there were two interfaces available. The first one, **UHCI** (**Universal Host Controller Interface**), was designed by Intel and put most of the burden on the software designers (read: Microsoft). The second one, **OHCI** (**Open Host Controller Interface**), was designed by Microsoft and put most of the burden on the hardware designers (read: Intel). In USB 2.0 everyone agreed to a single new interface called **EHCI** (**Enhanced Host Controller Interface**).

With USB now operating at 480 Mbps, it clearly competes with the IEEE 1394 serial bus popularly called FireWire, which runs at 400 Mbps. Although virtually every new Pentium system now comes with USB 2.0, 1394 is not likely to vanish because it has the backing of the consumer electronics industry. Camcorders, DVD players and similar devices will continue to be equipped with 1394 interfaces for the foreseeable future because the makers of these devices do not want to go to the expense of switching to a different standard that is hardly better than what they have now. Consumers, also, do not like changing standards.

3.7 INTERFACING

A typical small- to medium-sized computer system consists of a CPU chip, memory chips, and some I/O controllers, all connected by a bus. We have already studied memories, CPUs, and buses in some detail. Now it is time to look at the last part of the puzzle, the I/O chips. It is through these chips that the computer communicates with the external world.

3.7.1 I/O Chips

Numerous I/O chips are already available and new ones are being introduced all the time. Common chips include UARTs, USARTs, CRT controllers, disk controllers, and PIOs. A **UART** (**Universal Asynchronous Receiver Transmitter**) is a chip that can read a byte from the data bus and output it a bit at a time on a serial line for a terminal, or input data from a terminal. UARTs usually allow various speeds from 50 to 19,200 bps; character widths from 5 to 8 bits; 1, 1.5, or 2 stop bits; and provide even, odd, or no parity, all under program control. **USART**s (**Universal Synchronous Asynchronous Receiver Transmitters**) can handle synchronous transmission using a variety of protocols as well as performing all the UART functions. Since we already looked at UARTs in Chap. 2, let us now study the parallel interface as an example of an I/O chip.

PIO Chips

A typical **PIO** (**Parallel Input/Output**) chip is the Intel 8255A, shown in Fig. 3-60. It has 24 I/O lines that can interface to any TTL-compatible device, for example, keyboards, switches, lights, or printers. In a nutshell, the CPU program can write a 0 or 1 to any line, or read the input status of any line, providing great flexibility. A small CPU-based system using a PIO can often replace a complete board full of SSI or MSI chips, especially in embedded systems.

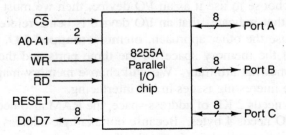

Figure 3-60. An 8255A PIO chip.

Although the CPU can configure the 8255A in many ways by loading status registers within the chip, we will concentrate on some of the simpler modes of operation. The simplest way of using the 8255A is as three independent 8-bit ports, A, B, and C. Associated with each port is an 8-bit latch register. To set the lines on a port, the CPU just writes an 8-bit number into the corresponding register, and the 8-bit number appears on the output lines and stays there until the register is rewritten. To use a port for input, the CPU just reads the corresponding register.

Other operating modes provide for handshaking with external devices. For example, to output to a device that is not always ready to accept data, the 8255A can present data on an output port and wait for the device to send a pulse back saying that it has accepted the data and wants more. The necessary logic for latching such pulses and making them available to the CPU is included in the 8255A hardware.

From the functional diagram of the 8255A we can see that in addition to 24 pins for the three ports, it has eight lines that connect directly to the data bus, a chip select line, read and write lines, two address lines, and a line for resetting the chip. The two address lines select one of the four internal registers, corresponding to ports A, B, C, and the status register, which has bits determining which ports are for input and which for output, and other functions. Normally, the two address lines are connected to the low-order bits of the address bus.

3.7.2 Address Decoding

Up until now we have been deliberately vague about how chip select is asserted on the memory and I/O chips we have looked at. It is now time to look more carefully at how this is done. Let us consider a simple 16-bit embedded computer consisting of a CPU, a 2KB × 8 byte EPROM for the program, a 2KB × 8 byte RAM for the data, and a PIO. This small system might be used as a prototype for the brain of a cheap toy or simple appliance. Once in production, the EPROM might be replaced by a ROM.

The PIO can be selected in one of two ways: as a true I/O device or as part of memory. If we choose to use it as an I/O device, then we must select it using an explicit bus line that indicates that an I/O device is being referenced, rather than memory. If we use the other approach, **memory-mapped I/O**, then we must assign it 4 bytes of the memory space for the three ports and the control register. The choice is somewhat arbitrary. We will choose memory-mapped I/O because it illustrates some interesting issues in I/O interfacing.

The EPROM needs 2 KB of address space, the RAM also needs 2K of address space, and the PIO needs 4 bytes. Because our example address space is 64K, we must make a choice about where to put the three devices. One possible choice is shown in Fig. 3-61. The EPROM occupies addresses to 2K, the RAM occupies addresses 32 KB to 34 KB, and the PIO occupies the highest 4 bytes of the address space, 65532 to 65535. From the programmer's point of view, it makes no difference which addresses are used; however, for interfacing it does matter. If we had chosen to address the PIO via the I/O space, it would not need any memory addresses (but it would need four I/O space addresses).

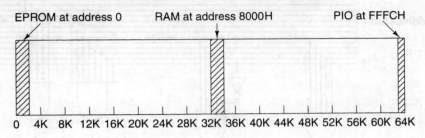

Figure 3-61. Location of the EPROM, RAM, and PIO in our 64 KB address space.

With the address assignments of Fig. 3-61, the EPROM should be selected by any 16-bit memory address of the form 00000xxxxxxxxxxx (binary). In other words, any address whose 5 high-order bits are all 0s falls in the bottom 2 KB of memory, hence in the EPROM. Thus the EPROM's chip select could be wired to a 5-bit comparator, one of whose inputs was permanently wired to 00000.

A better way to achieve the same effect is to use a five-input OR gate, with the five inputs attached to address lines A11 to A15. If and only if all five lines are 0 will the output be 0, thus asserting $\overline{CS}$ (which is asserted low). Unfortunately, no five-input OR gate exists in the standard SSI series. The closest we can come is an eight-input NOR gate. By grounding three inputs and inverting the output we can nevertheless produce the correct signal, as shown in Fig. 3-61(a). SSI chips are so cheap that except in exceptional circumstances, using one inefficiently is not an issue. By convention, unused inputs are not shown in circuit diagrams.

The same principle can be used for the RAM. However, the RAM should respond to binary addresses of the form 10000xxxxxxxxxxx, so an additional inverter is needed as shown in the figure. The PIO address decoding is somewhat more complicated, because it is selected by the four addresses of the form 11111111111111xx. A possible circuit that asserts $\overline{CS}$ only when the correct address appears on the address bus is shown in the figure. It uses two eight-input NAND gates to feed an OR gate. To build the address decoding logic of Fig. 3-62(a) using SSI requires six chips—the four eight-input chips, an OR gate, and a chip with three inverters.

However, if the computer really consists of only the CPU, two memory chips, and the PIO, we can use a trick to simplify greatly the address decoding. The trick is based on the fact that all EPROM addresses, and only EPROM addresses, have a 0 in the high-order bit, A15. Therefore, we can just wire $\overline{CS}$ to A15 directly, as shown in Fig. 3-62(b).

At this point the decision to put the RAM at 8000H may seem much less arbitrary. The RAM decoding can be done by noting that the only valid addresses of the form 10xxxxxxxxxxxxxx are in the RAM, so 2 bits of decoding are sufficient.

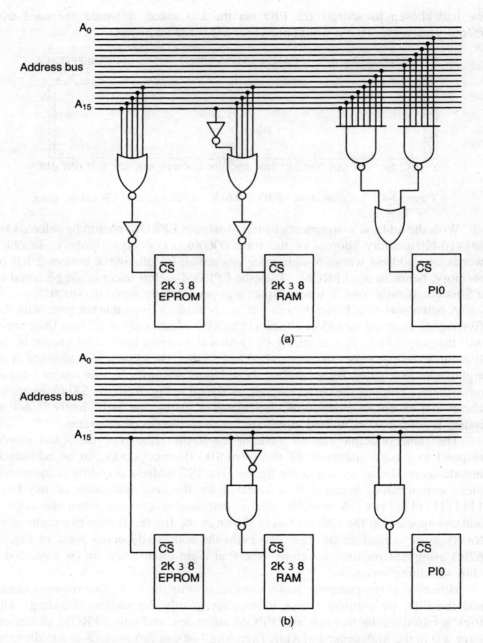

Figure 3-62. (a) Full address decoding. (b) Partial address decoding.

Similarly, any address starting with 11 must be a PIO address. The complete decoding logic is now two NAND gates and an inverter. Because an inverter can be made from a NAND gate by just tying the two inputs together, a single quad NAND chip is now more than sufficient.

The address decoding logic of Fig. 3-62(b) is called **partial address decoding**, because the full addresses are not used. It has the property that a read from addresses 0001000000000000, 0001100000000000, or 0010000000000000 will give the same result. In fact, every address in the bottom half of the address space will select the EPROM. Because the extra addresses are not used, no harm is done, but if one is designing a computer that may be expanded in the future (an unlikely occurrence in a toy), partial decoding should be avoided because it ties up too much address space.

Another common address decoding technique is to use a decoder, such as that shown in Fig. 3-13. By connecting the three inputs to the three high-order address lines, we get eight outputs, corresponding to addresses in the first 8K, second 8K, and so on. For a computer with eight RAMs, each $8K \times 8$, one such chip provides the complete decoding. For a computer with eight $2K \times 8$ memory chips, a single decoder is also sufficient, provided that the memory chips are each located in distinct 8-KB chunks of address space. (Remember our earlier remark that the position of the memory and I/O chips within the address space matters.)

3.8 SUMMARY

Computers are constructed from integrated circuit chips containing tiny switching elements called gates. The most common gates are AND, OR, NAND, NOR, and NOT. Simple circuits can be built up by directly combining individual gates.

More complex circuits are multiplexers, demultiplexers, encoders, decoders, shifters, and ALUs. Arbitrary Boolean functions can be programmed using a PLA. If many Boolean functions are needed, PLAs are often more efficient. The laws of Boolean algebra can be used to transform circuits from one form to another. In many cases more economical circuits can be produced this way.

Computer arithmetic is done by adders. A single-bit full adder can be constructed from two half adders. An adder for a multibit word can be built by connecting multiple full adders in such a way as to allow the carry out of each one feed into its left-hand neighbor.

The components of (static) memories are latches and flip-flops, each of which can store one bit of information. These can be combined linearly into octal latches and flip-flops or logarithmically into full-scale word-oriented memories. Memories are available as RAM, ROM, PROM, EPROM, EEPROM, and flash. Static RAMs need not be refreshed; they keep their stored values as long as the power remains on. Dynamic RAMs, on the other hand, must be refreshed periodically to compensate for leakage from the little capacitors on the chip.

The components of a computer system are connected by buses. Many, but not all, of the pins on a typical CPU chip directly drive one bus line. The bus lines can be divided into address, data, and control lines. Synchronous buses are driven by a master clock. Asynchronous buses use full handshaking to synchronize the slave to the master.

The Pentium 4 is an example of a modern CPU. Modern systems using it have a memory bus, a PCI bus, an ISA bus, and a USB bus. The PCI bus can transfer 64 bits at a time at a rate of 66 MHz, which makes it fast enough for nearly all peripherals, but not fast enough for memory.

Switches, lights, printers, and many other I/O devices can be interfaced to computers using parallel I/O chips such as the 8255A. These chips can be configured to be part of the I/O space or the memory space, as needed. They can be fully decoded or partially decoded, depending on the application.

PROBLEMS

1. A logician drives into a drive-in restaurant and says, "I want a hamburger or a hot dog and french fries." Unfortunately, the cook flunked out of sixth grade and does not know (or care) whether "and" has precedence over "or." As far as he is concerned, one interpretation is as good as the other. Which of the following cases are valid interpretations of the order? (Note that in English "or" means "exclusive or.")
   a. Just a hamburger.
   b. Just a hot dog.
   c. Just french fries.
   d. A hot dog and french fries.
   e. A hamburger and french fries.
   f. A hot dog and a hamburger.
   g. All three.
   h. Nothing—the logician goes hungry for being a wiseguy.

2. A missionary lost in Southern California stops at a fork in the road. He knows that two motorcycle gangs inhabit the area, one of which always tells the truth and one of which always lies. He wants to know which road leads to Disneyland. What question should he ask?

3. Use a truth table to show that $X = (X \text{ AND } Y) \text{ OR } (X \text{ AND NOT } Y)$.

4. There exist four Boolean functions of a single variable and 16 functions of two variables. How many functions of three variables are there? Of n variables?

5. Show how the AND function can be constructed from two NAND gates.

6. Using the three-variable multiplexer chip of Fig. 3-12, implement a function whose output is the parity of the inputs, that is, the output is 1 if and only if an even number of inputs are 1.

7. Put on your thinking cap. The three-variable multiplexer chip of Fig. 3-12 is actually capable of computing an arbitrary function of *four* Boolean variables. Describe how, and as an example, draw the logic diagram for the function that is 0 if the English word for the truth table row has an even number of letters, 1 if it has an odd number of letters (e.g., 0000 = zero = four letters $\rightarrow$ 0; 0111 = seven = five letters $\rightarrow$ 1; 1101 = thirteen = eight letters $\rightarrow$ 0). *Hint*: If we call the fourth input variable D, the eight input lines may be wired to V_{cc}, ground, D, or $\overline{D}$.

8. Draw the logic diagram of a 2-bit encoder, a circuit with four input lines, exactly one of which is high at any instant, and two output lines whose 2-bit binary value tells which input is high.

9. Draw the logic diagram of a 2-bit demultiplexer, a circuit whose single input line is steered to one of the four output lines depending on the state of the two control lines.

10. Redraw the PLA of Fig. 3-15 in enough detail to show how the majority logic function of Fig. 3-3 can be implemented. In particular, be sure to show which connections are present in both matrices.

11. What does this circuit do?

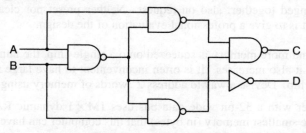

12. A common MSI chip is a 4-bit adder. Four of these chips can be hooked up to form a 16-bit adder. How many pins would you expect the 4-bit adder chip to have? Why?

13. An n-bit adder can be constructed by cascading n full adders in series, with the carry into stage i, C_i, coming from the output of stage $i - 1$. The carry into stage 0, C_0, is 0. If each stage takes T nsec to produce its sum and carry, the carry into stage i will not be valid until iT nsec after the start of the addition. For large n the time required for the carry to ripple through to the high-order stage may be unacceptably long. Design an adder that works faster. *Hint*: Each C_i can be expressed in terms of the operand bits A_{i-1} and B_{i-1} as well as the carry C_{i-1}. Using this relation it is possible to express C_i as a function of the inputs to stages 0 to $i - 1$, so all the carries can be generated simultaneously.

14. If all the gates in Fig. 3-19 have a propagation delay of 1 nsec, and all other delays can be ignored, what is the earliest time a circuit using this design can be sure of having a valid output bit?

15. The ALU of Fig. 3-20 is capable of doing 8-bit 2's complement additions. Is it also capable of doing 2's complement subtractions? If so, explain how. If not, modify it to be able to do subtractions.

16. A 16-bit ALU is built up of 16 1-bit ALUs, each one having an add time of 10 nsec. If there is an additional 1 nsec delay for propagation from one ALU to the next, how long does it take for the result of a 16-bit add to appear?

17. Sometimes it is useful for an 8-bit ALU such as Fig. 3-20 to generate the constant -1 as output. Give two different ways this can be done. For each way, specify the values of the six control signals.

18. What is the quiescent state of the S and R inputs to an SR latch built of two NAND gates?

19. The circuit of Fig. 3-26 is a flip-flop that is triggered on the rising edge of the clock. Modify this circuit to produce a flip-flop that is triggered on the falling edge of the clock.

20. The 4×3 memory of Fig. 3-29 uses 22 AND gates and three OR gates. If the circuit were to be expanded to 256×8, how many of each would be needed?

21. To help meet the payments on your new personal computer, you have taken up consulting for fledgling SSI chip manufacturers. One of your clients is thinking about putting out a chip containing four D flip-flops, each containing both Q and $\bar{Q}$, on request of a potentially important customer. The proposed design has all four clock signals ganged together, also on request. Neither preset nor clear is present. Your assignment is to give a professional evaluation of the design.

22. As more and more memory is squeezed onto a single chip, the number of pins needed to address it also increases. It is often inconvenient to have large numbers of address pins on a chip. Devise a way to address 2^n words of memory using fewer than n pins.

23. A computer with a 32-bit wide data bus uses $1M \times 1$ dynamic RAM memory chips. What is the smallest memory (in bytes) that this computer can have?

24. Referring to the timing diagram of Fig. 3-38, suppose that you slowed the clock down to a period of 20 nsec instead of 10 nsec as shown but the timing constraints remained unchanged. How much time would the memory have to get the data onto the bus during T_3 after $\overline{\text{MREQ}}$ was asserted, in the worst case?

25. Again referring to Fig. 3-38, suppose that the clock remained at 100 MHz, but T_{DS} was increased to 4 nsec. Could 10-nsec memory chips be used?

26. In Fig. 3-38(b), T_{ML} is specified to be at least 3 nsec. Can you envision a chip in which it is negative? Specifically, could the CPU assert $\overline{\text{MREQ}}$ before the address was stable? Why or why not?

27. Assume that the block transfer of Fig. 3-42 were done on the bus of Fig. 3-38. How much more bandwidth is obtained by using a block transfer over individual transfers for long blocks? Now assume that the bus is 32 bits wide instead of 8 bits wide. Answer the question again.

28. Denote the transition times of the address lines of Fig. 3-39 as T_{A1} and T_{A2}, and the transition times of $\overline{\text{MREQ}}$ as T_{MREQ1} and T_{MREQ2}, and so on. Write down all the inequalities implied by the full handshake.

29. Most 32-bit buses permit 16-bit reads and writes. Is there any ambiguity about where to place the data? Discuss.

30. Many CPUs have a special bus cycle type for interrupt acknowledge. Why?

31. A 64-bit computer with a 200-MHz bus requires four cycles to read a 64-bit word. How much bus bandwidth does the CPU consume in the worst case?

32. A 32-bit CPU with address lines A2–A31 requires all memory references to be aligned. That is, words have to be addressed at multiples of 4 bytes, and half-words have to be addressed at even bytes. Bytes can be anywhere. How many legal combinations are there for memory reads, and how many pins are needed to express them? Give two answers and make a case for each one.

33. Why is it impossible for the Pentium 4 to work on a 32-bit PCI bus without losing any functionality? After all, other computers with a 64-bit data bus can do 32-bit, 16-bit, and even 8-bit wide transfers.

34. Suppose that a CPU has a level 1 cache and a level 2 cache, with access times of 1 nsec and 2 nsec, respectively. The main memory access time is 10 nsec. If 20% of the accesses are level 1 cache hits and 60% are level 2 cache hits, what is the average access time?

35. Is it likely that an 8051-based embedded system would include an 8255A chip?

36. Calculate the bus bandwidth needed to display a VGA (640×480) true-color movie at 30 frames/sec. Assume that the data must pass over the bus twice, once from the CD-ROM to the memory and once from the memory to the screen.

37. Which Pentium 4 signal do you think drives the PCI bus FRAME# line?

38. Which of the signals of Fig. 3-56 is not strictly necessary for the bus protocol to work?

39. A PCI Express system has 5 Mbps links (gross capacity). How many signal wires are needed in each direction for 8x operation? What is the gross capacity each way? What is the net capacity each way?

40. A computer has instructions that each require two bus cycles, one to fetch the instruction and one to fetch the data. Each bus cycle takes 10 nsec and each instruction takes 20 nsec (i.e., the internal processing time is negligible). The computer also has a disk with 2048 512-byte sectors per track. Disk rotation time is 5 msec. To what percent of its normal speed is the computer reduced during a DMA transfer if each 32-bit DMA transfer takes one bus cycle?

41. The maximum payload of an isochronous data packet on the USB bus is 1023 bytes. Assuming that a device may send only one data packet per frame, what is the maximum bandwidth for a single isochronous device?

42. What would the effect be of adding a third input line to the NAND gate selecting the PIO of Fig. 3-62(b) if this new line were connected to A13?

43. Write a program to simulate the behavior of an $m \times n$ array of two-input NAND gates. This circuit, contained on a chip, has j input pins and k output pins. The values of j, k, m, and n are compile-time parameters of the simulation. The program should start off by reading in a "wiring list," each wire of which specifies an input and an output. An input is either one of the j input pins or the output of some NAND gate. An output is either one of the k output pins or an input to some NAND gate. Unused inputs are logical 1. After reading in the wiring list, the program should print the output for each of the 2^j possible inputs. Gate array chips like this one are widely used for putting custom circuits on a chip because most of the work (depositing the gate array on the chip) is independent of the circuit to be implemented. Only the wiring is specific to each design.

44. Write a program to read in two arbitrary Boolean expressions and see if they represent the same function. The input language should include single letters, as Boolean variables, the operands AND, OR, and NOT, and parentheses. Each expression should fit on one input line. The program should compute the truth tables for both functions and compare them.

45. Write a program to read in a collection of Boolean expressions and compute the 24×50 and 50×6 matrices needed to implement them with the PLA of Fig. 3-15. The input language should be the same as the previous problem. Print the matrices on the line printer.

4

THE MICROARCHITECTURE LEVEL

The level above the digital logic level is the microarchitecture level. Its job is to implement the ISA (Instruction Set Architecture) level above it, as illustrated in Fig. 1-2. The design of the microarchitecture level depends on the ISA being implemented, as well as the cost and performance goals of the computer. Many modern ISAs, particularly RISC designs, have simple instructions that can usually be executed in a single clock cycle. More complex ISAs, such as the Pentium 4, may require many cycles to execute a single instruction. Executing an instruction may require locating the operands in memory, reading them, and storing results back into memory. The sequencing of operations within a single instruction often leads to a different approach to control than that for simple ISAs.

4.1 AN EXAMPLE MICROARCHITECTURE

Ideally, we would like to introduce this subject by explaining the general principles of microarchitecture design. Unfortunately, there are no general principles; every one is a special case. Consequently, we will discuss a detailed example instead. For our example ISA, we have chosen a subset of the Java Virtual Machine, as we promised in Chap. 1. This subset contains only integer instructions, so we have named it **IJVM**. We will discuss the full JVM in Chap. 5.

We will start out by describing the microarchitecture on top of which we will implement IJVM. IJVM has some complex instructions. Many such architectures have often been implemented through microprogramming, as discussed in Chap. 1. Although IJVM is small, it is a good starting point for describing the control and sequencing of instructions.

Our microarchitecture will contain a microprogram (in ROM), whose job is to fetch, decode, and execute IJVM instructions. We cannot use the Sun JVM interpreter for the microprogram because we need a tiny microprogram that drives the individual gates in the actual hardware efficiently. In contrast, the Sun JVM interpreter was written in C for portability, and cannot control the hardware at the level of detail we need. Since the actual hardware used consists only of the basic components described in Chap. 3, in theory, after fully understanding this chapter, the reader should be able to go out and buy a large bag full of transistors and build this subset of the JVM machine. Students who successfully accomplish this task will be given extra credit (and a complete psychiatric examination).

A convenient model for the design of the microarchitecture is to think of the design as a programming problem, where each instruction at the ISA level is a function to be called by a master program. In this model, the master program is a simple, endless loop that determines a function to be invoked, calls the function, then starts over, very much like Fig. 2-3.

The microprogram has a set of variables, called the **state** of the computer, which can be accessed by all the functions. Each function changes at least some of the variables making up the state. For example, the Program Counter (PC) is part of the state. It indicates the memory location containing the next function (i.e., ISA instruction) to be executed. During the execution of each instruction, the PC is advanced to point to the next instruction to be executed.

IJVM instructions are short and sweet. Each instruction has a few fields, usually one or two, each of which has some specific purpose. The first field of every instruction is the **opcode** (short for **operation code**), which identifies the instruction, telling whether it is an ADD or a BRANCH, or something else. Many instructions have an additional field, which specifies the operand. For example, instructions that access a local variable need a field to tell *which* variable.

This model of execution, sometimes called the **fetch-execute cycle**, is useful in the abstract and may also be the basis for implementation for ISAs like IJVM that have complex instructions. Below we will describe how it works, what the microarchitecture looks like, and how it is controlled by the microinstructions, each of which controls the data path for one cycle. Together, the list of microinstructions forms the microprogram, which we will present and discuss in detail.

4.1.1 The Data Path

The **data path** is that part of the CPU containing the ALU, its inputs, and its outputs. The data path of our example microarchitecture is shown in Fig. 4-1. While it has been carefully optimized for interpreting IJVM programs, it is fairly similar to the data path used in most machines. It contains a number of 32-bit

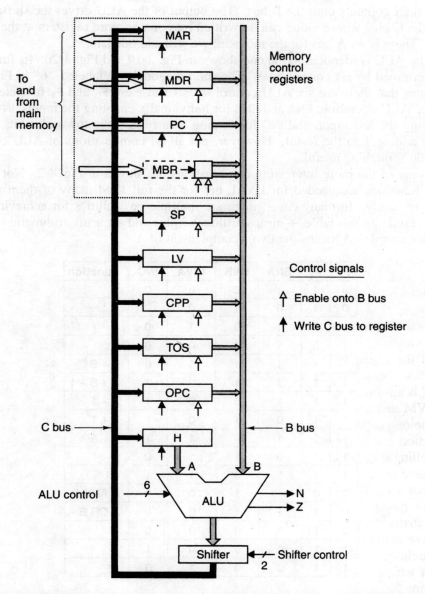

Figure 4-1. The data path of the example microarchitecture used in this chapter.

registers, to which we have assigned symbolic names such as PC, SP, and MDR. Though some of these names are familiar, it is important to understand that these registers are accessible only at the microarchitecture level (by the microprogram). They are given these names because they usually hold a value corresponding to the variable of the same name in the ISA level architecture. Most registers can drive their contents onto the B bus. The output of the ALU drives the shifter and then the C bus, whose value can be written into one or more registers at the same time. There is no A bus for the moment; we will add one later.

The ALU is identical to the one shown in Fig. 3-19 and Fig. 3-20. Its function is determined by six control lines. The short diagonal line labeled "6" in Fig. 4-1 indicates that there are six ALU control lines. These are F_0 and F_1 for determining the ALU operation, ENA and ENB for individually enabling the inputs, INVA for inverting the left input, and INC for forcing a carry into the low-order bit, effectively adding 1 to the result. However, not all 64 combinations of ALU control lines do something useful.

Some of the more interesting combinations are shown in Fig. 4-2. Not all of these functions are needed for IJVM, but for the full JVM many of them would come in handy. In many cases, there are multiple possibilities for achieving the same result. In this table, + means arithmetic plus and − means arithmetic minus, so, for example −A means the two's complement of A.

F_0	F_1	ENA	ENB	INVA	INC	Function
0	1	1	0	0	0	A
0	1	0	1	0	0	B
0	1	1	0	1	0	$\overline{A}$
1	0	1	1	0	0	$\overline{B}$
1	1	1	1	0	0	A + B
1	1	1	1	0	1	A + B + 1
1	1	1	0	0	1	A + 1
1	1	0	1	0	1	B + 1
1	1	1	1	1	1	B − A
1	1	0	1	1	0	B − 1
1	1	1	0	1	1	−A
0	0	1	1	0	0	A AND B
0	1	1	1	0	0	A OR B
0	1	0	0	0	0	0
1	1	0	0	0	1	1
1	1	0	0	1	0	−1

Figure 4-2. Useful combinations of ALU signals and the function performed.

The ALU of Fig. 4-1 needs two data inputs: a left input (A) and a right input (B). Attached to the left input is a holding register, H. Attached to the right input is the B bus, which can be loaded from any one of nine sources, indicated by the nine gray arrows touching it. An alternative design, with two full buses, has a different set of trade-offs and will be discussed later in this chapter.

H can be loaded by choosing an ALU function that just passes the right input (from the B bus) through to the ALU output. One such function is adding the ALU inputs, only with ENA negated so the left input is forced to zero. Adding zero to the value on the B bus just yields the value on the B bus. This result can then be passed through the shifter unmodified and stored in H.

In addition to the above functions, two other control lines can be used independently to control the output from the ALU. SLL8 (Shift Left Logical) shifts the contents left by 1 byte, filling the 8 least significant bits with zeros. SRA1 (Shift Right Arithmetic) shifts the contents right by 1 bit, leaving the most significant bit unchanged.

It is explicitly possible to read and write the same register on one cycle. For example, it is allowed to put SP onto the B bus, disable the ALU's left input, enable the INC signal, and store the result in SP, thus incrementing SP by 1 (see the eighth line in Fig. 4-2). How can a register be read and written on the same cycle without producing garbage? The solution is that reading and writing are actually performed at different times within the cycle. When a register is selected as the ALU's right input, its value is put onto the B bus early in the cycle and kept there continuously throughout the entire cycle. The ALU then does its work, producing a result that passes through the shifter onto the C bus. Near the end of the cycle, when the ALU and shifter outputs are known to be stable, a clock signal triggers the store of the contents of the C bus into one or more of the registers. One of these registers may well be the one that supplied the B bus with its input. The precise timing of the data path makes it possible to read and write the same register on one cycle, as described below.

Data Path Timing

The timing of these events is shown in Fig. 4-3. Here a short pulse is produced at the start of each clock cycle. It can be derived from the main clock, as shown in Fig. 3-21(c). On the falling edge of the pulse, the bits that will drive all the gates are set up. This takes a finite and known time, Δw. Then the register needed on the B bus is selected and driven onto the B bus. It takes Δx before the value is stable. Then the ALU and shifter begin to operate on valid data. After another Δy, the ALU and shifter outputs are stable. After an additional Δz, the results have propagated along the C bus to the registers, where they can be loaded on the rising edge of the next pulse. The load should be edge triggered and fast, so that even if some of the input registers are changed, the effects will not be felt on the C bus until long after the registers have been loaded. Also on the rising edge of the pulse, the register driving the B bus stops doing so, in preparation for the next cycle. MPC, MIR, and the memory are mentioned in the figure; their roles will be discussed shortly.

It is important to realize that even though there are no storage elements in the data path, there is a finite propagation time through it. Changing the value on the

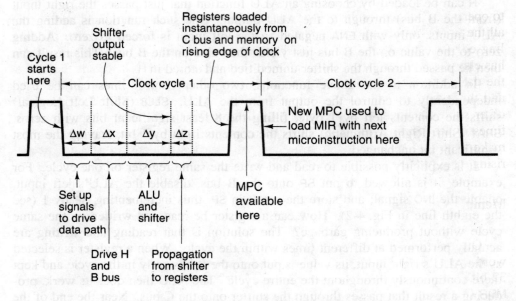

Figure 4-3. Timing diagram of one data path cycle.

B bus does not cause the C bus to change until a finite time later (due to the finite delays of each step). Consequently, even if a store changes one of the input registers, the value will be safely tucked away in the register long before the (now-incorrect) value being put on the B bus (or H) can reach the ALU.

Making this design work requires rigid timing, a long clock cycle, a known minimum propagation time through the ALU, and a fast load of the registers from the C bus. However, with careful engineering, the data path can be designed so that it functions correctly all the time. Actual machines work this way.

A somewhat different way to look at the data path cycle is to think of it as broken up into implicit subcycles. The start of subcycle 1 is triggered by the falling edge of the clock. The activities that go on during the subcycles are shown below along with the subcycle lengths (in parentheses).

1. The control signals are set up (Δw).

2. The registers are loaded onto the B bus (Δx).

3. The ALU and shifter operate (Δy).

4. The results propagate along the C bus back to the registers (Δz).

At the rising edge of the next clock cycle, the results are stored in the registers.

We said that the subcycles can be best thought of as being *implicit*. By this we mean there are no clock pulses or other explicit signals to tell the ALU when to operate or tell the results to enter the C bus. In reality, the ALU and shifter run all the time. However, their inputs are garbage until a time $\Delta w + \Delta x$ after the falling edge of the clock. Likewise, their outputs are garbage until $\Delta w + \Delta x + \Delta y$ has elapsed after the falling edge of the clock. The only explicit signals that drive the data path are the falling edge of the clock, which starts the data path cycle, and the rising edge of the clock, which loads the registers from the C bus. The other subcycle boundaries are implicitly determined by the inherent propagation times of the circuits involved. It is the responsibility of the design engineers to make sure that the time $\Delta w + \Delta x + \Delta y + \Delta z$ comes sufficiently in advance of the rising edge of the clock to have the register loads work all the time.

Memory Operation

Our machine has two different ways to communicate with memory: a 32-bit, word-addressable memory port and an 8-bit, byte-addressable memory port. The 32-bit port is controlled by two registers, MAR (**Memory Address Register**), and MDR (**Memory Data Register**), as shown in Fig. 4-1. The 8-bit port is controlled by one register, PC, which reads 1 byte into the low-order 8 bits of MBR. This port can only read data from memory; it cannot write data to memory.

Each of these registers (and all the other registers in Fig. 4-1) are driven by one or two **control signals**. An open arrow under a register indicates a control signal that enables the register's output onto the B bus. Since MAR does not have a connection to the B bus, it does not have an enable signal. H does not have one either because it is always enabled, it being the only possible left ALU input.

A solid black arrow under a register indicates a control signal that writes (i.e., loads) the register from the C bus. Since MBR cannot be loaded from the C bus, it does not have a write signal (although it does have two other enable signals, described below). To initiate a memory read or write, the appropriate memory registers must be loaded, then a read or write signal issued to the memory (not shown in Fig. 4-1).

MAR contains *word* addresses, so that the values 0, 1, 2, etc., refer to consecutive words. PC contains *byte* addresses, so that the values 0, 1, 2, etc. refer to consecutive bytes. Thus putting a 2 in PC and starting a memory read will read out byte 2 from memory and put it in the low-order 8 bits of MBR. Putting a 2 in MAR and starting a memory read will read out bytes 8–11 (i.e., word 2) from memory and put them in MDR.

This difference in functionality is needed because MAR and PC will be used to reference two different parts of memory. The need for this distinction will become clearer later. For the moment, suffice it to say that the MAR/MDR combination is used to read and write ISA-level data words and the PC/MBR combination is used to read the executable ISA-level program, which consists of a byte stream. All other registers that contain addresses use word addresses, like MAR.

In the actual physical implementation, there is only one real memory and it is byte oriented. Allowing MAR to count in words (needed due to the way JVM is defined) while the physical memory counts in bytes is handled by a simple trick. When MAR is placed on the address bus, its 32 bits do not map onto the 32 address lines, 0 – 31, directly. Instead MAR bit 0 is wired to address bus line 2, MAR bit 1 is wired to address bus line 3, and so on. The upper 2 bits of MAR are discarded since they are only needed for word addresses above 2^{32}, none of which are legal for our 4-GB machine. Using this mapping, when MAR is 1, address 4 is put onto the bus; when MAR is 2, address 8 is put onto the bus, and so forth. This trick is illustrated in Fig. 4-4.

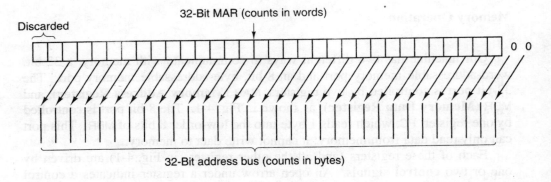

Figure 4-4. Mapping of the bits in MAR to the address bus.

As mentioned above, data read from memory through the 8-bit memory port are returned in MBR, an 8-bit register. MBR can be gated (i.e., copied) onto the B bus in one of two ways: unsigned or signed. When the unsigned value is needed, the 32-bit word put onto the B bus contains the MBR value in the low-order 8 bits and zeros in the upper 24 bits. Unsigned values are useful for indexing into a table, or when a 16-bit integer has to be assembled from 2 consecutive (unsigned) bytes in the instruction stream.

The other option for converting the 8-bit MBR to a 32-bit word is to treat it as a signed value between −128 and +127 and use this value to generate a 32-bit word with the same numerical value. This conversion is done by duplicating the MBR sign bit (leftmost bit) into the upper 24 bit positions of the B bus, a process known as **sign extension**. When this option is chosen, the upper 24 bits will either be all 0s or all 1s, depending on whether the leftmost bit of the 8-bit MBR is a 0 or a 1.

The choice of whether the 8-bit MBR is converted to an unsigned or a signed 32-bit value on the B bus is determined by which of the two control signals (open arrows below MBR in Fig. 4-1) is asserted. The need for these two options is why two arrows are present. The ability to have the 8-bit MBR act like a 32-bit source to the B bus is indicated by the dashed box to the left of MBR in the figure.

4.1.2 Microinstructions

To control the data path of Fig. 4-1, we need 29 signals. These can be divided into five functional groups, as described below.

    9 Signals to control writing data from the C bus into registers.

    9 Signals to control enabling registers onto the B bus for ALU input.

    8 Signals to control the ALU and shifter functions.

    2 Signals (not shown) to indicate memory read/write via MAR/MDR.

    1 Signal (not shown) to indicate memory fetch via PC/MBR.

The values of these 29 control signals specify the operations for one cycle of the data path. A cycle consists of gating values out of registers and onto the B bus, propagating the signals through the ALU and shifter, driving them onto the C bus, and finally writing the results in the appropriate register or registers. In addition, if a memory read data signal is asserted, the memory operation is started at the end of the data path cycle, after MAR has been loaded. The memory data are available at the very end of the *following* cycle in MBR or MDR and can be used in the cycle *after that*. In other words, a memory read on either port initiated at the end of cycle k delivers data that cannot be used in cycle $k + 1$, but only in cycle $k + 2$ or later.

This seemingly counterintuitive behavior is explained by Fig. 4-3. The memory control signals are not generated in clock cycle 1 until just after MAR and PC are loaded at the rising edge of the clock, toward the end of clock cycle 1. We will assume the memory puts its results on the memory buses within one cycle so that MBR and/or MDR can be loaded on the next rising clock edge, along with the other registers.

Put in other words, we load MAR at the end of a data path cycle and start the memory shortly thereafter. Consequently, we cannot really expect the results of a read operation to be in MDR at the start of the next cycle, especially if the width of the clock pulse is short. There is just not enough time if the memory takes one clock cycle. One data path cycle must intervene between starting a memory read and using the result. Of course, other operations can be performed during that cycle, just not ones that need the memory word.

The assumption that the memory takes one cycle to operate is equivalent to assuming that the level 1 cache hit rate is 100%. This assumption is never true, but the complexity introduced by a variable-length memory cycle time is more than we want to deal with here.

Since MBR and MDR are loaded on the rising edge of the clock, along with all the other registers, they may be read during cycles when a new memory read is being performed. They return the old values since the read has not yet had time to overwrite them. There is no ambiguity here; until new values are loaded into MBR and MDR at the rising edge of the clock, the previous values are still there and usable. Note that it is possible to perform back-to-back reads on two consecutive cycles since a read only takes 1 cycle. Also, both memories may operate at the same time. However, trying to read and write the same byte simultaneously gives undefined results.

While it may be desirable to write the output on the C bus into more than one register, it is never desirable to enable more than one register onto the B bus at a time. (In fact, some real implementations will suffer physical damage if this is done.) With a small increase in circuitry, we can reduce the number of bits needed to select among the possible sources for driving the B bus. There are only nine possible input registers that can drive the B bus (where the signed and unsigned versions of MBR each count separately). Therefore, we can encode the B bus information in 4 bits and use a decoder to generate the 16 control signals, 7 of which are not needed. In a commercial design, the architects would experience an overwhelming urge to get rid of one of the registers so that 3 bits would do the job. As academics, we have the enormous luxury of being able to waste 1 bit to give a cleaner and simpler design.

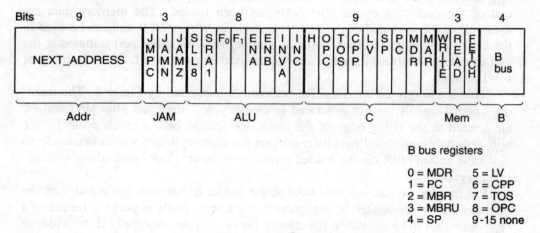

Figure 4-5. The microinstruction format for the Mic-1.

At this point we can control the data path with $9 + 4 + 8 + 2 + 1 = 24$ signals, hence 24 bits. However, these 24 bits only control the data path for one cycle. The second part of the control is to determine what is to be done on the following cycle. To include this in the design of the controller, we will create a format for describing the operations to be performed using the 24 control bits plus two additional fields: the NEXT_ADDRESS field and the JAM field. The contents of each of these fields will be discussed shortly. Figure 4-5 shows a possible format, divided into the six groups, and containing the following 36 signals:

Addr – Contains the address of a potential next microinstruction.

JAM – Determines how the next microinstruction is selected.

ALU – ALU and shifter functions.

C – Selects which registers are written from the C bus.

Mem – Memory functions.

B – Selects the B bus source; it is encoded as shown.

The ordering of the groups is, in principle, arbitrary although we have actually chosen it very carefully to minimize line crossings in Fig. 4-6. Line crossings in schematic diagrams like Fig. 4-6 often correspond to wire crossings on chips, which cause trouble in two-dimensional designs and are best minimized.

4.1.3 Microinstruction Control: The Mic-1

So far we have described how the data path is controlled, but we have not yet described how it is decided which of the control signals should be enabled on each cycle. This is determined by a **sequencer** that is responsible for stepping through the sequence of operations necessary for the execution of a single ISA instruction.

The sequencer must produce two kinds of information each cycle:

1. The state of every control signal in the system.

2. The address of the microinstruction that is to be executed next.

Figure 4-6 is a detailed block diagram of the complete microarchitecture of our example machine, which we will call the **Mic-1**. It may look imposing initially but it is worth studying carefully. When you fully understand every box and every line in this figure, you will be well on your way to understanding the microarchitecture level. The block diagram has two parts: the data path, on the left, which we have already discussed in detail, and the control section, on the right, which we will now look at.

The largest and most important item in the control portion of the machine is a memory called the **control store**. It is convenient to think of it as a memory that holds the complete microprogram, although it is sometimes implemented as a set of logic gates. In general, we will refer to it as the control store, to avoid confusion with the main memory, accessed through MBR and MDR. However, functionally, the control store is a memory that simply holds microinstructions instead of ISA instructions. For our example machine, it contains 512 words, each word consisting of one 36-bit microinstruction of the kind illustrated in Fig. 4-5. Actually, not all of these words are needed, but (for reasons to be explained shortly) we need addresses for 512 distinct words.

In one important way, the control store is quite different from the main memory: instructions in main memory are always executed in address order (except for

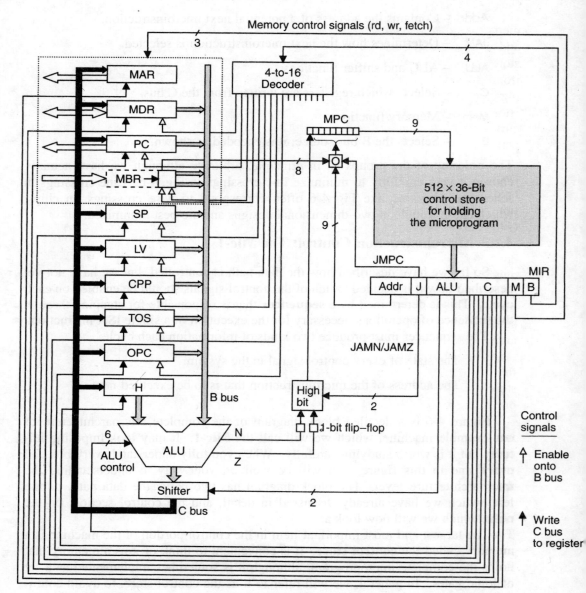

Figure 4-6. The complete block diagram of our example microarchitecture, the Mic-1.

branches); microinstructions are not. The act of incrementing the program counter in Fig. 2-3 expresses the fact that the default instruction to execute after the current one is the instruction following the current one in memory. Microprograms need more flexibility (because microinstruction sequences tend to be short), so they usually do not have this property. Instead, each microinstruction explicitly specifies its successor.

Since the control store is functionally a (read-only) memory, it needs its own memory address register and its own memory data register. It does not need read and write signals, because it is continuously being read. We will call the control store's memory address register **MPC** (**MicroProgram Counter**). This name is ironic since the locations in it are explicitly not ordered, so the concept of counting is not useful (but who are we to argue with tradition?). The memory data register is called **MIR** (**MicroInstruction Register**). Its function is to hold the current microinstruction, whose bits drive the control signals that operate the data path.

The MIR register in Fig. 4-6 holds the same six groups as Fig. 4-5. The Addr and J (for JAM) groups control the selection of the next microinstruction and will be discussed shortly. The ALU group contains the 8 bits that select the ALU function and drive the shifter. The C bits cause individual registers to load the ALU output from the C bus. The M bits control memory operations.

Finally, the last 4 bits drive the decoder that determines what goes onto the B bus. In this case we have chosen to use a standard 4-to-16 decoder, even though only nine possibilities are required. In a more finely-tuned design, a 4-to-9 decoder could be used. The trade-off here is using a standard circuit taken from a library of circuits versus designing a custom one. Using the standard circuit is simpler and is unlikely to introduce any bugs. Rolling your own uses less chip area but takes longer to design and you might get it wrong.

The operation of Fig. 4-6 is as follows. At the start of each clock cycle (the falling edge of the clock in Fig. 4-3), MIR is loaded from the word in the control store pointed to by MPC. The MIR load time is indicated in the figure by Δw. If one thinks in terms of subcycles, MIR is loaded during the first one.

Once the microinstruction is set up in MIR, the various signals propagate out into the data path. A register is put out onto the B bus, the ALU knows which operation to perform, and there is lots of activity out there. This is the second subcycle. After an interval $\Delta w + \Delta x$ from the start of the cycle, the ALU inputs are stable.

Another Δy later, everything has settled down and the ALU, N, Z, and shifter outputs are stable. The N and Z values are then saved in a pair of 1-bit flip-flops. These bits, like all the registers that are loaded from the C bus and from memory, are saved on the rising edge of the clock, near the end of the data path cycle. The ALU output is not latched but just fed into the shifter. The ALU and shifter activity occurs during subcycle 3.

After an additional interval, Δz, the shifter output has reached the registers via the C bus. Then the registers can be loaded near the end of the cycle (at the rising edge of the clock pulse in Fig. 4-3). Subcycle 4 consists of loading the registers and N and Z flip-flops. It terminates a little after the rising edge of the clock, when all the results have been saved and the results of the previous memory operations are available and MPC has been loaded. This process goes on and on until somebody gets bored with it and turns the machine off.

In parallel with driving the data path, the microprogram has to determine which microinstruction to execute next, as they need not be run in the order they appear in the control store. The calculation of the address of the next microinstruction begins after MIR has been loaded and is stable. First, the 9-bit NEXT_ADDRESS field is copied to MPC. While this copy is taking place, the JAM field is inspected. If it has the value 000, nothing else is done; when the copy of NEXT_ADDRESS completes, MPC will point to the next microinstruction.

If one or more of the JAM bits are 1, more work is needed. If JAMN is set, the 1-bit N flip-flop is ORed into the high-order bit of MPC. Similarly, if JAMZ is set, the 1-bit Z flip-flop is ORed there. If both are set, both are ORed there. The reason that the N and Z flip-flops are needed is that after the rising edge of the clock (while the clock is high), the B bus is no longer being driven, so the ALU outputs can no longer be assumed to be correct. Saving the ALU status flags in N and Z makes the correct values available and stable for the MPC computation, no matter what is going on around the ALU.

In Fig. 4-6, the logic that does this computation is labeled "High bit." The Boolean function it computes is

$$F = (JAMZ \text{ AND } Z) \text{ OR } (JAMN \text{ AND } N) \text{ OR } NEXT\_ADDRESS[8]$$

Note that in all cases, MPC can take on only one of two possible values:

1. The value of NEXT_ADDRESS.

2. The value of NEXT_ADDRESS with the high-order bit ORed with 1.

No other possibilities exist. If the high-order bit of NEXT_ADDRESS was already 1, using JAMN or JAMZ makes no sense.

Note that when the JAM bits are all zeros, the address of the next microinstruction to be executed is simply the 9-bit number in its NEXT_ADDRESS field. When either JAMN or JAMZ are 1, there are two potential successors: NEXT_ADDRESS and NEXT_ADDRESS ORed with 0x100 (assuming that NEXT_ADDRESS ≤ 0xFF). (Note that 0x indicates that the number following it is in hexadecimal.) This point is illustrated in Fig. 4-7. The current microinstruction, at location 0x75, has NEXT_ADDRESS = 0x92 and JAMZ set to 1. Consequently, the next address of the microinstruction depends on the Z bit stored on the previous ALU operation. If the Z bit is 0, the next microinstruction comes from 0x92. If the Z bit is 1, the next microinstruction comes from 0x192.

The third bit in the JAM field is JMPC. If it is set, the 8 MBR bits are bitwise ORed with the 8 low-order bits of the NEXT_ADDRESS field coming from the current microinstruction. The result is sent to MPC. The box with the label "O" in Fig. 4-6 does an OR of MBR with NEXT_ADDRESS if JMPC is 1 but just passes NEXT_ADDRESS through to MPC if JMPC is 0. When JMPC is 1, the low-order 8 bits of NEXT_ADDRESS are normally zero. The high-order bit can be 0 or 1, so the NEXT_ADDRESS value used with JMPC is normally 0x000 or 0x100. The reason for sometimes using 0x000 and sometimes using 0x100 will be discussed later.

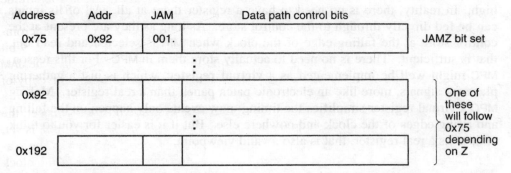

Figure 4-7. A microinstruction with JAMZ set to 1 has two potential successors.

The ability to OR MBR together with NEXT_ADDRESS and store the result in MPC allows an efficient implementation of a multiway branch (jump). Notice that any of 256 addresses can be specified, determined solely by the bits present in MBR. In a typical use, MBR contains an opcode, so the use of JMPC will result in a unique selection for the next microinstruction to be executed for every possible opcode. This method is useful for quickly branching directly to the function corresponding to the just-fetched opcode.

Understanding the timing of the machine is critical to what will follow, so it is perhaps worth repeating it again. We will do it in terms of subcycles, since this is easy to visualize, but the only real clock events are the falling edge, which starts the cycle, and the rising edge, which loads the registers and the N and Z flip-flops. Please refer to Fig. 4-3 once more.

During subcycle 1, initiated by the falling edge of the clock, MIR is loaded from the address currently held in MPC. During subcycle 2, the signals from MIR propagate out and the B bus is loaded from the selected register. During subcycle 3, the ALU and shifter operate and produce a stable result. During subcycle 4, the C bus, memory buses, and ALU values become stable. At the rising edge of the clock, the registers are loaded from the C bus, N and Z flip-flops are loaded, and MBR and MDR get their results from the memory operation started at the end of the previous data path cycle (if any). As soon as MBR is available, MPC is loaded in preparation for the next microinstruction. Thus MPC gets its value sometime during the middle of the interval when the clock is high but after MBR/MDR are ready. It could be either level triggered (rather than edge triggered), or edge trigger a fixed delay after the rising edge of the clock. All that matters is that MPC is not loaded until the registers it depends on (MBR, N, and Z) are ready. As soon as the clock falls, MPC can address the control store and a new cycle can begin.

Note that each cycle is self contained. It specifies what goes onto the B bus, what the ALU and shifter are to do, where the C bus is to be stored, and finally, what the next MPC value should be.

One final note about Fig. 4-6 is worth making. We have been treating MPC as a proper register, with 9 bits of storage capacity that is loaded while the clock is high. In reality, there is no need to have a register there at all. All of its inputs can be fed directly through to the control store. As long as they are present at the control store at the falling edge of the clock when MIR is selected and read out, that is sufficient. There is no need to actually store them in MPC. For this reason, MPC might well be implemented as a **virtual register**, which is just a gathering place for signals, more like an electronic patch panel, than a real register. Making MPC a virtual register simplifies the timing: now events only happen on the falling and rising edges of the clock and nowhere else. But if it is easier for you to think of MPC as a real register, that is also a valid viewpoint.

4.2 AN EXAMPLE ISA: IJVM

Let us continue our example by introducing the ISA level of the machine to be interpreted by the microprogram running on the microarchitecture of Fig. 4-6 (IJVM). For convenience, we will sometimes refer to the Instruction Set Architecture as the **macroarchitecture**, to contrast it with the microarchitecture. Before we describe IJVM, however, we will digress slightly to motivate it.

4.2.1 Stacks

Virtually all programming languages support the concept of procedures (methods), which have local variables. These variables can be accessed from inside the procedure but cease to be accessible once the procedure has returned. The question thus arises: "Where should these variables be kept in memory?"

The simplest solution, to give each variable an absolute memory address, does not work. The problem is that a procedure may call itself. We will study these recursive procedures in Chap. 5. For the moment, suffice it to say that if a procedure is active (i.e., called) twice, it is impossible to store its variables in absolute memory locations because the second invocation will interfere with the first.

Instead, a different strategy is used. An area of memory, called the **stack**, is reserved for variables, but individual variables do not get absolute addresses in it. Instead, a register, say, LV, is set to point to the base of the local variables for the current procedure. In Fig. 4-8(a), a procedure A, which has local variables a1, a2, and a3, has been called, so storage for its local variables has been reserved starting at the memory location pointed to by LV. Another register, SP, points to the highest word of A's local variables. If LV is 100 and words are 4 bytes, then SP will be 108. Variables are referred to by giving their offset (distance) from LV. The data structure between LV and SP (and including both words pointed to) is called A's **local variable frame**.

Now let us consider what happens if A calls another procedure, B. Where should B's four local variables (b1, b2, b3, b4) be stored? Answer: On the stack, on top of A's, as shown in Fig. 4-8(b). Notice that LV has been adjusted by the

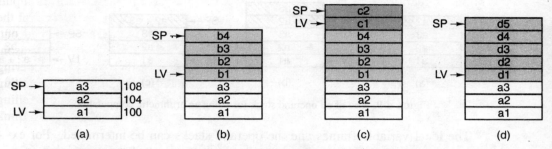

Figure 4-8. Use of a stack for storing local variables. (a) While *A* is active. (b) After *A* calls *B*. (c) After *B* calls *C*. (d) After *C* and *B* return and *A* calls *D*.

procedure call to point to *B*'s local variables instead of *A*'s. *B*'s local variables can be referred to by giving their offset from LV. Similarly, if *B* calls *C*, LV and SP are adjusted again to allocate space for *C*'s two variables, as shown in Fig. 4-8(c).

When *C* returns, *B* becomes active again, and the stack is adjusted back to Fig. 4-8(b) so that LV now points to *B*'s local variables again. Likewise, when *B* returns, we get back to the situation of Fig. 4-8(a). Under all conditions, LV points to the base of the stack frame for the currently active procedure, and SP points to the top of the stack frame.

Now suppose that *A* calls *D*, which has five local variables. We get the situation of Fig. 4-8(d), in which *D*'s local variables use the same memory that *B*'s did, as well as part of *C*'s. With this memory organization, memory is only allocated for procedures that are currently active. When a procedure returns, the memory used by its local variables is released.

Stacks have another use, in addition to holding local variables. They can be used for holding operands during the computation of an arithmetic expression. When used this way, the stack is referred to as the **operand stack**. Suppose, for example, that before calling *B*, *A* has to do the computation

    a1 = a2 + a3;

One way of doing this sum is to push *a2* onto the stack, as shown in Fig. 4-9(a). Here SP has been incremented by the number of bytes in a word, say, 4, and the first operand stored at the address now pointed to by SP. Next, *a3* is pushed onto the stack, as shown in Fig. 4-9(b). As an aside on notation, we will typeset all program fragments in Helvetica, as above. We will also use this font for assembly language opcodes and machine registers, but in running text, program variables and procedures will be given in *italics*. The difference is that variables and procedure names are chosen by the user; opcodes and register names are built in.

The actual computation can be done by now executing an instruction that pops two words off the stack, adds them together, and pushes the result back onto the stack, as shown in Fig. 4-9(c). Finally, the top word can be popped off the stack and stored back in local variable *a1*, as illustrated in Fig. 4-9(d).

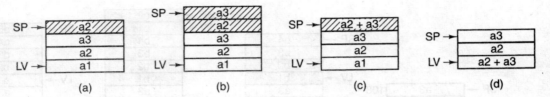

Figure 4-9. Use of an operand stack for doing an arithmetic computation.

The local variable frames and the operand stacks can be intermixed. For example, when computing an expression like $x^2 + f(x)$ part of the expression (e.g., x^2) may be on the operand stack when a function f is called. The result of the function is left on the stack, on top of x^2, so the next instruction can add them.

It is worth noting that while all machines use a stack for storing local variables, not all use an operand stack like this for doing arithmetic. In fact, most of them do not, but JVM and IJVM work like this, which is why we have introduced stack operations here. We will study them in more detail in Chap. 5.

4.2.2 The IJVM Memory Model

We are now ready to look at the IJVM's architecture. Basically, it consists of a memory that can be viewed in either of two ways: an array of 4,294,967,296 bytes (4 GB) or an array of 1,073,741,824 words, each consisting of 4 bytes. Unlike most ISAs, the Java Virtual Machine makes no absolute memory addresses directly visible at the ISA level, but there are several implicit addresses that provide the base for a pointer. IJVM instructions can only access memory by indexing from these pointers. At any time, the following areas of memory are defined:

1. *The Constant Pool.* This area cannot be written by an IJVM program and consists of constants, strings, and pointers to other areas of memory that can be referenced. It is loaded when the program is brought into memory and not changed afterward. There is an implicit register, CPP, that contains the address of the first word of the constant pool.

2. *The Local Variable Frame.* For each invocation of a method, an area is allocated for storing variables during the lifetime of the invocation. It is called the **local variable frame**. At the beginning of this frame reside the parameters (also called arguments) with which the method was invoked. The local variable frame does not include the operand stack, which is separate. However, for efficiency reasons, our implementation chooses to implement the operand stack immediately above the local variable frame. There is an implicit register that contains the address of the first location in the local variable frame. We will call this register LV. The parameters passed at the invocation of the method are stored at the beginning of the local variable frame.

3. *The Operand Stack.* The stack frame is guaranteed not to exceed a certain size, computed in advance by the Java compiler. The operand stack space is allocated directly above the local variable frame, as illustrated in Fig. 4-10. In our implementation, it is convenient to think of the operand stack as part of the local variable frame. In any case, there is an implicit register that contains the address of the top word of the stack. Notice that, unlike CPP and LV, this pointer, SP, changes during the execution of the method as operands are pushed onto the stack or popped from it.

4. *The Method Area.* Finally, there is a region of memory containing the program, referred to as the "text" area in a UNIX process. There is an implicit register that contains the address of the instruction to be fetched next. This pointer is referred to as the Program Counter, or PC. Unlike the other regions of memory, the Method Area is treated as a byte array.

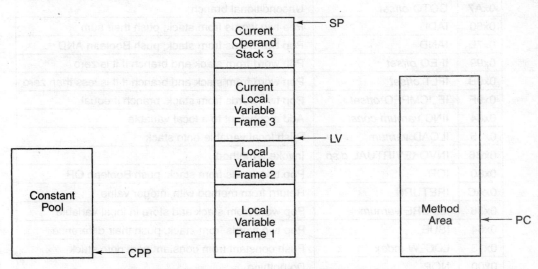

Figure 4-10. The various parts of the IJVM memory.

One point needs to be made regarding the pointers. The CPP, LV, and SP registers are all pointers to *words*, not *bytes*, and are offset by the number of words. For the integer subset we have chosen, all references to items in the constant pool, the local variables frame, and the stack are words, and all offsets used to index into these frames are word offsets. For example, LV, LV + 1, and LV + 2 refer to the first three words of the local variables frame. In contrast, LV, LV + 4, and LV + 8 refer to words at intervals of four words (16 bytes).

In contrast, PC contains a byte address, and an addition or subtraction to PC changes the address by a number of bytes, not a number of words. Addressing for

PC is different from the others, and this fact is apparent in the special memory port provided for PC on the Mic-1. Remember that it is only 1 byte wide. Incrementing PC by one and initiating a read results in a fetch of the next *byte*. Incrementing SP by one and initiating a read results in a fetch of the next *word*.

4.2.3 The IJVM Instruction Set

The IJVM instruction set is shown in Fig. 4-11. Each instruction consists of an opcode and sometimes an operand, such as a memory offset or a constant. The first column gives the hexadecimal encoding of the instruction. The second gives its assembly language mnemonic. The third gives a brief description of its effect.

Hex	Mnemonic	Meaning
0x10	BIPUSH *byte*	Push byte onto stack
0x59	DUP	Copy top word on stack and push onto stack
0xA7	GOTO *offset*	Unconditional branch
0x60	IADD	Pop two words from stack; push their sum
0x7E	IAND	Pop two words from stack; push Boolean AND
0x99	IFEQ *offset*	Pop word from stack and branch if it is zero
0x9B	IFLT *offset*	Pop word from stack and branch if it is less than zero
0x9F	IF_ICMPEQ *offset*	Pop two words from stack; branch if equal
0x84	IINC *varnum const*	Add a constant to a local variable
0x15	ILOAD *varnum*	Push local variable onto stack
0xB6	INVOKEVIRTUAL *disp*	Invoke a method
0x80	IOR	Pop two words from stack; push Boolean OR
0xAC	IRETURN	Return from method with integer value
0x36	ISTORE *varnum*	Pop word from stack and store in local variable
0x64	ISUB	Pop two words from stack; push their difference
0x13	LDC_W *index*	Push constant from constant pool onto stack
0x00	NOP	Do nothing
0x57	POP	Delete word on top of stack
0x5F	SWAP	Swap the two top words on the stack
0xC4	WIDE	Prefix instruction; next instruction has a 16-bit index

Figure 4-11. The IJVM instruction set. The operands *byte*, *const*, and *varnum* are 1 byte. The operands *disp*, *index*, and *offset* are 2 bytes.

Instructions are provided to push a word from various sources onto the stack. These sources include the constant pool (LDC_W), the local variable frame (ILOAD), and the instruction itself (BIPUSH). A variable can also be popped from the stack and stored into the local variable frame (ISTORE). Two arithmetic operations (IADD and ISUB) as well as two logical (Boolean) operations (IAND and IOR) can be performed using the two top words on the stack as operands. In all the arithmetic and logical operations, two words are popped from the stack and the result pushed back onto it. Four branch instructions are provided, one unconditional (GOTO) and three conditional ones (IFEQ, IFLT, and IF_ICMPEQ). All the branch instructions, if taken, adjust the value of PC by the size of their (16-bit signed) offset, which follows the opcode in the instruction. This offset is added to the address of the opcode. There are also IJVM instructions for swapping the top two words on the stack (SWAP), duplicating the top word (DUP), and removing it (POP).

Some instructions have multiple formats, allowing a short form for commonly-used versions. In IJVM we have included two of the various mechanisms JVM uses to accomplish this. In one case we have skipped the short form in favor of the more general one. In another case we show how the prefix instruction WIDE can be used to modify the ensuing instruction.

Finally, there is an instruction (INVOKEVIRTUAL) for invoking another method, and another instruction (IRETURN) for exiting the method and returning control to the method that invoked it. Due to the complexity of the mechanism we have slightly simplified the definition, making it possible to produce a straightforward mechanism for invoking a call and return. The restriction is that, unlike Java, we only allow a method to invoke a method existing within its own object. This restriction severely cripples the object orientation but allows us to present a much simpler mechanism, by avoiding the requirement to locate the method dynamically. (If you are not familiar with object-oriented programming, you can safely ignore this remark. What we have done is turn Java back into a nonobject-oriented language, such as C or Pascal.) On all computers except JVM, the address of the procedure to call is determined directly by the CALL instruction, so our approach is actually the normal case, not the exception.

The mechanism for invoking a method is as follows. First, the caller pushes onto the stack a reference (pointer) to the object to be called. (This reference is not needed in IJVM since no other object may be specified, but it is retained for consistency with JVM.) In Fig. 4-12(a) this reference is indicated by OBJREF. Then the caller pushes the method's parameters onto the stack, in this example, *Parameter 1*, *Parameter 2*, and *Parameter 3*. Finally, INVOKEVIRTUAL is executed.

The INVOKEVIRTUAL instruction includes a displacement which indicates the position in the constant pool that contains the start address within the Method Area for the method being invoked. However, while the method code resides at the location pointed to by this pointer, the first 4 bytes in the method area contain special data. The first 2 bytes are interpreted as a 16-bit integer indicating the number of parameters for the method (the parameters themselves have previously been pushed onto the stack). For this count, OBJREF is counted as a parameter:

parameter 0. This 16-bit integer, together with the value of SP, provides the location of OBJREF. Note that LV points to OBJREF rather than the first real parameter. The choice where LV points is somewhat arbitrary.

The second 2 bytes in the method area are interpreted as another 16-bit integer indicating the size of the local variable area for the method being invoked. This is necessary because a new stack will be established for the method, beginning immediately above the local variable frame. Finally, the fifth byte in the method area contains the first opcode to be executed.

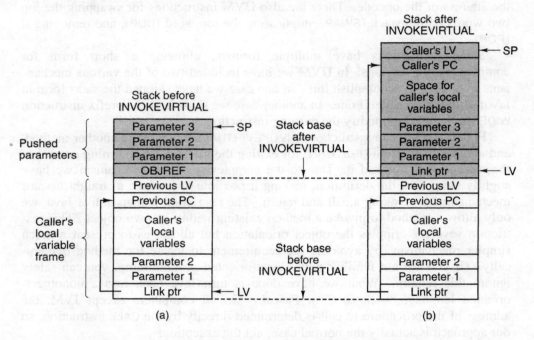

Figure 4-12. (a) Memory before executing INVOKEVIRTUAL. (b) After executing it.

The actual sequence that occurs for INVOKEVIRTUAL is as follows and is depicted in Fig. 4-12. The two unsigned index bytes that follow the opcode are used to construct an index into the constant pool table (the first byte is the high-order byte). The instruction computes the base address of the new local variable frame by subtracting off the number of parameters from the stack pointer and setting LV to point to OBJREF. At this location, overwriting OBJREF, the implementation stores the address of the location where the old PC is to be stored. This address is computed by adding the size of the local variable frame (parameters + local variables) to the address contained in LV. Immediately above the address where the old PC is to be stored is the address where the old LV is to be stored. Immediately above that address is the beginning of the stack for the newly-called procedure. SP is set to point to the old LV, which is the address immediately below the first empty location on the stack. Remember that SP always points to the top word on the stack. If the stack is empty, it points to the first location below the end of the stack because our stacks grow upward, toward higher addresses. In our figures, stacks always grow upward, toward the higher address at the top of the page.

The last operation needed to carry out INVOKEVIRTUAL is to set PC to point to the fifth byte in the method code space.

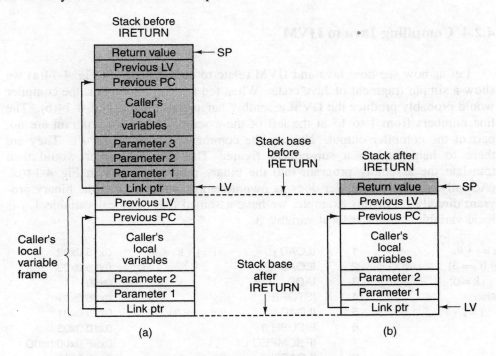

Figure 4-13. (a) Memory before executing IRETURN. (b) After executing it.

The IRETURN instruction reverses the operations of the INVOKEVIRTUAL instruction, as shown in Fig. 4-13. It deallocates the space used by the returning method. It also restores the stack to its former state, except that (1) the (now overwritten) OBJREF word and all the parameters have been popped from the stack, and (2) the returned value has been placed at the top of the stack, at the location formerly occupied by OBJREF. To restore the old state, the IRETURN instruction must be able to restore the PC and LV pointers to their old values. It does this by accessing the link pointer (which is the word identified by the current LV pointer). In this location, remember, where the OBJREF was originally stored, the INVOKEVIRTUAL instruction stored the address containing the old PC. This word and the word above it are retrieved to restore PC and LV, respectively, to their old values. The return value, which is stored at the top of the stack of the terminating method, is copied to the location where the OBJREF was originally stored, and SP is restored to point to this location. Control is therefore returned to the instruction immediately following the INVOKEVIRTUAL instruction.

So far, our machine does not have any input/output instructions. Nor are we going to add any. It does not need them any more than the Java Virtual Machine needs them, and the official specification for JVM never even mentions I/O. The theory is that a machine that does no input or output is "safe." (Reading and writing are performed in JVM by means of calls to special I/O methods.

4.2.4 Compiling Java to IJVM

Let us now see how Java and IJVM relate to one another. In Fig. 4-14(a) we show a simple fragment of Java code. When fed to a Java compiler, the compiler would probably produce the IJVM assembly language shown in Fig. 4-14(b). The line numbers from 1 to 15 at the left of the assembly language program are not part of the compiler output. Nor are the comments (starting with //). They are there to help explain a subsequent figure. The Java assembler would then translate the assembly program into the binary program shown in Fig. 4-14(c). (Actually, the Java compiler does its own assembly and produces the binary program directly.) For this example, we have assumed that *i* is local variable 1, *j* is local variable 2, and *k* is local variable 3.

i = j + k;	1	ILOAD j	// i = j + k	0x15 0x02
if (i == 3)	2	ILOAD k		0x15 0x03
k = 0;	3	IADD		0x60
else	4	ISTORE i		0x36 0x01
j = j - 1;	5	ILOAD i	// if (i == 3)	0x15 0x01
	6	BIPUSH 3		0x10 0x03
	7	IF_ICMPEQ L1		0x9F 0x00 0x0D
	8	ILOAD j	// j = j - 1	0x15 0x02
	9	BIPUSH 1		0x10 0x01
	10	ISUB		0x64
	11	ISTORE j		0x36 0x02
	12	GOTO L2		0xA7 0x00 0x07
	13 L1:	BIPUSH 0	// k = 0	0x10 0x00
	14	ISTORE k		0x36 0x03
	15 L2:			
(a)		(b)		(c)

Figure 4-14. (a) A Java fragment. (b) The corresponding Java assembly language. (c) The IJVM program in hexadecimal.

The compiled code is straightforward. First *j* and *k* are pushed onto the stack, added, and the result stored in *i*. Then *i* and the constant 3 are pushed onto the stack and compared. If they are equal, a branch is taken to *L1*, where *k* is set to 0. If they are unequal, the compare fails and code following IF_ICMPEQ is executed. When it is done, it branches to *L2*, where the then and else parts merge.

The operand stack for the IJVM program of Fig. 4-14(b) is shown in Fig. 4-15. Before the code starts executing, the stack is empty, indicated by the horizontal line above the 0. After the first ILOAD, j is on the stack, as indicated by the boxed j above the 1 (meaning instruction 1 has executed). After the second ILOAD, two words are on the stack, as shown above the 2. After the IADD, there is only one word on the stack, and it contains the sum $j + k$. When the top word is popped from the stack and stored in i, the stack is empty, as shown above the 4.

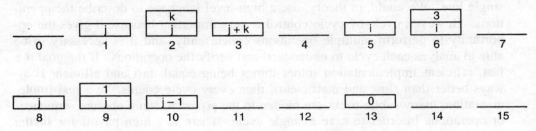

Figure 4-15. The stack after each instruction of Fig. 4-14(b).

Instruction 5 (ILOAD) starts the if statement by pushing i onto the stack (in 5) Next comes the constant 3 (in 6). After the comparison, the stack is empty again (7). Instruction 8 is the start of the else part of the Java program fragment. The else part continues until instruction 12, at which time it branches over the then part and goes to label *L2*.

4.3 AN EXAMPLE IMPLEMENTATION

Having specified both the microarchitecture and the macroarchitecture in detail, the remaining issue is the implementation. In other words, what does a program running on the former and interpreting the latter look like, and how does it work? Before we can answer these questions, we must carefully consider the notation we will use to describe the implementation.

4.3.1 Microinstructions and Notation

In principle, we could describe the control store in binary, 36 bits per word. But as in conventional programming languages, there is great benefit in introducing notation that conveys the essence of the issues we need to deal with while obscuring the details that can be ignored, or can be better handled automatically. It is important to realize here that the language we have chosen is intended to illustrate the concepts rather than to facilitate efficient designs. If the latter were our goal, we would use a different notation to maximize the flexibility available to the designer. One aspect where this issue is important is the choice of addresses.

Since the memory is not logically ordered, there is no natural "next instruction" to be implied as we specify a sequence of operations. Much of the power of this control organization derives from the ability of the designer (or the assembler) to select addresses efficiently. We therefore begin by introducing a simple symbolic language that fully describes each operation without explaining fully how all addresses may have been determined.

Our notation specifies all the activities that occur in a single clock cycle in a single line. We could, in theory, use a high-level language to describe the operations. However, cycle-by-cycle control is very important because it gives the opportunity to perform multiple operations concurrently, and it is necessary to be able to analyze each cycle to understand and verify the operations. If the goal is a fast, efficient implementation (other things being equal, fast and efficient is always better than slow and inefficient), then every cycle counts. In a real implementation, many subtle tricks are hidden in the program, using obscure sequences or operations in order to save a single cycle. There is a high payoff for saving cycles: a four-cycle instruction that can be reduced by two cycles now runs twice as fast. And this speedup is obtained every time we execute the instruction.

One possible approach is simply to list the signals that should be activated each clock cycle. Suppose that in one cycle we want to increment the value of SP. We also want to initiate a read operation, and we want the next instruction to be the one residing at location 122 in the control store. We might write

ReadRegister = SP, ALU = INC, WSP, Read, NEXT_ADDRESS = 122

where WSP means "write the SP register." This notation is complete, but hard to understand. Instead we will combine the operations in a natural and intuitive way to capture the effect of what is happening:

SP = SP + 1; rd

Let us call our high-level Micro Assembly Language "MAL" (French for "sick," something you become if you have to write too much code in it). MAL is tailored to reflect the characteristics of the microarchitecture. During each cycle, any of the registers can be written, but typically only one is. Only one register can be gated to the B side of the ALU. On the A side, the choices are +1, 0, −1, and the register H. Thus we can use a simple assignment statement, as in Java, to indicate the operation to be performed. For example, to copy something from SP to MDR, we can say

MDR = SP

To indicate the use of the ALU functions other than passing through the B bus, we can write, for example,

MDR = H + SP

which adds the contents of the H register to SP and writes the result into MDR.

The + operator is commutative (which means that the order of the operands does not matter), so the above statement can also be written as

    MDR = SP + H

and generate the same 36-bit microinstruction, even though strictly speaking H must be the left ALU operand.

We have to be careful to use only legal operations. The most important legal operations are shown in the Fig. 4-16, where SOURCE can be any of MDR, PC, MBR, MBRU, SP, LV, CPP, TOS, or OPC (MBRU implies the unsigned version of MBR). These registers can all act as sources to the ALU on the B bus. Similarly, DEST can be any of MAR, MDR, PC, SP, LV, CPP, TOS, OPC, or H, all of which are possible destinations for the ALU output on the C bus. This format is deceptive because many seemingly reasonable statements are illegal. For example,

    MDR = SP + MDR

looks perfectly reasonable, but there is no way to execute it on the data path of Fig. 4-6 in one cycle. This restriction exists because for an addition (other than increment or decrement) one of the operands must be the H register. Likewise,

    H = H – MDR

might be useful, but it, too, is impossible, because the only possible source of a subtrahend (the value being subtracted) is the H register. It is up to the assembler to reject statements that look valid but are, in fact, illegal.

We extend the notation to permit multiple assignments by the use of multiple equal signs. For example, adding 1 to SP and storing it back into SP as well as writing it into MDR can be accomplished by

    SP = MDR = SP + 1

To indicate memory reads and writes of 4-byte data words, we will just put rd and wr in the microinstruction. Fetching a byte through the 1-byte port is indicated by fetch. Assignments and memory operations can occur in the same cycle. This is indicated by writing them on the same line.

To avoid any confusion, let us repeat the fact that the Mic-1 has two ways of accessing memory. Reads and writes of 4-byte data words use MAR/MDR and are indicated in the microinstructions by rd and wr, respectively. Reads of 1-byte opcodes from the instruction stream use PC/MBR and are indicated by fetch in the microinstructions. Both kinds of memory operations can proceed simultaneously.

However, the same register may not receive a value from memory and the data path in the same cycle. Consider the code

    MAR = SP; rd
    MDR = H

The effect of the first microinstruction is to assign a value from memory to MDR at

DEST = H
DEST = SOURCE
DEST = $\overline{\text{H}}$
DEST = $\overline{\text{SOURCE}}$
DEST = H + SOURCE
DEST = H + SOURCE + 1
DEST = H + 1
DEST = SOURCE + 1
DEST = SOURCE − H
DEST = SOURCE − 1
DEST = −H
DEST = H AND SOURCE
DEST = H OR SOURCE
DEST = 0
DEST = 1
DEST = −1

Figure 4-16. All permitted operations. Any of the above operations may be extended by adding "<< 8" to them to shift the result left by 1 byte. For example, a common operation is H = MBR << 8.

the end of the second microinstruction. However, the second microinstruction also assigns a value to MDR at the same time. These two assignments are in conflict and are not permitted as the results are undefined.

Remember that each microinstruction must explicitly supply the address of the next microinstruction to be executed. However, it commonly occurs that a microinstruction is invoked only by one other microinstruction, namely, by the one on the line immediately above it. To ease the microprogrammer's job, the microassembler normally assigns an address to each microinstruction (not necessarily consecutive in the control store), and fills in the NEXT_ADDRESS field so that microinstructions written on consecutive lines are executed consecutively.

However, sometimes the microprogrammer wants to branch away, either unconditionally or conditionally. The notation for unconditional branches is easy:

    goto *label*

can be included in any microinstruction to explicitly name its successor. For example, most microinstruction sequences end with a return to the first instruction of the main loop, so the last instruction in each such sequence typically includes

    goto Main1

Note that the data path is available for normal operations even during a microinstruction that contains a goto. After all, every single microinstruction contains a

NEXT_ADDRESS field. All goto does is instruct the microassembler to put a specific value there instead of the address where it has decided to place the microinstruction on the next line. In principle, every line should have a goto statement, only as a convenience to the microprogrammer, when the target address is the next line, it may be omitted.

For conditional branches, we need a different notation. Remember that JAMN and JAMZ use the N and Z bits, which are set based on the ALU output. Sometimes it is needed to test a register to see if it is zero, for example. One way to do this would be to run it through the ALU and store it back in itself. Writing

    TOS = TOS

looks peculiar, although it does the job (setting the Z flip-flop based on TOS). However, to make microprograms look nicer, we now extend MAL, adding two new imaginary registers, N and Z, which can be assigned to. For example,

    Z = TOS

runs TOS through the ALU, thus setting the Z (and N) flip-flops, but it does not do a store into any register. What using Z or N as a destination really does is tell the microassembler to set all the bits in the C field of Fig. 4-5 to 0. The data path executes a normal cycle, with all normal operations allowed, but no registers are written to. Note that it does not matter whether the destination is N or Z; the microinstruction generated by the microassembler is identical. Programmers who intentionally choose the "wrong" one should be forced to work on a 4.77 MHz original IBM PC for a week as punishment.

The syntax for telling the microassembler to set the JAMZ bit is

    if (Z) goto L1; else goto L2

Since the hardware requires these two addresses to be identical in their low-order 8 bits, it is up to the microassembler to assign them such addresses. On the other hand, since *L2* can be anywhere in the bottom 256 words of the control store, the microassembler has a lot of freedom in finding an available pair.

Normally, these two statements will be combined, for example,

    Z = TOS; if (Z) goto L1; else goto L2

The effect of this statement is that MAL generates a microinstruction in which TOS is run through the ALU (but not stored anywhere) so that its value sets the Z bit. Shortly after Z has been loaded from the ALU condition bit, it is ORed into the high-order bit of MPC, forcing the address of the next microinstruction to be fetched from either *L2* or *L1* (which must be exactly 256 more than *L2*). MPC will be stable and ready to use for fetching the next microinstruction.

Finally, we need a notation for using the JMPC bit. The one we will use is

    goto (MBR OR *value*)

This syntax tells the microassembler to use *value* for NEXT_ADDRESS and set the

JMPC bit so that MBR is ORed into MPC along with NEXT_ADDRESS. If *value* is 0, which is the normal case, it is sufficient to just write

> goto (MBR)

Note that only the low-order 8 bits of MBR are wired to MPC (see Fig. 4-6), so the issue of sign extension (i.e., MBR versus MBRU) does not arise here. Also note that the MBR available at the end of the current cycle is the one used. A fetch started in *this* microinstruction is too late to affect the choice of the next microinstruction.

4.3.2 Implementation of IJVM Using the Mic-1

We have finally reached the point where we can put all the pieces together. Figure 4-17 is the microprogram that runs on Mic-1 and interprets IJVM. It is a surprisingly short program—only 112 microinstructions total. Three columns are given for each microinstruction: the symbolic label, the actual microcode, and a comment. Note that consecutive microinstructions are not necessarily located in consecutive addresses in the control store, as we have already pointed out.

By now the choice of names for most of the registers in Fig. 4-1 should be obvious: CPP, LV, and SP are used to hold the pointers to the constant pool, local variables, and the top of the stack, respectively, while PC holds the address of the next byte to be fetched from the instruction stream. MBR is a 1-byte register that sequentially holds the bytes of the instruction stream as they come in from memory to be interpreted. TOS and OPC are extra registers. Their use is described below.

At certain times, each of these registers is guaranteed to hold a certain value, but each can be used as a temporary register if needed. At the beginning and end of each instruction, TOS contains the value of the memory location pointed to by SP, the top word on the stack. This value is redundant since it can always be read from memory, but having it in a register often saves a memory reference. For a few instructions maintaining TOS means *more* memory operations. For example, the POP instruction throws away the top word, and therefore must fetch the new top-of-stack word from the memory into TOS.

The OPC register is a temporary (i.e., scratch) register. It has no preassigned use. It is used, for example, to save the address of the opcode for a branch instruction while PC is incremented to access parameters. It is also used as a temporary register in the IJVM conditional branch instructions.

Like all interpreters, the microprogram of Fig. 4-17 has a main loop that fetches, decodes, and executes instructions from the program being interpreted, in this case, IJVM instructions. Its main loop begins on the line labeled Main1. It starts with the invariant that PC has previously been loaded with an address of a memory location containing an opcode. Furthermore, that opcode has already been fetched into MBR. Note this implies however, that when we get back to this location, we must ensure that PC has been updated to point to the next opcode to be interpreted and the opcode byte itself has already been fetched into MBR.

This initial instruction sequence is executed at the beginning of every instruction, so it is important that it be as short as possible. Through very careful design of the Mic-1 hardware and software, we have managed to reduce the main loop to a single microinstruction. Once the machine has started, every time this microinstruction is executed, the IJVM opcode to execute is already present in MBR. What the microinstruction does is branch to the microcode for executing this IJVM instruction and also begin fetching the byte following the opcode, which may be either an operand byte or the next opcode.

Now we can reveal the real reason each microinstruction explicitly names its successor, instead of having them be executed sequentially. All the control store addresses corresponding to opcodes must be reserved for the first word of the corresponding instruction interpreter. Thus from Fig. 4-11 we see that the code that interprets POP starts at 0x57 and the code that interprets DUP starts at 0x59. (How MAL knows to put POP at 0x57 is one of the mysteries of the universe—presumably there is a file somewhere that tells it.)

Unfortunately, the code for POP is three microinstructions long, so if placed in consecutive words, it would interfere with the start of DUP. Since all the control store addresses corresponding to opcodes are effectively reserved, the microinstructions other than the initial one in each sequence must be stuffed away in the holes between reserved addresses. For this reason, there is a great deal of jumping around, so having an explicit microbranch (a microinstruction that branches) every few microinstructions to hop from hole to hole would be very wasteful.

To see how the interpreter works, let us assume, for example, that MBR contains the value 0x60, that is, the opcode for IADD (see Fig. 4-11). In the one-microinstruction main loop we accomplish three things:

1. Increment the PC, leaving it containing the address of the first byte after the opcode.

2. Initiate a fetch of the next byte into MBR. This byte will always be needed sooner or later, either as an operand for the current IJVM instruction or as the next opcode (as in the case of the IADD instruction, which has no operand bytes).

3. Perform a multiway branch to the address contained in MBR at the start of Main1. This address is equal to the numerical value of the opcode currently being executed. It was placed there by the previous microinstruction. Note carefully that the value being fetched in this microinstruction does not play any role in the multiway branch.

The fetch of the next byte is started here so it will be available by the start of the third microinstruction. It may or may not be needed then, but it will be needed eventually, so starting the fetch now cannot do any harm in any case.

Label	Operations	Comments
Main1	PC = PC + 1; fetch; goto (MBR)	MBR holds opcode; get next byte; dispatch
nop1	goto Main1	Do nothing
iadd1	MAR = SP = SP − 1; rd	Read in next-to-top word on stack
iadd2	H = TOS	H = top of stack
iadd3	MDR = TOS = MDR + H; wr; goto Main1	Add top two words; write to top of stack
isub1	MAR = SP = SP − 1; rd	Read in next-to-top word on stack
isub2	H = TOS	H = top of stack
isub3	MDR = TOS = MDR − H; wr; goto Main1	Do subtraction; write to top of stack
iand1	MAR = SP = SP − 1; rd	Read in next-to-top word on stack
iand2	H = TOS	H = top of stack
iand3	MDR = TOS = MDR AND H; wr; goto Main1	Do AND; write to new top of stack
ior1	MAR = SP = SP − 1; rd	Read in next-to-top word on stack
ior2	H = TOS	H = top of stack
ior3	MDR = TOS = MDR OR H; wr; goto Main1	Do OR; write to new top of stack
dup1	MAR = SP = SP + 1	Increment SP and copy to MAR
dup2	MDR = TOS; wr; goto Main1	Write new stack word
pop1	MAR = SP = SP − 1; rd	Read in next-to-top word on stack
pop2		Wait for new TOS to be read from memory
pop3	TOS = MDR; goto Main1	Copy new word to TOS
swap1	MAR = SP − 1; rd	Set MAR to SP − 1; read 2nd word from stack
swap2	MAR = SP	Set MAR to top word
swap3	H = MDR; wr	Save TOS in H; write 2nd word to top of stack
swap4	MDR = TOS	Copy old TOS to MDR
swap5	MAR = SP − 1; wr	Set MAR to SP − 1; write as 2nd word on stack
swap6	TOS = H; goto Main1	Update TOS
bipush1	SP = MAR = SP + 1	MBR = the byte to push onto stack
bipush2	PC = PC + 1; fetch	Increment PC, fetch next opcode
bipush3	MDR = TOS = MBR; wr; goto Main1	Sign-extend constant and push on stack
iload1	H = LV	MBR contains index; copy LV to H
iload2	MAR = MBRU + H; rd	MAR = address of local variable to push
iload3	MAR = SP = SP + 1	SP points to new top of stack; prepare write
iload4	PC = PC + 1; fetch; wr	Inc PC; get next opcode; write top of stack
iload5	TOS = MDR; goto Main1	Update TOS
istore1	H = LV	MBR contains index; Copy LV to H
istore2	MAR = MBRU + H	MAR = address of local variable to store into
istore3	MDR = TOS; wr	Copy TOS to MDR; write word
istore4	SP = MAR = SP − 1; rd	Read in next-to-top word on stack
istore5	PC = PC + 1; fetch	Increment PC; fetch next opcode
istore6	TOS = MDR; goto Main1	Update TOS
wide1	PC = PC + 1; fetch;	Fetch operand byte or next opcode
wide2	goto (MBR OR 0x100)	Multiway branch with high bit set
wide_iload1	PC = PC + 1; fetch	MBR contains 1st index byte; fetch 2nd
wide_iload2	H = MBRU << 8	H = 1st index byte shifted left 8 bits
wide_iload3	H = MBRU OR H	H = 16-bit index of local variable
wide_iload4	MAR = LV + H; rd; goto iload3	MAR = address of local variable to push
wide_istore1	PC = PC + 1; fetch	MBR contains 1st index byte; fetch 2nd
wide_istore2	H = MBRU << 8	H = 1st index byte shifted left 8 bits
wide_istore3	H = MBRU OR H	H = 16-bit index of local variable
wide_istore4	MAR = LV + H; goto istore3	MAR = address of local variable to store into
ldc_w1	PC = PC + 1; fetch	MBR contains 1st index byte; fetch 2nd
ldc_w2	H = MBRU << 8	H = 1st index byte << 8
ldc_w3	H = MBRU OR H	H = 16-bit index into constant pool
ldc_w4	MAR = H + CPP; rd; goto iload3	MAR = address of constant in pool

Label	Operations	Comments
iinc1	H = LV	MBR contains index; Copy LV to H
iinc2	MAR = MBRU + H; rd	Copy LV + index to MAR; Read variable
iinc3	PC = PC + 1; fetch	Fetch constant
iinc4	H = MDR	Copy variable to H
iinc5	PC = PC + 1; fetch	Fetch next opcode
iinc6	MDR = MBR + H; wr; goto Main1	Put sum in MDR; update variable
goto1	OPC = PC − 1	Save address of opcode.
goto2	PC = PC + 1; fetch	MBR = 1st byte of offset; fetch 2nd byte
goto3	H = MBR << 8	Shift and save signed first byte in H
goto4	H = MBRU OR H	H = 16-bit branch offset
goto5	PC = OPC + H; fetch	Add offset to OPC
goto6	goto Main1	Wait for fetch of next opcode
iflt1	MAR = SP = SP − 1; rd	Read in next-to-top word on stack
iflt2	OPC = TOS	Save TOS in OPC temporarily
iflt3	TOS = MDR	Put new top of stack in TOS
iflt4	N = OPC; if (N) goto T; else goto F	Branch on N bit
ifeq1	MAR = SP = SP − 1; rd	Read in next-to-top word of stack
ifeq2	OPC = TOS	Save TOS in OPC temporarily
ifeq3	TOS = MDR	Put new top of stack in TOS
ifeq4	Z = OPC; if (Z) goto T; else goto F	Branch on Z bit
if_icmpeq1	MAR = SP = SP − 1; rd	Read in next-to-top word of stack
if_icmpeq2	MAR = SP = SP − 1	Set MAR to read in new top-of-stack
if_icmpeq3	H = MDR; rd	Copy second stack word to H
if_icmpeq4	OPC = TOS	Save TOS in OPC temporarily
if_icmpeq5	TOS = MDR	Put new top of stack in TOS
if_icmpeq6	Z = OPC − H; if (Z) goto T; else goto F	If top 2 words are equal, goto T, else goto F
T	OPC = PC − 1; goto goto2	Same as goto1; needed for target address
F	PC = PC + 1	Skip first offset byte
F2	PC = PC + 1; fetch	PC now points to next opcode
F3	goto Main1	Wait for fetch of opcode
invokevirtual1	PC = PC + 1; fetch	MBR = index byte 1; inc. PC, get 2nd byte
invokevirtual2	H = MBRU << 8	Shift and save first byte in H
invokevirtual3	H = MBRU OR H	H = offset of method pointer from CPP
invokevirtual4	MAR = CPP + H; rd	Get pointer to method from CPP area
invokevirtual5	OPC = PC + 1	Save Return PC in OPC temporarily
invokevirtual6	PC = MDR; fetch	PC points to new method; get param count
invokevirtual7	PC = PC + 1; fetch	Fetch 2nd byte of parameter count
invokevirtual8	H = MBRU << 8	Shift and save first byte in H
invokevirtual9	H = MBRU OR H	H = number of parameters
invokevirtual10	PC = PC + 1; fetch	Fetch first byte of # locals
invokevirtual11	TOS = SP − H	TOS = address of OBJREF − 1
invokevirtual12	TOS = MAR = TOS + 1	TOS = address of OBJREF (new LV)
invokevirtual13	PC = PC + 1; fetch	Fetch second byte of # locals
invokevirtual14	H = MBRU << 8	Shift and save first byte in H
invokevirtual15	H = MBRU OR H	H = # locals
invokevirtual16	MDR = SP + H + 1; wr	Overwrite OBJREF with link pointer
invokevirtual17	MAR = SP = MDR;	Set SP, MAR to location to hold old PC
invokevirtual18	MDR = OPC; wr	Save old PC above the local variables
invokevirtual19	MAR = SP = SP + 1	SP points to location to hold old LV
invokevirtual20	MDR = LV; wr	Save old LV above saved PC
invokevirtual21	PC = PC + 1; fetch	Fetch first opcode of new method.
invokevirtual22	LV = TOS; goto Main1	Set LV to point to LV Frame

Figure 4-17. The microprogram for the Mic-1 (part 1 on facing page, part 2 above).

Label	Operations	Comments
ireturn1	MAR = SP = LV; rd	Reset SP, MAR to get link pointer
ireturn2		Wait for read
ireturn3	LV = MAR = MDR; rd	Set LV to link ptr; get old PC
ireturn4	MAR = LV + 1	Set MAR to read old LV
ireturn5	PC = MDR; rd; fetch	Restore PC; fetch next opcode
ireturn6	MAR = SP	Set MAR to write TOS
ireturn7	LV = MDR	Restore LV
ireturn8	MDR = TOS; wr; goto Main1	Save return value on original top of stack

Figure 4-17. The microprogram for the Mic-1 (part 3 of 3).

If the byte in MBR happens to be all zeros, the opcode for a NOP instruction, the next microinstruction is the one labeled nop1, fetched from location 0. Since this instruction does nothing, it simply branches back to the beginning of the main loop, where the sequence is repeated, but with a new opcode having been fetched into MBR.

Once again we emphasize that the microinstructions in Fig. 4-17 are not consecutive in memory and that Main1 is not at control store address 0 (because nop1 must be at address 0). It is up to the microassembler to place each microinstruction at a suitable address and link them together in short sequences using the NEXT_ADDRESS field. Each sequence starts at the address corresponding to the numerical value of the IJVM opcode it interprets (e.g., POP starts at 0x57), but the rest of the sequence can be anywhere in the control store, and not necessarily at consecutive addresses.

Now consider the IJVM IADD instruction. The microinstruction branched to by the main loop is the one labeled iadd1. This instruction starts the work specific to IADD:

1. The TOS is already present, but the next-to-top word of the stack must be fetched from memory.

2. The TOS must be added to the next-to-top word fetched from memory.

3. The result, which is to be pushed on the stack, must be stored back into memory, as well as stored in the TOS register.

In order to fetch the operand from memory, it is necessary to decrement the stack pointer and write it into MAR. Note that, conveniently, this address is also the address that will be used for the subsequent write. Furthermore, since this location will be the new top of stack, SP should be assigned this value. Therefore, a single operation can determine the new value of SP and MAR, decrement SP, and write it into both registers.

These things are accomplished in the first cycle, iadd1, and the read operation is initiated. In addition, MPC gets the value from iadd1's NEXT_ADDRESS field, which is the address of iadd2, wherever it may be. Then iadd2 is read from the control store. During the second cycle, while waiting for the operand to be read in from memory, we copy the top word of the stack from TOS into H, where it will be available for the addition when the read completes.

At the beginning of the third cycle, iadd3, MDR contains the addend fetched from memory. In this cycle it is added to the contents of H, and the result is stored back to MDR, as well as back into TOS. A write operation is also initiated, storing the new top-of-stack word back into memory. In this cycle the goto has the effect of assigning the address of Main1 to MPC, returning us to the starting point for the execution of the next instruction.

If the subsequent IJVM opcode, now contained in MBR, is 0x64 (ISUB), almost exactly the same sequence of events occurs again. After Main1 is executed, control is transferred to the microinstruction at 0x64 (isub1). This microinstruction is followed by isub2 and isub3, and then Main1 again. The only difference between this sequence and the previous one is that in isub3, the contents of H are subtracted from MDR rather than added to it.

The interpretation of IAND is almost identical to IADD and ISUB, except that the two top words of the stack are bitwise ANDed together instead of being added or subtracted. Something similar happens for IOR.

If the IJVC opcode is DUP, POP, or SWAP, the stack must be adjusted. The DUP instruction simply replicates the top word of the stack. Since value of this word is already stored in TOS, the operation is as simple as incrementing SP to point to the new location, and storing TOS to that location. The POP instruction is almost as simple, just decrementing SP to discard the top word on the stack. However, in order to maintain the top word in TOS it is now necessary to read the new top word in from memory and write it into TOS. Finally, the SWAP instruction involves swapping the values in two memory locations: the top two words on the stack. This is made somewhat easier by the fact that TOS already contains one of those values, so it need not be read from memory. This instruction will be discussed in more detail later.

The BIPUSH instruction is a little more complicated because the opcode is followed by a single byte, as shown in Fig. 4-18. The byte is to be interpreted as a signed integer. This byte, which has already been fetched into MBR in Main1, must be sign-extended to 32 bits and pushed onto the top of the stack. This sequence, therefore, must sign-extend the byte in MBR to 32 bits, and copy it to MDR. Finally, SP is incremented and copied to MAR, permitting the operand to be written out to the top of stack. Along the way, this operand must also be copied to TOS. Also, before returning to the main program, note that PC must be incremented so that the next opcode will be available in Main1.

BIPUSH (0x10)	BYTE

Figure 4-18. The BIPUSH instruction format.

Next consider the ILOAD instruction. ILOAD also has a byte following the opcode, as shown in Fig. 4-19(a), but this byte is an (unsigned) index to identify the word in the local variable space that is to be pushed onto the stack. Since there is only 1 byte, only 2^8=256 words can be distinguished, namely, the first 256 words in the local variable space. The ILOAD instruction requires both a read (to obtain the word) and a write (to push it onto the top of the stack). In order to determine the address for reading, however, the offset, contained in MBR, must be added to the contents of LV. Since both MBR and LV can only be accessed through the B bus, LV is first copied into H (in iload1), then MBR is added. The result of this addition is copied into MAR and a read initiated (in iload2).

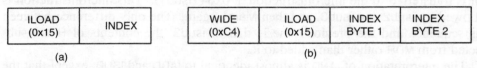

Figure 4-19. (a) ILOAD with a 1-byte index. (b) WIDE ILOAD with a 2-byte index.

However, the use of MBR for an index is slightly different than in BIPUSH, where it was sign-extended. In the case of an index, the offset is always positive, so the byte offset must be interpreted as an unsigned integer, unlike in BIPUSH, where it was interpreted as a signed 8-bit integer. The interface from MBR to the B bus is carefully designed to make both operations possible. In the case of BIPUSH (signed 8-bit integer), the proper operation is sign-extension, that is, the leftmost bit in the 1-byte MBR is copied into the upper 24 bits on the B bus. In the case of ILOAD (unsigned 8-bit integer), the proper operation is zero-fill. Here the upper 24 bits of the B bus are simply supplied with zeros. These two operations are distinguished by separate signals indicating which operation should be performed (see Fig. 4-6). In the microcode, this is indicated by MBR (sign-extended, as in BIPUSH 3) or MBRU (unsigned, as in iload2).

While waiting for memory to supply the operand (in iload3), SP is incremented to contain the value for storing the result, the new top of stack. This value is also copied to MAR in preparation for writing the operand out to the top of stack. PC again must be incremented to fetch the next opcode (in iload4). Finally, MDR is copied to TOS to reflect the new top of stack (in iload5).

ISTORE is the inverse operation of ILOAD, that is, a word is removed from the top of the stack and stored at the location specified by the sum of LV and the index contained in the instruction. It uses the same format as ILOAD, shown in Fig. 4-19(a), except with opcode 0x36 instead of opcode 0x15. This instruction is somewhat different than might be expected because the top word on the stack is already known (in TOS), so it can be stored away immediately. However, the new top of stack word must be fetched. So both a read and a write are required, but they can be performed in any order (or even in parallel, if that were possible).

Both ILOAD and ISTORE are restricted in that they can only access the first 256 local variables. While for most programs this may be all the local variable space needed, it is, of course, necessary to be able to access a variable wherever it is located in the local variable space. To achieve this, IJVM uses the same mechanism employed in JVM to achieve this: a special opcode WIDE, known as a **prefix byte**, followed by the ILOAD or ISTORE opcode. When this sequence occurs, the definitions of ILOAD and ISTORE are modified, with a 16-bit index following the opcode rather than an 8-bit index, as shown in Fig. 4-19(b).

WIDE is decoded in the usual way, leading to a branch to wide1 which handles the WIDE opcode. Although the opcode to widen is already available in MBR, wide1 fetches the first byte after the opcode, because the microprogram logic always expects that to be there. Then a second multiway branch is done in wide2 this time using the byte following WIDE for dispatching. However, since WIDE ILOAD requires different microcode than ILOAD, and WIDE ISTORE requires different microcode than ISTORE, etc., the second multiway branch cannot just use the opcode as the target address, the way Main1 does.

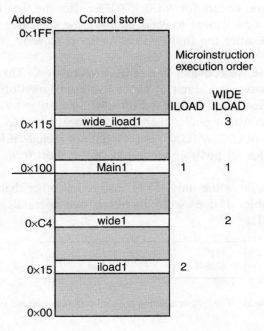

Figure 4-20. The initial microinstruction sequence for ILOAD and WIDE ILOAD. The addresses are examples.

Instead, wide2 ORs 0x100 with the opcode while putting it into MPC. As a result, the interpretation of WIDE ILOAD starts at 0x115 (instead of 0x15), the interpretation of WIDE ISTORE starts at 0x136 (instead of 0x36), and so on. In this way, every WIDE opcode starts at an address 256 (i.e., 0x100) words higher in the control store higher than the corresponding regular opcode. The initial sequence of microinstructions for both ILOAD and WIDE ILOAD is shown in Fig. 4-20.

Once the code is reached for implementing WIDE ILOAD (0x115), the code differs from normal ILOAD only in that the index must be constructed by concatenating 2 index bytes instead of simply sign-extending a single byte. The concatenation and subsequent addition must be accomplished in stages, first copying INDEX BYTE 1 into H shifted left by 8 bits. Since the index is an unsigned integer, MBR is zero-extended using MBRU. Now the second byte of the index is added (the addition operation is identical to concatenation since the low-order byte of H is now zero, guaranteeing that there will be no carry between the bytes), with the result again stored in H. From here on, the operation can proceed exactly as if it were a standard ILOAD. Rather than duplicate the final instructions of ILOAD (iload3 to iload5), we simply branch from wide_iload4 to iload3. Note, however, that PC must be incremented twice during the execution of the instruction in order to leave it pointing to the next opcode. The ILOAD instruction increments it once; the WIDE_ILOAD sequence also increments it once.

The same situation occurs for WIDE_ISTORE: after the first four microinstructions are executed (wide_istore1 to wide_istore4), the sequence is the same as the sequence for ISTORE after the first two instructions, so wide_istore4 branches to istore3.

The next example we consider is a LDC_W instruction. This opcode is different from ILOAD in two ways. First, it has a 16-bit unsigned offset (like the wide version of ILOAD). Second, it is indexed off CPP rather than LV, since its function is to read from the constant pool rather than the local variable frame. (Actually, there is a short form of LDC_W (LDC), but we did not include it in IJVM, since the long form incorporates all possible variations of the short form, but takes 3 bytes instead of 2.)

The IINC instruction is the only IJVM instruction other than ISTORE that can modify a local variable. It does so by including two operands, each 1 byte long, as shown in Fig. 4-21.

IINC (0x84)	INDEX	CONST

Figure 4-21. The IINC instruction has two different operand fields.

The IINC instruction uses INDEX to specify the offset from the beginning of the local variable frame. It reads that variable, incrementing it by CONST, a value contained in the instruction, and stores it back in the same location. Note that this instruction can increment by a negative amount, that is, CONST is a signed 8-bit constant, in the range −128 to +127. The full JVM includes a wide version of IINC where each operand is 2 bytes long.

We now come to the first IJVM branch instruction: GOTO. The sole function of this instruction is to change the value of PC, so that the next IJVM instruction executed is the one at the address computed by adding the (signed) 16-bit offset to the address of the branch opcode. A complication here is that the offset is relative to the value that PC had at the start of the instruction decoding, not the value it has after the 2 offset bytes have been fetched.

To make this point clear, in Fig. 4-22(a) we see the situation at the start of Main1. The opcode is already in MBR, but PC has not yet been incremented. In Fig. 4-22(b) we see the situation at the start of goto1. By now PC has been incremented but the first offset byte has not yet been fetched into MBR. One microinstruction later, we have Fig. 4-22(c), in which the old PC, which points to the opcode, has been saved in OPC and the first offset byte is in MBR. This value is needed because the offset of the IJVM GOTO instruction is relative to it, not to the current value of PC. In fact, this is the reason we needed the OPC register in the first place.

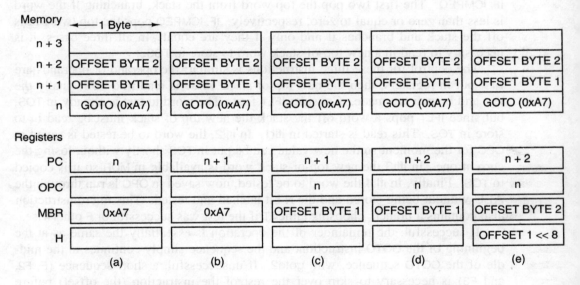

Figure 4-22. The situation at the start of various microinstructions. (a) Main1.
(b) goto1. (c) goto2. (d) goto3. (e) goto4.

The microinstruction at goto2 starts the fetch of the second offset byte, leading to Fig. 4-22(d) at the start of goto3. After the first offset byte has been shifted left 8 bits and copied to H, we arrive at goto4 and Fig. 4-22(e). Now we have the first offset byte shifted left in H, the second offset byte in MBR, and the base in OPC. By constructing the full 16-bit offset in H and then adding it to the base, we get the new address to put in PC, in goto5. Note carefully that we use MBRU in goto4 instead of MBR because we do not want sign extension of the second byte. The 16-bit offset is constructed, in fact, by ORing the two halves together. Finally, we have to fetch the next opcode before going back to Main1 because the code there expects the next opcode in MBR. The last cycle, goto6, is necessary because the memory data must be fetched in time to appear in MBR during Main1.

The offsets used in the goto IJVM instruction are signed 16-bit values, with a minimum of −32768 and a maximum of +32767. This means that branches either way to labels more distant than these values are not possible. This property can be regarded as either a bug or a feature in IJVM (and also in JVM). The bug-camp would say that the JVM definition should not restrict their programming style. The feature-camp would say that the work of many programmers would be radically improved if they had nightmares about the dreaded compiler message

Program is too big and hairy. You must rewrite it. Compilation aborted.

Unfortunately (in our view) this message only appears when a then or else clause exceeds 32 KB, typically at least 50 pages of Java.

Now consider the three IJVM conditional branch instructions: IFLT, IFEQ, and IF_ICMPEQ. The first two pop the top word from the stack, branching if the word is less than zero or equal to zero, respectively. IF_ICMPEQ pops the top two words off the stack and branches if and only if they are equal. In all three cases, it is necessary to read in a new top-of-stack word to store in TOS.

The control for these three instructions is similar: the operand or operands are first put in registers, then the new top-of-stack value is read into TOS, finally the test and branch are made. Consider IFLT first. The word to test is already in TOS, but since IFLT pops a word off the stack the new top of stack must be read in to store in TOS. This read is started in iflt1. In iflt2, the word to be tested is saved in OPC for the moment so the new value can be put in TOS shortly without losing the current one. In iflt3 the new top-of-stack word is available in MDR so it is copied to TOS. Finally, in iflt4 the word to be tested, now saved in OPC is run through the ALU without being stored and the N bit latched and tested. This microinstruction also contains a branch, choosing either T if the test was successful or F otherwise.

If successful, the remainder of the operation is essentially the same as at the beginning of the GOTO instruction, and the sequence simply continues in the middle of the GOTO sequence, with goto2. If unsuccessful, a short sequence (F, F2, and F3) is necessary to skip over the rest of the instruction (the offset) before returning to Main1 to continue with the next instruction.

The code in ifeq2 and ifeq3 follows the same logic, only using the Z bit instead of the N bit. In both cases, it is up to the assembler for MAL to recognize that the addresses T and F are special and to make sure that their addresses are placed at control store addresses that differ only in the leftmost bit.

The logic for IF_ICMPEQ is roughly similar to IFEQ except that here we need to read in the second operand as well. The second operand is stored in H in if_icmpeq3, where the read of the new top-of-stack word is started. Again the current top-of-stack word is saved in OPC and the new one installed in TOS. Finally, the test in if_icmpeq6 is similar to ifeq4.

Now, we consider the implementation of INVOKEVIRTUAL and IRETURN, the instructions for invoking a procedure call and return, as described in Sec. 4.2.3. INVOKEVIRTUAL is a sequence of 22 microinstructions, and is the most complex

IJVM instruction implemented. Its operation was shown in Fig 4-12. The instruction uses its 16-bit offset to determine the address of the method to be invoked. In our implementation, the offset is simply an offset into the Constant Pool. This location in the Constant Pool points to the method to be invoked. Remember, however, that the first 4 bytes of each method are *not* instructions. Instead they are two 16-bit pointers. The first one gives the number of parameter words (including OBJREF—see Fig. 4-12). The second one gives the size of the local variable area in words. These fields are fetched through the 8-bit port and assembled just as if they were two 16-bit offsets within an instruction.

Then, the linkage information necessary to restore the machine to its previous state—the address of the start of the old local variable area and the old PC—is stored immediately above the newly-created local variable area and below the new stack. Finally, the opcode of the next instruction is fetched and PC is incremented before returning to Main1 to begin the next instruction.

IRETURN is a simple instruction containing no operands. It simply uses the address stored in the first word of the local variable area to retrieve the linkage information. Then it restores SP, LV, and PC to their previous values and copies the return value from the top of the current stack onto the top of the original stack, as shown in Fig 4-13.

4.4 DESIGN OF THE MICROARCHITECTURE LEVEL

Like just about everything else in computer science, the design of the microarchitecture level is full of trade-offs. Computers have many desirable characteristics, including speed, cost, reliability, ease of use, energy requirements, and physical size. However, one trade-off drives the most important choices the CPU designer must make: speed versus cost. In this section we will look at this issue in detail to see what can be traded off against what, how high performance can be achieved, and at what price in hardware and complexity.

4.4.1 Speed versus Cost

While faster technology has resulted in the greatest speedup over any period of time, that is beyond the scope of this text. Speed improvements due to organization, while less amazing than that due to faster circuits, have nevertheless been impressive. Speed can be measured in a variety of ways, but given a circuit technology and an ISA, there are three basic approaches for increasing the speed of execution:

1. Reduce the number of clock cycles needed to execute an instruction.

2. Simplify the organization so that the clock cycle can be shorter.

3. Overlap the execution of instructions.

The first two are obvious, but there is a surprising variety of design opportunities that can dramatically affect either the number of clock cycles, the clock period, or—most often—both. In this section, we will give an example of how the encoding and decoding of an operation can affect the clock cycle.

The number of clock cycles needed to execute a set of operations is known as the **path length**. Sometimes the path length can be shortened by adding specialized hardware. For example, by adding an incrementer (conceptually, an adder with one side permanently wired to add 1) to PC, we no longer have to use the ALU to advance PC, eliminating cycles. The price paid is more hardware. However, this capability does not help as much as might be expected. For most instructions, the cycles consumed incrementing the PC are also cycles where a read operation is being performed. The following instruction could not be executed earlier anyway because it depends on the data coming from the memory.

Reducing the number of instruction cycles necessary for fetching instructions requires more than just an additional circuit to increment the PC. In order to speed up the instruction fetching to any significant degree, the third technique—overlapping the execution of instructions—must be exploited. Separating out the circuitry for fetching the instructions—the 8-bit memory port, and the MBR and PC registers— is most effective if the unit is made functionally independent of the main data path. In this way, it can fetch the next opcode or operand on its own, perhaps even performing asynchronously with respect to the rest of the CPU and fetching one or more instructions ahead.

One of the most time-consuming phases of the execution of many instructions is fetching a 2-byte offset, extending it appropriately, and accumulating it in the H register in preparation for an addition, for example, in a branch to PC $\pm n$ bytes. One potential solution—making the memory port 16 bits wide—greatly complicates the operation, because the memory is actually 32 bits wide. The 16 bits needed might span word boundaries, so that even a single read of 32 bits will not necessarily fetch both bytes needed.

Overlapping the execution of instructions is by far the most interesting and offers the most opportunity for dramatic increases in speed. Simple overlap of instruction fetch and execution is surprisingly effective. More sophisticated techniques go much further, however, overlapping execution of many instructions. In fact this idea is at the heart of modern computer design. We will discuss some of the basic techniques for overlapping instruction execution below and motivate some of the more sophisticated ones.

Speed is half the picture; cost is the other half. Cost can also be measured in a variety of ways, but a precise definition of cost is problematic. Some measures are as simple as a count of the number of components. This was particularly true in the days when processors were built of discrete components that were purchased and assembled. Today, the entire processor exists on a single chip, but bigger, more complex chips are much more expensive than smaller, simpler ones. Individual components—for example, transistors, gates, or functional units—can be counted, but often the count is not as important as the amount of area required on the integrated circuit. The more area required for the functions included, the larger the chip. And the manufacturing cost of the chip grows much faster than its area. For this reason, designers often speak of cost in terms of "real estate," that is, the area required for a circuit (presumably measured in pico-acres).

One of the most thoroughly studied circuits in history is the binary adder. There have been thousands of designs, and the fastest ones are much quicker than the slowest ones. They are also far more complex. The system designer has to decide whether the greater speed is worth the real estate.

Adders are not the only component with many choices. Nearly every component in the system can be designed to run faster or slower, with a cost differential. The challenge to the designer is to identify the components in the system that can improve the system the most by speeding them up. Interestingly enough, many an individual component can be replaced with a much faster component with little or no effect on speed. In the following sections we will look at some of the design issues and the corresponding trade-offs.

One of the key factors in determining how fast the clock can run is the amount of work that must be done on each clock cycle. Obviously, the more work to be done, the longer the clock cycle. It's not quite that simple, of course, because the hardware is quite good at doing things in parallel, so it's actually the sequence of operations that must be performed *serially* in a single clock cycle that determines how long the clock cycle must be.

One aspect that can be controlled is the amount of decoding that must be performed. Recall, for example, that in Fig. 4-6 we saw that while any of nine registers could be read into the ALU from the B bus, we required only 4 bits in the microinstruction word to specify which register was to be selected. Unfortunately, these savings come at a price. The decode circuit adds delay in the critical path. It means that whichever register is to enable its data onto the B bus will receive that command slightly later and will get its data on the bus slightly later. This effect cascades, with the ALU receiving its inputs a little later and producing its results a little later. Finally, the result is available on the C bus to be written to the registers a little later. Since this delay often is the factor that determines how long the clock cycle must be, this may mean that the clock cannot run quite as fast, and the entire computer must run a little slower. Thus there is a trade-off between speed and cost. Reducing the control store by 5 bits per word comes at the cost of slowing down the clock. The design engineer must take the design objectives into account when deciding which is the right choice. For a high-performance implementation, using a decoder is probably not a good idea; for a low-cost one, it might be.

4.4.2 Reducing the Execution Path Length

The Mic-1 was designed to be both moderately simple and moderately fast although there is admittedly an enormous tension between these two goals. Briefly stated, simple machines are not fast and fast machines are not simple. The Mic-1 CPU also uses a minimum amount of hardware: 10 registers, the simple

ALU of Fig. 3-19 replicated 32 times, a shifter, a decoder, a control store, and a bit of glue here and there. The whole system could be built with fewer than 5000 transistors plus whatever control store (ROM) and the main memory (RAM) take.

Having seen how IJVM can be implemented in a straightforward way in microcode with little hardware, it is now time to look at alternative, faster implementations. We will next look at ways to reduce the number of microinstructions per ISA instruction (i.e., reducing the execution path length). After that, we will consider other approaches.

Merging the Interpreter Loop with the Microcode

In the Mic-1, the main loop consists of one microinstruction that must be executed at the beginning of every IJVM instruction. In some cases it is possible to overlap it with the previous instruction. In fact, this has already been partially accomplished. Notice that when Main1 is executed, the opcode to be interpreted is already in MBR. The opcode is there because it was either fetched by the previous main loop (if the previous instruction had no operands), or during the execution of the previous instruction.

This concept of overlapping the beginning of the instruction can be carried further, and in fact, the main loop can in some cases be reduced to nothing. This can occur in the following way. Consider each sequence of microinstructions that terminates by branching to Main1. At each of these places, the main loop microinstruction can be tacked on to the end of the sequence (rather than at the beginning of the following sequence), with the multiway branch now replicated many places (but always with the same set of targets). In some cases the Main1 microinstruction can be merged with previous microinstructions, since those instructions are not always fully utilized.

In Fig. 4-23, the dynamic sequence of instructions is shown for a POP instruction. The main loop occurs before and after every instruction; in the figure we show only the occurrence after the POP instruction. Notice that the execution of this instruction takes four clock cycles: three for the specific microinstructions for POP and one for the main loop.

Label	Operations	Comments
pop1	MAR = SP = SP − 1; rd	Read in next-to-top word on stack
pop2		Wait for new TOS to be read from memory
pop3	TOS = MDR; goto Main1	Copy new word to TOS
Main1	PC = PC + 1; fetch; goto (MBR)	MBR holds opcode; get next byte; dispatch

Figure 4-23. Original microprogram sequence for executing POP.

In Fig. 4-24 the sequence has been reduced to three instructions by merging the main loop instructions, taking advantage of a clock cycle when the ALU is not used in pop2 to save a cycle and again in Main1. Be sure to note that the end of this sequence branches directly to the specific code for the subsequent instruction, so only three cycles are required total. This little trick reduces the execution time of the next microinstruction by one cycle, so for example, a subsequent IADD goes from four cycles to three. It is thus equivalent to speeding up the clock from 250 MHz (4 nsec microinstructions) to 333 MHz (3 nsec microinstructions) for free.

Label	Operations	Comments
pop1	MAR = SP = SP − 1; rd	Read in next-to-top word on stack
Main1.pop	PC = PC + 1; fetch	MBR holds opcode; fetch next byte
pop3	TOS = MDR; goto (MBR)	Copy new word to TOS; dispatch on opcode

Figure 4-24. Enhanced microprogram sequence for executing POP.

The POP instruction is particularly well suited for this treatment, because it has a dead cycle in the middle that does not use the ALU. The main loop, however, does use the ALU. Thus to reduce the instruction length by one within an instruction requires finding a cycle in the instruction where the ALU is not in use. Such dead cycles are not common, but they do occur, so merging Main1 into the end of each microinstruction sequence is worth doing. All it costs is a little control store. Thus we have our first technique for reducing path length:

Merge the interpreter loop into the end of each microcode sequence.

A Three-Bus Architecture

What else can we do to reduce execution path length? Another easy fix is to have two full input buses to the ALU, an A bus and a B bus, giving three buses in all. All (or at least most) of the registers should have access to both input buses. The advantage of having two input buses is that it then becomes possible to add any register to any other register in one cycle. To see the value of this feature, consider the Mic-1 implementation of ILOAD, shown again in Fig. 4-25.

Label	Operations	Comments
iload1	H = LV	MBR contains index; Copy LV to H
iload2	MAR = MBRU + H; rd	MAR = address of local variable to push
iload3	MAR = SP = SP + 1	SP points to new top of stack; prepare write
iload4	PC = PC + 1; fetch; wr	Inc PC; get next opcode; write top of stack
iload5	TOS = MDR; goto Main1	Update TOS
Main1	PC = PC + 1; fetch; goto (MBR)	MBR holds opcode; get next byte; dispatch

Figure 4-25. Mic-1 code for executing ILOAD.

We see here that in iload1 LV is copied into H. The only reason it is copied into H is so it can be added to MBRU in iload2. In our original two-bus design, there is no way to add two arbitrary registers, so one of them first has to be copied to H. With our new three-bus design, we can save a cycle, as shown in Fig. 4-26. We have added the interpreter loop to ILOAD here, but doing so neither increases nor decreases the execution path length. Still, the additional bus has reduced the total execution time of ILOAD from six cycles to five cycles. Now we have our second technique for reducing path length:

Go from a two-bus design to a three-bus design.

Label	Operations	Comments
iload1	MAR = MBRU + LV; rd	MAR = address of local variable to push
iload2	MAR = SP = SP + 1	SP points to new top of stack; prepare write
iload3	PC = PC + 1; fetch; wr	Inc PC; get next opcode; write top of stack
iload4	TOS = MDR	Update TOS
iload5	PC = PC + 1; fetch; goto (MBR)	MBR already holds opcode; fetch index byte

Figure 4-26. Three-bus code for executing ILOAD.

An Instruction Fetch Unit

Both of these techniques are worth using, but to get a dramatic improvement we need something much more radical. Let us step back and look at the common parts of every instruction: the fetching and decoding of the fields of the instruction. Notice that for every instruction the following operations may occur:

1. The PC is passed through the ALU and incremented.

2. The PC is used to fetch the next byte in the instruction stream.

3. Operands are read from memory.

4. Operands are written to memory.

5. The ALU does a computation and the results are stored back.

If an instruction has additional fields (for operands), each field must be explicitly fetched, 1 byte at a time, and assembled before it can be used. Fetching and assembling a field ties up the ALU for at least one cycle per byte to increment the PC, and then again to assemble the resulting index or offset. The ALU is used nearly every cycle for a variety of operations having to do with fetching the instruction and assembling the fields within the instruction, in addition to the real "work" of the instruction.

In order to overlap the main loop, it is necessary to free up the ALU from some of these tasks. This might be done by introducing a second ALU, though a full ALU is not necessary for much of the activity. Notice that in many cases the ALU is simply used as a path to copy a value from one register to another. These cycles might be eliminated by introducing additional data paths not going through the ALU. Some benefit may be derived, for example, by creating a path from TOS to MDR, or from MDR to TOS, since the top word of stack is frequently copied between those two registers.

In the Mic-1, much of the load can be removed from the ALU by creating an independent unit to fetch and process the instructions. This unit, called an **IFU** (**Instruction Fetch Unit**), can independently increment PC and fetch bytes from the byte stream before they are needed. This unit requires only an incrementer, a circuit far simpler than a full adder. Carrying this idea further, the IFU can also assemble 8- and 16-bit operands so that they are ready for immediate use whenever needed. There are at least two ways this can be accomplished:

1. The IFU can actually interpret each opcode, determining how many additional fields must be fetched, and assemble them into a register ready for use by the main execution unit.

2. The IFU can take advantage of the stream nature of the instructions, and make available at all times the next 8- and 16-bit pieces whether or not doing so makes any sense. The main execution unit can then ask for whatever it needs.

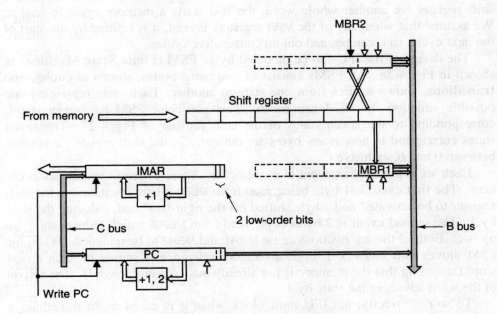

Figure 4-27. A fetch unit for the Mic-1.

We show the rudiments of the second scheme in Fig. 4-27. Rather than a single 8-bit MBR, there are now two MBRs: the 8-bit MBR1 and the 16-bit MBR2. The IFU keeps track of the most recent byte or bytes consumed by the main execution unit.

It also makes available in MBR1 the next byte, just as in the Mic-1, except that it automatically senses when the MBR1 is read, prefetches the next byte, and loads it into MBR1 immediately. As in the Mic-1, it has two interfaces to the B bus: MBR1 and MBR1U. The former is sign-extended to 32 bits; the latter is zero-extended.

Similarly, MBR2 provides the same functionality but holds the next 2 bytes. It also has two interfaces to the B bus: MBR2 and MBR2U, gating the 32-bit sign-extended and zero-extended values, respectively.

The IFU is responsible for fetching a stream of bytes. It does this by using a conventional 4-byte memory port, fetching entire 4-byte words ahead of time and loading the consecutive bytes into a shift register that supplies them one or two at a time, in the order fetched. The function of the shift register is to maintain a queue of bytes from memory, to feed MBR1 and MBR2.

At all times, MBR1 holds the oldest byte in the shift register and MBR2 holds the oldest 2 bytes (oldest byte on the left), to form a 16-bit integer [see Fig. 4-19(b)]. The 2 bytes in MBR2 may be from different memory words, because IJVM instructions do not align on word boundaries in memory.

Whenever MBR1 is read, the shift register shifts right 1 byte. Whenever MBR2 is read, it shifts right 2 bytes. Then MBR1 and MBR2 are reloaded from the oldest byte and pair of bytes, respectively. If there is now sufficient room left in the shift register for another whole word, the IFU starts a memory cycle to read it. We assume that when any of the MBR registers is read, it is refilled by the start of the next cycle, so it can be read out on consecutive cycles.

The design of the IFU can be modeled by an **FSM (Finite State Machine)** as shown in Fig. 4-28. All FSMs consist of two parts: **states**, shown as circles, and **transitions**, shown as arcs from one state to another. Each state represents one possible situation the FSM can be in. This particular FSM has seven states, corresponding to the seven states of the shift register of Fig. 4-27. The seven states correspond to how many bytes are currently in the shift register, a number between 0 and 6, inclusive.

Each arc represents an event that can occur. Three different events can occur here. The first event is 1 byte being read from MBR1. This event causes the shift register to be activated and 1 byte shifted off the right-hand end, reducing the state by 1. The second event is 2 bytes being read from MBR2, which reduces the state by two. Both of these transitions cause MBR1 and MBR2 to be reloaded. When the FSM moves into states 0, 1, or 2, a memory reference is started to fetch a new word (assuming that the memory is not already busy reading a word). The arrival of the word advances the state by 4.

To work correctly, the IFU must block when it is asked to do something it cannot do, such as supply the value of MBR2 when there is only 1 byte in the shift register and the memory is still busy fetching a new word. Also, it can do only one thing at a time, so incoming events must be serialized. Finally, whenever PC is changed, the IFU must be updated. Such details make it more complicated than we have shown. Still, many hardware devices are constructed as FSMs.

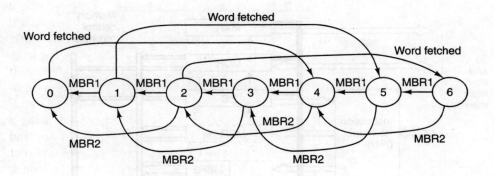

Transitions
MBR1: Occurs when MBR1 is read
MBR2: Occurs when MBR2 is read
Word fetched: Occurs when a memory word is read and 4 bytes are put into the shift register

Figure 4-28. A finite state machine for implementing the IFU.

The IFU has its own memory address register, called IMAR, which is used to address memory when a new word has to be fetched. This register has its own dedicated incrementer so that the main ALU is not needed to increment it to get the next word. The IFU must monitor the C bus so that whenever PC is loaded, the new PC value is also copied into IMAR. Since the new value in PC may not be on a word boundary, the IFU has to fetch the necessary word and adjust the shift register appropriately.

With the IFU, the main execution unit writes to PC only when it is necessary to change the sequential nature of the instruction byte stream. It writes on a successful branch instruction and on INVOKEVIRTUAL and IRETURN.

Since the microprogram no longer explicitly increments PC as opcodes are fetched, the IFU must keep PC current. It does this by sensing when a byte from the instruction stream has been consumed, that is, when MBR1 or MBR2 (or the unsigned versions) have been read. Associated with PC is a separate incrementer, capable of incrementing by 1 or 2, depending on how many bytes have been consumed. Thus the PC always contains the address of the first byte that has not been consumed. At the beginning of each instruction, MBR contains the address of the opcode for that instruction.

Note that there are two separate incrementers and they perform different functions. PC counts *bytes* and increments by 1 or 2. IMAR counts *words*, and increments only by 1 (for 4 new bytes). Like MAR, IMAR is wired to the address bus skew, with IMAR bit 0 connected to address line 2, and so on, to perform an implicit conversion of word addresses to byte addresses.

As we will see shortly in detail, not having to increment PC in the main loop is a big win, because the microinstruction in which PC is incremented often does

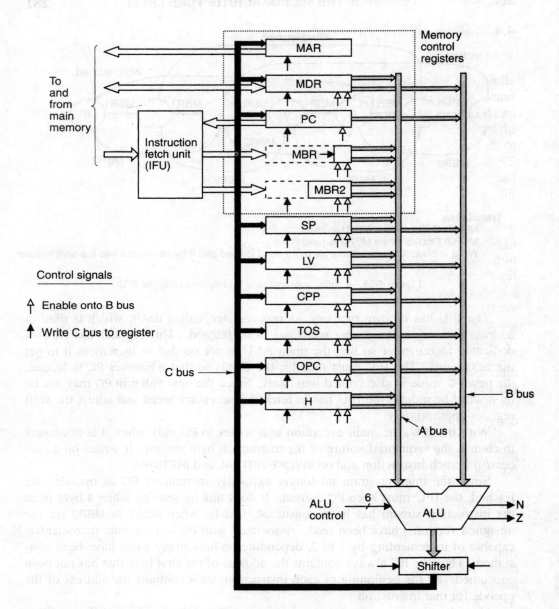

Figure 4-29. The datapath for Mic-2.

little else except increment PC. If this microinstruction can be eliminated, the execution path can be reduced. The trade-off here is more hardware for a faster machine, so our third technique for reducing path length is

Have instructions fetched from memory by a specialized functional unit.

4.4.3 A Design with Prefetching: The Mic-2

The IFU can greatly reduce the path length of the average instruction. First, it eliminates the main loop entirely, since the end of each instruction simply branches directly to the next instruction. Second, it avoids tying up the ALU incrementing PC. Third, it reduces the path length whenever a 16-bit index or offset is calculated, because it assembles the 16-bit value and supplies it directly to the ALU as a 32-bit value, avoiding the need for assembly in H. Figure Fig. 4-29 shows the Mic-2, an enhanced version of the Mic-1 where the IFU of Fig. 4-27 has been added. The microcode for the enhanced machine is shown in figure Fig. 4-30.

As an example of how the Mic-2 works, look at IADD. It fetches the second word on the stack and does the addition as before, only now it does not have to go to Main1 when it is done to increment PC and dispatch to the next microinstruction. When the IFU sees that MBR1 has been referenced in iadd3, its internal shift register pushes everything to the right and reloads MBR1 and MBR2. It also makes a transition to a state one lower than its current one. If the new state is 2, the IFU starts fetching a word from memory. All of this is in hardware. The microprogram does not have to do anything. That is why IADD can be reduced from four microinstructions to three microinstructions.

The Mic-2 improves some instructions more than others. LDC_W goes from nine microinstructions to only three, cutting its execution time by a factor of three. On the other hand, SWAP only goes from eight to six microinstructions. For overall performance, the gain for the more common instructions is what really counts. These include ILOAD (was 6, now 3), IADD (was 4, now 3), and IF_ICMPEQ (was 13, now 10 for the taken case; was 10, now 8 for the not taken case). To measure the improvement, one would have to choose and run some benchmarks, but it is clear there is a major gain here.

4.4.4 A Pipelined Design: The Mic-3

The Mic-2 is clearly an improvement over the Mic-1. It is faster and uses less control store, although the cost of the IFU will undoubtedly more than offset the real estate won by having a smaller control store. Thus it is a considerably faster machine at a marginally higher price. Let us see if we can make it faster still.

How about trying to decrease the cycle time? To a considerable extent, the cycle time is determined by the underlying technology. The smaller the transistors and the smaller the physical distances between them, the faster the clock can be run. For a given technology, the time required to perform a full data path operation is fixed (at least from our point of view). Nevertheless, we do have some freedom and we will exploit it to the fullest shortly.

Our other option is to introduce more parallelism into the machine. At the moment, the Mic-2 is highly sequential. It puts registers onto its buses, waits for

Label	Operations	Comments
nop1	goto (MBR)	Branch to next instruction
iadd1	MAR = SP = SP − 1; rd	Read in next-to-top word on stack
iadd2	H = TOS	H = top of stack
iadd3	MDR = TOS = MDR+H; wr; goto (MBR1)	Add top two words; write to new top of stack
isub1	MAR = SP = SP − 1; rd	Read in next-to-top word on stack
isub2	H = TOS	H = top of stack
isub3	MDR = TOS = MDR−H; wr; goto (MBR1)	Subtract TOS from Fetched TOS-1
iand1	MAR = SP = SP − 1; rd	Read in next-to-top word on stack
iand2	H = TOS	H = top of stack
iand3	MDR = TOS = MDR AND H; wr; goto (MBR1)	AND Fetched TOS-1 with TOS
ior1	MAR = SP = SP − 1; rd	Read in next-to-top word on stack
ior2	H = TOS	H = top of stack
ior3	MDR = TOS = MDR OR H; wr; goto (MBR1)	OR Fetched TOS-1 with TOS
dup1	MAR = SP = SP + 1	Increment SP; copy to MAR
dup2	MDR = TOS; wr; goto (MBR1)	Write new stack word
pop1	MAR = SP = SP − 1; rd	Read in next-to-top word on stack
pop2		Wait for read
pop3	TOS = MDR; goto (MBR1)	Copy new word to TOS
swap1	MAR = SP − 1; rd	Read 2nd word from stack; set MAR to SP
swap2	MAR = SP	Prepare to write new 2nd word
swap3	H = MDR; wr	Save new TOS; write 2nd word to stack
swap4	MDR = TOS	Copy old TOS to MDR
swap5	MAR = SP − 1; wr	Write old TOS to 2nd place on stack
swap6	TOS = H; goto (MBR1)	Update TOS
bipush1	SP = MAR = SP + 1	Set up MAR for writing to new top of stack
bipush2	MDR = TOS = MBR1; wr; goto (MBR1)	Update stack in TOS and memory
iload1	MAR = LV + MBR1U; rd	Move LV + index to MAR; read operand
iload2	MAR = SP = SP + 1	Increment SP; Move new SP to MAR
iload3	TOS = MDR; wr; goto (MBR1)	Update stack in TOS and memory
istore1	MAR = LV + MBR1U	Set MAR to LV + index
istore2	MDR = TOS; wr	Copy TOS for storing
istore3	MAR = SP = SP − 1; rd	Decrement SP; read new TOS
istore4		Wait for read
istore5	TOS = MDR; goto (MBR1)	Update TOS
wide1	goto (MBR1 OR 0x100)	Next address is 0x100 Ored with opcode
wide_iload1	MAR = LV + MBR2U; rd; goto iload2	Identical to iload1 but using 2-byte index
wide_istore1	MAR = LV + MBR2U; goto istore2	Identical to istore1 but using 2-byte index
ldc_w1	MAR = CPP + MBR2U; rd; goto iload2	Same as wide_iload1 but indexing off CPP
iinc1	MAR = LV + MBR1U; rd	Set MAR to LV + index for read
iinc2	H = MBR1	Set H to constant
iinc3	MDR = MDR + H; wr; goto (MBR1)	Increment by constant and update
goto1	H = PC − 1	Copy PC to H
goto2	PC = H + MBR2	Add offset and update PC
goto3		Have to wait for IFU to fetch new opcode
goto4	goto (MBR1)	Dispatch to next instruction
iflt1	MAR = SP = SP − 1; rd	Read in next-to-top word on stack
iflt2	OPC = TOS	Save TOS in OPC temporarily
iflt3	TOS = MDR	Put new top of stack in TOS
iflt4	N = OPC; if (N) goto T; else goto F	Branch on N bit

Figure 4-30. The microprogram for the Mic-2 (part 1 of 2).

Label	Operations	Comments
ifeq1	MAR = SP = SP − 1; rd	Read in next-to-top word of stack
ifeq2	OPC = TOS	Save TOS in OPC temporarily
ifeq3	TOS = MDR	Put new top of stack in TOS
ifeq4	Z = OPC; if (Z) goto T; else goto F	Branch on Z bit
if_icmpeq1	MAR = SP = SP − 1; rd	Read in next-to-top word of stack
if_icmpeq2	MAR = SP = SP − 1	Set MAR to read in new top-of-stack
if_icmpeq3	H = MDR; rd	Copy second stack word to H
if_icmpeq4	OPC = TOS	Save TOS in OPC temporarily
if_icmpeq5	TOS = MDR	Put new top of stack in TOS
if_icmpeq6	Z = H − OPC; if (Z) goto T; else goto F	If top 2 words are equal, goto T, else goto F
T	H = PC − 1; goto goto2	Same as goto1
F	H = MBR2	Touch bytes in MBR2 to discard
F2	goto (MBR1)	
invokevirtual1	MAR = CPP + MBR2U; rd	Put address of method pointer in MAR
invokevirtual2	OPC = PC	Save Return PC in OPC
invokevirtual3	PC = MDR	Set PC to 1st byte of method code.
invokevirtual4	TOS = SP − MBR2U	TOS = address of OBJREF − 1
invokevirtual5	TOS = MAR = H = TOS + 1	TOS = address of OBJREF
invokevirtual6	MDR = SP + MBR2U + 1; wr	Overwrite OBJREF with link pointer
invokevirtual7	MAR = SP = MDR	Set SP, MAR to location to hold old PC
invokevirtual8	MDR = OPC; wr	Prepare to save old PC
invokevirtual9	MAR = SP = SP + 1	Inc. SP to point to location to hold old LV
invokevirtual10	MDR = LV; wr	Save old LV
invokevirtual11	LV = TOS; goto (MBR1)	Set LV to point to zeroth parameter.
ireturn1	MAR = SP = LV; rd	Reset SP, MAR to read Link ptr
ireturn2		Wait for link ptr
ireturn3	LV = MAR = MDR; rd	Set LV, MAR to link ptr; read old PC
ireturn4	MAR = LV + 1	Set MAR to point to old LV; read old LV
ireturn5	PC = MDR; rd	Restore PC
ireturn6	MAR = SP	
ireturn7	LV = MDR	Restore LV
ireturn8	MDR = TOS; wr; goto (MBR1)	Save return value on original top of stack

Figure 4-30. The microprogram for the Mic-2 (part 2 of 2).

the ALU and shifter to process them, and then writes the results back to the registers. Except for the IFU, little parallelism is present. Adding parallelism is a real opportunity.

As mentioned earlier, the clock cycle is limited by the time needed for the signals to propagate through the data path. Figure 4-3 shows a breakdown of the delay through the various components during each cycle. There are three major components to the actual data path cycle:

1. The time to drive the selected registers onto the A and B buses.

2. The time for the ALU and shifter to do their work.

3. The time for the results to get back to the registers and be stored.

In Fig. 4-31 we show a new three-bus architecture, including the IFU, but with three additional latches (registers), one inserted in the middle of each bus.

The latches are written on every cycle. In effect, the registers partition the data path into distinct parts that can now operate independently of one another. We will refer to this as **Mic-3**, or the **pipelined** model.

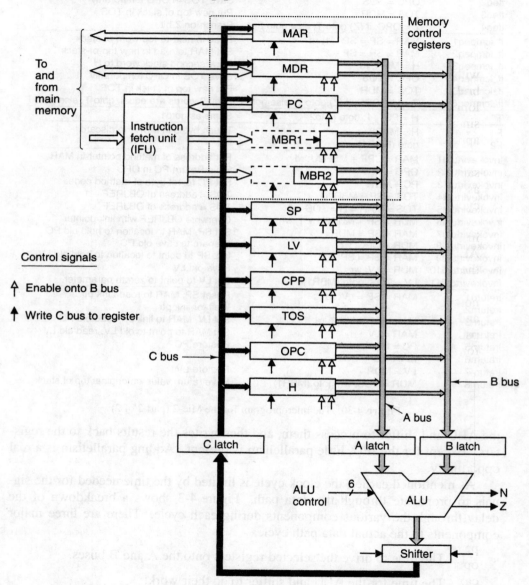

Figure 4-31. The three-bus data path used in the Mic-3.

How can these extra registers possibly help? Now it takes three clock cycles to use the data path: one for loading the A and B latches, one for running the ALU and shifter and loading the C latch, and one for storing the C latch back into the registers. Are we crazy? (*Hint*: No.) The point of inserting the latches is twofold:

1. We can speed up the clock because the maximum delay is now shorter.

2. We can use all parts of the data path during every cycle.

By breaking up the data path into three parts, the maximum delay is reduced, with the result that the clock frequency can be higher. Let us suppose that by breaking the data path cycle into three time intervals, each one is about 1/3 as long as the original, so we can triple the clock speed. (This is not totally realistic since we have also added two more registers into the data path, but as a first approximation it will do.)

Because we have been assuming that all memory reads and writes can be satisfied out of the level 1 cache, and this cache is made out of the same material as the registers, we will continue to assume that a memory operation takes one cycle. In practice this may not be so easy to achieve, though.

The second point deals with throughput rather than the speed of an individual instruction. In the Mic-2, during the first and third parts of each clock cycle the ALU is idle. By breaking the data path up into three pieces, we will be able to use the ALU on every cycle, getting three times as much work out of the machine.

Let us now see how the Mic-3 data path works. Before starting, we need a notation for dealing with the latches. The obvious one is to call the latches A, B, and C and treat them like registers, keeping in mind the constraints of the data path. Figure 4-32 shows an example code sequence, the implementation of SWAP for the Mic-2.

Label	Operations	Comments
swap1	MAR = SP − 1; rd	Read 2nd word from stack; set MAR to SP
swap2	MAR = SP	Prepare to write new 2nd word
swap3	H = MDR; wr	Save new TOS; write 2nd word to stack
swap4	MDR = TOS	Copy old TOS to MDR
swap5	MAR = SP − 1; wr	Write old TOS to 2nd place on stack
swap6	TOS = H; goto (MBR1)	Update TOS

Figure 4-32. The Mic-2 code for SWAP.

Now let us reimplement this sequence on the Mic-3. Remember that the data path now requires three cycles to operate: one to load A and B, one to perform the operation and load C, and one to write the results back to the registers. We will call each of these pieces a **microstep**.

The implementation of SWAP for the Mic-3 is shown in Fig. 4-33. In cycle 1, we start on swap1 by copying SP to B. It does not matter what goes in A because to subtract 1 from B ENA is negated (see Fig. 4-2). For simplicity, we will not show assignments that are not used. In cycle 2 we do the subtraction. In cycle 3 the result is stored in MAR and the read operation is started at the end of cycle 3 (after MAR has been stored). Since memory reads now take one cycle, this one will not complete until the end of cycle 4, indicated by showing the assignment to MDR in cycle 4. The value in MDR may be read no earlier than cycle 5.

Cy	Swap1 MAR=SP−1;rd	Swap2 MAR=SP	Swap3 H=MDR;wr	Swap4 MDR=TOS	Swap5 MAR=SP−1;wr	Swap6 TOS=H;goto (MBR1)
1	B=SP					
2	C=B−1	B=SP				
3	MAR=C; rd	C=B				
4	MDR=Mem	MAR=C				
5			B=MDR			
6			C=B	B=TOS		
7			H=C; wr	C=B	B=SP	
8			Mem=MDR	MDR=C	C=B−1	B=H
9					MAR=C; wr	C=B
10					Mem=MDR	TOS=C
11						goto (MBR1)

Figure 4-33. The implementation of SWAP on the Mic-3.

Now let us go back to cycle 2. We can now begin breaking up swap2 into microsteps and starting them too. In cycle 2, we can copy SP to B, then run it through the ALU in cycle 3 and finally store it in MAR in cycle 4. So far, so good. It should be clear that if we can keep going at this rate, starting a new microinstruction every cycle, we have tripled the speed of the machine. This gain comes from the fact that we can issue a new microinstruction on every clock cycle, and the Mic-3 has three times as many clock cycles per second as the Mic-2 has. In fact, we have built a pipelined CPU.

Unfortunately, we hit a snag in cycle 3. We would like to start working on swap3, but the first thing it does is run MDR through the ALU, and MDR will not be available from memory until the start of cycle 5. The situation that a microstep cannot start because it is waiting for a result that a previous microstep has not yet produced is called a **true dependence** or a **RAW dependence**. Dependences are often referred to as **hazards**. RAW stands for Read After Write and indicates that a microstep wants to read a register that has not yet been written. The only sensible thing to do here is delay the start of swap3 until MDR is available, in cycle 5. Stopping to wait for a needed value is called **stalling**. After that, we can continue starting microinstructions every cycle as there are no more dependences, although swap6 just barely makes it, since it reads H in the cycle after swap3 writes it. If swap5 had tried to read H, it would have stalled for one cycle.

Although the Mic-3 program takes more cycles than the Mic-2 program, it still runs faster. If we call the Mic-3 cycle time ΔT nsec, then the Mic-3 requires

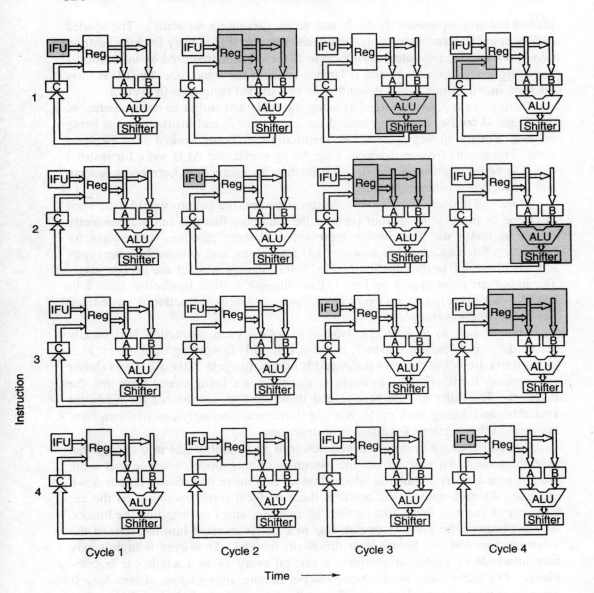

Instruction

Cycle 1   Cycle 2   Cycle 3   Cycle 4

Time ⟶

Figure 4-34. Graphical illustration of how a pipeline works.

11ΔT nsec to execute SWAP. In contrast, the Mic-2 takes 6 cycles at 3ΔT each, for a total of 18ΔT. Pipelining has made the machine faster, even though we had to stall once to avoid a dependence.

Pipelining is a key technique in all modern CPUs, so it is important to understand it well. In Fig. 4-34 we see the data path of Fig. 4-31 graphically illustrated as a pipeline. The first column represents what is going on during cycle 1, the second column represents cycle 2, and so on (assuming no stalls). The shaded region in cycle 1 for instruction 1 indicates that the IFU is busy fetching instruction 1. One clock tick later, during cycle 2, the registers required by instruction 1 are being loaded into the A and B latches while at the same time the IFU is busy fetching instruction 2, again shown by the two shaded rectangles in cycle 2.

During cycle 3, instruction 1 is using the ALU and shifter to do its operation, the A and B latches are being loaded for instruction 2, and instruction 3 is being fetched. Finally, during cycle 4, four instructions are being worked on at the same time. The results from instruction 1 are being stored, the ALU work for instruction 2 is being performed, the A and B latches for instruction 3 are being loaded, and instruction 4 is being fetched.

If we had shown cycle 5 and subsequent cycles, the pattern would have been the same as in cycle 4: all four parts of the data path that can run independently would be doing so. This design represents a 4-stage pipeline, with stages for instruction fetching, operand access, ALU operations, and writeback to the registers. It is similar to the pipeline of Fig. 2-4(a), except without the decode stage. The important point to pick up here is that although a single instruction takes four clock cycles to carry out, on every clock cycle, one new instruction is started and one old instruction completes.

Another way to look at Fig. 4-34 is to follow each instruction horizontally across the page. For instruction 1, in cycle 1 the IFU is working on it. In cycle 2, its registers are being put onto the A and B buses. In cycle 3, the ALU and shifter are working for it. Finally, in cycle 4, its results are being stored back into the registers. The thing to note here is that there are four sections of the hardware available, and during each cycle, a given instruction uses only one of them, freeing up the other sections for different instructions.

A useful analogy to our pipelined design is an assembly line in a factory that assembles cars. To abstract out the essentials of this model, imagine that a big gong is struck every minute, at which time all cars move one station further down the line. At each station, the workers there perform some operation on the car currently in front of them, like adding the steering wheel or installing the brakes. At each beat of the gong (1 cycle), one new car is injected into the start of the assembly line and one finished car drives off the end. Thus even though it may take hundreds of cycles to complete a car, on every cycle a whole car is completed. The factory can produce one car per minute, independent of how long it actually takes to assemble a car. This is the power of pipelining, and it applies equally well to CPUs as to car factories.

4.4.5 A Seven-Stage Pipeline: The Mic-4

One point that we have glossed over is the fact that every microinstruction selects its own successor. Most of them just select the next one in the current sequence, but the last one, such as **swap6**, often does a multiway branch, which gums up the pipeline since continuing to prefetch after it is impossible. We need a better way of dealing with this point.

Our next (and last) microarchitecture is the Mic-4. The main parts of it are illustrated in Fig. 4-35, but a substantial amount of detail has been suppressed for clarity. Like the Mic-3, it has an IFU that prefetches words from memory and maintains the various MBRs.

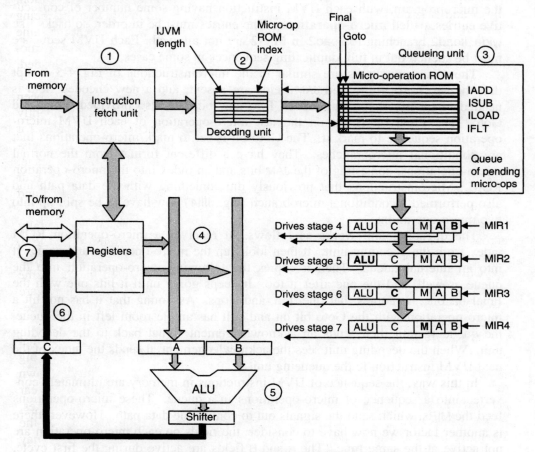

Figure 4-35. The main components of the Mic-4.

The IFU also feeds the incoming byte stream to a new component, the **decoding unit**. This unit has an internal ROM indexed by IJVM opcode. Each entry (row) contains two parts: the length of that IJVM instruction and an index into another ROM, the micro-operation ROM. The IJVM instruction length is used to allow the decoding unit to parse the incoming byte stream into instructions, so it always knows which bytes are opcodes and which are operands. If the current instruction length is 1 byte (e.g., POP), then the decoding unit knows that the next byte is an opcode. If, however, the current instruction length is 2 bytes, the decoding unit knows that the next byte is an operand, followed immediately by another opcode. When the WIDE prefix is seen, the following byte is transformed into a special wide opcode, for example, WIDE + ILOAD becomes WIDE_ILOAD.

The decoding unit ships the index into the micro-operation ROM that it found in its table to the next component, the **queueing unit**. This unit contains some logic plus two internal tables, one in ROM and one in RAM. The ROM contains the microprogram, with each IJVM instruction having some number of consecutive entries, called **micro-operations**. The entries must be in order, so tricks like wide_iload2 branching to iload2 in Mic-2 are not allowed. Each IJVM sequence must be spelled out in full, duplicating sequences in some cases.

The micro-operations are similar to the microinstructions of Fig. 4-5 except that the NEXT_ADDRESS and JAM fields are absent, and a new encoded field is needed to specify the A bus input. Two new bits are also provided: Final and Goto. The Final bit is set on the last micro-operation of each IJVM micro-operation sequence to mark it. The Goto bit is set to mark micro-operations that are conditional microbranches. They have a different format from the normal micro-operations, consisting of the JAM bits and an index into the micro-operation ROM. Microinstructions that previously did something with the data path and also performed a conditional microbranch (e.g., iflt4) now have to be split up into two micro-operations.

The queueing unit works as follows. It receives a micro-operation ROM index from the decoding unit. It then looks up the micro-operation and copies it into an internal queue. Then it copies the following micro-operation into the queue as well, and the one after it too. It keeps going until it hits one with the Final bit one. It copies that one, too, and stops. Assuming that it has not hit a micro-operation with the Goto bit on and still has ample room left in the queue, the queueing unit then sends an acknowledgement signal back to the decoding unit. When the decoding unit sees the acknowledgement, it sends the index of the next IJVM instruction to the queueing unit.

In this way, the sequence of IJVM instructions in memory are ultimately converted into a sequence of micro-operations in a queue. These micro-operations feed the MIRs, which send the signals out to control the data path. However, there is another factor we now have to consider: the fields on each micro-operation are not active at the same time. The A and B fields are active during the first cycle, the ALU field is active during the second cycle, the C field is active during the third cycle, and any memory operations take place in the fourth cycle.

To make this work properly, we have introduced four independent MIRs into Fig. 4-35. At the start of each clock cycle (the Δw time in Fig. 4-3), MIR3 is copied to MIR4, MIR2 is copied to MIR3, MIR1 is copied to MIR2, and MIR1 is loaded with a fresh micro-operation from the micro-operation queue. Then each MIR puts out its control signals, but only some of them are used. The A and B fields from MIR1 are used to select the registers that drive the A and B latches, but the ALU field in MIR1 is not used and is not connected to anything else in the data path.

One clock cycle later, this micro-operation has moved on to MIR2 and the registers that it selected are now safely sitting in the A and B latches waiting for the adventures to come. Its ALU field is now used to drive the ALU. In the next cycle, its C field will write the results back into the registers. After that, it will move on to MIR4 and initiate any memory operations needed using the now-loaded MAR (and MDR, for a write).

One last aspect of the Mic-4 needs some discussion now: microbranches. Some IJVM instructions, such as IFLT, need to conditionally branch based on, say, the N bit. When a microbranch occurs, the pipeline cannot continue. To deal with that, we have added the Goto bit to the micro-operation. When the queueing unit hits a micro-operation with this bit set while copying it to the queue, it realizes that there is trouble ahead and refrains from sending an acknowledgement to the decoding unit. As a result, the machine will stall at this point until the microbranch has been resolved.

Conceivably, some IJVM instructions beyond the branch have already been fed into the decoding unit (but not into the queueing unit), since it does not send back an acknowledge (i.e., continue) signal when it hits a micro-operation with the Goto bit on. Special hardware and mechanisms are needed to clean up the mess and get back on track, but they are beyond the scope of this book. When Edsger Dijkstra wrote his famous letter "GOTO Statement Considered Harmful," (Dijkstra, 1968a), he had no idea how right he was.

We have come a long way since the Mic-1. The Mic-1 was a very simple piece of hardware, with nearly all the control in software. The Mic-4 is a highly pipelined design, with seven stages and far more complex hardware. The pipeline is shown schematically in Fig. 4-36, with the circled numbers keyed back to components in Fig. 4-35. The Mic-4 automatically prefetches a stream of bytes from memory, decodes them into IJVM instructions, converts them to a sequence of micro-operations using a ROM, and queues them for use as needed. The first three stages of the pipeline can be tied to the data path clock if desired, but there will not always be work to do. For example, the IFU can certainly not feed a new IJVM opcode to the decoding unit on every clock cycle because IJVM instructions take several cycles to execute and the queue would rapidly overflow.

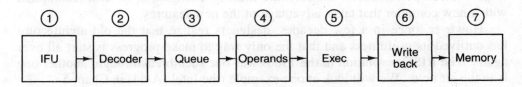

Figure 4-36. The Mic-4 pipeline.

On each clock cycle, the MIRs are shifted forward and the micro-operation at the bottom of the queue is copied into MIR1 to start its execution. The control signals from the four MIRs then spread out through the data path causing actions to occur. Each MIR controls a different portion of the data path and thus different microsteps.

In this design we have a deeply pipelined CPU, which allows the individual steps to be very short and thus the clock frequency high. Many CPUs are designed in essentially this way, especially those that have to implement an older (CISC) instruction set. For example, the Pentium II implementation is conceptually similar to the Mic-4 in some ways, as we will see later in this chapter.

4.5 IMPROVING PERFORMANCE

All computer manufacturers want their systems to run as fast as possible. In this section, we will look at a number of advanced techniques currently being investigated to improve system (primarily CPU and memory) performance. Due to the highly competitive nature of the computer industry, the lag between new research ideas that can make a computer faster and their incorporation into products is surprisingly short. Consequently, most of the ideas we will discuss are already in use in a wide variety of existing products.

The ideas to be discussed fall into roughly two categories: implementation improvements and architectural improvements. Implementation improvements are ways of building a new CPU or memory to make the system run faster without changing the architecture. Modifying the implementation without changing the architecture means that old programs will run on the new machine, a major selling point. One way to improve the implementation is to use a faster clock, but this is not the only way. The performance gains from the 80386 through the 80486, Pentium, and Pentium Pro, to the Pentium II are due to better implementations, as the architecture has remained essentially the same through all of them.

Some kinds of improvements can be made only by changing the architecture. Sometimes these changes are incremental, such as adding new instructions or registers, so that old programs will continue to run on the new models. In this case, to get the full performance, the software must be changed, or at least recompiled with a new compiler that takes advantage of the new features.

However, once in a few decades, designers realize that the old architecture has outlived its usefulness and that the only way to make progress is start all over again. The RISC revolution in the 1980s was one such breakthrough; another one is in the air now. We will look at one example (the Intel IA-64) in Chap. 5.

In the rest of this section we will look at four different techniques for improving CPU performance. We will start with three well-established implementation improvements and then move on to one that needs a little architectural support to work best. These techniques are cache memory, branch prediction, out-of-order execution with register renaming, and speculative execution.

4.5.1 Cache Memory

One of the most challenging aspects of computer design throughout history has been to provide a memory system able to provide operands to the processor at the speed it can process them. The recent high rate of growth in processor speed has not been accompanied by a corresponding speedup in memories. Relative to CPUs, memories have been getting slower for decades. Given the enormous importance of primary memory, this situation has greatly limited the development of high-performance systems, and has stimulated research on ways to get around the problem of memory speeds that are much slower than CPU speeds, and relatively speaking, getting worse every year.

Modern processors place overwhelming demands on a memory system, both in terms of latency (the delay in supplying an operand) and bandwidth (the amount of data supplied per unit of time). Unfortunately, these two aspects of a memory system are largely at odds. Many techniques for increasing bandwidth do so only by increasing latency. For example, the pipelining techniques used in the Mic-3 can be applied to a memory system, with multiple, overlapping memory requests handled efficiently. Unfortunately, as with the Mic-3, this results in greater latency for individual memory operations. As processor clock speeds get faster, it becomes more and more difficult to provide a memory system capable of supplying operands in one or two clock cycles.

One way to attack this problem is by providing caches. As we saw in Sec. 2.2.5, a cache holds the most recently used memory words in a small, fast memory, speeding up access to them. If a large enough percentage of the memory words needed are in the cache, the effective memory latency can be reduced enormously.

One of the most effective techniques for improving both bandwidth and latency comes from the use of multiple caches. A basic technique that works very effectively is to introduce a separate cache for instructions and data. There are several benefits from having separate caches for instructions and data, often called a **split cache**. First, memory operations can be initiated independently in each cache, effectively doubling the bandwidth of the memory system. This is the reason that it makes sense to provide two separate memory ports, as we did in the Mic-1: each port has its own cache. Note that each cache has independent access to the main memory.

Today, many memory systems are more complicated than this, and an additional cache, called a **level 2 cache**, may reside between the instruction and data caches and main memory. In fact, there may be three or more levels of cache as more sophisticated memory systems are required. In Fig. 4-37 we see a system with three levels of cache. The CPU chip itself contains a small instruction cache and a small data cache, typically 16 KB to 64 KB. Then there is the level 2 cache, which is not on the CPU chip, but may be included in the CPU package, next to the CPU chip and connected to it by a high-speed path. This cache is generally unified, containing a mix of data and instructions. A typical size for the L2 cache is 512 KB to 1 MB. The third-level cache is on the processor board and consists of a few megabytes of SRAM, which is much faster than the main DRAM memory. Caches are generally inclusive, with the full contents of the level 1 cache being in the level 2 cache and the full contents of the level 2 cache being in the level 3 cache.

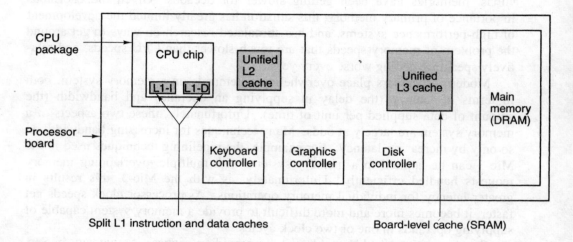

Figure 4-37. A system with three levels of cache.

Caches depend on two kinds of address locality to achieve their goal. **Spatial locality** is the observation that memory locations with addresses numerically similar to a recently accessed memory location are likely to be accessed in the near future. Caches exploit this property by bringing in more data than have been requested, with the expectation that future requests can be anticipated. **Temporal locality** occurs when recently accessed memory locations are accessed again. This may occur, for example, to memory locations near the top of the stack, or instructions inside a loop. Temporal locality is exploited in cache designs primarily by the choice of what to discard on a cache miss. Many cache replacement algorithms exploit temporal locality by discarding those entries that have not been recently accessed.

All caches use the following model. Main memory is divided up into fixed-size blocks called **cache lines**. A cache line typically consists of 4 to 64 consecutive bytes. Lines are numbered consecutively starting at 0, so with a 32-byte line size, line 0 is bytes 0 to 31, line 1 is bytes 32 to 63, and so on. At any instant, some lines are in the cache. When memory is referenced, the cache controller circuit checks to see if the word referenced is currently in the cache. If so, the value there can be used, saving a trip to main memory. If the word is not there, some line entry is removed from the cache and the line needed is fetched from memory or lower level cache to replace it. Many variations on this scheme exist, but in all of them the idea is to keep the most heavily-used lines in the cache as much as possible, to maximize the number of memory references satisfied out of the cache.

Direct-Mapped Caches

The simplest cache is known as a **direct-mapped cache**. An example single-level direct-mapped cache is shown in Fig. 4-38(a). This example cache contains 2048 entries. Each entry (row) in the cache can hold exactly one cache line from main memory. With a 32-byte cache line size (for this example), the cache can hold 64 KB. Each cache entry consists of three parts:

1. The Valid bit indicates whether there is any valid data in this entry or not. When the system is booted (started), all entries are marked as invalid.

2. The Tag field consists of a unique, 16-bit value identifying the corresponding line of memory from which the data came.

3. The Data field contains a copy of the data in memory. This field holds one cache line of 32 bytes.

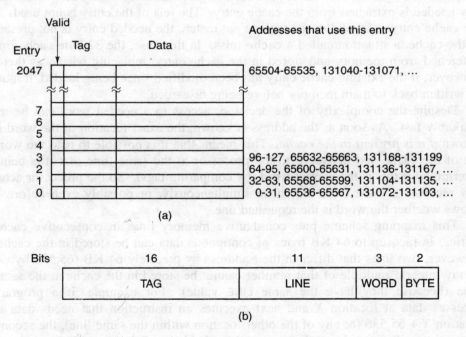

Figure 4-38. (a) A direct-mapped cache. (b) A 32-bit virtual address.

In a direct-mapped cache, a given memory word can be stored in exactly one place within the cache. Given a memory address, there is only one place to look for it in the cache. If it is not there, then it is not in the cache. For storing and retrieving data from the cache, the address is broken into four components, as shown in Fig. 4-38(b):

1. The TAG field corresponds to the Tag bits stored in a cache entry.

2. The LINE field indicates which cache entry holds the corresponding data, if they are present.

3. The WORD field tells which word within a line is referenced.

4. The BYTE field is usually not used, but if only a single byte is requested, it tells which byte within the word is needed. For a cache supplying only 32-bit words, this field will always be 0.

When the CPU produces a memory address, the hardware extracts the 11 LINE bits from the address and uses these to index into the cache to find one of the 2048 entries. If that entry is valid, the TAG field of the memory address and the Tag field in cache entry are compared. If they agree, the cache entry holds the word being requested, a situation called a **cache hit**. On a hit, a word being read can be taken from the cache, eliminating the need to go to memory. Only the word actually needed is extracted from the cache entry. The rest of the entry is not used. If the cache entry is invalid or the tags do not match, the needed entry is not present in the cache, a situation called a **cache miss**. In this case, the 32-byte cache line is fetched from memory and stored in the cache entry, replacing what was there. However, if the existing cache entry has been modified since being loaded, it must be written back to main memory before being discarded.

Despite the complexity of the decision, access to a needed word can be remarkably fast. As soon as the address is known, the exact location of the word is known *if it is present in the cache*. This means that it is possible to read the word out of the cache and deliver it to the processor at the same time that it is being determined if this is the correct word (by comparing tags). So the processor actually receives a word from the cache simultaneously, or possibly even before it knows whether the word is the requested one.

This mapping scheme puts consecutive memory lines in consecutive cache entries, In fact, up to 64 KB bytes of contiguous data can be stored in the cache. However, two lines that differ in their address by precisely 64 KB (65,536 bytes) or any integral multiple of that number cannot be stored in the cache at the same time (because they have the same LINE value). For example, if a program accesses data at location X and next executes an instruction that needs data at location $X + 65,536$ (or any of the other location within the same line), the second instruction will force the cache entry to be reloaded, overwriting what was there. If this happens often enough, it can result in poor behavior. In fact, the worst-case behavior of a cache is worse than if there were no cache at all, since each memory operation involves reading in an entire cache line instead of just one word.

Direct-mapped caches are the most common kind of cache, and they perform quite effectively, because collisions such as the one described above can be made to occur only rarely, or not at all. For example, a very clever compiler can take cache collisions into account when placing instructions and data in memory. Notice that the particular case described would not occur in a system with separate instruction and data caches, because the colliding requests would be serviced by different caches. Thus we see a second benefit of two caches rather than one: more flexibility in dealing with conflicting memory patterns.

Set-Associative Caches

As mentioned above, many different lines in memory compete for the same cache slots. If a program using the cache of Fig. 4-38(a) heavily uses words at addresses 0 and at 65,536, there will be constant conflicts, with each reference potentially evicting the other one from the cache. A solution to this problem is to allow two or more lines in each cache entry. A cache with *n* possible entries for each address is called an **n-way set-associative cache**. A four-way set-associative cache is illustrated in Fig. 4-39.

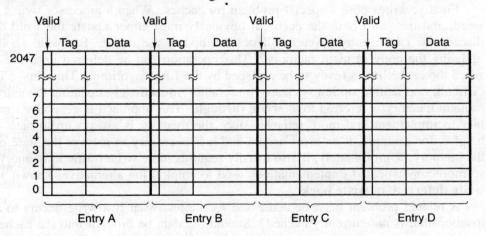

Figure 4-39. A four-way set-associative cache.

A set-associative cache is inherently more complicated than a direct-mapped cache because although the correct cache entry to examine can be computed from the memory address being referenced, a set of *n* cache entries must be checked to see if the needed line is present. Nevertheless, experience shows that two-way and four-way caches perform well enough to make this extra circuitry worthwhile.

The use of a set-associative cache presents the designer with a choice. When a new entry is to be brought into the cache, which of the present items should be discarded? The optimal decision, of course, requires a peek into the future, but a pretty good algorithm for most purposes is **LRU** (**Least Recently Used**). This algorithm keeps an ordering of each set of locations that could be accessed from a given memory location. Whenever any of the present lines are accessed, it updates the list, marking that entry the most recently accessed. When it comes time to replace an entry, the one at the end of the list—the least recently accessed—is the one discarded.

Carried to the extreme, a 2048-way cache containing a single set of 2048 line entries is also possible. Here all memory addresses map onto the single set, so the lookup requires comparing the address against all 2048 tags in the cache. Note that each entry must now have tag-matching logic. Since the LINE field is of 0 length, the TAG field is the entire address except for the WORD and BYTE fields. Furthermore, when a cache line is replaced, all 2048 locations are possible candidates for replacement. Maintaining an ordered list of 2048 entries requires a great deal of bookkeeping, making LRU replacement infeasible. (Remember that this list has to be updated on every memory operation, not just on a miss). Surprisingly, high-associativity caches do not improve performance much over low-associativity caches under most circumstances, and in some cases actually perform worse. For these reasons, set associativity beyond four-way is relatively unusual.

Finally, writes pose a special problem for caches. When a processor writes a word, and the word is in the cache, it obviously must either update the word or discard the cache entry. Nearly all designs update the cache. But what about updating the copy in main memory? This operation can be deferred until later, when the cache line is ready to be replaced by the LRU algorithm. This choice is difficult, and neither option is clearly preferable. Immediately updating the entry in main memory is referred to as **write through**. This approach is generally simpler to implement and more reliable, since the memory is always up to date—helpful, for example, if an error occurs and it is necessary to recover the state of the memory. Unfortunately, it also usually requires more write traffic to memory, so more sophisticated implementations tend to employ the alternative, known as **write deferred**, or **write back**.

A related problem must be addressed for writes: what if a write occurs to a location that is not currently cached? Should the data be brought into the cache, or just written out to memory? Again, neither answer is always best. Most designs that defer writes to memory tend to bring data into the cache on a write miss, a technique known as **write allocation**. Most designs employing write through, on the other hand, tend not to allocate an entry on a write because this option complicates an otherwise simple design. Write allocation wins only if there are repeated writes to the same or different words within a cache line.

Cache performance is critical to system performance because the gap between CPU speed and memory speed is very large. Consequently, research on better caching strategies is still a hot topic (Alameldeen and Wood, 2004; Huh et al., 2004; Min et al., 2004; Nesbit and Smith, 2004; and Suh et al., 2004).

4.5.2 Branch Prediction

Modern computers are highly pipelined. The pipeline of Fig. 4-35 has seven stages; high-end computers sometimes have 10-stage pipelines or even more. Pipelining works best on linear code, so the fetch unit can just read in consecutive words from memory and send them off to the decode unit in advance of their being needed.

The only minor problem with this wonderful model is that it is not the slightest bit realistic. Programs are not linear code sequences. They are full of branch instructions. Consider the simple statements of Fig. 4-40(a). A variable, i, is compared to 0 (probably the most common test in practice). Depending on the result, another variable, k, gets assigned one of two possible values.

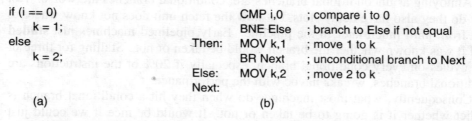

```
if (i == 0)              CMP i,0    ; compare i to 0
    k = 1;               BNE Else   ; branch to Else if not equal
else             Then:   MOV k,1    ; move 1 to k
    k = 2;               BR Next    ; unconditional branch to Next
                 Else:   MOV k,2    ; move 2 to k
                 Next:
(a)                             (b)
```

Figure 4-40. (a) A program fragment. (b) Its translation to a generic assembly language.

A possible translation to assembly language is shown in Fig. 4-40(b). We will study assembly language later in this book, and the details are not important now, but depending on the machine and the compiler, code more-or-less like that of Fig. 4-40(b) is likely. The first instruction compares i to 0. The second one branches to the label *Else* (the start of the else clause) if i is not 0. The third instruction assigns 1 to k. The fourth instruction branches to the code for the next statement. The compiler has conveniently planted a label, *Next*, there, so there is a place to branch to. The fifth instruction assigns 2 to k.

The thing to observe here is that two of the five instructions are branches. Furthermore, one of these, BNE, is a conditional branch (a branch that is taken if and only if some condition is met, in this case, that the two operands in the previous CMP are unequal). The longest linear code sequence here is two instructions. As a consequence, fetching instructions at a high rate to feed the pipeline is very difficult.

At first glance, it might appear that unconditional branches, such as the instruction BR Next in Fig. 4-40(b), are not a problem. After all, there is no ambiguity about where to go. Why can the fetch unit not just continue to read instructions from the target address (the place that will be branched to)?

The trouble lies in the nature of pipelining. In Fig. 4-35, for example, we see that instruction decoding occurs in the second stage. Thus the fetch unit has to decide where to fetch from next before it knows what kind of instruction it just got. Only one cycle later can it learn that it just picked up an unconditional branch, and by then it has already started to fetch the instruction following the unconditional branch. As a consequence, a substantial number of pipelined machines (such as the UltraSPARC III) have the property that the instruction *following* an unconditional branch is executed, even though logically it should not be. The position after a branch is called a **delay slot**. The Pentium II [and the machine used in Fig. 4-40(b)] do not have this property, but the internal complexity to get around this problem is often enormous. An optimizing compiler will try to find some useful instruction to put in the delay slot, but frequently there is nothing available, so it is forced to insert a NOP instruction there. Doing so keeps the program correct, but makes it bigger and slower.

Annoying as unconditional branches are, conditional branches are worse. Not only do they also have delay slots, but now the fetch unit does not know where to read from until much later in the pipeline. Early pipelined machines just **stalled** until it was known whether the branch would be taken or not. Stalling for three or four cycles on every conditional branch, especially if 20% of the instructions are conditional branches, wreaks havoc with the performance.

Consequently, what most machines do when they hit a conditional branch is predict whether it is going to be taken or not. It would be nice if we could just plug a crystal ball into a free PCI slot to help out with the prediction, but so far this approach has not borne fruit.

Lacking such a peripheral, various ways have been devised to do the prediction. One very simple way is as follows: assume that all backward conditional branches will be taken and that all forward ones will not be taken. The reasoning behind the first part is that backward branches are frequently located at the end of a loop. Most loops are executed multiple times, so guessing that a branch back to the top of the loop will be taken is generally a good bet.

The second part is shakier. Some forward branches occur when error conditions are detected in software (e.g., a file cannot be opened). Errors are rare, so most of the branches associated with them are not taken. Of course, there are plenty of forward branches not related to error handling, so the success rate is not nearly as good as with backward branches. While not fantastic, this rule is at least better than nothing.

If a branch is correctly predicted, there is nothing special to do. Execution just continues at the target address. The trouble comes when a branch is predicted wrongly. Figuring out where to go and going there is not difficult. The hard part is undoing instructions that have already been executed and should not have been.

There are two ways of going about this. The first way is to allow instructions fetched after a predicted conditional branch to execute until they try to change the machine's state (e.g., storing into a register). Instead of overwriting the register, the value computed is put into a (secret) scratch register and only copied to the real register after it is known that the prediction was correct. The second way is to record the value of any register about to be overwritten (e.g., in a secret scratch register), so the machine can be rolled back to the state it had at the time of the mispredicted branch. Both solutions are complex and require industrial-strength bookkeeping to get them right. And if a second conditional branch is hit before it is known whether the first one was predicted right, things can get really messy.

Dynamic Branch Prediction

Clearly, having the predictions be accurate is of great value, since it allows the CPU to proceed at full speed. As a consequence, much ongoing research aims at improving branch prediction algorithms (Chen et al., 2003; Falcon et al., 2004; Jimenez, 2003; and Parikh et al., 2004). One approach is for the CPU to maintain a history table (in special hardware), in which it logs conditional branches as they occur, so they can be looked up when they occur again. The simplest version of this scheme is shown in Fig. 4-41(a). Here the history table contains one entry for each conditional branch instruction. The entry contains the address of the branch instruction along with a bit telling whether it was taken the last time it was executed. Using this scheme, the prediction is simply that the branch will go the same way it went last time. If the prediction is wrong, the bit in the history table is changed.

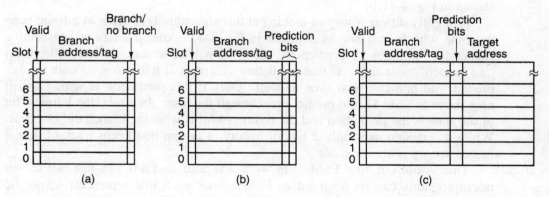

Figure 4-41. (a) A 1-bit branch history. (b) A 2-bit branch history. (c) A mapping between branch instruction address and target address.

There are several ways to organize the history table. In fact, these are precisely the same ways used to organize a cache. Consider a machine with 32-bit instructions that are word aligned so that the low-order 2 bits of each memory address are 00. With a direct-mapped history table containing 2^n entries, the low-order $n + 2$ bits of a branch instruction can be extracted and shifted right 2 bits. This n-bit number can be used as an index into the history table where a check is made to see if the address stored there matches the address of the branch. As with a cache, there is no need to store the low-order $n + 2$ bits, so they can be omitted (i.e., just the upper address bits—the tag—are stored). If there is a hit, the prediction bit is used to predict the branch. If the wrong tag is present or the entry is invalid, a miss occurs, just as with a cache. In this case, the forward/backward branch rule can be used.

If the branch history table has, say, 4096 entries, then branches at addresses 0, 16384, 32768, ... will conflict, analogous to the same problem with a cache. The same solution is possible: a two-way, four-way, or *n*-way associative entry. As with a cache, the limiting case is a single *n*-way associative entry, which requires full associativity of lookup.

Given a large enough table size and enough associativity, this scheme works well in most situations. However, one systematic problem always occurs. When a loop is finally exited, the branch at the end will be mispredicted, and worse yet, the misprediction will change the bit in the history table to indicate a future prediction of "no branch." The next time the loop is entered, the branch at the end of the first iteration will be predicted wrong. If the loop is inside an outer loop, or in a frequently-called procedure, this error can occur often.

To eliminate this misprediction, we can give the table entry a second chance. With this method, the prediction is only changed after two consecutive incorrect predictions. This approach requires having two prediction bits in the history table, one for what the branch is "supposed" to do, and one for what it did last time, as shown in Fig. 4-41(b).

A slightly different way of looking at this algorithm is to see it as a finite-state machine with four states, as depicted in Fig. 4-42. After a series of consecutive successful "no branch" predictions, the FSM will be in state 00 and will predict "no branch" next time. If that prediction is wrong, it will move to state 01, but predict "no branch" next time as well. Only if this prediction is wrong will it now move to state 11 and predict branches all the time. In effect, the leftmost bit of the state is the prediction and the rightmost bit is what the branch did last time. While this design uses only 2 bits of history, a design that keeps track of 4 or 8 bits of history is also possible.

This is not our first FSM. Fig. 4-28 was also an FSM. In fact, all of our microprograms can be regarded as FSMs, since each line represents a specific state the machine can be in, with well-defined transitions to a finite set of other states. FSMs are very widely used in all aspects of hardware design.

So far, we have assumed that the target of each conditional branch was known, typically either as an explicit address to branch to (contained within the instruction itself), or as a relative offset from the current instruction (i.e., a signed number to add to the program counter). Often this assumption is valid, but some conditional branch instructions compute the target address by doing arithmetic on registers, and then going there. Even if the FSM of Fig. 4-42 accurately predicts the branch will be taken, such a prediction is of no use if the target address is unknown. One way of dealing with this situation is to store the actual address branched to last time in the history table, as shown in Fig. 4-41(c). In this way, if

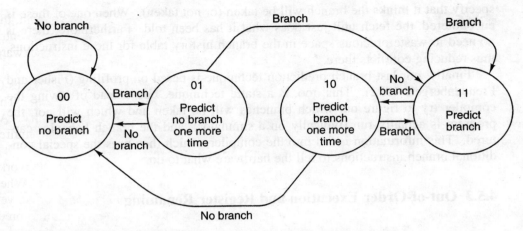

Figure 4-42. A 2-bit finite-state machine for branch prediction.

the table says that the last time the branch at address 516 was taken it went to address 4000, if the prediction is now for "branch," the working assumption will be a branch to 4000 again.

A different approach to branch prediction is to keep track of whether the last k conditional branches encountered were taken, irrespective of which instructions they were. This k-bit number, kept in the **branch history shift register**, is then compared in parallel to all the entries of a history table with a k-bit key and if a hit occurs, the prediction found there used. Somewhat surprisingly, this technique works quite well.

Static Branch Prediction

All of the branch prediction techniques discussed so far are dynamic, that is, carried out at run time while the program is running. They also adapt to the program's current behavior, which is good. The down side is that they require specialized and expensive hardware and a great deal of chip complexity.

A different way to go is to have the compiler help out. When the compiler sees a statement like

for (i = 0; i < 1000000; i++) { ... }

it knows very well that the branch at the end of the loop will be taken nearly all the time. If only there were a way for it to tell the hardware, a lot of effort could be saved.

Although this is an architectural change (and not just an implementation issue), some machines, such as the UltraSPARC III, have a second set of conditional branch instructions, in addition to the regular ones (which are needed for backward compatibility). The new ones contain a bit in which the compiler can specify that it thinks the branch will be taken (or not taken). When one of these is encountered, the fetch unit just does what it has been told. Furthermore, there is no need to waste precious space in the branch history table for these instructions, thus reducing conflicts there.

Finally, our last branch prediction technique is based on profiling (Fisher and Freudenberger, 1992). This, too, is a static technique, but instead of having the compiler try to figure out which branches will be taken and which will not, the program is actually run (typically on a simulator), and the branch behavior captured. This information is fed into the compiler, which then uses the special conditional branch instructions to tell the hardware what to do.

4.5.3 Out-of-Order Execution and Register Renaming

Most modern CPUs are both pipelined and superscalar, as shown in Fig. 2-6. What this generally means is that there is a fetch unit that pulls instruction words out of memory before they are needed in order to feed a decode unit. The decode unit issues the decoded instructions to the proper functional units for execution. In some cases it may break individual instructions into micro-ops before issuing them to the functional units, depending on what the functional units can do.

Clearly, the machine design is simplest if all instructions are executed in the order they are fetched (assuming for the moment that the branch prediction algorithm never guesses wrong). However, in-order execution does not always give optimal performance due to dependences between instructions. If an instruction needs a value computed by the previous instruction, the second one cannot begin executing until the first one has produced the needed value. In this situation (a RAW dependence), the second instruction has to wait. Other kinds of dependences also exist, as we will soon see.

In an attempt to get around these problems and produce better performance, some CPUs allow dependent instructions to be skipped over, to get to future instructions that are not dependent. Needless to say, the internal instruction scheduling algorithm used must deliver the same effect as if the program were executed in the order written. We will now demonstrate how instruction reordering works using a detailed example.

To illustrate the nature of the problem, we will start with a machine that always issues instructions in program order and also requires them to complete execution in program order. The significance of the latter will become clear later.

Our example machine has eight registers visible to the programmer, R0 through R7. All arithmetic instructions use three registers: two for the operands and one for the result, the same as the Mic-4. We will assume that if an instruction is decoded in cycle n, execution starts in cycle $n + 1$. For a simple instruction, such as an addition or subtraction, the writeback to the destination register occurs at the end of cycle $n + 2$. For a more complicated instruction, such as a multiplication, the writeback occurs at the end of cycle $n + 3$. To make the example realistic, we will allow the decode unit to issue up to two instructions per clock cycle. Commercial superscalar CPUs often can issue four or even six instructions per clock cycle.

Our example execution sequence is shown in Fig. 4-43. Here the first column gives the number of the cycle and the second one gives the instruction number. The third column lists the instruction decoded. The fourth one tells which instruction is being issued (with a maximum of two per clock cycle). The fifth one tells which instruction has been retired (completed). Remember that in this example we are requiring both in-order issue and in-order completion, so instruction $k + 1$ cannot be issued until instruction k has been issued, and instruction $k + 1$ cannot be retired (meaning the writeback to the destination register is performed) until instruction k has been retired. The other 16 columns are discussed below.

After decoding an instruction, the decode unit has to decide whether or not it can be issued immediately. To make this decision, the decode unit needs to know the status of all the registers. If, for example, the current instruction needs a register whose value has not yet been computed, the current instruction cannot be issued and the CPU must stall.

We will keep track of register use with a device called a **scoreboard**, which was first present in the CDC 6600. The scoreboard has a small counter for each register telling how many times that register is in use as a source by currently-executing instructions. If a maximum of, say, 15 instructions may be executing at once, then a 4-bit counter will do. When an instruction is issued, the scoreboard entries for its operand registers are incremented. When an instruction is retired, the entries are decremented.

The scoreboard also has a counters to keep track of registers being used as destinations. Since only one write at a time is allowed, these counters can be 1-bit wide. The rightmost 16 columns in Fig. 4-43 show the scoreboard.

In real machines, the scoreboard also keeps track of functional unit usage, to avoid issuing an instruction for which no functional unit is available. For simplicity, we will assume there is always a suitable functional unit available, so we will not show the functional units on the scoreboard.

The first line of Fig. 4-43 shows I1 (instruction 1), which multiplies R0 by R1 and puts the result in R3. Since none of these registers are in use yet, the instruction is issued and the scoreboard is updated to reflect that R0 and R1 are being read and R3 is being written. No subsequent instruction can write into any of these or can read R3 until I1 has been retired. Since this instruction is a multiplication, it will be finished at the end of cycle 4. The scoreboard values shown on each line reflect their state after the instruction on that line has been issued. Blank entries are 0s.

Since our example is a superscalar machine that can issue two instructions per cycle, a second instruction (I2) is issued during cycle 1. It adds R0 and R2, storing the result in R4. To see if this instruction can be issued, these rules are applied:

Cy	#	Decoded	Iss	Ret	Registers being read								Registers being written							
					0	1	2	3	4	5	6	7	0	1	2	3	4	5	6	7
1	1	R3=R0*R1	1		1	1										1				
	2	R4=R0+R2	2		2	1	1									1	1			
2	3	R5=R0+R1	3		3	2	1									1	1	1		
	4	R6=R1+R4	–		3	2	1									1	1	1		
3					3	2	1									1	1	1		
4				1	2	1	1										1	1		
				2	1	1												1		
				3																
5			4			1			1										1	
	5	R7=R1*R2	5			2	1		1										1	1
6	6	R1=R0−R2	–			2	1		1										1	1
7				4	1	1														1
8				5																
9			6		1		1							1						
	7	R3=R3*R1	–		1		1							1						
10					1		1							1						
11				6																
12			7			1		1								1				
	8	R1=R4+R4	–			1		1								1				
13						1		1								1				
14						1		1								1				
15				7																
16			8						2					1						
17									2					1						
18				8																

Figure 4-43. A superscalar CPU with in-order issue and in-order completion.

1. If any operand is being written, do not issue (RAW dependence).

2. If the result register is being read, do not issue (WAR dependence).

3. If the result register is being written, do not issue (WAW dependence).

We have already seen RAW dependences, which occur when an instruction needs to use as a source a result that a previous instruction has not yet produced. The other two dependences are less serious. They are essentially resource conflicts. In a **WAR dependence** (Write After Read), one instruction is trying to overwrite a register that a previous instruction may not yet have finished reading. A **WAW**

dependence (Write After Write) is similar. These can often be avoided by having the second instruction put its results somewhere else (perhaps temporarily). If none of the above three dependences exist, and the functional unit it needs is available, the instruction is issued. In this case, I2 uses a register (R0) that is being read by a pending instruction, but this overlap is permitted so I2 is issued. Similarly, I3 is issued during cycle 2.

Now we come to I4, which needs to use R4. Unfortunately, we see from line 3 that R4 is being written. Here we have a RAW dependence, so the decode unit stalls until R4 becomes available. While stalled, it stops pulling instructions from the fetch unit. When the fetch unit's internal buffers fill up, it stops prefetching.

It is worth noting that the next instruction in program order, I5, does not have conflicts with any of the pending instructions. It could have been decoded and issued were it not for the fact that this design requires issuing instructions in order.

Now let us look at what happens during cycle 3. I2, being an addition (two cycles), finishes at the end of cycle 3. Unfortunately, it cannot be retired (thus freeing up R4 for I4). Why not? The reason is that this design also requires in-order retirement. Why? What harm could possibly come from doing the store into R4 now and marking it as available?

The answer is subtle, but important. Suppose that instructions could complete out of order. Then if an interrupt occurred, it would be very difficult to save the state of the machine so it could be restored later. In particular, it would not be possible to say that all instructions up to some address had been executed and all instructions beyond it had not. This is called a **precise interrupt** and is a desirable characteristic in a CPU (Moudgill and Vassiliadis, 1996). Out-of-order retirement makes interrupts imprecise, which is why some machines require in-order instruction completion.

Getting back to our example, at the end of cycle 4, all three pending instructions can be retired, so in cycle 5 I4 can finally be issued, along with the newly decoded I5. Whenever an instruction is retired, the decode unit has to check to see if there is a stalled instruction that can now be issued.

In cycle 6, I6 stalls because it needs to write into R1 and R1 is busy. It is finally started in cycle 9. The entire sequence of eight instructions takes 18 cycles to complete due to many dependences, even though the hardware is capable of issuing two instructions on every cycle. Notice, however, that when reading down the *Iss* column of Fig. 4-43, all the instructions have been issued in order. Likewise, the *Ret* column shows that they have been retired in order as well.

Now let us consider an alternative design: out-of-order execution. In this design, instructions may be issued out of order and may be retired out of order as well. The same sequence of eight instructions is shown in Fig. 4-44, only now with out-of-order issue and out-of-order retirement permitted.

The first difference occurs in cycle 3. Even though I4 has stalled, we are allowed to decode and issue I5 since it does not conflict with any pending

Cy	#	Decoded	Iss	Ret	Registers being read								Registers being written							
					0	1	2	3	4	5	6	7	0	1	2	3	4	5	6	7
1	1	R3=R0*R1	1		1	1										1				
	2	R4=R0+R2	2		2	1	1									1	1			
2	3	R5=R0+R1	3		3	2	1									1	1	1		
	4	R6=R1+R4	–		3	2	1									1	1	1		
3	5	R7=R1*R2	5		3	3	2									1	1	1		1
	6	S1=R0–R2	6		4	3	3									1	1	1		1
				2	3	3	2									1		1		1
4			4		3	4	2		1							1		1	1	1
	7	R3=R3*S1	–		3	4	2		1							1		1	1	1
	8	S2=R4+R4	8		3	4	2		3							1		1	1	1
				1	2	3	2		3									1	1	1
				3	1	2	2		3										1	1
5				6		2	1		3										1	1
6			7			2	1	1	3							1			1	1
				4		1	1	1	2							1				1
				5				1	2							1				
				8				1								1				
7								1								1				
8								1								1				
9				7																

Figure 4-44. Operation of a superscalar CPU with out-of-order issue and out-of-order completion.

instruction. However, skipping over instructions causes a new problem. Suppose that I5 had used an operand computed by the skipped instruction, I4. With the current scoreboard, we would not have noticed this. As a consequence, we have to extend the scoreboard to keep track of stores done by skipped-over instructions. This can be done by adding a second bit map, 1 bit per register, to keep track of stores done by stalled instructions. (These counters are not shown in the figure.) The rule for issuing instructions now has to be extended to prevent the issue of any instruction with an operand scheduled to be stored into by an instruction that came before it but was skipped over.

Now let us look back at I6, I7, and I8 in Fig. 4-43. Here we see that I6 computes a value in R1 that is used by I7. However, we also see that the value is never used again because I8 overwrites R1. There is no real reason to use R1 as the place to hold the result of I6. Worse yet, R1 is a terrible choice of intermediate register, although a perfectly reasonable one for a compiler or programmer used to the idea of sequential execution with no instruction overlap.

In Fig. 4-44 we introduce a new technique for solving this problem: **register renaming**. The wise decode unit changes the use of R1 in I6 (cycle 3) and I7 (cycle 4) to a secret register, S1, not visible to the programmer. Now I6 can be issued concurrently with I5. Modern CPUs often have dozens of secret registers for use with register renaming. This technique can often eliminate WAR and WAW dependences.

At I8, we use register renaming again. This time R1 is renamed into S2 so the addition can be started before R1 is free, at the end of cycle 6. If it turns out that the result really has to be in R1 this time, the contents of S2 can always be copied back there just in time. Even better, all future instructions needing it can have their sources renamed to the register where it really is stored. In any case, the I8 addition got to start earlier this way.

On many real machines, renaming is deeply embedded in the way the registers are organized. There are many secret registers and a table that maps the registers visible to the programmer onto the secret registers. Thus the real register being used for, say, R0 is located by looking at entry 0 of this mapping table. In this way, there is no real register R0, just a binding between the name R0 and one of the secret registers. This binding changes frequently during execution to avoid dependences.

Notice that in Fig. 4-44 when reading down the fourth column, the instructions have not been issued in order. Nor they have been retired in order. The conclusion of this example is simple: using out-of-order execution and register renaming, we were able to speed up the computation by a factor of two.

4.5.4 Speculative Execution

In the previous section we introduced the concept of reordering instructions in order to improve performance. Although we did not mention it explicitly, the focus there was on reordering instructions within a single basic block. It is now time to look at this point more closely.

Computer programs can be broken up into **basic blocks**, with each basic block consisting of a linear sequence of code with one entry point on top and one exit on the bottom. A basic block does not contain any control structures (e.g., if statements or while statements) so that its translation into machine language does not contain any branches. The basic blocks are connected by control statements.

A program in this form can be represented as a directed graph, as shown in Fig. 4-45. Here we compute the sum of the cubes of the even and odd integers up to some limit and accumulate them in *evensum* and *oddsum*, respectively. Within each basic block, the reordering techniques of the previous section work fine.

The trouble is that most basic blocks are short and there is insufficient parallelism in them to exploit effectively. Consequently, the next step is to allow the reordering to cross basic block boundaries in an attempt to fill all the issue slots. The biggest gains come when a potentially slow operation can be moved upward

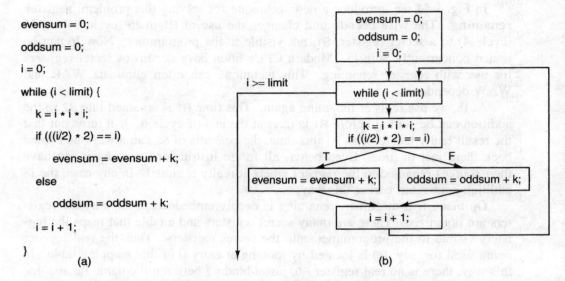

```
evensum = 0;

oddsum = 0;

i = 0;

while (i < limit) {

    k = i * i * i;

    if (((i/2) * 2) == i)

        evensum = evensum + k;

    else

        oddsum = oddsum + k;

    i = i + 1;

}
```

(a)

Figure 4-45. (a) A program fragment. (b) The corresponding basic block graph.

in the graph to start it early. This might be a LOAD instruction, a floating-point operation, or even the start of a long dependence chain. Moving code upward over a branch is called **hoisting**.

Imagine that in Fig. 4-45 all the variables were kept in registers except *evensum* and *oddsum* (for lack of registers). It might make sense then to move their LOAD instructions to the top of the loop, before computing k, to get them started early on, so the values will be available when they are needed. Of course, only one of them will be needed on each iteration, so the other LOAD will be wasted, but if the cache and memory are pipelined and there are issue slots available, it might still be worth doing this. Executing code before it is known if it is even going to be needed is called **speculative execution**. Using this technique requires support from the compiler and the hardware as well as some architectural extensions. Normally, reordering instructions over basic block boundaries is beyond the capability of hardware, so the compiler must move the instructions explicitly.

Speculative execution introduces some interesting problems. For one, it is essential that none of the speculative instructions have irrevocable results because it may turn out later that they should not have been executed. In Fig. 4-45, it is fine to fetch *evensum* and *oddsum*, and it is also fine to do the addition as soon as k is available (even before the if statement), but it is not fine to store the results back in memory. In more complicated code sequences, one common way of preventing speculative code from overwriting registers before it is known if this is desired is to rename all the destination registers used by the speculative code. In this way, only scratch registers are modified, so there is no problem if the code ultimately is not needed. If the code is needed, the scratch registers are copied to the true destination registers. As you can imagine, the scoreboarding to keep track of all this is not simple, but given enough hardware, it can be done.

However, there is another problem introduced by speculative code that cannot be solved by register renaming. What happens if a speculatively executed instruction causes an exception? A painful, but not fatal, example is a LOAD instruction that causes a cache miss on a machine with a large cache line size (say, 256 bytes) and a memory far slower than the CPU and cache. If a LOAD that is actually needed stops the machine dead in its tracks for many cycles while the cache line is being loaded, well, that's life, since the word is needed. However, stalling the machine to fetch a word that turns out not to be needed is counterproductive. Too many of these "optimizations," may make the CPU slower than if it did not have them at all. (If the machine has virtual memory, which is discussed in Chap. 6, a speculative LOAD might even cause a page fault, which requires a disk operation to bring in the needed page. False page faults can have a terrible effect on performance, so it is important to avoid them.)

One solution present in a number of modern machines is to have a special SPECULATIVE-LOAD instruction that tries to fetch the word from the cache, but if it is not there, just gives up. If the value is there when it is actually needed, it can be used, but if it is not, the hardware must go out and get it on the spot. If the value turns out not to be needed, no penalty has been paid for the cache miss.

A far worse situation can be illustrated with the following statement:

if (x > 0) z = y/x;

where x, y, and z are floating-point variables. Suppose that the variables are all fetched into registers in advance and that the (slow) floating-point division is hoisted above the if test. Unfortunately, x is 0 and the resulting divide-by-zero trap terminates the program. The net result is that speculation has caused a correct program to fail. Worse yet, the programmer put in explicit code to prevent this situation and it happened anyway. This situation is not likely to lead to a happy programmer.

One possible solution is to have special versions of instructions that might cause exceptions. In addition, a bit, called a **poison bit**, is added to each register. When a special speculative instruction fails, instead of causing a trap, it sets the poison bit on the result register. If that register is later touched by a regular instruction, the trap occurs then (as it should). However, if the result is never used, the poison bit is eventually cleared and no harm is done.

4.6 EXAMPLES OF THE MICROARCHITECTURE LEVEL

In this section, we will show brief examples of three state-of-the-art processors, showing how they employ the concepts explored in this chapter. These will of necessity be brief because real machines are enormously complex, containing millions of gates. The examples are the same ones we have been using so far: the Pentium 4, the UltraSPARC III, and the 8051.

4.6.1 The Microarchitecture of the Pentium 4 CPU

On the outside, the Pentium 4 appears to be a traditional CISC machine, with a huge and unwieldy instruction set supporting 8-, 16-, and 32-bit integer operations as well as 32-bit and 64-bit floating-point operations. It has only eight visible registers and no two of them are quite the same. Instruction lengths vary from 1 to 17 bytes. In short, it is a legacy architecture that seems to do everything wrong.

However, on the inside, the Pentium 4 contains a modern, lean-and-mean, deeply-pipelined RISC core that runs at an extremely fast clock rate that is likely to increase in the years ahead. It is quite amazing how the Intel engineers managed to build a state-of-the-art processor to implement an ancient architecture. In this section we will look at the Pentium 4 microarchitecture to see how it works.

Overview of the NetBurst Microarchitecture

The Pentium 4 microarchitecture, called the **NetBurst** microarchitecture, is a complete break from the previous P6 microarchitecture used in the Pentium Pro, Pentium II, and Pentium III, and represents the base on which Intel will build for the next few years. A rough overview of the Pentium 4 microarchitecture is given in Fig. 4-46. This diagram corresponds to Fig. 1-12, more or less.

The Pentium 4 consists of four major subsections: the memory subsystem, the front end, the out-of-order control, and the execution units. Let us examine these one at a time starting at the upper left and going counter clockwise around the chip.

The memory subsystem contains the a unified L2 (level 2) cache as well as the logic for accessing the external RAM over the memory bus. In the first generation Pentium 4, it was 256 KB; in the second it was 512 MB; in the third it was 1 MB. The L2 cache is an 8-way associative cache based on 128-byte cache lines. When a request to the L2 cache misses, it initiates a pair of 64-byte transfers to main memory to fetch the needed blocks. The L2 cache is a write-back cache. This means that when a line is modified, the new contents are not written back to memory until the line is flushed to memory.

Associated with the cache is a prefetch unit (not shown in the figure) that attempts to prefetch data from the main memory into the L2 cache before it is needed. From the L2 cache, data can migrate into the other caches at high speed. A new L2 cache fetch can begin every other clock cycle, so with, for example, a 3-GHz clock, theoretically the L2 cache can supply up to 1.5 billion 64-byte blocks per second to the other caches, for a bandwidth of 96 GB/sec.

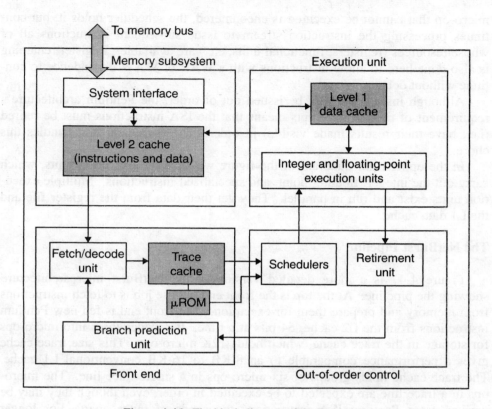

Figure 4-46. The block diagram of the Pentium 4.

Below the memory subsystem in Fig. 4-46 is the front end, which fetches instructions from the L2 cache and decodes them in program order. Each Pentium ISA instruction is broken down into a sequence of RISC-like micro-ops. For the simpler instructions, the fetch/decode unit determines which micro-ops are needed internally. For the more complex ones, the sequence of micro-ops needed is looked up in the micro-ROM. Either way, every Pentium 4 ISA instruction is converted to a sequence of micro-ops for execution by the chip's RISC core. This mechanism is how the gap is bridged between an ancient CISC instruction set and a modern RISC data path.

The decoded micro-ops are fed into the **trace cache**, which is the level 1 instruction cache. By caching the decoded micro-ops rather than the raw instructions, when an instruction is executed out of the trace cache, there is no need to decode it a second time. This approach is one of the key differences between the NetBurst microarchitecture and the P6 (which just held Pentium 4 instructions in the level 1 instruction cache). Branch prediction is also done here.

Instructions are fed from the trace cache to the scheduler in the order dictated by the program, but they are not necessarily issued in program order. When a micro-op that cannot be executed is encountered, the scheduler holds it, but continues processing the instruction stream to issue subsequent instructions all of whose resources (registers, functional units, etc.) are available. Register renaming is also done here to allow instructions with a WAR or WAW dependence to continue without delay.

Although instructions can be issued out of order, the Pentium architecture's requirement of precise interrupts means that the ISA instructions must be retired (i.e., have their results made visible) in order. The retirement unit handles this chore.

In the upper right quadrant of the figure we have the execution units, which carry out the integer, floating point, and specialized instructions. Multiple execution units exist and run in parallel. They get their data from the register file and the L1 data cache.

The NetBurst Pipeline

Figure 4-47 is a more detailed version of the NetBurst microarchitecture showing the pipeline. At the top is the front end, whose job is to fetch instructions from memory and prepare them for execution. The front end is fed new Pentium instructions from the L2 cache, 64 bits at a time. It decodes them into micro-ops for storage in the trace cache, which holds 12K micro-ops. This size trace cache gives a performance comparable to an 8-KB to 16-KB conventional L1 cache. The trace cache holds groups of six micro-ops in a single trace line. The micro-ops in a trace line are expected to be executed in order, even though they may be derived from Pentium ISA instructions thousands of bytes apart. For longer sequences of micro-ops, multiple trace lines can be linked together.

If a Pentium ISA instruction requires more than four micro-ops, it is not decoded into the trace cache. Instead, a marker is placed there telling the logic to look up the micro-ops in the microcode ROM. In this way, micro-ops are fed into the out-of-order logic, either by using previously decoded ISA instructions from the trace cache or by looking up complex ISA instructions, such as string moves, on the fly in the microcode ROM.

If the decode unit hits a conditional branch, it looks up the predicted target in the **L1 BTB** (**Branch Target Buffer**), and continues from the predicted address. The L1 BTB holds 4K of the most recent branches. If the branch instruction is not in the table, static prediction is used. A backward branch is assumed to be part of a loop and assumed to be taken. The accuracy of these static predictions is extremely high. A forward branch is assumed to be part of an if statement and is assumed not to be taken. The accuracy of these static predictions is much lower than that of the backward branches. The **trace BTB** is used for predicting where branch micro-ops will go.

The second part of the pipeline, the out-of-order control logic, is fed from the trace cache, which holds 12K micro-ops. As each micro-op comes in from the

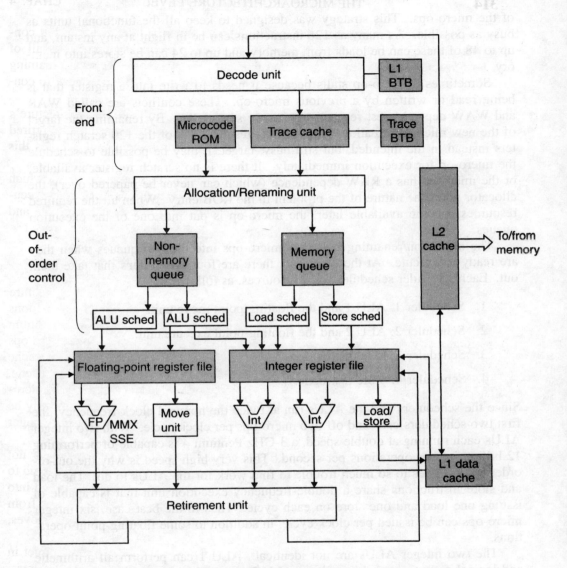

Figure 4-47. A simplified view of the Pentium 4 data path.

front end, three per cycle, the **allocation/renaming unit** logs it in a 128-entry table called the **ROB (ReOrder Buffer)**. This entry keeps track of the status of the micro-op until it is retired. The allocation/renaming unit then checks to see if the resources the micro-op needs are available. If so, the micro-op is enqueued for execution in one of the execution queues. Separate queues are maintained for memory and nonmemory micro-ops. If a micro-op cannot be executed, it is delayed, but subsequent micro-ops are processed, leading to out-of-order execution of the micro-ops. This strategy was designed to keep all the functional units as busy as possible. As many as 126 instructions can be in flight at any instant, and up to 48 of these can be loads from memory and up to 24 can be stores into memory.

Sometimes a micro-op stalls because it needs to write into a register that is being read or written by a previous micro-op. These conflicts are called WAR and WAW dependences, respectively, as we saw earlier. By renaming the target of the new micro-op to allow it to write its result in one of the 120 scratch registers instead in the intended, but still-busy, target, it may be possible to schedule the micro-op for execution immediately. It there is no scratch register available, or the micro-op has a RAW dependence (which can never be papered over), the allocator notes the nature of the problem in the ROB entry. When all the required resources become available later, the micro-op is put into one of the execution queues.

The allocation/renaming unit puts micro-ops into the two queues when they are ready to execute. At the other end, there are four **schedulers** that take them out. Each scheduler schedules some resources, as follows:

1. Scheduler 1: ALU 1 and the floating-point move unit.

2. Scheduler 2: ALU 2 and the floating-point execute unit.

3. Scheduler 3: Load instructions.

4. Scheduler 4: Store instructions.

Since the schedulers and the ALUs run at twice the nominal clock frequency, the first two schedulers can send off two micro-ops per clock cycle. With two integer ALUs each running at double speed, a 3-GHz Pentium 4 is capable of performing 12 billion integer operations per second. This very high speed is why the out-of-order control goes to so much trouble to find work for the ALUs to do. The load and store instructions share a double-frequency execution unit that is capable of issuing one load and one store on each cycle. Thus in the best case, six integer micro-ops can be issued per clock cycle, in addition to some floating-point operations.

The two integer ALUs are not identical. ALU 1 can perform all arithmetic and logical operations and branches. ALU 2 can perform only addition, subtraction, shift, and rotate instructions. Similarly, the two floating-point units are not identical either. The first one can perform moves and the SSE instructions. The second one can perform floating-point arithmetic, MMX instructions, and SSE instructions.

The ALU and floating-point units are fed by a pair of 128-entry register files, one for integers and one for floating-point numbers. These provide all the operands for the instructions to be executed and provide a repository for results. Due to the register renaming, eight of them contain the registers visible at the ISA level (EAX, EBX, *ECX*, *EDX*, etc.), but which eight hold the "real" values varies over time as the mapping changes during execution.

The L1 data cache is part of the high-speed (2x) circuitry. It is an 8-KB cache, and holds integers, floating-point numbers, and other kinds of data. Unlike the trace cache, it is not decoded in any way. It just holds a copy of the bytes in memory. The L1 data cache is a 4-way associative cache with 64 bytes per cache line. It is a write-through cache, meaning that when a cache line is modified, that line is immediately copied back to the L2 cache. The cache can handle one read and one write operation per clock cycle. When a needed word is not present in the L1 cache, a request is sent to the L2 cache, which either responds immediately or fetches the cache line from memory and then responds. Up to four requests from the L1 cache to the L2 cache can be in progress at any instant.

Because micro-ops are executed out of a order, stores into the L1 cache are not permitted until all instructions preceding the one causing the store have been retired. The **retirement unit** has the task of retiring instructions, in order, and keeping track of where it is. If an interrupt occurs, instructions not yet retired are aborted, so the Pentium 4 retains the property that upon an interrupt, all instructions up to a certain point have been completed and no instruction beyond that has any effect.

If a store instruction has been retired, but earlier instructions are still in progress, the L1 cache cannot be updated, so the results are put into a special pending-store buffer. This buffer has 24 entries, corresponding to the 24 stores that might be in execution at once. If a subsequent load tries to read the stored data, it can be passed from the pending-store buffer to the instruction, even though it is not yet in the L1 data cache. This process is called **store-to-load** forwarding.

It should be clear by now that the Pentium 4 has a highly complex microarchitecture whose design was driven by the need to execute the old Pentum instruction set on a modern, highly-pipelined RISC core. It accomplishes this goal by breaking Pentium instructions into micro-ops, caching them, and feeding them into the pipeline three at time for execution on a set of ALUs capable of executing up to six micro-ops per cycle under optimal conditions. Micro-ops are executed out of order, but retired in order and results are stored into the L1 and L2 caches in order. More information about the NetBurst microarchitecture can be found in Hinton et al. (2004).

4.6.2 The Microarchitecture of the UltraSPARC-III Cu CPU

The UltraSPARC series is Sun's implementation of the Version 9 SPARC architecture. From the user's or programmer's point of view (i.e., at the ISP level), the various models are quite similar, differing mainly in performance and price. However, at the level of the microarchitecture, they differ considerably. In this section we will describe the UltraSPARC III Cu processor. The Cu in the designation refers to the use of copper wiring on chip, as opposed to the aluminum wiring used in its predecessor. Copper has lower resistance than aluminum, which allows thinner wires and faster operation.

The UltraSPARC III Cu is a full 64-bit machine, with 64-bit registers and a 64-bit data path, although for reasons of backward compatibility with Version 8 (i.e., 32-bit) SPARCs, it can also handle 32-bit operands, and, in fact, run unmodified 32-bit SPARC software. Although the internal architecture is 64 bits, the memory bus is 128 bits wide, analogous to the Pentium II's having a 32-bit architecture and a 64-bit memory bus, in both cases, the bus being one generation ahead of the CPU itself.

Unlike the Pentium 4, the UltraSPARC is a true RISC architecture, which means that it does not need a complex mechanism to convert old CISC instructions into micro-ops for execution. The core instructions are in fact already micro-ops. However, in recent years, graphics and multimedia instructions have been added, which requires special hardware facilities for their execution.

Overview of the UltraSPARC III Cu Microarchitecture

The block diagram of the UltraSPARC III Cu is given in Fig. 4-48. On the whole, it is much simpler than the Pentium 4's NetBurst microarchitecture because the UltraSPARC has a simpler ISA architecture to implement. Nevertheless, some of the key components are similar to those used in the Pentium 4. The similarities are mostly driven by technology and economics. For example, at the time these chips were designed, L1 data caches in the range of 8 KB to 16 KB made sense, so that is what they have. If at some point in the future, 64-MB L1 caches make technological and economic sense, all CPUs will have them. The differences, in contrast, are mostly due to the difference between having to bridge the gap between an old CISC instruction set and a modern RISC core and not having to do so.

At the top left of Fig. 4-48 is the 32-KB 4-way associative instruction cache, which uses 32-byte cache lines. Since most UltraSPARC instructions are 4 bytes, there is room for about 8K instructions here, slightly smaller than the NetBurst's trace cache.

The **instruction issue unit** prepares up to four instructions for execution per clock cycle. If there is a miss on the L1 cache, fewer instructions will be issued. When a conditional branch is encountered, a **branch table** with 16K entries is consulted to predict whether to fetch the next instruction or the one at the target address. In addition, an extra bit associated with each word in the instruction cache also helps improve branch prediction. Prepared instructions are fed into a 16-instruction buffer that smoothes out the flow of instructions into the pipelines.

The output of the instruction buffer flows into the integer, floating-point, and load/store units, as shown in Fig. 4-48. The integer execution unit contains two ALUs and as well as a short pipeline for branch instructions. Both the ISA registers and some scratch registers are also contained there.

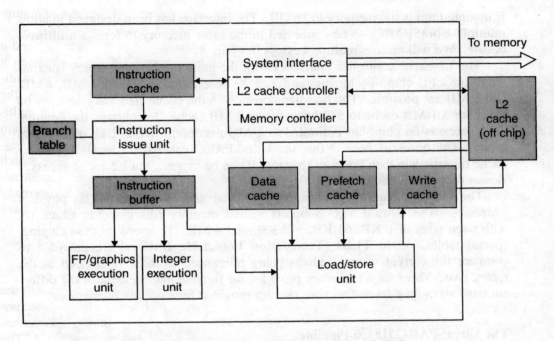

Figure 4-48. The block diagram of the UltraSPARC III Cu.

The floating-point unit contains 32 registers and three separate ALUs, for addition/subtraction, multiplication, and division, respectively. Graphical instructions are also executed here.

The load/store unit handles various load and store instructions. It has data paths to three different caches. The **data cache** is a traditional 64-KB 4-way associative L1 data cache using a 32-byte line size. The 2-KB **prefetch cache** is provided because the UltraSPARC ISA contains prefetch instructions which allow a compiler to fetch data words before they are needed. When a compiler thinks it might need a certain word, it can issue a prefetch instruction, which causes the cache line addressed to be loaded into the prefetch cache ahead of time, thus speeding up access when the word is needed a few instructions later. Under certain circumstances, hardware prefetching is also done, in order to improve the performance of legacy programs that do not do prefetching. The **write cache** is a small (2-KB) cache that is used to combine write results to make better use of the wide (256-bit) bus into the L2 cache. Its only function is to improve performance.

The chip also contains logic for controlling memory access. This logic is split into three parts: the system interface, the L2 cache controller, and the memory controller. The system interface interfaces with the memory over a 128-bit wide bus. All requests to the outside world, except to the L2 cache, pass through this interface. With a 43-bit physical memory address, in theory, the main memory can be up to 8 TB, but the size of the printed circuit board on which the processor is mounted limits the memory to 16 GB. The interface has been designed to allow multiple UltraSPARCs to be connected to the same memory to form a **multiprocessor**. We will discuss multiprocessors in Chap. 8.

The L2 cache controller interfaces with the unified L2 cache, which is external to the CPU chip. By having the L2 cache be external, caches of 1 MB, 4 MB, and 8 MB are possible. The line size depends on the cache size, ranging from 64 bytes for a 1-MB cache to 512 bytes for an 8-MB cache. In contrast, the Pentium 4 L2 cache is on chip, but is limited to 1 MB maximum due to lack of chip real estate. The trade-off here is that the UltraSPARC can have a much higher L2 cache hit rate than then Pentium (because it can be bigger), but L2 cache access is slower (because it is off chip).

The memory controller maps 64-bit virtual addresses onto 43-bit physical addresses. The UltraSPARC supports virtual memory (discussed in Chap. 6), with page sizes of 8 KB, 64 KB, 512 KB, and 4 MB. To speed up the mapping, special tables, called **TLBs** (**Translation Lookaside Buffers**) are provided to compare the current virtual address being referenced to those referenced in the recent past. Three such tables are provided for flexible management of the different page sizes for data and another two are provided for mapping instructions.

The UltraSPARC III Cu Pipeline

The UltraSPARC III Cu has a 14-stage pipeline, illustrated in simplified form in Fig. 4-49. The 14 stages are designated by the letters A through D on the left-hand side of the figure. Let us now briefly examine each of the stages. The A (Address generation) stage is at the beginning of the pipeline. It is here that the address of the next instruction to be fetched is determined. Normally, this address is the one following the current instruction. However, this sequential order can be broken for a variety of reasons, such as when a previous instruction is a branch that has been predicted to be taken, or a trap or interrupt needs to be serviced. Because branch prediction cannot be done in one cycle, the instruction following a conditional branch is always executed, no matter which way the branch goes.

The P (Preliminary fetch) stage uses the address provided by the A stage to start fetching up to four instructions from the L1 I-cache per cycle. The branch table is also consulted here to see if any of them are conditional branches, and if so, whether they are predicted to be taken. The F (Fetch) stage completes fetching the instructions for the I-cache.

The B (Branch target) stage decodes the instructions just fetched. If any of them are branches predicted to be taken, that information is available in this stage and fed back into the A stage to direct future instruction fetching.

The I (Instruction group formation) stage groups the incoming instruction depending on which of the six functional units they use:

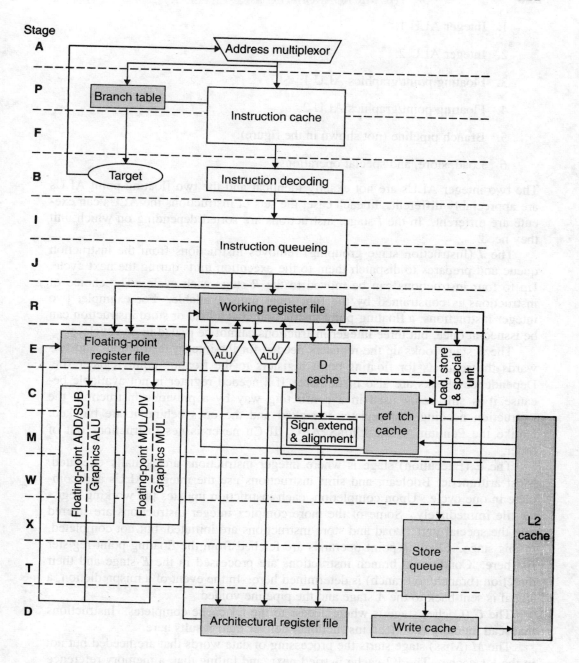

Figure 4-49. A simplified representation of the UltraSPARC III Cu pipeline.

1. Integer ALU 1.

2. Integer ALU 2.

3. Floating point/graphics ALU 1.

4. Floating point/graphics ALU 2.

5. Branch pipeline (not shown in the figure).

6. Load, store, and special operations.

The two integer ALUs are not exactly identical and the two floating-point ALUs are appreciably different. In each case, the sets of instructions the ALUs can execute are different. In the *I* stage, instructions are sorted depending on which unit they need.

The *J* (Instruction stage grouping) removes instructions from the instruction queue and prepares to dispatch them to the execution units during the next cycle. Up to four instructions can be moved to the *R* stage each cycle. The choice of instructions is constrained by the functional units available. For example, two integer instructions, a floating-point instruction, and a load or store instruction can be issued at once, but three integer instructions cannot be issued in one cycle.

The *R* stage looks up the registers needed for the integer instructions and forwards the requests for floating-point registers to the floating-point register file. Dependence checks are also made here. If a needed register is not available because it is still being used in a conflicting way by a previous instruction, the instruction needing that register is stalled and the ones behind it are blocked. Unlike the Pentium 4, the UltraSPARC III Cu never issues instructions out of order.

The *E* (Execution) stage is where integer instructions are actually executed. Most arithmetic, Boolean, and shift instructions use the integer ALUs and complete in one cycle. Upon completion, each instruction updates the working register file immediately. Some of the more complex integer instructions are steered into the special unit. Load and store instructions are initiated, but not completed, in this stage. Floating-point operands are fetched from the floating-point register file here. Conditional branch instructions are processed in the *E* stage and their direction (branch/no branch) is determined here. In the event of a misprediction, a signal is sent back to the *A* stage and the pipeline voided.

The *C* (Cache) stage is where access to the L1 cache completes. Instructions that read memory (i.e., load instructions) deliver their results here.

The *M* (Miss) stage starts the processing of data words that are needed but not in the L1 cache. The L2 cache is tried next, and failing that, a memory reference is issued, which takes a large number of cycles. Any bytes, quarter-words, or half-words that are hits on the L1 cache but need to be aligned or sign extended are also processed in this stage. Floating-point loads that hit the prefetch cache also get their results here. The prefetch cache is not used for integer data for somewhat complicated timing reasons.

The *W* (Write) stage is where the results from the special unit are written back to the working register file.

The *X* (eXtend) stage is where most of the floating-point and graphics instructions complete. The results are available to subsequent instructions via store-to-load forwarding before the instructions are formally retired in the *D* stage.

The *T* (Trap) stage is where integer and floating-point traps are detected. This stage is responsible for making traps and interrupts precise. In other words, after a trap or interrupt, the state of the machine that is saved must be such that all instructions before the trap or interrupt have fully completed and none of the instructions following it having started.

The *D* stage commits the integer and floating-point registers to their respective architectural register files. If a trap or interrupt occurs, it is these values, not those in the working registers, that are made visible. The act of storing the register in the architectural file is equivalent to retirement in the Pentium. In addition, in the *D* stage, any store instructions now complete write their results to the write cache rather than the L1 data cache. Ultimately, lines in this cache are written back to the L2 cache, bypassing the L1 cache (whose contents are disjoint from the L2 cache). This arrangement relates to making it easier to build UltraSPARC multiprocessors.

This description of the UltraSPARC III is far from complete, but should give a reasonable idea of how it works and how it differs from the Pentium 4 microarchitecture.

4.6.3 The Microarchitecture of the 8051 CPU

Our last example of a microarchitecture is the 8051's, shown in Fig. 4-50. This one is considerably simpler than that of the Pentium and UltraSPARC. The reason for this simplicity is that the chip is very small (60,000 transistors) and was designed long before pipelining became common. Also, the primary design goal was to make the chip cheap, not fast. Cheap and Simple are good friends. Cheap and Fast are not good friends.

The heart of the 8051 is the main bus. Attached to it are a number of registers, most of which can be read and written under program control. Let us briefly describe them now. The ACC register is the **ACCumulator**, the main arithmetic register where most computational results are stored. Most of the arithmetic instructions use it. The B register is used in multiplication and division as well as being a scratch register for holding temporary results. The SP register is the stack pointer, and points to the top of the stack, as in most machines. The IR register is the **Instruction Register**. It holds the instruction currently being executed.

The TMP1 and TMP2 registers are latches for the ALU. To perform an ALU operation, the operands are first copied to these latches, then the ALU is started.

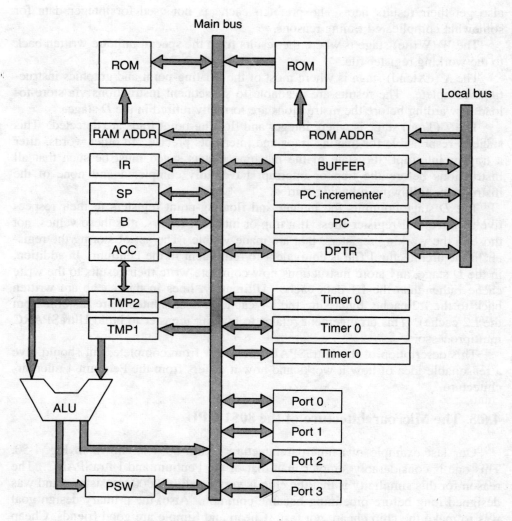

Figure 4-50. The microarchitecture of the 8051.

The ALU output can be written to any of the writable registers via the main bus. In addition, the condition codes, which indicate if the result was zero, negative, etc., are written to the PSW (**Program Status Word**).

The 8051 has separate memories for data and code. The data RAM is 128 bytes (8051) or 256 bytes (8052), so the 8-bit RAM ADDR register is sufficiently wide to address all of it. To address the RAM, the address of the byte desired is put in the RAM ADDR register, and the memory operation started. The code memory can be as large as 64 KB (when off-chip memory is used), so the ROM ADDR register used to address it is 16 bits wide. In a similar way, the ROM ADDR register addresses the program code in the ROM.

The DPTR (**Double PoinTeR**) register is a 16-bit scratch register for managing and assembling 16-bit addresses. The PC register is the 16-bit **Program Counter**, that is, the address of the next instruction to fetch and execute. The PC INCREMENTER register is a special piece of hardware that acts like a pseudoregister. When the PC is copied into it and then read back, the value is automatically incremented. Neither PC nor PC INCREMENTER are reachable from the main bus. Finally, BUFFER is another 16-bit scratch register. All these 16-bit registers actually consist of a pair of 8-bit registers that can be independently manipulated, but the effect is a 16-bit register.

In addition, the 8051 has three on-chip 16-bit timers, which are essential for real-time applications. There are also four 8-bit I/O ports, which allow the 8051 to control up to 32 external buttons, lights, sensors, actuators, and so on. It is the presence of the timers and I/O ports more than anything else that make it possible to use the 8051 for embedded applications without any additional chips.

The 8051 is a synchronous processor, with most instructions taking one clock cycle, although some take more. Each clock cycle can be divided into six parts, called states. During the first state, the next instruction is fetched from the ROM, put on the main bus, and routed into the IR register. During the second state, the instruction is decoded and the PC incremented. During the third state, the operands are prepared. During the fourth state, one of the operands is put on the main bus, usually for shipment to TMP1 where it can be latched for use as an ALU operand. The ACC register can also be copied to TMP2 during this state so both ALU inputs are ready to go. During the fifth state, the ALU executes. Finally, during the sixth state, the ALU output is written back to its destination on the main bus. Meanwhile, the ROM ADDR register is set up to fetch the next instruction.

While we could go into more detail about the 8051, the description above and Fig. 4-50 give the basic idea. The 8051 has a single main bus (to reduce chip area), a heterogeneous set of registers, and three timers and four ports hanging off the main bus, plus a few extra registers on the local bus. On each data path cycle, two operands are run through the ALU and the results stored back into a register, just as on more modern computers.

4.7 COMPARISON OF THE PENTIUM, ULTRASPARC, AND 8051

Our three examples are very different, yet even they exhibit a certain amount of commonality. The Pentium 4 has an ancient CISC instruction set that Intel's engineers would dearly love to toss into San Francisco Bay, except that doing so would violate California's water pollution laws. The UltraSPARC III is a pure RISC design, with a lean and mean instruction set. The 8051 is a simple 8-bit processors for embedded applications. Yet the heart of each of them is a set of registers and one or more ALUs that perform simple arithmetic and Boolean operands on register operands.

Despite their obvious external differences, the Pentium 4 and the Ultra-SPARC III have fairly similar execution units. Both of the execution units accept micro-operations that contain an opcode, two source registers, and a destination register. Both of them can execute a micro-operation in one cycle. Both of them have deep pipelines, branch prediction, and split I- and D-caches.

This internal similarity is not an accident or even due to the endless job-hopping by Silicon Valley engineers. As we saw with our Mic-3 and Mic-4 examples, it is easy and natural to build a pipelined data path that takes two source registers, runs them through an ALU, and stores the results in a register. Figure 4-34 shows this pipeline graphically. With current technology, this is the most effective design.

The main difference between the Pentium 4 and the UltraSPARC III is how they get from their ISA instruction set to the execution unit. The Pentium 4 has to break up its CISC instructions to get them into the three-register format needed by the execution unit. That is what the front end in Fig. 4-47 is all about—hacking big instructions into nice, neat micro-operations. The UltraSPARC III does not have to do anything because its native instructions are already nice, neat micro-operations. This is why most new ISAs are of the RISC type—to provide a better match between the ISA instruction set and the internal execution engine.

It is instructive to compare our final design, the Mic-4, to these two real-world examples. The Mic-4 is most like the Pentium 4. Both of them have the job of interpreting a non-RISC ISA instruction set. Both of them do this by breaking the ISA instructions into micro-operations with an opcode, two source registers, and a destination register. In both cases, the micro-operations are deposited in a queue for execution later. The Mic-4 has a strict in-order issue, in-order execute, in-order retire design, whereas the Pentium 4 has an in-order issue, out-of-order execute, in-order retire policy.

The Mic-4 and the UltraSPARC II are not really comparable at all because the UltraSPARC III has RISC instructions (i.e., three-register micro-operations) as its ISA instruction set. They do not have to be broken up. They can be executed as is, each one in a single data path cycle.

In contrast to the Pentium 4 and the UltraSPARC III, the 8051 is a simple machine indeed. It is more RISC-like than CISC-like because most of its simple instructions can be executed in one clock cycle and do not need to be decomposed. It has no pipelining, no caching, and has in-order issue, in-order execute, and in-order retirement. In its simplicity, it is much akin to the Mic-1.

4.8 SUMMARY

The heart of every computer is the data path. It contains some registers, one, two or three buses, and one or more functional units such as ALUs and shifters. The main execution loop consists of fetching some operands from the registers and sending them over the buses to the ALU and other functional unit for execution. The results are then stored back in the registers.

The data path can be controlled by a sequencer that fetches microinstructions from a control store. Each microinstruction contains bits that control the data path for one cycle. These bits specify which operands to select, which operation to perform, and what to do with the results. In addition, each microinstruction specifies its successor, typically explicitly by containing its address. Some microinstructions modify this base address by ORing bits into the address before it is used.

The IJVM machine is a stack machine with 1-byte opcodes that push words onto the stack, pop words from the stack, and combine (e.g., add) words on the stack. A microprogrammed implementation was given for the Mic-1 microarchitecture. By adding an instruction fetch unit to preload the bytes in the instruction stream, many references to the program counter could be eliminated and the machine greatly speeded up.

There are many ways to design the microarchitecture level. Many trade-offs exist, including two-bus versus three-bus designs, encoded versus decoded microinstruction fields, presence or absence of prefetching, shallow or deep pipelines, and much more. The Mic-1 is a simple, software-controlled machine with sequential execution and no parallelism. In contrast, the Mic-4 is a highly parallel microarchitecture with a seven-stage pipeline.

Performance can be improved in a variety of ways. Cache memory is a major one. Direct-mapped caches and set-associative caches are commonly used to speed up memory references. Branch prediction, both static and dynamic, is important, as is out-of-order execution, and speculative execution.

Our three example machines, the Pentium 4, UltraSPARC III, and 8051, all have microarchitectures not visible to the ISA assembly language programmers. The Pentium 4 has a complex scheme for converting the ISA instructions into micro-operations, caching them, and feeding them into a superscalar RISC core for out-of-order execution, register renaming, and every other trick in the book to get the last possible drop of speed out of the hardware. The UltraSPARC III Cu has a deep pipeline, but is further relatively simple, with in-order issue, in-order execution, and in-order retirement. The 8051 is very simple, with a straightforward single main bus to which a handful of registers and one ALU are attached.

PROBLEMS

1. In Fig. 4-6, the B bus register is encoded in a 4-bit field, but the C bus is represented as a bit map. Why?

2. In Fig. 4-6 there is a box labeled "High bit." Give a circuit diagram for it.

3. When the JMPC field in a microinstruction is enabled, MBR is ORed with NEXT_ADDRESS to form the address of the next microinstruction. Are there any circumstances in which it makes sense to have NEXT_ADDRESS be 0x1FF and use JMPC?

4. Suppose that in the example of Fig. 4-14(a) the statement

    k = 5;

   is added after the if statement. What would the new assembly code be? Assume that the compiler is an optimizing compiler.

5. Give two different IJVM translations for the following Java statement:

    i = k + n + 5;

6. Give the Java statement that produced the following IJVM code:

    ILOAD j
    ILOAD n
    ISUB
    BIPUSH 7
    ISUB
    DUP
    IADD
    ISTORE i

7. In the text we mentioned that when translating the statement

    if (Z) goto L1; else goto L2

   to binary, L2 has to be in the bottom 256 words of the control store. Would it not be equally possible to have L1 at, say, 0x40 and L2 at 0x140? Explain your answer.

8. In the microprogram for Mic-1, in if_icmpeq3, MDR is copied to H. A few lines later it is subtracted from TOS to check for equality. Surely it is better to have one statement here:

    if_cmpeq3   Z = TOS – MDR; rd

   Why is this not done?

9. How long does a 2.5-GHz Mic-1 take to execute the Java statement

    i = j + k;

   Give your answer in nanoseconds.

10. Repeat the previous question, only now for a 2.5-GHz Mic-2. Based on this calculation, how long would a program that runs for 100 sec on the Mic-1 take on the Mic-2?

11. Write microcode for the Mic-1 to implement the JVM POPTWO instruction. This instruction removes two words from the top of the stack.

12. On the full JVM machine, there are special 1-byte opcodes for loading locals 0 through 3 onto the stack instead of using the general ILOAD instruction. How should IJVM be modified to make the best use of these instructions?

13. The instruction ISHR (arithmetic shift right integer) exists in JVM but not in IJVM. It uses the top two values on the stack, replacing the two with a single value, the result. The second from top word of the stack is the operand to be shifted. Its content is shifted right by a value between 0 and 31, inclusive, depending on the value of the 5 least significant bits of the top word on the stack (the other 27 bits of the top word are ignored). The sign bit is replicated to the right for as many bits as the shift count. The opcode for ISHR is 122 (0x7A).

    a. What is the arithmetic operation equivalent to left right with a count of 2?
    b. Extend the microcode to include this instruction as a part of IJVM.

14. The instruction ISHL (shift left integer) exists in JVM but not in IJVM. It uses the top two values on the stack, replacing the two with a single value, the result. The second from top word of the stack is the operand to be shifted. Its content is shifted left by a value between 0 and 31, inclusive, depending on the value of the 5 least significant bits of the top word on the stack (the other 27 bits of the top word are ignored). Zeros are shifted in from the right for as many bits as the shift count. The opcode for ISHL is 120 (0x78).

    a. What is the arithmetic operation equivalent to shifting left with a count of 2?
    b. Extend the microcode to include this instruction as a part of IJVM.

15. The JVM INVOKEVIRTUAL instruction needs to know how many parameters it has. Why?

16. Implement the JVM DLOAD instruction for the Mic-2. It has a 1-byte index and pushes the local variable at this position onto the stack. Then it pushes the next higher word onto the stack as well.

17. Draw a finite state machine for tennis scoring. The rules of tennis are as follows. To win, you need at least four points and you must have at least two points more than your opponent. Start with a state (0, 0) indicating that no one has scored yet. Then add a state (1, 0) meaning that *A* has scored. Label the arc from (0, 0) to (1, 0) with an *A*. Now add a state (0, 1) indicating that *B* has scored, and label the arc from (0, 0) with a *B*. Continue adding states and arcs until all the possible states have been included.

18. Reconsider the previous problem. Are there any states that could be collapsed without changing the result of any game? If so, which ones are equivalent?

19. Draw a finite state machine for branch prediction that is more tenacious than Fig. 4-42. It should only change predictions after three consecutive mispredictions.

20. The shift register of Fig. 4-27 has a maximum capacity of 6 bytes. Could a cheaper version of the IFU be built with a 5-byte shifter register? How about a 4-byte one?

21. Having examined cheaper IFUs in the previous question, now let us examine more expensive ones. Would there ever be any point to have a much larger shift register in it, say 12 bytes? Why or why not?

22. In the microprogram for the Mic-2, the code for if_icmpeq6 goes to T when Z is set to 1. However, the code at T is the same as goto1. Would it have been possible to go to goto1 directly? Would doing so have made the machine faster?

23. In the Mic-4, the decoding unit maps the IJVM opcode onto the ROM index where the corresponding micro-operations are stored. It would seem to be simpler to just omit the decoding stage and feed the IJVM opcode into the queueing directly. It could use the IJVM opcode as an index into the ROM, the same way as the Mic-1 works. What is wrong with this plan?

24. A computer has a two-level cache. Suppose that 60% of the memory references hit on the first level cache, 35% hit on the second level, and 5% miss. The access times are 5 nsec, 15 nsec, and 60 nsec, respectively, where the times for the level 2 cache and memory start counting at the moment it is known that they are needed (e.g., a level 2 cache access does not even start until the level 1 cache miss occurs). What is the average access time?

25. At the end of Sec. 4.5.1, we said that write allocation wins only if there are likely to be multiple writes to the same cache line in a row. What about the case of a write followed by multiple reads? Would that not also be a big win?

26. In the first draft of this book, Fig. 4-39 showed a three-way associative cache instead of a four-way associative cache. One of the reviewers threw a temper tantrum, claiming that students would be horribly confused by this because three is not a power of two and computers do everything in binary. Since the customer is always right, the figure was changed to a four-way associative cache. Was the reviewer right? Discuss your answer.

27. A computer with a five-stage pipeline deals with conditional branches by stalling for the next three cycles after hitting one. How much does stalling hurt the performance if 20% of all instructions are conditional branches? Ignore all sources of stalling except conditional branches.

28. Suppose that a computer prefetches up to 20 instructions in advance. However, on the average, four of these are conditional branches, each with a probability of 90% of being predicted correctly. What is the probability that the prefetching is on the right track?

29. Suppose that we were to change the design of the machine used in Fig. 4-43 to have 16 registers instead of 8. Then we change I6 to use R8 as its destination. What happens in the cycles starting at cycle 6?

30. Normally, dependences cause trouble with pipelined CPUs. Are there any optimizations that can be done with WAW dependences that might actually improve matters? What?

31. Rewrite the Mic-1 interpreter but having LV now point to the first local variable instead of to the link pointer.

32. Write a simulator for a 1-way direct mapped cache. Make the number of entries and the line size parameters of the simulation. Experiment with it and report on your findings.

5

THE INSTRUCTION SET
ARCHITECTURE LEVEL

This chapter discusses the Instruction Set Architecture (ISA) level in detail. This level is positioned between the microarchitecture level and the operating system level, as we saw in Fig. 1-2. Historically, this level was developed before any of the other levels, and, in fact, was originally the only level. To this day it is not unusual to hear this level referred to simply as "the architecture" of a machine or sometimes (incorrectly) as "assembly language."

The ISA level has a special significance that makes it important for system architects: it is the interface between the software and the hardware. While it might be possible to have the hardware directly execute programs written in C, C++, Java, or some other high-level language, it would not be a good idea. The performance advantage of compiling over interpreting would then be lost. Furthermore, to be of much practical use, most computers have to be able to execute programs written in multiple languages, not just one.

The approach that essentially all system designers take is to have programs in various high-level languages be translated to a common intermediate form—the ISA level—and build hardware that can execute ISA-level programs directly. The ISA level defines the interface between the compilers and the hardware. It is the language that both of them have to understand. The relationship among the compilers, the ISA level, and the hardware is shown in Fig. 5-1.

Ideally, when designing a new machine, the architects will talk to both the compiler writers and the hardware engineers to find out what features each of them want in the ISA level. If the compiler writers want some feature that the

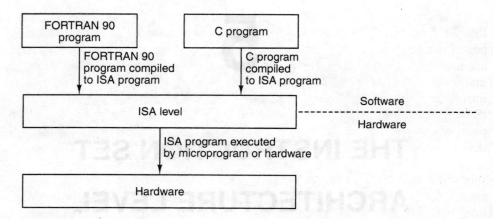

Figure 5-1. The ISA level is the interface between the compilers and the hardware.

engineers cannot implement in a cost-effective way (e.g., a branch-and-do-payroll instruction), it does not go in. Similarly, if the hardware folks have some nifty new feature they want to put in (e.g., a memory in which the words whose addresses are prime numbers are super fast), but the software folks cannot figure out how to generate code to use it, it will die on the drawing board. After much negotiation and simulation, an ISA perfectly optimized for the intended programming languages will emerge and be implemented.

That is the theory. Now the grim reality. When a new machine comes along, the first question all the potential customers ask is: "Is it compatible with its predecessor?" The second one is: "Can I run my old operating system on it?" The third one is: "Will it run all my existing application programs unmodified?" If any of the answers are "no," the designers will have a lot of explaining to do. Customers are rarely keen on throwing out all their old software and starting all over again.

This attitude puts a great deal of pressure on ccmputer architects to keep the ISA the same between models, or at least make it **backward compatible**. By this we mean that the new machine must be able to run old programs without change. However, it is completely acceptable for the new machine to have new instructions and other features that can only be exploited by new software. In terms of Fig. 5-1, as long as the designers make the ISA backward compatible with the previous models, they are pretty much free to do whatever they want with the hardware as hardly anyone cares about the real hardware (or even knows what it does). They can switch from a microprogrammed design to direct execution, or add pipelines or superscalar facilities or anything else they want, provided that they maintain backward compatibility with the previous ISA. The goal is to make sure that old programs run on the new machine. The challenge then becomes building better machines subject to the backward compatibility constraint.

The above is not intended to imply that ISA design does not matter. A good ISA has significant advantages over a poor one, particularly in raw computing power versus cost. For otherwise equivalent designs, different ISAs might account for a difference of as much as 25% in performance. Our point is just that market forces make it hard (but not impossible) to throw out an ancient ISA and introduce a new one. Nevertheless, every once in a while a new general-purpose ISA emerges, and in specialized markets (e.g., embedded systems or multimedia processors) they occur much more frequently. Consequently, understanding ISA design is important.

What makes a good ISA? There are two primary factors. First, a good ISA should define a set of instructions that can be implemented efficiently in current and future technologies, resulting in cost-effective designs over several generations. A poor design is more difficult to implement and may require many more gates to implement a processor and more memory for executing programs. It also may run slower because the ISA obscures opportunities to overlap operations, requiring much more sophisticated designs to achieve equivalent performance. A design that takes advantage of the peculiarities of a particular technology may be a flash in the pan, providing a single generation of cost-effective implementations, only to be surpassed by more forward-looking ISAs.

Second, a good ISA should provide a clean target for compiled code. Regularity and completeness of a range of choices are important traits that are not always present in an ISA. These are important properties for a compiler, which may have trouble making the best choice among limited alternatives, particularly when some seemingly obvious alternatives are not permitted by the ISA. In short, since the ISA is the interface between the hardware and the software, it should make the hardware designers happy (easy to implement efficiently) and make the software designers happy (easy to generate good code for).

5.1 OVERVIEW OF THE ISA LEVEL

Let us start our study of the ISA level by asking what it is. This may seem like a simple question, but it has more complications than one might at first imagine. In the following section we will raise some of these issues. Then we will look at memory models, registers, and instructions.

5.1.1 Properties of the ISA Level

In principle, the ISA level is defined by how the machine appears to a machine language programmer. Since no (sane) person does much programming in machine language any more, let us redefine this to say that ISA-level code is what a compiler outputs (ignoring operating system calls and ignoring symbolic assembly language for the moment). To produce ISA level code, the compiler writer has to know what the memory model is, what registers there are, what data types and instructions are available, and so on. The collection of all this information is what defines the ISA level.

According to this definition, issues such as whether the microarchitecture is microprogrammed or not, whether it is pipelined or not, whether it is superscalar or not, and so on are not part of the ISA level because they are not visible to the compiler writer. However, this remark is not entirely true because some of these properties do affect performance, and that is visible to the compiler writer. Consider, for example, a superscalar design that can issue back-to-back instructions in the same cycle provided that one is an integer instruction and one is a floating-point instruction. If the compiler alternates integer and floating-point instructions, it will get observably better performance than if it does not. Thus the details of the superscalar operation *are* visible at the ISA level, so the separation between the layers is not quite as clean as it might appear at first.

For some architectures, the ISA level is specified by a formal defining document, often produced by an industry consortium. For others it is not For example, the V9 SPARC (Version 9 SPARC) has an official definition (Weaver and Germond, 1994). The purpose of a defining document is to make it possible for different implementers to build the machine and have them all run exactly the same software and get exactly the same results.

In the case of the SPARC, the idea is to allow multiple chip vendors to manufacture SPARC chips that are functionally identical, differing only in performance and price. To make this idea work, the chip vendors have to know what a SPARC chip is supposed to do (at the ISA level). Therefore the defining document tells what the memory model is, what registers are present, what the instructions do, and so on, but not what the microarchitecture is like.

Such defining documents contain **normative** sections, which impose requirements, and **informative** sections, that are intended to help the reader but are not part of the formal definition. The normative sections constantly use words like *shall*, *may not*, and *should* to require, prohibit, and suggest aspects of the architecture, respectively. For example, a sentence like

> *Executing a reserved opcode shall cause a trap.*

says that if a program executes an opcode that is not defined, it must cause a trap and not be just ignored. An alternative approach might be to leave this open, in which case the sentence might read

> *The effect of executing a reserved opcode is implementation defined.*

This means that the compiler writer cannot count on any particular behavior, thus giving different implementers the freedom to make different choices. Most architectural specifications are accompanied by test suites that check to see if an implementation that claims to conform to the specification really does.

It is clear why the V9 SPARC has a document that defines its ISA level: so that all V9 SPARC chips will run the same software. There is no formal defining document for the Pentium 4's ISA level because Intel does not want to make it easy for other vendors to make Pentium 4 chips. In fact, Intel has gone to court to try to stop other vendors from cloning its chips, although it lost the case.

Another important property of the ISA level is that on most machines there are at least two modes. **Kernel mode** is intended to run the operating system and allows all instructions to be executed. **User mode** is intended to run application programs and does not permit certain sensitive instructions (such as those that manipulate the cache directly) to be executed. In this chapter we will primarily focus on user mode instructions and properties.

5.1.2 Memory Models

All computers divide memory up into cells that have consecutive addresses. The most common cell size at the moment is 8 bits, but cell sizes from 1 bit to 60 bits have been used in the past (see Fig. 2-10). An 8-bit cell is called a **byte**. The reason for using 8-bit bytes is that ASCII characters are 7 bits, so one ASCII character plus a parity bit fits into a byte. If UNICODE comes to dominate the industry in the future, then future computers may be based on 16-bit consecutively numbered units. After all, 2^4 is an even nicer number than 2^3, since 4 is a power of 2 and 3 is not.

Bytes are generally grouped into 4-byte (32-bit) or 8-byte (64-bit) words with instructions available for manipulating entire words. Many architectures require words to be aligned on their natural boundaries, so, for example, a 4-byte word may begin at address 0, 4, 8, etc., but not at address 1 or 2. Similarly, an 8-byte word may begin at address 0, 8, or 16, but not at address 4 or 6. Alignment of 8-byte words is illustrated in Fig. 5-2.

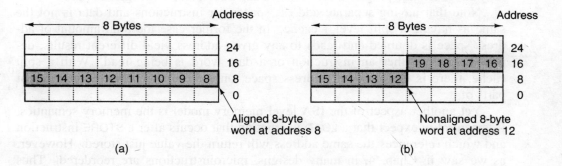

Figure 5-2. An 8-byte word in a little-endian memory. (a) Aligned. (b) Not aligned. Some machines require that words in memory be aligned.

Alignment is often required because memories operate more efficiently that way. The Pentium 4, for example, which fetches 8 bytes at a time from memory, uses 36-bit physical addresses, but it has only 33 address bits, as shown in Fig. 3-44. Thus the Pentium 4 could not even make a nonaligned memory reference if it wanted to because the low-order 3 bits are not explicitly specified. They are always 0s, forcing all memory addresses to be multiples of 8 bytes.

However, this alignment requirement sometimes causes problems. On the Pentium 4, ISA programs are allowed to reference words starting at any address, a property that goes back to the 8088, which had a 1-byte wide data bus (and thus no requirement about aligning memory references on 8-byte boundaries). If a Pentium 4 program reads a 4-byte word at address 7, the hardware has to make one memory reference to get bytes 0 through 7, and a second memory reference to get bytes 8 through 15. Then the CPU has to extract the required 4 bytes from the 16 bytes read from memory and assemble them in the right order to form a 4-byte word.

Having the ability to read words at arbitrary addresses requires extra logic on the chip, which makes it bigger and more expensive. The design engineers would love to get rid of it and simply require all programs to make word-aligned references to memory. The trouble is, whenever the engineers say "Who cares about running musty old 8088 programs that reference memory wrong?" the folks in marketing have a succinct answer: "Our customers."

Most machines have a single linear address space at the ISA level, extending from address 0 up to some maximum, often 2^{32} bytes or 2^{64} bytes. However, a few machines have separate address spaces for instructions and data, so that an instruction fetch at address 8 goes to a different address space than a data fetch at address 8. This scheme is more complex than having a single address space, but it has two advantages. First, it becomes possible to have 2^{32} bytes of program and an additional 2^{32} bytes of data while using only 32-bit addresses. Second, because all writes automatically go to data space, it becomes impossible to accidentally overwrite the program, thus eliminating one source of program bugs.

Note that having separate address spaces for instructions and data is not the same as having a split level 1 cache. In the former case the total amount of address space is doubled and reads to any given address yield different results, depending on whether an instruction or a data word is being read. With a split cache, there is still just one address space, only different caches store different parts of it.

Yet another aspect of the ISA level memory model is the memory semantics. It is natural to expect that a LOAD instruction that occurs after a STORE instruction and which references the same address will return the value just stored. However, as we saw in Chap. 4, in many designs, microinstructions are reordered. Thus there is a real danger that the memory will not have the expected behavior. The problem gets even worse on a multiprocessor, with each of multiple CPUs sending a stream of (possibly reordered) read and write requests to a shared memory.

System designers can take any one of several approaches to this problem. At one extreme, all memory requests can be serialized, so each one is completed before the next one is issued. This strategy hurts performance but gives the simplest memory semantics (all operations are executed in strict program order).

At the other extreme, no guarantees of any kind are given. To force an ordering on memory, the program must execute a SYNC instruction, which blocks the issuing of all new memory operations until all the previous ones have completed. This design puts a great burden on the compilers because they have to understand how the underlying microarchitecture works in detail, but it gives the hardware designers the maximum freedom to optimize memory usage.

Intermediate memory models are also possible, in which the hardware automatically blocks the issuing of certain memory references (e.g., those involving a RAW or WAR dependence) but not others. While having all these peculiarities caused by the microarchitecture be exposed to the ISA level is annoying (at least to the compiler writers and assembly language programmers), it is very much the trend. This trend is caused by the underlying implementations such as microinstruction reordering, deep pipelines, multiple cache levels, and so on. We will see more examples of such unnatural effects later in this chapter.

5.1.3 Registers

All computers have some registers visible at the ISA level. They are there to control execution of the program, hold temporary results, and for other purposes. In general, the registers visible at the microarchitecture level, such as TOS and MAR in Fig. 4-1, are not visible at the ISA level. However, a few of them, such as the program counter and stack pointer, are visible at both levels. On the other hand, registers visible at the ISA level are always visible at the microarchitecture level since that is where they are implemented.

ISA-level registers can be roughly divided into two categories: special-purpose registers and general-purpose registers The special-purpose registers include things like the program counter and stack pointer, as well as other registers with a specific function. In contrast, the general-purpose registers are there to hold key local variables, and intermediate results of calculations. Their main function is to provide rapid access to heavily-used data (basically, avoiding memory accesses). RISC machines, with their fast CPUs and (relatively) slow memories, usually have at least 32 general-purpose registers, and the trend in new CPU designs is to have even more.

On some machines, the general-purpose registers are completely symmetric and interchangeable. If the registers are all equivalent, a compiler can use R1 to hold a temporary result, but it can equally well use R25. The choice of register does not matter.

However, on other machines some of the general-purpose registers may be somewhat special. For example, on the Pentium 4, there is a register called EDX that can be used as a general register, but which also receives half the product in a multiplication and which holds half the dividend in a division.

Even when the general-purpose registers are completely interchangeable, it is common for the operating system or compilers to adopt conventions about how they are used. For example, some registers may hold parameters to procedures called and others may be used as scratch registers. If a compiler puts an important local variable in R1 and then calls a library procedure that thinks R1 is a scratch register available to it, when the library procedure returns, R1 may contain garbage. If there are system-wide conventions on how the registers are to be used, compilers and assembly-language programmers are advised to adhere to them to avoid trouble.

In addition to the ISA-level registers visible to user programs, there are always a substantial number of special-purpose registers available only in kernel mode. These registers control the various caches, memory, I/O devices, and other hardware features of the machine. They are used only by the operating system, so compilers and users do not have to know about them.

One control register that is something of a kernel/user hybrid is the **flags register** or PSW (**Program Status Word**). This register holds various miscellaneous bits that are needed by the CPU. The most important bits are the **condition codes**. These bits are set on every ALU cycle and reflect the status of the result of the most recent operation. Typical condition code bits include

N — Set when the result was Negative.

Z — Set when the result was Zero.

V — Set when the result caused an oVerflow.

C — Set when the result caused a Carry out of the leftmost bit.

A — Set when there was a carry out of bit 3 (Auxiliary carry).

P — Set when the result had even Parity.

The condition codes are important because the comparison and conditional branch instructions (i.e., conditional jump instructions) use them. For example, the CMP instruction typically subtracts two operands and sets the condition codes based on the difference. If the operands are equal, then the difference will be zero and the Z condition code bit in the PSW register will be set. A subsequent BEQ (Branch Equal) instruction tests the Z bit and branches if it is set.

The PSW contains more than just the condition codes, but the full contents varies from machine to machine. Typical additional fields are the machine mode (e.g., user or kernel), trace bit (used for debugging), CPU priority level, and interrupt enable status. Often the PSW is readable in user mode, but some of the fields can be written only in kernel mode (e.g., the user/kernel mode bit).

5.1.4 Instructions

The main feature of the ISA level is its set of machine instructions. These control what the machine can do. There are always LOAD and STORE instructions (in one form or another) for moving data between memory and registers and MOVE instructions for copying data among the registers. Arithmetic instructions are always present, as are Boolean instructions and instructions for comparing data items and branching on the results. We have seen some typical ISA instructions already (see Fig. 4-11) and will study many more in this chapter.

5.1.5 Overview of the Pentium 4 ISA Level

In this chapter we will discuss three widely different ISAs: Intel's IA-32, as embodied in the Pentium 4, the Version 9 SPARC architecture, implemented in the UltraSPARC processors, and the 8051. The intent is not to provide an exhaustive description of any of the ISAs, but rather to demonstrate important aspects of an ISA, and to show how these aspects can vary from one ISA to another. Let us start with the Pentium 4.

The Pentium 4 processor has evolved over many generations, tracing its lineage back to some of the earliest microprocessors ever built, as we discussed in Chap. 1. While the basic ISA maintains full support for execution of programs written for the 8086 and 8088 processors (which had the same ISA), it even contains remnants of the 8080, an 8-bit processor popular in the 1970s. The 8080, in turn, was strongly influenced by compatibility constraints with the still-earlier 8008, which was based on the 4004, a 4-bit chip used back when dinosaurs roamed the earth.

From a software standpoint, the 8086 and 8088 were straightforward 16-bit machines (although the 8088 had an 8-bit data bus). Their successor, the 80286 was also a 16-bit machine. Its main advantage was a larger address space, although few programs ever used it because it consisted of 16,384 64 KB segments rather than a linear 2^{30}-byte memory.

The 80386 was the first 32-bit machine in the Intel family. All the subsequent machines (80486, Pentium, Pentium Pro, Pentium II, Pentium III, Pentium 4, Celeron, Xeon, Pentium M, Centrino, etc) have essentially the same 32-bit architecture as the 80386, called **IA-32**, so it is this architecture that we will focus on here. The only major architectural change since the 80386 was the introduction of the MMX, SSE, and SSE2 instructions in later versions of the Pentium series. These instructions are highly specialized and designed to improve performance on multimedia applications.

The Pentium 4 has three operating modes, two of which make it act like an 8088. In **real mode**, all the features that have been added since the 8088 are turned off and the Pentium 4 behaves like a simple 8088. If any program does something wrong, the whole machine just crashes. If Intel had designed human beings, it would have put in a bit that made them revert back to chimpanzee mode (most of the brain disabled, no speech, sleeps in trees, eats mostly bananas, etc.)

One step up is **virtual 8086 mode**, which makes it possible to run old 8088 programs in a protected way. In this mode, a real operating system is in control of the whole machine. To run an old 8088 program, the operating system creates a special isolated environment that acts like an 8088, except that if its program crashes, the operating system is notified instead of the machine crashing. When a Windows user starts an MS-DOS window, the program run there is started in virtual 8086 mode to protect Windows itself from misbehaving MS-DOS programs.

The final mode is protected mode, in which the Pentium 4 actually acts like a Pentium 4 instead of a very expensive 8088. Four privilege levels are available and controlled by bits in the PSW. Level 0 corresponds to kernel mode on other computers and has full access to the machine. It is used by the operating system. Level 3 is for user programs. It blocks access to certain critical instructions and control registers to prevent a rogue user program from bringing down the entire machine. Levels 1 and 2 are rarely used.

The Pentium 4 has a huge address space, with memory divided into 16,384 segments, each going from address 0 to address $2^{32} - 1$. However, most operating systems (including UNIX and all versions of Windows) support only one segment, so most application programs effectively see a linear address space of 2^{32} bytes, and sometimes part of this is occupied by the operating system. Every byte in the address space has its own address, with words being 32 bits long. Words are stored in little endian format (the low-order byte has the lowest address).

The Pentium 4's registers are shown in Fig. 5-3. The first four registers, EAX, EBX, ECX, and EDX, are 32-bit, more-or-less general-purpose registers, although each one has its own peculiarities. EAX is the main arithmetic register; EBX is good for holding pointers (memory addresses); ECX plays a role in looping; EDX is needed for multiplication and division, where, together with EAX, it holds 64-bit products and dividends. Each of these registers contains a 16-bit register in the low-order 16 bits and an 8-bit register in the low-order 8 bits. These registers make it easy to manipulate 16- and 8-bit quantities, respectively. The 8088 and 80286 had only the 8- and 16-bit registers. The 32-bit registers were added with the 80386, along with the E prefix, which stands for Extended.

The next three are also somewhat general purpose, but with more peculiarities. The ESI and EDI registers are intended to hold pointers into memory, especially for the hardware string manipulation instructions, where ESI points to the source string and EDI points to the destination string. The EBP register is also a pointer register. It is typically used to point to the base of the current stack frame, the same as LV in IJVM. When a register (like EBP) is used to point to the base of the local stack frame, it is usually called the **frame pointer**. Finally, ESP is the stack pointer.

The next group of registers, CS through GS, are segment registers. To some extent, they are electronic trilobites, ancient fossils left over from the time the

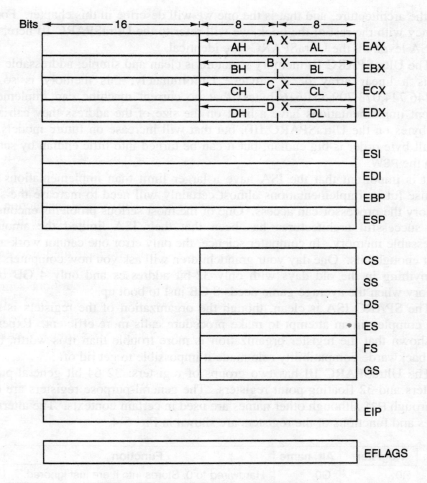

Figure 5-3. The Pentium 4's primary registers.

8088 attempted to address 2^{20} bytes of memory using 16-bit addresses. Suffice it to say that when the Pentium 4 is set up to use a single linear 32-bit address space, they can be safely ignored. Next is EIP, which is the program counter (Extended Instruction Pointer). Finally, we come to EFLAGS, which is the PSW.

5.1.6 Overview of the UltraSPARC III ISA Level

The SPARC Architecture was first introduced in 1987 by Sun Microsystems. The architecture was one of the first commercial architectures labeled a RISC architecture. It was closely based on the research done at Berkeley in the 1980s (Patterson, 1985; and Patterson and Séquin, 1982). The original SPARC was a 32-bit architecture, but the UltraSPARC III is a 64-bit machine, based on Version

9 of the architecture, and that is the one we will describe in this chapter. For consistency with the rest of the book, we will refer to the UltraSPARC III here, but at the ISA level, all the UltraSPARCs are identical.

The UltraSPARC III memory structure is clean and simple: addressable memory is a linear array of 2^{64} bytes. Unfortunately, this memory is so large (18,446,744,073,709,551,616 bytes) that no current machine can implement it. Current implementations have a limit on the size of the address they can access (2^{44} bytes on the UltraSPARC III), but that will increase on future models. The default byte order is big endian, but it can be turned into little endian by setting a bit in the PSW.

It is important that the ISA have a larger limit than implementations need, because future implementations almost certainly will need to increase the size of memory the processor can access. One of the most serious problems encountered with successful architectures has been that their ISA limited the amount of addressable memory. In computer science, the only error one cannot work around is not enough bits. One day your grandchildren will ask you how computers could do anything in the old days with only 32-bit addresses and only 4 GB of real memory when the average game needs 8 GB just to boot up.

The SPARC ISA is clean, though the organization of the registers is somewhat complex in an attempt to make procedure calls more efficient. Experience has shown that the register organization is more trouble than it is worth, but ye olde backwarde compatibility rule made it impossible to get rid of.

The UltraSPARC III has two groups of registers: 32 64-bit general-purpose registers and 32 floating-point registers. The general-purpose registers are called R0 through R31 although other names are used in certain contexts. The alternative names and functions of the registers are shown in Fig. 5-4.

Register	Alt. name	Function
R0	G0	Hardwired to 0. Stores into it are just ignored.
R1 – R7	G1 – G7	Holds global variables
R8 – R13	O0 – O5	Holds parameters to the procedure being called
R14	SP	Stack pointer
R15	O7	Scratch register
R16 – R23	L0 – L7	Holds local variables for the current procedure
R24 – R29	I0 – I5	Holds incoming parameters
R30	FP	Pointer to the base of the current stack frame
R31	I7	Holds return address for the current procedure

Figure 5-4. The UltraSPARC III's general registers.

All the general registers are 64 bits wide, and except for R0, which is truly 0, can be read and written by a variety of load and store instructions. The uses given in Fig. 5-4 are partly based on convention, but also partly based on how the hardware treats them. In general, it is unwise to deviate from the uses listed in the figure unless you have a Black Belt in SPARC Guru and really, really know what you are doing. It is the responsibility of the compiler or programmer to be sure that the program accesses the registers correctly and performs the correct kind of arithmetic on them. For example, it is very easy to load floating-point numbers into the general registers and then perform integer addition on them, an operation that will produce utter nonsense, but which the CPU will cheerfully perform when so instructed.

The global variables are used to hold constants, variables, and pointers that are needed in all procedures, although they can be stored and reloaded at procedure entries and exits if need be. The Ix and Ox registers are used for passing parameters to procedures to avoid memory references. We will explain how this works below.

Three dedicated registers are used for special purposes. The FP and SP registers bound the current frame. The former points to the base of the current frame and is used for addressing local variables, precisely the same way as LV in Fig. 4-10. The latter indicates the current top of the stack and fluctuates as words are pushed onto the stack or popped from it. In contrast, FP only changes on procedure calls and returns. The third special-purpose register is R31. It is used for procedure calls to hold the return address.

The UltraSPARC III actually has more than 32 general-purpose registers, although only 32 are visible to the program at any instant of time. This feature, known as **register windows**, is intended for the efficient support of procedure calls. It is illustrated in Fig. 5-5. The basic idea is to emulate a stack, but using the registers. That is, there are actually multiple sets of registers, just as there are multiple frames on a stack. Precisely 32 general registers are visible at any instant. The register CWP (Current Window Pointer) keeps track of which register set is currently in use.

The procedure call instruction hides the old set of registers and provides a new set for use by the called procedure by decrementing CWP. However, some registers are carried over from the calling procedure to the called procedure, providing an efficient way of passing parameters between procedures. This technique works by renaming some of the registers: after the procedure call, the old output registers, R8 to R15, are still visible, but they are now the input registers, R24 to R31. However, the eight global registers do not change, that is, they are always the same set of registers.

Unlike memory, which is quasi-infinite (at least as far as the stack goes), when procedures get nested too deeply, the machine will run out of register windows to use. At that point the oldest set is spilled into memory to free up a new set. Similarly, after many procedure returns, a register set may have to be fetched from memory. On the whole, this complexity is a big nuisance and probably more trouble than it is worth. It only helps when calls are not deeply nested.

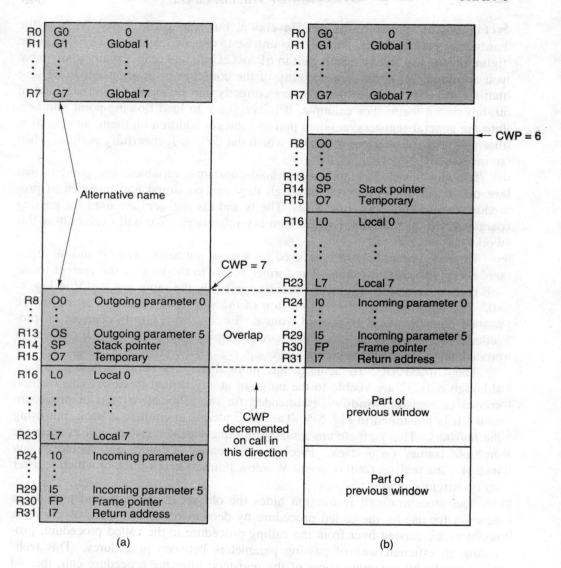

Figure 5-5. Operation of the UltraSPARC III register windows.

The UltraSPARC III also has 32 floating-point registers, which can hold either 32-bit (single-precision) or 64-bit (double-precision) values. It is also possible to use pairs of these registers to support 128-bit (quad-precision) values.

The UltraSPARC III architecture is a **load/store architecture**. That is, the only operations that access memory directly are LOADs and STOREs, instructions to move data between the registers and the memory. All operands for arithmetic and logical instructions must come from registers, or be supplied by the instruction (not memory), and all results must be saved in a register (not memory).

5.1.7 Overview of the 8051 ISA Level

Our third example is the 8051. Unlike the Pentium 4 (which is primarily used in desktop machines and server farms), and the UltraSPARC III (which is primarily used in large server configurations, especially multiprocessor servers), the 8051 is used in embedded systems such as traffic lights and clock radios to control the device and manage the buttons, lights, and other parts of the user interface. Its history is simple and straightforward. When Intel came out with the 8080 single chip CPU in 1974, it was an instant success. Manufacturers of all kinds embedded it in their products and then asked Intel if it could produce a single chip containing not only the CPU, but also the memory and I/O device controllers in order to reduce chip count. Intel complied and launched the 8048, which soon became the 8051. Despite its great age (or maybe, on account of its great age), it is now still widely used, in no small part because it is very cheap and in embedded systems, low cost is critical. In this section, we will give a brief technical introduction to the 8051 and its brothers and sisters.

The 8051 has one mode and no protection hardware since it never runs multiple programs owned by potentially hostile users. The memory model is extremely simple. There is a 64-KB address space for programs and a second 64-KB address space for data. The program and data spaces are split to make it possible to implement the program space in ROM and the data space in RAM.

Several different implementations of memory are possible. In the simplest one, there is a 4-KB ROM for the program and a 128-byte RAM for data. Both the ROM and the RAM are on chip. For small applications, this amount of memory is often enough and having all the memory on the CPU chip is a big win. The 8052 has twice as much memory on chip: 8 KB of ROM and 256 bytes of RAM. When this model is used for either chip, the program is burned into the ROM at the factory and never changed by the user.

At the other extreme, it is possible to have an 8051 system with an external program memory of 64 KB ROM or EPROM and an additional 64 KB of RAM for data. It is also possible to have a single external RAM of 64 KB that holds both the program and the data.

The 8051 also supports an intermediate model, with the lower 4 KB of program memory and 128 bytes of data memory on chip and the rest off chip. The voltage applied to certain pins on the chip determines which of these models holds.

The 8051 has an unusual way of dealing with registers. Most 8051 programs are written as though the 8051 had eight registers, each 8-bits wide. This is a natural way of viewing the CPU because many instructions contain a 3-bit field specifying which register to use. The registers are called R0 through R7. However, there are four sets of these registers, although at any instant, only one of them is current. A 2-bit field in the PSW determines which register set is the current one. The real purpose of having multiple register sets is to enable very rapid interrupt processing. When a interrupt occurs, the interrupt handler need not save all the registers; it can just switch to a different set. This property makes the 8051 capable of handling a very large number of interrupts per second, an important feature for a processor designed for embedded real-time systems.

Another peculiar property of the 8051 registers is that they are present in the memory space. Byte 0 of the data space is equivalent to R0 of register set 0. When an instruction changes R0 and then later reads out byte 0, it finds the new value of R0 there. Similarly, byte 1 of memory is R1 and so on. Bytes 8 through 15 of memory correspond to register set 1, and so on up through byte 31, which is R7 in register set 3. This arrangement is shown in Fig. 5-6(a).

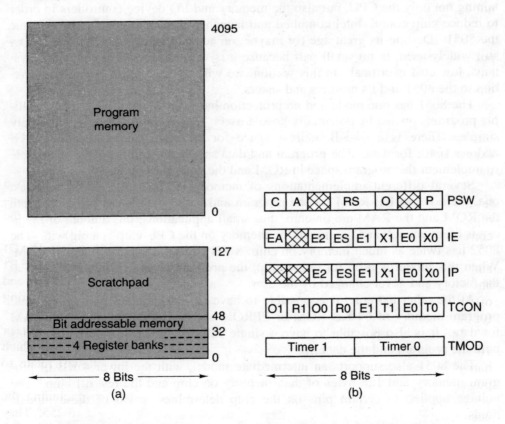

Figure 5-6. (a) On-chip memory organization for the 8051. (b) Major 8051 registers.

Directly above the four register banks, at memory addresses 32 through 47, are 16 bytes of memory that are bit addressable as bits 0 through 127. The 8051 has a set of instructions for setting, clearing, ANDing, ORing, and testing specific bits addressed by a number in the range from 0 through 127. Those instructions operate on bytes 32 through 47. Such instructions are useful because embedded processors often need bit variables for recording or setting the status of switches, lamps, and other I/O devices. These special memory locations allow the 8051 to access these bit variables without fetching whole bytes, shifting them into position, and masking off unwanted bits. For such a small processor, it is exceedingly good at managing Boolean variables.

In addition to the four sets of eight registers, the 8051 has a small number of special purpose registers, the most important of which are illustrated in Fig. 5-6(b). The PSW contains, from left to right, the carry bit, the auxiliary carry bit, the register set to use, the overflow bit, and the parity bit. All of these except the register set are set as a result of arithmetic operations. The crosshatched fields are not defined.

The IE register allows interrupts to be enabled or disabled individually or collectively. If the EA bit is 0, all interrupts are disabled. Clearing this bit makes it possible to disable any further interrupts in a single instruction. Setting the bit enables any interrupts whose individual bits are set. The E2, E1, and E0 bits enable or disable the three timer channels. With three timer channels, up to three counters can be running at once, each of which generates an interrupt when it expires. The ES bit enables or disables the serial channel interrupt. The other two bits enable or disable the externally generated interrupts. When they are enabled, external devices attached to two of the 8051's pins can cause interrupts. When they are disabled, these interrupts cannot occur.

The IP register determines the priority level for each interrupt. There are two levels, low and high. If a low priority interrupt is being serviced, it can be interrupted by a high priority one, but not vice versa. When a bit is set here, the corresponding interrupt is set to high priority, otherwise it is low priority.

The TCON register controls timers 0 and 1, which are the main timers. The O1 and O0 bits are set by hardware when the corresponding timer overflows. The R1 and R0 bits are the run control bits, allowing the program to turn the timers on and off in software. The other bits related to edge triggering versus level triggering for both timers.

The final register, TMOD, determines the mode of each timer, (8-bit, 13-bit, or 16-bit), whether it is to be a true timer or just a counter, and the degree to which hardware signals can control the timers. Other registers (not shown) relate to power management and controlling the serial port.

All the special registers mentioned above, and a few others including the accumulator and the I/O ports, are located in the memory range 128 to 255. They can be addressed just like memory in the same way R0 through R7 can be. For example, the **accumulator**, which is used in most arithmetic instructions, is located at address 240. On the 8052, which has real memory in the range 128 to 255, the special registers overlay the memory space. When direct addressing is used on the 8052, the special registers are addressed whereas indirect references to memory (via a pointer in a register) go to the real RAM.

5.2 DATA TYPES

All computers need data. In fact, for many computer systems, the whole purpose is to process financial, commercial, scientific, engineering, or other data. The data have to be represented in some specific form inside the computer. At the ISA level, a variety of different data types are used. These data types will be explained below.

A key issue is whether or not there is hardware support for a particular data type. Hardware support means that one or more instructions expect data in a particular format, and the user is not free to pick a different format. For example, accountants have the peculiar habit of writing negative numbers with the minus sign to the right of the number rather than to the left, where computer scientists put it. Suppose that in an effort to impress his boss, the head of the computer center at an accounting firm changed all the numbers in all the computers to use the rightmost bit (instead of the leftmost bit) as the sign bit. This would no doubt make a big impression on the boss—because all the software would cease to function correctly. The hardware expects a certain format for integers and does not work properly when given anything else.

Now consider another accounting firm, this one just having gotten a contract to verify the federal debt (how much the U.S. government owes everyone). Using 32-bit arithmetic would not work here because the numbers involved are larger than 2^{32} (about 4 billion). One solution is to use two 32-bit integers to represent each number, giving 64 bits in all. If the machine does not support this kind of **double precision** number, all arithmetic on them will have to be done in software, but the two parts can be in either order since the hardware does not care. This is an example of a data type without hardware support and thus without a required hardware representation. In the following sections we will look at data types that are supported by the hardware, and thus for which specific formats are required.

5.2.1 Numeric Data Types

Data types can be divided into two categories: numeric and nonnumeric. Chief among the numeric data types are the integers. They come in many lengths, typically 8, 16, 32, and 64 bits. Integers count things (e.g., the number of screwdrivers a hardware store has in stock), identify things (e.g., bank account numbers), and much more. Most modern computers store integers in two's complement binary notation, although other systems have also been used in the past. Binary numbers are discussed in Appendix A.

Some computers support unsigned integers as well as signed integers. For an unsigned integer, there is no sign bit and all the bits contain data. This data type has the advantage of an extra bit, so for example, a 32-bit word can hold a single unsigned integer in the range from 0 to $2^{32} - 1$, inclusive. In contrast, a two's complement signed 32-bit integer can only handle numbers up to $2^{31} - 1$, but, of course, it can also handle negative numbers.

For numbers that cannot be expressed as an integer, such as 3.5, floating-point numbers are used. These are discussed in Appendix B. They have lengths of 32, 64, or sometimes 128 bits. Most computers have instructions for doing floating-point arithmetic. Many computers have separate registers for holding integer operands and for holding floating-point operands.

Some programming languages, notably COBOL, allow decimal numbers as a data type. Machines that wish to be COBOL-friendly often support decimal numbers in hardware, typically by encoding a decimal digit in 4 bits and then packing two decimal digits per byte (binary code decimal format). However, arithmetic does not work correctly on packed decimal numbers, so special decimal-arithmetic-correction instructions are needed. These instructions need to know the carry out of bit 3. This is why the condition code often holds an auxiliary carry bit. As an aside, the infamous Y2K (Year 2000) problem was caused by COBOL programmers who decided that it would be cheaper to represent the year as two decimal digits rather than as a 16-bit binary number. Some optimization.

5.2.2 Nonnumeric Data Types

Although most early computers earned their living crunching numbers, modern computers are often used for nonnumerical applications, such as e-mail, surfing the Web, digital photography, and multimedia creation and playback. For these applications, other data types are needed and are frequently supported by ISA-level instructions. Characters are clearly important here although not every computer provides hardware support for them. The most common character codes are ASCII and UNICODE. These support 7-bit characters and 16-bit characters, respectively. Both were discussed in Chap. 2.

It is not uncommon for the ISA level to have special instructions that are intended for handling character strings, that is, consecutive runs of characters. These strings are sometimes delimited by a special character at the end. Alternatively a string length field can be used to keep track of the end. The instructions can perform copy, search, edit and other functions on the strings.

Boolean values are also important. A Boolean value can take on one of two values: true or false. In theory, a single bit can represent a Boolean, with 0 as false and 1 as true (or vice versa). In practice, a byte or word is used per Boolean value because individual bits in a byte do not have their own addresses and thus are hard to access. A common system uses the convention that 0 means false and everything else means true.

The one situation in which a Boolean value is normally represented by 1 bit is when there is an entire array of them, so a 32-bit word can hold 32 **Boolean** values. Such a data structure is called a **bit map** and occurs in many contexts.

For example, a bit map can be used to keep track of free blocks on a disk. If the disk has *n* blocks, then the bit map has *n* bits.

Our last data type is the pointer, which is just a machine address. We have already seen pointers repeatedly. In the Mic-*x* machines, SP, PC, LV, and CPP are all examples of pointers. Accessing a variable at a fixed distance from a pointer, which is the way ILOAD works, is extremely common on all machines.

5.2.3 Data Types on the Pentium 4

The Pentium 4 supports signed two's complement integers, unsigned integers, binary coded decimal numbers, and IEEE 754 floating-point numbers, as listed in Fig. 5-7. Due to its origins as a humble 8-bit/16-bit machine, it handles integers of these lengths well, with numerous instructions for doing arithmetic, Boolean operations, and comparisons on them. Operands do not have to be aligned in memory, but better performance is achieved if word addresses are multiples of 4 bytes.

Type	1 Bit	8 Bits	16 Bits	32 Bits	64 Bits	128 Bits
Bit						
Signed integer		×	×	×		
Unsigned integer		×	×	×		
Binary coded decimal integer		×				
Floating point					×	×

Figure 5-7. The Pentium 4 numeric data types. Supported types are marked with ×.

The Pentium 4 is also good at manipulating 8-bit ASCII characters: there are special instructions for copying and searching character strings. These instructions can be used both with strings whose length is known in advance and with strings whose end is marked. They are often used in string manipulation libraries.

5.2.4 Data Types on the UltraSPARC III

The UltraSPARC III supports a wide range of data formats, as shown in Fig. 5-8. For integers alone, it can support 8-, 16-, 32-, and 64-bit operands, both signed and unsigned. Signed integers use two's complement. Floating-point operands of 32, 64, and 128 bits are included and conform to the IEEE 754 standard (for the 32-bit and 64-bit numbers). Binary coded decimal numbers are not supported. All operands must be aligned in memory.

The UltraSPARC III is highly register oriented and nearly all instructions operate on 64-bit registers. Character and string data types are not supported by special hardware instructions. They are manipulated entirely in software.

Type	1 Bit	8 Bits	16 Bits	32 Bits	64 Bits	128 Bits
Bit						
Signed integer		×	×	×	×	
Unsigned integer		×	×	×	×	
Binary coded decimal integer						
Floating point				×	×	×

Figure 5-8. The UltraSPARC III numeric data types. Supported types are marked with ×.

5.2.5 Data Types on the 8051

The 8051 has a very limited number of data types. With one exception, all the registers are 8 bits wide, so integers are also 8 bits wide. Characters are also 8 bits wide. In essence the only data type that is really supported by the hardware for arithmetic operations is the 8-bit byte, as shown in Fig. 5-9.

Type	1 Bit	8 Bits	16 Bits	32 Bits	64 Bits	128 Bits
Bit	×					
Signed integer		×				
Unsigned integer						
Binary coded decimal integer						
Floating point						

Figure 5-9. The 8051 numeric data types. Supported types are marked with ×.

The 8051 also has another hardware supported data type not used for arithmetic: the bit. A block of 16 bytes starting at address 32 is bit-oriented memory. Every bit can be individually addressed using an offset from 0 to 127. Bit 0 is the rightmost bit in byte 32, bit 1 is the bit next to it, and so on. There are instructions to set, clear, AND, OR, and complement individual bits, move to bits, and test bits. For embedded systems, individual bits are used to store the status of switches, lights, etc., so the ability to manipulate them directly is very useful.

5.3 INSTRUCTION FORMATS

An instruction consists of an opcode, usually along with some additional information such as where operands come from, and where results go to. The general subject of specifying where the operands are (i.e., their addresses) is called **addressing** and will be discussed in detail later in this section.

Figure 5-10 shows several possible formats for level 2 instructions. Instructions always have an opcode to tell what the instruction does. There can be zero, one, two, or three addresses present.

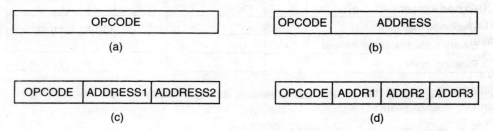

Figure 5-10. Four common instruction formats: (a) Zero-address instruction. (b) One-address instruction (c) Two-address instruction. (d) Three-address instruction.

On some machines, all instructions have the same length; on others there may be many different lengths. Instructions may be shorter than, the same length as, or longer than the word length. Having all the instructions be the same length is simpler and makes decoding easier but often wastes space, since all instructions then have to be as long as the longest one. Figure 5-11 shows some possible relationships between instruction length and word length.

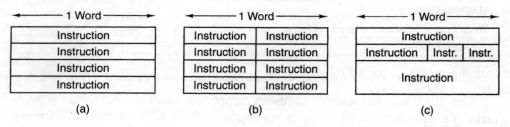

Figure 5-11. Some possible relationships between instruction and word length.

5.3.1 Design Criteria for Instruction Formats

When a computer design team has to choose instruction formats for its machine, they must consider a number of factors. The difficulty of this decision should not be underestimated. The decision about the instruction format must be made early in the design of a new computer. If the computer is commercially successful, the instruction set may survive for 20 years or more. The ability to add new instructions and exploit other opportunities that arise over an extended period are of great importance, but only if the architecture—and the company building it—survive long enough for the architecture to be a success.

The efficiency of a particular ISA is highly dependent on the technology with which the computer is to be implemented. Over a long period of time, this technology will undergo vast changes, and some of the ISA choices will be seen (with 20-20 hindsight) as unfortunate. For example, if memory accesses are fast, a stack-based design (like IJVM) is a good one, but if they are slow, then having many registers (like the UltraSPARC III) is the way to go. Readers who think this choice is easy are invited to find a slip of paper and write down their predictions for (1) a typical CPU clock speed, and (2) a typical RAM access time for computers 20 years in the future. Fold this slip neatly and keep it for 20 years. Then unfold and read it. The humility-challenged can forget the slip of paper and just post their predictions to the Internet now.

Of course, even far-sighted designers may not be able to make all the right choices. And even if they could, they have to deal with the short term, too. If this elegant ISA is a little more expensive than its current ugly competitors, the company may not survive long enough for the world to appreciate the elegance of the ISA.

All things being equal, short instructions are better than long ones. A program consisting of n 16-bit instructions takes up only half as much memory space as n 32-bit instructions. With ever declining memory prices, this factor might be less important in the future, were it not for the fact that software is metastasizing even faster than memory prices are dropping.

Furthermore, minimizing the size of the instructions may make them harder to decode or harder to overlap. Therefore, achieving the minimum instruction size must be weighed against the time required to decode and execute the instructions.

Another reason for minimizing instruction length is already important and becoming more important with faster processors: memory bandwidth (the number of bits/sec the memory can supply). The impressive growth in processor speeds over the last decade has not been matched by equal increases in memory bandwidth. One of the increasingly common constraints on processors stems from the inability of the memory system to supply instructions and operands as rapidly as the processor can consume them. Each memory has a bandwidth that is determined by its technology and engineering design. The bandwidth bottleneck applies not only to the main memory, but also to all the caches.

If the bandwidth of an instruction cache is t bps and the average instruction length is r bits, the cache can deliver at most t/r instructions per second. Notice that this is an *upper limit* on the rate at which the processor can execute instructions, though there are current research efforts to breach even this seemingly impossible barrier. Clearly, the rate at which instructions can be executed (i.e., the processor speed) may be limited by the instruction length. Shorter instructions means a faster processor. Since modern processors are capable of executing multiple instructions every clock cycle, fetching multiple instructions per clock cycle is imperative. This aspect of the instruction cache makes the size of instructions an important design criterion that has major implications for performance.

A second design criterion is sufficient room in the instruction format to express all the operations desired. A machine with 2^n operations with all instructions smaller than n bits is impossible. There simply will not be enough room in the opcode to indicate which instruction is needed. And history has shown over and over the folly of not leaving a substantial number of opcodes free for future additions to the instruction set.

A third criterion concerns the number of bits in an address field. Consider the design of a machine with an 8-bit character and a main memory that must hold 2^{32} characters. The designers could choose to assign consecutive addresses to units of 8, 16, 24, or 32 bits, as well as other possibilities.

Imagine what would happen if the design team degenerated into two warring factions, one advocating making the 8-bit byte the basic unit of memory, and the other advocating the 32-bit word. The former group would propose a memory of 2^{32} bytes, numbered 0, 1, 2, 3, ..., 4,294,967,295. The latter group would propose a memory of 2^{30} words numbered 0, 1, 2, 3, ..., 1,073,741,823.

The first group would point out that in order to compare two characters in the 32-bit word organization, the program would not only have to fetch the words containing the characters but would also have to extract each character from its word in order to compare them. Doing so costs extra instructions and therefore wastes space. The 8-bit organization, on the other hand, provides an address for every character, thus making the comparison much easier.

The 32-bit word supporters would retaliate by pointing out that their proposal requires only 2^{30} separate addresses, giving an address length of only 30 bits, whereas the 8-bit byte proposal requires 32 bits to address the same memory. A shorter address means a shorter instruction, which not only takes up less space but also requires less time to fetch. Alternatively, they could retain the 32-bit address to reference a 16 GB memory instead of a puny 4 GB memory.

This example demonstrates that in order to gain a finer memory resolution, one must pay the price of longer addresses and thus longer instructions. The ultimate in resolution is a memory organization in which every bit is directly addressable (e.g., the Burroughs B1700). At the other extreme is a memory consisting of very long words (e.g., the CDC Cyber series had 60-bit words).

Modern computer systems have arrived at a compromise that, in some sense, captures the worst of both. They require all the bits necessary to address individual bytes, but memory accesses read one, two, or sometimes four words at a time. Reading 1 byte from memory on the UltraSPARC III, for example, brings in a minimum of 16 bytes (see Fig. 3-47) and probably an entire 64-byte cache line.

5.3.2 Expanding Opcodes

In the preceding section we saw how short addresses and good memory resolution could be traded off against each other. In this section we will examine new trade-offs, involving both opcodes and addresses. Consider an $(n + k)$ bit instruction with a k-bit opcode and a single n-bit address. This instruction allows 2^k different operations and 2^n addressable memory cells. Alternatively, the same $n + k$ bits could be broken up into a $(k - 1)$ bit opcode, and an $(n + 1)$ bit address, meaning only half as many instructions but either twice as much memory addressable, or the same amount of memory but with twice the resolution. A $(k + 1)$ bit opcode and an $(n - 1)$ bit address gives more operations, but the price is either a smaller number of cells addressable, or poorer resolution and the same amount of memory addressable. Quite sophisticated trade-offs are possible between opcode bits and address bits as well as the simpler ones just described. The scheme discussed in the following paragraphs is called an **expanding opcode**.

The concept of an expanding opcode can be most clearly seen by a simple example. Consider a machine in which instructions are 16 bits long and addresses are 4 bits long, as shown in Fig. 5-12. This situation might be reasonable for a machine that has 16 registers (hence a 4-bit register address) on which all arithmetic operations take place. One design would be a 4-bit opcode and three addresses in each instruction, giving 16 three-address instructions.

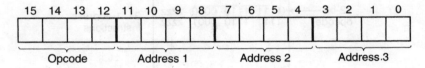

Figure 5-12. An instruction with a 4-bit opcode and three 4-bit address fields.

However, if the designers need 15 three-address instructions, 14 two-address instructions, 31 one-address instructions, and 16 instructions with no address at all, they can use opcodes 0 to 14 as three-address instructions but interpret opcode 15 differently (see Fig. 5-13).

Opcode 15 means that the opcode is contained in bits 8 to 15 instead of 12 to 15. Bits 0 to 3 and 4 to 7 form two addresses, as usual. The 14 two-address instructions all have 1111 in the leftmost 4 bits, and numbers from 0000 to 1101 in bits 8 to 11. Instructions with 1111 in the leftmost 4 bits and either 1110 or 1111 in bits 8 to 11 will be treated specially. They will be treated as though their opcodes were in bits 4 to 15. The result is 32 new opcodes. Because only 31 are needed, opcode 111111111111 is interpreted to mean that the real opcode is in bits 0 to 15, giving 16 instructions with no address.

As we proceeded through this discussion, the opcode got longer and longer: the three-address instructions have a 4-bit opcode, the two-address instructions have an 8-bit opcode, the one-address instructions have a 12-bit opcode, and the zero-address instructions have a 16-bit opcode.

The idea of expanding opcodes demonstrates a trade-off between the space for opcodes and space for other information. In practice, expanding opcodes are not quite as clean and regular as in our example. In fact, the ability to use variable sizes of opcodes can be exploited in either of two ways. First, the instructions can

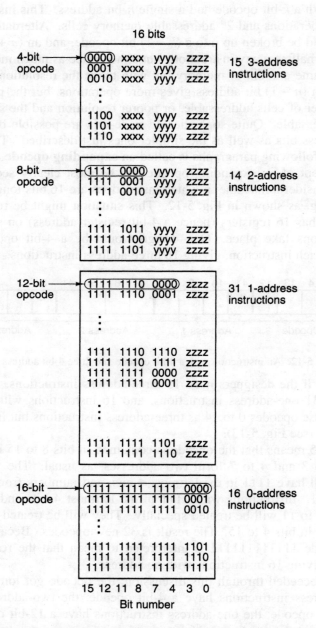

Figure 5-13. An expanding opcode allowing 15 three-address instructions, 14 two-address instructions, 31 one-address instructions, and 16 zero-address instructions. The fields marked *xxxx*, *yyyy*, and *zzzz* are 4-bit address fields.

all be kept the same length, by assigning the shortest opcodes to the instructions that need the most bits to specify other things. Second, the size of the *average* instruction can be minimized by choosing opcodes that are shortest for common instructions, and longest for rare instructions.

Carrying the idea of variable-length opcodes to an extreme, it is possible to minimize the average instruction length by encoding every instruction to minimize the number of bits needed. Unfortunately, this would result in instructions of various sizes not even aligned on byte boundaries. While there have been ISAs that had this property (for example, the ill-fated Intel 432), the importance of alignment is so important for the rapid decoding of instructions that this degree of optimization is almost certainly counterproductive. Nevertheless, it is often employed at the byte level.

5.3.3 The Pentium 4 Instruction Formats

The Pentium 4 instruction formats are highly complex and irregular, with up to six variable-length fields, five of which are optional. The general pattern is shown in Fig. 5-14. This state of affairs occurred because the architecture evolved over many generations and included some poor choices early on. In the name of backward compatibility, these early decisions could not be reversed later. In general, for two-operand instructions, if one operand is in memory, the other may not be in memory. Thus instructions exist to add two registers, add a register to memory, and add memory to a register, but not to add a memory word to another memory word.

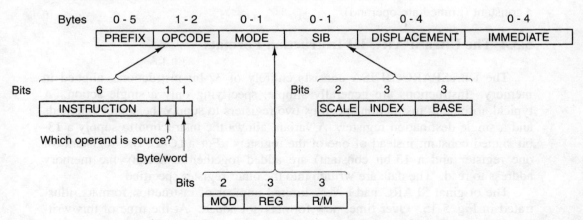

Figure 5-14. The Pentium 4 instruction formats.

On earlier Intel architectures, all opcodes were 1 byte, though the concept of a prefix byte was used extensively for modifying some instructions. A **prefix byte** is an extra opcode stuck onto the front of an instruction to change its action. The WIDE instruction in IJVM is an example of a prefix byte. Unfortunately, at some point during the evolution, Intel ran out of opcodes, so one opcode, 0xFF, was designated as an **escape code** to permit a second instruction byte.

The individual bits in the Pentium 4 opcodes do not give much information about the instruction. The only structure in the opcode field is the use of the low-order bit in some instructions to indicate byte/word, and the use of the adjoining bit to indicate whether the memory address (if it is present) is the source or the destination. Thus in general, the opcode must be fully decoded to determine what class of operation is to be performed—and thus how long the instruction is. This makes high-performance implementations difficult, since extensive decoding is necessary before it can even be determined where the next instruction starts.

Following the opcode byte in most instructions that reference an operand in memory is a second byte that tells all about the operand. These 8 bits are split up into a 2-bit MOD field and two 3-bit register fields, REG and R/M. Sometimes the first 3 bits of this byte are used as an extension for the opcode, giving a total 11 bits for the opcode. However, the 2-bit mode field means that there are only four ways to address operands and one of the operands must always be a register. Logically, any of EAX, EBX, ECX, EDX, ESI, EDI, EBP, ESP should be specifiable as either register, but the encoding rules prohibit some combinations and use them for special cases. Some modes require an additional byte, called **SIB** giving**Scale, Index, Base**), This scheme is not ideal, but a compromise given the competing demands of backward compatibility and the desire to add new features not originally envisioned.

In addition to all this, some instructions have 1, 2, or 4 more bytes specifying a memory address (displacement) and possibly another 1, 2, or 4 bytes containing a constant (immediate operand).

5.3.4 The UltraSPARC III Instruction Formats

The UltraSPARC III ISA consists entirely of 32-bit instructions, aligned in memory. Instructions are generally simple, specifying only a single action. A typical arithmetic instruction specifies two registers to supply the source operands and a single destination register. A variant allows the instruction to supply a 13-bit signed constant instead of one of the registers. For a LOAD, two registers (or one register and a 13-bit constant) are added together to specify the memory address to read. The data are written into the other register specified.

The original SPARC had a very limited number of instruction formats, illustrated in Fig. 5-15. Over time, new formats got added. At the time of this writing, the count was 31 and rising. (Can it be long before we see some company advertising the "World's most complex RISC machine"?) Most of the new variants were obtained by chopping a few bits off some field. For example, the original branches used format 3, with a 22-bit offset. When predicted branches were added, 3 of the 22 bits were removed, 1 being used for the prediction (taken/not taken), and 2 being used for specifying which set of condition code bits to use.

This left a 19-bit displacement. As another example, there are many instructions for converting between data types (integer to floating point, etc.). Many of these use a variant of format 1b, with the IMMEDIATE field broken up into a 5-bit field giving the source register and an 8-bit field providing more opcode bits. The majority of instructions, however, still use the formats shown in the figure.

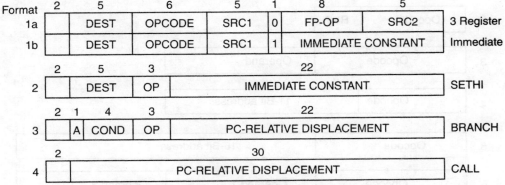

Figure 5-15. The original SPARC instruction formats.

The first 2 bits of every instruction help determine the instruction format and tell hardware where to find the rest of the opcode, if there is more. In format 1a, both sources are registers; in format 1b, one source is a register and one is a constant in the range −4096 to +4095. Bit 13 selects between them. (The rightmost bit is bit 0.) In both cases, the destination is always a register. Sufficient encoding space is provided for up to 64 instructions, some of which are currently reserved for future use.

With only 32-bit instructions, it is not possible to include a 32-bit constant in the instruction. The SETHI instruction sets 22 bits, leaving room for another instruction to set the remaining 10. It is the only instruction to use this format.

The nonpredictive conditional branches use format 3, with the COND field telling which condition to test. The A bit has to do with avoiding delay slots under certain conditions. The predictive branches use the same format, except with a 19-bit displacement, as mentioned above.

The last format is for the CALL instruction, used for making a procedure call. This instruction is special, because it is the only one where 30 bits of data are needed to specify an address. For this ISA, there is a single, 2-bit opcode. The address is the target address divided by four, making the range approximately $\pm 2^{31}$ bytes relative to the current instruction.

5.3.5 The 8051 Instruction Formats

The 8051 has six simple instruction formats, as illustrated in Fig. 5-16. Instructions are 1, 2, or 3 bytes. Format one consists of just an opcode. The instruction that increments the accumulator uses it, for example.

Format

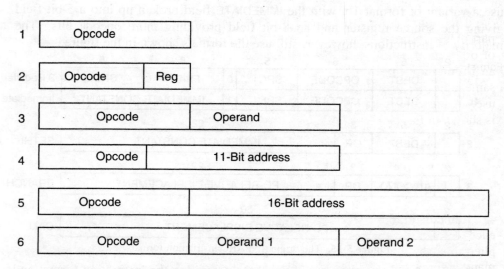

Figure 5-16. The 8051 instruction formats.

Format 2 is also one byte, consisting of a 5-bit opcode and a 3-bit register number. Instructions that use this format include many that do something involving the accumulator and a register, such as adding a register to the accumulator or moving data between a register and the accumulator.

Format 3 has a 1-byte operand. The operand can be an immediate constant, for example, to be loaded into the accumulator, an offset, for example, the distance to jump, or a bit number for example, to set, clear, or test bit *n*.

Formats 4 and 5 are used for jumps and subroutine calls. The 11-bit address version can be used when there is no external memory so all program addresses must be below 4096 (8051) or 8192 (8052). When more than 8 KB of external memory is used, the 16-bit form is needed.

Format 6 contains two 8-bit operands. A variety of instructions use it, for example, moving an 8-bit immediate constant to an on-chip memory address.

5.4 ADDRESSING

Most instructions have operands, so some way is needed to specify where they are. This subject, which we will now discuss, is called **addressing**.

5.4.1 Addressing Modes

Up to this point, we have paid little attention to how the bits of an address field are interpreted to find the operand. It is now time to investigate this subject, called **address modes**.

5.4.2 Immediate Addressing

The simplest way for an instruction to specify an operand is for the address part of the instruction actually to contain the operand itself rather than an address or other information describing where the operand is. Such an operand is called an **immediate operand** because it is automatically fetched from memory at the same time the instruction itself is fetched; hence it is immediately available for use. A possible immediate instruction for loading register R1 with the constant 4 is shown in Fig. 5-17.

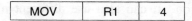

| MOV | R1 | 4 |

Figure 5-17. An immediate instruction for loading 4 into register 1.

Immediate addressing has the virtue of not requiring an extra memory reference to fetch the operand. It has the disadvantage that only a constant can be supplied this way. Also, the number of values is limited by the size of the field. Still, many architectures use this technique for specifying small integer constants.

5.4.3 Direct Addressing

A method for specifying an operand in memory is just to give its full address. This mode is called **direct addressing**. Like immediate addressing, direct addressing is restricted in its use: the instruction will always access exactly the same memory location. So while the value can change, the location cannot. Thus direct addressing can only be used to access global variables whose address is known at compile time. Nevertheless, many programs have global variables, so this mode is widely used. The details of how the computer knows which addresses are immediate and which are direct will be discussed later.

5.4.4 Register Addressing

Register addressing is conceptually the same as direct addressing but specifies a register instead of a memory location. Because registers are so important (due to fast access and short addresses) this addressing mode is the most common one on most computers. Many compilers go to great lengths to determine which variables will be accessed most often (for example, a loop index) and put these variables in registers.

This addressing mode is known simply as **register mode**. In load/store architectures such as the UltraSPARC III, nearly all instructions use this addressing mode exclusively. The only time this addressing mode is not used is when an operand is moved from memory into a register (LOAD instruction) or from a register to memory (STORE instruction). Even for those instructions, one of the operands is a register—where the memory word is to come from or go to.

5.4.5 Register Indirect Addressing

In this mode, the operand being specified comes from memory or goes to memory, but its address is not hardwired into the instruction, as in direct addressing. Instead, the address is contained in a register. When an address is used in this manner, it is called a **pointer**. A big advantage of register indirect addressing is that it can reference memory without paying the price of having a full memory address in the instruction. It can also use different memory words on different executions of the instruction.

To see why using a different word on each execution might be useful, imagine a loop that steps through the elements of a 1024-element one-dimensional integer array to compute the sum of the elements in register R1. Outside the loop, some other register, say. R2, can be set to point to the first element of the array, and another register, say, R3 can be set to point to the first address beyond the array. With 1024 integers of 4 bytes each, if the array begins at A, the first address beyond the array will be A + 4096. Typical assembly code for doing this calculation is shown in Fig. 5-18 for a two-address machine.

```
            MOV R1,#0          ; accumulate the sum in R1, initially 0
            MOV R2,#A          ; R2 = address of the array A
            MOV R3,#A+4096     ; R3 = address of the first word beyond A
    LOOP:   ADD R1,(R2)        ; register indirect through R2 to get operand
            ADD R2,#4          ; increment R2 by one word (4 bytes)
            CMP R2,R3          ; are we done yet?
            BLT LOOP           ; if R2 < R3, we are not done, so continue
```

Figure 5-18. A generic assembly program for computing the sum of the elements of an array.

In this little program, we use several addressing modes. The first three instructions use register mode for the first operand (the destination), and immediate mode for the second operand (a constant indicated by the # sign). The second instruction puts the *address* of A in R2, not the contents. That is what the # sign tells the assembler. Similarly, the third instruction puts the address of the first word beyond the array in R3.

What is interesting to note is that the body of the loop itself does not contain any memory addresses. It uses register and register indirect mode in the fourth instruction. It uses register and immediate mode in the fifth instruction, and register mode twice in the sixth instruction. The BLT might use a memory address, but more likely it specifies the address to branch to with an 8-bit offset relative to the BLT instruction itself. By avoiding the use of memory addresses completely, we have produced a short, fast loop. As an aside, this program is really for the Pentium 4, except that we have renamed the instructions and registers and changed the notation to make it easy to read because the Pentium 4's standard assembly language syntax (MASM) verges on the bizarre, a remnant of the machine's former life as an 8088.

It is worth noting that, in theory, there is another way to do this computation without using register indirect addressing. The loop could have contained an instruction to add A to R1, such as

```
ADD R1,A
```

Then on each iteration of the loop, the instruction itself could be incremented by 4, so that after one iteration it read

```
ADD R1,A+4
```

and so on until it was done.

A program that modifies itself like this is called a **self-modifying** program. The idea was thought of by none other than John von Neumann and made sense on early computers, which did not have register indirect addressing. Nowadays, self-modifying programs are considered horrible style and hard to understand. They also cannot be shared among multiple processes at the same time. Furthermore, they will not even work correctly on machines with a split level 1 cache if the I-cache has no circuitry for doing writebacks (because the designers assumed that programs do not modify themselves).

5.4.6 Indexed Addressing

It is frequently useful to be able to reference memory words at a known offset from a register. We saw some examples with IJVM where local variables are referenced by giving their offset from LV. Addressing memory by giving a register (explicit or implicit) plus a constant offset is called **indexed addressing**.

Local variable access in IJVM uses a pointer into memory (LV) in a register plus a small offset in the instruction itself, as shown in Fig. 4-19(a). However, it is also possible to do it the other way: the memory pointer in the instruction and the small offset in the register. To see how that works, consider the following calculation. We have two one-dimensional arrays of 1024 words each, A and B, and we wish to compute A_i AND B_i for all the pairs and then OR these 1024 Boolean products together to see if there is at least one nonzero pair in the set. One approach would be to put the address of A in one register, the address of B in a second register, and then step through them together in lockstep, analogous to what we did in Fig. 5-18. This way of doing it would certainly work, but it can be done in a better, more general way, as illustrated in Fig. 5-19.

```
        MOV R1,#0          ; accumulate the OR in R1, initially 0
        MOV R2,#0          ; R2 = index, i, of current product: A[i] AND B[i]
        MOV R3,#4096       ; R3 = first index value not to use
LOOP:   MOV R4,A(R2)       ; R4 = A[i]
        AND R4,B(R2)       ; R4 = A[i] AND B[i]
        OR R1,R4           ; OR all the Boolean products into R1
        ADD R2,#4          ; i = i + 4 (step in units of 1 word = 4 bytes)
        CMP R2,R3          ; are we done yet?
        BLT LOOP           ; if R2 < R3, we are not done, so continue
```

Figure 5-19. A generic assembly program for computing the OR of A_i AND B_i for two 1024-element arrays.

Operation of this program is straightforward. We need four registers here:

1. R1 – Holds the accumulated OR of the Boolean product terms.

2. R2 – The index, i, that is used to step through the arrays.

3. R3 – The constant 4096, which is the lowest value of i not to use.

4. R4 – A scratch register for holding each product as it is formed.

After initializing the registers, we enter the six-instruction loop. The instruction at *LOOP* fetches A_i into R4. The calculation of the source here uses indexed mode. A register, R2, and a constant, the address of A, are added together and used to reference memory. The sum of these two quantities goes to the memory, but is not stored in any user-visible register. The notation

    MOV R4,A(R2)

means that the destination uses register mode with R4 as the register and the source uses indexed mode, with A as the offset and R2 as the register. If A has the value, say, 124300, the actual machine instruction for this is likely to look something like the one shown in Fig. 5-20.

MOV	R4	R2	124300

Figure 5-20. A possible representation of MOV R4,A(R2).

The first time through the loop, R2 is 0 (due to it being initialized that way), so the memory word addressed is A_0, at address 124300. This word is loaded into R4. The next time though the loop, R2 is 4, so the memory word addressed is A_1, at 124304, and so on.

As we promised earlier, here the offset in the instruction itself is the memory pointer and the value in the register is a small integer that is incremented during the calculation. This form requires an offset field in the instruction large enough to hold an address, of course, so it is less efficient than doing it the other way; however, it is nevertheless frequently the best way.

5.4.7 Based-Indexed Addressing

Some machines have an addressing mode in which the memory address is computed by adding up two registers plus an (optional) offset. Sometimes this mode is called **based-indexed addressing**. One of the registers is the base and the other is the index. Such a mode would have been useful here. Outside the loop we could have put the address of *A* in R5 and the address of *B* in R6. Then we could have replaced the instruction at *LOOP* and its successor with

```
LOOP:     MOV R4,(R2+R5)
          AND R4,(R2+R6)
```

If there were an addressing mode for indirecting through the sum of two registers with no offset, that would be ideal. Alternatively, even an instruction with an 8-bit offset would have been an improvement over the original code since we could set both offsets to 0. If, however, the offsets are always 32 bits, then we have not gained anything by using this mode. In practice, however, machines that have this mode usually have a form with an 8-bit or 16-bit offset.

5.4.8 Stack Addressing

We have already noted that making machine instructions as short as possible is highly desirable. The ultimate limit in reducing address lengths is having no addresses at all. As we saw in Chap. 4, zero-address instructions, such as IADD, are possible in conjunction with a stack. In this section we will look at stack addressing more closely.

Reverse Polish Notation

It is an ancient tradition in mathematics to put the operator between the operands, as in $x + y$, rather than after the operands, as in $x\ y\ +$. The form with the operator "in" between the operands is called **infix** notation. The form with the operator after the operands is called **postfix** or **reverse Polish notation**, after the Polish logician J. Lukasiewicz (1958), who studied the properties of this notation.

Reverse Polish notation has a number of advantages over infix for expressing algebraic formulas. First, any formula can be expressed without parentheses. Second, it is convenient for evaluating formulas on computers with stacks. Third, infix operators have precedence, which is arbitrary and undesirable. For example, we know that $a \times b + c$ means $(a \times b) + c$ and not $a \times (b + c)$ because multiplication has been arbitrarily defined to have precedence over addition. But does left shift have precedence over Boolean AND? Who knows? Reverse Polish notation eliminates this nuisance.

Several algorithms for converting infix formulas into reverse Polish notation exist. The one given below is an adaptation of an idea due to E. W. Dijkstra. Assume that a formula is composed of the following symbols: variables, the dyadic (two-operand) operators + − * /, and left and right parentheses. To mark the ends of a formula, we will insert the symbol ⊥ after the last symbol and before the first symbol.

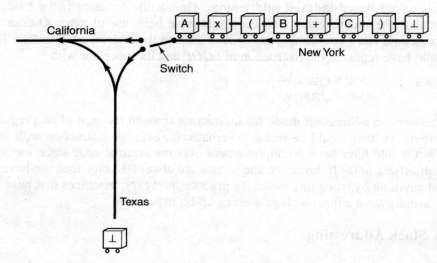

Figure 5-21. Each railroad car represents one symbol in the formula to be converted from infix to reverse Polish notation.

Figure 5-21 shows a railroad track from New York to California, with a spur in the middle that heads off in the direction of Texas. Each symbol in the formula is represented by one railroad car. The train moves westward (to the left). When each car arrives at the switch, it must stop just before it and ask if it should go to California directly or take a side trip to Texas. Cars containing variables always go directly to California and never to Texas. Cars containing all other symbols must inquire about the contents of the nearest car on the Texas line before entering the switch.

The table of Fig. 5-22 shows what happens, depending on the contents of the nearest car on the Texas line and the car poised at the switch. The first ⊥ always goes to Texas. The numbers refer to the following situations:

1. The car at the switch heads toward Texas.

2. The most recent car on the Texas line turns and goes to California.

3. Both the car at the switch and the most recent car on the Texas line are diverted and disappear (i.e., both are deleted).

   4. Stop. The symbols now in California represent the reverse Polish notation formula when read from left to right.

   5. Stop. An error has occurred. The original formula was not correctly balanced.

Car at the switch

	⊥	+	–	x	/	(	)
⊥	4	1	1	1	1	1	5
+	2	2	2	1	1	1	2
–	2	2	2	1	1	1	2
x	2	2	2	2	2	1	2
/	2	2	2	2	2	1	2
(	5	1	1	1	1	1	3

Most recently arrived car on the Texas line

Figure 5-22. Decision table used by the infix-to-reverse Polish notation algorithm

After each action is taken, a new comparison is made between the car currently at the switch, which may be the same car as in the previous comparison or may be the next car, and the car that is now the last one on the Texas line. The process continues until step 4 is reached. Notice that the Texas line is being used as a stack, with routing a car to Texas being a push operation, and turning a car already on the Texas line around and sending it to California being a pop operation.

Infix	Reverse Polish notation
A + B × C	A B C × +
A × B + C	A B × C +
A × B + C × D	A B × C D × +
(A + B) / (C – D)	A B + C D – /
A × B / C	A B × C /
((A + B) × C + D)/(E + F + G)	A B + C × D + E F + G + /

Figure 5-23. Some examples of infix expressions and their reverse Polish notation equivalents.

The order of the variables is the same in infix and in reverse Polish notation. The order of the operators, however, is not always the same. Operators appear in reverse Polish notation in the order they will actually be executed during the evaluation of the expression. Figure 5-23 gives several examples of infix formulas and their reverse Polish notation equivalents.

Evaluation of Reverse Polish notation Formulas

Reverse Polish notation is the ideal notation for evaluating formulas on a computer with a stack. The formula consists of n symbols, each one either an operand or an operator. The algorithm for evaluating a reverse Polish notation formula using a stack is simple. Scan the reverse Polish notation string from left to right. When an operand is encountered, push it onto the stack. When an operator is encountered, execute the corresponding instruction.

Figure 5-24 shows the evaluation of

$$(8 + 2 \times 5) / (1 + 3 \times 2 - 4)$$

in IJVM. The corresponding reverse Polish notation formula is

$$8 \; 2 \; 5 \times + 1 \; 3 \; 2 \times + 4 - /$$

In the figure, we have introduced IMUL and IDIV as the multiplication and division instructions, respectively. The number on top of the stack is the right operand, not the left operand. This point is important for division (and subtraction) since the order of the operands is significant (unlike addition and multiplication). In other words, IDIV has been carefully defined so that first pushing the numerator, then pushing the denominator, and then doing the operation gives the correct result. Notice how easy code generation is from reverse Polish notation to IJVM: just scan the reverse Polish notation formula and output one instruction per symbol. If the symbol is a constant or variable, output an instruction to push it onto the stack. If the symbol is an operator, output an instruction to perform the operation.

Step	Remaining string	Instruction	Stack
1	$8 \; 2 \; 5 \times + 1 \; 3 \; 2 \times + 4 - /$	BIPUSH 8	8
2	$2 \; 5 \times + 1 \; 3 \; 2 \times + 4 - /$	BIPUSH 2	8, 2
3	$5 \times + 1 \; 3 \; 2 \times + 4 - /$	BIPUSH 5	8, 2, 5
4	$\times + 1 \; 3 \; 2 \times + 4 - /$	IMUL	8, 10
5	$+ 1 \; 3 \; 2 \times + 4 - /$	IADD	18
6	$1 \; 3 \; 2 \times + 4 - /$	BIPUSH 1	18, 1
7	$3 \; 2 \times + 4 - /$	BIPUSH 3	18, 1, 3
8	$2 \times + 4 - /$	BIPUSH 2	18, 1, 3, 2
9	$\times + 4 - /$	IMUL	18, 1, 6
10	$+ 4 - /$	IADD	18, 7
11	$4 - /$	BIPUSH 4	18, 7, 4
12	$- /$	ISUB	18, 3
13	$/$	IDIV	6

Figure 5-24. Use of a stack to evaluate a reverse Polish notation formula.

5.4.9 Addressing Modes for Branch Instructions

So far we have been looking only at instructions that operate on data. Branch instructions (and procedure calls) also need addressing modes for specifying the target address. The modes we have examined so far also work for branches for the most part. Direct addressing is certainly a possibility, with the target address simply being included in the instruction in full.

However, other addressing modes also make sense. Register indirect addressing allows the program to compute the target address, put it in a register, and then go there. This mode gives the most flexibility since the target address is computed at run time. It also presents the greatest opportunity for creating bugs that are nearly impossible to find.

Another reasonable mode is indexed mode, which offsets a known distance from a register. It has the same properties as register indirect mode.

Another option is PC-relative addressing. In this mode, the (signed) offset in the instruction itself is added to the program counter to get the target address. In fact, this is simply indexed mode, using PC as the register.

5.4.10 Orthogonality of Opcodes and Addressing Modes

From a software point of view, instructions and addressing should have a regular structure, with a minimum number of instruction formats. Such a structure makes it much easier for a compiler to produce good code. All opcodes should permit all addressing modes wherever that makes sense. Furthermore, all registers should be available for all register modes [including the frame pointer (FP), stack pointer (SP), and program counter (PC)].

As an example of a clean design for a three-address machine, consider the 32-bit instruction formats of Fig. 5-25. Up to 256 opcodes are supported. In format 1, each instruction has two source registers and a destination register. All arithmetic and logical instructions use this format.

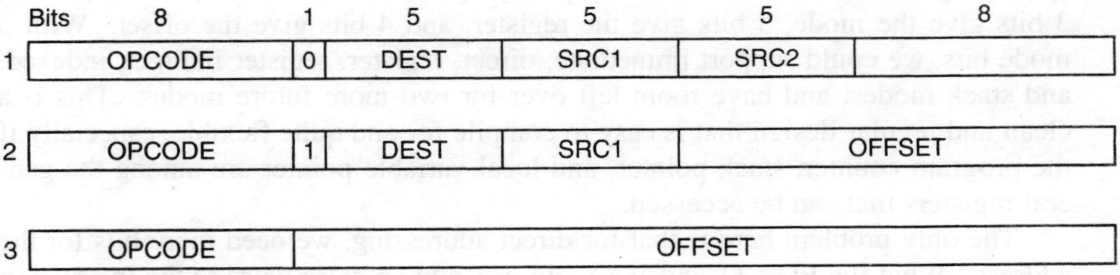

Bits	8	1	5	5	5	8
1	OPCODE	0	DEST	SRC1	SRC2	
2	OPCODE	1	DEST	SRC1	OFFSET	
3	OPCODE			OFFSET		

Figure 5-25. A simple design for the instruction formats of a three-address machine.

The unused 8-bit field at the end can be used for further instruction differentiation. For example, one opcode could be allocated for all the floating-point operations, with the extra field distinguishing among them. In addition, if bit 23 is set, format 2 is used and the second operand is no longer a register, but a 13-bit signed immediate constant. LOAD and STORE instructions can also use this format to reference memory in indexed mode.

A small number of additional instructions are needed, such as conditional branches, but they could easily fit in format 3. For example, one opcode could be assigned to each (conditional) branch, procedure call, etc., leaving 24 bits for a PC relative offset. Assuming that this offset counted in words, the range would be ±32 MB. Also a few opcodes could be reserved for LOADs and STOREs that need the long offsets of format 3. These would not be fully general (e.g., only R0 could be loaded or stored), but they would rarely be used.

Now consider a design for a two-address machine that can use a memory word for either operand. It is shown in Fig. 5-26. Such a machine can add a memory word to a register, add a register to a memory word, add a register to a register, or add a memory word to a memory word. At present, memory accesses are relatively expensive, so this design is not currently popular, but if advances in cache or memory technology make memory accesses cheap in the future, it is a particularly easy and efficient design to compile to. The PDP-11 and VAX were highly successful machines that dominated the minicomputer world for two decades using designs similar to this one.

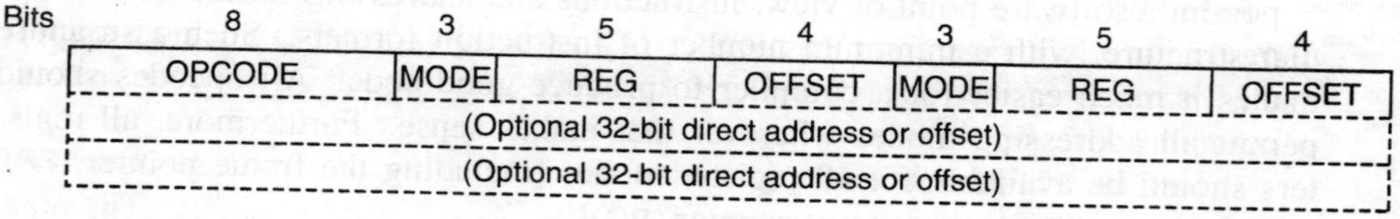

Figure 5-26. A simple design for the instruction formats of a two-address machine.

In this design, we again have an 8-bit opcode, but now we have 12 bits for specifying the source and 12 bits for specifying the destination. For each operand, 3 bits give the mode, 5 bits give the register, and 4 bits give the offset. With 3 mode bits, we could support immediate, direct, register, register indirect, indexed, and stack modes, and have room left over for two more future modes. This is a clean and regular design that is easy to compile for and quite flexible, especially if the program counter, stack pointer, and local variable pointer are among the general registers that can be accessed.

The only problem here is that for direct addressing, we need more bits for the address. What the PDP-11 and VAX did was add an extra word to the instruction for the address of each directly addressed operand. We could also use one of the two available addressing modes for an indexed mode with a 32-bit offset following the instruction. Thus in the worst case, say, a memory-to-memory ADD with both operands directly addressed or using the long indexed form, the instruction would be 96 bits long and use three bus cycles (one for the instruction, two for data). On the other hand, most RISC designs would require at least 96 bits, probably more, to add an arbitrary word in memory to another arbitrary word in memory and use at least four bus cycles.

Many alternatives to Fig. 5-26 are possible. In this design, it is possible to execute the statement

    i = j;

in one 32-bit instruction, provided that both *i* and *j* are among the first 16 local variables. On the other hand, for variables beyond 16, we have to go to 32-bit offsets. One option would be another format with a single 8-bit offset instead of two 4-bit offsets, plus a rule saying that either the source or the destination could use it, but not both. The possibilities and trade-offs are unlimited, and machine designers must juggle many factors to get a good result.

5.4.11 The Pentium 4 Addressing Modes

The Pentium 4's addressing modes are highly irregular and are different depending whether a particular instruction is in 16-bit mode or 32-bit mode. Below we will ignore 16-bit mode; 32-bit mode is bad enough. The modes supported include immediate, direct, register, register indirect, indexed, and a special mode for addressing array elements. The problem is that not all modes apply to all instructions and not all registers can be used in all modes. This makes the compiler writer's job much more difficult and leads to worse code.

The MODE byte in Fig. 5-14 controls the addressing modes. One of the operands is specified by the combination of the MOD and R/M fields. The other is always a register, and is given by the value of the REG field. The 32 combinations that can be specified by the 2-bit MOD field and the 3-bit R/M field are listed in Fig. 5-27. If both fields are zero, for example, the operand is read from the memory address contained in the EAX register.

The 01 and 10 columns involve modes in which a register is added to an 8- or 32-bit offset that follows the instruction. If an 8-bit offset is selected, it is first sign-extended to 32 bits before being added. For example, an ADD instruction with R/M = 011, MOD = 01, and an offset of 6 computes the sum of EBX and 6 and reads the memory word at that address for one of the operands. EBX is not modified.

The MOD = 11 column gives a choice of two registers. For word instructions, the first choice is used; for byte instructions, the second choice is used. Observe that the table is not entirely regular. For example there is no way to indirect through EBP and no way to offset from ESP.

In some modes, an additional byte, called **SIB (Scale, Index, Base)** follows the MODE byte (see Fig. 5-14). The SIB byte specifies a scale factor as well as two registers. When a SIB byte is present, the operand address is computed by

R/M	MOD			
	00	**01**	**10**	**11**
000	M[EAX]	M[EAX + OFFSET8]	M[EAX + OFFSET32]	EAX or AL
001	M[ECX]	M[ECX + OFFSET8]	M[ECX + OFFSET32]	ECX or CL
010	M[EDX]	M[EDX + OFFSET8]	M[EDX + OFFSET32]	EDX or DL
011	M[EBX]	M[EBX + OFFSET8]	M[EBX + OFFSET32]	EBX or BL
100	SIB	SIB with OFFSET8	SIB with OFFSET32	ESP or AH
101	Direct	M[EBP + OFFSET8]	M[EBP + OFFSET32]	EBP or CH
110	M[ESI]	M[ESI + OFFSET8]	M[ESI + OFFSET32]	ESI or DH
111	M[EDI]	M[EDI + OFFSET8]	M[EDI + OFFSET32]	EDI or BH

Figure 5-27. The Pentium 4 32-bit addressing modes. M[x] is the memory word at x.

multiplying the index register by 1, 2, 4, or 8 (depending on SCALE), adding it to the base register, and finally possibly adding an 8- or 32-bit displacement, depending on MOD. Almost all the registers can be used as either index or base.

The SIB modes are useful for accessing array elements. For example, consider the Java statement

    for (i = 0; i < n; i++) a[i] = 0;

where a is an array of 4-byte integers local to the current procedure. Typically, EBP is used to point to the base of the stack frame containing the local variables and arrays, as shown in Fig. 5-28. The compiler might keep i in EAX. To access $a[i]$, it would use an SIB mode whose operand address was the sum of $4 \times$ EAX, EBP, and 8. This instruction could store into $a[i]$ in a single instruction.

Is this mode worth the trouble? It is hard to say. Undoubtedly this instruction, when properly used, saves a few cycles. How often it is used depends on the compiler and the application. The problem is that this instruction occupies a certain amount of chip area that could have been used in a different way had this instruction not been present. For example, the level 1 cache could have been made bigger, or the chip could have been made smaller, possibly allowing a slightly higher clock speed.

These are the kinds of trade-offs that designers are faced with constantly. Usually, extensive simulation runs are made before casting anything in silicon, but these simulations require having a good idea of what the workload is like. It is a safe bet that the designers of the 8088 did not include a Web browser in their test set. Nevertheless, quite a few of that product's descendants are now used primarily for Web surfing so the decisions made 20 years ago may be completely wrong for current applications. However, in the name of backward compatibility, once a feature gets in there, it is impossible to get it out.

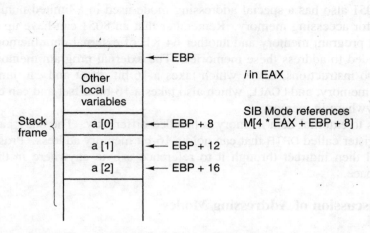

Figure 5-28. Access to *a*[*i*].

5.4.12 The UltraSPARC III Addressing Modes

In the UltraSPARC ISA, all instructions use immediate or register addressing except for those that address memory. For register mode, the 5 bits simply tell which register to use. For immediate mode, a (signed) 13-bit constant provides the data. No other modes are present for the arithmetic, logical, and similar instructions.

Three kinds of instructions address memory: LOADs, STOREs, and one multiprocessor synchronization instruction. LOAD and STORE instructions have two modes for addressing memory. The first mode computes the sum of two registers and then indirects through it. The other is traditional indexing, with a (signed) 13-bit offset.

5.4.13 The 8051 Addressing Modes

The 8051 has a fairly regular addressing structure. There are five basic modes. The simplest one is in implicit mode that uses the accumulator. Many instructions combine an operand with the accumulator, such as adding, subtracting, ANDing or ORing an operand with it. Instructions that use the accumulator do not have special bits to indicate the accumulator is being used. This fact is implicit in the opcode.

The second mode is register mode, in which the operand is in a register. Registers can be used as both sources and destinations. The third mode is direct addressing, where the operand is in memory at an address contained in the instruction itself. The fourth mode is register indirect, in which a register contains a pointer to the operand. Since the normal registers are 8 bits wide, operands addressed this way must be in the bottom 256 bytes of memory. The fifth mode is immediate, where the operand is part of the instruction itself.

The 8051 also has a special addressing mode used in a limited number of instructions for accessing memory. Remember that an 8051 can have up to 64 KB of external program memory and another 64 KB of external data memory. Some way is needed to address these memories. The external program memory is handled by two instructions, LJMP, which takes a 16-bit offset and can jump to any address in memory, and LCALL, which also takes a 16-bit offset and can call a subroutine anywhere in memory.

Access to external data memory is handled differently. The 8051 has a 16-bit pointer register called DPTR that can hold a 16-bit memory address. Programs can load it and then indirect through it to reference a byte anywhere in the 64 KB memory space.

5.4.14 Discussion of Addressing Modes

We have now studied quite a few addressing modes. The ones used by the Pentium 4, UltraSPARC III, and 8051 are summarized in Fig. 5-29. As we have pointed out, however, not every mode can be used in every instruction.

Addressing mode	Pentium 4	UltraSPARC III	8051
Accumulator			×
Immediate	×	×	×
Direct	×		×
Register	×	×	×
Register indirect	×	×	×
Indexed	×	×	
Based-indexed		×	
Stack			

Figure 5-29. A comparison of addressing modes.

In practice, not many addressing modes are needed for an effective ISA. Since most code written at this level these days will be generated by compilers (except possibly for the 8051), the most important aspect of an architecture's addressing modes is that the choices be few and clear, with costs (in terms of execution time and code size) that are readily computable. What that generally means is that a machine should take an extreme position: either it should offer every possible choice, or it should offer only one. Anything in between means that the compiler is faced with choices that it may not have the knowledge or sophistication to make.

Thus the cleanest architectures generally have only a very small number of addressing modes, with strict limits on their use. In practice, having immediate, direct, register, and indexed mode is generally enough for almost all applications.

Also, every register (including local variable pointer, stack pointer, and program counter) should be usable wherever a register is called for. More complicated addressing modes may reduce the number of instructions, but at the expense of introducing sequences of operations that cannot easily be parallelized with other sequential operations.

We have now completed our study of the various trade-offs possible between opcodes and addresses, and various forms of addressing. When approaching a new computer, you should examine the instructions and addressing modes not only to see which ones are available but also to understand why those choices were made and what the consequences of alternative choices would have been.

5.5 INSTRUCTION TYPES

ISA level instructions can be approximately divided into a half dozen groups that are relatively similar from machine to machine, even though they may differ in the details. In addition, every computer has a few unusual instructions, added for compatibility with previous models, or because the architect had a brilliant idea, or possibly because a government agency paid the manufacturer to include it. We will try to briefly cover all the common categories below, without any attempt at being exhaustive.

5.5.1 Data Movement Instructions

Copying data from one place to another is the most fundamental of all operations. By copying we mean the creating of a new object, with the identical bit pattern as the original. This use of the word "movement" is somewhat different from its normal usage in English. When we say that Marvin Mongoose has moved from New York to California, we do not mean that an identical copy of Mr. Mongoose was created in California and that the original is still in New York. When we say that the contents of memory location 2000 have been moved to some register, we always mean that an identical copy has been created there and that the original is still undisturbed in location 2000. Data movement instructions would better be called "data duplication" instructions, but the term "data movement" is already established.

There are two reasons that data may be copied from one location to another. One is fundamental: the assignment of values to variables. The assignment

    A = B

is implemented by copying the value at memory address B to location A because the programmer has said to do this. The second reason for copying data is to stage it for efficient access and use. As we have seen, many instructions can only access variables when they are available in registers. Since there are two possible sources for a data item (memory or register), and there are two possible destinations for a data item (memory or register), there are four different kinds of copying possible. Some computers have four instructions for the four cases. Others have one instruction for all four cases. Still others use LOAD to go from memory to a register, STORE to go from a register to memory, MOVE to go from one register to another register, and no instruction for a memory-to-memory copy.

Data movement instructions must somehow indicate the amount of data to be moved. Instructions exist for some ISAs to move variable quantities of data ranging from 1 bit to the entire memory. On fixed-word-length machines, the amount to be moved is often exactly one word. Any more or less must be performed by a software routine using shifting and merging. Some ISAs provide additional capability both for copying less than a word (usually in increments of bytes) and for multiple words. Copying multiple words is tricky, particularly if the maximum number of words is large, because such an operation can take a long time, and may have to be interrupted in the middle. Some variable-word-length machines have instructions specifying only the source and destination addresses but not the amount. The move continues until an end-of-data field mark is found in the data.

5.5.2 Dyadic Operations

Dyadic operations are those that combine two operands to produce a result. All ISAs have instructions to perform addition and subtraction on integers. Multiplication and division of integers are nearly standard as well. It is presumably unnecessary to explain why computers are equipped with arithmetic instructions.

Another group of dyadic operations includes the Boolean instructions. Although 16 Boolean functions of two variables exist, few, if any, machines have instructions for all 16. Usually, AND, OR, and NOT are present; sometimes EXCLUSIVE OR, NOR, and NAND are there as well.

An important use of AND is for extracting bits from words. Consider, for example, a 32-bit-word-length machine in which four 8-bit characters are stored per word. Suppose that it is necessary to separate the second character from the other three in order to print it; that is, it is necessary to create a word which contains that character in the rightmost 8 bits, referred to as **right justified**, with zeros in the leftmost 24 bits.

To extract the character, the word containing the character is ANDed with a constant, called a **mask**. The result of this operation is that the unwanted bits are all changed into zeros—that is, masked out—as shown below.

```
10110111 10111100 11011011 10001011  A
00000000 11111111 00000000 00000000  B (mask)
00000000 10111100 00000000 00000000  A AND B
```

The result would then be shifted 16 bits to the right to isolate the character to be extracted at the right end of the word.

An important use of OR is to pack bits into a word, packing being the inverse of extracting. To change the rightmost 8 bits of a 32-bit word without disturbing the other 24 bits, first the unwanted 8 bits are masked out and then the new character is ORed in, as shown below.

```
10110111 10111100 11011011 10001011  A
11111111 11111111 11111111 00000000  B (mask)
10110111 10111100 11011011 00000000  A AND B
00000000 00000000 00000000 01010111  C
10110111 10111100 11011011 01010111  (A AND B) OR C
```

The AND operation tends to remove 1s, because there are never more 1s in the result than in either of the operands. The OR operation tends to insert 1s, because there are always at least as many 1s in the result as in the operand with the most 1s. EXCLUSIVE OR, on the other hand, is symmetric, tending, on the average, neither to insert nor remove 1s. This symmetry with respect to 1s and 0s is occasionally useful, for example, in generating random numbers.

Most computers today also support a set of floating-point instructions, roughly corresponding to the integer arithmetic operations. Most machines provide at least two lengths of floating-point numbers, the shorter ones for speed and the longer ones for occasions when many digits of accuracy are needed. While there are lots of possible variations for floating-point formats, a single standard has now been almost universally adopted: IEEE 754. Floating-point numbers and IEEE 754 are discussed in Appendix B.

5.5.3 Monadic Operations

Monadic operations have one operand and produce one result. Because one fewer address has to be specified than with dyadic operations, the instructions are sometimes shorter, though often other information must be specified.

Instructions to shift or rotate the contents of a word or byte are quite useful and are often provided in several variations. Shifts are operations in which the bits are moved to the left or right, with bits shifted off the end of the word being lost. Rotates are shifts in which bits pushed off one end reappear on the other end. The difference between a shift and a rotate is illustrated below.

```
00000000 00000000 00000000 01110011  A
00000000 00000000 00000000 00011100  A shifted right 2 bits
11000000 00000000 00000000 00011100  A rotated right 2 bits
```

Both left and right shifts and rotates are useful. If an n-bit word is left rotated k bits, the result is the same as if it had been right rotated $n - k$ bits.

Right shifts are often performed with sign extension. This means that positions vacated on the left end of the word are filled up with the original sign bit, 0 or 1. It is as though the sign bit were dragged along to the right. Among other things, it means that a negative number will remain negative. This situation is illustrated below for 2-bit right shifts.

```
11111111 11111111 11111111 11110000  A
00111111 11111111 11111111 11111100  A shifted without sign extension
11111111 11111111 11111111 11111100  A shifted with sign extension
```

An important use of shifting is multiplication and division by powers of 2. If a positive integer is left shifted k bits, the result, barring overflow, is the original number multiplied by 2^k. If a positive integer is right shifted k bits, the result is the original number divided by 2^k.

Shifting can be used to speed up certain arithmetic operations. Consider, for example, computing $18 \times n$ for some positive integer n. Because $18 \times n = 16 \times n + 2 \times n$, $16 \times n$ can be obtained by shifting a copy of n 4 bits to the left. $2 \times n$ can be obtained by shifting n 1 bit to the left. The sum of these two numbers is $18 \times n$. The multiplication has been accomplished by a move, two shifts, and an addition, which is often faster than a multiplication. Of course, the compiler can only use this trick when one factor is a constant.

Shifting negative numbers, even with sign extension, gives quite different results, however. Consider, for example, the one's complement number, -1. Shifted 1 bit to the left it yields -3. Another 1-bit shift to the left yields -7:

```
11111111 11111111 11111111 11111110  −1 in one's complement
11111111 11111111 11111111 11111100  −1 shifted left 1 bit = −3
11111111 11111111 11111111 11111000  −1 shifted left 2 bits = −7
```

Left shifting one's complement negative numbers does not multiply by 2. Right shifting does simulate division correctly, however.

Now consider a two's complement representation of -1. When right shifted 6 bits with sign extension, it yields -1, which is incorrect because the integral part of $-1/64$ is 0:

```
11111111 11111111 11111111 11111111  −1 in two's complement
11111111 11111111 11111111 11111111  −1 shifted right 6 bits = −1
```

In general, right shifting introduces errors because it truncates down (toward the more negative integer), which is incorrect for integer arithmetic on negative numbers. Left shifting does, however, simulate multiplication by 2.

Rotate operations are useful for packing and unpacking bit sequences from words. If it is desired to test all the bits in a word, rotating the word 1 bit at a time either way successively puts each bit in the sign bit, where it can be easily tested, and also restores the word to its original value when all bits have been tested. Rotate operations are more pure than shift operations because no information is lost: an arbitrary rotate operation can be negated with another rotate operation.

Certain dyadic operations occur so frequently with particular operands that ISAs sometimes have monadic instructions to accomplish them quickly. Moving zero to a memory word or register is extremely common when initializing a calculation. Moving zero is, of course, a special case of the general move data instructions. For efficiency, a CLR operation, with only one address, the location to be cleared (i.e., set to zero), is often provided.

Adding 1 to a word is also commonly used for counting. A monadic form of the ADD instruction is the INC operation, which adds 1. The NEG operation is another example. Negating X is really computing $0 - X$, a dyadic subtraction, but again, because of its frequent use, a separate NEG instruction is sometimes provided. It is important to note here the difference between the arithmetic operation NEG and the logical operation NOT. The NEG operation produces the **additive inverse** of a number (the number which when added to the original gives 0). The NOT operation simply inverts all the individual bits in the word. The operations are very similar, and in fact, for a system using 1's complement representation, they are identical. (In 2's complement arithmetic, the NEG instruction is carried out by first inverting all the individual bits, then adding 1.)

Dyadic and monadic instructions are often grouped together by their use, rather than by the number of operands they require. One group includes the arithmetic operations, including negation. The other group includes logical operations and shifting, since these two categories are most often used together to accomplish data extraction.

5.5.4 Comparisons and Conditional Branches

Nearly all programs need the ability to test their data and alter the sequence of instructions to be executed based on the results. A simple example is the square root function, $\sqrt{x}$. If x is negative, the procedure gives an error message; otherwise, it computes the square root. A function *sqrt* has to test x and then branch, depending on whether it is negative or not.

A common method for doing so is to provide conditional branch instructions that test some condition and branch to a particular memory address if the condition is met. Sometimes a bit in the instruction indicates whether the branch is to occur if the condition is met or the condition is not met, respectively. Often the target address is not absolute, but relative to the current instruction.

The most common condition to be tested is whether a particular bit in the machine is 0 or not. If an instruction tests the sign bit of a number and branches to *LABEL* if it is 1, the statements beginning at *LABEL* will be executed if the number was negative, and the statements following the conditional branch will be executed if it was 0 or positive.

Many machines have condition code bits that are used to indicate specific conditions. For example, there may be an overflow bit that is set to 1 whenever an arithmetic operation gives an incorrect result. By testing this bit, one checks for overflow on the previous arithmetic operation, so that if an overflow occurred, a branch can be made to an error routine and corrective action taken.

Similarly, some processors have a carry bit that is set when a carry spills over from the leftmost bit, for example, if two negative numbers are added. A carry from the leftmost bit is quite normal and should not be confused with an overflow. Testing of the carry bit is needed for multiple-precision arithmetic (i.e., where an integer is represented in two or more words).

Testing for zero is important for loops and many other purposes. If all the conditional branch instructions tested only 1 bit, to test a particular word for 0, one would need a separate test for each bit, to ensure that none was a 1. To avoid this situation, many machines have an instruction to test a word and branch if it is zero. Of course, this solution merely passes the buck to the microarchitecture. In practice, the hardware usually contains a register all of whose bits are ORed together, to give a single bit telling whether the register contains any 1 bits. The Z bit in Fig. 4-1 would normally be computed by ORing all the ALU output bits together and then inverting the result.

Comparing two words or characters to see if they are equal or, if not, which one is greater is also important, in sorting for example. To perform this test, three addresses are needed: two for the data items, and one for the address to branch to if the condition is true. Computers whose instruction format allows three addresses per instruction have no trouble but those that do not must do something to get around this problem.

One common solution is to provide an instruction that performs a comparison and sets one or more condition bits to record the result. A subsequent instruction can test the condition bits and branch if the two compared values were equal, or unequal, or if the first was greater, and so on. Both the Pentium 4 and Ultra-SPARC III use this approach.

Some subtle points are involved in comparing two numbers. For example, comparison is not quite as simple as subtraction. If a very large positive number is compared to a very large negative number, the subtraction will result in overflow, since the result of the subtraction cannot be represented. Nevertheless, the comparison instruction must determine whether the specified test is met, and return the correct answer—there is no overflow on comparisons.

Another subtle point relating to comparing numbers is deciding whether or not the numbers should be considered signed or not. Three-bit binary numbers can be ordered in one of two ways. From smallest to largest:

Unsigned	Signed	
000	100	(smallest)
001	101	
010	110	
011	111	
100	000	
101	001	
110	010	
111	011	(largest)

The column on the left shows the positive integers 0 to 7 in increasing order. The column on the right shows the two's complement signed integers −4 to +3. The answer to the question "Is 011 greater than 100?" depends on whether or not the numbers are regarded as being signed. Most ISAs have instructions to handle both orderings.

5.5.5 Procedure Call Instructions

A procedure is a group of instructions that performs some task and that can be invoked (called) from several places in the program. The term **subroutine** is often used instead of procedure, especially when referring to assembly language programs. In Java, the term used is **method**. When the procedure has finished its task, it must return to the statement after the call. Therefore, the return address must be transmitted to the procedure or saved somewhere so that it can be located when it is time to return.

The return address may be placed in any of three places: memory, a register, or the stack. Far and away the worst solution is putting it in a single, fixed memory location. In this scheme, if the procedure called another procedure, the second call would cause the return address from the first one to be lost.

A slight improvement is having the procedure call instruction store the return address in the first word of the procedure, with the first executable instruction being in the second word. The procedure can then return by branching indirectly to the first word or, if the hardware puts the opcode for branch in the first word along with the return address, branching directly to it. The procedure may call other procedures, because each procedure has space for one return address. If the procedure calls itself, this scheme fails, because the first return address will be destroyed by the second call. The ability for a procedure to call itself, called **recursion**, is exceedingly important for both theorists and practical programmers. Furthermore, if procedure A calls procedure B, and procedure B calls procedure C, and procedure C calls procedure A (indirect or daisy-chain recursion), this scheme also fails.

A bigger improvement is to have the procedure call instruction put the return address in a register, leaving the responsibility for storing it in a safe place to the procedure. If the procedure is recursive, it will have to put the return address in a different place each time it is called.

The best thing for the procedure call instruction to do with the return address is to push it onto a stack. When the procedure has finished, it pops the return address off the stack and stuffs it into the program counter. If this form of procedure call is available, recursion does not cause any special problems; the return address will automatically be saved in such a way as to avoid destroying previous return addresses. Recursion works just fine under these conditons. We saw this form of saving the return address in IJVM in Fig. 4-12.

5.5.6 Loop Control

The need to execute a group of instructions a fixed number of times occurs frequently and thus some machines have instructions to facilitate doing this. All the schemes involve a counter that is increased or decreased by some constant once each time through the loop. The counter is also tested once each time through the loop. If a certain condition holds, the loop is terminated.

One method initializes a counter outside the loop and then immediately begins executing the loop code. The last instruction of the loop updates the counter and, if the termination condition has not yet been satisfied, branches back to the first instruction of the loop. Otherwise, the loop is finished and it falls through, executing the first instruction beyond the loop. This form of looping is characterized as test-at-the-end type looping, and is illustrated in C in Fig. 5-30(a). (We could not use Java here because it does not have a goto statement.)

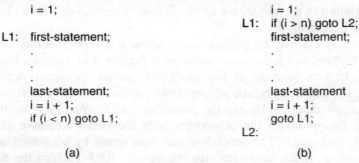

Figure 5-30. (a) Test-at-the-end loop. (b) Test-at-the-beginning loop.

Test-at-the-end looping has the property that the loop will always be executed at least once, even if n is less than or equal to 0. Consider, as an example, a program that maintains personnel records for a company. At a certain point in the program, it is reading information about a particular employee. It reads in n, the number of children the employee has, and executes a loop n times, once per child, reading the child's name, sex, and birthday, so that the company can send him or her a birthday present, one of the company's fringe benefits. If the employee does not have any children, n will be 0 but the loop will still be executed once sending presents and giving erroneous results.

Figure 5-30(b) shows another way of performing the test that works properly even for n less than or equal to 0. Notice that the testing is different in the two cases, so that if a single ISA instruction does both the increment and the test, the designers are forced to choose one method or the other.

Consider the code that should be produced for the statement

for (i = 0; i < n; i++) { statements }

If the compiler does not have any information about n, it must use the approach of Fig. 5-30(b) to correctly handle the case of $n \le 0$. If, however, it can determine that $n > 0$, for example, by seeing where n is assigned, it may use the better code of Fig. 5-30(a). The FORTRAN standard formerly stated that all loops were to be executed once, to allow the more efficient code of Fig. 5-30(a) to be generated all the time. In 1977, that defect was corrected when even the FORTRAN community began to realize that having a loop statement with outlandish semantics that sometimes gave the wrong answer was not a good idea, even if it did save one branch instruction per loop. C and Java have always done it right.

5.5.7 Input/Output

No other group of instructions exhibits as much variety from machine to machine as the I/O instructions. Three different I/O schemes are in current use in personal computers. These are

1. Programmed I/O with busy waiting.

2. Interrupt-driven I/O.

3. DMA I/O.

We will now discuss each of these in turn.

The simplest possible I/O method is **programmed I/O**, which is commonly used in low-end microprocessors, for example, in embedded systems or in systems that must respond quickly to external changes (real-time systems). These CPUs usually have a single input instruction and a single output instruction. Each of these instructions selects one of the I/O devices. A single character is transferred between a fixed register in the processor and the selected I/O device. The processor must execute an explicit sequence of instructions for each and every character read or written.

As a simple example of this method, consider a terminal with four 1-byte registers, as shown in Fig. 5-31. Two registers are used for input, status and data, and two are used for output, also status and data. Each one has a unique address. If memory-mapped I/O is being used, all four registers are part of the computer's memory address space and can be read and written using ordinary instructions. Otherwise, special I/O instructions, say, IN and OUT, are provided to read and write them. In both cases, I/O is performed by transferring data and status information between the CPU and these registers.

The keyboard status register has 2 bits that are used and 6 bits that are not used. The leftmost bit (7) is set to 1 by the hardware whenever a character arrives. If the software has previously set bit 6, an interrupt is generated, otherwise it is not (interrupts will be discussed shortly). When using programmed I/O, to get input, the CPU normally sits in a tight loop repeatedly reading the keyboard status register, waiting for bit 7 to go on. When this happens, the software reads in the keyboard buffer register to get the character. Reading the keyboard data register causes the CHARACTER AVAILABLE bit to be reset to 0.

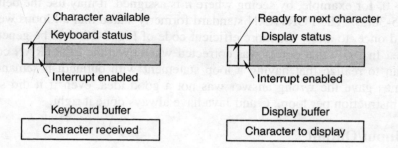

Figure 5-31. Device registers for a simple terminal.

Output works in a similar way. To write a character to the screen, the software first reads the display status register to see if the READY bit is 1. If not, it loops until the bit goes to 1, indicating that the device is ready to accept a character. As soon as the terminal is ready, the software writes a character to the display buffer register, which causes it to be transmitted to the screen, and also causes the device to clear the READY bit in the display status register. When the character has been displayed and the terminal is prepared to handle the next character, the READY bit is automatically set to 1 again by the controller.

As an example of programmed I/O, consider the Java procedure of Fig. 5-32. This procedure is called with two parameters: a character array to be output, and the count of characters present in the array, up to 1K. The body of the procedure is a loop that outputs characters one at a time. For each character, first the CPU must wait until the device is ready, then the character is output. The procedures *in* and *out* would typically be assembly language routines to read and write the device registers specified by the first parameter from or to the variable specified as the second parameter. The division by 128 gets rid of the low-order 7 bits, leaving the READY bit in bit 0.

```
public static void output_buffer(char buf[ ], int count) {
    // Output a block of data to the device
    int status, i, ready;

    for (i = 0; i < count; i++) {
        do {
            status = in(display_status_reg);        // get status
            ready = (status >> 7) & 0x01;           // isolate ready bit
        } while (ready != 1);
        out(display_buffer_reg, buf[i]);
    }
}
```

Figure 5-32. An example of programmed I/O.

The primary disadvantage of programmed I/O is that the CPU spends most of its time in a tight loop waiting for the device to become ready. This approach is called **busy waiting**. If the CPU has nothing else to do (e.g., the CPU in a washing machine), busy waiting may be OK (though even a simple controller often needs to monitor multiple, concurrent events). However, if there is other work to do, such as running other programs, busy waiting is wasteful, so a different I/O method is needed.

The way to get rid of busy waiting is to have the CPU start the I/O device and tell it to generate an interrupt when it is done. Looking at Fig. 5-31, we show how this is done. By setting the INTERRUPT ENABLE bit in a device register, the software can request that the hardware give it a signal when the I/O is completed. We will study interrupts in detail later in this chapter when we come to flow of control.

It is worth mentioning that in many computers, the interrupt signal is generated by ANDing the INTERRUPT ENABLE bit with the READY bit. If the software first enables interrupts (before starting I/O), an interrupt will happen immediately, because the READY bit will be 1. Thus it may be necessary to first start the device, then immediately afterward enable interrupts. Writing a byte to the status register does not change the READY bit, which is read only.

Although interrupt-driven I/O is a big step forward compared to programmed I/O, it is far from perfect. The problem is that an interrupt is required for every character transmitted. Processing an interrupt is expensive. A way is needed to get rid of most of the interrupts.

The solution lies in going back to programmed I/O, but having somebody else do it. (The solution to many problems lies in having somebody else do the work.) Figure 5-33 shows how this is arranged. Here we have added a new chip, a **DMA (Direct Memory Access)** controller to the system, with direct access to the bus.

The DMA chip has (at least) four registers inside it, all of which can be loaded by software running on the CPU. The first one contains the memory address to be read or written. The second one contains the count of how many bytes (or words) are to be transferred. The third one specifies the device number or I/O space address to use, thus specifying which I/O device is desired. The fourth one tells whether data are to be read from or written to the I/O device.

To write a block of 32 bytes from memory address 100 to a terminal (say, device 4), the CPU writes the numbers 32, 100, and 4 into the first three DMA registers, and then the code for WRITE (say, 1) in the fourth one, as shown in Fig. 5-33. Once initialized like this, the DMA controller makes a bus request to read byte 100 from the memory, the same way the CPU would read from the memory. Having gotten this byte, the DMA controller then makes an I/O request to device 4 to write the byte to it. After both of these operations have been completed, the DMA controller increments its address register by 1 and decrements its count register by 1. If the count register is still greater than 0, another byte is read from memory and then written to the device.

When the count finally goes to 0, the DMA controller stops transferring data and asserts the interrupt line on the CPU chip. With DMA, the CPU only has to

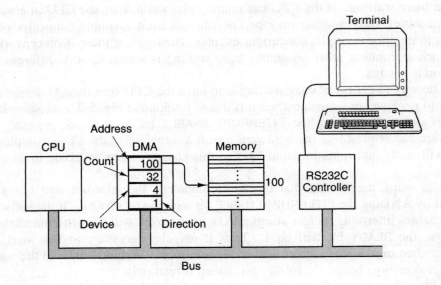

Figure 5-33. A system with a DMA controller.

initialize a few registers. After that, it is free to do something else until the complete transfer is finished, at which time it gets an interrupt from the DMA controller. Some DMA controllers have two, or three, or more sets of registers, so they can control multiple simultaneous transfers.

While DMA greatly relieves the CPU from the burden of I/O, the process is not totally free. If a high-speed device, such as a disk, is being run by DMA, many bus cycles will be needed, both for memory references and device references. During these cycles the CPU will have to wait (DMA always has a higher bus priority than the CPU because I/O devices frequently cannot tolerate delays). The process of having a DMA controller take bus cycles away from the CPU is called **cycle stealing**. Nevertheless, the gain in not having to handle one interrupt per byte (or word) transferred far outweighs the loss due to cycle stealing.

5.5.8 The Pentium 4 Instructions

In this section and the next two, we will look at the instruction sets of our three example machines: the Pentium 4, the UltraSPARC, and the 8051. Each of these has a core of instructions that compilers normally generate, plus a set of instructions that are rarely used, or are used only by the operating system. In our discussion, we will focus on the common instructions. Let us start with the Pentium 4.

The Pentium 4 instruction set is a mixture of instructions that make sense in 32-bit mode and those that hark back to its former life as an 8088. In Fig. 5-34 we show a small selection of the more common integer instructions that compilers and programmers are likely to use these days. This list is far from complete, as it does not include any floating-point instructions, control instructions, or even some of the more exotic integer instructions (such as using an 8-bit byte in AL to perform table lookup). Nevertheless, it does give a good feel for what the Pentium 4 can do.

Many of the Pentium 4 instructions reference one or two operands, either in registers or in memory. For example the two-operand ADD instruction adds the source to the destination and the one operand INC instruction increments (adds 1 to) its operand. Some of the instructions have several closely related variants. For example, the shift instructions can shift either left or right and can treat the sign bit specially or not. Most of the instructions have a variety of different encodings, depending on the nature of the operands.

In Fig. 5-34, the SRC fields are sources of information and are not changed. In contrast, the DST fields are destinations and are normally modified by the instruction. There are some rules about what is allowed as a source or a destination, which vary somewhat erratically from instruction to instruction, but we will not go into them here. Many instructions have three variants, for 8-, 16-, and 32-bit operands, respectively. These are distinguished by different opcodes and/or a bit in the instruction. The list of Fig. 5-34 emphasizes the 32-bit instructions.

For convenience, we have divided the instructions into several groups. The first group contains instructions that move data around the machine, among registers, memory, and the stack. The second group does arithmetic, both signed and unsigned. For multiplication and division, the 64-bit product or dividend is stored in EAX (low-order part) and EDX (high-order part).

The third group does Binary Coded Decimal (BCD) arithmetic, treating each byte as two 4-bit **nibbles**. Each nibble holds one decimal digit (0 to 9). Bit combinations 1010 to 1111 are not used. Thus a 16-bit integer can hold a decimal number from 0 to 9999. While this form of storage is inefficient, it eliminates the need to convert decimal input to binary and then back to decimal for output. These instructions are used for doing arithmetic on the BCD numbers. They are heavily used by COBOL programs.

The Boolean and shift/rotate instructions manipulate the bits in a word or byte in various ways. Several combinations are provided.

The next two groups deal with testing and comparing, and then jumping based on the results. The results of test and compare instructions are stored in various bits of the EFLAGS register. Jxx stands for a set of instructions that conditionally jump, depending on the results of the previous comparison (i.e., bits in EFLAGS).

The Pentium 4 has several instructions for loading, storing, moving, comparing, and scanning strings of characters or words. These instructions can be prefixed by a special byte called REP, which cause them to be repeated until a certain condition is met, such as ECX, which is decremented after each iteration, reaching 0. In this way, arbitrary blocks of data can be moved, compared, and so on. The next group manages the condition codes.

Moves

MOV DST,SRC	Move SRC to DST
PUSH SRC	Push SRC onto the stack
POP DST	Pop a word from the stack to DST
XCHG DS1,DS2	Exchange DS1 and DS2
LEA DST,SRC	Load effective addr of SRC into DST
CMOVcc DST,SRC	Conditional move

Arithmetic

ADD DST,SRC	Add SRC to DST
SUB DST,SRC	Subtract SRC from DST
MUL SRC	Multiply EAX by SRC (unsigned)
IMUL SRC	Multiply EAX by SRC (signed)
DIV SRC	Divide EDX:EAX by SRC (unsigned)
IDIV SRC	Divide EDX:EAX by SRC (signed)
ADC DST,SRC	Add SRC to DST, then add carry bit
SBB DST,SRC	Subtract SRC & carry from DST
INC DST	Add 1 to DST
DEC DST	Subtract 1 from DST
NEG DST	Negate DST (subtract it from 0)

Binary coded decimal

DAA	Decimal adjust
DAS	Decimal adjust for subtraction
AAA	ASCII adjust for addition
AAS	ASCII adjust for subtraction
AAM	ASCII adjust for multiplication
AAD	ASCII adjust for division

Boolean

AND DST,SRC	Boolean AND SRC into DST
OR DST,SRC	Boolean OR SRC into DST
XOR DST,SRC	Boolean Exclusive OR SRC to DST
NOT DST	Replace DST with 1's complement

Shift/rotate

SAL/SAR DST,#	Shift DST left/right # bits
SHL/SHR DST,#	Logical shift DST left/right # bits
ROL/ROR DST,#	Rotate DST left/right # bits
RCL/RCR DST,#	Rotate DST through carry # bits

Test/compare

TEST SRC1,SRC2	Boolean AND operands, set flags
CMP SRC1,SRC2	Set flags based on SRC1 - SRC2

Transfer of control

JMP ADDR	Jump to ADDR
Jxx ADDR	Conditional jumps based on flags
CALL ADDR	Call procedure at ADDR
RET	Return from procedure
IRET	Return from interrupt
LOOPxx	Loop until condition met
INT n	Initiate a software interrupt
INTO	Interrupt if overflow bit is set

Strings

LODS	Load string
STOS	Store string
MOVS	Move string
CMPS	Compare two strings
SCAS	Scan Strings

Condition codes

STC	Set carry bit in EFLAGS register
CLC	Clear carry bit in EFLAGS register
CMC	Complement carry bit in EFLAGS
STD	Set direction bit in EFLAGS register
CLD	Clear direction bit in EFLAGS reg
STI	Set interrupt bit in EFLAGS register
CLI	Clear interrupt bit in EFLAGS reg
PUSHFD	Push EFLAGS register onto stack
POPFD	Pop EFLAGS register from stack
LAHF	Load AH from EFLAGS register
SAHF	Store AH in EFLAGS register

Miscellaneous

SWAP DST	Change endianness of DST
CWQ	Extend EAX to EDX:EAX for division
CWDE	Extend 16-bit number in AX to EAX
ENTER SIZE,LV	Create stack frame with SIZE bytes
LEAVE	Undo stack frame built by ENTER
NOP	No operation
HLT	Halt
IN AL,PORT	Input a byte from PORT to AL
OUT PORT,AL	Output a byte from AL to PORT
WAIT	Wait for an interrupt

SRC = source   # = shift/rotate count
DST = destination   LV = # locals

Figure 5-34. A selection of the Pentium 4 integer instructions.

The last group is a hodge-podge of instructions that do not fit in anywhere else. These include conversions, stack frame management, stopping the CPU, and I/O.

The Pentium 4 has a number of **prefixes**, of which we have mentioned one (REP) already. Each of these prefixes is a special byte that can precede most instructions, analogous to WIDE in IJVM. REP causes the instruction following it to be repeated until ECX hits 0, as mentioned above. REPZ and REPNZ repeatedly execute the following instruction until the Z condition code is set, or not set, respectively. LOCK reserves the bus for the entire instruction, to permit multiprocessor synchronization. Other prefixes are used to force an instruction to operate in 16-bit mode, or in 32-bit mode, which not only changes the length of the operands but also completely redefines the addressing modes. Finally, the Pentium 4 has a complex segmentation scheme with code, data, stack, and extra segments, a holdover from the 8088. Prefixes are provided to force memory references to use specific segments, but these will not be of concern to us (fortunately).

5.5.9 The UltraSPARC III Instructions

All the user-mode integer UltraSPARC III instructions that a compiler might generate are listed in Fig. 5-35. Floating-point instructions are not given here, nor are control instructions (e.g., cache management, system reset), instructions involving address spaces other than the user's, or obsolete instructions. The set is surprisingly small: the UltraSPARC III really is a reduced instruction set computer.

The LOAD and STORE instructions are straightforward, with versions for 1, 2, 4, and 8 bytes. When a number less than 64 bits is loaded into a (64-bit) register, the number can be either sign extended or zero extended. Instructions for both choices exist.

The next group is for arithmetic. The instructions with CC in their name set the NZVC condition code bits. The others do not. On CISC machines, most instructions set the condition codes, but on a RISC machine that is undesirable because it restricts the compiler's freedom to move instructions around when trying to fill delay slots. If the original instruction order is A ... B ... C with A setting the condition codes and B testing them, the compiler cannot insert C between A and B if C sets the condition codes. For this reason, two versions of many instructions are provided, with the compiler normally using the one that does not set the condition codes, unless it is planning to test them later. Multiplication, signed division, and unsigned division are all supported.

Tagged arithmetic is a special self-identifying format of 30-bit numbers. It can be used for languages like Smalltalk and Prolog in which variables are not typed at compile time and can change types at run time. With tagged numbers, the compiler can generate an ADD instruction, and at run time the machine determines whether it needs an integer ADD or a floating-point ADD.

Loads

LDSB ADDR,DST	Load signed byte (8 bits)
LDUB ADDR,DST	Load unsigned byte (8 bits)
LDSH ADDR,DST	Load signed halfword (16 bits)
LDUH ADDR,DST	Load unsigned halfword (16)
LDSW ADDR,DST	Load signed word (32 bits)
LDUW ADDR,DST	Load unsigned word (32 bits)
LDX ADDR,DST	Load extended (64-bits)

Stores

STB SRC,ADDR	Store byte (8 bits)
STH SRC,ADDR	Store halfword (16 bits)
STW SRC,ADDR	Store word (32 bits)
STX SRC,ADDR	Store extended (64 bits)

Arithmetic

ADD R1,S2,DST	Add
ADDCC "	Add and set icc
ADDC "	Add with carry
ADDCCC "	Add with carry and set icc
SUB R1,S2,DST	Subtract
SUBCC "	Subtract and set icc
SUBC "	Subtract with carry
SUBCCC "	Subtract with carry and set icc
MULX R1,S2,DST	Multiply
SDIVX R1,S2,DST	Signed divide
UDIVX R1,S2,DST	Unsigned divide
TADCC R1,S2,DST	Tagged add

Shifts/rotates

SLL R1,S2,DST	Shift left logical (32 bits)
SLLX R1,S2,DST	Shift left logical extended (64)
SRL R1,S2,DST	Shift right logical (32 bits)
SRLX R1,S2,DST	Shift right logical extended (64)
SRA R1,S2,DST	Shift right arithmetic (32 bits)
SRAX R1,S2,DST	Shift right arithmetic ext. (64)

Boolean

AND R1,S2,DST	Boolean AND
ANDCC "	Boolean AND and set icc
ANDN "	Boolean NAND
ANDNCC "	Boolean NAND and set icc
OR R1,S2,DST	Boolean OR
ORCC "	Boolean OR and set icc
ORN "	Boolean NOR
ORNCC "	Boolean NOR and set icc
XOR R1,S2,DST	Boolean XOR
XORCC "	Boolean XOR and set icc
XNOR "	Boolean EXCLUSIVE NOR
XNORCC "	Boolean EXCL. NOR and set icc

Transfer of control

BPcc ADDR	Branch with prediction
BPr SRC,ADDR	Branch on register
CALL ADDR	Call procedure
RETURN ADDR	Return from procedure
JMPL ADDR,DST	Jump and link
SAVE R1,S2,DST	Advance register windows
RESTORE "	Restore register windows
Tcc CC,TRAP#	Trap on condition
PREFETCH FCN	Prefetch data from memory
LDSTUB ADDR,R	Atomic load/store
MEMBAR MASK	Memory barrier

Miscellaneous

SETHI CON,DST	Set bits 10 to 31
MOVcc CC,S2,DST	Move on condition
MOVr R1,S2,DST	Move on register
NOP	No operation
POPC S1,DST	Population count
RDCCR V,DST	Read condition code register
WRCCR R1,S2,V	Write condition code register
RDPC V,DST	Read program counter

SRC = source register
DST = destination register
R1 = source register
S2 = source: register or immediate
ADDR = memory address

TRAP# = trap number
FCN = function code
MASK = operation type
CON = constant
V = register designator

CC = condition code set
R = destination register
cc = condition
r = LZ,LEZ,Z,NZ,GZ,GEZ

Figure 5-35. The primary UltraSPARC III integer instructions.

The shift group contains one left shift and two right shifts, each with a 32-bit version and a 64-bit extended version. For SLL, the whole 64 bits are shifted, since this is still compatible with old software. The shifts are mostly used for bit manipulation. Most CISC machines have a vast number of shift and rotate instructions, nearly all of them totally useless. Few compiler writers will spend restless nights mourning their absence.

The Boolean instruction group is analogous to the arithmetic group. It includes AND, OR, EXCLUSIVE OR, ANDN, ORN, and XNORN. The latter three are of questionable value, but they can be done in one cycle and require almost no additional hardware so they got thrown in. Even RISC machine designers sometimes succumb to temptation.

The next instruction group contains the control transfers. BPcc represents a set of instructions that branch on the various conditions, and specify in the instruction whether the compiler thinks the branch will be taken or not. BPr tests a register and branches on the condition detected.

Two ways are provided for calling procedures. The CALL instruction uses format 4 of Fig. 5-15 with a 30-bit PC-relative *word* offset. This value is enough to reach any instruction within 2 gigabytes of the caller in either direction. The CALL instruction deposits the return address in R15, which becomes R31 after the call.

The other way to call a procedure is by using JMPL, which uses format 1a or 1b, and allows the return address to be put in any register. This form is useful when the target address is computed during execution.

SAVE and RESTORE manipulate the register window and stack pointer. Both of them trap when the next (previous) window is not available.

Instruction	How to do it
MOV SRC,DST	OR SRC with G0 and store the result DST
CMP SRC1,SRC2	SUBCC SRC2 from SRC1 and store the result in G0
TST SRC	ORCC SRC with G0 and store the result in G0
NOT DST	XNOR DST with G0
NEG DST	SUB DST from G0 and store in DST
INC DST	ADD 1 to DST (immediate operand)
DEC DST	SUB 1 from DST (immediate operand)
CLR DST	OR G0 with G0 and store in DST
NOP	SETHI G0 to 0
RET	JMPL %I7+8,%G0

Figure 5-36. Some simulated UltraSPARC III instructions.

The last group contains some miscellaneous **instructions**. SETHI is needed because there is no way to get a 32-bit immediate **operand** into a register. The way it is done is to use SETHI to set bits 10 through 31 and then have the next instruction supply the remaining bits using the immediate format.

The population count instruction is a mystery. It counts the number of 1 bits in a word. Rumor has it that it is good for simulating bomb explosions, and that Los Alamos National Laboratory (a big spender) looks favorably upon machines that have it. The last three instructions are for reading and writing special registers.

A number of familiar CISC instructions that are missing from this list can be easily simulated using either G0 or a constant operand (format 1b). A few of them are given in Fig. 5-36. They are recognized by the UltraSPARC III assembler and are frequently generated by compilers. Many of them use the fact that G0 is hardwired to 0 and that stores into it have no effect.

5.5.10 The 8051 Instructions

The 8051 has a simple instruction set, the first part of which is shown in Fig. 5-36. Each line gives the mnemonic, a brief description, and the applicable addressing modes for either the source or destination, depending on whether *src* or dstfR appears in the description. As to be expected, there are a variety of MOV instructions for moving data between the ACC (accumulator), registers, and memory. There are instructions for pushing and popping from a stack, which is pointed to by a dedicated register Memory above address 256, which is always external since the 8051 has only 128 bytes of memory and the 8052 has only 256 bytes, is always addressed indirectly via the 16-bit DPTR register. Some miscellaneous instructions for swapping parts of registers fill out the move group.

The 8051 has simple arithmetic instructions for adding, subtracting, multiplying and dividing, the latter two of which use fixed registers. Incrementing and decrementing are also possible and commonly used. Boolean and rotate instructions are also present.

The rest of the 8051 instructions are shown in Fig. 5-36. Here we have the bit operations. for example,

    SETB 43

sets bit number 43 and does not affect the other bits in the same byte. Next come the instructions that transfer control including the jumps and the subroutine calls plus two conditional jumps that compare a source to something and an instruction, *DJNZ* used for looping.

5.5.11 Comparison of Instruction Sets

The three example instruction sets are very different. The Pentium 4 is a classic two-address 32-bit CISC machine, with a long history, eculiar and highly irregular addressing modes, and many instructions that reference memory. The

Inst.	Description	ACC	Reg	Dir	@R	#	C	Bit
MOV	Move *src* to ACC		×	×	×	×		
MOV	Move *src* to register	×		×		×		
MOV	Move *src* to memory	×	×	×	×	×		
MOV	Move *src* to indirect RAM	×		×		×		
MOV	Move 16-bit constant to DPTR							
MOVC	Move code to ACC offset from DPTR							
MOVC	Move code to ACC offset from PC							
MOVX	Move external RAM byte to ACC				×			
MOVX	Move ext. RAM byte to ACC @DPTR							
MOVX	Move to ext. RAM byte from ACC				×			
MOVX	Move to ext. RAM byte from ACC @DPTR							
PUSH	Push *src* byte to stack			×				
POP	Pop stack byte to dst			×				
XCH	Exchange ACC and dst	×		×	×			
XCHD	Exchange low-order digit ACC and dst			×				
SWAP	Swap nibbles of dst	×						
ADD	Add *src* to ACC		×	×	×	×		
ADDC	Add *src* to ACC with carry		×	×	×	×		
SUBB	Subtract *src* from ACC with borrow		×	×	×	×		
INC	Increment dst	×	×	×	×			
DEC	Decrement dst	×	×	×	×			
INC	DPTR							
MUL	Multiply							
DIV	Divide							
DA	Decimal adjust dst	×						
ANL	AND *src* to ACC		×	×	×	×		
ANL	AND ACC to dst			×				
ANL	AND immediate to dst			×				
ORL	OR *src* to ACC		×	×	×	×		
ORL	OR ACC to dst			×				
ORL	OR immediate to dst			×				
XRL	XOR *src* to ACC		×	×	×	×		
XRL	XOR ACC to dst			×				
XRL	XOR immediate to dst			×				
CLR	Clear dst	×						
CPL	Complement dst	×						
RL	Rotate dst left	×						
RLC	Rotate dst left through carry	×						
RR	Rotate dst right	×						
RRC	Rotate dst right through carry	×						

Figure 5-37. The 8051 instruction set, part 1.

The UltraSPARC III is a modern three-address 64-bit RISC, with a load/store architecture, hardly any addressing modes, and a compact and efficient instruction set. The 8051 architecture is a tiny embedded processor designed to fit on a single chip.

Inst.	Description	ACC	Reg	Dir	@R	#	C	Bit
CLR	Clear bit						×	×
SETB	Set bit						×	×
CPL	Complement bit						×	×
ANL	AND src to carry							×
ANL	AND complement of src to carry							×
ORL	OR src to carry							×
ORL	OR complement of src to carry							×
MOV	Move src to carry							×
MOV	Move carry to src							×
JV	Jump relative if carry set							
JNC	Jump relative if carry not set							
JB	Jump relative if direct bit set							×
JNB	Jump relative if direct bit not set							×
JBC	Jump rel. if direct bit set and carry clear							×
ACALL	Call subroutine (11-bit addr)							
LCALL	Call subroutine (16-bit addr)							
RET	Return from subroutine							
RETI	Return from interrupt							
SJMP	Short relative jump (8-bit addr)							
AJMP	Absolute jump (11-bit addr)							
LJMP	Absolute jump (16-bit addr)							
JMP	Jump indirect rel. to DPR+ACC							
JZ	Jump if ACC is zero							
JNZ	Jump if ACC is nonzero							
CJNE	Comp. src to ACC, jump unequal			×		×		
CJNE	Comp. src to immediate, jump unequal		×			×		
DJNZ	Decrement dst and jump nonzero							
NOP	No operation							

Figure 5-38. The 8051 instruction set, part 2.

Each machine is the way it is for a good reason. The Pentium 4's design was determined by three major factors:

1. Backward compatibility.

2. Backward compatibility.

3. Backward compatibility.

Given the current state of the art, no one would now design such an irregular machine with so few registers, all of them different. This makes compilers hard to write. The lack of registers also forces compilers to constantly spill variables into memory and then reload them, an expensive business, even with two or three levels of caching. It is a testimonial to the quality of Intel's engineers that the Pentium 4 is so fast, even with the constraints of this ISA. But as we saw in Chap. 4, the implementation is exceedingly complex.

The UltraSPARC III represents a state-of-the-art in ISA design. It has a full 64-bit ISA (with a 128-bit bus). It has many registers, and an instruction set that emphasizes three-register operations, plus a small group of LOAD and STORE instructions. All instructions are the same size, although the number of formats has gotten a bit out of hand. Still, it lends itself to a straightforward and efficient implementation. Most new designs tend to look like the UltraSPARC III, but with fewer instruction formats.

The 8051 has a simple and fairly regular instruction set with relatively few instructions and few addressing modes. It is distinguished by having four register sets for rapid interrupt processing, a way to access registers in the memory space, and surprisingly powerful bit manipulation instructions. Its main claim to fame is that it can be implemented with a very small number of transistors, thus making it possible to put a large number on a die, which keeps the cost per CPU very low.

5.6 FLOW OF CONTROL

Flow of control refers to the sequence in which instructions are executed dynamically, that is, during program execution. In general, in the absence of branches and procedure calls, successively-executed instructions are fetched from consecutive memory locations. Procedure calls cause the flow of control to be altered, stopping the procedure currently executing and starting the called procedure. Coroutines are related to procedures and cause similar alterations in the flow of control. They are useful for simulating parallel processes. Traps and interrupts also cause the flow of control to be altered when special conditions occur. All these topics will be discussed in the following sections.

5.6.1 Sequential Flow of Control and Branches

Most instructions do not alter the flow of control. After an instruction is executed, the one following it in memory is fetched and executed. After each instruction, the program counter is increased by the instruction length. If observed over an interval of time that is long compared to the average instruction time, the program counter is approximately a linear function of time, increasing by the average instruction length per average instruction time. Stated another way, the dynamic order in which the processor actually executes the instructions is the same as the order in which they appear on the program listing, as shown in Fig. 5-39(a). If a program contains branches, this simple relation between the order in which instructions appear in memory and the order in which they are executed is no longer true. When branches are present, the program counter is no longer a monotonically increasing function of time, as shown in Fig. 5-39(b). As a result; it becomes difficult to visualize the instruction execution sequence from the program listing.

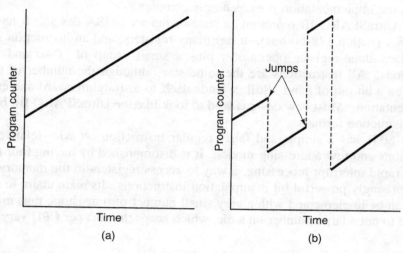

Figure 5-39. Program counter as a function of time (smoothed). (a) Without branches. (b) With branches.

When programmers have trouble keeping track of the sequence in which the processor will execute the instructions, they are prone to make errors. This observation led Dijkstra (1968a) to write a then-controversial letter entitled "GO TO Statement Considered Harmful," in which he suggested avoiding goto statements. That letter gave birth to the structured programming revolution, one of whose tenets is the replacement of goto statements with more structured forms of flow control, such as while loops. Of course, these programs compile down to level 2 programs that may contain many branches, because the implementation of if, while, and other high-level control structures requires branching around.

5.6.2 Procedures

The most important technique for structuring programs is the procedure. From one point of view, a procedure call alters the flow of control just as a branch does, but unlike the branch, when finished performing its task, it returns control to the statement or instruction following the call.

However, from another point of view, a procedure body can be regarded as defining a new instruction on a higher level. From this standpoint, a procedure call can be thought of as a single instruction, even though the procedure may be quite complicated. To understand a piece of code containing a procedure call, it is only necessary to know *what* it does, not *how* it does it.

One particularly interesting kind of procedure is the **recursive procedure**, that is, a procedure that calls itself, either directly or indirectly via a chain of other procedures. Studying recursive procedures gives considerable insight into how procedure calls are implemented, and what local variables really are. Now we will give an example of a recursive procedure.

The "Towers of Hanoi" is an ancient problem that has a simple solution involving recursion. In a certain monastery in Hanoi, there are three gold pegs. Around the first one were a series of 64 concentric gold disks, each with a hole in the middle for the peg. Each disk is slightly smaller in diameter than the disk directly below it. The second and third pegs were initially empty. The monks there are busily transferring all the disks to peg 3, one disk at a time, but at no time may a larger disk rest on a smaller one. When they finish, it is said the world will come to an end. If you wish to get hands-on experience, it is all right to use plastic disks and fewer of them, but when you solve the problem, nothing will happen. To get the end-of-world effect, you need 64 of them and in gold. Figure 5-40 shows the initial configuration for $n = 5$ disks.

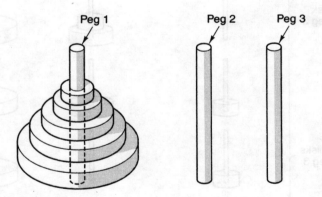

Figure 5-40. Initial configuration for the Towers of Hanoi problem for five disks.

The solution of moving n disks from peg 1 to peg 3 consists first of moving $n - 1$ disks from peg 1 to peg 2, then moving 1 disk from peg 1 to peg 3, then moving $n - 1$ disks from peg 2 to peg 3. This solution is illustrated in Fig. 5-41.

To solve the problem we need a procedure to move n disks from peg i to peg j. When this procedure is called, by

    towers(n, i, j)

the solution is printed out. The procedure first makes a test to see if $n = 1$. If so,

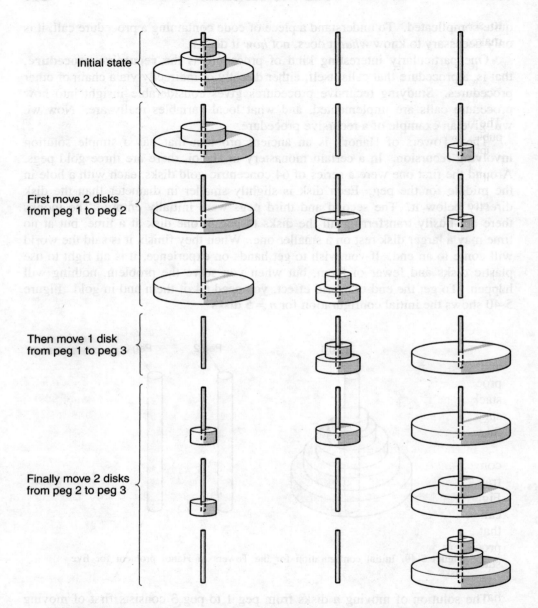

Initial state

First move 2 disks
from peg 1 to peg 2

Then move 1 disk
from peg 1 to peg 3

Finally move 2 disks
from peg 2 to peg 3

Figure 5-41. The steps required to solve the Towers of Hanoi for three disks.

the solution is trivial, just move the one disk from i to j. If $n \neq 1$, the solution consists of three parts as discussed above, each being a recursive procedure call.

The complete solution is shown in Fig. 5-42. The call

    towers(3, 1, 3)

to solve the problem of Fig. 5-41 generates three more calls. Specifically, it makes the calls

```
towers(2, 1, 2)
towers(1, 1, 3)
towers(2, 2, 3)
```

The first and third will generate three calls each, for a total of seven.

```
public void towers(int n, int i, int j) {
    int k;

    if (n == 1)
        System.out.println("Move a disk from " + i + " to " + j);
    else {
        k = 6 – i – j;
        towers(n – 1, i, k);
        towers(1, i, j);
        towers(n – 1, k, j);
    }
}
```

Figure 5-42. A procedure for solving the Towers of Hanoi.

In order to have recursive procedures, we need a stack to store the parameters and local variables for each invocation, the same as we had in IJVM. Each time a procedure is called, a new stack frame is allocated for the procedure on top of the stack. The frame most recently created is the current frame. In our examples, the stack grows upward, from low memory addresses to high ones, just like in IJVM. So the most recent frame has higher addresses than all the others.

In addition to the stack pointer, which points to the top of the stack, it is often convenient to have a frame pointer, FP, which points to a fixed location within the frame. It could point to the link pointer, as in IJVM, or to the first local variable. Figure 5-43 shows the stack frame for a machine with a 32-bit word. The original call to *towers* pushes *n, i,* and *j* onto the stack and then executes a CALL instruction that pushes the return address onto the stack, at address 1012. On entry, the called procedure stores the old value of FP on the stack at 1016 and then advances the stack pointer to allocate storage for the local variables. With only one 32-bit local variable (*k*), SP is incremented by 4 to 1020. The situation, after all these things have been done, is shown in Fig. 5-43(a).

The first thing a procedure must do when called is save the previous FP (so it can be restored at procedure exit), copy SP into FP, and possibly increment by one word, depending on where in the new frame FP points. In this example, FP points to the first local variable, but in IJVM, LV pointed to the link pointer. Different machines handle the frame pointer slightly differently, sometimes putting it at the bottom of the stack frame, sometimes at the top, and sometimes in the middle as in Fig. 5-43. In this respect, it is worth comparing Fig. 5-43 with Fig. 4-12 to see

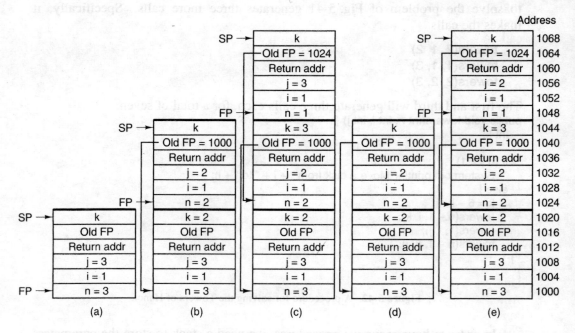

Figure 5-43. The stack at several points during the execution of Fig. 5-42.

two different ways to manage the link pointer. Other ways are also possible. In all cases, the key is the ability to later be able to do a procedure return and restore the state of the stack to what it was just prior to the current procedure invocation.

The code that saves the old frame pointer, sets up the new frame pointer, and advances the stack pointer to reserve space for local variables is called the **procedure prolog**. Upon procedure exit, the stack must be cleaned up again, something called the **procedure epilog**. One of the most important characteristics of any computer is how short and fast it can make the prolog and epilog. If they are long and slow, procedure calls will be expensive. Programmers who worship at the altar of efficiency will learn to avoid writing many short procedures and write large, monolithic, unstructured programs instead. The Pentium 4 ENTER and LEAVE instructions have been designed to do most of the procedure prolog and epilog work efficiently. Of course, they have a particular model of how the frame pointer should be managed, and if the compiler has a different model, they cannot be used.

Now let us get back to the Towers of Hanoi problem. Each procedure call adds a new frame to the stack and each procedure return removes a frame from the stack. In order to illustrate the use of a stack in implementing recursive procedures, we will trace the calls starting with

towers(3, 1, 3)

Figure 5-43(a) shows the stack just after this call has been made. The procedure first tests to see if $n = 1$, and on discovering that $n = 3$, fills in k and makes the call

   towers(2, 1, 2)

After this call is completed the stack is as shown in Fig. 5-43(b), and the procedure starts again at the beginning (a called procedure always starts at the beginning). This time the test for $n = 1$ fails again, so it fills in k again and makes the call

   towers(1, 1, 3)

The stack then is as shown in Fig. 5-43(c) and the program counter points to the start of the procedure. This time the test succeeds and a line is printed. Next, the procedure returns by removing one stack frame, resetting FP and SP to Fig. 5-43(d). It then continues executing at the return address, which is the second call:

   towers(1, 1, 2)

This adds a new frame to the stack as shown in Fig. 5-43(e). Another line is printed; after the return a frame is removed from the stack. The procedure calls continue in this way until the original call completes execution and the frame of Fig. 5-43(a) is removed from the stack. To best understand how recursion works, it is recommended that you simulate the complete execution of

   towers(3, 1, 3)

using pencil and paper.

5.6.3 Coroutines

In the usual calling sequence, there is a clear distinction between the calling procedure and the called procedure. Consider a procedure A, which calls a procedure B in Fig. 5-44.

Procedure B computes for a while and then returns to A. At first sight you might consider this situation symmetric, because neither A nor B is a main program, both being procedures. (Procedure A may have been called by the main program but that is irrelevant.) Furthermore, first control is transferred from A to B—the call—and later control is transferred from B to A—the return.

The asymmetry arises from the fact that when control passes from A to B, procedure B begins executing at the beginning; when B returns to A, execution starts not at the beginning of A but at the statement following the call. If A runs for a while and calls B again, execution starts at the beginning of B again, not the statement following the previous return. If, in the course of running, A calls B many times, B starts at the beginning all over again each and every time, whereas A never starts over again.

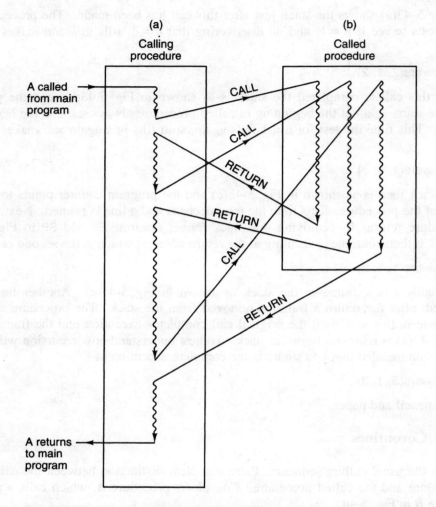

Figure 5-44. When a procedure is called, execution of the procedure always begins at the first statement of the procedure.

This difference is reflected in the method by which control is passed between *A* and *B*. When *A* calls *B*, it uses the procedure call instruction, which puts the return address (i.e., the address of the statement following the call) somewhere useful, for example, on top of the stack. It then puts the address of *B* into the program counter to complete the call. When *B* returns, it does not use the call instruction but instead it uses the return instruction, which simply pops the return address from the stack and puts it into the program counter.

Sometimes it is useful to have two procedures, *A* and *B*, each of which calls the other as a procedure, as shown in Fig. 5-45. When *B* returns to *A*, it branches to the statement following the call to *B*, as above. When *A* transfers control to *B*,

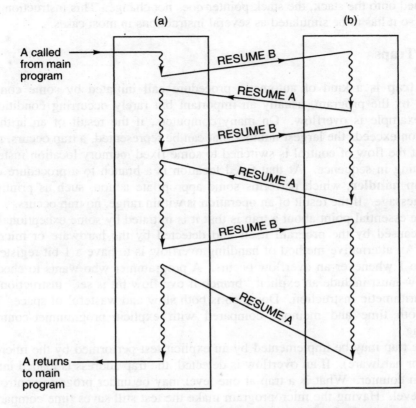

Figure 5-45. When a coroutine is resumed, execution begins at the statement where it left off the previous time, not at the beginning.

it does not go to the beginning (except the first time) but to the statement following the most recent "return," that is, the most recent call of *A*. Two procedures that work this way are called **coroutines**.

A common use for coroutines is to simulate parallel processing on a single CPU. Each coroutine runs in pseudo-parallel with the others, as though it had its own CPU. This style of programming makes programming some applications easier. It also is useful for testing software that will later actually run on a multiprocessor.

Neither the usual CALL nor the usual RETURN instruction works for calling coroutines, because the address to branch to comes from the stack like a return, but, unlike a return, the coroutine call itself puts a return address somewhere for the subsequent return to it. It would be nice if there were an instruction to exchange the top of the stack with the program counter. In detail, this instruction would first pop the old return address off the stack into an internal register, then push the program counter onto the stack, and finally, copy the internal register into the program counter. Because one word is popped off the stack and one word is pushed onto the stack, the stack pointer does not change. This instruction rarely exists, so it has to be simulated as several instructions in most cases.

5.6.4 Traps

A **trap** is a kind of automatic procedure call initiated by some condition caused by the program, usually an important but rarely occurring condition. A good example is overflow. On many computers, if the result of an arithmetic operation exceeds the largest number that can be represented, a trap occurs, meaning that the flow of control is switched to some fixed memory location instead of continuing in sequence. At that fixed location is a branch to a procedure called the **trap handler**, which performs some appropriate action, such as printing an error message. If the result of an operation is within range, no trap occurs.

The essential point about a trap is that it is initiated by some exceptional condition caused by the program itself and detected by the hardware or microprogram. An alternative method of handling overflow is to have a 1-bit register that is set to 1 whenever an overflow occurs. A programmer who wants to check for overflow must include an explicit "branch if overflow bit is set" instruction after every arithmetic instruction. Doing so is both slow and wasteful of space. Traps save both time and memory compared with explicit programmer-controlled checking.

The trap may be implemented by an explicit test performed by the microprogram (or hardware). If an overflow is detected, the trap address is loaded into the program counter. What is a trap at one level may be under program control at a lower level. Having the microprogram make the test still saves time compared to a programmer test, because it can be easily overlapped with something else. It also saves memory, because it need only occur in one place, for example, the main loop of the microprogram, independent of how many arithmetic instructions occur in the main program.

A few of the common conditions that can cause traps are floating-point overflow, floating-point underflow, integer overflow, protection violation, undefined opcode, stack overflow, attempt to start nonexistent I/O device, attempt to fetch a word from an odd-numbered address, and division by zero.

5.6.5 Interrupts

Interrupts are changes in the flow of control caused not by the running program, but by something else, usually related to I/O. For example, a program may instruct the disk to start transferring information, and set the disk up to provide an interrupt as soon as the transfer is finished. Like the trap, the interrupt stops the running program and transfers control to an interrupt handler, which performs some appropriate action. When finished, the interrupt handler returns control to the interrupted program. It must restart the interrupted process in exactly the same state that it was in when the interrupt occurred, which means restoring all the internal registers to their preinterrupt state.

The essential difference between traps and interrupts is this: *traps* are synchronous with the program and *interrupts* are asynchronous. If the program is rerun a million times with the same input, the traps will reoccur in the same place each time but the interrupts may vary, depending, for example, on precisely when a person at a terminal hits carriage return. The reason for the reproducibility of traps and irreproducibility of interrupts is that traps are caused directly by the program and interrupts are, at best, indirectly caused by the program.

To see how interrupts really work, let us consider a common example: a computer wants to output a line of characters to a terminal. The system software first collects all the characters to be written to the terminal together in a buffer, initializes a global variable *ptr*, to point to the start of the buffer, and sets a second global variable *count* equal to the number of characters to be output. Then it checks to see if the terminal is ready and if so, outputs the first character (e.g., using registers like those of Fig. 5-31). Having started the I/O, the CPU is then free to run another program or do something else.

In due course of time, the character is displayed on the screen. The interrupt can now begin. In simplified form, the steps are as follows.

HARDWARE ACTIONS

1. The device controller asserts an interrupt line on the system bus to start the interrupt sequence.

2. As soon as the CPU is prepared to handle the interrupt, it asserts an interrupt acknowledge signal on the bus.

3. When the device controller sees that its interrupt signal has been acknowledged, it puts a small integer on the data lines to identify itself. This number is called the **interrupt vector**.

4. The CPU removes the interrupt vector from the bus and saves it temporarily.

5. Then the CPU pushes the program counter and PSW onto the stack.

6. The CPU then locates a new program counter by using the interrupt vector as an index into a table at the bottom of memory. If the program counter is 4 bytes, for example, then interrupt vector n corresponds to address $4n$. This new program counter points to the start of the interrupt service routine for the device causing the interrupt. Often the PSW is loaded or modified as well (e.g., to disable further interrupts).

SOFTWARE ACTIONS

7. The first thing the interrupt service routine does is save all the registers it uses so they can be restored later. They can be saved on the stack or in a system table.

8. Each interrupt vector is generally shared by all the devices of a given type, so it is not yet known which terminal caused the interrupt. The terminal number can be found by reading some device register.

9. Any other information about the interrupt, such as status codes, can now be read in.

10. If an I/O error occurred, it can be handled here.

11. The global variables, *ptr* and *count*, are updated. The former is incremented, to point to the next byte, and the latter is decremented, to indicate that 1 byte fewer remains to be output. If *count* is still greater than 0, there are more characters to output. Copy the one now pointed to by *ptr* to the output buffer register.

12. If required, a special code is output to tell the device or the interrupt controller that the interrupt has been processed.

13. Restore all the saved registers.

14. Execute the RETURN FROM INTERRUPT instruction, putting the CPU back into the mode and state it had just before the interrupt happened. The computer then continues from where it was.

A key concept related to interrupts is **transparency**. When an interrupt happens, some actions are taken and some code runs, but when everything is finished, the computer should be returned to exactly the same state it had before the interrupt. An interrupt routine with this property is said to be transparent. Having all interrupts be transparent makes interrupts much easier to understand.

If a computer only has one I/O device, then interrupts always work as we have just described, and there is nothing more to say about them. However, a large computer may have many I/O devices, and several may be running at the same time, possibly on behalf of different users. A nonzero probability exists that while an interrupt routine is running, a second I/O device wants to generate *its* interrupt.

Two approaches can be taken to this problem. The first one is for all interrupt routines to disable subsequent interrupts as the very first thing they do, even before saving the registers. This approach keeps things simple, as interrupts are then taken strictly sequentially, but it can lead to problems for devices that cannot tolerate much delay. For example, on a 9600-bps communication line, characters arrive every 1042 μsec, ready or not. If the first one has not yet been processed when the second one arrives, data may be lost.

When a computer has time-critical I/O devices, a better design approach is to assign each I/O device a priority, high for very critical devices and low for less critical devices. Similarly, the CPU should also have priorities, typically determined by a field in the PSW. When a priority n device interrupts, the interrupt routine should also run at priority n.

While a priority n interrupt routine is running, any attempt by a device with a lower priority to cause an interrupt is ignored until the interrupt routine is finished and the CPU goes back to running lower priority code. On the other hand, interrupts from higher-priority devices should be allowed to happen with no delay.

With interrupt routines themselves subject to interrupt, the best way to keep the administration straight is to make sure that all interrupts are transparent. Let us consider a simple example of multiple interrupts. A computer has three I/O devices, a printer, a disk, and an RS232 (serial) line, with priorities 2, 4, and 5, respectively. Initially, ($t = 0$) a user program is running, when suddenly at $t = 10$ a printer interrupt occurs. The printer Interrupt Service Routine (ISR) is started up, as shown in Fig. 5-46.

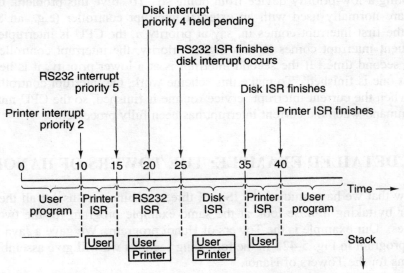

Figure 5-46. Time sequence of multiple interrupt example.

At $t = 15$, the RS232 line wants attention and generates an interrupt. Since the RS232 line has a higher priority (5) than the printer (2), the interrupt happens. The state of the machine, which is now running the printer interrupt service routine, is pushed onto the stack, and the RS232 interrupt service routine is started.

A little later, at $t = 20$, the disk is finished and wants service. However, its priority (4) is lower than that of the interrupt routine currently running (5), so the CPU hardware does not acknowledge the interrupt, and it is held pending. At $t = 25$, the RS232 routine is finished, so it returns to the state it was in just before the RS232 interrupt happened, namely, running the printer interrupt service routine at priority 2. As soon as the CPU switches to priority 2, before even one instruction can be executed, the disk interrupt at priority 4 now is allowed in, and the disk service routine runs. When it finishes, the printer routine gets to continue. Finally, at $t = 40$, all the interrupt service routines have completed and the user program continues from where it left off.

Since the 8088, the Intel CPU chips have had two interrupt levels (priorities): maskable and nonmaskable. Nonmaskable interrupts are generally only used for signaling near-catastrophes, such as memory parity errors. All the I/O devices use the one maskable interrupt.

When an I/O device issues an interrupt, the CPU uses the interrupt vector to index into a 256-entry table to find the address of the interrupt service routine. The table entries are 8-byte segment descriptors and the table can begin anywhere in memory. A global register points to its start.

With only one usable interrupt level, there is no way for the CPU to let a high-priority device interrupt a medium-priority interrupt service routine while prohibiting a low-priority device from doing so. To solve this problem, the Intel CPUs are normally used with an external interrupt controller (e.g., an 8259A). When the first interrupt comes in, say at priority n, the CPU is interrupted. If a subsequent interrupt comes in at a higher priority, the interrupt controller interrupts a second time. If the second interrupt is at a lower priority, it is held until the first one is finished. To make this scheme work, the interrupt controller must know when the current interrupt service routine is finished, so the CPU must send it a command when the current interrupt has been fully processed.

5.7 A DETAILED EXAMPLE: THE TOWERS OF HANOI

Now that we have studied the ISA of three machines, let us put all the pieces together by taking a close look at the same example program for the two larger machines. Our example is the Towers of Hanoi program. We gave a Java version of this program in Fig. 5-42. In the following sections we will give assembly code programs for the Towers of Hanoi.

However, we will cheat a tiny bit. Rather than give the translation of the Java version, for the Pentium 4 and UltraSPARC III we will give the translation of a C version to avoid some problems with Java I/O. The only difference is the replacement of the Java call to *println* with the standard C statement

```
printf("Move a disk from %d to %d\n", i, j)
```

For our purposes, the syntax of *printf* format strings is unimportant (basically, the string is printed literally except that %d means print the next integer in decimal). The only thing that is relevant here is that the procedure is called with three parameters: a format string and two integers.

The reason for using the C version for the Pentium 4 and UltraSPARC III is that the Java I/O library is not available in native form for these machines, whereas the C library is. The difference is minimal, affecting only the one print statement.

5.7.1 The Towers of Hanoi in Pentium 4 Assembly Language

Figure 5-47 gives a possible translation of the C version of the Towers of Hanoi for the Pentium 4. For the most part, it is fairly straightforward. The EBP register is used as the frame pointer. The first two words are used for linkage, so the first actual parameter, *n* (or *N* here, as MASM is case insensitive) is at EBP + 8, followed by *i* and *j* at EBP +12 and EBP + 16, respectively. The local variable, *k*, is in EBP + 20.

The procedure begins by establishing the new frame at the end of the old one. It does this by copying ESP to the frame pointer, EBP. Then it compares *n* to 1, branching off to the else clause if *n* > 1. The then code pushes three values on the stack: the address of the format string, *i*, and *j*, and calls itself.

The parameters are pushed in reverse order, which is required for C programs. This is necessary to put the pointer to the format string on top of the stack. Since *printf* has a variable number of parameters, if the parameters were pushed in forward order, *printf* would not know how deep in the stack the format string was.

After the call, 12 is added to ESP to remove the parameters from the stack. Of course, they are not really erased from memory, but the adjustment of ESP makes them inaccessible via the normal stack operations.

The else clause, which starts at *L1*, is straightforward. It first computes $6 - i - j$ and stores this value in *k*. No matter what values *i* and *j* have, the third peg is always $6 - i - j$. Saving it in *k* saves the trouble of recomputing it the second time.

Next, the procedure calls itself three times, with different parameters each time. After each call, the stack is cleaned up. That is all there is to it.

Recursive procedures sometimes confuse people at first, but when viewed at this level, they are straightforward. All that happens is that the parameters are pushed onto the stack and the procedure itself is called.

5.7.2 The Towers of Hanoi in UltraSPARC III Assembly Language

Now let us try again, only this time for the UltraSPARC III. The code is listed in Fig. 5-48. Because the UltraSPARC III code is especially unreadable, even for assembly code and even after a lot of practice, we have taken the liberty to define a few symbols in the beginning to clean it up. To make this work, the program has to be run through a program called *cpp*, the C preprocessor, before assembling it. Also we have used lowercase letters here because the UltraSPARC III assembler insists on them (in case any readers wish to type the program in).

```
                .586                              ; compile for Pentium (as opposed to 8088 etc.)
.MODEL FLAT
PUBLIC _towers                                    ; export 'towers'
EXTERN _printf:NEAR                               ; import printf
.CODE
_towers:  PUSH EBP                                ; save EBP (frame pointer) and decrement ESP
          MOV EBP, ESP                            ; set new frame pointer above ESP
          CMP [EBP+8], 1                          ; if (n == 1)
          JNE L1                                  ; branch if n is not 1
          MOV EAX, [EBP+16]                       ; printf(" ...", i, j);
          PUSH EAX                                ; note that parameters i, j and the format
          MOV EAX, [EBP+12]                       ; string are pushed onto the stack
          PUSH EAX                                ; in reverse order. This is the C calling convention
          PUSH OFFSET FLAT:format                 ; offset flat means the address of format
          CALL _printf                            ; call printf
          ADD ESP, 12                             ; remove params from the stack
          JMP Done                                ; we are finished
L1:       MOV EAX, 6                              ; start k = 6 – i – j
          SUB EAX, [EBP+12]                       ; EAX = 6 – i
          SUB EAX, [EBP+16]                       ; EAX = 6 – i – j
          MOV [EBP+20], EAX                       ; k = EAX
          PUSH EAX                                ; start towers(n – 1, i, k)
          MOV EAX, [EBP+12]                       ; EAX = i
          PUSH EAX                                ; push i
          MOV EAX, [EBP+8]                        ; EAX = n
          DEC EAX                                 ; EAX = n – 1
          PUSH EAX                                ; push n – 1
          CALL _towers                            ; call towers(n – 1, i, 6 – i – j)
          ADD ESP, 12                             ; remove params from the stack
          MOV EAX, [EBP+16]                       ; start towers(1, i, j)
          PUSH EAX                                ; push j
          MOV EAX, [EBP+12]                       ; EAX = i
          PUSH EAX                                ; push i
          PUSH 1                                  ; push 1
          CALL _towers                            ; call towers(1, i, j)
          ADD ESP, 12                             ; remove params from the stack
          MOV EAX, [EBP+12]                       ; start towers(n – 1, 6 – i – j, i)
          PUSH EAX                                ; push i
          MOV EAX, [EBP+20]                       ; EAX = k
          PUSH EAX                                ; push k
          MOV EAX, [EBP+8]                        ; EAX = n
          DEC EAX                                 ; EAX = n–1
          PUSH EAX                                ; push n – 1
          CALL _towers                            ; call towers(n – 1, 6 – i – j, i)
          ADD ESP, 12                             ; adjust stack pointer
Done:     LEAVE                                   ; prepare to exit
          RET 0                                   ; return to the caller
.DATA
format    DB "Move disk from %d to %d\n"          ; format string
END
```

Figure 5-47. The Towers of Hanoi for the Pentium 4.

Algorithmically, the UltraSPARC III version is identical to the Pentium 4 version. Both test *n* to start with, branching to the else clause if *n* > 1. The main complexity of the UltraSPARC version is due to some properties of the ISA.

To start with, the UltraSPARC III has to pass the address of the format string to *printf*, but the machine cannot just move the address to the register that holds the outgoing parameter because there is no way to put a 32-bit constant in a register in one instruction. It takes two instructions to do this, SETHI and OR.

The next thing to notice is that there is no need to do a stack adjustment after the call because the register window is adjusted by the RESTORE instruction at the end of the procedure. The ability to put the outgoing parameters in registers and not have to go to memory is a big performance win if the depth of calling does not get too deep, but in general, the whole register window mechanism is probably not worth the complexity.

Now notice the NOP instruction following the branch to *Done*. This is a delay slot. This instruction will always be executed, even though it follows an unconditional branch instruction. The problem is that the UltraSPARC III has a deep pipeline and by the time the hardware discovers it has a branch on its hands, the next instruction is practically finished. Welcome to the Wonder World of RISC Programming.

This fun feature also extends to procedure calls. Observe the first call to *towers* in the else clause. It puts *n* − 1 in %o0 and *i* in %o1, but it makes the procedure call to *towers* before it puts the last parameter in place. On the Pentium 4, first you pass the parameters, then you make the call. Here, first you pass some of the parameters, then you make the call, and finally you pass the last parameter. Again, here, by the time the machine realizes it is dealing with a *CALL* instruction, the instruction following it is so deep in the pipeline that it has to be executed. In that case, why not use the delay slot to pass the last parameter? Even if the very first instruction of the called procedure uses that parameter, it will be there on time.

Finally, at *Done*, we see that the RET instruction also has a delay slot. This one is used for the RESTORE instruction, which increments CWP to put the register window back the way the caller expects it.

5.8 THE IA-64 ARCHITECTURE AND THE ITANIUM 2

Intel is rapidly getting to the point where it has just about squeezed every last drop of juice out of the IA-32 ISA and the Pentium 4 line of processors. New models can still benefit from advances in manufacturing technology, which means smaller transistors (hence faster clock speeds). However, finding new tricks to speed up the implementation even more is getting harder and harder as the constraints imposed by the IA-32 ISA are looming larger all the time.

```
#define N %i0              /* N is input parameter 0 */
#define I %i1              /* I is input parameter 1 */
#define J %i2              /* J is input parameter 2 */
#define K %l0              /* K is local variable 0 */
#define Param0 %o0         /* Param0 is output parameter 0 */
#define Param1 %o1         /* Param1 is output parameter 1 */
#define Param2 %o2         /* Param2 is output parameter 2 */
#define Scratch %l1        /* as an aside, cpp uses the C comment convention */
          .proc 04
          .global towers

towers:   save %sp, −112, %sp
          cmp N, 1                            ! if (n == 1)
          bne Else                            ! if (n != 1) goto Else

          sethi %hi(format), Param0           ! printf("Move a disk from %d to %d\n", i, j)
          or Param0, %lo(format), Param0      ! Param0 = address of format string
          mov I, Param1                       ! Param1 = i
          call printf                         ! call printf BEFORE parameter 2 (j) is set up
          mov J, Param2                       ! use the delay slot after call to set up parameter 2
          b Done                              ! we are done now
          nop                                 ! fill delay slot

Else:     mov 6, K                            ! start k = 6 −i − j
          sub K, J, K                         ! k = 6 − j
          sub K, I, K                         ! k = 6 − i − j

          add N, −1, Scratch                  ! start towers(n − 1, i, k)
          mov Scratch, Param0                 ! Scratch = n − 1
          mov I, Param1                       ! parameter 1 = i
          call towers                         ! call towers BEFORE parameter 2 (k) is set up
          mov K, Param2                       ! use the delay slot after call to set up parameter 2

          mov 1, Param0                       ! start towers(1, i, j)
          mov I, Param1                       ! parameter 1 = i
          call towers                         ! call towers BEFORE parameter 2 (j) is set up
          mov J, Param2                       ! parameter 2 = j

          mov Scratch, Param0                 ! start towers(n − 1, k, j)
          mov K, Param1                       ! parameter 1 = k
          call towers                         ! call towers BEFORE parameter 2 (j) is set up
          mov J, Param2                       ! parameter 2 = j

Done:     ret                                 ! return
          restore                             ! use the delay slot after ret to restore windows

format:   .asciz "Move a disk from %d to %d\n"
```

Figure 5-48. The Towers of Hanoi for the UltraSPARC III.

The only real solution is to abandon the IA-32 as the main line of development and go to a completely new ISA. This is, in fact, what Intel intends to do. In fact, it has plans for two new lines. The EMT-64 is a wider version of the Pentium 4, with 64-bit registers and a 64-bit address space. This processor solves the address space problem but still has all the implementation complexities of the Pentium 4. It can best be thought of as a wider Pentium.

The other new architecture, developed jointly by Intel and Hewlett Packard, is called the **IA-64**. It is a full 64-bit machine from beginning to end, not an extension of an existing 32-bit machine. Furthermore, it is a radical departure from the Pentium 4 in many ways. The initial market is for high-end servers, but it may catch on in the desktop world eventually. In any case, the architecture is so radically different from anything we have studied so far that it is worth examining it just for that reason. The first implementation of the IA-64 architecture is the Itanium series. In the remainder of this section we will study the IA-64 architecture and the Itanium 2 CPU that implements it.

5.8.1 The Problem with the Pentium 4

Before getting into the details of the IA-64 and Itanium 2, it is useful to review what is wrong with the Pentium 4 to see what problems Intel was trying to solve with the new architecture. The main fact of life that causes all the trouble is that IA-32 is an ancient ISA with all the wrong properties for current technology. It is a CISC ISA with variable-length instructions and a myriad of different formats that are hard to decode quickly on the fly. Current technology works best with RISC ISAs that have one instruction length and a fixed-length opcode that is easy to decode. The IA-32 instructions can be broken up into RISC-like micro-operations at execution time, but doing so requires hardware (chip area), takes time, and adds complexity to the design. That is strike one.

The IA-32 is also a two-address memory-oriented ISA. Most instructions reference memory, and most programmers and compilers think nothing of referencing memory all the time. Current technology favors load/store ISAs that only reference memory to get the operands into registers but otherwise perform all their calculations using three-address memory register instructions. And with CPU clock speeds going up much faster than memory speeds, the problem will get worse with time. That is strike two.

The IA-32 also has a small and irregular register set. Not only does this tie compilers in knots, but the small number of general-purpose registers (four or six, depending on how you count ESI and EDI) requires intermediate results to be spilled into memory all the time, generating extra memory references even when they are not logically needed. That is strike three. The IA-32 is out.

Now let us start the second inning. The small number of registers causes many dependences, especially unnecessary WAR dependences, because results have to go somewhere and there are no extra registers available. Getting around the lack of registers requires the implementation to do renaming internally—a terrible hack if ever there was one—to secret registers inside the reorder buffer. To avoid blocking on cache misses too often, instructions have to be executed out of order. However, the IA-32's semantics specify precise interrupts, so the out-of-order instructions have to be retired in order. All of these things require a lot of very complex hardware. Strike four.

Doing all this work quickly requires a deep pipeline. In turn, the deep pipeline means that instructions are entered into it take many cycles before they are finished. Consequently, very accurate branch prediction is essential to make sure the right instructions are being entered into the pipeline. Because a misprediction requires the pipeline to be flushed, at great cost, even a fairly low misprediction rate can cause a substantial performance degradation. Strike five.

To alleviate the problems with mispredictions, the processor has to do speculative execution, with all the problems that entails, especially when memory references on the wrong path cause an exception. Strike six.

We are not going to play the whole baseball game here, but it should be clear by now that there is a real problem. And we have not even mentioned the fact that IA-32's 32-bit addresses limit individual programs to 4 GB of memory, which is a growing problem on high-end servers. The EMT-64 solves this problem but not all the others.

All in all, the situation with IA-32 can be favorably compared to the state of celestial mechanics just prior to Copernicus. The then-current theory dominating astronomy was that the earth was fixed and motionless in space and that the planets moved in circles with epicycles around it. However, as observations got better and more deviations from this model could be clearly observed, epicycles were added to the epicycles until the whole model just collapsed from its internal complexity.

Intel is in the same pickle now. A huge fraction of all the transistors on the Pentium 4 are devoted to decomposing CISC instructions, figuring out what can be done in parallel, resolving conflicts, making predictions, repairing the consequences of incorrect predictions and other bookkeeping, leaving surprisingly few over for doing the real work the user asked for. The conclusion that Intel is being inexorably driven to is the only sane conclusion: junk the whole thing (IA-32) and start all over with a clean slate (IA-64). The EMT-64 provides some breathing room, but it really papers over the complexity issue.

5.8.2 The IA-64 Model: Explicitly Parallel Instruction Computing

The key idea behind the IA-64 is moving work from run time to compile time. On the Pentium 4, during execution the CPU reorders instructions, renames registers, schedules functional units, and does a lot of other work to determine how to keep all the hardware resources fully occupied. In the IA-64 model, the compiler figures out all these things in advance and produces a program that can be run as is, without the hardware having to juggle everything during execution. For example, rather than tell the compiler that the machine has eight registers when it actually has 128 and then try to figure out at run time how to avoid dependences, in the IA-64 model, the compiler is told how many registers the machine really has so it can produce a program that does not have any register conflicts to start with. Similarly, in this model, the compiler keeps track of which functional units are busy and does not issue instructions that use functional units that are not available. The model of making the underlying parallelism in the hardware visible to the compiler is called **EPIC** (**Explicitly Parallel Instruction Computing**). To some extent, EPIC can be thought of as the successor to RISC.

The IA-64 model has a number of features that speed up performance. These include reducing memory references, instruction scheduling, reducing conditional branches, and speculation. We will now examine each of these in turn and discuss how they are implemented in the Itanium 2.

5.8.3 Reducing Memory References

The Itanium 2 has a simple memory model. Memory consists of up to 2^{64} bytes of linear memory. Instructions are available to access memory in units of 1, 2, 4, 8, 16, and 10 bytes, the latter for 80-bit IEEE 745 floating-point numbers. Memory references need not be aligned on their natural boundaries, but a performance penalty is incurred if they are not. Memory can be either big endian or little endian, determined by a bit in a register loadable by the operating system.

Memory access is a huge bottleneck in all modern computers because CPUs are so much faster than memory. One way to reduce memory references is to have a large level 1 cache on chip and an even larger level 2 cache close to the chip. All modern designs have these two caches. But one can go beyond caching to look for other ways to reduce memory references and the IA-64 uses some of these ways.

The best way to speed up memory references is to avoid having them in the first place. The Itanium 2 implementation of the IA-64 model has 128 general-purpose 64-bit registers. The first 32 of these are static, but the remaining 96 are used as a register stack, very similar to the register window scheme in the UltraSPARC III. However, unlike the UltraSPARC III, the number of registers visible to the program is variable and can change from procedure to procedure. Thus each procedure has access to 32 static registers and some (variable) number of dynamically allocated registers.

When a procedure is called, the register stack pointer is advanced so the input parameters are visible in registers, but no registers are allocated for local variables. The procedure itself decides how many registers it needs and advances the register stack pointer to allocate them. These registers need not be saved on entry or restored on exit although if the procedure needs to modify a static register it must take care to explicitly save it first and restore it later. By making the number of registers available variable and tailored to what each procedure needs, scarce registers are not wasted and procedure calls can go deeper before registers have to be spilled to memory.

The Itanium 2 also has 128 floating-point registers in IEEE 745 format. They do not operate as a register stack. This very large number of registers means that many floating-point computations can keep all their intermediate results in registers and avoid having to store temporary results in memory.

There are also 64 1-bit predicate registers, eight branch registers, and 128 special-purpose application registers used for various purposes, such as passing parameters between application programs and the operating system. An overview of the Itanium 2's registers is given in Fig. 5-49.

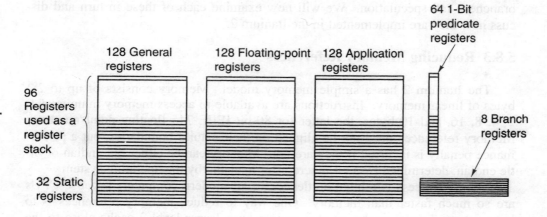

Figure 5-49. The Itanium 2's registers.

5.8.4 Instruction Scheduling

One of the main problems in the Pentium 4 is the difficulty of scheduling the various instructions over the various functional units and avoiding dependences. Exceedingly complex mechanisms are needed to handle these issues at run time, and a large fraction of the chip area is devoted to managing them. The IA-64 and Itanium 2 avoid all these problems by having the compiler do the work. The key idea is that a program consists of a sequence of **instruction groups**. Within certain boundaries, all the instructions within a group do not conflict with one another, do not use more functional units and resources than the machine has, do not contain RAW and WAW dependences, and have only restricted WAR dependences. Consecutive instruction groups give the appearance of being executed strictly sequentially with the second group not starting until the first one has completed. The CPU may, however, start the second group (in part) as soon as it feels it is safe to.

As a consequence of these rules, the CPU is free to schedule the instructions within a group in any order it chooses, possibly in parallel if it can, without having to worry about conflicts. If the instruction group violates the rules, program behavior is undefined. It is up to the compiler to reorder the assembly code generated from the source program to meet all these requirements. For rapid compilation while a program is being debugged, the compiler can put every instruction in a different group, which is easy to do but gives poor performance. When it is time to produce production code, the compiler can spend a long time optimizing it.

Instructions are organized into 128-bit **bundles** as shown at the top of Fig. 5-50. Each bundle contains three 41-bit instructions and a 5-bit template. An instruction group need not be an integral number of bundles; it can start and end in the middle of a bundle.

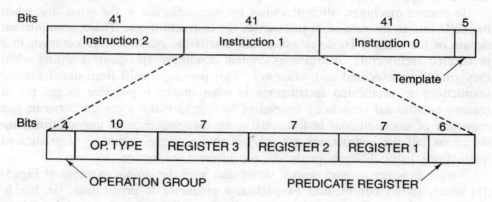

Figure 5-50. An IA-64 bundle contains three instructions.

Over 100 instruction formats exist. A typical one, in this case for ALU operations such as ADD, which sums two registers into a third one, is shown in Fig. 5-50. The first field OPERATION GROUP is the major group and mostly tells the broad class of the instruction, such as an integer ALU operation. The next field, the OPERATION TYPE gives the specific operation required, such as ADD or SUB. Then come the three register fields. Finally, we have the PREDICATE REGISTER, to be described shortly.

The bundle template essentially tells which functional units the bundle needs and also the position of an instruction group boundary present, if any. The major functional units are the integer ALU, non-ALU integer instructions, memory operations, floating-point operations, branching, and other. Of course, with six units and three instructions, complete orthogonality would require 216 combinations, plus another 216 to indicate an instruction group marker after instruction 0, another 216 to indicate an instruction group marker after instruction 1, and yet another 216 to indicate an instruction marker after instruction 2. With only 5 bits available, only a very limited number of these combinations are allowed. On the other hand, allowing three floating-point instructions in a bundle would not work, not even if there were a way to specify this since the CPU cannot initiate three floating-point instructions simultaneously. The allowed combinations are the ones that are actually feasible.

5.8.5 Reducing Conditional Branches: Predication

Another important feature of IA-64 is the new way it deals with conditional branches. If there were a way to get rid of most of them, CPUs could be made much simpler and faster. At first thought it might seem that getting rid of conditional branches would be impossible because programs are full of if statements. However, IA-64 uses a technique called **predication** that can greatly reduce their number (August et al., 1998; and Hwu, 1998). We will now briefly describe it.

In current machines, all instructions are unconditional in the sense that when the CPU hits an instruction, it just carries the instruction out. There is no internal debate of the form: "To do or not to do, that is the question." In contrast, in a predicated architecture, instructions contain conditions (predicates) telling when they should be executed and when not. This paradigm shift from unconditional instructions to predicated instructions is what makes it possible to get rid of (many) conditional branches. Instead of having to make a choice between one sequence of unconditional instructions or another sequence of unconditional instructions, all the instructions are merged into a single sequence of predicated instructions, using different predicates for different instructions.

To see how predication works, let us start with the simple example of Fig. 5-51, which shows **conditional execution**, a precursor to predication. In Fig. 5-51(a) we see an if statement. In Fig. 5-51(b) we see its translation into three instructions: a comparison, a conditional branch, and a move instruction.

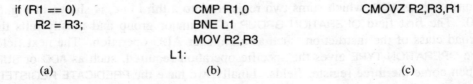

```
   if (R1 == 0)          CMP R1,0          CMOVZ R2,R3,R1
      R2 = R3;           BNE L1
                         MOV R2,R3
                 L1:
      (a)                 (b)                    (c)
```

Figure 5-51. (a) An if statement. (b) Generic assembly code for (a). (c) A conditional instruction.

In Fig. 5-51(c) we get rid of the conditional branch by using a new instruction, CMOVZ, which is a conditional move. What it does is check to see if the third register, R1, is 0. If so, it copies R3 to R2. If not, it does nothing.

Once we have an instruction that can copy data when some register is 0, it is a small step to an instruction that can copy data when some register is not 0, say CMOVN. With both of these instructions available, we are on our way to full conditional execution. Imagine an if statement with several assignments in the then part and several other assignments in the else part. The whole statement can be translated into code to set some register to 0 if the condition is false and another value if it is true. Following the register setup, the then part assignments can be compiled into a sequence of CMOVN instructions and the else part assignments could be compiled into a sequence of CMOVZ instructions.

All of these instructions, the register setup, the CMOVNs and the CMOVZs form a single basic block with no conditional branch. The instructions can even be reordered, either by the compiler (including hoisting the assignments before the test), or during execution. The only catch is that the condition has to be known by the time the conditional instructions have to be retired (near the end of the pipeline). A simple example showing a then part and an else part is given in Fig. 5-52.

if (R1 == 0) {	CMP R1,0	CMOVZ R2,R3,R1
R2 = R3;	BNE L1	CMOVZ R4,R5,R1
R4 = R5;	MOV R2,R3	CMOVN R6,R7,R1
} else {	MOV R4.R5	CMOVN R8,R9,R1
R6 = R7;	BR L2	
R8 = R9;	L1: MOV R6,R7	
}	MOV R8,R9	
	L2:	
(a)	(b)	(c)

Figure 5-52. (a) An if statement. (b) Generic assembly code for (a). (c) Conditional execution.

Although we have shown only very simple conditional instructions here (taken from the Pentium 4, actually), on the IA-64 all instructions are predicated. What this means is that the execution of every instruction can be made conditional. The extra 6-bit field referred to earlier selects one of 64 1-bit predicate registers. Thus an if statement will be compiled into code that sets one of the predicate registers to 1 if the condition is true and to 0 if it is false. Simultaneously and automatically, it sets another predicate register to the inverse value. Using predication, the machine instructions forming the then and else clauses will be merged into a single stream of instructions, the former ones using the predicate and the latter ones using its inverse.

Although simple, the example of Fig. 5-53 shows the basic idea of how predication can be used to eliminate branches. The CMPEQ instruction compares two registers and sets the predicate register P4 to 1 if they are equal and to 0 if they are different. It also sets a paired register, say, P5, to the inverse condition. Now the instructions for the if and then parts can be put after one another, each one conditioned on some predicate register (shown in angle brackets). Arbitrary code can be put here provided that each instruction is properly predicated.

In the IA-64, this idea is taken to the extreme, with comparison instructions for setting the predicate registers as well as arithmetic and other instructions whose execution is dependent on some predicate register. Predicated instructions

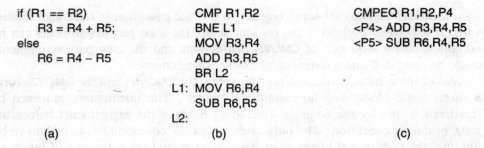

```
if (R1 == R2)          CMP R1,R2          CMPEQ R1,R2,P4
    R3 = R4 + R5;      BNE L1             <P4> ADD R3,R4,R5
else                   MOV R3,R4          <P5> SUB R6,R4,R5
    R6 = R4 - R5       ADD R3,R5
                       BR L2
                   L1: MOV R6,R4
                       SUB R6,R5
                   L2:
        (a)                (b)                   (c)
```

Figure 5-53. (a) An if statement. (b) Generic assembly code for (a). (c) Predicated execution.

can be stuffed into the pipeline in sequence, with no stalls and no problems. That is why they are so useful.

The way predication really works on the IA-64 is that every instruction is actually executed. At the very end of the pipeline, when it is time to retire an instruction, a check is made to see if the predicate is true. If so, the instruction is retired normally and its results are written back to the destination register. If the predicate is false, no writeback is done so the instruction has no effect. Predication is discussed further in Dulong (1998).

5.8.6 Speculative Loads

Another feature of the IA-64 that speeds up execution is the presence of speculative LOADs. If a LOAD is speculative and it fails, instead of causing an exception, it just stops and a bit associated with the register to be loaded is set marking the register as invalid. This is just the poison bit introduced in Chap. 4. If it turns out that the poisoned register is later used, the exception occurs at that time; otherwise, it never happens.

The way speculation is normally used is for the compiler to hoist LOADs to positions before they are needed. By starting early, they may be finished before the results are needed. At the place where the compiler needs to use the register just loaded, it inserts a CHECK instruction. If the value is there, CHECK acts like a NOP and execution continues immediately. If the value is not there yet, the next instruction must stall. If an exception occurred and the poison bit is on, the pending exception occurs at that point.

In summary, a machine implementing the IA-64 architecture gets its speed from several sources. At the core is a state-of-the-art pipelined, load/store, three-address RISC engine. In addition, IA-64 has a model of explicit parallelism that requires the compiler to figure out which instructions can be executed at the same time without conflicts and group them together in bundles. In this way the CPU can just blindly schedule a bundle without having to do any heavy thinking. Next, predication allows the statements in both branches of an if statement to be merged together in a single stream, eliminating the conditional branch and thus the prediction of which way it will go. Finally, speculative LOADs make it possible to fetch operands in advance, without penalty if it turns out later that they are not needed after all.

For more information about the Itanium 2 and its microarchitecture, see (McNairy and Soltis, 200virtual memorycrypto3; and Rusu et al., 2004).

5.9 SUMMARY

The instruction set architecture level is what most people think of as "machine language." At this level the machine has a byte- or word-oriented memory consisting of some tens of megabytes, and instructions such as MOVE, ADD, and BEQ.

Most modern computers have a memory that is organized as a sequence of bytes, with 4 or 8 bytes grouped together into words. There are normally also between 8 and 32 registers present, each one containing one word. On some machines (e.g., Pentium 4), references to words in memory do not have to be aligned on natural boundaries in memory while on others (e.g., UltraSPARC III), they must be.

Instructions generally have one, two, or three operands, which are addressed using immediate, direct, register, indexed, or other addressing modes. Some machines have a large number of complex addressing modes. Instructions are generally available for moving data, dyadic and monadic operations, including arithmetic and Boolean operations, branches, procedure calls, and loops, and sometimes for I/O. Typical instructions move a word from memory to a register (or vice versa), add, subtract, multiply, or divide two registers or a register and a memory word, or compare two items in registers or memory. It is not unusual for a computer to have well over 200 instructions in its repertoire. CISC machines often have many more.

Control flow at level 2 is achieved using a variety of primitives, including branches, procedure calls, coroutine calls, traps, and interrupts. Branches are used to terminate one instruction sequence and begin a new one. Procedures are used as an abstraction mechanism, to allow a part of the program to be isolated as a unit and called from multiple places. Coroutines allow two threads of control to work simultaneously. Traps are used to signal exceptional situations, such as arithmetic overflow. Interrupts allow I/O to take place in parallel with the main computation, with the CPU getting a signal as soon as the I/O has been completed.

The Towers of Hanoi is a fun little problem with a nice recursive solution that we examined.

Last, the IA-64 architecture uses the EPIC model of computing to make it easy for programs to exploit parallelism. It uses instruction groups, predication and speculative LOADs to gain speed. All in all, it may represent a significant advance over the Pentium 4, but it puts much of the burden of parallelization on the compiler.

PROBLEMS

1. A word on a little-endian computer has the numerical value of 3. If it is transmitted to a big-endian computer byte by byte and stored there, with byte 0 in byte 0, and so on, what is its numerical value on the big endian machine?

2. On the Pentium 4, instructions can contain any number of bytes, even or odd. On the UltraSPARC III, all instructions contain an integral number of words, that is, an even number of bytes. Give one advantage of the Pentium 4 scheme.

3. Design an expanding opcode to allow all the following to be encoded in a 36-bit instruction:

   7 instructions with two 15-bit addresses and one 3-bit register number
   500 instructions with one 15-bit address and one 3-bit register number
   40 instructions with no addresses or registers

4. A certain machine has 16-bit instructions and 6-bit addresses. Some instructions have one address and others have two. If there are n two-address instructions, what is the maximum number of one-address instructions?

5. Is it possible to design an expanding opcode to allow the following to be encoded in a 12-bit instruction? A register is 3 bits.

   4 instructions with three registers
   255 instructions with one register
   16 instructions with zero registers

6. Given the memory values below and a one-address machine with an accumulator, what values do the following instructions load into the accumulator?

   word 20 contains 40
   word 30 contains 50
   word 40 contains 60
   word 50 contains 70

   a. LOAD IMMEDIATE 20
   b. LOAD DIRECT 20
   c. LOAD INDIRECT 20
   d. LOAD IMMEDIATE 30
   e. LOAD DIRECT 30
   f. LOAD INDIRECT 30

7. Compare 0-, 1-, 2-, and 3-address machines by writing programs to compute

$$X = (A + B \times C) / (D - E \times F)$$

for each of the four machines. The instructions available for use are as follows:

0 Address	1 Address	2 Address		3 Address	
PUSH M	LOAD M	MOV	(X = Y)	MOV	(X = Y)
POP M	STORE M	ADD	(X = X+Y)	ADD	(X = Y+Z)
ADD	ADD M	SUB	(X = X−Y)	SUB	(X = Y−Z)
SUB	SUB M	MUL	(X = X∗Y)	MUL	(X = Y∗Z)
MUL	MUL M	DIV	(X = X/Y)	DIV	(X = Y/Z)
DIV	DIV M				

M is a 16-bit memory address, and *X*, *Y*, and *Z* are either 16-bit addresses or 4-bit registers. The 0-address machine uses a stack, the 1-address machine uses an accumulator, and the other two have 16 registers and instructions operating on all combinations of memory locations and registers. SUB X,Y subtracts *Y* from *X* and SUB X,Y,Z subtracts Z from *Y* and puts the result in *X*. With 8-bit opcodes and instruction lengths that are multiples of 4 bits, how many bits does each machine need to compute *X*?

8. Devise an addressing mechanism that allows an arbitrary set of 64 addresses, not necessarily contiguous, in a large address space to be specifiable in a 6-bit field.

9. Give a disadvantage of self-modifying code that was not mentioned in the text.

10. Convert the following formulas from infix to reverse Polish notation.

a. $A + B + C + D - E$
b. $(A - B) \times (C + D) + E$
c. $(A \times B) + (C \times D) + E$
d. $(A - B) \times (((C - D \times E) / F) / G) \times H$

11. Which of the following pairs of reverse Polish notation formulas are mathematically equivalent?

a. $A\ B + C +$ and $A\ B\ C + +$
b. $A\ B - C -$ and $A\ B\ C - -$
c. $A\ B \times C +$ and $A\ B\ C + \times$

12. Convert the following reverse Polish notation formulas to infix.

a. $A\ B - C + D \times$
b. $A\ B / C\ D / +$
c. $A\ B\ C\ D\ E + \times \times /$
d. $A\ B\ C\ D\ E \times F / + G - H / \times +$

13. Write three reverse Polish notation formulas that cannot be converted to infix.

14. Convert the following infix Boolean formulas to reverse Polish notation.

a. (A AND B) OR C
b. (A OR B) AND (A OR C)
c. (A AND B) OR (C AND D)

15. Convert the following infix formula to reverse Polish notation and generate IJVM code to evaluate it.

$$(5 \times 2 + 7) - (4 / 2 + 1)$$

16. The assembly language instruction

    MOV REG,ADDR

means load a register from memory on the Pentium 4. However, on the UltraSPARC III, to load a register from memory one writes

    LOAD ADDR,REG

Why is the operand order different?

17. How many registers does the machine whose instruction formats are given in Fig. 5-25 have?

18. In Fig. 5-25, bit 23 is used to distinguish the use of format 1 from format 2. No bit is provided to distinguish the use of format 3. How does the hardware know to use it?

19. It is common in programming for a program to need to determine where a variable X is with respect to the interval A to B. If a three-address instruction were available with operands A, B, and X, how many condition code bits would have to be set by this instruction?

20. The Pentium 4 has a condition code bit that keeps track of the carry out of bit 3 after an arithmetic operation. What good is it?

21. The UltraSPARC III has no instruction to load a 32-bit number into a register. Instead a sequence of two instructions, SETHI and ADD, are normally used. Is there more than one way to load a 32-bit number into a register? Discuss your answer.

22. One of your friends has just come bursting into your room at 3 A.M., out of breath, to tell you about his brilliant new idea: an instruction with two opcodes. Should you send your friend off to the patent office or back to the drawing board?

23. The 8051 does not have instructions with offsets longer than 8 bits. Does this mean it cannot address memory above 255? If it can, how does it do it?

24. Tests of the form

        if (k == 0) ...
        if (a > b) ...
        if (k < 5) ...

are common in programming. Devise an instruction to perform these tests efficiently. What fields are present in your instruction?

25. For the 16-bit binary number 1001 0101 1100 0011, show the effect of:

a. A right shift of 4 bits with zero fill.
b. A right shift of 4 bits with sign extension.
c. A left shift of 4 bits.
d. A left rotate of 4 bits.
e. A right rotate of 4 bits.

26. How can you clear a memory word on a machine with no CLR instruction?

27. Compute the Boolean expression (A AND B) OR C for

A = 1101 0000 1010 0011
B = 1111 1111 0000 1111
C = 0000 0000 0010 0000

28. Devise a way to interchange two variables A and B without using a third variable or register. *Hint*: Think about the EXCLUSIVE OR instruction.

29. On a certain computer it is possible to move a number from one register to another, shift each of them left by different amounts, and add the results in less time than a multiplication takes. Under what condition is this instruction sequence useful for computing "constant × variable"?

30. Different machines have different instruction densities (number of bytes required to perform a certain computation). For the following Java code fragments, translate each one into Pentium 4 assembly language, UltraSPARC III assembly language, and IJVM. Then compute how many bytes each expression requires for each machine. Assume that i and j are local variables in memory, but otherwise make the most optimistic assumptions in all cases

a. i = 3;
b. i = j;
c. i = j − 1;

31. The loop instructions discussed in the text were for handling for loops. Design an instruction that might be useful for handling common while loops instead.

32. Assume that the monks in Hanoi can move 1 disk per minute (they are in no hurry to finish the job because employment opportunities for people with this particular skill are limited in Hanoi). How long will it take them to solve the entire 64-disk problem? Express your result in years.

33. Why do I/O devices place the interrupt vector on the bus? Would it be possible to store that information in a table in memory instead?

34. A computer uses DMA to read from its disk. The disk has 64 512-byte sectors per track. The disk rotation time is 16 msec. The bus is 16 bits wide, and bus transfers take 500 nsec each. The average CPU instruction requires two bus cycles. How much is the CPU slowed down by DMA?

35. Why do interrupt service routines have priorities associated with them whereas normal procedures do not have priorities?

36. The IA-64 architecture contains an unusually large number of registers (64). Was the choice to have so many of them related to the use of predication? If so, in what way? If not, why are there so many?

37. In the text, the concept of speculative LOAD instructions is discussed. However, there is no mention of speculative STORE instructions. Why not? Are they essentially the same as speculative LOAD instructions or is there another reason not to discuss them?

38. When two local area networks are to be connected, a computer called a bridge is inserted between them, connected to both. Each packet transmitted on either network causes an interrupt on the bridge, to let the bridge see if the packet has to be forwarded. Suppose that it takes 250 μsec per packet to handle the interrupt and inspect the packet, but forwarding it, if need be, is done by DMA hardware without burdening the CPU. If all packets are 1 KB, what is the maximum data rate on each of the networks that can be tolerated without having the bridge lose packets?

39. In Fig. 5-43, the frame pointer points to the first local variable. What information does the program need in order to return from a procedure?

40. Write an assembly language subroutine to convert a signed binary integer to ASCII.

41. Write an assembly language subroutine to convert an infix formula to reverse Polish notation.

42. The towers of Hanoi is not the only little recursive procedure much loved by computer scientists. Another all-time favorite is $n!$, where $n! = n(n-1)!$ subject to the limiting condition that $0! = 1$. Write a procedure in your favorite assembly language to compute $n!$.

43. If you are not convinced that recursion is at times indispensable, try programming the Towers of Hanoi without using recursion and without simulating the recursive solution by maintaining a stack in an array. Be warned, however, that you will probably not be able to find the solution.

6

THE OPERATING SYSTEM
MACHINE LEVEL

The theme of this book is that a modern computer is built as a series of levels, each one adding functionality to the one below it. We have seen the digital logic level, microarchitecture level, and instruction set architecture level so far. Now it is time to move up another level, into the realm of the operating system.

An **operating system** is a program that, from the programmer's point of view, adds a variety of new instructions and features, above and beyond what the ISA level provides. Normally, the operating system is implemented largely in software, but there is no theoretical reason why it could not be put into hardware, just as microprograms normally are (when they are present). For short, we will call the level that it implements the **OSM** (**Operating System Machine**) level. It is shown in Fig. 6-1.

Although the OSM level and the ISA level are both abstract (in the sense that they are not the true hardware level), there is an important difference between them. The OSM level instruction set is the complete set of instructions available to application programmers. It contains nearly all of the ISA level instructions, as well as the set of new instructions that the operating system adds. These new instructions are called **system calls**. A system call invokes a predefined operating system service, effectively, one of its instructions. A typical system call is reading some data from a file. We will typeset system calls in lowercase Helvetica.

The OSM level is always interpreted. When a user program executes an OSM instruction, such as reading some data from a file, the operating system carries out this instruction step by step, the same way as a microprogram would carry out an

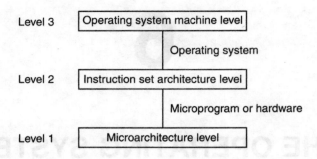

Figure 6-1. Positioning of the operating system machine level.

ADD instruction step by step. However, when a program executes an ISA level instruction, it is carried out directly by the underlying microarchitecture level, without any assistance from the operating system.

In this book we can only provide the briefest of introductions to the subject of operating systems. We will focus on three topics of importance. The first is virtual memory, a technique provided by many modern operating systems to make the machine appear to have more memory than it in reality has. The second is file I/O, a higher-level concept than the I/O instructions that we studied in the previous chapter. The third topic is parallel processing—how multiple processes can execute, communicate, and synchronize. The concept of a process is an important one, and we will describe it in detail later in this chapter. For the time being, a process can be thought of as a running program and all its state information (memory, registers, program counter, I/O status, and so on). After discussing these principles in general, we will show how they apply to the operating systems of two of our example machines, the Pentium 4 (Windows XP) and the Ultra-SPARC III UNIX). Since the 8051 is normally used for embedded systems, it does not have an operating system.

6.1 VIRTUAL MEMORY

In the early days of computers, memories were small and expensive. The IBM 650, the leading scientific computer of its day (late 1950s), had only 2000 words of memory. One of the first ALGOL 60 compilers was written for a computer with only 1024 words of memory. An early timesharing system ran quite well on a PDP-1 with a total memory size of only 4096 18-bit words for the operating system and user programs combined. In those days the programmer spent a lot of time trying to squeeze programs into the tiny memory. Often it was necessary to use an algorithm that ran a great deal slower than another, better algorithm simply because the better algorithm was too big—that is, a program using the better algorithm could not be squeezed into the computer's memory.

The traditional solution to this problem was the use of secondary memory, such as disk. The programmer divided the program up into a number of pieces, called **overlays**, each of which could fit in the memory. To run the program, the first overlay was brought in and it ran for a while. When it finished, it read in the next overlay and called it, and so on. The programmer was responsible for breaking the program into overlays, deciding where in the secondary memory each overlay was to be kept, arranging for the transport of overlays between main memory and secondary memory, and in general managing the whole overlay process without any help from the computer.

Although widely used for many years, this technique involved much work in connection with overlay management. In 1961 a group of researchers at Manchester, England, proposed a method for performing the overlay process automatically, without the programmer even knowing that it was happening (Fotheringham, 1961). This method, now called **virtual memory**, had the obvious advantage of freeing the programmer from a lot of annoying bookkeeping. It was first used on a number of computers during the 1960s, mostly associated with research projects in computer systems design. By the early 1970s virtual memory had become available on most computers. Now even single-chip computers, including the Pentium 4 and UltraSPARC III, have highly sophisticated virtual memory systems. We will look at these later in this chapter.

6.1.1 Paging

The idea put forth by the Manchester group was to separate the concepts of address space and memory locations. Consider, as an example, a typical computer of that era, which might have had a 16-bit address field in its instructions and 4096 words of memory. A program on this computer could address 65536 words of memory. The reason is that 65536 (2^{16}) 16-bit addresses exist, each corresponding to a different memory word. Please note that the number of addressable words depends only on the number of bits in an address and is in no way related to the number of memory words actually available. The **address space** for this computer consists of the numbers 0, 1, 2, ..., 65535, because that is the set of possible addresses. The computer may well have had fewer than 65535 words of memory, however.

Before virtual memory was invented, people would have made a distinction between the addresses below 4096 and those equal to or above 4096. Although rarely stated in so many words, these two parts were regarded as the useful address space and the useless address space, respectively (the addresses above 4095 being useless because they did not correspond to actual memory addresses). People did not make a distinction between address space and memory addresses, because the hardware enforced a one-to-one correspondence between them.

The idea of separating the address space and the memory addresses is as follows. At any instant of time, 4096 words of memory can be directly accessed, but they need not correspond to memory addresses 0 to 4095. We could, for example, "tell" the computer that henceforth whenever address 4096 is referenced, the memory word at address 0 is to be used. Whenever address 4097 is referenced, the memory word at address 1 is to be used; whenever address 8191 is referenced, the memory word at address 4095 is to be used, and so forth. In other words, we have defined a mapping from the address space onto the actual memory addresses, as shown in Fig. 6-2.

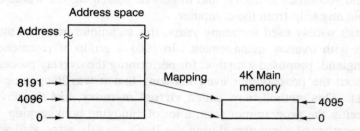

Figure 6-2. A mapping in which virtual addresses 4096 to 8191 are mapped onto main memory addresses 0 to 4095.

In terms of this picture of mapping addresses from the address space onto the actual memory locations, a 4-KB machine without virtual memory simply has a fixed mapping between the addresses 0 to 4095 and the 4096 words of memory. An interesting question is: "What happens if a program branches to an address between 8192 and 12287?" On a machine that lacks virtual memory, the program would cause an error trap that would print a suitably rude message, for example: "Nonexistent memory referenced" and terminate the program. On a machine with virtual memory, the following sequence of steps would occur:

1. The contents of main memory would be saved on disk.

2. Words 8192 to 12287 would be located on disk.

3. Words 8192 to 12287 would be loaded into main memory.

4. The address map would be changed to map addresses 8192 to 12287 onto memory locations 0 to 4095.

5. Execution would continue as though nothing unusual had happened.

This technique for automatic overlaying is called **paging** and the chunks of program read in from disk are called **pages**.

A more sophisticated way of mapping addresses from the address space onto the actual memory addresses is also possible. For emphasis, we will call the addresses that the program can refer to the **virtual address space**, and the actual, hardwired (physical) memory addresses the **physical address space**. A **memory map** or **page table** specifies for each virtual address what the corresponding physical address is. We presume that there is enough room on disk to store the entire virtual address space (or at least that portion of it that is being used) there.

Programs are written just as though there were enough main memory for the whole virtual address space, even though that is not the case. Programs may load from, or store into, any word in the virtual address space, or branch to any instruction located anywhere within the virtual address space, without regard to the fact that there really is not enough physical memory. In fact, the programmer can write programs without even being aware that virtual memory exists. The computer just looks as if it has a big memory.

This point is crucial and will be contrasted later with segmentation, where the programmer must be aware of the existence of segments. To emphasize it once more, paging gives the programmer the illusion of a large, continuous, linear main memory, the same size as the virtual address space. In reality, the main memory available may be smaller (or larger) than the virtual address space. The simulation of this large main memory by paging cannot be detected by the program (except by running timing tests). Whenever an address is referenced, the proper instruction or data word appears to be present. Because the programmer can program as though paging did not exist, the paging mechanism is said to be **transparent**.

The idea that a programmer may use some nonexistent feature without being concerned with how it works is not new to us, after all. The ISA-level instruction set often includes a MUL instruction, even though the underlying microarchitecture does not have a multiplication device in the hardware. The illusion that the machine can multiply is typically sustained by microcode. Similarly, the virtual machine provided by the operating system can provide the illusion that all the virtual addresses are backed up by real memory, even though this is not true. Only operating system writers (and students of operating systems) have to know how the illusion is supported.

6.1.2 Implementation of Paging

One essential requirement for a virtual memory is a disk on which to keep the whole program and all the data. It is conceptually simpler if one thinks of the copy of the program on the disk as the original one and the pieces brought into main memory every now and then as copies rather than the other way around. Naturally, it is important to keep the original up to date. When changes are made to the copy in main memory, they should also be reflected in the original (eventually).

The virtual address space is broken up into a number of equal-sized pages. Page sizes ranging from 512 to 64 KB per page are common at present, although sizes as large as 4 MB are used occasionally. The page size is always a power of 2. The physical address space is broken up into pieces in a similar way, each piece being the same size as a page, so that each piece of main memory is capable of holding exactly one page. These pieces of main memory into which the pages go are called **page frames**. In Fig. 6-2 the main memory contains only one page frame. In practical designs it will usually contain thousands of them.

Figure 6-3(a) illustrates one possible way to divide up the first 64 KB of a virtual address space—in 4-KB pages. (Note that we are talking about 64 KB and 4K of addresses here. An address might be a byte but could equally well be a word on a computer in which consecutive words had consecutive addresses.) The virtual memory of Fig. 6-3 would be implemented by means of a page table with as many entries as there are pages in the virtual address space. We have shown only the first 16 entries here for simplicity. When the program tries to reference a word in the first 64 KB of its virtual address space, whether to fetch instructions, fetch data, or store data, it first generates a virtual address between 0 and 65532 (assuming that word addresses must be divisible by 4). Indexing, indirect addressing, and all the usual techniques may be used to generate this address.

Page	Virtual addresses
15	61440 – 65535
14	57344 – 61439
13	53248 – 57343
12	49152 – 53247
11	45056 – 49151
10	40960 – 45055
9	36864 – 40959
8	32768 – 36863
7	28672 – 32767
6	24576 – 28671
5	20480 – 24575
4	16384 – 20479
3	12288 – 16383
2	8192 – 12287
1	4096 – 8191
0	0 – 4095

(a)

Bottom 32K of main memory

Page frame	Physical addresses
7	28672 – 32767
6	24576 – 28671
5	20480 – 24575
4	16384 – 20479
3	12288 – 16383
2	8192 – 12287
1	4096 – 8191
0	0 – 4095

(b)

Figure 6-3. (a) The first 64 KB of virtual address space divided into 16 pages, with each page being 4K. (b) A 32 KB main memory divided up into eight page frames of 4 KB each.

Figure 6-3(b) shows a physical memory consisting of eight 4-KB page frames. This memory might be limited to 32 KB because (1) that is all the machine had (a processor embedded in a washing machine or microwave oven might not need more), or (2) the rest of the memory was allocated to other programs.

Now consider how a 32-bit virtual address can be mapped onto a physical main memory address. After all, the only thing the memory understands are main memory addresses, not virtual addresses, so that is what it must be given. Every computer with virtual memory has a device for doing the virtual-to-physical mapping. This device is called the **MMU** (**Memory Management Unit**). It may be on the CPU chip, or it may be on a separate chip that works closely with the CPU chip. Since our sample MMU maps from a 32-bit virtual address to a 15-bit physical address, it needs a 32-bit input register and a 15-bit output register.

To see how the MMU works, consider the example of Fig. 6-4. When the MMU is presented with a 32-bit virtual address, it separates the address into a 20-bit virtual page number and a 12-bit offset within the page (because the pages in our example are 4K). The virtual page number is used as an index into the page table to find the entry for the page referenced. In Fig. 6-4, the virtual page number is 3, so entry 3 of the page table is selected, as shown.

The first thing the MMU does with the page table entry is check to see if the page referenced is currently in main memory. After all, with 2^{20} virtual pages and only eight page frames, not all virtual pages can be in memory at once. The MMU makes this check by examining the **present/absent bit** in the page table entry. In our example, the bit is 1, meaning the page is currently in memory.

The next step is to take the page frame value from the selected entry (6 in this case) and copy it into the upper 3 bits of the 15-bit output register. Three bits are needed because there are eight page frames in physical memory. In parallel with this operation, the low-order 12 bits of the virtual address (the page offset field) are copied into the low-order 12 bits of the output register, as shown. This 15-bit address is now sent to the cache or memory for lookup.

Figure 6-5 shows a possible mapping between virtual pages and physical page frames. Virtual page 0 is in page frame 1. Virtual page 1 is in page frame 0. Virtual page 2 is not in main memory. Virtual page 3 is in page frame 2. Virtual page 4 is not in main memory. Virtual page 5 is in page frame 6, and so on.

6.1.3 Demand Paging and the Working Set Model

In the preceding discussion it was assumed that the virtual page referenced was in main memory. However, that assumption will not always be true because there is not enough room in main memory for all the virtual pages. When a reference is made to an address on a page not present in main memory, it is called a **page fault**. After a page fault has occurred, it is necessary for the operating system to read in the required page from the disk, enter its new physical memory location in the page table, and then repeat the instruction that caused the fault.

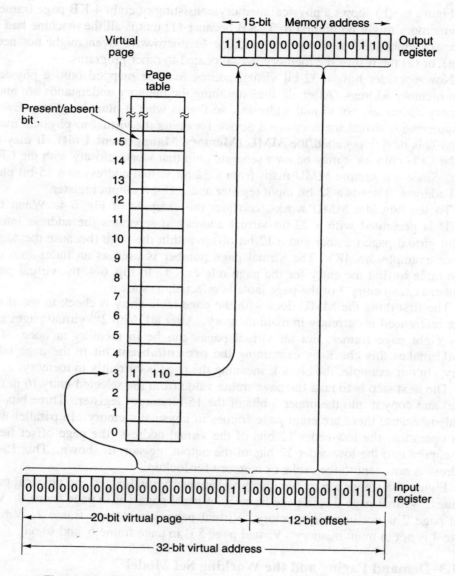

Figure 6-4. Formation of a main memory address from a virtual address.

It is possible to start a program running on a machine with virtual memory even when none of the program is in main memory. The page table merely has to be set to indicate that each and every virtual page is in the secondary memory and not in main memory. When the CPU tries to fetch the first instruction, it immediately gets a page fault, which causes the page containing the first instruction to be loaded into memory and entered in the page table. Then the first instruction can

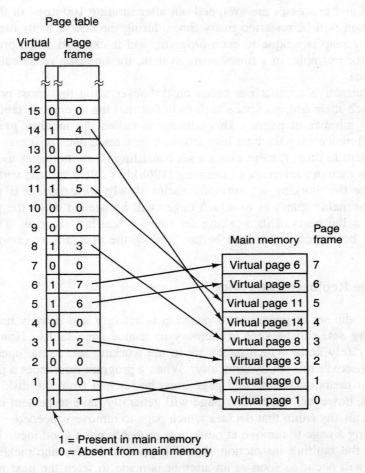

Figure 6-5. A possible mapping of the first 16 virtual pages onto a main memory with eight page frames.

begin. If the first instruction has two addresses, with the two addresses on different pages, both different from the instruction page, two more page faults will occur, and two more pages will be brought in before the instruction can finally execute. The next instruction may cause some more page faults, and so on.

This method of operating a virtual memory is called **demand paging**, in analogy to the well-known demand feeding algorithm for babies: when the baby cries, you feed it (as opposed to feeding it on a precise schedule). In demand paging, pages are brought into memory only when an actual request for a page occurs, not in advance.

The question of whether demand paging should be used or not is only relevant when a program first starts up. Once it has been running for a while, the needed pages will already have been collected in main memory. If the computer is timeshared and processes are swapped out after running 100 msec or thereabouts, each program will be restarted many times during the course of its run. Because the memory map is unique to each program, and is changed when programs are switched, for example, in a timesharing system, the question repeatedly becomes a critical one.

The alternative approach is based on the observation that most programs do not reference their address space uniformly but that the references tend to cluster on a small number of pages. This concept is called the **locality principle**. A memory reference may fetch an instruction, it may fetch data, or it may store data. At any instant in time, t, there exists a set consisting of all the pages used by the k most recent memory references. Denning (1968) has called this the **working set**.

Because the working set normally varies slowly with time, it is possible to make a reasonable guess as to which pages will be needed when the program is restarted, on the basis of its working set when it was last stopped. These pages could then be loaded in advance before starting the program up (assuming they fit).

6.1.4 Page Replacement Policy

Ideally, the set of pages that a program is actively and heavily using, called the **working set**, can be kept in memory to reduce page faults. However, programmers rarely know which pages are in the working set, so the operating system must discover this set dynamically. When a program references a page that is not in main memory, the needed page must be fetched from the disk. To make room for it, however, some other page will generally have to be sent back to the disk. Thus an algorithm that decides which page to remove is needed.

Choosing a page to remove at random is probably not a good idea. If the page containing the faulting instruction should happen to be the one picked, another page fault will occur as soon as an attempt is made to fetch the next instruction. Most operating systems try to predict which of the pages in memory is the least useful in the sense that its absence would have the smallest adverse effect on the running program. One way of doing so is to make a prediction when the next reference to each page will occur and remove the page whose predicted next reference lies furthest in the future. In other words, rather than evict a page that will be needed shortly, try to select one that will not be needed for a long time.

One popular algorithm evicts the page least recently used because the a priori probability of its not being in the current working set is high. It is called the **LRU (Least Recently Used)** algorithm. Although it usually performs well, there are pathological situations, such as the one described below, where LRU fails miserably.

Imagine a program executing a large loop that extends over nine virtual pages on a machine with room for only eight pages in physical memory. After the program gets to page 7, the main memory will be as shown in Fig. 6-6(a). An attempt is eventually made to fetch an instruction from virtual page 8, which causes a page fault. A decision has to be made about which page to evict. The LRU algorithm will choose virtual page 0, because it has been used least recently. Virtual page 0 is removed and virtual page 8 is brought in to replace it, giving the situation in Fig. 6-6(b).

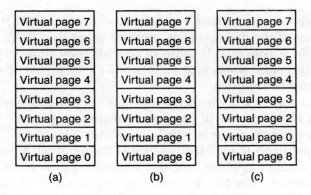

Figure 6-6. Failure of the LRU algorithm.

After executing the instructions on virtual page 8, the program branches back to the top of the loop, to virtual page 0. This step causes another page fault. Virtual page 0, which was just thrown out, has to be brought back in. The LRU algorithm chooses page 1 to be thrown out, producing the situation in Fig. 6-6(c). The program continues on page 0 for a little while. Then it tries to fetch an instruction from virtual page 1, causing a page fault. Page 1 has to be brought back in again and page 2 will be thrown out.

It should be apparent by now that here the LRU algorithm is consistently making the worst choice every time (other algorithms also fail under similar conditions). If, however, the available main memory exceeds the size of the working set, LRU tends to minimize the number of page faults.

Another page replacement algorithm is **FIFO** (**First-In First-Out**). FIFO removes the least recently loaded page, independent of when this page was last referenced. Associated with each page frame is a counter. Initially, all the counters are set to 0. After each page fault has been handled, the counter for each page presently in memory is increased by one, and the counter for the page just brought in is set to 0. When it becomes necessary to choose a page to remove, the page whose counter is highest is chosen. Since its counter is the highest, it has witnessed the largest number of page faults. This means that it was loaded prior to the loading of any of the other pages in memory and therefore (hopefully) has a large a priori chance of no longer being needed.

If the working set is larger than the number of available page frames, no algorithm that is not an oracle will give good results, and page faults will be frequent. A program that generates page faults frequently and continuously is said to be

thrashing. Needless to say, thrashing is an undesirable characteristic to have in your system. If a program uses a large amount of virtual address space but has a small, slowly changing working set that fits in available main memory, it will give little trouble. This observation is true, even if, over its lifetime, the program uses hundreds of times as many words of virtual memory as the machine has words of main memory.

If a page about to be evicted has not been modified since it was read in (a likely occurrence if the page contains program rather than data), it is not necessary to write it back onto disk, because an accurate copy already exists there. If it has been modified since it was read in, the copy on the disk is no longer accurate, and the page must be rewritten.

If there is a way to tell whether a page has not changed since it was read in (page is clean) or whether it, in fact, has been stored into (page is dirty), all the rewriting of clean pages can be avoided, thus saving a lot of time. Many computers have 1 bit per page, in the MMU, which is set to 0 when a page is loaded and set to 1 by the microprogram or hardware whenever it is stored into (i.e., is made dirty). By examining this bit, the operating system can find out if the page is clean or dirty, and hence whether it need be rewritten or not.

6.1.5 Page Size and Fragmentation

If the user's program and data accidentally happen to fill an integral number of pages exactly, there will be no wasted space when they are in memory. If, on the other hand, they do not fill an integral number of pages exactly, there will be some unused space on the last page. For example, if the program and data need 26,000 bytes on a machine with 4096 bytes per page, the first six pages will be full, totaling $6 \times 4096 = 24,576$ bytes, and the last page will contain $26,000 - 24576 = 1424$ bytes. Since there is room for 4096 bytes per page, 2672 bytes will be wasted. Whenever the seventh page is present in memory, those bytes will occupy main memory but will serve no useful function. The problem of these wasted bytes is called **internal fragmentation** (because the wasted space is internal to some page).

If the page size is n bytes, the average amount of space wasted in the last page of a program by internal fragmentation will be $n/2$ bytes—a situation that suggests using a small page size to minimize waste. On the other hand, a small page size means many pages, as well as a large page table. If the page table is maintained in hardware, a large page table means that more registers are needed to store it, which increases the cost of the computer. In addition, more time will be required to load and save these registers whenever a program is started or stopped.

Furthermore, small pages make inefficient use of disk bandwidth. Given that one is going to wait 10 msec or so before the transfer can begin (seek + rotational delay), large transfers are more efficient than small ones. With a 10-MB/sec transfer rate, transferring 8 KB adds only 0.7 msec compared to transferring 1 KB.

However, small pages also have the advantage that if the working set consists of a large number of small, separated regions in the virtual address space, there may be less thrashing with a small page size than with a big one. For example, consider a $10,000 \times 10,000$ matrix, A, stored with $A[1,1]$, $A[2,1]$, $A[3,1]$, and so on, in consecutive 8-byte words. This column-ordered storage means that the elements of row 1, $A[1,1]$, $A[1,2]$, $A[1,3]$, and so on, will begin 80,000 bytes apart. A program performing an extensive calculation on all the elements of this row would use 10,000 regions, each separated from the next one by 79,992 bytes. If the page size were 8 KB, a total storage of 80 MB would be needed to hold all the pages being used.

On the other hand, a page size of 1 KB would require only 10 MB of RAM to hold all the pages. If the available memory were 32 MB, with an 8-KB page size, the program would thrash, but with a 1-KB page size it would not. All things considered, the trend is towards larger page sizes.

6.1.6 Segmentation

The virtual memory discussed above is one-dimensional because the virtual addresses go from 0 to some maximum address, one address after another. For many problems, having two or more separate virtual address spaces may be much better than having only one. For example, a compiler might have many tables that are built up as compilation proceeds, including

1. The symbol table, containing the names and attributes of variables.

2. The source text being saved for the printed listing.

3. A table containing all the integer and floating-point constants used.

4. The parse tree, containing the syntactic analysis of the program.

5. The stack used for procedure calls within the compiler.

Each of the first four tables grows continuously as compilation proceeds. The last one grows and shrinks in unpredictable ways during compilation. In a one-dimensional memory, these five tables would have to be allocated as contiguous chunks of virtual address space, as in Fig. 6-7.

Consider what happens if a program has an exceptionally large number of variables. The chunk of address space allocated for the symbol table may fill up, even if there is lots of room in the other tables. The compiler could, of course, simply issue a message saying that the compilation cannot continue due to too many variables, but doing so does not seem very sporting when unused space is left in the other tables.

Another possibility is to have the compiler play Robin Hood, taking space from the tables with much room and giving it to the tables with little room. This shuffling can be done, but it is analogous to managing one's own overlays—a nuisance at best and a great deal of tedious, unrewarding work at worst.

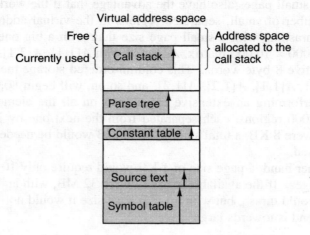

Figure 6-7. In a one-dimensional address space with growing tables, one table may bump into another.

What is really needed is a way of freeing the programmer from having to manage the expanding and contracting tables, in the same way that virtual memory eliminates the worry of organizing the program into overlays.

A straightforward solution is to provide many completely independent address spaces, called **segments**. Each segment consists of a linear sequence of addresses, from 0 to some maximum. The length of each segment may be anything from 0 to the maximum allowed. Different segments may, and usually do, have different lengths. Moreover, segment lengths may change during execution. The length of a stack segment may be increased whenever something is pushed onto the stack and decreased whenever something is popped off the stack.

Because each segment constitutes a separate address space, different segments can grow or shrink independently, without affecting each other. If a stack in a certain segment needs more address space to grow, it can have it, because there is nothing else in its address space to bump into. Of course, a segment can fill up completely but segments are usually very large, so this occurrence is rare. To specify an address in this segmented or two-dimensional memory, the program must supply a two-part address: a segment number, and an address within the segment. Figure 6-8 illustrates a segmented memory being used for the compiler tables discussed earlier.

We emphasize that a segment is a *logical* entity, which the programmer is aware of and uses as a single logical entity. A segment might contain a procedure, or an array, or a stack, or a collection of scalar variables, but usually it does not contain a mixture of different types.

A segmented memory has other advantages besides simplifying the handling of data structures that are growing or shrinking. If each procedure occupies a separate segment, with address 0 as its starting address, the linking up of procedures

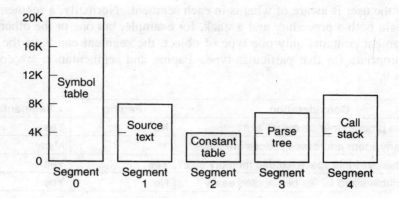

Figure 6-8. A segmented memory allows each table to grow or shrink independently of the other tables.

compiled separately is greatly simplified. After all the procedures that constitute a program have been compiled and linked up, a procedure call to the procedure in segment n will use the two-part address $(n, 0)$ to address word 0 (the entry point).

If the procedure in segment n is subsequently modified and recompiled, no other procedures need be changed (because no starting addresses have been modified), even if the new version is larger than the old one. With a one-dimensional memory, the procedures are normally packed tightly next to each other, with no address space between them. Consequently, changing one procedure's size can affect the starting address of other, unrelated, procedures. This, in turn, requires modifying all procedures that call any of the moved procedures, in order to incorporate their new starting addresses. If a program contains hundreds of procedures, this process can be costly.

Segmentation also facilitates sharing procedures or data between several programs. If a computer has several programs running in parallel (either true or simulated parallel processing), all of which use certain library procedures, it is wasteful of main memory to provide each one with its own private copy. By making each procedure a separate segment, they can be shared easily, thus eliminating the need for more than one physical copy of any shared procedure to be in main memory. As a result, memory is saved.

Because each segment forms a logical entity of which the programmer is aware, such as a procedure, or an array, or a stack, different segments can have different kinds of protection. A procedure segment could be specified as execute only, prohibiting attempts to read from it or store into it. A floating-point array could be specified as read/write but not execute, and attempts to branch to it would be caught. Such protection is frequently helpful in catching programming errors.

You should try to understand why protection makes sense in a segmented memory but not in a one-dimensional (i.e., linear) paged memory. In a segmented memory the user is aware of what is in each segment. Normally, a segment would not contain both a procedure and a stack, for example, but one or the other. Since each segment contains only one type of object, the segment can have the protection appropriate for that particular type. Paging and segmentation are compared in Fig. 6-9.

Consideration	Paging	Segmentation
Need the programmer be aware of it?	No	Yes
How many linear addresses spaces are there?	1	Many
Can virtual address space exceed memory size?	Yes	Yes
Can variable-sized tables be handled easily?	No	Yes
Why was the technique invented?	To simulate large memories	To provide multiple address spaces

Figure 6-9. Comparison of paging and segmentation.

The contents of a page are, in a sense, accidental. The programmer is unaware of the fact that paging is even occurring. Although putting a few bits in each entry of the page table to specify the access allowed would be possible, to utilize this feature the programmer would have to keep track of where in his address space the page boundaries were. The trouble with this idea is that this is precisely the sort of administration that paging was invented to eliminate. Because the user of a segmented memory has the illusion that all segments are in main memory all the time, they can be addressed without having to be concerned with the administration of overlaying them.

6.1.7 Implementation of Segmentation

Segmentation can be implemented in one of two ways: swapping and paging. In the former scheme, some set of segments is in memory at a given instant. If a reference is made to a segment not currently in memory, that segment is brought in. If there is no room for it, one or more segments must be written to disk first (unless a clean copy already exists there, in which case the memory copy can just be abandoned). In a certain sense, segment swapping is not unlike demand paging: segments come and segments go as needed.

However, the implementation of segmentation differs from paging in an essential way: pages are fixed size and segments are not. Figure 6-10(a) shows an example of physical memory initially containing five segments. Now consider what happens if segment 1 is evicted and segment 7, which is smaller, is put in its place. We arrive at the memory configuration of Fig. 6-10(b). Between segment 7 and segment 2 is an unused area—that is, a hole. Then segment 4 is replaced by segment 5, as in Fig. 6-10(c), and segment 3 is replaced by segment 6, as in Fig. 6-10(d). After the system has been running for a while, memory will be divided up into a number of chunks, some containing segments and some containing holes. This phenomenon is called **external fragmentation** (because space is wasted external to the segments, in the holes between them). Sometimes external fragmentation is called **checkerboarding**.

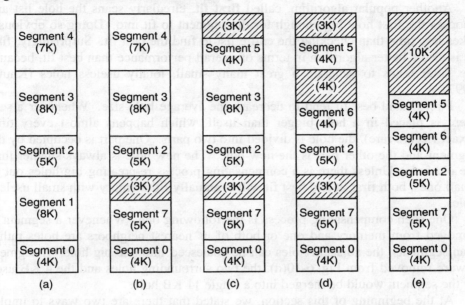

Figure 6-10. (a)-(d) Development of external fragmentation (e) Removal of the external fragmentation by compaction.

Consider what would happen if the program referenced segment 3 at the time memory was suffering from external fragmentation, as in Fig. 6-10(d). The total space in the holes is 10K, more than enough for segment 3, but because the space is distributed in small, useless pieces, segment 3 cannot simply be loaded. Instead, another segment must be removed first.

One way to avoid external fragmentation is as follows: every time a hole appears, move the segments following the hole closer to memory location 0, thereby eliminating that hole but leaving a big hole at the end. Alternatively, one could wait until the external fragmentation became quite serious (e.g., more than a certain percentage of the total memory wasted in holes) before performing the compaction (squeezing out the holes). Figure 6-10(e) shows how the memory of Fig. 6-10(d) would look after compaction. The intention of compacting memory is to collect all the small useless holes into one big hole, into which one or more segments can be placed. Compacting has the obvious drawback that some time is wasted doing the compacting. Compacting after every hole is created is usually too time consuming.

If the time required for compacting memory is unacceptably large, an algorithm is needed to determine which hole to use for a particular segment. Hole management requires maintaining a list of the addresses and sizes of all holes. One popular algorithm, called **best fit**, chooses the smallest hole into which the needed segment will fit. The idea is to match holes and segments so as to avoid breaking off a piece of a big hole, which may be needed later for a big segment.

Another popular algorithm, called **first fit**, circularly scans the hole list and chooses the first hole big enough for the segment to fit into. Doing so obviously takes less time than checking the entire list to find the best fit. Surprisingly, first fit is also a better algorithm in terms of overall performance than best fit, because the latter tends to generate a great many small, totally useless holes (Knuth, 1997).

First fit and best fit tend to decrease the average hole size. Whenever a segment is placed in a hole bigger than itself, which happens almost every time (exact fits are rare), the hole is divided into two parts. One part is occupied by the segment and the other part is the new hole. The new hole is always smaller than the old hole. Unless there is a compensating process re-creating big holes out of small ones, both first fit and best fit will eventually fill memory with small useless holes.

One such compensating process is the following one. Whenever a segment is removed from memory and one or both of its nearest neighbors are holes rather than segments, the adjacent holes can be coalesced into one big hole. If segment 5 were removed from Fig. 6-10(d), the two surrounding holes and the 4 KB used by the segment would be merged into a single 11 KB hole.

At the beginning of this section, we stated that there are two ways to implement segmentation: swapping and paging. The discussion so far has centered on swapping. In this scheme, whole segments are shuttled back and forth between memory and disk on demand. The other way to implement segmentation is by dividing each segment up into fixed size pages and demand paging them. In this scheme, some of the pages of a segment may be in memory and some may be on disk. To page a segment, a separate page table is needed for each segment. Since a segment is just a linear address space, all the techniques we have seen so far for paging apply to each segment. The only new feature here is that each segment gets its own page table.

An early operating system that combined segmentation with paging was **MULTICS** (**MULTiplexed Information and Computing Service**), initially a joint effort of M.I.T., Bell Labs, and General Electric (Corbató and Vyssotsky, 1965; and Organick, 1972). MULTICS addresses had two parts: a segment number and an address within the segment. There was a descriptor segment for each process, which contained a descriptor for each segment. When a virtual address was presented to the hardware, the segment number was used as an index into the descriptor segment to locate the descriptor for the segment being accessed, as shown in Fig. 6-11. The descriptor pointed to the page table, allowing each segment to be paged in the usual way. To speed up performance, the most recently used segment/page combinations were held in a 16-entry hardware **associative**

memory that allowed them to be looked up quickly. Although MULTICS is long gone, its spirit lives on because the virtual memory of all the Intel CPUs since the 386 have been closely modeled on it.

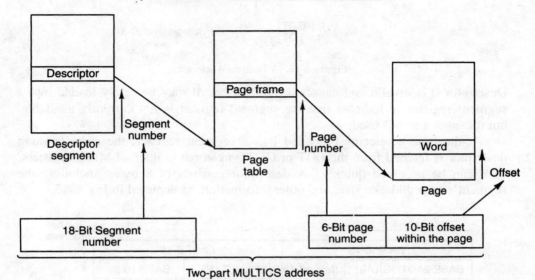

Figure 6-11. Conversion of a two-part MULTICS address into a main memory address.

6.1.8 Virtual Memory on the Pentium 4

The Pentium 4 has a sophisticated virtual memory system that supports demand paging, pure segmentation, and segmentation with paging. The heart of the Pentium 4 virtual memory consists of two tables: the **LDT** (**Local Descriptor Table**) and the **GDT** (**Global Descriptor Table**). Each program has its own LDT, but there is a single GDT, shared by all the programs on the computer. The LDT describes segments local to each program, including its code, data, stack, and so on, whereas the GDT describes system segments, including the operating system itself.

As we described in Chap. 5, to access a segment, a Pentium 4 program first loads a selector for that segment into one of the segment registers. During execution, CS holds the selector for the code segment, DS holds the selector for the data segment, and so on. Each selector is a 16-bit number, as shown in Fig. 6-12.

One of the selector bits tells whether the segment is local or global (i.e., whether it is in the LDT or GDT). Thirteen other bits specify the LDT or GDT entry number, so these tables are each restricted to holding 8 KB (2^{13}) segment descriptors. The other 2 bits relate to protection and will be described later.

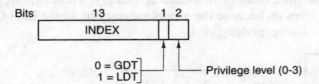

Figure 6-12. A Pentium 4 selector.

Descriptor 0 is invalid and causes a trap if used. It may be safely loaded into a segment register to indicate that the segment register is not currently available, but it causes a trap if used.

At the time a selector is loaded into a segment register, the corresponding descriptor is fetched from the LDT or GDT and stored in internal MMU registers, so it can be accessed quickly. A descriptor consists of 8 bytes, including the segment's base address, size, and other information, as depicted in Fig. 6-13.

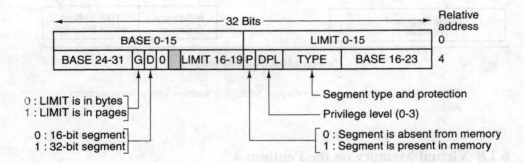

Figure 6-13. A Pentium 4 code segment descriptor. Data segments differ slightly.

The format of the selector has been cleverly chosen to make locating the descriptor easy. First either the LDT or GDT is selected, based on selector bit 2. Then the selector is copied to an MMU scratch register, and the 3 low-order bits are set to 0, effectively multiplying the 13-bit selector number by eight. Finally, the address of either the LDT or GDT table (kept in internal MMU registers) is added to it, to give a direct pointer to the descriptor. For example, selector 72 refers to entry 9 in the GDT, which is located at address GDT + 72.

Let us trace the steps by which a (selector, offset) pair is converted to a physical address. As soon as the hardware knows which segment register is being used, it can find the complete descriptor corresponding to that selector in its internal registers. If the segment does not exist (selector 0), or is currently not in memory (P is 0), a trap occurs. The former case is a programming error; the latter case requires the operating system to go get it.

It then checks to see if the offset is beyond the end of the segment, in which case a trap also occurs. Logically, there should simply be a 32-bit field in the descriptor giving the size of the segment, but there are only 20 bits available, so a different scheme is used. If the G (Granularity) field is 0, the LIMIT field is the exact segment size, up to 1 MB. If it is 1, the LIMIT field gives the segment size in pages instead of bytes. The Pentium 4 page size is never smaller than 4 KB, so 20 bits is enough for segments up to 2^{32} bytes.

Assuming that the segment is in memory and the offset is in range, the Pentium 4 then adds the 32-bit BASE field in the descriptor to the offset to form what is called a **linear address**, as shown in Fig. 6-14. The BASE field is broken up into three pieces and spread all over the descriptor for compatibility with the 80286, in which the BASE is only 24 bits. In effect, the BASE field allows each segment to start at an arbitrary place within the 32-bit linear address space.

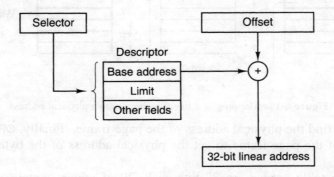

Figure 6-14. Conversion of a (selector, offset) pair to a linear address.

If paging is disabled (by a bit in a global control register), the linear address is interpreted as the physical address and sent to the memory for the read or write. Thus with paging disabled, we have a pure segmentation scheme, with each segment's base address given in its descriptor. Segments are permitted to overlap, incidentally, probably because it would be too much trouble and take too much time to verify that they were all disjoint.

On the other hand, if paging is enabled, the linear address is interpreted as a virtual address and mapped onto the physical address using page tables, pretty much as in our examples. The only complication is that with a 32-bit virtual address and a 4 KB page, a segment might contain 1 million pages, so a two-level mapping is used to reduce the page table size for small segments.

Each running program has a **page directory** consisting of 1024 32-bit entries. It is located at an address pointed to by a global register. Each entry in this directory points to a page table also containing 1024 32-bit entries. The page table entries point to page frames. The scheme is shown in Fig. 6-15.

In Fig. 6-15(a) we see a linear address broken up into three fields: DIR, PAGE, and OFF. The DIR field is first used as an index into the page directory to locate a pointer to the proper page table. Then the PAGE field is used as an index into the

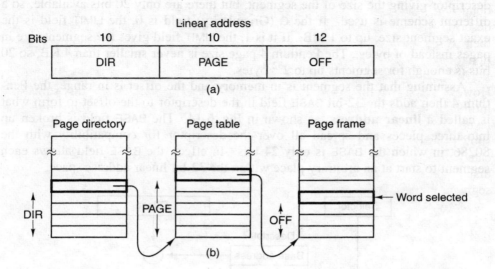

Figure 6-15. Mapping of a linear address onto a physical address.

page table to find the physical address of the page frame. Finally, OFF is added to the address of the page frame to get the physical address of the byte or word addressed.

The page table entries are 32 bits each, 20 of which contain a page frame number. The remaining bits contain access and dirty bits, set by the hardware for the benefit of the operating system, protection bits, and other utility bits.

Each page table has entries for 1024 4 KB page frames, so a single page table handles 4 megabytes of memory. A segment shorter than 4M will have a page directory with a single entry, a pointer to its one and only page table. In this way, the overhead for short segments is only two pages, instead of the million pages that would be needed in a one-level page table.

To avoid making repeated references to memory, the Pentium 4 MMU has special hardware support to look up the most recently used DIR–PAGE combinations quickly and map them onto the physical address of the corresponding page frame. Only when the current combination has not been used recently are the steps shown in Fig. 6-15 actually carried out.

A little thought will reveal the fact that when paging is used, there is really no point in having the BASE field in the descriptor be nonzero. All that BASE does is cause a small offset to use an entry in the middle of the page directory, instead of at the beginning. The real reason for including BASE at all is to allow pure (non-paged) segmentation, and for backward compatibility with the old 80286, which did not have paging.

It is also worth mentioning that if a particular application does not need segmentation, but is content with a single, paged, 32-bit address space, that is easy to obtain. All the segment registers can then be set up with the same selector, whose descriptor has BASE = 0 and LIMIT set to the maximum. The instruction offset will then be the linear address, with only a single address space used—in effect, traditional paging.

We are now finished with our treatment of virtual memory on the Pentium 4. However, it is worth saying a few words about protection, since this subject is intimately related to the virtual memory. The Pentium 4 supports four protection levels, with level 0 being the most privileged and level 3 the least. These are shown in Fig. 6-16. At each instant, a running program is at a certain level, indicated by a 2-bit field in its **PSW (Program Status Word)**, a hardware register that holds the condition codes and various other status bits. Furthermore, each segment in the system also belongs to a certain level.

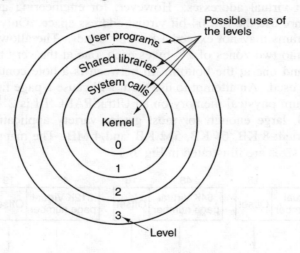

Figure 6-16. Protection on the Pentium 4.

As long as a program restricts itself to using segments at its own level, everything works fine. Attempts to access data at a higher level are permitted. Attempts to access data at a lower level are illegal and cause traps. Attempts to call procedures at a different level (higher or lower) are allowed, but in a carefully controlled way. To make an interlevel call, the CALL instruction must contain a selector instead of an address. This selector designates a descriptor called a **call gate**, which gives the address of the procedure to be called. Thus it is not possible to branch into the middle of an arbitrary code segment at a different level. Only official entry points may be used.

A possible use for this mechanism is suggested in Fig. 6-16. At level 0, we find the kernel of the operating system, which handles I/O, memory management, and other critical matters. At level 1, the system call handler is present. User programs may call procedures here to have system calls carried out, but only a specific and protected list of procedures may be called. Level 2 contains library procedures, possibly shared among many running programs. User programs may call these procedures, but they may not modify them. Finally, user programs run at level 3, which has the least protection. Like the Pentium 4's memory management scheme, the protection system is closely based on MULTICS.

Traps and interrupts use a mechanism similar to the call gates. They, too, reference descriptors, rather than absolute addresses, and these descriptors point to specific procedures to be executed. The TYPE field in Figure 6-13 distinguishes between code segments, data segments, and the various kinds of gates.

6.1.9 Virtual Memory on the UltraSPARC III

The UltraSPARC III is a 64-bit machine and supports a paged virtual memory based on 64-bit virtual addresses. However, for engineering and cost reasons, programs may not use the full 64-bit virtual address space. Only 44 bits are supported, so programs may not exceed 1.8×10^{13} bytes. The allowed virtual memory is divided into two zones of 2^{43} bytes each, one at the very top of the virtual address space and one at the bottom. In between is a hole containing addresses that may not be used. An attempt to use them will cause a page fault.

The maximum physical memory on an UltraSPARC III is 2^{41} bytes, which is about 2200 GB, large enough for most garden-variety applications. Four page sizes are supported: 8 KB, 64 KB, 512 KB, and 4 MB. The mappings implied by these four page sizes are illustrated in Fig. 6-17.

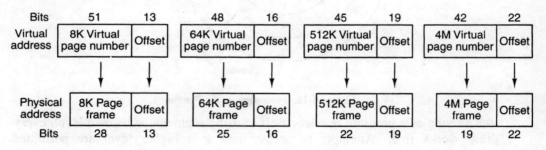

Figure 6-17. Virtual to physical mappings on the UltraSPARC.

Due to its extremely large virtual address space, a straightforward page table like the Pentium 4 has would not be practical. Instead, the UltraSPARC III MMU is forced to use a very different approach. It contains a hardware table called a **TLB (Translation Lookaside Buffer)** that maps virtual page numbers onto physical page frame numbers. For the 8-KB page size, there are 2^{31} virtual page numbers, which is over 2 billion. Clearly, not all of them can be mapped.

Instead, the TLB holds only the most recently used virtual page numbers. Instruction and data pages are kept track of separately, with the TLB holding the 64 most recently used virtual page numbers in each category. Each TLB entry holds a virtual page number and the corresponding physical page frame number.

When a process number, called a **context**, and a virtual address within that context is presented to the MMU, it uses special circuitry to compare the virtual page number contained in it to all the TLB entries for that context at once. If a match is found, the page frame number in that TLB entry is combined with the offset taken from the virtual address to form a 41-bit physical address and produce some flags, such as protection bits. The TLB is illustrated in Fig. 6-18(a).

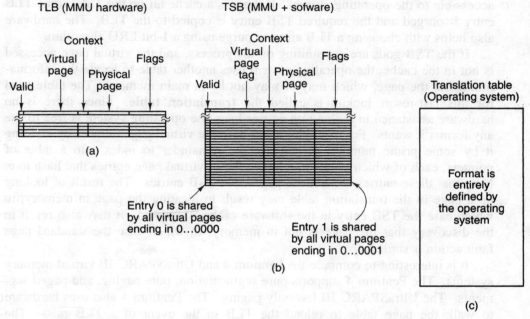

Figure 6-18. Data structures used in translating virtual addresses on the UltraSPARC. (a) TLB. (b) TSB. (c) Translation table.

However, if no match is found, a **TLB miss** occurs, which causes a trap to the operating system. Handling the fault is up to the operating system. Note that a TLB miss is very different from a page fault. A TLB miss can happen even if the page referenced is in memory. In theory, the operating system can do whatever it wants to in order to load a new TLB entry for the virtual page required. However, to speed up this crucial operation, some hardware assistance is provided if the software cooperates.

In particular, the operating system is expected to maintain a software cache of heavily used TLB entries in a table called the **TSB** (**Translation Storage Buffer**). This table is organized as a direct-mapped cache of virtual pages. Each 16-byte TSB entry refers to one virtual page and contains a validity bit, the context number, the virtual address tag, the physical page number, and some flag bits. If the size of the cache is say, 8192 entries, then all virtual pages whose low-order 13 bits map onto 0000000000000 compete for entry 0 in the TSB. Similarly, all virtual pages whose low-order bits map onto 0000000000001 compete for entry 1 in the TSB, as shown in Fig. 6-18(b). The TSB size is determined by software and communicated to the MMU via special registers accessible only to the operating system.

On a TLB miss, the operating system checks to see if the corresponding entry in the TSB contains the virtual page needed. The MMU conveniently helps here by computing the address of this entry and putting it in an internal MMU register accessible to the operating system. If there is a cache hit on the TSB, some TLB entry is purged and the required TSB entry is copied to the TLB. The hardware also helps with choosing a TLB entry to purge using a 1-bit LRU algorithm.

If the TSB gods are not smiling on the process, and the virtual page accessed is not in the cache, the operating system uses another table to locate the information about the page, which may or may not be in main memory. The table used for this last-resort lookup is called the **translation table**. Since there is no hardware assistance in looking up entries here, the operating system is free to use any format it wants. For example, it can hash the virtual page number by dividing it by some prime number, p, and use the remainder to index into a table of pointers, each of which points to a linked list of virtual page entries that hash to p. Note that these entries are not the pages, but TSB entries. The result of looking up a page in the translation table may result in locating the page in memory, in which case the TSB entry in the software cache is updated. It may also result in the discovery that the page is not in memory, in which case the standard page fault action is started.

It is interesting to compare the Pentium 4 and UltraSPARC III virtual memory systems. The Pentium 4 supports pure segmentation, pure paging, and paged segments. The UltraSPARC III has only paging. The Pentium 4 also uses hardware to walk the page table to reload the TLB in the event of a TLB miss. The UltraSPARC III just gives control to the operating system on a TLB miss.

The primary reason for this difference is that the Pentium 4 uses 32-bit segments, and such small segments (only 1 million pages) can be handled with conventional page tables. In theory, the Pentium 4 would have a problem if a program used thousands of segments, but since no versions of Windows or UNIX support more than one segment per process, the problem does not arise. In contrast, the UltraSPARC III is a 64-bit machine and can have up to 2 billion pages, so conventional page tables will not work. In the future, all machines will have 64-bit virtual address spaces, so schemes like the UltraSPARC's will become the norm.

6.1.10 Virtual Memory and Caching

Although at first glance, (demand-paged) virtual memory and caching may look unrelated, they are conceptually very similar. With virtual memory, the entire program is kept on disk and broken up into fixed-size pages. Some subset of these pages are in main memory. If the program mostly uses the pages in memory, there will be few page faults and the program will run fast. With caching, the entire program is kept in main memory and broken up into fixed-size cache blocks. Some subset of these blocks are in the cache. If the program mostly uses the blocks in the cache, there will be few cache misses and the program will run fast. Conceptually, the two are identical, only operating at different levels in the hierarchy.

Of course, virtual memory and caching also have some differences. For one, cache misses are handled by the hardware, whereas page faults are handled by the operating system. Also, cache blocks are typically much smaller than pages (e.g., 64 bytes vs. 8 KB). In addition, the mapping between virtual pages and page frames is different, with page tables organized by indexing on the high-order bits of the virtual address, whereas caches index on the low-order bits of the memory address. Nevertheless, it is important to realize that these are implementation differences. The underlying concept is very similar.

6.2 VIRTUAL I/O INSTRUCTIONS

The ISA-level instruction set is completely different from the microarchitecture instruction set. Both the operations that can be performed and the formats for the instructions are quite different at the two levels. The occasional existence of a few instructions that are the same at both levels is essentially accidental.

In contrast, the OSM level instruction set contains most of the ISA level instructions, with a few new, but important, instructions added and a few potentially damaging instructions removed. Input/output is one of the areas where the two levels differ considerably. The reason for this difference is simple: a user who could execute the real ISA level I/O instructions could read confidential data stored anywhere in the system, write on other users' terminals, and, in general, make a big nuisance of himself or herself as threaten the security of the system itself. Second, normal, sane programmers do not want to do I/O at the ISA level themselves because doing so is extremely tedious and complex. It is done by setting fields and bits in a number of device registers, waiting until the operation is completed, and then checking to see what happened. As an example of the latter, disks typically have device register bits to detect the following errors, among many others:

1. Disk arm failed to seek properly.

2. Nonexistent memory specified as buffer.

3. Disk I/O started before previous one finished.

4. Read timing error.

5. Nonexistent disk addressed.

6. Nonexistent cylinder addressed.

7. Nonexistent sector addressed.

8. Checksum error on read.

9. Write check error after write operation.

When one of these errors occurs, the corresponding bit in a device register is set. Few users want to be bothered keeping track of all these error bits and a great deal of additional status information.

6.2.1 Files

One way of organizing the virtual I/O is to use an abstraction called a **file**. In its simplest form, a file consists of a sequence of bytes written to an I/O device. If the I/O device is a storage device, such as a disk, the file can be read back later; if the device is not a storage device (e.g., a printer), it cannot be read back, of course. A disk can hold many files, each with some particular kind of data, for example, a picture, a spreadsheet, or the text of a book chapter. Different files have different lengths and other properties. The abstraction of a file allows virtual I/O to be organized in a simple way.

To the operating system, a file is normally just a sequence of bytes, as we have described above. Any further structure is up to the application programs. File I/O is done by system calls for opening, reading, writing, and closing files. Before reading a file, it must be opened. The process of opening a file allows the operating system to locate the file on disk and bring into memory information necessary to access it.

Once a file has been opened, it can be read. The read system call must have the following parameters, at a minimum:

1. An indication of which open file is to be read.

2. A pointer to a buffer in memory in which to put the data.

3. The number of bytes to be read.

The read call puts the requested data in the buffer. Usually, it returns the count of the number of bytes actually read, which may be smaller than the number requested (you cannot read 2000 bytes from a 1000-byte file).

Associated with each open file is a pointer telling which byte will be read next. After a read it is advanced by the number of bytes read, so consecutive reads read consecutive blocks of data from the file. Usually, there is a way to set this pointer to a specific value, so programs can randomly access any part of the file. When a program is done reading a file, it can close it, to inform the operating system that it will not be using the file any more, thus allowing the operating system to free up the table space being used to hold information about the file.

Mainframe operating systems have a more sophisticated idea of what a file is. There, a file can be a sequence of **logical records**, each with a well-defined structure. For example, a logical record might be a data structure consisting of five items: two character strings, "Name," and "Supervisor"; two integers, "Department" and "Office"; and a Boolean, "SexIsFemale." Some operating systems make a distinction between files in which all the records in a file have the same structure and files which contain a mixture of different record types.

The basic virtual input instruction reads the next record from the specified file and puts it into main memory beginning at a specified address, as illustrated in Fig. 6-19. To perform this operation, the virtual instruction must be told which file to read and where in memory to put the record. Often there are options to read a specific record, specified either by its position in the file, or by its key.

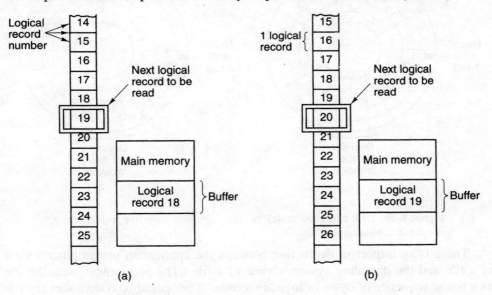

Figure 6-19. Reading a file consisting of logical records. (a) Before reading record 19. (b) After reading record 19.

The basic virtual output instruction writes a logical record from memory onto a file. Consecutive sequential write instructions produce consecutive logical records on the file.

6.2.2 Implementation of Virtual I/O Instructions

To understand how virtual I/O instructions are implemented, it is necessary to examine how files are organized and stored. A basic issue that must be dealt with by all file systems is allocation of storage. The allocation unit can be a single disk sector, but often it consists of a block of consecutive sectors.

Another fundamental property of a file system implementation is whether a file is stored in consecutive allocation units or not. Figure 6-20 depicts a simple disk with one surface consisting of five tracks of 12 sectors each. Figure 6-20(a) shows an allocation scheme in which the sector is the basic unit of space allocation and in which a file consists of consecutive sectors. Consecutive allocation of file blocks is commonly used on CD-ROMs. Figure 6-20(b) shows an allocation scheme in which the sector is the basic allocation unit but in which a file need not occupy consecutive sectors. This scheme is the norm on hard disks.

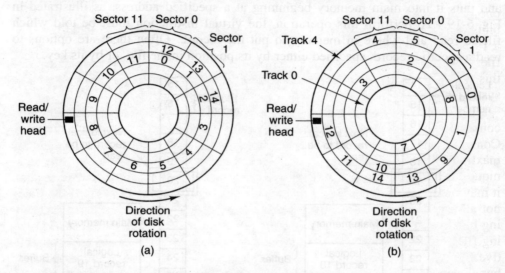

Figure 6-20. Disk allocation strategies. (a) A file in consecutive sectors. (b) A file not in consecutive sectors.

There is an important distinction between the application programmer's view of a file and the operating system's view of a file. The programmer sees the file as a linear sequence of bytes or logical records. The operating system sees the file as an ordered, although not necessarily consecutive, collection of allocation units on disk.

In order for the operating system to deliver byte or logical record n of some file on request, it must have some method for locating the data. If the file is allocated consecutively, the operating system need only know the location of the start of the file in order to calculate the position of the byte or logical record needed.

If the file is not allocated consecutively, it is not possible to calculate the position of an arbitrary byte or logical record in the file from the position of the start of the file alone. In order to locate any arbitrary byte or logical record, a table called a **file index**, giving the allocation units and their actual disk addresses is needed. The file index can be organized either as a list of disk block addresses (used by UNIX), or as a list of logical records, giving the disk address and offset for each one. Sometimes each logical record has a **key** and programs can refer to a record by its key, rather than by its logical record number. In this case, the latter organization is required, with each entry containing not only the location of the record on disk, but also its key. This organization is common on mainframes.

An alternative method of locating the allocation units of a file is to organize the file as a linked list. Each allocation unit contains the address of its successor. One way to implement this scheme efficiently is to keep the table with all the successor addresses in main memory. For example, for a disk with 64 KB allocation units, the operating system could have a table in memory with 64 KB entries, each one giving the index of its successor. For example, if a file occupied allocation units 4, 52, and 19, entry 4 in the table would contain a 52, entry 52 would contain a 19, and entry 19 would contain a special code (e.g., 0 or −1) to indicate end of file. The file systems used by MS-DOS and Windows 95 and Windows 98 worked this way. Windows XP supports this file system but also has its own native file system that works more like UNIX.

Up until now we have discussed both consecutively allocated files and non-consecutively allocated files but we have not specified why both kinds are used. Consecutively allocated files have simpler block administration, but when the maximum file size is not known in advance, it is rarely possible to use this technique. If a file is started at sector j and allowed to grow into consecutive sectors, it may bump into another file at sector k and have no room to expand. If the file is not allocated consecutively, this situation presents no problem, because succeeding blocks can be put anywhere on the disk. If a disk contains a number of growing files, none of whose final sizes is known, storing each of them as a consecutive file will be nearly impossible. Moving an existing file is sometimes possible but always expensive.

On the other hand, if the maximum size of all files is known in advance, as it is when a CD-ROM is burned, the recording program can preallocate a run of sectors exactly equal in length to each file. Thus if files with lengths of 1200, 700, 2000, and 900 sectors are to be put on a CD-ROM, they can be simply begun at sectors 0, 1200, 1900, and 3900, respectively (ignoring the table of contents here). Finding any part of any file is simple once the file's first sector is known.

In order to allocate space on the disk for a file, the operating system must keep track of which blocks are available, and which are already in use storing other files. For a CD-ROM, the calculation is done once and for all in advance, but for a hard disk, files come and go all the time. One method consists of maintaining a list of all the holes, a hole being any number of contiguous allocation units. This list is called the **free list**. Figure 6-21(a) illustrates the free list for the disk of Fig. 6-20(b).

An alternative method is to maintain a bit map, with 1 bit per allocation unit, as shown in Fig. 6-21(b). A 1 bit indicates that the allocation unit is already occupied and a 0 bit indicates that it is available.

The first method has the advantage of making it easy to find a hole of a particular length. However, it has the disadvantage of being variable sized. As files are

Track	Sector	Number of sectors in hole
0	0	5
0	6	6
1	0	10
1	11	1
2	1	1
2	3	3
2	7	5
3	0	3
3	9	3
4	3	8

(a)

	Sector											
Track	0	1	2	3	4	5	6	7	8	9	10	11
0	0	0	0	0	0	1	0	0	0	0	0	0
1	0	0	0	0	0	0	0	0	0	0	1	0
2	1	0	1	0	0	0	0	1	0	0	0	0
3	0	0	0	1	1	1	1	1	1	0	0	0
4	1	1	1	0	0	0	0	0	0	0	0	1

(b)

Figure 6-21. Two ways of keeping track of available sectors. (a) A free list. (b) A bit map.

created and destroyed, the length of the list will fluctuate, an undesirable characteristic. The bit table has the advantage of being constant in size. In addition, changing the status of an allocation unit from available to occupied is just a matter of changing 1 bit. However, finding a block of a given size is difficult. Both methods require that when any file on the disk is allocated or returned, the allocation list or table be updated.

Before leaving the subject of file system implementation, it is worth commenting about the size of the allocation unit. Several factors play an key role here. First, seek time and rotational delay dominate disk accesses. Having invested 10 msec to get to the start of an allocation unit, it is far better to read 8 KB (about 1 msec) than 1 KB (about 0.125 msec), since reading 8 KB as eight 1-KB units will require eight seeks. Transfer efficiency argues for large units.

Also arguing for large allocation units is the fact that having small allocation units means having many of them. Many allocation units, in turn, means large file indices or large linked list tables in memory. In fact, the reason MS-DOS had to go to multisector allocation units was the fact that disk addresses were stored as 16-bit numbers. When disks grew beyond 64 KB sectors, the only way to represent them was to use bigger allocation units, so the number of allocation units did not exceed 64K. The first release of Windows 95 had the same problem, but a subsequent release used 32-bit numbers. Windows 98 supported both sizes.

However, arguing for small allocation units is the fact that few files occupy exactly an integral number of allocation units. Therefore, some space will be wasted in the last allocation unit of nearly every file. If the file is much larger than the allocation unit, the average space wasted will be half of an allocation unit. The larger the allocation unit, the larger the amount of wasted space. If the average file is much smaller than the allocation unit, most of the disk space will be wasted. For example, on an MS-DOS or Windows 95 release 1 disk partition of

2 GB, the allocation units were 32 KB, so a 100-character file wasted 32,668 bytes of disk space. Storage efficiency argues for small allocation units. All in all, at present, transfer efficiency tends to be the most important factor nowadays, so block sizes tend to be increasing over time.

6.2.3 Directory Management Instructions

In the early days of computing, people kept their programs and data on punched cards in file cabinets in their offices. As the programs and data grew in size and number, this situation became less and less desirable. It eventually led to the idea of using the computer's secondary memory (e.g., disk) as a storage place for programs and data as an alternative to file cabinets. Information that is directly accessible to the computer without the need for human intervention is said to be **on-line**, as contrasted with **off-line** information, which requires human intervention (e.g., inserting a CD-ROM) before the computer can access it.

On-line information is stored in files, making it accessible to programs via the file I/O instructions discussed above. However, additional instructions are needed to keep track of the information stored on-line, collect it into convenient units, and to protect it from unauthorized use.

The usual way for an operating system to organize on-line files is to group them into **directories**. Figure 6-22 shows an example directory organization. System calls are provided for at least the following functions:

1. Create a file and enter it in a directory.

2. Delete a file from a directory.

3. Rename a file.

4. Change the protection status of a file.

Various protection schemes are in use. One possibility is for the owner of each file to specify a secret password for each file. When attempting to access a file, a program must supply the password, which the operating system then checks to see if it is correct before permitting the access. Another protection method is for the owner of each file to provide an explicit list of people whose programs may access that file.

All modern operating systems allow users to maintain more than one file directory. Each directory is typically itself a file and, as such, may be listed in another directory, thus giving rise to a tree of directories. Multiple directories are particularly useful for programmers working on several projects. They can then group all the files related to one project together in one directory. While working on that project, they will not be distracted by unrelated files. Directories are also a convenient way for people to share files with members of their group.

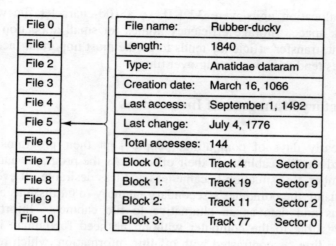

File 0
File 1
File 2
File 3
File 4
File 5
File 6
File 7
File 8
File 9
File 10

File name:	Rubber-ducky	
Length:	1840	
Type:	Anatidae dataram	
Creation date:	March 16, 1066	
Last access:	September 1, 1492	
Last change:	July 4, 1776	
Total accesses:	144	
Block 0:	Track 4	Sector 6
Block 1:	Track 19	Sector 9
Block 2:	Track 11	Sector 2
Block 3:	Track 77	Sector 0

Figure 6-22. A user file directory and the contents of a typical entry in a file directory.

6.3 VIRTUAL INSTRUCTIONS FOR PARALLEL PROCESSING

Some computations can be most conveniently programmed for two or more cooperating processes running in parallel (i.e., simultaneously, on different processors) rather than for a single process. Other computations can be divided into pieces, which can then be carried out in parallel to decrease the elapsed time required for the total computation. In order for several processes to work together in parallel, certain virtual instructions are needed. These instructions will be discussed in the following sections.

The laws of physics provide yet another reason for the current interest in parallel processing. According to Einstein's special theory of relativity, it is impossible to transmit electrical signals faster than the speed of light, which is nearly 1 ft/nsec in vacuum, less in copper wire or optical fiber. This limit has important implications for computer organization. For example, if a CPU needs data from the main memory 1 ft away, it will take at least 1 nsec for the request to arrive at the memory and another nanosecond for the reply to get back to the CPU. Consequently, subnanosecond computers will need to be extremely tiny. An alternative approach to speeding up computers is to build machines with many CPUs. A computer with a thousand 1-nsec CPUs may have the same computing power as one CPU with a cycle time of 0.001 nsec, but the former may be much easier and cheaper to construct.

On a computer with more than one CPU each of several cooperating processes can be assigned to its own CPU, to allow the processes to progress simultaneously. If only one processor is available, the effect of parallel processing can be simulated by having the processor run each process in turn for a short time. In other words, the processor can be shared among several processes.

Figure 6-23 shows the difference between true parallel processing, with more than one physical processor, and simulated parallel processing, with only one physical processor. Even when parallel processing is simulated, it is useful to regard each process as having its own dedicated virtual processor. The same communication problems that arise when there is true parallel processing also arise in the simulated case.

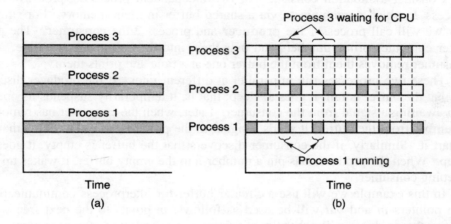

Figure 6-23. (a) True parallel processing with multiple CPUs. (b) Parallel processing simulated by switching one CPU among three processes.

6.3.1 Process Creation

When a program is to be executed, it must run as part of some process. This process, like all other processes, is characterized by a state and an address space through which the program and data can be accessed. The state includes at the very least the program counter, a program status word, a stack pointer, and the general registers.

Most modern operating systems allow processes to be created and terminated dynamically. To take full advantage of this feature to achieve parallel processing, a system call to create a new process is needed. This system call may just make a clone of the caller, or it may allow the creating process to specify the initial state of the new process, including its program, data, and starting address.

In some cases, the creating (parent) process maintains partial or even complete control over the created (child) process. To this end, virtual instructions exist for a parent to stop, restart, examine, and terminate its children. In other cases, a parent has less control over its children: once a process has been created, there is no way for the parent to forcibly stop, restart, examine, or terminate it. The two processes then run independently of one another.

6.3.2 Race Conditions

In many cases, parallel processes need to communicate and synchronize in order to get their work done. In this section, process synchronization will be examined and some of the difficulties explained by means of a detailed example. A solution to these difficulties will be given in the following section.

Consider a situation consisting of two independent processes, process 1 and process 2, which communicate via a shared buffer in main memory. For simplicity we will call process 1 the **producer** and process 2 the **consumer**. The producer computes prime numbers and puts them into the buffer one at a time. The consumer removes them from the buffer one at a time and prints them.

These two processes run in parallel at different rates. If the producer discovers that the buffer is full, it goes to sleep; that is, it temporarily suspends its operation awaiting a signal from the consumer. Later, when the consumer has removed a number from the buffer, it sends a signal to the producer to wake it up—that is, restart it. Similarly, if the consumer discovers that the buffer is empty, it goes to sleep. When the producer has put a number into the empty buffer, it wakes up the sleeping consumer.

In this example we will use a circular buffer for interprocess communication. The pointers *in* and *out* will be used as follows: *in* points to the next free word (where the producer will put the next prime) and *out* points to the next number to be removed by the consumer. When *in* = *out*, the buffer is empty, as shown in Fig. 6-24(a). After the producer has generated some primes, the situation is as shown in Fig. 6-24(b). Figure 6-24(c) illustrates the buffer after the consumer has removed some of these primes for printing. Figure 6-24(d)-(f) depict the effect of continued buffer activity. The top of the buffer is logically contiguous with the bottom; that is, the buffer wraps around. When there has been a sudden burst of input and *in* has wrapped around and is only one word behind *out* (e.g., *in* = 52, and *out* = 53), the buffer is full. The last word is not used; if it were, there would be no way to tell if *in* = *out* meant a full buffer or an empty one.

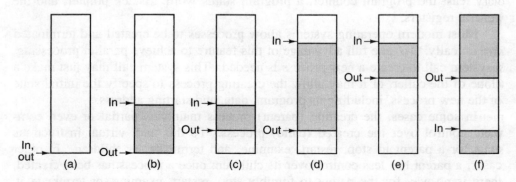

Figure 6-24. Use of a circular buffer.

Figure 6-25 shows a simple way to implement the producer-consumer problem in Java. This solution uses three classes, *m*, *producer*, and *consumer*. The *m* (main) class contains some constant definitions, the buffer pointers *in* and *out*, and the buffer itself, which in this example holds 100 primes, going from *buffer*[0] to *buffer*[99].

This solution uses Java threads to simulate parallel processes. With this solution we have a class *producer* and a class *consumer*, which are instantiated in the variables *p* and *c* respectively. Each of these classes is derived from a base class *Thread*, which has a method *run*. The *run* method contains the code for the thread. When the *start* method of an object derived from *Thread* is invoked, a new thread is started.

Each thread is like a process, except that all threads within a single Java program run in the same address space. This feature is convenient for having them share a common buffer. If the computer has two or more CPUs, each thread can be scheduled on a different CPU, allowing true parallelism. If there is only one CPU, the threads are timeshared on the same CPU. We will continue to refer to the producer and consumer as processes (since we are really interested in parallel processes), even though Java supports only parallel threads and not true parallel processes.

The utility function *next* allows *in* and *out* to be incremented easily, without having to write code to check for the wraparound condition every time. If the parameter to *next* is 98 or lower, the next higher integer is returned. If, however, the parameter is 99, we have hit the end of the buffer, so 0 is returned.

We need a way for either process to put itself to sleep when it cannot continue. The Java designers understood the need for this ability and included the methods *suspend* (sleep) and *resume* (wakeup) in the *Thread* class right from the first version of Java. They are used in Fig. 6-25.

Now we come to the actual code for the producer and consumer. First, the producer generates a new prime in P1. Notice the use of *m.MAX_PRIME* here. The prefix *m.* is needed to indicate that we mean the *MAX_PRIME* defined in class *m*. For the same reason, this prefix is needed for *in*, *out*, *buffer*, and *next*, as well.

Then the producer checks (in P2) to see if *in* is one behind *out*. If it is (e.g., *in* = 62 and *out* = 63), the buffer is full and the producer goes to sleep by calling *suspend* in P2. If the buffer is not full, the new prime is inserted into the buffer (P3) and *in* is incremented (P4). If the new value of *in* is 1 ahead of *out* (P5) (e.g., *in* = 17 and *out* = 16), *in* and *out* must have been equal before *in* was incremented. The producer concludes that the buffer was empty and that the consumer was, and still is, sleeping. Therefore, the producer calls *resume* to wake the consumer up (P5). Finally, the producer begins looking for the next prime.

The consumer's program is structurally similar. First, a test is made (C1) to see if the buffer is empty. If it is, there is no work for the consumer to do, so it goes to sleep. If the buffer is not empty, it removes the next number to be printed

```
public class m {
    final public static int BUF_SIZE = 100;              // buffer runs from 0 to 99
    final public static long MAX_PRIME = 100000000000L;  // stop here
    public static int in = 0, out = 0;                   // pointers to the data
    public static long buffer[ ] = new long[BUF_SIZE];   // primes stored here
    public static producer p;                            // name of the producer
    public static consumer c;                            // name of the consumer

    public static void main(String args[ ]) {            // main class
        p = new producer( );                             // create the producer
        c = new consumer( );                             // create the consumer
        p.start( );                                      // start the producer
        c.start( );                                      // start the consumer
    }

    // This is a utility function for circularly incrementing in and out
    public static int next(int k) {if (k < BUF_SIZE − 1) return(k+1); else return(0);}
}

class producer extends Thread {                          // producer class
    public void run( ) {                                 // producer code
        long prime = 2;                                  // scratch variable

        while (prime < m.MAX_PRIME) {
            prime = next_prime(prime);                   // statement P1
            if (m.next(m.in) == m.out) suspend( );       // statement P2
            m.buffer[m.in] = prime;                      // statement P3
            m.in = m.next(m.in);                         // statement P4
            if (m.next(m.out) == m.in) m.c.resume( );    // statement P5
        }
    }

    private long next_prime(long prime){ ... }           // function that computes next prime
}


class consumer extends Thread {                          // consumer class
    public void run( ) {                                 // consumer code
        long emirp = 2;                                  // scratch variable

        while (emirp < m.MAX_PRIME) {
            if (m.in == m.out) suspend( );               // statement C1
            emirp = m.buffer[m.out];                     // statement C2
            m.out = m.next(m.out);                       // statement C3
            if (m.out == m.next(m.next(m.in))) m.p.resume( ); // statement C4
            System.out.println(emirp);                   // statement C5
        }
    }
}
```

Figure 6-25. Parallel processing with a fatal race condition.

(C2) and increments *out* (*C*3). If *out* is two positions ahead of *in* at this point (C4), it must have been one position ahead of *in* before it was just incremented. Because *in* = *out* − 1 is the "buffer full" condition, the producer must have been sleeping, and thus the consumer wakes it up with *resume*. Finally, the number is printed (C5) and the cycle repeats.

Unfortunately, this design contains a fatal flaw, as illustrated in Fig. 6-26. Remember that the two processes run asynchronously and at different, possibly varying, speeds. Consider the case where only one number is left in the buffer, in entry 21, and *in* = 22 and *out* = 21, as shown in Fig. 6-26(a). The producer is at statement P1 looking for a prime and the consumer is busy at C5 printing out the number in position 20. The consumer finishes printing the number, makes the test at C1, and takes the last number out of the buffer at C2. It then increments *out*. At this instant, both *in* and *out* have the value 22. The consumer prints the number and then goes to C1, where it fetches *in* and *out* from memory in order to compare them, as shown in Fig. 6-26(b).

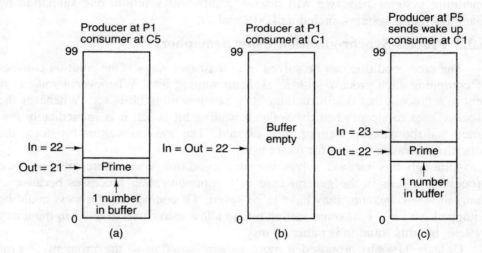

Figure 6-26. Failure of the producer-consumer communication mechanism.

At this very moment, after the consumer has fetched *in* and *out* but before it has compared them, the producer finds the next prime. It puts the prime into the buffer at P3 and increments *in* at P4. Now *in* = 23 and *out* = 22. At P5 the producer discovers that *in* = *next*(*out*). In other words, *in* is one higher than *out*, signifying that there is now one item in the buffer. The producer therefore (incorrectly) concludes that the consumer must be sleeping, so it sends a wakeup signal (i.e., calls *resume*), as shown in Fig. 6-26(c). Of course, the consumer is still awake, so the wakeup signal is lost. The producer begins looking for the next prime.

At this point in time the consumer continues. It has already fetched *in* and *out* from memory before the producer put the last number in the buffer. Because they both have the value 22, the consumer goes to sleep. Now the producer finds another prime. It checks the pointers and finds $in = 24$ and $out = 22$, therefore it assumes that there are two numbers in the buffer (true) and that the consumer is awake (false). The producer continues looping. Eventually, it fills the buffer and goes to sleep. Now both processes are sleeping and will remain so forever.

The difficulty here is that between the time when the consumer fetched in and out and the time it went to sleep, the producer snuck in, discovered that $in = out + 1$, assumed that the consumer was sleeping (which it was not yet), and sent a wakeup signal that was lost because the consumer was still awake. This difficulty is known as a **race condition**, because the method's success depends on who wins the race to test in and out after out is incremented.

The problem of race conditions is well known. In fact it is so serious that several years after Java was introduced, Sun changed the *Thread* class and depre-cated the *suspend* and *resume* calls because they led to race conditions so often. The solution offered was a language-based solution, but since we are studying operating systems here, we will discuss a different solution, one supported by many operating systems, including UNIX and XP.

6.3.3 Process Synchronization Using Semaphores

The race condition can be solved in at least two ways. One solution consists of equipping each process with a "wakeup waiting bit." Whenever a wakeup is sent to a process that is still running, its wakeup waiting bit is set. Whenever the process goes to sleep when the wakeup waiting bit is set, it is immediately res-tarted and the wakeup waiting bit is cleared. The wakeup waiting bit stores the superfluous wakeup signal for future use.

Although this method solves the race condition when there are only two processes, it fails in the general case of n communicating processes because as many as $n - 1$ wakeups may have to be saved. Of course, each process could be equipped with $n - 1$ wakeup waiting bits to allow it to count to $n - 1$ in the unary system, but this solution is rather clumsy.

Dijkstra (1968b) proposed a more general solution to the problem of syn-chronizing parallel processes. Somewhere in the memory are some nonnegative integer variables called **semaphores**. Two system calls that operate on sema-phores, up and down, are provided by the operating system. Up adds 1 to a sema-phore and down subtracts 1 from a semaphore.

If a down operation is performed on a semaphore that is currently greater than 0, the semaphore is decremented by 1 and the process doing the down continues. If, however, the semaphore is 0, the down cannot complete; the process doing the down is put to sleep and remains asleep until the other process performs an up on that semaphore. Usually sleeping processes are strung together in a queue to keep track of them.

The up instruction checks to see if the semaphore is 0. If it is and the other process is sleeping on it, the semaphore is increased by 1. The sleeping process can then complete the down operation that suspended it, resetting the semaphore to 0 and allowing both processes to continue. An up instruction on a nonzero semaphore simply increases it by 1. In essence, a semaphore provides a counter to store wakeups for future use, so that they will not be lost. An essential property of semaphore instructions is that once a process has initiated an instruction on a semaphore, no other process may access the semaphore until the first one has either completed its instruction, or been suspended trying to perform a down on a 0. Figure 6-27 summarizes the essential properties of the up and down system calls.

Instruction	Semaphore = 0	Semaphore > 0
Up	Semaphore = semaphore + 1; if the other process was halted attempting to complete a down instruction on this semaphore, it may now complete the down and continue running	Semaphore = semaphore + 1
Down	Process halts until the other process ups this semaphore	Semaphore = semaphore − 1

Figure 6-27. The effect of a semaphore operation.

As mentioned above, Java has a language-based solution for dealing with race conditions, and we are discussing operating systems now. Thus we need a way to express semaphore usage in Java, even though it is not in the language or the standard classes. We will do this by assuming that two native methods have been written, *up* and *down*, which make the up and down system calls, respectively. By calling these with ordinary integers as parameters, we have a way to express the use of semaphores in Java programs.

Figure 6-28 shows how the race condition can be eliminated through the use of semaphores. Two semaphores are added to the *m* class, *available*, which is initially 100 (the buffer size), and *filled*, which is initially 0. The producer starts executing at P1 in Fig. 6-28 and the consumer starts executing at C1 as before. The *down* call on *filled* halts the consumer processor immediately. When the producer has found the first prime, it calls *down* with *available* as parameter, setting *available* to 99. At P5 it calls *up* with *filled* as parameter, making *filled* 1. This action releases the consumer, which is now able to complete its suspended *down* call. At this point, *filled* is 0 and both processes are running.

Let us now reexamine the race condition. At a certain point in time, *in* = 22, *out* = 21, the producer is at P1, and the consumer is at C5. The consumer finishes what it was doing and gets to C1 where it calls *down* on *filled*, which had the value 1 before the call and 0 after it. The consumer then takes the last number out of the buffer and ups *available*, making it 100. The consumer prints the number and goes to C1. Just before the consumer can call *down*, the producer finds the next prime and in quick succession executes statements P2, P3, and P4.

At this point, *filled* is 0. The producer is about to up it and the consumer is about to call *down*. If the consumer executes its instruction first, it will be suspended until the producer releases it (by calling *up*). On the other hand, if the producer goes first, the semaphore will be set to 1 and the consumer will not be suspended at all. In both cases, no wakeup is lost. This, of course, was our goal in introducing semaphores in the first place.

The essential property of the semaphore operations is that they are indivisible. Once a semaphore operation has been initiated, no other process can use the semaphore until the first process has either completed the operation or been suspended trying. Furthermore, with semaphores, no wakeups are lost. In contrast, the if statements of Figure 6-25 are not indivisible. Between the evaluation of the condition and the execution of the selected statement, another process can send a wakeup signal.

In effect the problem of process synchronization has been eliminated by declaring the up and down system calls made by *up* and *down* to be indivisible. In order for these operations to be indivisible, the operating system must prohibit two or more processes from using the same semaphore at the same time. At the very least, once an up or down system call has been made, no other user code will be run until the call has been completed. On single-processor systems, semaphores are sometimes implemented by disabling interrupts during semaphore operations. On multiple-processor systems, this trick does not work.

Synchronization using semaphores is a technique that works for arbitrarily many processes. Several processes may be sleeping, attempting to complete a down system call on the same semaphore. When some other process finally performs an up on that semaphore, one of the waiting processes is allowed to complete its down and continue running. The semaphore value remains 0 and the other processes continue waiting.

An analogy may make the nature of semaphores clearer. Imagine a picnic with 20 volleyball teams divided into 10 games (processes) each playing on its own court, and a large basket (the semaphore) for the volleyballs. Unfortunately, only seven volleyballs are available. At any instant, there are between zero and seven volleyballs in the basket (the semaphore has a value between 0 and 7). Putting a ball in the basket is an up because it increases the value of the semaphore; taking a ball out of the basket is a down because it decreases the value.

At the start of the picnic, each court sends a player to the basket to get a volleyball. Seven of them successfully manage to get a volleyball (complete the down); three are forced to wait for a volleyball (i.e., fail to complete the down). Their games are suspended temporarily. Eventually, one of the other games finishes and puts a ball into the basket (executes an up). This operation allows one of the three players waiting around the basket to get a ball (complete an unfinished down), allowing one game to continue. The other two games remain suspended until two more balls are put into the basket. When two more balls come back (two more ups are executed), the last two games can proceed.

```
public class m {
    final public static int BUF_SIZE = 100;              // buffer runs from 0 to 99
    final public static long MAX_PRIME = 100000000000L;  // stop here
    public static int in = 0, out = 0;                   // pointers to the data
    public static long buffer[ ] = new long[BUF_SIZE];   // primes stored here
    public static producer p;                            // name of the producer
    public static consumer c;                            // name of the consumer
    public static int filled = 0, available = 100;       // semaphores

    public static void main(String args[ ]) {            // main class
        p = new producer( );                             // create the producer
        c = new consumer( );                             // create the consumer
        p.start( );                                      // start the producer
        c.start( );                                      // start the consumer
    }

    // This is a utility function for circularly incrementing in and out
    public static int next(int k) {if (k < BUF_SIZE – 1) return(k+1); else return(0);}
}

class producer extends Thread {                          // producer class
    native void up(int s); native void down(int s);      // methods on semaphores
    public void run( ) {                                 // producer code
        long prime = 2;                                  // scratch variable

        while (prime < m.MAX_PRIME) {
            prime = next_prime(prime);                   // statement P1
            down(m.available);                           // statement P2
            m.buffer[m.in] = prime;                      // statement P3
            m.in = m.next(m.in);                         // statement P4
            up(m.filled);                                // statement P5
        }
    }

    private long next_prime(long prime){ ... }           // function that computes next prime
}

class consumer extends Thread {                          // consumer class
    native void up(int s); native void down(int s);      // methods on semaphores
    public void run( ) {                                 // consumer code
        long emirp = 2;                                  // scratch variable

        while (emirp < m.MAX_PRIME) {
            down(m.filled);                              // statement C1
            emirp = m.buffer[m.out];                     // statement C2
            m.out = m.next(m.out);                       // statement C3
            up(m.available);                             // statement C4
            System.out.println(emirp);                   // statement C5
        }
    }
}
```

Figure 6-28. Parallel processing using semaphores.

6.4 EXAMPLE OPERATING SYSTEMS

In this section we will continue discussing our example systems, the Pentium 4 and the UltraSPARC III. For each one we will look at an operating system used on that processor. For the Pentium 4 we will use Windows XP (called XP for short below); for the UltraSPARC III we will use UNIX. Since UNIX is simpler and in many ways more elegant, we will begin with it. Also, UNIX was designed and implemented first and had a major influence on XP, so this order makes more sense than the reverse.

6.4.1 Introduction

In this section we will give a brief introduction to our two example operating systems, UNIX and XP, focusing on the history, structure, and system calls.

UNIX

UNIX was developed at Bell Labs in the early 1970s. The first version was written by Ken Thompson in assembler for the PDP-7 minicomputer. This was soon followed by a version for the PDP-11, written in a new language called C that was devised and implemented by Dennis Ritchie. In 1974, Ritchie and his colleague Ken Thompson published a landmark paper about UNIX (Ritchie and Thompson, 1974). For the work described in this paper they were later given the prestigious ACM Turing Award (Ritchie, 1984; Thompson, 1984). The publication of this paper stimulated many universities to ask Bell Labs for a copy of UNIX. Since Bell Labs' parent company, AT&T, was a regulated monopoly at the time and was not permitted to be in the computer business, it had no objection to licensing UNIX to universities for a modest fee.

In one of those coincidences that often shape history, the PDP-11 was the computer of choice at nearly all university computer science departments, and the operating systems that came with the PDP-11 were widely regarded as being dreadful by professors and students alike. UNIX quickly filled the void, not in the least because it was supplied with the complete source code, so people could, and did, tinker with it endlessly.

One of the many universities that acquired UNIX early on was the University of California at Berkeley. Because the complete source code was available, Berkeley was able to modify the system substantially. Foremost among the changes was a port to the VAX minicomputer and the addition of paged virtual memory, the extension of file names from 14 characters to 255 characters, and the inclusion of the TCP/IP networking protocol, which is now used on the Internet (largely due to the fact that it was in Berkeley UNIX).

While Berkeley was making all these changes, AT&T itself continued to develop UNIX, leading to System III in 1982 and then System V in 1984. By the late 1980s, two different, and quite incompatible, versions of UNIX were in widespread use: Berkeley UNIX and System V. This split in the UNIX world, together with the fact that there were no standards for binary program formats, greatly inhibited the commercial success of UNIX because it was impossible for software vendors to write and package UNIX programs with the expectation that they would run on any UNIX system (as was routinely done with MS-DOS). After much bickering, a standard called **POSIX** (**Portable Operating System-IX**) was created by the IEEE Standards Board. is also known by its IEEE Standards number, P1003. It later became an International Standard.

The standard is divided into many parts, each covering a different area of UNIX. The first part, P1003.1, defines the system calls; the second part, P1003.2, defines the basic utility programs, and so on. The P1003.1 standard defines about 60 system calls that all conformant systems must support. These are the basic calls for reading and writing files, creating new processes, and so on. Nearly all UNIX systems now support the P1003.1 system calls. However many UNIX systems also support extra system calls, especially those defined by System V and/or those in Berkeley UNIX. Typically these add up to 200 system calls to the set.

In 1987, the author released the source code for a small version of UNIX, called MINIX, for use at universities (Tanenbaum, 1987). One of the students who studied MINIX at his university in Helsinki and ran it on his home PC was Linus Torvalds. After becoming thoroughly familiar with MINIX, Torvalds decided to write his own clone of MINIX, which was called Linux and has become quite popular. Both MINIX and Linux are conformant, and nearly everything said about UNIX in this chapter also applies to them unless stated otherwise. Although all these UNIX variants different greatly inside, for the most part in this chapter we will be discussing their system call interface, which is a superset of in all cases.

The operating system for the UltraSPARC III is based on System V and is called **Solaris**. It also supports many of the Berkeley system calls.

A rough breakdown of the Solaris system calls by category is given in Fig. 6-29. The file and directory management system calls are largest and the most important categories. Most of these come from P1003.1. A relatively large fraction of the others are derived from System V.

One area that is largely due to Berkeley UNIX rather than System V is networking. Berkeley invented the concept of a **socket**, which is the endpoint of a network connection. The four-pin wall plugs to which telephones can be connected served as the model for this concept. It is possible for a UNIX process to create a socket, attach to it, and establish a connection to a socket on a distant machine. Over this connection it can then exchange data in both directions, typically using the TCP/IP protocol. Since networking technology has been in UNIX for decades and is very stable and mature, a substantial fraction of the servers on the Internet run UNIX.

Category	Some examples
File management	Open, read, write, close, and lock files
Directory management	Create and delete directories; move files around
Process management	Spawn, terminate, trace, and signal processes
Memory management	Share memory among processes; protect pages
Getting/setting parameters	Get user, group, process ID; set priority
Dates and times	Set file access times; use interval timer; profile execution
Networking	Establish/accept connection; send/receive message
Miscellaneous	Enable accounting; manipulate disk quotas; reboot the system

Figure 6-29. A rough breakdown of the UNIX system calls.

Since there are many implementations of UNIX, it is difficult to say much about the structure of the operating system since each one is somewhat different from all the others. However, in general, Fig. 6-30 applies to most of them. At the bottom, there is a layer of device drivers that shield the file system from the bare hardware. Originally, each device driver was written as an independent entity, separate from all the others. This arrangement led to a lot of duplicated effort, since many drivers must deal with flow control, error handling, priorities, separating data from control, and so on. This observation led Dennis Ritchie to develop a framework called **streams** for writing drivers in a modular way. With a stream, it is possible to establish a two-way connection from a user process to a hardware device and to insert one or more modules along the path. The user process pushes data into the stream, which then is processed or transformed by each module until it gets to the hardware. The inverse processing occurs for incoming data.

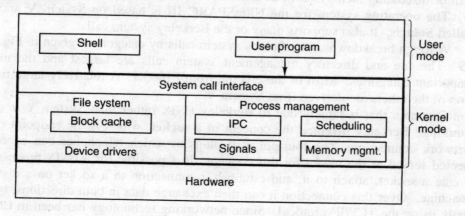

Figure 6-30. The structure of a typical UNIX system.

On top of the device drivers comes the file system. It manages file names, directories, disk block allocation, protection, and much more. Part of the file system is a **block cache**, for holding the blocks most recently read in from disk, in case they are needed again soon. A variety of file systems have been used over the years, including the Berkeley fast file system (McKusick et al., 1984), and log-structured file systems (Rosenblum and Ousterhout, 1991; and Seltzer et al., 1993).

The other part of the UNIX kernel is the process management portion. Among its various other functions, it handles IPC (InterProcess Communication), which allows processes to communicate with one another and synchronize to avoid race conditions. A variety of mechanisms are provided. The process management code also handles process scheduling, which is based on priorities. Signals, which are a form of (asynchronous) software interrupt, are also managed here. Finally, memory management is done here as well. Most UNIX systems support demand-paged virtual memory, sometimes with a few extra features, such as the ability of multiple processes to share common regions of address space.

From its inception, UNIX has tried to be a small system, in order to enhance reliability and performance. The first versions of UNIX were entirely text-based, using terminals that could display 24 or 25 lines of 80 ASCII characters. The user interface was handled by a user-level program called the **shell**, which offered a command line interface. Since the shell was not part of the kernel, adding new shells to UNIX was easy, and over time a number of increasingly sophisticated ones were invented.

Later on, when graphics terminals came into existence, a windowing system for UNIX, called **X Windows**, was developed at M.I.T. Still later, a full-fledged **GUI** (**Graphical User Interface**), called **Motif**, was put on top of X Windows. In keeping with the UNIX philosophy of having a small kernel, nearly all the code of X Windows and Motif runs in user mode, outside the kernel.

Windows XP

When the original IBM PC was launched in 1981, it came equipped with a 16-bit real-mode, single-user, command-line oriented operating system called MS-DOS 1.0 This operating system consisted of 8 KB of memory resident code. Two years later, a much more powerful 24-KB system, MS-DOS 2.0, appeared. It contained a command line processor (shell), with a number of features borrowed from UNIX. When IBM released the 286-based PC/AT in 1984, it came equipped with MS-DOS 3.0, by now 36 KB. Over the years, MS-DOS continued to acquire new features, but it was still a command-line oriented system.

Inspired by the success of the Apple Macintosh, Microsoft decided to give MS-DOS a graphical user interface that it called **Windows**. The first three versions of Windows, culminating in Windows 3.x, were not true operating systems, but graphical user interfaces on top of MS-DOS, which was still in control of the machine. All programs ran in the same address space and a bug in any one of them could bring the whole system to a grinding halt.

The release of Windows 95 in 1995 still did not eliminate MS-DOS, although it introduced a new version, 7.0. Together, Windows 95 and MS-DOS 7.0 contained most of the features of a full-blown operating system, including virtual memory, process management, and multiprogramming. However, Windows 95 was not a full 32-bit program. It contained large chunks of old 16-bit code (as well as some 32-bit code) and still used the MS-DOS file system, with nearly all its limitations. The only major changes to the file system were the addition of long file names in place of the 8 + 3 character file names allowed in MS-DOS and the ability to have more than 65,536 blocks on a disk.

Even with the release of Windows 98 in 1998, MS-DOS was still there (now called version 7.1) and running 16-bit code. Although a bit more functionality migrated from the MS-DOS part to the Windows part, and a disk layout suitable for larger disks was now standard, under the hood, Windows 98 was not very different from Windows 95. The main difference was the user interface, which integrated the desktop, the Internet, and television more closely. It was precisely this integration that attracted the attention of the U.S. Dept. of Justice, which then sued Microsoft claiming that it was an illegal monopoly. Windows 98 was followed by the short-lived Windows Millennium Edition (ME), which was a slightly improved Windows 98.

While all these developments were going on, Microsoft was also busy with a completely new 32-bit operating system being written from the ground up. This new system was called **Windows New Technology**, or **Windows NT**. It was initially hyped as the replacement for all other operating systems for Intel-based PCs, but it was somewhat slow to catch on and was later redirected to the upper end of the market, where it found a niche. The second version of NT was called Windows 2000 and became the mainstream version, also for the desktop market. The successor to Windows 2000 was XP, but the changes here were relatively minor. XP is essentially a slightly improved Windows 2000.

XP is sold in two versions: server and client. These two versions are nearly identical and are generated from the same source code. The server version is intended for machines that run as LAN-based file and print servers and has more elaborate management features than the client version, which is intended for desktop computing for a single user. The server version has a variant (enterprise) intended for large sites. The various versions are tuned differently, each one optimized for its expected environment. Other than these minor differences, all the versions are essentially the same. In fact, nearly all the executable files are identical for all versions. XP itself discovers which version it is by looking at a variable in an internal data structure (the registry). Users are forbidden by the license from changing this variable and thus converting the (inexpensive) client version into the (much more expensive) server or enterprise versions. We will not make any further distinction between these versions.

MS-DOS and all previous versions of Windows were single-user systems. XP, however, supports multiprogramming, so several users can work on the same machine at the same time. For example, a network server may have multiple users logged in simultaneously over a network, each accessing its own files.

XP is a true 32-bit multiprogramming operating system. It supports multiple user processes, each of which has a full 32-bit demand-paged virtual address space. In addition, the system itself is written as 32-bit code everywhere.

One of NT's original improvements over Windows 95 was its modular structure. It consisted of a moderately small kernel that ran in kernel mode, plus a number of server processes that ran in user mode. User processes interacted with the server processes using the client-server model: a client sent a request message to a server, and the server did the work and returned the result to the client via a second message. This modular structure made it easier to port it to several computers besides the Intel line, including the DEC Alpha, IBM PowerPC, and SGI MIPS. However, for performance reasons, starting with NT 4.0, most of the system was put back into the kernel.

Although we could go on for a long time both about how XP is structured internally and what its system call interface is like. Since our primary interest here is the virtual machine presented by various operating systems (i.e., the system calls), we will give a brief summary of the system structure and then move on to the system call interface.

The structure of XP is illustrated in Fig. 6-31. It consists of a number of modules that are structured in layers and work together to implement the operating system. Each module has some particular function and a well-defined interface to the other modules. Nearly all the modules are written in C, although part of the graphics device interface is written in C++ and a tiny bit of the lowest layers are written in assembly language.

At the bottom is a thin layer called the **hardware abstraction layer**. Its job is to present the rest of the operating system with abstract hardware devices, devoid of the warts and idiosyncracies with which real hardware is so richly endowed. Among the devices modeled are off-chip caches, timers, I/O buses, interrupt controllers, and DMA controllers. By exposing these to the rest of the operating system in idealized form, it becomes easier to port XP to other hardware platforms, since most of the modifications required are concentrated in one place.

Above the hardware abstraction layer is a layer containing the kernel and the device drivers. The kernel and all the device drivers have direct access to the hardware when needed, as they contain hardware-dependent code.

The **kernel** supports the primitive kernel objects, interrupt, trap, and exception handling, process scheduling and synchronization, multiprocessor synchronization, and time management. The purpose of this layer is to make the rest of the operating system completely independent of the hardware, and thus highly portable. The kernel is permanently resident in main memory and is not preemptible, although it can temporarily give up control to service I/O interrupts.

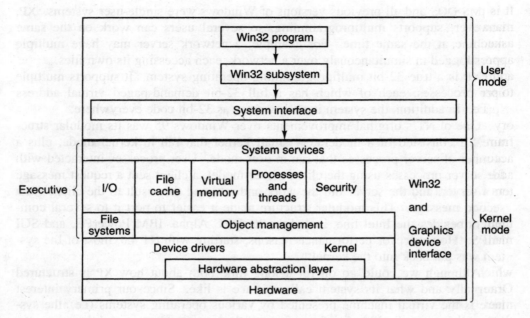

Figure 6-31. The structure of Windows XP.

Each **device driver** can control one or more I/O devices, but a device driver can also do things not related to a specific device, such as encrypting a data stream or even just providing access to kernel data structures. Since users can install new device drivers, they have the power to affect the kernel and corrupt the system. For this reason, drivers must be written with great care.

Above the kernel and device drivers is the upper portion of the operating system, called the **executive**. The executive is architecture independent and can be ported to new machines with only a relatively small amount of effort. It consists of three layers.

The lowest layer contains the file systems and the object manager. The **file systems** support the use of files and directories The **object manager** handles objects known to the kernel. These include processes, threads (lightweight processes within an address space), files, directories, semaphores, I/O devices, timers, and many others. The object manager also manages a namespace in which newly created objects can be placed so they can be referred to later.

The next layer consists of six major parts, as shown in Fig. 6-31. The **I/O manager** provides a framework for managing I/O devices and provides generic I/O services. It uses the services of the file system, which in turn uses the device drivers, as well as the services of the object manager.

The **file cache manager** is involved with managing file blocks and helping the virtual memory manager to determine which ones to keep in memory for future use. It is also involved with managing files that are mapped onto memory.

It is possible to configure XP with multiple file systems, in which case the cache manager works for all of them. When a block is needed, the cache manager is asked to supply it. If it does not have the block, the cache manager calls upon the appropriate file system to get it. Since files can be mapped into processes' address spaces, the cache manager must interact with the virtual memory manager to provide the necessary consistency.

The **virtual memory manager** implements XP's demand-paged virtual memory architecture. It manages the mapping of virtual pages onto physical page frames. It thereby enforces the protection rules that restrict each process to only access those pages belonging to its address space and not to other processes' address spaces (except under special circumstances). It also handles certain system calls that relate to virtual memory.

The **process and thread manager** handles processes and threads, including their creation and destruction. It is concerned about the mechanisms used to manage them, rather than policies about how they are used.

The **security reference monitor** enforces XP's elaborate security mechanism, which meets the U.S. Dept. of Defense's Orange Book C2 requirements. The Orange Book specifies a large number of rules that a conforming system must meet, starting with authenticated login through how access control is handled to the fact that virtual pages must be zeroed out before being reused.

The **graphics device interface** handles image management for the monitor and printers. It provides system calls to allow user programs to write on the monitor or printers in a device-independent way. It also contains the hardware device drivers for graphical output. In versions of XP prior to XP 4.0, it was in user space but the performance was disappointing, so Microsoft moved it into the kernel to speed it up. The Win32 module also handles most of the system calls. It, too, was originally in user space but was also moved to the kernel to improve performance.

On the top of the executive is a thin layer called **system services**. Its function is to provide an interface to the executive. It accepts the true XP system calls and calls other parts of the executive to have them executed.

Outside the kernel are the user programs and the environment subsystem. The **environmental subsystem** is provided because user programs are not encouraged to make system calls directly (although they are technically capable of it). Instead, the environmental subsystem exports a set of function calls that user programs can use. Originally there were three environmental subsystems, Win32 (for NT, Windows 2000, XP or even Windows 95/98/ME programs), POSIX (for UNIX programs that have been ported), and OS/2 (for OS/2 programs that have been ported). Of these, only Win32 is supported. However, a new Services for UNIX module now exists and provides modest UNIX support.

Windows applications use the Win32 functions and communicate with the Win32 subsystem to make system calls. The **Win32 subsystem** accepts the Win32 function calls (see below) and uses the **system interface** library module (actually, a DLL file—see Chap. 7) to make the necessary true XP system calls to carry them out. This is how system calls are made in XP.

Having looked briefly at the structure of XP, let us now turn to our main subject, the services offered by XP. This interface is the programmer's main connection to the system. Unfortunately, Microsoft has never made the complete list of XP system calls public, and it also changes them from release to release. Under such conditions, writing programs that make system calls directly is nearly impossible.

What Microsoft did do was define a set of calls called the **Win32 API** (**Application Programming Interface**) that are publicly known. These are library procedures that either make system calls to get the work done, or, in some case, do the work right in the user-space library procedure or in the Win32 subsystem. The Win32 API calls do not change with new releases, to promote stability. However, there are also XP API calls that may change between releases of XP. Although the Win32 API calls are not all XP system calls, it is better to focus on these here rather than the true XP system calls because the Win32 API calls are well documented and more stable over time. When Windows was ported to 64-bit machines, Microsoft changed the name of Win32 to cover both the 32-bit and 64-bit versions, but for our purposes, looking at the 32-bit version is sufficient.

The Win32 API philosophy is completely different from the UNIX philosophy. In the latter, the system calls are all publicly known and form a minimal interface: removing even one of them would reduce the functionality of the operating system. The Win32 philosophy is to provide a very comprehensive interface, often with three or four ways of doing the same thing, and including many functions that clearly should not be (and are not) system calls, such as an API call to copy an entire file.

Many Win32 API calls create kernel objects of one kind or another, including files, processes, threads, pipes, etc. Every call creating a kernel object returns a result called a **handle** to the caller. This handle can be subsequently used to perform operations on the object. Handles are specific to the process that created the object referred to by the handle. They cannot be passed directly to another process and used there (just as UNIX file descriptors cannot be passed to other processes and used there). However, under certain circumstances, it is possible to duplicate a handle and pass it to other processes in a protected way, allowing them controlled access to objects belonging to other processes. Every object can have a security descriptor associated with it, telling in detail who may and may not perform what kinds of operations on the object.

XP is sometimes said to be object-oriented because the only way to manipulate kernel objects is by invoking methods (API functions) on their handles. On the other hand, it lacks some of the most basic properties of object-oriented systems such as inheritance and polymorphism.

The Win32 API was also available on Windows 95/98/ME (as well as on the consumer electronics operating system, Windows CE), with a small number of exceptions. For example, Windows 95/98 did not have any security, so those API calls that relate to security just return error codes on Windows 95/98. Also, XP file names use the Unicode character set, which was not available on Windows 95/98. There are also differences in parameters to some API function calls. On XP, for example, all the screen coordinates given in the graphics functions are true 32-bit numbers; on Windows 95/98, only the low-order 16 bits were used (for backward compatibility with Windows 3.1). The existence of the Win32 API on multiple operating systems makes it easier to port programs between them but also points out more clearly that it is somewhat decoupled from the actual system calls.

6.4.2 Examples of Virtual Memory

In this section we will look at virtual memory in both UNIX and XP. For the most part, they are fairly similar from the programmer's point of view.

UNIX Virtual Memory

The UNIX memory model is simple. Each process has three segments: code, data, and stack, as illustrated in Fig. 6-32. In a machine with a single, linear address space, the code is generally placed near the bottom of memory, followed by the data. The stack is placed at the top of memory. The code size is fixed, but the data and stack may each grow, in opposite directions. This model is easy to implement on almost any machine and is the model used by Solaris.

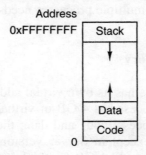

Figure 6-32. The address space of a single UNIX process.

Furthermore, if the machine has paging, the entire address space can be paged, without user programs even being aware of it. The only thing they notice is that it is permitted to have programs larger than the machine's physical memory. UNIX systems that do not have paging generally swap entire processes between memory and disk to allow an arbitrarily large number of processes to be timeshared.

For Berkeley UNIX, the above description (demand-paged virtual memory) is basically the entire story. However, System V (and also Solaris) include several features that allow users to manage their virtual memory in more sophisticated ways. Most important of these is the ability of a process to map a (portion of a) file onto part of its address space. For example, if a 12-KB file is mapped at virtual address 144K, a read to the word at address 144 KB reads the first word of the file. In this way file I/O can be done without making system calls. Since some files may exceed the size of the virtual address space, it is also possible to map in only a portion of a file instead of the whole file. The mapping is done first opening the file and getting back a file descriptor, *fd*, which is used to identify the file to be mapped. Then the process makes a call

paddr = mmap(virtual_address, length, protection, flags, fd, file_offset)

which maps *length* bytes starting at *file_offset* in the file onto the virtual address space starting at *virtual_address*. Alternatively, the *flags* parameter can be set to ask the system to choose a virtual address, which it then returns as *paddr*. The mapped region must be an integral number of pages and aligned at a page boundary. The *protection* parameter can specify any combination of read, write, or execute permission. The mapping can be removed later with unmap.

Multiple processes can map onto the same file at the same time. Two options are provided for sharing. In the first one, all the pages are shared, so writes done by one process are visible to all the others. This option provides a high-bandwidth communication path between processes. The other option shares the pages as long as no process modifies them. However, as soon as any process attempts to write on a page, it gets a protection fault, which causes the operating system to give it a private copy of the page to write on. This scheme, known as **copy on write**, is used when each of multiple processes needs the illusion it is the only one mapped onto a file.

Windows XP Virtual Memory

In XP, every user process has its own virtual address space. Virtual addresses are 32 bits long, so each process has 4 GB of virtual address space. The lower 2 GB are available for the process' code and data; the upper 2 GB allow (limited) access to kernel memory, except in Server versions of Windows, in which the split can be 3 GB for the user and 1 GB for the kernel. The virtual address space is demand paged, with a fixed page size (4 KB on the Pentium 4).

Each virtual page can be in one of three states: free, reserved, or committed. A **free page** is not currently in use and a reference to it causes a page fault. When a process is started, all of its pages are in free state until the program and initial data are mapped into its address space. Once code or data is mapped onto a page, the page is said to be **committed**. A reference to a committed page is mapped using the virtual memory hardware and succeeds if the page is in main memory. If the page is not in main memory, a page fault occurs and the operating system finds and brings in the page from disk. A virtual page can also be in **reserved** state, meaning it is not available for being mapped until the reservation is explicitly removed. In addition to the free, reserved, and committed attributes, pages also have other attributes, such as being readable, writable, and executable. The top 64 KB and bottom 64 KB of memory are always free, to catch pointer errors (uninitialized pointers are often 0 or −1).

Each committed page has a shadow page on the disk where it is kept when it is not in main memory. Free and reserved pages do not have shadow pages, so references to them cause page faults (the system cannot bring in a page from disk if there is no page on disk). The shadow pages on the disk are arranged into one or more paging files. The operating system keeps track of which virtual page maps onto which part of which paging file. For (execute only) program text, the executable binary file contains the shadow pages; for data pages, special paging files are used.

XP, like System V, allows files to be mapped directly onto regions of the virtual address spaces (i.e., runs of pages). Once a file has been mapped onto the address space, it can be read or written using ordinary memory references.

Memory-mapped files are implemented in the same way as other committed pages, only the shadow pages can be in the disk file instead of in the paging file. As a result, when a file is mapped in, the version in memory may not be identical to the disk version (due to recent writes to the virtual address space). However, when the fileunmapped or is explicitly flushed, the disk version is updated.

XP explicitly allows two or more processes to map in the same file at the same time, possibly at different virtual addresses. By reading and writing memory words, the processes can now communicate with each other and pass data back and forth at very high bandwidth, since no copying is required. Different processes may have different access permissions. Since all the processes using a mapped file share the same pages, changes made by one of them are immediately visible to all the others, even if the disk file has not yet been updated.

The Win32 API contains a number of functions that allow a process to manage its virtual memory explicitly. The most important of these functions are listed in Fig. 6-33. All of them operate on a region consisting either of a single page or a sequence of two or more pages that are consecutive in the virtual address space.

The first four API functions are self-explanatory. The next two give a process the ability to hardwire some numbe of pages in memory so they will not be paged out and to undo this property. A real-time program might need this ability, for example. Only programs run on behalf of the system administrator may pin pages in memory. And a limit is enforced by the operating system to prevent even these processes from getting too greedy. Although not shown in Fig. 6-33, XP also has API functions to allow a process to access the virtual memory of a different process over which it has been given control (i.e., for which it has a handle).

The last four API functions listed are for managing memory-mapped files. To map a file, a file mapping object must first be created, with **CreateFileMapping**.

API function	Meaning
VirtualAlloc	Reserve or commit a region
VirtualFree	Release or decommit a region
VirtualProtect	Change the read/write/execute protection on a region
VirtualQuery	Inquire about the status of a region
VirtualLock	Make a region memory resident (i.e., disable paging for it)
VirtualUnlock	Make a region pageable in the usual way
CreateFileMapping	Create a file-mapping object and (optionally) assign it a name
MapViewOfFile	Map (part of) a file into the address space
UnmapViewOfFile	Remove a mapped file from the address space
OpenFileMapping	Open a previously created file mapping object

Figure 6-33. The principal Windows XP API calls for managing virtual memory

This function returns a handle to the file mapping object and optionally enters a name for it into the file system so another process can use it. The next two functions map and unmap files, respectively. The last one can be used by a process to map in a file currently also mapped in by a different process. In this way, two or more processes can share regions of their address spaces.

These API functions are the basic ones upon which the rest of the memory management system is built. For example, there are API functions for allocating and freeing data structures on one or more heaps. Heaps are used for storing data structures that are dynamically created and destroyed. The heaps are not garbage collected, so it is up to user software to free blocks of virtual memory that are no longer in use. (Garbage collection is the automatic removal of unused data structures by the system.) Heap usage in XP is similar to the use of the *malloc* function in UNIX systems, except that there can be multiple independently managed heaps.

6.4.3 Examples of Virtual I/O

The heart of any operating system is providing services to user programs, mostly I/O services such as reading and writing files. Both UNIX and XP offer a wide variety of I/O services to user programs. For most UNIX system calls, XP has an equivalent call, but the reverse is not true, as XP has far more calls and each of them is far more complicated than its UNIX counterpart.

UNIX Virtual I/O

Much of the popularity of the UNIX system can be traced directly to its simplicity, which, in turn, is a direct result of the organization of the file system. An ordinary file is a linear sequence of 8-bit bytes starting at 0 and going up to a maximum of $2^{32} - 1$ bytes. The operating system itself imposes no record structure on files, although many user programs regard ASCII text files as sequences of lines, each line terminated by a line feed.

Associated with every open file is a pointer to the next byte to be read or written. The read and write system calls read and write data starting at the file position indicated by the pointer. Both calls advance the pointer after the operation by an amount equal to the number of bytes transferred. However, random access to files is possible by explicitly setting the file pointer to a specific value.

In addition to ordinary files, the UNIX system also supports special files, which are used to access I/O devices. Each I/O device typically has one or more special files assigned to it. By reading and writing from the associated special file, a program can read or write from the I/O device. Disks, printers, terminals, and many other devices are handled this way.

The major UNIX file system calls are listed in Fig. 6-34. The creat call (without the *e*) can be used to create a new file. It is not strictly necessary any more, because open can also create a new file now. Unlink removes a file, assuming that the file is in only one directory.

System call	Meaning
creat(name, mode)	Create a file; *mode* specifies the protection mode
unlink(name)	Delete a file (assuming that there is only 1 link to it)
open(name, mode)	Open or create a file and return a file descriptor
close(fd)	Close a file
read(fd, buffer, count)	Read *count* bytes into *buffer*
write(fd, buffer, count)	Write *count* bytes from *buffer*
lseek(fd, offset, w)	Move the file pointer as required by *offset* and *w*
stat(name, buffer)	Return information about a file
chmod(name, mode)	Change the protection mode of a file
fcntl(fd, cmd, ...)	Do various control operations such as locking (part of) a file

Figure 6-34. The principal UNIX file system calls.

Open is used to open existing files (and create new ones). The mode flag tells how to open it (for reading, for writing, etc.). The call returns a small integer called a **file descriptor** that identifies the file in subsequent calls. When the file is no longer needed, close is called to free up the file descriptor.

The actual file I/O is done with read and write, each of which has a file descriptor indicating which file to use, a buffer for the data to go to or come from, and a byte count telling how much data to transmit. Lseek is used to position the file pointer, making random access to files possible.

Stat returns information about a file, including its size, time of last access, owner, and more. Chmod changes the protection mode of a file, for example, allowing or forbidding users other than the owner from reading it. Finally, fcntl does various miscellaneous operations on a file, such as locking or unlocking it.

Figure 6-35 illustrates how the major file I/O calls work. This code is minimal and does not include the necessary error checking. Before entering the loop, the program opens an existing file, *data*, and creates a new file, *newf*. Each call returns a file descriptor, *infd*, and *outfd*, respectively. The second parameters to the two calls are protection bits that specify that the files are to be read and written, respectively. Both calls return a file descriptor. If either open or creat fails, a negative file descriptor is returned, telling that the call failed.

```
/* Open the file descriptors. */
infd = open("data", 0);
outfd = creat("newf", ProtectionBits);

/* Copy loop. */
do {
       count = read(infd, buffer, bytes);
       if (count > 0) write(outfd, buffer, count);
} while (count > 0);

/* Close the files. */
close(infd);
close(outfd);
```

Figure 6-35. A program fragment for copying a file using the UNIX system calls. This fragment is in C because Java hides the low-level system calls and we are trying to expose them.

The call to read has three parameters: a file descriptor, a buffer, and a byte count. The call tries to read the desired number of bytes from the indicated file into the buffer. The number of bytes actually read is returned in *count*, which will be smaller than *bytes* if the file was too short. The write call deposits the newly read bytes on the output file. The loop continues until the input file has been completely read, at which time the loop terminates and both files are closed.

File descriptors in UNIX are small integers (usually below 20). File descriptors 0, 1, and 2 are special and correspond to **standard input**, **standard output**, and **standard error**, respectively. Normally, these refer to the keyboard, the display, and the display, respectively, but they can be redirected to files by the user. Many UNIX programs get their input from standard input and write the processed output on standard output. Such programs are often called **filters**.

Closely related to the file system is the directory system. Each user may have multiple directories, with each directory containing both files and subdirectories. UNIX systems normally are configured with a main directory, called the **root directory**, containing subdirectories *bin* (for frequently executed programs), *dev* (for the special I/O device files), *lib* (for libraries), and *usr* (for user directories), as shown in Fig. 6-36. In this example, the *usr* directory contains subdirectories for *ast* and *jim*. The *ast* directory contains two files, *data* and *foo.c*, and a sub-directory, *bin*, containing four games.

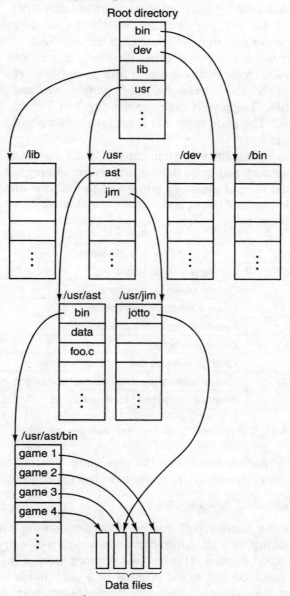

Figure 6-36. Part of a typical UNIX directory system.

Files can be named by giving their **path** from the root directory. A path contains a list of all the directories traversed from the root to the file, with directory names separated by slashes. For example, the absolute path name of *game2* is */usr/ast/bin/game2*. A path starting at the root is called an **absolute path**.

At every instant, each running program has a **working directory**. Path names may also be relative to the working directory, in which case they do not begin with a slash, to distinguish them from absolute path names. Such paths are called **relative paths**. When */usr/ast* is the working directory, *game3* can be accessed using the path *bin/game3*. A user may create a **link** to someone else's file using the link system call. In the above example, */usr/ast/bin/game3* and */usr/jim/jotto* both access the same file. To prevent cycles in the directory system, links are not permitted to directories. The calls open and creat take either absolute or relative path names as arguments.

The major directory management system calls in UNIX are listed in Fig. 6-37. Mkdir creates a new directory and rmdir deletes an existing (empty) directory. The next three calls are used to read directory entries. The first one opens the directory, the next one reads entries from it, and the last one closes the directory. Chdir changes the working directory.

System call	Meaning
mkdir(name, mode)	Create a new directory
rmdir(name)	Delete an empty directory
opendir(name)	Open a directory for reading
readdir(dirpointer)	Read the next entry in a directory
closedir(dirpointer)	Close a directory
chdir(dirname)	Change working directory to *dirname*
link(name1, name2)	Create a directory entry *name2* pointing to *name1*
unlink(name)	Remove *name* from its directory

Figure 6-37. The principal UNIX directory management calls.

Link makes a new directory entry with the new entry pointing to an existing file. For example, the entry */usr/jim/jotto* might have been created by the call

    link("/usr/ast/bin/game3", "/usr/jim/jotto")

or an equivalent call using relative path names, depending on the working directory of the program making the call. Unlink removes a directory entry. If the file has only one link, the file is deleted. If it has two or more links, it is kept. It does not matter whether a removed link is the original or a copy made later. Once a link is made, it is a first-class citizen, indistinguishable from the original. The call

    unlink("/usr/ast/bin/game3")

makes *game3* only accessible via the path */usr/jim/jotto* henceforth. Link and unlink can be used in this way to "move" files from one directory to another.

Associated with every file (including directories, because they are also files) is a bit map telling who may access the file. The map contains three RWX fields, the first controlling the Read, Write, eXecute permissions for the owner, the second for others in the owner's group, and the third for everybody else. Thus RWX R-X --X means that the owner can read the file, write the file, and execute the file (obviously, it is an executable program, or execute would be off), whereas others in his group can read or execute it and strangers can only execute it. With these permissions, strangers can use the program but not steal (copy) it because they do not have read permission. The assignment of users to groups is done by the system administrator, usually called the **superuser**. The superuser also has the power to override the protection mechanism and read, write, or execute any file.

Let us now briefly examine how files and directories are implemented in UNIX. For a more complete treatment, see Vahalia (1996). Associated with each file (and each directory, because a directory is also a file) is a 64-byte block of information called an **i-node**. The i-node tells who owns the file, what the permissions are, where to find the data, and similar things. The i-nodes for the files on each disk are located either in numerical sequence at the beginning of the disk, or if the disk is split up into groups of cylinders, at the start of a cylinder group. Thus given an i-node number, the UNIX system can locate the i-node by simply calculating its disk address.

A directory entry consists of two parts: a file name and an i-node number. When a program executes

    open("foo.c", 0)

the system searches the working directory for the file name, "foo.c," in order to locate the i-node number for that file. Having found the i-node number, it can then read in the i-node, which tells it all about the file.

When a longer path name is specified, the basic steps outlined above are repeated several times until the full path has been parsed. For example, to locate the i-node number for */usr/ast/data*, the system first searches the root directory for an entry *usr*. Having found the i-node for *usr*, it can read that file (a directory is a file in UNIX). In this file it looks for an entry *ast*, thus locating the i-node number for the file */usr/ast*. By reading */usr/ast*, the system can then find the entry for *data*, and thus the i-node number for */usr/ast/data*. Given the i-node number for the file, it can then find out everything about the file from the i-node.

The format, contents, and layout of an i-node vary somewhat from system to system (especially when networking is in use), but the following items are typically found in each i-node.

1. The file type, the 9 RWX protection bits, and a few other bits.

2. The number of links to the file (number of directory entries for it).

3. The owner's identity.

4. The owner's group.

5. The file length in bytes.

6. Thirteen disk addresses.

7. The time the file was last read.

8. The time the file was last written.

9. The time the i-node was last changed.

The file type distinguishes ordinary files, directories, and two kinds of special files, for block-structured and unstructured I/O devices, respectively. The number of links and the owner identification have already been discussed. The file length is a 32-bit integer giving the highest byte that has a value. It is perfectly legal to create a file, do an lseek to position 1,000,000, and write 1 byte, which yields a file of length 1,000,001. The file would *not*, however, require storage for all the "missing" bytes.

The first 10 disk addresses point to data blocks. With a block size of 1024 bytes, files up to 10,240 bytes can be handled this way. Address 11 points to a disk block, called an **indirect block**, which contains 256 disk addresses. Files up to $10,240 + 256 \times 1024 = 272,384$ bytes are handled this way. For still larger files, address 12 points to a block containing the addresses of 256 indirect blocks, which takes care of files up to $272,384 + 256 \times 256 \times 1024 = 67,381,248$ bytes. If this **double indirect block** scheme is still too small, disk address 13 is used to point to a **triple indirect block** containing the addresses of 256 double indirect blocks. Using the direct, single, double, and triple indirect addresses, up to 16,843,018 blocks can be addressed giving a theoretical maximum file size of 17,247,250,432 bytes. Since file pointers are limited to 32 bits, the practical upper limit is actually 4,294,967,295 bytes. Free disk blocks are kept on a linked list. When a new block is needed, the next block is plucked from the list. As a result, the blocks of each file are scattered randomly around the disk.

To make disk I/O more efficient, when a file is opened, its i-node is copied to a table in main memory and is kept there for handy reference as long as the file remains open. In addition, a pool of recently referenced disk blocks is maintained in memory. Because most files are read sequentially, it often happens that a file reference requires the same disk block as the previous reference. To strengthen this effect, the system also tries to read the *next* block in a file, before it is referenced, in order to speed up processing. All this optimization is hidden from the user; when a user issues a read call, the program is suspended until the requested data are available in the buffer.

With this background information, we can now take a look to see how file I/O works. Open causes the system to search the directories for the specified path. If the search is successful, the i-node is read into an internal table. Reads and writes require the system to compute the block number from the current file position.

The disk addresses of the first 10 blocks are always in main memory (in the i-node); higher-numbered blocks require one or more indirect blocks to be read first. Lseek just changes the current position pointer without doing any I/O.

Link and unlink are also simple to understand now. Link looks up its first argument to find the i-node number. Then it creates a directory entry for the second argument, putting the i-node number of the first file in that entry. Finally, it increases the link count in the i-node by one. Unlink removes a directory entry and decrements the link count in the i-node. If it is zero, the file is removed and all the blocks are put back on the free list.

Windows XP Virtual I/O

XP supports several file systems, the most important of which are **NTFS** (**NT File System**) and the **FAT** (**File Allocation Table**) file system. The former is a new file system developed specifically for XP; the latter is the old MS-DOS file system, which was also used on Windows 95/98 (albeit with support for longer file names). Since the FAT file system is basically obsolete, we will study NTFS below.

File names in NTFS can be up to 255 characters long. File names are in Unicode, allowing people in countries not using the Latin alphabet (e.g., Japan, India, and Israel) to write file names in their native language. (In fact, XP uses Unicode throughout internally; versions starting with Windows 2000 have a single binary that can be used in any country and still use the local language because all the menus, error messages, etc., are kept in country-dependent configuration files.) NTFS fully supports case-sensitive names (so *foo* is different from *FOO*). Unfortunately, the Win32 API does not fully support case-sensitivity for file names and not at all for directory names, so this advantage is lost to programs using Win32.

As with UNIX, a file is just a linear sequence of bytes, although up to a maximum of $2^{64} - 1$. File pointers also exist, as in UNIX, but are 64 bits wide rather than 32 bits, to handle the maximum length file. The Win32 API function calls for file and directory manipulation are roughly similar to their UNIX counterparts, except most have more parameters and the security model is different. Opening a file returns a handle, which is then used for reading and writing the file. However, unlike in UNIX, handles are not small integers, and standard input, standard output, and standard error have to be acquired explicitly rather than being predefined as 0, 1, and 2 (except in console mode, where they are preopened). The principal Win32 API functions for file management are listed in Fig. 6-38.

Let us now examine these calls briefly. CreateFile can be used to create a new file and return a handle to it. This API function is also used to open existing files as there is no open API function. We have not listed the parameters for the XP API functions because they are so voluminous. As an example, CreateFile has seven parameters, as follows:

API function	UNIX	Meaning
CreateFile	open	Create a file or open an existing file; return a handle
DeleteFile	unlink	Destroy an existing file
CloseHandle	close	Close a file
ReadFile	read	Read data from a file
WriteFile	write	Write data to a file
SetFilePointer	lseek	Set the file pointer to a specific place in the file
GetFileAttributes	stat	Return the file properties
LockFile	fcntl	Lock a region of the file to provide mutual exclusion
UnlockFile	fcntl	Unlock a previously locked region of the file

Figure 6-38. The principal Win32 API functions for file I/O. The second column gives the nearest UNIX equivalent.

1. A pointer to the name of the file to create or open.

2. Flags telling whether the file can be read, written, or both.

3. Flags telling whether multiple processes can open the file at once.

4. A pointer to the security descriptor, telling who can access the file.

5. Flags telling what to do if the file exists/does not exist.

6. Flags dealing with attributes such as archiving, compression, etc.

7. The handle of a file whose attributes should be cloned for the new file.

The next six API functions in Fig. 6-38 are fairly similar to the corresponding UNIX system calls. The last two allow a region of a file to be locked and unlocked to permit a process to get guaranteed mutual exclusion to it.

Using these API functions, it is possible to write a procedure to copy a file, analogous to the UNIX version of Figure 6-35. Such a procedure (without any error checking) is shown in Fig. 6-39. It has been designed to mimic the structuré of Figure 6-35. In practice, one would not have to program a copy file program since CopyFile is an API function (which executes something close to this program as a library procedure).

XP supports a hierarchical file system, similar to the UNIX file system. The separator between component names is \ however, instead of /, a fossil inherited from MS-DOS. There is a concept of a current working directory and path names can be relative or absolute. One significant difference with UNIX, however, is that UNIX allows the file systems on different disks and machines to be mounted together in a single naming tree, thus hiding the disk structure from all software. XP 4.0 does not have this property, so absolute file names must begin with a drive

```
/* Open files for input and output. */
inhandle = CreateFile("data"; GENERIC_READ, 0, NULL, OPEN_EXISTING, 0, NULL);
outhandle = CreateFile("newf", GENERIC_WRITE, 0, NULL, CREATE_ALWAYS,
        FILE_ATTRIBUTE_NORMAL, NULL);

/* Copy the file. */
do {
        s = ReadFile(inhandle, buffer, BUF_SIZE, &count, NULL);
        if (s > 0 && count > 0) WriteFile(outhandle, buffer, count, &ocnt, NULL);
} while (s > 0 && count > 0);

/* Close the files. */
CloseHandle(inhandle);
CloseHandle(outhandle);
```

Figure 6-39. A program fragment for copying a file using the Windows XP API functions. This fragment is in C because Java hides the low-level system calls and we are trying to expose them.

letter indicating which logical disk is meant, as in *C:\windows\system\foo.dll*. Starting with Windows 2000 UNIX-style mounting of file systems was added.

The major directory management API functions are given in Fig. 6-40, again along with their nearest UNIX equivalents. The functions are hopefully self-explanatory.

API function	UNIX	Meaning
CreateDirectory	mkdir	Create a new directory
RemoveDirectory	rmdir	Remove an empty directory
FindFirstFile	opendir	Initialize to start reading the entries in a directory
FindNextFile	readdir	Read the next directory entry
MoveFile		Move a file from one directory to another
SetCurrentDirectory	chdir	Change the current working directory

Figure 6-40. The principal Win32 API functions for directory management. The second column gives the nearest UNIX equivalent, when one exists.

XP has a much more elaborate security mechanism than most UNIX systems. Although there are hundreds of API functions relating to security, the following brief description gives the general idea. When a user logs in, his or her initial process is given an **access token** by the operating system. The access token contains the user's **SID (Security ID)**, a list of the security groups to which the user belongs, any special privileges available, and a few other items. The point of the access token is to concentrate all the security information in one easy-to-find place. All processes created by this process inherit the same access token.

One of the parameters that can be supplied when any object is created is its **security descriptor**. The security descriptor contains a list of entries called an **ACL (Access Control List)**. Each entry permits or prohibits some set of the operations on the object by some SID or group. For example, a file could have a security descriptor specifying that Elinor has no access to the file at all, Ken can read the file, Linda can read or write the file, and that all members of the XYZ group can read the file's length but nothing else.

When a process tries to perform some operation on an object using the handle it got when it opened the object, the security manager gets the process' access token and goes down the list of entries in the ACL in order. As soon as it finds an entry that matches the caller's SID or one of the caller's groups, the access found there is taken as definitive. For this reason, it is usual to put entries denying access ahead of entries granting access in the ACL, so that a user who is specifically denied access cannot get in via a back door by being a member of a group that has legitimate access. The security descriptor also contains information used for auditing accesses to the object.

Let us now take a quick look at how files and directories are implemented in XP. Each disk is statically divided up into self-contained volumes, which are the same as disk partitions in UNIX. Each volume contains bit maps, files, directories, and other data structures for managing its information. Each volume is organized as a linear sequence of **clusters**, with the cluster size being fixed for each volume and ranging from 512 bytes to 64 KB, depending on the volume size. Clusters are referred to by their offset from the start of the volume using 64-bit numbers.

The main data structure in each volume is the **MFT (Master File Table)**, which has an entry for each file and directory in the volume. These entries are analogous to the i-nodes in UNIX. The MFT is itself a file, and as such can be placed anywhere within the volume, thus eliminating the problem that UNIX has with bad disk blocks in the middle of the i-nodes.

The MFT is shown in Fig. 6-41. It begins with a header containing information about the volume, such as (pointers to) the root directory, the boot file, the bad-block file, the free-list administration, etc. After that comes an entry per file or directory, 1 KB except when the cluster size is 2 KB or more. Each entry contains all the metadata (administrative information) about the file or directory. Several formats are allowed, one of which is shown in Fig. 6-41.

The standard information field contains information such as the time stamps needed by the hard link count, the read-only and archive bits, etc. It is a fixed-length field and always present. The file name is variable length, up to 255 Unicode characters. In order to make such files accessible to old 16-bit programs, files can also have a MS-DOS name, which consists of eight alphanumeric characters optionally followed by a dot and an extension of up to three alphanumeric characters. If the actual file name conforms to the MS-DOS 8+3 naming rule, a secondary MS-DOS name is not used.

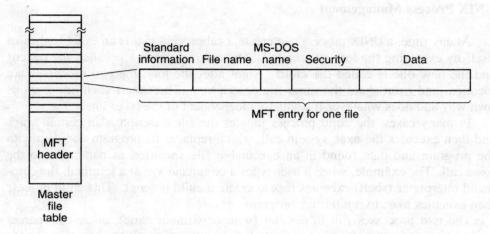

Figure 6-41. The Windows XP master file table.

Next comes the security information. In versions up to and including XP 4.0, the security field contained the actual security descriptor. Starting with Windows 2000, all the security information was centralized in a single file, with the security field simply pointing to the relevant part of this file.

For small files, the file data itself is actually contained in the MFT entry, saving a disk access to fetch it. This idea is called an **immediate file** (Mullender and Tanenbaum, 1984). For somewhat larger files, this field contains pointers to the clusters containing the data, or more commonly, runs of consecutive clusters so a single cluster number and a length can represent an arbitrary amount of file data. If a single MFT entry is insufficiently large to hold whatever information it is supposed to hold, one or more additional entries can be chained to it.

The maximum file size is 2^{64} bytes. To get an idea of how big a 2^{64}-byte file is, imagine that the file were written out in binary, with each 0 or 1 occupying 1 mm of space. The 2^{67}-mm listing would be 15 light-years long, reaching far beyond the solar system, to Alpha Centauri and back.

The NTFS file system has many other interesting properties including data compression and fault tolerance using atomic transactions. Additional information about it can be found in (Russinovich and Solomon 2005).

6.4.4 Examples of Process Management

Both UNIX and XP allow a job to be split up into multiple processes that can run in (pseudo)parallel and communicate with each other, in the style of the producer-consumer example discussed earlier. In this section we will discuss how processes are managed in both systems. Both systems also support parallelism within a single process using threads, so that will also be discussed.

UNIX Process Management

At any time, a UNIX process can create a subprocess that is an exact replica of itself by executing the fork system call. The original process is called the **parent** and the new one is called the **child**. Right after the fork, the two processes are identical and even share the same file descriptors. Thereafter, each one goes its own way and does whatever it wants to, independent of the other one.

In many cases, the child process juggles the file descriptors in certain ways and then executes the exec system call, which replaces its program and data with the program and data found in an executable file specified as parameter to the exec call. For example, when a user types a command *xyz* at a terminal, the command interpreter (shell) executes fork to create a child process. This child process then executes exec to run the *xyz* program.

The two processes run in parallel (with or without exec), unless the parent wishes to wait for the child to terminate before continuing. If the parent wishes to wait, it executes either the wait or waitpid system call, which causes it to be suspended until the child finishes by executing exit. After the child finishes, the parent continues.

Processes can execute fork as often as they want, giving rise to a tree of processes. In Fig. 6-42, for example, process *A* has executed fork twice, creating two children, *B* and *C*. Then *B* also executed fork twice, and *C* executed it once, giving the final tree of six processes.

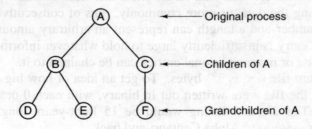

Figure 6-42. A process tree in UNIX.

Processes in UNIX can communicate with each other via a structure called a **pipe**. A pipe is a kind of buffer into which one process can write a stream of data and another can take it out. Bytes are always retrieved from a pipe in the order they were written. Random access is not possible. Pipes do not preserve message boundaries, so if one process does four 128-byte writes and the other does a 512-byte read, the reader will get all the data at once, with no indication that they were written in multiple operations.

In System V and Solaris, another way for processes to communicate is by using **message queues**. A process can create a new message queue or open an existing one using msgget. Using a message queue, a process can send messages using msgsnd and receive them using msgrecv. Messages sent this way differ from data stuffed into a pipe in several ways. First, message boundaries are preserved, whereas a pipe is just a byte stream. Second, messages have priorities, so urgent ones can skip ahead of less important ones. Third, messages are typed, and a msgrecv can specify a particular type, if desired.

Another communication mechanism is the ability of two or more processes to share a region of their respective address spaces. UNIX handles this shared memory by mapping the same pages into the virtual address space of all the sharing processes. As a result, a write by one process into the shared region is immediately visible to the other processes. This mechanism provides a very high bandwidth communication path between processes. The system calls involved in shared memory go by names like shmat and shmop.

Another feature of System V and Solaris is the availability of semaphores. These work essentially as described in the producer-consumer example given in the text.

Another facility provided by all UNIX systems is the ability to have multiple threads of control within a single process. These threads of control, usually just called **threads**, are like lightweight processes that share a common address space and everything associated with that address space, such as file descriptors, environment variables, and outstanding timers. However, each thread has its own program counter, own registers, and own stack. When a thread blocks (i.e., has to stop temporarily until I/O completes or some other event happens), other threads in the same process are still able to run. Two threads in the same process operating as a producer and consumer are similar, but not identical, to two single-thread processes that are sharing a memory segment containing a buffer. The differences have to do with the fact that in the latter case, each process has its own file descriptors, etc., whereas in the former case all of these items are shared. We saw the use of Java threads in our producer-consumer example earlier. Often the Java runtime system uses an operating system thread for each of its threads, but it does not have to do this.

As an example of where threads might be useful, consider a World Wide Web server. Such a server might keep a cache of commonly-used Web pages in main memory. If a request is for a page in the cache, the Web page is returned immediately. Otherwise, it is fetched from disk. Unfortunately, waiting for the disk takes a long time (typically 20 msec), during which the process is blocked and cannot serve new incoming requests, even those for Web pages in the cache.

The solution is to have multiple threads within the server process, all of which share the common Web page cache. When one thread blocks, other threads can handle new requests. To prevent blocking without threads, one could have multiple server processes, but this would probably entail replicating the cache, thus wasting valuable memory.

The UNIX standard for threads is called **pthreads**, and is defined by (P1003.1C). It contains calls for managing and synchronizing threads. It is not defined whether threads are managed by the kernel or entirely in user space. The most commonly-used thread calls are listed in Fig. 6-43.

Thread call	Meaning
pthread_create	Create a new thread in the caller's address space
pthread_exit	Terminate the calling thread
pthread_join	Wait for a thread to terminate
pthread_mutex_init	Create a new mutex
pthread_mutex_destroy	Destroy a mutex
pthread_mutex_lock	Lock a mutex
pthread_mutex_unlock	Unlock a mutex
pthread_cond_init	Create a condition variable
pthread_cond_destroy	Destroy a condition variable
pthread_cond_wait	Wait on a condition variable
pthread_cond_signal	Release one thread waiting on a condition variable

Figure 6-43. The principal POSIX thread calls.

Let us briefly examine the thread calls shown in Fig. 6-43. The first call, pthread_create, creates a new thread. After successful completion, one more thread is running in the caller's address space than was before the call. A thread that has done its job and wants to terminate calls pthread_exit. A thread can wait for another thread to exit by calling pthread_join. If the thread waited for has already exited, the pthread_join finishes immediately. Otherwise it blocks.

Threads can synchronize using locks called **mutexes**. Typically a mutex guards some resource, such as a buffer shared by two threads. To make sure that only one thread at a time accesses the shared resource, threads are expected to lock the mutex before touching the resource and unlock it when they are done. As long as all threads obey this protocol, race conditions can be avoided. Mutexes are like binary semaphores, that is, semaphores that can take on only the values of 0 and 1. The name "mutex" comes from the fact that mutexes are used to ensure mutual exclusion on some resource.

Mutexes can be created and destroyed by the calls pthread_mutex_init and pthread_mutex_destroy, respectively. A mutex can be in one of two states: locked or unlocked. When a thread needs to set a lock on an unlocked mutex (using pthread_mutex_lock), the lock is set and the thread continues. However, when a thread tries to lock a mutex that is already locked, it blocks. When the locking thread is finished with the shared resource, it is expected to unlock the corresponding mutex by calling pthread_mutex_unlock.

Mutexes are intended for short-term locking, such as protecting a shared variable. They are not intended for long-term synchronization, such as waiting for a tape drive to become free. For long-term synchronization, **condition variables** are provided. These are created and destroyed by calls to pthread_cond_init and pthread_cond_destroy, respectively.

A condition variable is used by having one thread wait on it, and another signal it. For example, having discovered that the tape drive it needs is busy, a thread would do pthread_cond_wait on a condition variable that all the threads have agreed to associate with the tape drive. When the thread using the tape drive is finally done with it (possibly hours later), it uses pthread_cond_signal to release exactly one thread waiting on that condition variable (if any). If no thread is waiting, the signal is lost. Condition variables do not count like semaphores. A few other operations are also defined on threads, mutexes, and condition variables.

Windows XP Process Management

XP supports multiple processes, which can communicate and synchronize. Each process contains at least one thread, which in turn contains at least one fiber (lightweight thread). Together, processes, threads, and fibers provide a very general set of tools for managing parallelism, both on uniprocessors (single-CPU machines) and on multiprocessors (multi-CPU machines).

New processes are created using the API function CreateProcess. This function has 10 parameters, each of which has many options. This design is clearly a lot more complicated that the UNIX scheme, in which fork has no parameters, and exec has just three: pointers to the name of the file to execute, the (parsed) command line parameter array, and the environment strings. Roughly speaking, the 10 parameters to CreateProcess are as follows:

1. A pointer to the name of the executable file.

2. The command line itself (unparsed).

3. A pointer to a security descriptor for the process.

4. A pointer to a security descriptor for the initial thread.

5. A bit telling whether the new process inherits the creator's handles.

6. Miscellaneous flags (e.g., error mode, priority, debugging, consoles).

7. A pointer to the environment strings.

8. A pointer to the name of the new process' current working directory.

9. A pointer to a structure describing the initial window on the screen.

10. A pointer to a structure that returns 18 values to the caller.

XP does not enforce any kind of parent-child or other hierarchy. All processes are created equal. However, since 1 of the 18 parameters returned to the creating process is a handle to the new process (allowing considerable control over the new process), there is an implicit hierarchy in terms of who has a handle to whom. Although these handles cannot just be passed directly to other processes, there is a way for a process to make a handle suitable for another process and then give it the handle, so the implicit process hierarchy may not last long.

Each process in XP is created with a single thread, but a process can create more threads later on. Thread creation is simpler than process creation: CreateThread has only six parameters instead of 10: the security descriptor, the stack size, the starting address, a user-defined parameter, the initial state of the thread (ready or blocked), and the thread's ID. The kernel does the thread creation, so it is clearly aware of threads (i.e., they are not implemented purely in user space as is the case in some other systems).

When the kernel does scheduling, it not only picks the process to run next but also which thread in that process. This means that the kernel is always aware of which threads are ready and which ones are blocked. Because threads are kernel objects, they have security descriptors and handles. Since a handle for a thread can be passed to another process, it is possible to have one process control the threads in a different process. This feature is useful for debuggers, for example.

Threads in XP are relatively expensive because doing a thread switch requires entering and later leaving the kernel. To provide very lightweight pseudoparallelism, XP provides **fibers**, which are like threads, but are scheduled in user space by the program that created them (or its runtime system). Each thread can have multiple fibers, the same way a process can have multiple threads, except that when a fiber logically blocks, it puts itself on the queue of blocked fibers and selects another fiber to run in the context of its thread. The kernel is not aware of this transition because the thread keeps running, even though it may be first running one fiber, then another. The kernel just manages processes and threads, not fibers. Fibers are useful, for example, when programs that manage their own threads are ported to XP.

Processes can communicate in a wide variety of ways, including pipes, named pipes, mailslots, sockets, remote procedure calls, and shared files. Pipes have two modes: byte and message, selected at creation time. Byte-mode pipes work the same way as in UNIX. Message-mode pipes are somewhat similar but preserve message boundaries, so that four writes of 128 bytes will be read as four 128-byte messages, and not as one 512-byte message, as would happen with byte-mode pipes. Named pipes also exist and have the same two modes as regular pipes. Named pipes can also be used over a network; regular pipes cannot.

Mailslots are a feature of XP not present in UNIX. They are similar to pipes in some ways, but not all. For one thing, they are one-way, whereas pipes are two-way. They can also be used over a network but do not provide guaranteed delivery. Finally, they allow the sending process to broadcast a message to many receivers, instead of to just one.

Sockets are like pipes, except that they normally connect processes on different machines. However, they can also be used to connect processes on the same machine. In general, there is usually little advantage to using a socket connection over a pipe or named pipe for intramachine communication.

Remote procedure calls are a way for process *A* to have process *B* call a procedure in *B*'s address space on *A*'s behalf and return the result to *A*. Various restrictions on the parameters exist. For example, it makes no sense to pass a pointer to a different process.

Finally, processes can share memory by mapping onto the same file at the same time. All writes done by one process then appear in the address spaces of the other processes. Using this mechanism, the shared buffer used in our producer-consumer example can be easily implemented.

Just as XP provides numerous interprocess communication mechanisms, it also provides numerous synchronization mechanisms, including semaphores, mutexes, critical sections, and events. All of these mechanisms work on threads, not processes, so that when a thread blocks on a semaphore, other threads in that process (if any) are not affected and can continue to run.

A semaphore is created using the CreateSemaphore API function, which can initialize it to a given value and define a maximum value as well. Semaphores are kernel objects and thus have security descriptors and handles. The handle for a semaphore can be duplicated using DuplicateHandle and passed to another process so that multiple processes can synchronize on the same semaphore. Calls for up and down are present, although they have the somewhat peculiar names of ReleaseSemaphore (up) and WaitForSingleObject (down). It is also possible to give WaitForSingleObject a timeout, so the calling thread can be released eventually, even if the semaphore remains at 0 (although timers reintroduce races).

Mutexes are also kernel objects used for synchronization, but simpler than semaphores because they do not have counters. They are essentially locks, with API functions for locking (WaitForSingleObject) and unlocking (ReleaseMutex). Like semaphore handles, mutex handles can be duplicated and passed between processes so that threads in different processes can access the same mutex.

The third synchronization mechanism is based on **critical sections**, which are similar to mutexes, except local to the address space of the creating thread. Because critical sections are not kernel objects, they do not have handles or security descriptors and cannot be passed between processes. Locking and unlocking is done with EnterCriticalSection and LeaveCriticalSection, respectively. Because these API functions are performed entirely in user space, they are much faster than mutexes.

The last synchronization mechanism uses kernel objects called **events**. A thread can wait for an event to occur with WaitForSingleObject. A thread can release a single thread waiting on an event with SetEvent or it can release all threads waiting on an event with PulseEvent. Events come in several flavors and have a variety of options, too.

Events, mutexes, and semaphores can all be named and stored in the file system, like named pipes. Two or more processes can synchronize by opening the same event, mutex, or semaphore, rather than having one of them create the object and then make duplicate handles for the others, although the latter approach is certainly an option as well.

6.5 SUMMARY

The operating system can be regarded as an interpreter for certain architectural features not found at the ISA level. Chief among these are virtual memory, virtual I/O instructions, and facilities for parallel processing.

Virtual memory is an architectural feature whose purpose is to allow programs to use more address space than the machine has physical memory, or to provide a consistent and flexible mechanism for memory protection and sharing. It can be implemented as pure paging, pure segmentation, or a combination of the two. In pure paging, the address space is broken up into equal-sized virtual pages. Some of these are mapped onto physical page frames. Others are not mapped. A reference to a mapped page is translated by the MMU into the correct physical address. A reference to an unmapped page causes a page fault. Both the Pentium 4 and the UltraSPARC III have MMUs that support virtual memory and paging.

The most important I/O abstraction present at this level is the file. A file consists of a sequence of bytes or logical records that can be read and written without knowledge of how disks, tapes, and other I/O devices work. Files can be accessed sequentially, randomly by record number, or randomly by key. Directories can be used to group files together. Files can be stored in consecutive sectors or scattered around the disk. In the latter case, normal on hard disks, data structures are needed to locate all the blocks of a file. Free disk storage can be kept track of using a list or a bit map.

Parallel processing is often supported and is implemented by simulating multiple processors by timesharing a single CPU. Uncontrolled interaction between processes can lead to race conditions. To solve this problem, synchronization primitives are introduced, of which semaphores are a simple example. Using semaphores, producer-consumer problems can be solved simply and elegantly.

Two examples of sophisticated operating systems are UNIX and XP. Both support paging and memory-mapped files. They also both support hierarchical file systems, with files consisting of byte sequences. Finally, both support processes and threads and provide ways to synchronize them.

PROBLEMS

1. Why does an operating system interpret only some of the level 3 instructions, whereas a microprogram interprets all the ISA level instructions?

2. A machine has a 32-bit byte-addressable virtual address space. The page size is 4 KB. How many pages of virtual address space exist?

3. Is it necessary to have the page size be a power of 2? Could a page of size, say, 4000 bytes be implemented in theory? If so, would it be practical?

4. A virtual memory has a page size of 1024 words, eight virtual pages, and four physical page frames. The page table is as follows:

Virtual page	Page frame
0	3
1	1
2	not in main memory
3	not in main memory
4	2
5	not in main memory
6	0
7	not in main memory

a. Make a list of all virtual addresses that will cause page faults.
b. What are the physical addresses for 0, 3728, 1023, 1024, 1025, 7800, and 4096?

5. A computer has 16 pages of virtual address space but only four page frames. Initially, the memory is empty. A program references the virtual pages in the order

0, 7, 2, 7, 5, 8, 9, 2, 4

a. Which references cause a page fault with LRU?
b. Which references cause a page fault with FIFO?

6. In Sec. 6.1.4 an algorithm was presented for implementing a FIFO page replacement strategy. Devise a more efficient one. *Hint:* It is possible to update the counter in the newly-loaded page, leaving all the others alone.

7. In the paged systems discussed in the text, the page fault handler was part of the ISA level and thus was not present in any OSM level program's address space. In reality, the page fault handler also occupies pages, and might, under some circumstances (e.g., FIFO page replacement policy), itself be removed. What would happen if the page fault handler were not present when a page fault occurred? How could this be fixed?

8. Not all computers have a hardware bit that is automatically set when a page is written to. Nevertheless, it is useful to keep track of which pages have been modified, to avoid having to assume worst case and write all pages back to the disk after use. Assuming that each page has hardware bits to separately enable access for reading, writing, and execution, how can the operating system keep track of which pages are clean and which are dirty?

9. A segmented memory has paged segments. Each virtual address has a 2-bit segment number, a 2-bit page number, and an 11-bit offset within the page. The main memory contains 32 KB, divided up into 2-KB pages. Each segment is either read-only, read/execute, read/write, or read/write/execute. The page tables and protection are as follows:

Segment 0		Segment 1		Segment 2	Segment 3	
Read only		Read/execute		Read/write/execute	Read/write	
Virtual page	Page frame	Virtual page	Page frame		Virtual page	Page frame
0	9	0	On disk	Page table	0	14
1	3	1	0	not in	1	1
2	On disk	2	15	main	2	6
3	12	3	8	memory	3	On disk

For each of the following accesses to virtual memory, tell what physical address is computed. If a fault occurs, tell which kind.

Access	Segment	Page	Offset within page
1. fetch data	0	1	1
2. fetch data	1	1	10
3. fetch data	3	3	2047
4. store data	0	1	4
5. store data	3	1	2
6. store data	3	0	14
7. branch to it	1	3	100
8. fetch data	0	2	50
9. fetch data	2	0	5
10. branch to it	3	0	60

10. Some computers allow I/O directly to user space. For example, a program could start up a disk transfer to a buffer inside a user process. Does this cause any problems if compaction is used to implement the virtual memory? Discuss.

11. Operating systems that allow memory-mapped files always require files to be mapped at page boundaries. For example, with 4-KB pages, a file can be mapped in starting at virtual address 4096, but not starting at virtual address 5000. Why?

12. When a segment register is loaded on the Pentium 4, the corresponding descriptor is fetched and loaded into an invisible part of the segment register. Why do you think the Intel designers decided to do this?

13. A program on the Pentium 4 references local segment 10 with offset 8000. The BASE field of LDT segment 10 contains 10000. Which page directory entry does the Pentium 4 use? What is the page number? What is the offset?

14. Discuss some possible algorithms for removing segments in an unpaged, segmented memory.

15. Compare internal fragmentation to external fragmentation. What can be done to alleviate each?

16. Supermarkets are constantly faced with a problem similar to page replacement in virtual memory systems. They have a fixed amount of shelf space to display an ever-increasing number of products. If an important new product comes along, say, 100%

efficient dog food, some existing product must be dropped from the inventory to make room for it. The obvious replacement algorithms are LRU and FIFO. Which of these would you prefer?

17. In some ways, caching and paging are very similar. In both cases there are two levels of memory (the cache and main memory in the former and main memory and disk in the latter). In this chapter we looked at some of the arguments in favor of large disk pages and small disk pages. Do the same arguments hold for cache line sizes?

18. Why do many file systems require that a file be explicitly opened with an open system call before being read?

19. Compare the bit-map and hole-list methods for keeping track of free space on a disk with 800 cylinders, each one having 5 tracks of 32 sectors. How many holes would it take before the hole list would be larger than the bit map? Assume that the allocation unit is the sector and that a hole requires a 32-bit table entry.

20. To be able to make some predictions of disk performance, it is useful to have a model of storage allocation. Suppose that the disk is viewed as a linear address space of $N \gg 1$ sectors, consisting of a run of data blocks, then a hole, then another run of data blocks, and so on. If empirical measurements show that the probability distributions for data and hole lengths are the same, with the chance of either being i sectors as 2^{-i}, what is the expected number of holes on the disk?

21. On a certain computer, a program can create as many files as it needs, and all files may grow dynamically during execution without giving the operating system any advance information about their ultimate size. Do you think that files are stored in consecutive sectors? Explain.

22. Studies of different file systems have shown that more than half the files are a few KB or smaller, with the vast majority of files less than something like 8 KB. On the other hand, the largest 10 percent of all files usually occupies about 95 percent of the entire disk space in use. From this data, what conclusion can you draw about disk block size?

23. Consider the following method by which an operating system might implement semaphore instructions. Whenever the CPU is about to do an up or down on a semaphore (an integer variable in memory), it first sets the CPU priority or mask bits in such a way as to disable all interrupts. Then it fetches the semaphore, modifies it, and branches accordingly. Finally, it enables interrupts again. Does this method work if

   a. There is a single CPU that switches between processes every 100 msec?
   b. Two CPUs share a common memory in which the semaphore is located?

24. The Nevercrash Operating System Company has been receiving complaints from some of its customers about its latest release, which includes semaphore operations. They feel it is immoral for processes to block (they call it "sleeping on the job"). Since it is company policy to give the customers what they want, it has been proposed to add a third operation, peek, to supplement up and down. peek simply examines the semaphore without changing it or blocking the process. In this way, programs that feel it is immoral to block can first inspect the semaphore to see if it is safe to do a down. Will this idea work if three or more processes use the semaphore? If two processes use the semaphore?

25. Make a table showing which of the processes P1, P2, and P3 are running and which are blocked as a function of time from 0 to 1000 msec. All three processes perform up and down instructions on the same semaphore. When two processes are blocked and an up is done, the process with the lower number is restarted, that is, P1 gets preference over P2 and P3, and so on. Initially, all three are running and the semaphore is 1.

   At $t = 100$ P1 does a down
   At $t = 200$ P1 does a down
   At $t = 300$ P2 does an up
   At $t = 400$ P3 does a down
   At $t = 500$ P1 does a down
   At $t = 600$ P2 does an up
   At $t = 700$ P2 does a down
   At $t = 800$ P1 does an up
   At $t = 900$ P1 does an up

26. In an airline reservation system, it is necessary to ensure that while one process is busy using a file, no other process can also use it. Otherwise, two different processes, working for two different ticket agents, might each inadvertently sell the last seat on some flight. Devise a synchronization method using semaphores that makes sure that only one process at a time accesses each file (assuming that the processes obey the rules).

27. To make it possible to implement semaphores on a computer with multiple CPUs that share a common memory, computer architects often provide a Test and Set Lock instruction. TSL X tests the location X. If the contents are zero, they are set to 1 in a single, indivisible memory cycle, and the next instruction is skipped. If it is nonzero, the TSL acts like a no-op. Using TSL it is possible to write procedures *lock* and *unlock* with the following properties. *lock* (x) checks to see if x is locked. If not, it locks x and returns control. If x is already locked, it just waits until it becomes unlocked, then it locks x and returns control. *unlock* releases an existing lock. If all processes lock the semaphore table before using it, only one process at a time can fiddle with the variables and pointers, thus preventing races. Write *lock* and *unlock* in assembly language. (Make any reasonable assumptions you need.)

28. Show the values of *in* and *out* for a circular buffer of length 65 words after each of the following operations. Both start at 0.

   a. 22 words are put in
   b. 9 words are removed
   c. 40 words are put in
   d. 17 words are removed
   e. 12 words are put in
   f. 45 words are removed
   g. 8 words are put in
   h. 11 words are removed

29. Suppose that a version of UNIX uses 2-KB disk blocks and stores 512 disk addresses per indirect block (single, double, and triple). What would the maximum file size be? (Assume that file pointers are 64 bits wide).

30. Suppose that the UNIX system call

unlink("/usr/ast/bin/game3")

were executed in the context of Figure 6-36. Describe carefully what changes are made in the directory system.

31. Imagine that you had to implement the UNIX system on a microcomputer where main memory was in short supply. After a considerable amount of shoehorning, it still did not quite fit, so you picked a system call at random to sacrifice for the general good. You picked pipe, which creates the pipes used to send byte streams from one process to another. Is it still possible to implement I/O redirection somehow? What about pipelines? Discuss the problems and possible solutions.

32. The Committee for Fairness to File Descriptors is organizing a protest against the UNIX system because whenever the latter returns a file descriptor, it always returns the lowest number not currently in use. Consequently, higher-numbered file descriptors are hardly ever used. Their plan is to return the lowest number not yet used by the program rather than the lowest number currently not in use. They claim that it is trivial to implement, will not affect existing programs, and is fairer. What do you think?

33. In XP it is possible to set up an access control list in such a way that Roberta has no access at all to a file, but everyone else has full access to it. How do you think this is implemented?

34. Describe two different ways to program producer-consumer problems using shared buffers and semaphores in XP. Think about how to implement the shared buffer in each case.

35. It is common to test out page replacement algorithms by simulation. For this exercise, you are to write a simulator for a page-based virtual memory for a machine with 64 1-KB pages. The simulator should maintain a single table of 64 entries, one per page, containing the physical page number corresponding to that virtual page. The simulator should read in a file containing virtual addresses in decimal, one address per line. If the corresponding page is memory, just record a page hit. If it is not in memory, call a page replacement procedure to pick a page to evict (i.e., an entry in the table to overwrite) and record a page miss. No page transport actually occurs. Generate a file consisting of random addresses and test the performance for both LRU and FIFO. Now generate an address file in which x percent of the addresses are four bytes higher than the previous one (to simulate locality). Run tests for various values of x and report on your results.

36. The program of Fig. 6-25 has a fatal race condition because two threads access shared variables in an uncontrolled way, without using semaphores or any other mutual exclusion technique. Run this program and see how long it takes to hang. If you cannot make it hang, modify it to increase the size of the window of vulnerability by putting some computing between adjusting *m.in* and *m.out* and testing them. How much computing do you have to put in before it fails, say, once an hour?

37. Write a program for UNIX or XP that takes as input the name of a directory. The program should print a list of the files in the directory, one line per file, and after the file name, print the size of the file. Print the file names in the order they occur in the directory. Unused slots in the directory should be listed as (unused).

7

THE ASSEMBLY LANGUAGE LEVEL

In Chapters 4, 5, and 6 we discussed three different levels present on most contemporary computers. This chapter is concerned primarily with another level that is also present on essentially all modern computers: the assembly language level. The assembly language level differs in a significant respect from the microarchitecture, ISA, and operating system machine levels—it is implemented by translation rather than by interpretation.

Programs that convert a user's program written in some language to another language are called **translators**. The language in which the original program is written is called the **source language** and the language to which it is converted is called the **target language**. Both the source language and the target language define levels. If a processor that can directly execute programs written in the source language is available, there is no need to translate the source program into the target language.

Translation is used when a processor (either hardware or an interpreter) is available for the target language but not for the source language. If the translation has been performed correctly, running the translated program will give precisely the same results as the execution of the source program would have given had a processor for it been available. Consequently, it is possible to implement a new level for which there is no processor by first translating programs written for that level to a target level and then executing the resulting target-level programs.

It is important to note the difference between translation, on the one hand, and interpretation, on the other hand. In translation, the original program in the source language is not directly executed. Instead, it is converted to an equivalent program called an **object program** or **executable binary program** whose execution is carried out only after the translation has been completed. In translation, there are two distinct steps:

1. Generation of an equivalent program in the target language.

2. Execution of the newly generated program.

These two steps do not occur simultaneously. The second step does not begin until the first has been completed. In interpretation, there is only one step: executing the original source program. No equivalent program need be generated first, although sometimes the source program is converted to an intermediate form (e.g., Java byte code) for easier interpretation.

While the object program is being executed, only three levels are in evidence: the microarchitecture level, the ISA level, and the operating system machine level. Consequently, three programs—the user's object program, the operating system, and the microprogram (if any)—can be found in the computer's memory at run time. All traces of the original source program have vanished. Thus the number of levels present at execution time may differ from the number of levels present before translation. It should be noted, however, that although we define a level by the instructions and linguistic constructs available to its programmers (and not by the implementation technique), other authors sometimes make a greater distinction between levels implemented by execution-time interpreters and levels implemented by translation.

7.1 INTRODUCTION TO ASSEMBLY LANGUAGE

Translators can be roughly divided into two groups, depending on the relation between the source language and the target language. When the source language is essentially a symbolic representation for a numerical machine language, the translator is called an **assembler** and the source language is called an **assembly language**. When the source language is a high-level language such as Java or C and the target language is either a numerical machine language or a symbolic representation for one, the translator is called a **compiler**.

7.1.1 What Is an Assembly Language?

A pure assembly language is a language in which each statement produces exactly one machine instruction. In other words, there is a one-to-one correspondence between machine instructions and statements in the assembly program. If each line in the assembly language program contains exactly one statement and each machine word contains exactly one machine instruction, then an n-line assembly program will produce an n-word machine language program.

The reason that people use assembly language, as opposed to programming in machine language (in hexadecimal), is that it is much easier to program in assembly language. The use of symbolic names and symbolic addresses instead of binary or octal ones makes an enormous difference. Most people can remember that the abbreviations for add, subtract, multiply, and divide are ADD, SUB, MUL, and DIV, but few can remember the corresponding numerical values the machine uses. The assembly language programmer need only remember the symbolic names because the assembler translates them to the machine instructions.

The same remarks apply to addresses. The assembly language programmer can give symbolic names to memory locations and have the assembler worry about supplying the correct numerical values. The machine language programmer must always work with the numerical values of the addresses. As a consequence, no one programs in machine language today, although people did so decades ago, before assemblers had been invented.

Assembly languages have another property, besides the one-to-one mapping of assembly language statements onto machine instructions, that distinguishes them from high-level languages. The assembly programmer has access to all the features and instructions available on the target machine. The high-level language programmer does not. For example, if the target machine has an overflow bit, an assembly language program can test it, but a Java program cannot directly test it. Such a program can execute every instruction in the instruction set of the target machine, but the high-level language program cannot. In short, everything that can be done in machine language can be done in assembly language, but many instructions, registers, and similar features are not available for the high-level language programmer to use. Languages for system programming, like C, are often a cross between these types, with the syntax of a high-level language but with much of the access to the machine of an assembly language.

One final difference that is worth making explicit is that an assembly language program can run only on one family of machines, whereas a program written in a high-level language can potentially run on many machines. For many applications, this ability to move software from one machine to another is of great practical importance.

7.1.2 Why Use Assembly Language?

Assembly language programming is difficult. Make no mistake about that. It is not for wimps and weaklings. Furthermore, writing a program in assembly language takes much longer than writing the same program in a high-level language. It also takes much longer to debug and is much harder to maintain.

Under these conditions, why would anyone ever program in assembly language? There are two reasons: performance and access to the machine. First of all, an expert assembly language programmer can often produce code that is much smaller and much faster than a high-level language programmer can. For some applications, speed and size are critical. Many embedded applications, such as the code on a smart card, the code in a cellular telephone, device drivers, BIOS routines, and the inner loops of performance-critical applications fall in this category.

Second, some procedures need complete access to the hardware, something usually impossible in high-level languages. For example, the low-level interrupt and trap handlers in an operating system, and the device controllers in many embedded real-time systems fall into this category.

The first reason for programming in assembly language (to get high performance) is usually the most important one, so let us look at that more closely. In most programs, a small percentage of the total code is responsible for a large percentage of the execution time. It is common to have 1% of the program be responsible for 50% of the execution time and 10% of the program be responsible for 90% of the execution time.

Assume, for example, that it requires 10 programmer-years to write some program in a high-level language and that the resulting program requires 100 sec to execute a certain typical benchmark. (A **benchmark** is a test program used to compare computers, compilers, etc.) Writing the whole program in assembly language might require 50 programmer-years, due to the lower productivity of assembler language programmers. The final program might run the benchmark in about 33 sec, because a clever programmer can outdo a clever compiler by a factor of 3 (although you can get endless arguments about these ratios). This situation is illustrated in Fig. 7-1.

Based on the above observation that only a tiny fraction of the code is responsible for most of the execution time, another approach is possible. The program is first written in a high-level language. Then a series of measurements is performed to determine which parts of the program account for most of the execution time. Such measurements would normally include using the system clock to compute the amount of time spent in each procedure, keeping track of the number of times each loop is executed, and similar steps.

As an example, let us assume that 10% of the total program accounts for 90% of the execution time. This means that for a 100-sec job, 90 sec is spent in this critical 10% and 10 sec is spent in the remaining 90% of the program. The critical 10% can now be improved by rewriting it in assembly language. This process is called **tuning** and is illustrated in Fig. 7-1. Here an additional five programmer-years are needed to rewrite the critical procedures but their execution time is reduced from 90 sec to 30 sec.

It is instructive to compare the mixed high-level language/assembly language approach with the pure assembly language version (see Fig. 7-1). The latter is about 20% faster (33 sec versus 40 sec) but at more than triple the price (50 programmer-years versus 15 programmer years). Furthermore, the advantage of

	Programmer-years to produce the program	Program execution time in seconds
Assembly language	50	33
High-level language	10	100
Mixed approach before tuning		
Critical 10%	1	90
Other 90%	9	10
Total	10	100
Mixed approach after tuning		
Critical 10%	6	30
Other 90%	9	10
Total	15	40

Figure 7-1. Comparison of assembly language and high-level language programming, with and without tuning.

the mixed approach is really more than indicated, because recoding an already debugged high-level language procedure in assembly code is, in fact, much easier than writing the same assembly code procedure from scratch. In other words, the estimate of 5 programmer-years to rewrite the critical procedures is exceedingly conservative. If this recoding actually took only 1 programmer-year, the cost ratio between the mixed approach and the pure assembly language approach would be more than 4 to 1 in favor of the mixed approach.

A programmer who uses a high-level language is not immersed in moving bits around and sometimes obtains insights into the problem that allow *real* improvements in performance. This situation rarely occurs with assembly language programmers, who are usually trying to juggle instructions to save a few cycles.

All in all, there are still at least four good reasons for studying assembly language. First, because the success or failure of a large project may depend on being able to squeeze a factor of 2 or 3 improvement in performance out of some critical procedure, it is important to be able to write good assembly language code when it is really necessary.

Second, assembly code is sometimes the only alternative due to lack of memory. Smart cards contain a CPU, but few have a megabyte of memory, and fewer yet have a hard disk for paging. Yet they must perform complex cryptographic calculations with limited resources. Processors embedded in appliances often have minimal memory for reasons of cost. Personal digital assistants and other battery-powered wireless electronic devices often have small memories to conserve battery power, so small, efficient code is a necessity here, too.

Third, a compiler must either produce output used by an assembler or perform the assembly process itself. Thus understanding assembly language is essential to understanding how compilers work. And someone has to write the compiler (and its assembler) after all.

Finally, studying assembly language exposes the real machine to view. For students of computer architecture, writing some assembly code is the only way to get a feel for what machines are really like at the architectural level.

7.1.3 Format of an Assembly Language Statement

Although the structure of an assembly language statement closely mirrors the structure of the machine instruction that it represents, assembly languages for different machines and different levels have sufficient resemblance to one another to allow a discussion of assembly language in general. Figure 7-2 shows fragments of assembly language programs for the Pentium 4, Motorola 680x0, and the (Ultra)SPARC which perform the computation $N = I + J$. In all three examples, the statements above the blank line perform the computation. The statements below the blank line are commands to the assembler to reserve memory for the variables I, J, and N and are not symbolic representations of machine instructions.

Several assemblers exist for the Intel family, each with a different syntax. In this chapter we will use the Microsoft MASM assembly language for our examples. Although we are focusing on the Pentium 4, all of what we have to say about it applies equally well to the 386, 486, Pentium, and Pentium Pro. For the SPARC, we are basing our examples on the Sun assembler. Here, too, everything we say applies to the earlier (32-bit) versions of the SPARC as well. For the sake of uniformity, we will use uppercase for opcodes and registers throughout (Pentium 4 convention) even though the Sun assembler expects lowercase.

Assembly language statements have four parts: a label field, an operation (opcode) field, an operands field, and a comments field. Labels, which are used to provide symbolic names for memory addresses, are needed on executable statements so that the statements can be branched to. They are also needed for data words to permit the data stored there to be accessible by symbolic name. If a statement is labeled, the label (usually) begins in column 1.

Each of the three parts of Fig. 7-2 has four labels: *FORMULA*, *I*, *J*, and *N*. Notice that the SPARC assembly languages requires a colon after each label, but the Motorola one does not. The Intel one requires colons on code labels but not on data labels. There is nothing fundamental about this difference. The designers of different assemblers often have different tastes. Nothing in the underlying architecture suggests one choice or the other. One advantage of the colon notation is that with it a label can appear by itself on a line, with the opcode in column 1 of the next line. This style is sometimes convenient for compilers. Without the colon, there would be no way to tell a label on a line all by itself from an opcode on a line all by itself. The colon eliminates this potential ambiguity.

Label	Opcode	Operands	Comments
FORMULA:	MOV	EAX,I	; register EAX = I
	ADD	EAX,J	; register EAX = I + J
	MOV	N,EAX	; N = I + J
I	DD	3	; reserve 4 bytes initialized to 3
J	DD	4	; reserve 4 bytes initialized to 4
N	DD	0	; reserve 4 bytes initialized to 0

(a)

Label	Opcode	Operands	Comments
FORMULA	MOVE.L	I, D0	; register D0 = I
	ADD.L	J, D0	; register D0 = I + J
	MOVE.L	D0, N	; N = I + J
I	DC.L	3	; reserve 4 bytes initialized to 3
J	DC.L	4	; reserve 4 bytes initialized to 4
N	DC.L	0	; reserve 4 bytes initialized to 0

(b)

Label	Opcode	Operands	Comments
FORMULA:	SETHI	%HI(I),%R1	! R1 = high-order bits of the address of I
	LD	[%R1+%LO(I)],%R1	! R1 = I
	SETHI	%HI(J),%R2	! R2 = high-order bits of the address of J
	LD	[%R2+%LO(J)],%R2	! R2 = J
	NOP		! wait for J to arrive from memory
	ADD	%R1,%R2,%R2	! R2 = R1 + R2
	SETHI	%HI(N),%R1	! R1 = high-order bits of the address of N
	ST	%R2,[%R1+%LO(N)]	
I:	.WORD 3		! reserve 4 bytes initialized to 3
J:	.WORD 4		! reserve 4 bytes initialized to 4
N:	.WORD 0		! reserve 4 bytes initialized to 0

(c)

Figure 7-2. Computation of $N = I + J$. (a) Pentium 4. (b) Motorola 680x0. (c) SPARC.

It is an unfortunate characteristic of some assemblers that labels are restricted to six or eight characters. In contrast, most high-level languages allow the use of arbitrarily long names. Long, well-chosen names make programs much more readable and understandable by other people.

Each of the machines has some registers, but they have been given very different names. The Pentium 4 registers have names like EAX, EBX, ECX, and so on.

The Motorola registers are called D0, D1, D2, among others. The SPARC registers have multiple names. Here we have used %R1 and %R2 for them.

The opcode field contains either a symbolic abbreviation for the opcode—if the statement is a symbolic representation for a machine instruction—or a command to the assembler itself. The choice of an appropriate name is just a matter of taste, and different assembly language designers often make different choices. The designers of the Intel assembler decided to use MOV for both loading a register from memory and storing a register into memory. The designers of the Motorola assembler chose MOVE for both of them. In contrast, the designers of the SPARC assembler decided to use LD for the former and ST for the latter. Here, too, these choices have nothing to do with the underlying machine.

In contrast, the need to use two machine instructions, starting with SETHI, to access memory, is an inherent property of the SPARC architecture because virtual addresses are 32 bits (SPARC Version 8) or 44 (SPARC Version 9) bits and instructions can hold at most 22 bits of immediate data. Thus it always takes two instructions to provide all the bits of a full virtual address. What

    SETHI %HI(I),%R1

does is zero the upper 32 bits and lower 10 bits of (the 64-bit) register R1, then put the upper 22 bits of the 32-bit address of I in bit positions 10 through 31 of R1. The next instruction,

    LD [%R1+%LO(I)],%R1

adds R1 and the low-order 10 bits of the address of I to form the full address of I, fetch that word from memory, and put it in R1. In a beauty contest using a scale of 1 to 10, these instructions would score about −20, but the SPARC was not designed for the beauty of its assembly language. It was designed for high-speed execution, and it achieves that goal well.

The Pentium family, 680x0, and SPARC all allow byte, word, and long operands. How does the assembler know which length to use? Again, the assembler designers chose different solutions. On the Pentium 4, different length registers have different names, so EAX is used to move 32-bit items, AX is used to move 16-bit items, and AL and AH are used to move 8-bit items. The Motorola assembler designers, in contrast decided to add a suffix .L for long, .W for word, or .B for byte to each opcode rather than giving subsets of D0, etc., different names. The SPARC uses different opcodes for the different lengths (e.g., LDSB, LDSH, and LDSW to load signed bytes, halfwords, and words into a 64-bit register, respectively). All three ways are valid, but again they point out the arbitrary nature of language design.

The three assemblers also differ in how they reserve space for data. The Intel assembly language designers chose DD (Define Double), since a word on the 8088 was 16 bits. The Motorola ones liked DC (Define Constant). The SPARC folks preferred .WORD from the beginning. Once again, the differences are arbitrary.

The operands field of an assembly language statement is used to specify the addresses and registers used as operands by the machine instruction. The operands field of an integer addition instruction tells what is to be added to what. The operands field of a branch instruction tells where to branch to. Operands can be registers, constants, memory locations, and so on.

The comments field provides a place for programmers to put helpful explanations of how the program works for the benefit of other programmers who may subsequently use or modify the program (or for the benefit of the original programmer a year later). An assembly language program without such documentation is nearly incomprehensible to all programmers, frequently including the author as well. The comments field is solely for human consumption; it has no effect on the assembly process or on the generated program.

7.1.4 Pseudoinstructions

In addition to specifying which machine instructions to execute, an assembly language program can also contain commands to the assembler itself, for example, asking it to allocate some storage or to eject to a new page on the listing. Commands to the assembler itself are called **pseudoinstructions** or sometimes **assembler directives**. We have already seen a typical pseudoinstruction in Fig. 7-2(a): DW. Some other pseudoinstructions are listed in Fig. 7-3. These are taken from the Microsoft MASM assembler for the Intel family.

The SEGMENT pseudoinstruction starts a new segment, and ENDS terminates one. It is allowed to start a text segment, with code, then start a data segment, then go back to the text segment, and so on.

ALIGN forces the next line, usually data, to an address that is a multiple of its argument. For example, if the current segment has 61 bytes of data already, then after ALIGN 4 the next address allocated will be 64.

EQU is used to give a symbolic name to an expression. For example, after the pseudoinstruction

    BASE EQU 1000

the symbol BASE can be used everywhere instead of 1000. The expression that follows the EQU can involve multiple defined symbols combined with arithmetic and other operators, as in

    LIMIT EQU 4 * BASE + 2000

Most assemblers, including MASM, require that a symbol be defined before it is used in an expression like this.

The next four pseudoinstructions, DB, DW, DD, and DQ, allocate storage for one or more variables of size 1, 2, 4, or 8 bytes, respectively. For example,

    TABLE DB 11, 23, 49

Pseudoinstruction	Meaning
SEGMENT	Start a new segment (text, data, etc.) with certain attributes
ENDS	End the current segment
ALIGN	Control the alignment of the next instruction or data
EQU	Define a new symbol equal to a given expression
DB	Allocate storage for one or more (initialized) bytes
DW	Allocate storage for one or more (initialized) 16-bit (word) data items
DD	Allocate storage for one or more (initialized) 32-bit (double) data items
DQ	Allocate storage for one or more (initialized) 64-bit (quad) data items
PROC	Start a procedure
ENDP	End a procedure
MACRO	Start a macro definition
ENDM	End a macro definition
PUBLIC	Export a name defined in this module
EXTERN	Import a name from another module
INCLUDE	Fetch and include another file
IF	Start conditional assembly based on a given expression
ELSE	Start conditional assembly if the IF condition above was false
ENDIF	End conditional assembly
COMMENT	Define a new start-of-comment character
PAGE	Generate a page break in the listing
END	Terminate the assembly program

Figure 7-3. Some of the pseudoinstructions available in the Pentium 4 assembler (MASM).

allocates space for 3 bytes and initializes them to 11, 23, and 49, respectively. It also defines the symbol *TABLE* and sets it equal to the address where 11 is stored.

The PROC and ENDP pseudoinstructions define the start and end of assembly language procedures, respectively. Procedures in assembly language have the same function as procedures in other programming languages. Similarly, MACRO and ENDM delimit the scope of a macro definition. We will study macros later in this chapter.

The next two pseudoinstructions, PUBLIC and EXTERN, control the visibility of symbols. It is common to write programs as a collection of files. Frequently, a procedure in one file needs to call a procedure or access a data word defined in another file. To make this cross-file referencing possible, a symbol that is to be made available to other files is exported using PUBLIC. Similarly, to prevent the assembler from complaining about the use of a symbol that is not defined in the current file, the symbol can be declared as EXTERN, which tells the assembler that it will be defined in some other file. Symbols that are not declared in either of these pseudoinstructions have a scope of the local file. This default means that using, say, *FOO* in multiple files does not generate a conflict because each definition is local to its own file.

The INCLUDE pseudoinstruction causes the assembler to fetch another file and include it bodily into the current one. Such included files often contain definitions, macros, and other items needed in multiple files.

Many assemblers, including MASM, support conditional assembly. For example,

```
WORDSIZE EQU 16
IF WORDSIZE GT 16
WSIZE:   DD  32
ELSE
WSIZE:   DD  16
ENDIF
```

allocates a single 32-bit word and calls its address *WSIZE*. The word is initialized to either 32 or 16, depending on the value of *WORDSIZE*, in this case, 16. Typically this construction would be used to write a program that could be assembled on either 16-bit machines (like the 8088) or 32-bit machines (like the Pentium 4). By bracketing all the machine-dependent code within IF and ENDIF, then by changing a single definition, *WORDSIZE*, the program can automatically be set to assemble for either size. Using this approach, it is possible to maintain one source program for multiple (different) target machines, which makes software development and maintenance easier. In many cases, all the machine-dependent definitions, like *WORDSIZE*, are collected into a single file, with different versions for different machines. By including the right definitions file, the program can be easily recompiled for different machines.

The COMMENT pseudoinstruction allows the user to change the comment delimiter to something other than semicolon. PAGE is used to control the listing the assembler can produce, if requested. Finally, END marks the end of the program.

Many other pseudoinstructions exist in MASM. Other Pentium 4 assemblers have a different collection of pseudoinstructions available because they are dictated not by the underlying architecture, but by the taste of the assembler writer.

7.2 MACROS

Assembly language programmers frequently need to repeat sequences of instructions several times within a program. The most obvious way to do so is simply to write the required instructions wherever they are needed. If a sequence is long, however, or must be used a large number of times, writing it repeatedly becomes tedious.

An alternative approach is to make the sequence into a procedure and call it wherever it is needed. This strategy has the disadvantage of requiring a procedure call instruction and a return instruction to be executed every time a sequence is needed. If the sequences are short—for example, two instructions—but are used frequently, the procedure call overhead may significantly slow the program down. Macros provide an easy and efficient solution to the problem of repeatedly needing the same or nearly the same sequences of instructions.

7.2.1 Macro Definition, Call, and Expansion

A **macro definition** is a way to give a name to a piece of text. After a macro has been defined, the programmer can write the macro name instead of the piece of program. A macro is, in effect, an abbreviation for a piece of text. Figure 7-4(a) shows an assembly language program for the Pentium 4 that exchanges the contents of the variables *p* and *q* twice. These sequences could be defined as macros, as shown in Fig. 7-4(b). After its definition, every occurrence of *SWAP* causes it to be replaced by the four lines:

```
MOV EAX,P
MOV EBX,Q
MOV Q,EAX
MOV P,EBX
```

The programmer has defined *SWAP* as an abbreviation for the four statements shown above.

MOV	EAX,P	SWAP	MACRO
MOV	EBX,Q		MOV EAX,P
MOV	Q,EAX		MOV EBX,Q
MOV	P,EBX		MOV Q,EAX
			MOV P,EBX
MOV	EAX,P		ENDM
MOV	EBX,Q		
MOV	Q,EAX		SWAP
MOV	P,EBX		
			SWAP

(a)	(b)

Figure 7-4. Assembly language code for interchanging P and Q twice. (a) Without a macro. (b) With a macro.

Although different assemblers have slightly different notations for defining macros, all require the same basic parts in a macro definition:

1. A macro header giving the name of the macro being defined.

2. The text comprising the body of the macro.

3. A pseudoinstruction marking the end of the definition (e.g., ENDM).

When the assembler encounters a macro definition, it saves it in a macro definition table for subsequent use. From that point on, whenever the name of the macro (*SWAP* in the example of Fig. 7-4) appears as an opcode, the assembler replaces it by the macro body. The use of a macro name as an opcode is known as a **macro call** and its replacement by the macro body is called **macro expansion**.

Macro expansion occurs during the assembly process and not during execution of the program. This point is important. The program of Fig. 7-4(a) and that of Fig. 7-4(b) will produce precisely the same machine language code. Looking only at the machine language program, it is impossible to tell whether or not any macros were involved in its generation. The reason is that once macro expansion has been completed the macro definitions are discarded by the assembler. No trace of them is left in the generated program.

Macro calls should not be confused with procedure calls. The basic difference is that a macro call is an instruction to the assembler to replace the macro name with the macro body. A procedure call is a machine instruction that is inserted into the object program and that will later be executed to call the procedure. Figure 7-5 compares macro calls with procedure calls.

Item	Macro call	Procedure call
When is the call made?	During assembly	During program execution
Is the body inserted into the object program every place the call is made?	Yes	No
Is a procedure call instruction inserted into the object program and later executed?	No	Yes
Must a return instruction be used after the call is done?	No	Yes
How many copies of the body appear in the object program?	One per macro call	One

Figure 7-5. Comparison of macro calls with procedure calls.

Conceptually, it is best to think of the assembly process as taking place in two passes. On pass one, all the macro definitions are saved and the macro calls expanded. On pass two, the resulting text is processed as though it was in the original program. In this view, the source program is read in and is then transformed into another program from which all macro definitions have been removed, and in which all macro calls have been replaced by their bodies. The resulting output, an assembly language program containing no macros at all, is then fed into the assembler.

It is important to keep in mind that a program is a string of characters including letters, digits, spaces, punctuation marks, and "carriage returns" (change to a new line). Macro expansion consists of replacing certain substrings of this string with other character strings. A macro facility is a technique for manipulating character strings, without regard to their meaning.

7.2.2 Macros with Parameters

The macro facility previously described can be used to shorten programs in which precisely the same sequence of instructions occurs repeatedly. Frequently, however, a program contains several sequences of instructions that are almost but not quite identical, as illustrated in Fig. 7-6(a). Here the first sequence exchanges P and Q, and the second sequence exchanges R and S.

```
        MOV     EAX,P              CHANGE   MACRO P1, P2
        MOV     EBX,Q                       MOV EAX,P1
        MOV     Q,EAX                       MOV EBX,P2
        MOV     P,EBX                       MOV P2,EAX
                                            MOV P1,EBX
        MOV     EAX,R                       ENDM
        MOV     EBX,S
        MOV     S,EAX              CHANGE P, Q
        MOV     R,EBX

                                   CHANGE R, S

              (a)                            (b)
```

Figure 7-6. Nearly identical sequences of statements. (a) Without a macro. (b) With a macro.

Macro assemblers handle the case of nearly identical sequences by allowing macro definitions to provide **formal parameters** and by allowing macro calls to supply **actual parameters**. When a macro is expanded, each formal parameter appearing in the macro body is replaced by the corresponding actual parameter. The actual parameters are placed in the operand field of the macro call. Figure 7-6(b) shows the program of Fig. 7-6(a) rewritten using a macro with two parameters. The symbols P1 and P2 are the formal parameters. Each occurrence of P1 within a macro body is replaced by the first actual parameter when the macro is expanded. Similarly, P2 is replaced by the second actual parameter. In the macro call

    CHANGE P, Q

P is the first actual parameter and Q is the second actual parameter. Thus the executable programs produced by both parts of Fig. 7-6 are identical. They contain precisely the same instructions with the same operands.

7.2.3 Advanced Features

Most macro processors have a whole raft of advanced features to make life easier for the assembly language programmer. In this section we will take a look at a few of MASM's advanced features. One problem that occurs with all assemblers that support macros is label duplication. Suppose that a macro contains a conditional branch instruction and a label that is branched to. If the macro is called two or more times, the label will be duplicated, causing an assembly error. One solution is to have the programmer supply a different label on each call as a parameter. A different solution (used by MASM) is to allow a label to be declared LOCAL, with the assembler automatically generating a different label on each expansion of the macro. Some other assemblers have a rule that numeric labels are automatically local.

MASM and most other assemblers allow macros to be defined within other macros. This feature is most useful in combination with conditional assembly. Typically, the same macro is defined in both parts of an IF statement, like this:

```
M1    MACRO
          IF WORDSIZE GT 16
M2        MACRO
              ...
          ENDM
      ELSE
M2        MACRO
      ...
          ENDM
      ENDIF
      ENDM
```

Either way, the macro *M2* will be defined, but the definition will depend on whether the program is being assembled on a 16-bit machine or a 32-bit machine. If *M1* is not called, *M2* will not be defined at all.

Finally, macros can call other macros, including themselves. If a macro is recursive, that is, it calls itself, it must pass itself a parameter that is changed on each expansion and the macro must test the parameter and terminate the recursion when it reaches a certain value. Otherwise the assembler can be put into an infinite loop. If this happens, the assembler must be killed explicitly by the user.

7.2.4 Implementation of a Macro Facility in an Assembler

To implement a macro facility, an assembler must be able to perform two functions: save macro definitions and expand macro calls. We will examine these functions in turn.

The assembler must maintain a table of all macro names and, along with each name, a pointer to its stored definition so that it can be retrieved when needed.

Some assemblers have a separate table for macro names and some have a combined opcode table in which all machine instructions, pseudoinstructions, and macro names are kept.

When a macro definition is encountered, a table entry is made giving the name of the macro, the number of formal parameters, and a pointer to another table—the macro definition table—where the macro body will be kept. A list of the formal parameters is also constructed at this time for use in processing the definition. The macro body is then read and stored in the macro definition table. Formal parameters occurring within the body are indicated by some special symbol. As an example, the internal representation of the macro definition of *CHANGE* with semicolon as "carriage return" and ampersand as the formal parameter symbol is shown below:

        MOV EAX,&P1; MOV EBX,&P2; MOV &P2,EAX; MOV &P1,EBX;

Within the macro definition table the macro body is simply a character string.

During pass one of the assembly, opcodes are looked up and macros expanded. Whenever a macro definition is encountered, it is stored in the macro table. When a macro is called, the assembler temporarily stops reading input from the input device and starts reading from the stored macro body instead. Formal parameters extracted from the stored macro body are replaced by the actual parameters provided in the call. The presence of an ampersand in front of the formal parameters makes it easy for the assembler to recognize them.

7.3 THE ASSEMBLY PROCESS

In the following sections we will briefly describe how an assembler works. Although each machine has a different assembly language, the assembly process is sufficiently similar on different machines that it is possible to describe it in general terms.

7.3.1 Two-Pass Assemblers

Because an assembly language program consists of a series of one-line statements, it might at first seem natural to have an assembler that read one statement, then translated it to machine language, and finally output the generated machine language onto a file, along with the corresponding piece of the listing, if any, onto another file. This process would then be repeated until the whole program had been translated. Unfortunately, this strategy does not work.

Consider the situation where the first statement is a branch to *L*. The assembler cannot assemble this statement until it knows the address of statement *L*. Statement *L* may be near the end of the program, making it impossible for the assembler to find the address without first reading almost the entire program.

This difficulty is called the **forward reference problem**, because a symbol, *L*, has been used before it has been defined; that is, a reference has been made to a symbol whose definition will only occur later.

Forward references can be handled in two ways. First, the assembler may in fact read the source program twice. Each reading of the source program is called a **pass**; any translator that reads the input program twice is called a **two-pass translator**. On pass one of a two-pass assembler, the definitions of symbols, including statement labels, are collected and stored in a table. By the time the second pass begins, the values of all symbols are known; thus no forward reference remains and each statement can be read, assembled, and output. Although this approach requires an extra pass over the input, it is conceptually simple.

The second approach consists of reading the assembly program once, converting it to an intermediate form, and storing this intermediate form in a table in memory. Then a second pass is made over the table instead of over the source program. If there is enough memory (or virtual memory), this approach saves I/O time. If a listing is to be produced, then the entire source statement, including all the comments, has to be saved. If no listing is needed, then the intermediate form can be reduced to the bare essentials.

Either way, another task of pass one is to save all macro definitions and expand the calls as they are encountered. Thus defining the symbols and expanding the macros are generally combined into one pass.

7.3.2 Pass One

The principal function of pass one is to build up a table called the **symbol table**, containing the values of all symbols. A symbol is either a label or a value that is assigned a symbolic name by means of a pseudoinstruction such as

BUFSIZE EQU 8192

In assigning a value to a symbol in the label field of an instruction, the assembler must know what address that instruction will have during execution of the program. To keep track of the execution-time address of the instruction being assembled, the assembler maintains a variable during assembly, known as the **ILC** (**Instruction Location Counter**). This variable is set to 0 at the beginning of pass one and incremented by the instruction length for each instruction processed, as shown in Fig. 7-7. This example is for the Pentium 4. We will not give SPARC (or Motorola) examples henceforth since the differences between the assembly languages are not very important, and one example should be enough. Besides, if there a contest for the world's least readable assembly language, the SPARC's would be a real contender.

Pass one of most assemblers uses at least three internal tables: the symbol table, the pseudoinstruction table, and the opcode table. If needed, a literal table is also kept. The symbol table has one entry for each symbol, as illustrated in

Label	Opcode	Operands	Comments	Length	ILC
MARIA:	MOV	EAX, I	EAX = I	5	100
	MOV	EBX, J	EBX = J	6	105
ROBERTA:	MOV	ECX, K	ECX = K	6	111
	IMUL	EAX, EAX	EAX = I * I	2	117
	IMUL	EBX, EBX	EBX = J * J	3	119
	IMUL	ECX, ECX	ECX = K * K	3	122
MARILYN:	ADD	EAX, EBX	EAX = I * I + J * J	2	125
	ADD	EAX, ECX	EAX = I * I + J * J + K * K	2	127
STEPHANY:	JMP	DONE	branch to DONE	5	129

Figure 7-7. The instruction location counter (ILC) keeps track of the address where the instructions will be loaded in memory. In this example, the statements prior to MARIA occupy 100 bytes.

Fig. 7-8. Symbols are defined either by using them as labels or by explicit definition (e.g., EQU). Each symbol table entry contains the symbol itself (or a pointer to it), its numerical value, and sometimes other information. This additional information may include

1. The length of data field associated with symbol.

2. The relocation bits. (Does the symbol change value if the program is loaded at a different address than the assembler assumed?)

3. Whether or not the symbol is to be accessible outside the procedure.

Symbol	Value	Other information
MARIA	100	
ROBERTA	111	
MARILYN	125	
STEPHANY	129	

Figure 7-8. A symbol table for the program of Fig. 7-7.

The opcode table contains at least one entry for each symbolic opcode (mnemonic) in the assembly language. Figure 7-9 shows part of an opcode table. Each entry contains the symbolic opcode, two operands, the opcode's numerical value, the instruction length, and a type number that separates the opcodes into groups depending on the number and kind of operands.

As an example, consider the opcode ADD. If an ADD instruction contains EAX as the first operand and a 32-bit constant (immed32) as the second one, then opcode 0x05 is used and the instruction length is 5 bytes. (Constants that can be expressed in 8 or 16 bits use different opcodes, not shown.) If ADD is used with two registers as operands, the instruction is 2 bytes, with opcode 0x01. The

Opcode	First operand	Second operand	Hexadecimal opcode	Instruction length	Instruction class
AAA	—	—	37	1	6
ADD	EAX	immed32	05	5	4
ADD	reg	reg	01	2	19
AND	EAX	immed32	25	5	4
AND	reg	reg	21	2	19

Figure 7-9. A few excerpts from the opcode table for a Pentium 4 assembler.

(arbitrary) instruction class 19 would be given to all opcode-operand combinations that follow the same rules and should be processed the same way as ADD with two register operands. The instruction class effectively designates a procedure within the assembler that is called to process all instructions of a given type.

Some assemblers allow programmers to write instructions using immediate addressing even though no corresponding target language instruction exists. Such "pseudoimmediate" instructions are handled as follows. The assembler allocates memory for the immediate operand at the end of the program and generates an instruction that references it. For instance, the IBM 3090 mainframe has no immediate instructions. Nevertheless, programmers may write

    L 14,=F'5'

to load register 14 with a full word constant 5. In this way, the programmer avoids explicitly writing a pseudoinstruction to allocate a word initialized to 5, giving it a label, and then using that label in the L instruction. Constants for which the assembler automatically reserves memory are called **literals**. In addition to saving the programmer a little writing, literals improve the readability of a program by making the value of the constant apparent in the source statement. Pass one of the assembler must build a table of all literals used in the program. All three of our example computers have immediate instructions, so their assemblers do not provide literals. Immediate instructions are quite common nowadays, but formerly they were unusual. It is likely that the widespread use of literals made it clear to machine designers that immediate addressing was a good idea. If literals are needed, a literal table is maintained during assembly, with a new entry made each time a literal is encountered. After the first pass, this table is sorted and duplicates removed.

Figure 7-10 shows a procedure that could serve as a basis for pass one of an assembler. The style of programming is noteworthy in itself. The procedure names have been chosen to give a good indication of what the procedures do. Most important, Fig. 7-10 represents an outline of pass one which, although not complete, forms a good starting point. It is short enough to be easily understood and it makes clear what the next step must be—namely, to write the procedures used in it.

```
public static void pass_one( ) {
    // This procedure is an outline of pass one of a simple assembler.
    boolean more_input = true;              // flag that stops pass one
    String line, symbol, literal, opcode;   // fields of the instruction
    int location_counter, length, value, type;  // misc. variables
    final int END_STATEMENT = -2;           // signals end of input

    location_counter = 0;                   // assemble first instruction at 0
    initialize_tables( );                   // general initialization

    while (more_input) {                    // more_input set to false by END
        line = read_next_line( );           // get a line of input
        length = 0;                         // # bytes in the instruction
        type = 0;                           // which type (format) is the instruction

        if (line_is_not_comment(line)) {
            symbol = check_for_symbol(line);       // is this line labeled?
            if (symbol != null)                    // if it is, record symbol and value
                enter_new_symbol(symbol, location_counter);
            literal = check_for_literal(line);     // does line contain a literal?
            if (literal != null)                   // if it does, enter it in table
                enter_new_literal(literal);

            // Now determine the opcode type.  -1 means illegal opcode.
            opcode = extract_opcode(line);         // locate opcode mnemonic
            type = search_opcode_table(opcode);    // find format, e.g. OP REG1,REG2
            if (type < 0)                          // if not an opcode, is it a pseudoinstruction?
                type = search_pseudo_table(opcode);
            switch(type) {                         // determine the length of this instruction
                case 1: length = get_length_of_type1(line);  break;
                case 2: length = get_length_of_type2(line);  break;
                // other cases here
            }
        }
        write_temp_file(type, opcode, length, line);    // useful info for pass two
        location_counter = location_counter + length;   // update loc_ctr
        if (type == END_STATEMENT) {           // are we done with input?
            more_input = false;                // if so, perform housekeeping tasks
            rewind_temp_for_pass_two( );       // like rewinding the temp file
            sort_literal_table( );             // and sorting the literal table
            remove_redundant_literals( );      // and removing duplicates from it
        }
    }
}
```

Figure 7-10. Pass one of a simple assembler.

Some of these procedures will be relatively short, such as *check_for_symbol*, which just returns the symbol as a character string if there is one and null if there is not. Other procedures, such as *get_length_of_type1* and *get_length_of_type2*, may be longer and may call other procedures. In general, the number of types will not be two, of course, but will depend on the language being assembled and how many types of instructions it has.

Structuring programs in this way has other advantages in addition to ease of programming. If the assembler is being written by a group of people, the various procedures can be parceled out among the programmers. All the (nasty) details of getting the input are hidden away in *read_next_line*. If they should change—for example, due to an operating system change—only one subsidiary procedure is affected, and no changes are needed to the *pass_one* procedure itself.

As it reads the program, pass one has to parse each line to find the opcode (e.g., ADD), look up its type (basically, the pattern of operands), and compute the instruction's length. This information is also needed on the second pass, so it is possible to write it out explicitly to eliminate the need to parse the line from scratch next time. However, rewriting the input file causes more I/O to occur. Whether it is better to do more I/O to eliminate parsing or less I/O and more parsing depends on the relative speed of the CPU and disk, the efficiency of the file system, and other factors. In this example we will write out a temporary file containing the type, opcode, length, and actual input line. It is this line that pass two reads instead of the raw input file.

When the END pseudoinstruction is read, pass one is over. The symbol table and literal tables can be sorted at this point if needed. The sorted literal table can be checked for duplicate entries, which can be removed.

7.3.3 Pass Two

The function of pass two is to generate the object program and possibly print the assembly listing. In addition, pass two must output certain information needed by the linker for linking up procedures assembled at different times into a single executable file. Figure 7-11 shows a sketch of a procedure for pass two.

The operation of pass two is more-or-less similar to that of pass one: it reads the lines one at a time and processes them one at a time. Since we have written the type, opcode, and length at the start of each line (on the temporary file), all of these are read in to save some parsing. The main work of the code generation is done by the procedures *eval_type1*, *eval_type2*, and so on. Each one handles a particular pattern, such as an opcode and two register operands. It generates the binary code for the instruction and returns it in *code*. Then it is written out. More likely, *write_output* just buffers the accumulated binary code and writes the file to disk in large chunks to reduce disk traffic.

The original source statement and the object code generated from it (in hexadecimal) can then be printed or put into a buffer for later printing. After the ILC has been adjusted, the next statement is fetched.

```
public static void pass_two( ) {
  // This procedure is an outline of pass two of a simple assembler.
  boolean more_input = true;              // flag that stops pass two
  String line, opcode;                     // fields of the instruction
  int location_counter, length, type;      // misc. variables
  final int END_STATEMENT = -2;            // signals end of input
  final int MAX_CODE = 16;                 // max bytes of code per instruction
  byte code[] = new byte[MAX_CODE];        // holds generated code per instruction

  location_counter = 0;                    // assemble first instruction at 0

  while (more_input) {                     // more_input set to false by END
    type = read_type( );                   // get type field of next line
    opcode = read_opcode( );               // get opcode field of next line
    length = read_length( );               // get length field of next line
    line = read_line( );                   // get the actual line of input

    if (type != 0) {                       // type 0 is for comment lines
      switch(type) {                       // generate the output code
        case 1: eval_type1(opcode, length, line, code);  break;
        case 2: eval_type2(opcode, length, line, code);  break;
        // other cases here
      }
    }

    write_output(code);                    // write the binary code
    write_listing(code, line);             // print one line on the listing
    location_counter = location_counter + length;   // update loc_ctr
    if (type == END_STATEMENT) {           // are we done with input?
      more_input = false;                  // if so, perform housekeeping tasks
      finish_up( );                        // odds and ends
    }
  }
}
```

Figure 7-11. Pass two of a simple assembler.

Up until now it has been assumed that the source program does not contain any errors. Anyone who has ever written a program, in any language, knows how realistic that assumption is. Some of the common errors are as follows:

1. A symbol has been used but not defined.

2. A symbol has been defined more than once.

3. The name in the opcode field is not a legal opcode.

4. An opcode is not supplied with enough operands.

5. An opcode is supplied with too many operands.

6. An octal number contains an 8 or a 9.

7. Illegal register use (e.g., a branch to a register).

8. The END statement is missing.

Programmers are most ingenious at thinking up new kinds of errors to make. Undefined symbol errors are frequently caused by typing errors, so a clever assembler could try to figure out which of the defined symbols most resembles the undefined one and use that instead. Little can be done about correcting most other errors. The best thing for the assembler to do with an errant statement is to print an error message and try to continue assembly.

7.3.4 The Symbol Table

During pass one of the assembly process, the assembler accumulates information about symbols and their values that must be stored in the symbol table for lookup during pass two. Several different ways are available for organizing the symbol table. We will briefly describe some of them below. All of them attempt to simulate an **associative memory**, which conceptually is a set of (symbol, value) pairs. Given the symbol, the associative memory must produce the value.

The simplest implementation technique is indeed to implement the symbol table as an array of pairs, the first element of which is (or points to) the symbol and the second of which is (or points to) the value. Given a symbol to look up, the symbol table routine just searches the table linearly until it finds a match. This method is easy to program but is slow, because, on the average, half the table will have to be searched on each lookup.

Another way to organize the symbol table is to sort it on the symbols and use the **binary search** algorithm to look up a symbol. This algorithm works by comparing the middle entry in the table to the symbol. If the symbol comes before the middle entry alphabetically, the symbol must be located in the first half of the table. If the symbol comes after the middle entry, it must be in the second half of the table. If the symbol is equal to the middle entry, the search terminates.

Assuming that the middle entry is not equal to the symbol sought, we at least know which half of the table to look for it in. Binary search can now be applied to the correct half, which yields either a match, or the correct quarter of the table. Applying the algorithm recursively, a table of size n entries can be searched in about $\log_2 n$ attempts. Obviously, this way is much faster than searching linearly, but it requires maintaining the table in sorted order.

A completely different way of simulating an associative memory is a technique known as **hash coding** or **hashing**. This approach requires having a "hash" function that maps symbols onto integers in the range 0 to $k - 1$. One possible function is to multiply the ASCII codes of the characters in the symbols together, ignoring overflow, and taking the result modulo k or dividing it by a prime number. In fact, almost any function of the input that gives a uniform distribution of the hash values will do. Symbols can be stored by having a table consisting of k **buckets** numbered 0 to $k - 1$. All the (symbol, value) pairs whose symbol hashes to i are stored on a linked list pointed to by slot i in the hash table. With n symbols and k slots in the hash table, the average list will have length n/k.

By choosing k approximately equal to n, symbols can be located with only about one lookup on the average. By adjusting k we can reduce table size at the expense of slower lookups. Hash coding is illustrated in Fig. 7-12.

Andy	14025	0
Anton	31253	4
Cathy	65254	5
Dick	54185	0
Erik	47357	6
Frances	56445	3
Frank	14332	3
Gerrit	32334	4
Hans	44546	4
Henri	75544	2
Jan	17097	5
Jaco	64533	6
Maarten	23267	0
Reind	63453	1
Roel	76764	7
Willem	34544	6
Wiebren	34344	1

(a)

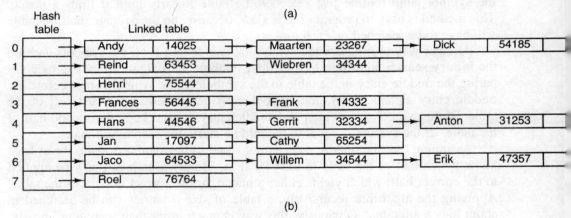

(b)

Figure 7-12. Hash coding. (a) Symbols, values, and the hash codes derived from the symbols. (b) Eight-entry hash table with linked lists of symbols and values.

7.4 LINKING AND LOADING

Most programs consist of more than one procedure. Compilers and assemblers generally translate one procedure at a time and put the translated output on disk. Before the program can be run, all the translated procedures must be found and linked together properly. If virtual memory is not available, the linked program must be explicitly loaded into main memory as well. Programs that perform these functions are called by various names, including **linker**, **linking loader**, and **linkage editor**. The complete translation of a source program requires two steps, as shown in Fig. 7-13:

1. Compilation or assembly of the source procedures.
2. Linking of the object modules.

The first step is performed by the compiler or assembler and the second one is performed by the linker.

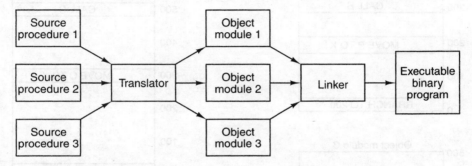

Figure 7-13. Generation of an executable binary program from a collection of independently translated source procedures requires using a linker.

The translation from source procedure to object module represents a change of level because the source language and target language have different instructions and notation. The linking process, however, does not represent a change of level, since both the linker's input and the linker's output are programs for the same virtual machine. The linker's function is to collect procedures translated separately and link them together to be run as a unit called an **executable binary program**. On MS-DOS, Windows 95/98, and NT the object modules have extension *.obj* and the executable binary programs have extension *.exe*. On UNIX, the object modules have extension *.o*; executable binary programs have no extension.

Compilers and assemblers translate each source procedure as a separate entity for a good reason. If a compiler or assembler were to read a series of source procedures and directly produce a ready-to-run machine language program, changing one statement in one source procedure would require that all the source procedures be retranslated.

If the separate-object-module technique of Fig. 7-13 is used, it is only necessary to retranslate the modified procedure and not the unchanged ones, although it is necessary to relink all the object modules again. Linking is usually much faster than translating, however; thus the two-step process of translating and linking can save a great deal of time during the development of a program. This gain is especially important for programs with hundreds or thousands of modules.

7.4.1 Tasks Performed by the Linker

At the start of pass one of the assembly process, the instruction location counter is set to 0. This step is equivalent to assuming that the object module will be located at (virtual) address 0 during execution. Figure 7-14 shows four object modules for a generic machine. In this example, each module begins with a BRANCH instruction to a MOVE instruction within the module.

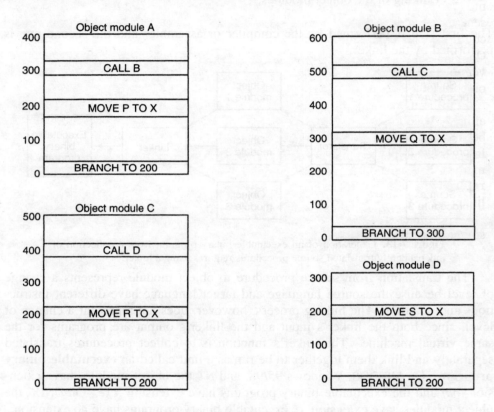

Figure 7-14. Each module has its own address space, starting at 0.

In order to run the program, the linker brings the object modules into main memory to form the image of the executable binary program, as shown in Fig. 7-15(a). The idea is to make an exact image of the executable program's virtual address space inside the linker and position all the object modules at their correct locations. If there is not enough (virtual) memory to form the image, a disk file can be used. Typically, a small section of memory starting at address zero is used for interrupt vectors, communication with the operating system, catching uninitialized pointers, or other purposes, so programs often start above 0. In this figure we have (arbitrarily) started programs at address 100.

The program of Fig. 7-15(a), although loaded into the image of the executable binary file, is not yet ready for execution. Consider what would happen if execution began with the instruction at the beginning of module *A*. The program would not branch to the MOVE instruction as it should, because that instruction is now at 300. In fact, all memory reference instructions will fail for the same reason. Clearly something has to be done.

This problem, called the **relocation problem**, occurs because each object module in Fig. 7-14 represents a separate address space. On a machine with a segmented address space, such as the Pentium 4, theoretically each object module could have its own address space by being placed in its own segment. However, OS/2 is the only operating system for the Pentium 4 that supports this concept. All versions of Windows and UNIX support only one linear address space, so all the object modules must be merged together into a single address space.

Furthermore, the procedure call instructions in Fig. 7-15(a) will not work either. At address 400, the programmer had intended to call object module *B*, but because each procedure is translated by itself, the assembler has no way of knowing what address to insert into the CALL B instruction. The address of object module *B* is not known until linking time. This problem is called the **external reference** problem. Both of these problems can be solved in a simple way by the linker.

The linker merges the separate address spaces of the object modules into a single linear address space in the following steps:

1. It constructs a table of all the object modules and their lengths.

2. Based on this table, it assigns a starting address to each object module.

3. It finds all the instructions that reference memory and adds to each a **relocation constant** equal to the starting address of its module.

4. It finds all the instructions that reference other procedures and inserts the address of these procedures in place.

The object module table constructed in step 1 is shown for the modules of Fig. 7-15 below. It gives the name, length, and starting address of each module.

Module	Length	Starting address
A	400	100
B	600	500
C	500	1100
D	300	1600

Figure 7-15(b) shows how the address space of Fig. 7-15(a) looks after the linker has performed these steps.

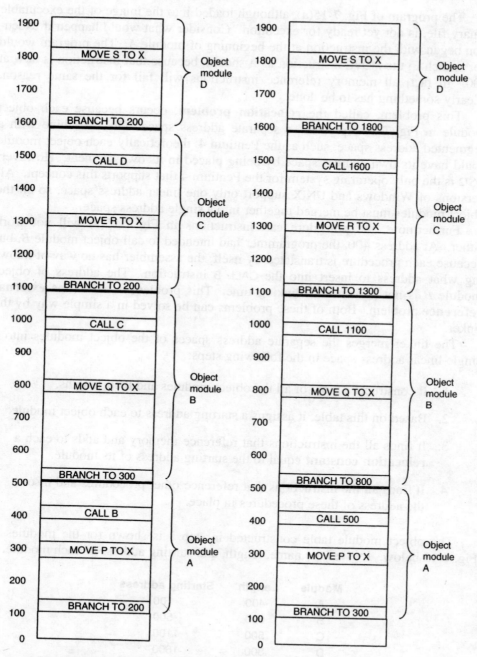

Figure 7-15. (a) The object modules of Fig. 7-14 after being positioned in the binary image but before being relocated and linked. (b) The same object modules after linking and after relocation has been performed.

7.4.2 Structure of an Object Module

Object modules often contain six parts, as shown in Fig. 7-16. The first part contains the name of the module, certain information needed by the linker, such as the lengths of the various parts of the module, and sometimes the assembly date.

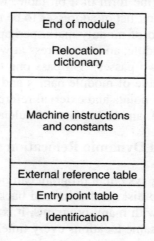

Figure 7-16. The internal structure of an object module produced by a translator.

The second part of the object module is a list of the symbols defined in the module that other modules may reference, together with their values. For example, if the module consists of a procedure named *bigbug*, the entry point table will contain the character string "bigbug" followed by the address to which it corresponds. The assembly language programmer indicates which symbols are to be declared as **entry points** by using a pseudoinstruction such as PUBLIC in Fig. 7-3.

The third part of the object module consists of a list of the symbols that are used in the module but which are defined in other modules, along with a list of which machine instructions use which symbols. The linker needs the latter list in order to be able to insert the correct addresses into the instructions that use external symbols. A procedure can call other independently translated procedures by declaring the names of the called procedures to be external. The assembly language programmer indicates which symbols are to be declared as **external symbols** by using a pseudoinstruction such as EXTERN in Fig. 7-3. On some computers entry points and external references are combined into one table.

The fourth part of the object module is the assembled code and constants. This part of the object module is the only one that will be loaded into memory to be executed. The other five parts will be used by the linker to help it do its work and then discarded before execution begins.

The fifth part of the object module is the relocation dictionary. As shown in Fig. 7-15, instructions that contain memory addresses must have a relocation constant added. Since the linker has no way of telling by inspection which of the data words in part four contain machine instructions and which contain constants, information about which addresses are to be relocated is provided in this table. The information may take the form of a bit table, with 1 bit per potentially relocatable address, or an explicit list of addresses to be relocated.

The sixth part is an end-of-moduly mark, perhaps a checksum to catch errors made while reading the module, and the address at which to begin execution.

Most linkers require two passes. On pass one the linker reads all the object modules and builds up a table of module names and lengths, and a global symbol table consisting of all entry points and external references. On pass two the object modules are read, relocated, and linked one module at a time.

7.4.3 Binding Time and Dynamic Relocation

In a multiprogramming system, a program can be read into main memory, run for a little while, written to disk, and then read back into main memory to be run again. In a large system, with many programs, it is difficult to ensure that a program is read back into the same locations every time.

Figure 7-17 shows what would happen if the already relocated program of Fig. 7-15(b) were reloaded at address 400 instead of address 100 where the linker put it originally. All the memory addresses are incorrect; moreover, the relocation information has long since been discarded. Even if the relocation information were still available, the cost of having to relocate all the addresses every time the program was swapped would be too high.

The problem of moving programs that have already been linked and relocated is intimately related to the time at which the final binding of symbolic names onto absolute physical memory addresses is completed. When a program is written it contains symbolic names for memory addresses, for example, BR L. The time at which the actual main memory address corresponding to L is determined is called the **binding time**. At least six possibilities for the binding time exist:

1. When the program is written.

2. When the program is translated.

3. When the program is linked but before it is loaded.

4. When the program is loaded.

5. When a base register used for addressing is loaded.

6. When the instruction containing the address is executed.

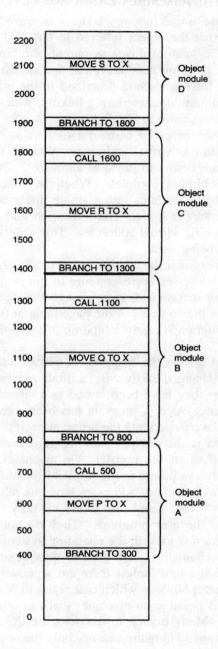

2200	
2100	MOVE S TO X
2000	
1900	BRANCH TO 1800
1800	
	CALL 1600
1700	
1600	MOVE R TO X
1500	
1400	BRANCH TO 1300
1300	CALL 1100
1200	
1100	MOVE Q TO X
1000	
900	
800	BRANCH TO 800
700	CALL 500
600	MOVE P TO X
500	
400	BRANCH TO 300
0	

Object module D

Object module C

Object module B

Object module A

Figure 7-17. The relocated binary program of Fig. 7-15(b) moved up 300 addresses. Many instructions now refer to an incorrect memory address.

If an instruction containing a memory address is moved after binding, it will be incorrect (assuming that the object referred to has also been moved). If the translator produces an executable binary as output, the binding has occurred at translation time, and the program must be run at the address the translator expected it to be run at. The linking method described in the preceding section binds symbolic names to absolute addresses during linking, which is why moving programs after linking fails, as shown in Fig. 7-17.

Two related issues are involved here. First, there is the question of when symbolic names are bound to virtual addresses. Second, there is a question of when virtual addresses are bound to physical addresses. Only when both operations have taken place is binding complete. When the linker merges the separate address spaces of the object modules into a single linear address space, it is, in fact, creating a virtual address space. The relocation and linking serve to bind symbolic names onto specific virtual addresses. This observation is true whether or not virtual memory is being used.

Assume for the moment that the address space of Fig. 7-15(b) were paged. It is clear that the virtual addresses corresponding to the symbolic names A, B, C, and D have already been determined, even though their physical main memory addresses will depend on the contents of the page table at the time they are used. An executable binary program is really a binding of symbolic names onto virtual addresses.

Any mechanism that allows the mapping of virtual addresses onto physical memory addresses to be changed easily will facilitate moving programs around in main memory, even after they have been bound to a virtual address space. One such mechanism is paging. After a program has been moved in main memory, only its page table need be changed, not the program itself.

A second mechanism is the use of a runtime relocation register. The CDC 6600 and its successors had such a register. On machines using this relocation technique, the register always points to the physical memory address of the start of the current program. All memory addresses have the relocation register added to them by the hardware before being sent to the memory. The entire relocation process is transparent to the user programs. They do not even know that it is occurring. When a program is moved, the operating system must update the relocation register. This mechanism is less general than paging because the entire program must be moved as a unit (unless there are separate code and data relocation registers, as on the Intel 8088, in which case it has to be moved as two units).

A third mechanism is possible on machines that can refer to memory relative to the program counter. Many branch instructions are PC relative, which helps. Whenever a program is moved in main memory only the program counter need be updated. A program, all of whose memory references are either relative to the program counter or absolute (e.g., to I/O device registers at absolute addresses) is said to be **position independent**. A position-independent procedure can be placed anywhere within the virtual address space without the need for relocation.

7.4.4 Dynamic Linking

The linking strategy discussed in Sec. 7.4.1 has the property that all procedures that a program might call are linked before the program can begin execution. On a computer with virtual memory, completing all linking before beginning execution does not take advantage of the full capabilities of the virtual memory. Many programs have procedures that are called only under unusual circumstances. For example, compilers have procedures for compiling rarely used statements, plus procedures for handling error conditions that seldom occur.

A more flexible way to link separately compiled procedures is to link each procedure at the time it is first called. This process is known as **dynamic linking**. It was pioneered by MULTICS whose implementation is in some ways still unsurpassed. In the next sections we will look at dynamic linking in several systems.

Dynamic Linking in MULTICS

In the MULTICS form of dynamic linking, associated with each program is a segment, called the **linkage segment**, which contains one block of information for each procedure that might be called. This block of information starts with a word reserved for the virtual address of the procedure and it is followed by the procedure name, which is stored as a character string.

When dynamic linking is being used, procedure calls in the source language are translated into instructions that indirectly address the first word of the corresponding linkage block, as shown in Fig. 7-18(a). The compiler fills this word with either an invalid address or a special bit pattern that forces a trap.

When a procedure in a different segment is called, the attempt to address the invalid word indirectly causes a trap to the dynamic linker. The linker then finds the character string in the word following the invalid address and searches the user's file directory for a compiled procedure with this name. That procedure is then assigned a virtual address, usually in its own private segment, and this virtual address overwrites the invalid address in the linkage segment, as indicated in Fig. 7-18(b). Next, the instruction causing the linkage fault is re-executed, allowing the program to continue from the place it was before the trap.

All subsequent references to that procedure will be executed without causing a linkage fault, for the indirect word now contains a valid virtual address. Consequently, the dynamic linker is invoked only the first time a procedure is called and not thereafter.

Dynamic Linking in Windows

All versions of the Windows operating system, including NT, support dynamic linking and rely heavily on it. Dynamic linking uses a special file format called a **DLL (Dynamic Link Library)**. DLLs can contain procedures, data, or both.

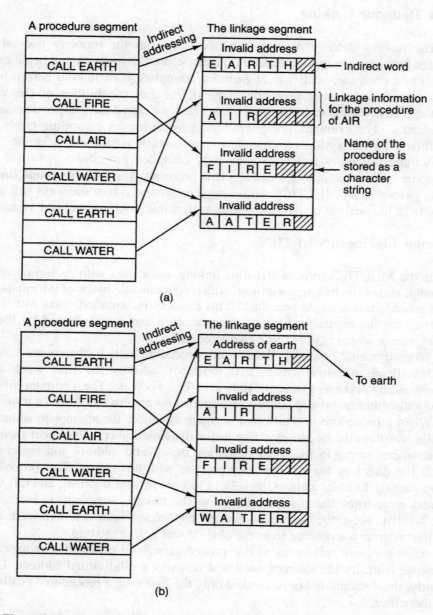

Figure 7-18. Dynamic linking. (a) Before *EARTH* is called. (b) After *EARTH* has been called and linked.

They are commonly used to allow two or more processes to share library procedures or data. Many DLLs have extension *.dll*, but other extensions are also in use, including *.drv* (for driver libraries) and *.fon* (for font libraries).

The most common form of a DLL is a library consisting of a collection of procedures that can be loaded into memory and accessed by multiple processes at the same time. Figure 7-19 illustrates two programs sharing a DLL file that contains four procedures, *A*, *B*, *C*, and *D*. Program 1 uses procedure *A*; program 2 uses procedure *C*, although they could equally well have used the same procedure.

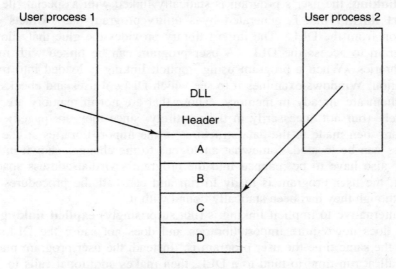

Figure 7-19. Use of a DLL file by two processes.

A DLL is constructed by the linker from a collection of input files. In fact, building a DLL file is very much like building an executable binary program, except that a special flag is given to the linker to tell it to make a DLL. DLLs are commonly constructed from collections of library procedures that are likely to be needed by multiple processes. The interface procedures to the Windows system call library and large graphics libraries are common examples of DLLs. The advantage of using DLLs is saving space in memory and on disk. If some common library were statically bound to each program using it, it would appear in many executable binaries on the disk and in memory, wasting space. With DLLs, each library only appears once on disk and once in memory.

In addition to saving space, this approach makes it easy to update library procedures, even after the programs using them have been compiled and linked. For commercial software packages, where the users rarely have the source code, using DLLs means that the software vendor can fix bugs in the libraries by just distributing new DLL files over the Internet, without requiring any changes to the main program binaries.

The main difference between a DLL and an executable binary is that a DLL cannot be started and run on its own (because it has no main program). It also has different information in its header. In addition, the DLL as a whole has several extra procedures not related to the procedures in the library. For example, there is one procedure that is automatically called whenever a new process is bound to the DLL and another one that is automatically called whenever a process is unbound from it. These procedures can allocate and deallocate memory or manage other resources needed by the DLL.

There are two ways for a program to bind to a DLL. In the first way, called **implicit linking**, the user's program is statically linked with a special file called an **import library** that is generated by a utility program that extracts certain information from the DLL. The import library provides the glue that allows the user program to access the DLL. A user program can be linked with multiple import libraries. When a program using implicit linking is loaded into memory for execution, Windows examines it to see which DLLs it uses and checks to see if all of them are already in memory. Those that are not in memory are loaded immediately (but not necessarily in their entirety, since they are paged). Some changes are then made to the data structures in the import libraries so the called procedures can be located, somewhat analogous to the changes shown in Fig. 7-18. They also have to be mapped into the program's virtual address space. At this point, the user program is ready to run and can call the procedures in the DLLs as though they had been statically bound with it.

The alternative to implicit linking is (not surprisingly) **explicit linking**. This approach does not require import libraries and does not cause the DLLs to be loaded at the same time the user program is. Instead, the user program makes an explicit call at run time to bind to a DLL, then makes additional calls to get the addresses of procedures it needs. Once these have been found, it can call the procedures. When it is all done, it makes a final call to unbind from the DLL. When the last process unbinds from a DLL, the DLL can be removed from memory.

It is important to realize that a procedure in a DLL does not have any identity of its own (as a thread or process does). It runs in the caller's thread and uses the caller's stack for its local variables. It can have process-specific static data (as well as shared data) and otherwise behaves the same as a statically-linked procedure. The only essential difference is how the binding to it is performed.

Dynamic Linking in UNIX

The UNIX system has a mechanism similar in essence to DLLs in Windows. It is called a **shared library**. Like a DLL file, a shared library is an archive file containing multiple procedures or data modules that are present in memory at run time and can be bound to multiple processes at the same time. The standard C library and much of the networking code are shared libraries.

UNIX supports only implicit linking, so a shared library consist of two parts: a **host library**, which is statically linked with the executable file, and a **target library**, which is called at run time. While the details differ, the concepts are essentially the same as with DLLs.

7.5 SUMMARY

Although most programs can and should be written in a high-level language, occasional situations exist in which assembly language is needed, at least in part. Programs for resource-poor portable computers such as smart cards, embedded processors in appliances, and wireless portable digital assistants are potential candidates. An assembly language program is a symbolic representation for some underlying machine language program. It is translated to the machine language by a program called an assembler.

When extremely fast execution is critical to the success of some application, a better approach than writing everything in assembly language is to first write the whole program in a high-level language, then measure where it is spending its time, and finally rewrite only those portions of the program that are heavily used. In practice, a small fraction of the code is usually responsible for a large fraction of the execution time.

Many assemblers have a macro facility that allows the programmer to give commonly used code sequences symbolic names for subsequent inclusion. Usually, these macros can be parameterized in a straightforward way. Macros are implemented by a kind of literal string-processing algorithm.

Most assemblers are two pass. Pass one is devoted to building up a symbol table for labels, literals, and explicitly declared identifiers. The symbols can either be kept unsorted and then searched linearly, first sorted and then searched using binary search, or hashed. If symbols do not need to be deleted during pass one, hashing is usually the best method. Pass two does the code generation. Some pseudoinstructions are carried out on pass one and some on pass two.

Independently-assembled programs can be linked together to form an executable binary program that can be run. This work is done by the linker. Its primary tasks are relocation and binding of names. Dynamic linking is a technique in which certain procedures are not linked until they are actually called. Windows DLLs and UNIX shared libraries use dynamic linking.

PROBLEMS

1. For a certain program, 2% of the code accounts for 50% of the execution time. Compare the following three strategies with respect to programming time and execution time. Assume that it would take 100 man-months to write it in C, and that assembly code is 10 times slower to write and four times more efficient.

   a. Entire program in C.
   b. Entire program in assembler.
   c. First all in C, then the key 2% rewritten in assembler.

2. Do the considerations that hold for two-pass assemblers also hold for compilers?

   a. Assume that the compilers produce object modules, not assembly code.
   b. Assume that the compilers produce symbolic assembly language.

3. Most assemblers for the Intel CPUs have the destination address as the first operand and the source address as the second operand. What problems would have to be solved to do it the other way?

4. Can the following program be assembled in two passes? EQU is a pseudoinstruction that equates the label to the expression in the operand field.

```
P EQU Q
Q EQU R
R EQU S
S EQU 4
```

5. The Dirtcheap Software Company is planning to produce an assembler for a computer with a 48-bit word. To keep costs down, the project manager, Dr. Scrooge, has decided to limit the length of allowed symbols so that each symbol can be stored in a single word. Scrooge has declared that symbols may consist only of letters, except the letter Q, which is forbidden (to demonstrate their concern for efficiency to the customers). What is the maximum length of a symbol? Describe your encoding scheme.

6. What is the difference between an instruction and a pseudoinstruction?

7. What is the difference between the instruction location counter and the program counter, if any? After all, both keep track of the next instruction in a program.

8. Show the symbol table after the following Pentium 4 statements have been encountered. The first statement is assigned to address 1000.

EVEREST:	POP BX	(1 BYTE)
K2:	PUSH BP	(1 BYTE)
WHITNEY:	MOV BP,SP	(2 BYTES)
MCKINLEY:	PUSH X	(3 BYTES)
FUJI:	PUSH SI	(1 BYTE)
KIBO:	SUB SI,300	(3 BYTES)

9. Can you envision circumstances in which an assembly language permits a label to be the same as an opcode (e.g., *MOV* as a label)? Discuss.

10. Show the steps needed to look up Berkeley using binary search on the following list: Ann Arbor, Berkeley, Cambridge, Eugene, Madison, New Haven, Palo Alto, Pasadena, Santa Cruz, Stony Brook, Westwood, and Yellow Springs. When computing the middle element of a list with an even number of elements, use the element just after the middle index.

11. Is it possible to use binary search on a table whose size is prime?

12. Compute the hash code for each of the following symbols by adding up the letters (A = 1, B = 2, etc.) and taking the result modulo the hash table size. The hash table has 19 slots, numbered 0 to 18.

    els, jan, jelle, maaike

Does each symbol generate a unique hash value? If not, how can the collision problem be dealt with?

13. The hash coding method described in the text links all the entries having the same hash code together on a linked list. An alternative method is to have only a single n-slot table, with each table slot having room for one key and its value (or pointers to them). If the hashing algorithm generates a slot that is already full, a second hashing algorithm is used to try again. If that one is also full, another is used, and so on, until an empty is found. If the fraction of the slots that are full is R, how many probes will be needed, on the average, to enter a new symbol?

14. As technology progresses, it may one day be possible to put thousands of identical CPUs on a chip, each CPU having a few words of local memory. If all CPUs can read and write three shared registers, how can an associative memory be implemented?

15. The Pentium 4 has a segmented architecture, with multiple independent segments. An assembler for this machine might well have a pseudoinstruction SEG N that would direct the assembler to place subsequent code and data in segment N. Does this scheme have any influence on the ILC?

16. Programs often link to multiple DLLs. Would it not be more efficient just to put all the procedures in one big DLL and then link to it?

17. Can a DLL be mapped into two process' virtual address spaces at different virtual addresses? If so, what problems arise? Can they be solved? If not, what can be done to eliminate them?

18. One way to do (static) linking is as follows. Before scanning the library, the linker builds a list of procedures needed, that is, names defined as EXTERN in the modules being linked. Then the linker goes through the library linearly, extracting every procedure that is in the list of names needed. Does this scheme work? If not, why not and how can it be remedied?

19. Can a register be used as the actual parameter in a macro call? How about a constant? Why or why not?

20. You are to implement a macro assembler. For esthetic reasons, your boss has decided that macro definitions need not precede their calls. What implications does this decision have on the implementation?

21. Think of a way to put a macro assembler into an infinite loop.

22. A linker reads five modules, whose lengths are 200, 800, 600, 500, and 700 words, respectively. If they are loaded in that order, what are the relocation constants?

23. Write a symbol table package consisting of two routines: *enter(symbol, value)* and *lookup(symbol, value)*. The former enters new symbols in the table and the latter looks them up. Use some form of hash coding.

24. Write a simple assembler for the Mic-1 computer of Chap. 4. In addition to handling the machine instructions, provide a facility for assigning constants to symbols at assembly time, and a way to assemble a constant into a machine word.

25. Add a simple macro facility to the assembler of the preceding problem.

8

PARALLEL COMPUTER
ARCHITECTURES

Although computers keep getting faster, the demands placed on them are increasing at least as fast. Astronomers want to simulate the entire history of the universe, from the big bang until the show is over. Pharmaceutical engineers would love to be able to design medicines to order for specific diseases on their computers instead of having to sacrifice legions of rats. Aircraft designers could come up with more fuel-efficient products if computers could do all the work, without the need for constructing physical wind tunnel prototypes. In short, however much computing power is available, for many users, especially in science, engineering, and industry, it is never enough.

Although clock rates are continually rising, circuit speed cannot be increased indefinitely. The speed of light is already a major problem for designers of high-end computers, and the prospects of getting electrons and photons to move faster are dim. Heat-dissipation issues are turning supercomputers into state-of-the-art air conditioners. Finally, as transistor sizes continue to shrink, at some point each transistor will have so few atoms in it that quantum mechanical effects (e.g., the Heisenberg uncertainty principle) may become a major problem.

Therefore, in order to handle larger and larger problems, computer architects are turning increasingly to parallel computers. While it may not be possible to build a computer with one CPU and a cycle time of 0.001 nsec, it may well be possible to build one with 1000 CPUs each with a cycle time of 1 nsec. Although the latter design uses slower CPUs than the former one, its total computing capacity is theoretically the same. Herein lies the hope.

Parallelism can be introduced at various levels. At the lowest level, it can be added to the CPU chip, by pipelining and superscalar designs with multiple functional units. It can also be added by having very long instruction words with implicit parallelism. Special features can be added to a CPU to allow it to handle multiple threads of control at once. Finally, multiple CPUs can be put together on the same chip. Together, these features can pick up perhaps a factor of 10 in performance over purely sequential designs.

At the next level, extra CPU boards with additional processing capacity can be added to a system. Usually, these plug-in CPUs have specialized functions, such as network packet processing, multimedia processing, or cryptography. For specialized applications, they can also gain a factor of perhaps 5 to 10.

However, to win a factor of a hundred or a thousand or a million, it is necessary to replicate entire CPUs and to make them all work together efficiently. This idea leads to large multiprocessors and multicomputers (cluster computers). Needless to say, hooking up thousands of processors into a big system leads to its own problems that need to be solved.

Finally, it is now possible to lash together entire organizations over the Internet to form very loosely coupled compute grids. These systems are only starting to emerge, but have interesting potential for the future.

When two CPUs or processing elements are close together, have a high bandwidth and low delay between them, and are computationally intimate, they are said to be **tightly coupled**. Conversely, when they are far apart, have a low bandwidth and high delay and are computationally remote, they are said to be **loosely coupled**. In this chapter we will look at the design principles for these various forms of parallelism and study a variety of examples. We will start with the most tightly-coupled systems, those that use on-chip parallelism, and gradually move to more and more loosely coupled systems, ending with a few words on grid computing. This spectrum is crudely illustrated in Fig. 8-1.

The whole issue of parallelism, from one end of the spectrum to the other, is a hot topic of research. Accordingly, many more references are given in this chapter, primary to recent papers on the subject. More introductory references are given in Sec. 9.1.8.

8.1 ON-CHIP PARALLELISM

One way to increase the throughput of a chip is to have it do more things at the same time. In this section, we will look at some of the ways of achieving speedup through parallelism at the chip level, including instruction-level parallelism, multithreading, and putting more than one CPU on the chip. These techniques are quite different, but each of them helps in its own way. But in all cases the idea is to get more activity going at the same time.

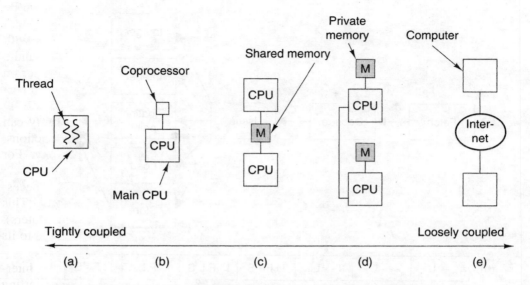

Figure 8-1. (a) On-chip parallelism. (b) A coprocessor. (c) A multiprocessor. (d) A multicomputer. (e) A grid.

8.1.1 Instruction-Level Parallelism

At the lowest level, one way to achieve parallelism is to issue multiple instructions per clock cycle. Multiple-issue CPUs come in two varieties: superscalar processors and VLIW processors. We have actually touched on both earlier in the book, but it may be useful to review this material here.

We have seen superscalar CPUs before (e.g., Fig. 2-5). In the most common configuration, at a certain point in the pipeline an instruction is ready to be executed. Superscalar CPUs are capable of issuing multiple instructions to the execution units in a single clock cycle. The number of instructions actually issued depends on both the processor design and on current circumstances. The hardware determines the maximum number that can be issued, usually two to six instructions. However, if an instruction needs a functional unit that is not available or a result that has not yet been computed, the instruction will not be issued.

The other form of instruction-level parallelism is found in **VLIW** (**Very Long Instruction Word**) processors. In the original form, VLIW machines indeed had long words containing instructions that used multiple functional units. Consider, for example, the pipeline of Fig. 8-2(a), where the machine has five functional units and can perform two integer operations, one floating-point operation, one load, and one store simultaneously. A VLIW instruction for this machine would contain five opcodes and five pairs of operands, one opcode and operand pair per functional unit. With 6 bits per opcode, 5 bits per register, and 32 bits per memory address, instructions could easily be 134 bits—quite long indeed.

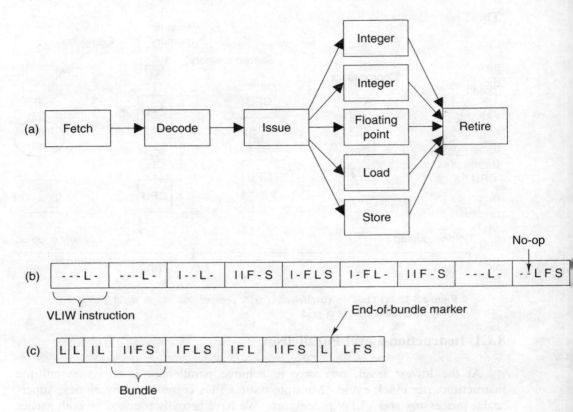

Figure 8-2. (a) A CPU pipeline. (b) A sequence of VLIW instructions. (c) An instruction stream with bundles marked.

However, this design proved too rigid because not every instruction was able to utilize every functional unit, leading to many useless NO-OPs used as filler, as illustrated in Fig. 8-2(b). Consequently, modern VLIW machines have a way of marking a bundle of instructions as belonging together, for example with an "end of bundle" bit, as shown in Fig. 8-2(c). The processor can then fetch the entire bundle and issue it all at once. It is up to the compiler to prepare bundles of compatible instructions.

In effect, VLIW shifts the burden of determining which instructions can be issued together from run time to compile time. Not only does this choice make the hardware simpler and faster, but since an optimizing compiler can run for a long time if need be, better bundles can be assembled than what the hardware could do at run time. Of course, such a radical change in CPU architecture will be difficult to introduce, as demonstrated by the slow acceptance of the Itanium.

It is worth noting in passing that instruction-level parallelism is not the only form of low-level parallelism. Another is memory-level parallelism, in which multiple memory operations are in flight at the same time (Chou et al., 2004).

The TriMedia VLIW CPU

We studied one example of a VLIW CPU, the Itanium-2, in Chap. 5. Let us now look at a very different VLIW processor, the **TriMedia**, designed by Philips, the Dutch electronics company that also invented the audio CD and CD-ROM. The TriMedia is intended for use as an embedded processor in image-, audio-, and video-intensive applications such as CD, DVD, and MP3 players, CD and DVD recorders, interactive TV sets, digital cameras, camcorders, and so on. Given these application areas, it is not surprising that it differs considerably from the Itanium-2, which is a general-purpose CPU intended for high-end servers.

The TriMedia is a true VLIW processor with every instruction holding as many as five **operations**. Under completely optimal conditions, every clock cycle one instruction is started and the five operations are issued. The clock runs at 266 MHz or 300 MHz, but since it can issue five operations per cycle, the effective clock speed is as much as five times higher. In the discussion below, we will focus on the TM3260 implementation of the TriMedia; other versions differ in minor ways from it.

A typical instruction is illustrated in Fig. 8-3. The instructions vary from standard 8-, 16-, and 32-bit integer instructions, through IEEE 754 floating-point instructions to parallel multimedia instructions. As a consequence of the five issues per cycle and the parallel multimedia instructions, the TriMedia is fast enough to decode streaming DV from a camcorder at full size and full frame rate in software.

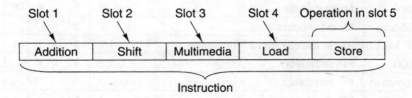

Figure 8-3. A typical TriMedia instruction, showing five possible operations.

The TriMedia has a byte-oriented memory, with the I/O registers mapped into the memory space. Half words (16 bits) and full words (32 bits) must be aligned on their natural boundaries. It can run either as little endian or big endian, depending on a PSW bit that the operating system can set. This bit affects only the way load operations and store operations transfer between memory and registers. The CPU contains a split 8-way set-associative cache, with a 64-byte line size for both the instruction cache and the data cache. The instruction cache is 64 KB; the data cache is 16 KB.

There are 128 general-purpose 32-bit registers. Register R0 is hardwired to 0. Register R1 is hardwired to 1. Attempting to change either one gives the CPU a heart attack. The remaining 126 registers are all functionally equivalent and can be used for any purpose. In addition, four special-purpose, 32-bit registers also exist. These are the program counter, program status word, and two registers that relate to interrupts. Finally, a 64-bit register counts the number of CPU cycles since the CPU was last reset. At 300 MHz, it takes nearly 2000 years for the counter to wrap around.

The Trimedia TM3260 has 11 different functional units for doing arithmetic, logical, and control flow operations (as well as one for cache control that we will not discuss here). They are listed in Fig. 8-4. The first two columns name the unit and give a brief description of what it does. The third column tells how many hardware copies of the unit exist. The fourth column gives the latency, that is, how many clock cycles it takes to complete. In this context, it is worth nothing that all the functional units except the FP square root/divide unit are pipelined. The latency given in the table tells how long before the result of an operation is available, but a new operation can be initiated every cycle. Thus, for example, each of three consecutive instructions can hold two load operations, resulting in six loads in various stages of execution at the same time.

Finally, the last five columns show which instruction slots can be used for which functional unit. For example, floating-point compare operations must appear only in the third slot of an instruction

Unit	Description	#	Lat.	1	2	3	4	5
Constant	Immediate operations	5	1	x	x	x	x	x
Integer ALU	32-Bit arithmetic, Boolean ops	5	1	x	x	x	x	x
Shifter	Multibit shifts	2	1	x	x	x	x	x
Load/Store	Memory operations	2	3				x	x
Int/FP MUL	32-Bit integer and FP multiplies	2	3		x	x		
FP ALU	FP arithmetic	2	3	x			x	
FP compare	FP compares	1	1			x		
FP sqrt/div	FP division and square root	1	17	x				
Branch	Control flow	3	3		x	x	x	
DSP ALU	Dual 16-bit, quad 8-bit multimedia arithmetic	2	3	x		x		x
DSP MUL	Dual 16-bit, quad 8-bit multimedia multiplies	2	3		x	x		

Figure 8-4. The TM3260 functional units, their quantity, latency, and which instruction slots they can use.

The constant unit is used for immediate operations, such as loading a number stored in the operation itself into a register. The integer ALU does addition, subtraction, the usual Boolean operations, and pack/unpack operations. The shifter can shift a register in either direction a specified number of bits.

The load/store unit fetches memory words into registers and writes them back. The TriMedia is basically an augmented RISC CPU, so normal operations operate on registers and the load/store unit is used to access memory. Transfers can be 8, 16, or 32 bits. Arithmetic and logical instructions do not access memory.

The multiply unit handles both integer and floating-point multiplications. The next three units handle floating-point additions/subtractions, compares, and square roots and divisions, respectively.

Branch operations are executed by the branch unit. There is a fixed 3-cycle delay after a branch, so the three instructions (up to 15 operations) following a branch are always executed, even for unconditional branches.

Finally, we come to the two multimedia units, which handle the special multimedia operations. The DSP in the name of the functional unit refers to Digital Signal Processor, which the multimedia operations effectively replace. We will describe the multimedia operations briefly below. One noteworthy feature is that they all use **saturated arithmetic** instead of twos complement arithmetic used by the integer operations When an operation produces a result that cannot be expressed due to overflow, instead of generating an exception or giving a garbage result, the closest valid number is used. For example, with 8-bit unsigned numbers, adding 130 and 130 gives 255.

Because not every operation can appear in every slot, it frequently happens that an instruction does not contain all five potential operations. When a slot is not used, it is compacted to minimized the amount of space wasted. Operations that are present occupy 26, 34, or 42 bits. Depending on the number of operations actually present, TriMedia instructions vary from 2 to 28 bytes, including some fixed overhead.

The TriMedia does not make runtime checks to see if the operations in an instruction are compatible. If they are not, it just executes them anyway and gets the wrong answer. Leaving the check out was a deliberate decision to save a time and transistors. The Pentium does do runtime checking to make sure all the superscalar operations are compatible, but at a huge cost in complexity, time, and transistors. The TriMedia avoids this expense by putting the burden of scheduling on the compiler, which has all the time in the world to carefully optimize the placement of operations in instruction words. On the other hand, if an operation needs a functional unit that is not available, the instruction will stall until it becomes available.

As in the Itanium-2, TriMedia operations are predicated. Each operation (with two minor exceptions) specifies a register that is tested before the operation is executed. If the low-order bit of the register is set, the operation is executed; otherwise, it is skipped. Each of the (up to) five operations is individually predicated. An example of a predicated operation is

    IF R2 IADD R4, R5 -> R8

which tests R2 and, if the low-order bit is 1, adds R4 to R5 and stores the result in R8. An operation can be made unconditional by using R1 (which is always 1) as the predicate register. Using R0 (which is always 0) makes it a no-op.

The TriMedia multimedia operations can be grouped into the 15 groups listed in Fig. 8-5. Many of the operations involving clipping, which specifies an operand and a range, and forces the operand into the range, using the lowest or highest values for operands that fall outside it. Clipping can be done on 8-, 16-, or 32-bit operands. For example, when clipping is performed with a range of 0 to 255 on 40 and 340, the clipped results are 40 and 255, respectively. The clip group performs clip operations.

Group	Description
Clip	Clip 4 bytes or 2 halfwords
DSP absolute value	Clipped, signed, absoluted value
DSP add	Clipped signed addition
DSP subtract	Clipped signed subtraction
DSP multiply	Clipped signed multiplication
Min, max	Get minimum or maximum of four byte pairs
Compare	Bytewise compare of two registers
Shift	Shift a pair of 16-bit operands
Sum of products	Signed sum of 8- or 16-bit products
Merge, pack, swap	Byte and halfword manipulation
Byte quad averages	Unsigned byte-wise quad averaging
Byte averages	Unsigned byte-wise average of four elements
Byte multiplies	Unsigned 8-bit multiply
Motion estimation	Unsigned sum of absolute values of signed 8-bit diffs
Miscellaneous	Other arithmetic operations

Figure 8-5. The major groups of TriMedia custom operations.

The next four groups in Fig. 8-5 perform the indicated operation on operands of various sizes, clipping the results into a specific range. The min, max group examines two registers and for each byte finds the smallest or largest value. Similarly, the compare group regards two registers as four pairs of bytes and compares each pair.

Multimedia operations are rarely performed on 32-bit integers because most images are composed of RGB pixels with 8-bit values for each of the red, green, and blue colors. When an image is being processed (e.g., compressed), it is normally represented by three components, one for each color (RGB space) or a logically equivalent form (YUV space, discussed later in this chapter). Either way, a lot of processing is done on rectangular arrays containing 8-bit unsigned integers.

The TriMedia has a large number of operations specifically designed for processing arrays of 8-bit unsigned integers efficiently. As a simple example, consider the upper left-hand corner of an array of 8-bit values stored in (big endian) memory as illustrated in Fig. 8-6(a). The 4×4 block shown in the corner contains 16 8-bit values labeled A through P. Suppose, for example, that the image needs to be transposed, to produce Fig. 8-6(b). How can this task be achieved?

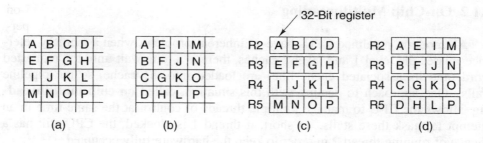

Figure 8-6. (a) An array of 8-bit elements. (b) The transposed array. (c) The original array fetched into four registers. (d) The transposed array in four registers.

One way to do the transposition is to use 12 operations that each load a byte into a different register, followed by 12 more operations that each store a byte in its correct locations. (Note: the four bytes on the diagonal do not move in the transposition.) The problem with this approach is that it requires 24 (long and slow) operations that reference memory.

An alternative approach is to start with four operations that each load a word into four different registers, R2 through R5, as shown in Fig. 8-6(c). Then the four output words are assembled by masking and shifting operations to achieve the desired output, as shown in Fig. 8-6(d). Finally, these words are stored in memory. Although this way of doing it reduces the number of memory references from 24 to 8, the masking and shifting is expensive due to the many operations required to extract and insert each byte in the correct position.

The TriMedia provides a better solution than either of these. It begins by fetching the four words into registers. However, instead of building the output using masking and shifting, special operations that extract and insert bytes within registers are used to build the output. The result is that with eight memory references and eight of these special multimedia operations, the transposition can be accomplished. The code first contains an operation with two load operations in slots 4 and 5, respectively, to load words into R2 and R3, followed by another such operation to load R4 and R5. The instructions holding these operations can use slots 1, 2, and 3 for other purposes. When all the words have been loaded, the eight special multimedia operations can be packed into two instructions to build the output, followed by two operations to store them. All in all, only six instructions are needed, and 14 of the 30 slots in these instructions are available for other operations. In effect, the entire job can be done with the effective equivalent of about three or so instructions. Other multimedia operations are equally efficient.

Between these powerful operations and the five issue slots per instruction, the Tri-Media is highly efficient at doing the kinds of calculations needed in multimedia processing.

8.1.2 On-Chip Multithreading

All modern, pipelined CPUs have an inherent problem: when a memory reference misses the level 1 and level 2 caches, there is a long wait until the requested word (and its associated cache line) are loaded into the cache, so the pipeline stalls. One approach to dealing with this situation, called **on-chip multithreading**, allows the CPU to manage multiple threads of control at the same time in an attempt to mask these stalls. In short, if thread 1 is blocked, the CPU still has a chance of running thread 2 in order to keep the hardware fully occupied.

Although the basic idea is fairly simple, multiple variants exist, which we will now examine. The first approach, called **fine-grained multithreading**, is illustrated in Fig. 8-7 for a CPU with the ability to issue one instruction per clock cycle. In Fig. 8-7(a)–(c), we see three threads, A, B, and C, for 12 machine cycles. During the first cycle, thread A executes instruction A1. This instruction completes in one cycle, so in the second cycle instruction A2 is started. Unfortunately, this instruction misses on the level 1 cache so two cycles are wasted while the word needed is fetched from the level 2 cache. The thread continues in cycle 5. Similarly, threads B and C also stall occasional as well, as illustrated in the figure. In this model if an instruction stalls, subsequent instructions cannot be issued. Of course, with a more sophisticated scoreboard, sometimes new instructions can still be issued, but we will ignore that possibility in this discussion.

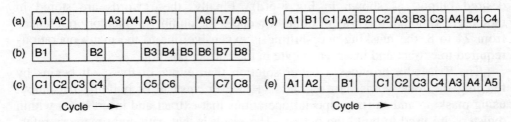

Figure 8-7. (a)–(c) Three threads. The empty boxes indicated that the thread has stalled waiting for memory. (d) Fine-grained multithreading. (e) Coarse-grained multithreading.

Fine-grained multithreading masks the stalls by running the threads round robin, with a different thread in consecutive cycles, as shown in Fig. 8-7(d). By the time the fourth cycle comes up, the memory operation initiated in A1 has completed, so instruction A2 can be run, even if it needs the result of A1. In this case the maximum stall is two cycles, so with three threads the stalled operation always completes in time. If a memory stall took four cycles, we would need four threads to insure continuous operation, and so on.

Since different threads have nothing to do with one another, each one needs its own set of registers. When an instruction is issued, a pointer to its register set has to be included along with the instruction so that if a register is referenced, the hardware will know which register set to use. Consequently, the maximum number of threads that can be run at once is fixed at the time the chip is designed.

Memory operations are not the only reason for stalling. Sometimes an instruction needs a result computed by a previous instruction that is not yet complete. Sometimes an instruction cannot start because it follows a conditional branch whose direction is not yet known. In general, if the pipeline has k stages but there are at least k threads to run round robin, there will never be more than one instruction per thread in the pipeline at any moment so no conflicts can occur. In this situation, the CPU can run at full speed, never stalling.

Of course, there may not be as many threads available as there are pipeline stages, so some designers prefer a different approach, known as **coarse-grained multithreading**, and illustrated in Fig. 8-7(e). Here thread A starts and continues to issue instructions until it stalls, wasting one cycle. At that point a switch occurs and $B1$ is executed. Since the first instruction of thread B stalls, another thread switch happens and $C1$ is executed in cycle 6. Since a cycle is lost whenever an instruction stalls, coarse-grained multithreading is potentially less efficient than fine-grained multithreading, but it has the big advantage that many fewer threads are needed to keep the CPU busy. In situations with an insufficient number of active threads, to be sure of finding a runnable one, coarse-grained multithreading works better.

Although we have depicted coarse-grained multithreading as doing thread switches on a stall, that is not the only option. Another possibility is to switch immediately on any instruction that might cause a stall, such as a load, store, or branch, before even finding out if it does cause a stall. The latter strategy allows a switch to occur earlier (as soon as the instruction is decoded), and may make it possible to avoid dead cycles. In effect, it is saying: "Run until there might be a problem, then switch just in case." Doing so makes coarse-grained multithreading somewhat more like fine-grained multithreading with its frequent switches.

No matter which kind of multithreading is used, some way is needed to keep track of which operation belongs to which thread. With fine-grained multithreading, the only serious possibility is to attach a thread identifier to each operation, so as it moves through the pipeline, its identity is clear. With coarse-grained multithreading, another possibility exists: when switching threads, let the pipeline clear and only then start the next thread. In that way, only one thread at a time is in the pipeline and its identity is never in doubt. Of course, letting the pipeline run dry on a thread switch only makes sense if thread switches take place at intervals very much longer than the time it takes to empty the pipeline.

So far we have assumed that the CPU can issue only one instruction per cycle. As we have seen, however, modern CPUs can issue multiple instructions per cycle. In Fig. 8-8 we assume the CPU can issue two instructions per clock cycle, but we maintain the rule that when an instruction stalls, subsequent instructions cannot be issued. In Fig. 8-8(a) we see how fine-grained multithreading works with a dual-issue superscalar CPU. For thread *A*, the first two instructions can be issued in the first cycle, but for thread *B* we immediately hit a problem in the next cycle, so only one instruction can be issued, and so on.

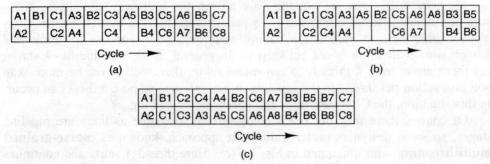

Figure 8-8. Multithreading with a dual-issue superscalar CPU. (a) Fine-grained multithreading. (b) Coarse-grained multithreading. (c) Simultaneous multithreading.

In Fig. 8-8(b), we see how coarse-grained multithreading works with a dual-issue CPU, but now with a static scheduler that does not introduce a dead cycle after an instruction that stalls. Basically, the threads are run in turn, with the CPU issuing two instructions per thread until it hits one that stalls, at which point it switches to the next thread at the start of the next cycle.

With superscalar CPUs, a third possible way of doing multithreading is available, called **simultaneous multithreading** and illustrated in Fig. 8-8(c). This approach can be seen as a refinement to coarse-grained multithreading, in which a single thread is allowed to issue two instructions per cycle as long as it can, but when it stalls, instructions are immediately taken from the next thread in sequence to keep the CPU fully occupied. Simultaneous multithreading can also help keep all the functional units busy. When an instruction cannot be started because a functional unit it needs is occupied, an instruction from a different thread can be chosen instead. In this figure, we are assuming that *B8* stalls in cycle 11, so *C7* is started in cycle 12.

For more information about multithreading, see (Dean, 2004; Kalla et al., 2004; and Kapil et al., 2004). The combination of multithreading and speculative execution is examined in Sohi and Roth (2001).

Hyperthreading on the Pentium 4

Having looked at multithreading in the abstract, let us now consider a practical example of multithreading: the Pentium 4 CPU. After the Pentium 4 was already in production, the architects at Intel looked for various ways to speed it up without changing the programmers' interface, something that would never have been accepted. Five ways quickly popped up:

1. Increasing the clock speed.

2. Putting two CPUs on a chip.

3. Adding functional units.

4. Making the pipeline longer.

5. Using multithreading.

An obvious way to improve performance is to increase the clock speed without changing anything else. Doing this is relatively straightforward and well understood, so each new chip that comes out is generally slightly faster than its predecessor. Unfortunately, a faster clock also has two main drawbacks that limit how much of an increase can be tolerated. First, a faster clock uses more energy, which is a huge problem for notebook computers and other battery-powered devices. Second, the extra energy input means the chip gets hotter and there is more heat to dissipate.

Putting two CPUs on a chip is relatively straightforward, but it comes close to doubling the chip area if each one has its own caches and thus reduces the number of chips per wafer by a factor of two, which essentially doubles the unit manufacturing cost. If the two chips share a common cache as big as the original one, the chip area is not doubled, but cache size per CPU is halved, cutting into performance. Also, while high-end server applications can often fully utilize multiple CPUs, not all desktop applications have enough inherent parallelism to warrant two full CPUs.

Adding additional functional units is also fairly easy, but it is important to get the balance right. Having 10 ALUs does little good if the chip is incapable of feeding instructions into the pipeline fast enough to keep them all busy.

A longer pipeline with more stages, each doing a smaller piece of work in a shorter time period, also increases performance, but also increases the negative effects of branch mispredictions, cache misses, interrupts, and other factors that interrupt normal pipeline flow. Furthermore, to take full advantage of a longer pipeline, the clock speed has to be increased, which means more energy is consumed and more heat is produced.

Finally, multithreading can be added. Its value is in having a second thread utilize hardware that would otherwise have lain fallow. After some experimentation, it became clear that a 5% increase in chip area for multithreading support gave a 25% performance gain in many applications, making this a good choice. Intel's first multithreaded CPU was the Xeon in 2002, but multithreading was later added to the Pentium 4, starting with the 3.06 GHz version and continuing with faster versions of the Pentium processor. Intel calls the implementation of multithreading used in the Pentium 4 **hyperthreading**.

The basic idea is to allow two threads (or possibly processes, since the CPU cannot tell what is a thread and what is a process) to run at once. To the operating system, a hyperthreaded Pentium 4 chip looks like a dual processor in which both CPUs share a common cache and main memory. The operating system schedules the threads independently. If two applications are running at the same time, the operating system can run each one at the same time. For example, if a mail daemon is sending or receiving e-mail in the background while a user is interacting with some program in the foreground, the daemon and the user program can be run in parallel, as though there were two CPUs available.

Application software that has been designed to run as multiple threads can use both virtual CPUs. For example, video editing programs usually allow users to specify certain filters to apply to each frame in some range. These filters can modify the brightness, contrast, color balance, or other properties of each frame. The program can then assign one CPU to process the even-numbered frames and the other CPU to process the odd-numbered frames, and the two of them can run completely independently of each other.

Since the two threads share all the hardware resources, a strategy is needed to manage the sharing. Intel identified four useful strategies for resource sharing in conjunction with hyperthreading: resource duplication, partitioned resources, threshold sharing, and full sharing. We will now touch on each of these in turn.

To start with, some resources are duplicated just for threading. For example, since each thread has its own flow of control, a second program counter had to be added. In addition, the table that maps the architectural registers (*EAX*, *EBX*, etc.) onto the physical registers also had to be duplicated, as did the interrupt controller, since the threads can be independently interrupted.

Next we have **partitioned resource sharing**, in which the hardware resources are rigidly divided between the threads. For example, if the CPU has a queue between two functional pipeline stages, half the slots could be dedicated to thread 1 and the other half to thread 2. Partitioning is easy to accomplish, has no overhead, and keeps the threads out of each other's hair. If all the resources are partitioned, we effectively have two separate CPUs. On the down side, it can easily happen that at some point one thread is not using some of its resources that the other one wants but is forbidden from accessing. As a consequence, resources that could have been used productively lie idle.

The opposite of partitioned sharing is **full resource sharing**. When this scheme is used, either thread can acquire any resources it needs, first come, first served. However, imagine a fast thread consisting primarily of additions and subtractions and a slow thread consisting primarily of multiplications and divisions. If instructions are fetched from memory faster than multiplications and divisions can be carried out, the backlog of instructions fetched for the slow thread and queued but not yet fed into the pipeline will grow in time. Eventually, this backlog will occupy the entire instruction queue, bringing the fast thread to a halt for lack of space in the instruction queue. Full resource sharing solves the problem of a resource lying idle while another thread wants it, but creates a new problem of one thread potentially hogging so many resources as to slow the other one down or stop it altogether.

An intermediate scheme is **threshold sharing**, in which a thread can acquire resources dynamically (no fixed partitioning) but only up to some maximum. For resources that are replicated, this approach allows flexibility without the danger that one thread will starve due to its inability to acquire any of the resource. If, for example, no thread can acquire more than 3/4 of the instruction queue, no matter what the slow thread does, the fast thread will be able to run.

The Pentium 4 hyperthreading uses different sharing strategies for different resources in an attempt to address the various problems alluded to above. Duplication is used for resources that each thread requires all the time, such as the program counter, register map, and interrupt controller. Duplicating these resources increases the chip area by only 5%, a modest price to pay for multithreading. Resources available in such large abundance that there is no danger of one thread capturing them all, such as cache lines, are fully shared in a dynamic way. On the other hand, resources that control the operation of the pipeline, such as the various queues within the pipeline, are partitioned, giving each thread half of the slots. The main pipeline of the Netburst microarchitecture used in the Pentium 4 is illustrated in Fig. 8-9, with the white and gray boxes indicating how the resources are allocated between the white and gray threads.

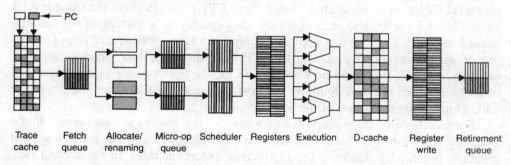

Figure 8-9. Resource sharing between threads in the Pentium 4 NetBurst microarchitecture.

In this figure we can see that all the queues are partitioned, with half the slots in each queue reserved for each thread. In this one, neither thread can choke off the other one. The register allocator and renamer is also partitioned. The scheduler is dynamically shared, but with a threshold, to prevent either thread from claiming all of the slots. The remaining pipeline stages are fully shared.

All is not sweetness and light with multithreading, however. There is also a downside. While partitioning is cheap, dynamic sharing of any resource and especially with a limit on how much a thread can take, requires bookkeeping at run time to monitor usage. In addition, situations can arise in which programs work much worse with multithreading than without it. For example, imagine two threads that each need 3/4 of the cache to function well. Run separately, each one works fine and has few (expensive) cache misses. Run together, each one has large numbers of cache misses and the net result may be far worse than without multithreading.

More information about multithreading in the Pentium 4 is given in (Gerber and Binstock, 2004; Koufaty and Marr, 2003; and Tuck and Tullsen, 2003).

8.1.3 Single-Chip Multiprocessors

While multithreading provides significant performance gains at modest cost, for some applications a much larger performance gain is needed than multithreading can provide. To get this gain, multiprocessor chips are being developed. Two areas where these chips, which contain two or more CPUs, are of interest are high-end servers and in consumer electronics. We will now briefly touch on each of them.

Homogeneous Multiprocessors on a Chip

With advances in VLSI technology, it is now possible to put two or more powerful CPUs on a single chip. Since these CPUs always share the same level 1 cache, level 2 cache, and main memory, they qualify as a multiprocessor, as discussed in Chap. 2. A typical application area is a large Web server farm consisting of many servers. By putting two CPUs in the same box, sharing not only memory, but also disks and network interfaces, the performance of the server can often be doubled without doubling the cost (because even at twice the price, the CPU chip is only a fraction of the total system cost).

For small-scale single-chip multiprocessors, two designs are prevalent. In the first one, shown in Fig. 8-10(a), there is really only one chip, but it has a second pipeline, potentially doubling the instruction execution rate. In the second one, shown in Fig. 8-10(b), there are separate cores on the chip, each one containing a full CPU. A **core** is large circuit, such as a CPU, I/O controller, or cache, that can be placed on a chip in a modular way, usually next to other cores.

The former design allows resources, such as functional units, to be shared between the processors, thus allowing one CPU to use resources the other does not need. On the other hand, this approach requires redesigning the chip and it does not scale well much above two CPUs. In contrast, just putting two or more CPU cores on the same chip is relatively easy to do.

We will discuss multiprocessors later in the chapter. While that discussion is somewhat focused on multiprocessors built from single-CPU chips, much of it is also applicable to multi-CPU chips as well.

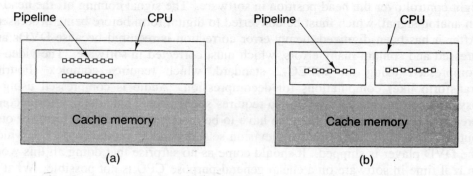

Figure 8-10. Single-chip multiprocessors. (a) A dual-pipeline chip. (b) A chip with two cores.

Heterogeneous Multiprocessors on a Chip

A completely different application area calling for single-chip multiprocessors is embedded systems, especially in audio-visual consumer electronics, such as television sets, DVD players, camcorders, game consoles, cell phones, and so on. These systems have demanding performance requirements and tight constraints. Although these devices look different, in reality, more and more of them are simply small computers, with one or more CPUs, memories, I/O controllers, and some custom I/O devices. A cell phone, for example, is merely a PC with a CPU, memory, dwarf keyboard, microphone, loudspeaker, and a wireless network connection in a small package.

Consider, as an example, a portable DVD player. The computer inside of it has to handle the following functions:

1. Control of a cheap, unreliable servomechanism for head tracking.

2. Analog to digital conversion.

3. Error correction.

4. Decryption and digital rights management.

5. MPEG-2 video decompression.

6. Audio decompression.

7. Encoding the output for NTSC, PAL, or SECAM television sets.

This work must be done subject to stringent real time, quality of service, energy, heat dissipation, size, weight, and price constraints.

DVD disks contain a long spiral containing the information, as illustrated in Fig. 2-24 (for a CD). The read head must accurately track the spiral as the disk rotates. The price is kept low by using a relatively simple mechanical design and tight control over the head position in software. The signal coming off the head is an analog signal, which must be converted to digital form before being processed. After it has been digitized, heavy error correction is required because DVDs are pressed and contain many errors, which must corrected in software. The video is compressed using the MPEG-2 standard, which requires complex (Fourier transform like) computations for decompression. Audio is compressed using a psycho-acoustic model, which also requires sophisticated calculations for decompression. Finally, audio and video have to be rendered in a suitable form for output to NTSC, PAL, or SECAM television sets, depending on the country to which the DVD player is shipped. It should come as no surprise that doing all this work in real time in software on a cheap general-purpose CPU is not possible. What is needed is a heterogeneous multiprocessor containing multiple cores, each specialized for one particular task. An example DVD player is given in Fig. 8-11.

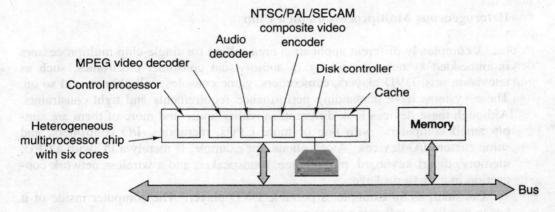

Figure 8-11. The logical structure of a simple DVD player contains a heterogeneous multiprocessor containing multiple cores for different functions.

The functions of the cores in Fig. 8-11 are all different, with each one being carefully designed to be extremely good at what it does for the lowest possible price. For example, DVD video is compressed using a scheme known as **MPEG-2** (after the **Motion Picture Experts Group** that invented it). It consists of dividing each frame up into blocks of pixels and doing a complex transformation on each one. A frame can consist entirely of transformed blocks or it can specify that a certain block is the same as one found in the previous frame but located at an offset of $(\Delta x, \Delta y)$ from its current position except with a couple of pixels changed. Doing this calculation in software is extremely slow, but it is possible to build an MPEG-2 decoding engine that can do it in hardware quite rapidly. Similarly, audio decoding and reencoding the composite audio-video signal to conform to one of the world's television standards can be done better by dedicated hardware processors. These observations quickly lead to heterogeneous multiprocessor chips containing multiple cores specifically designed for audio-

visual applications. However, because the control processor is a general-purpose programmable CPU, the multiprocessor chip can also be used in other, similar applications, such as a DVD recorder.

Another device requiring a heterogeneous multiprocessor is the engine inside an advanced cell phone. Current ones sometimes have still cameras, video cameras, game machines, web browsers, e-mail readers, and digital satellite radio receivers, using either cell phone technology (CDMA or GSM) or wireless Internet (IEEE 802.11, also called WiFi) built in; future ones may include all of these. As devices take on more and more functionality, with watches becoming GPS-based maps and eyeglasses becoming radios, the need for heterogeneous multiprocessors will only increase.

Fairly soon chips will have 500 million transistors. Such chips are far too large to design one gate and one wire at a time. The human effort required would render the chips obsolete by the time they were finished. The only feasible way is to use cores (essentially libraries) containing fairly large subassemblies and then to place and interconnect them on the chip as needed. Designers then have to determine which CPU core to use for the control processor and which special-purpose processors to throw in to help it. Putting more of the burden on software running on the control processor makes the system slower but yields a smaller (and cheaper) chip. Having multiple special-purpose processors for audio and video processing takes up chip area, increasing the cost, but produces higher performance at a lower clock rate, which means lower power consumption and less heat dissipation. Thus chip designers are increasingly faced with these macroscopic trade-offs rather than worrying about where to place each transistor.

Audio-visual applications are very data intensive. Huge amounts of data have to be processed quickly, so typically 50% to 75% of the chip area is devoted to memory in one form or another and the amount is rising. The design issues here are numerous. How many levels of cache should be used? Should the cache(s) be split or unified? How big should each cache be? How fast should each one be? Should some actual memory go on the chip too? Should it be SRAM or SDRAM? The answers to each of these questions have major implications for the performance, energy consumption, and heat dissipation of the chip.

Besides design of the processors and memory system, another issue of considerable consequence is the communication system—how do all the cores communicate with each other? For small systems, a single bus will usually do the trick, but for larger ones it rapidly becomes a bottleneck. Often the problem can be solved by going to multiple buses or possibly a ring going from core to core. In the latter case, arbitration is handled by passing a small packet called a **token** around the ring. To transmit, a core must first capture the token. When it is done, it puts the token back on the ring so it can continue circulating. This protocol prevents collisions on the ring.

As an example of an on-chip interconnect, look at the IBM **CoreConnect**, illustrated in Fig. 8-12. It is an architecture for connecting cores on a single-chip heterogeneous multiprocessor, especially complete system-on-a-chip designs. In a sense, CoreConnect is to one-chip multiprocessors what the PCI bus is to the Pentium—the glue that holds all the parts together. However, unlike the PCI bus, CoreConnect was designed without any requirements to be backward compatible with legacy equipment or protocols and without the constraints of board-level buses, such as limits on the number of pins the edge connector can have.

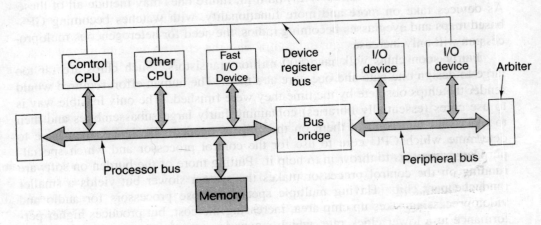

Figure 8-12. An example of the IBM CoreConnect architecture.

CoreConnect consists of three buses. The **processor bus** is a high-speed, synchronous, pipelined bus with 32, 64, or 128 data lines clocked at 66, 133, or 183 MHz. The maximum throughput is thus 23.4 Gbps (vs. 4.2 Gbps for the PCI bus). The pipelining features allow cores to request the bus while a transfer is going on, and to allow different cores to use different lines at the same time, similar to the PCI bus. The processor bus is optimized for short block transfers. It is intended to connect fast cores, such as CPUs, MPEG-2 decoders, high-speed networks, and similar items.

Stretching the processor bus over the entire chip would reduce its performance, so a second bus is present for low-speed I/O devices, such as UARTs, timers, USB controllers, serial I/O devices, and so forth. This **peripheral bus** has been designed with the goal of making it simple to interface 8-, 16-, and 32-bit peripherals to it using no more than a few hundred gates. It, too, is a synchronous bus, with a maximum throughput is 300 Mbps. The two buses are connected by a bridge, not unlike the bridges that were used to connect the PCI and ISA buses in PCs until the ISA bus was phased out a number of years ago.

The third bus is the **device register bus**, a very low-speed, asynchronous, handshaking bus used to allow the processors to access the device registers of all the peripherals in order to control the corresponding devices. It is intended for infrequent transfers of only a few bytes at a time.

By providing a standard on-chip bus, interface, and framework, IBM hopes to create a miniature version of the PCI world, in which many manufacturers produce processors and controllers that plug together easily. One difference, however, is that in the PCI world the manufacturers produce and sell actual boards that PC vendors and end users buy. In the CoreConnect world, third parties design cores, but do not manufacture them. Instead, they license them as intellectual property to consumer electronics and other companies, which then design custom heterogeneous multiprocessor chips based on their own and licensed third-party cores. Since manufacturing such large and complex chips requires a massive investment in fabrication facilities, in most cases the consumer electronics company just does the design, subcontracting the chip manufacturing out to a semiconductor vendor. Cores for numerous CPUs (ARM, MIPS, PowerPC, etc.) exist, as well as for MPEG decoders, digital signal processors, and all the standard I/O controllers.

The IBM CoreConnect is not the only popular on-chip bus on the market. The **AMBA** (**Advanced Microcontroller Bus Architecture**), is also widely used (Flynn, 1997). Other, somewhat less popular on-chip buses are the **VCI** (**Virtual Component Interconnect**) and **OCP-IP** (**Open Core Protocol-International Partnership**), which are also competing for market share (Kogel and Meyr, 2004; and Ouadjaout and Houzet, 2004). On-chip buses are only the start; people are now even thinking of complete networks on a chip (Benini and De Micheli, 2002).

With chip manufacturers having increasing difficulty in raising clock frequencies due to heat dissipation problems, single-chip multiprocessors are a very hot topic. More information can be found in (Claasen, 2003; Jerraya and Wolf, 2005; Kumar et al., 2004; Lavagno, 2002; Lines, 2004; and Ravikumar, 2004).

8.2 COPROCESSORS

Having examined some of the ways of achieving on-chip parallelism, let us now move up a step and look at how the computer can be speeded up by adding a second, specialized processor. These **coprocessors** some in many varieties, from small to large. On the IBM 360 mainframes and all of its successors, independent I/O channels exist for doing input/output. Similarly, the CDC 6600 had 10 independent processors for doing I/O. Graphics and floating-point arithmetic are other areas where coprocessors have been used. Even a DMA chip can be seen as a coprocessor. In some cases, the CPU gives the coprocessor an instruction or set of instructions and tells it to execute them; in other cases, the coprocessor is more independent and runs pretty much on its own.

Physically, coprocessors can range from a separate cabinet (the 360 I/O channels) to a plug-in board (network processors) to an area on the main chip (floating-point). In all cases, what distinguishes them is the fact that some other processor is the main processor and the coprocessors are there to help it. We will now examine thre areas where speedups are possible: network processing, multimedia, and cryptography.

8.2.1 Network Processors

Most computers nowadays are connected to a network or to the Internet. As a result of technological progress in network hardware, networks are now so fast that it has become increasingly difficult to process all the incoming and outgoing data in software. As a consequence, special network processors have been developed to handle the traffic, and many high-end computers now have one of these processors. In this section we will first give a brief introduction to networking and then discuss how network processors work.

Introduction to Networking

Computer networks come in two general types: **local-area networks**, or **LAN**s, which connect multiple computers within a building or campus, and **wide-area networks** or **WAN**s, which connect computers spread over a large geographic area. The most popular LAN is called **Ethernet**. The original Ethernet consisted of a fat cable into which a wire coming from each computer was forcibly inserted using what was euphemistically referred to a **vampire tap**. Modern Ethernets have the computers attached to a central switch, as illustrated in the right-hand portion of Fig. 8-13. The original Ethernet crawled along at 3 Mbps, but the first commercial version was 10 Mbps. It was eventually replaced by fast Ethernet at 100 Mbps and then by gigabit Ethernet at 1 Gbps. A 10-gigabit Ethernet is already on the market and a 40-gigabit Ethernet is in the pipeline.

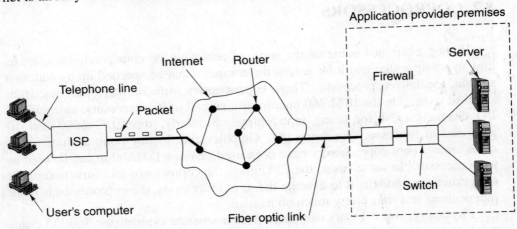

Figure 8-13. How users are connected to servers on the Internet.

WANs are organized differently. They consist of specialized computers called **routers** connected by wires or optical fibers, as shown in the middle of Fig. 8-13. Chunks of data called **packets**, typically 64 to about 1500 bytes, are moved from the source machine through one or more routers until they reach their destination. At each hop, a packet is stored in the router's memory and then forwarded to the next router along the path as soon as the needed transmission line is available. This technique is called **store-and-forward packet switching**.

Although many people think of the Internet as a single WAN, technically it is a collection of many WANs connected together. However, for our purposes, that distinction is not important. Figure 8-13 gives a bird's eye view of the Internet from the perspective of a home user. The user's computer is typically connected to a Web server via the telephone system, either a 56 kbps dial-up modem or ADSL, which was discussed in Chap. 2. (Alternatively, cable TV can be used, in which case the left-hand part of Fig. 8-13 is slightly different and the cable company is the ISP.) The user's computer breaks the data to be sent to the server into packets and sends these packets to the user's **ISP (Internet Service Provider)**, a company that offers Internet access to its customers. The ISP has a high-speed (usually fiber optic) connection to one of the regional or backbone networks that comprise the Internet. The user's packets are forwarded hop-by-hop across the Internet until they arrive at the Web server.

Most companies offering Web service have a specialized computer called a **firewall** that filters all incoming traffic in an attempt to remove unwanted packets (e.g., from hackers trying to break in). The firewall is connected to the local LAN, typically an Ethernet switch, which routes packets to the desired server. Of course, reality is a lot more complicated than we have shown, but the basic idea of Fig. 8-13 is still valid.

Network software consists of multiple **protocols**, each one being a set of formats, exchange sequences, and rules about what the packets mean. For example, when a user wants to fetch a Web page from a server, the user's browser sends a packet containing a *GET PAGE* request using the **HTTP (HyperText Transfer Protocol)** to the server, which understands how to process such requests. Many protocols are in use and often combined. In most situations, protocols are structured as a series of layers, with upper layers handing packets to lower layers for processing, with the bottom layer doing the actual transmission. At the receiving side, the packets work their way up the layers in the reverse order.

Since protocol processing is what network processors do for a living, it is necessary to explain a little bit about protocols before looking at the network processors themselves. Let us go back to the *GET PAGE* request for a moment. How is that sent to the Web server? What happens is that the browser first establishes a connection to the Web server using a protocol called **TCP (Transmission Control Protocol)**. The software that implements this protocol checks that all packets have been correctly received and in the proper order. If a packet gets lost, the TCP software assures that it is retransmitted as often as need be until it received.

In practice, what happens is that the Web browser formats the *GET PAGE* request as a correct HTTP message and then hands it to the TCP software to transmit over the connection. The TCP software adds a header in front of the message containing a sequence number and other information. This header is naturally called the **TCP header**.

When it is done, the TCP software takes the TCP header and payload (containing the *GET PAGE* request) and passes it to another piece of software that implements the **IP protocol** (**Internet Protocol**). This software attaches an **IP header** to the front containing the source address (the machine the packet is coming from), the destination address (the machine the packet is supposed to go to), how many more hops the packet may live (to prevent lost packets from living forever), a checksum (to detect transmission and memory errors), and other fields.

Next the resulting packet (now consisting of the IP header, TCP header, and *GET PAGE* request), is passed down to the data link layer. where a data link header is attached to the front for actual transmission. The data link layer also adds a checksum to the end called a **CRC** (**Cyclic Redundancy Code**) used to detect transmission errors. It might seem that having checksums in the data link layer and the IP layer is redundant, but it improves reliability. At each hop, the CRC is checked and the header and CRC stripped and regenerated, with a format being chosen that is appropriate for the outgoing link. Figure 8-14 shows what the packet looks like when on the Ethernet; on the telephone line, it is similar except with a "telephone line header" instead of an Ethernet header. Header management is important and is one of the things network processors can do. Needless to say, we have only scratched the surface of the subject of computer networking. For a more comprehensive treatment, see (Tanenbaum, 2003).

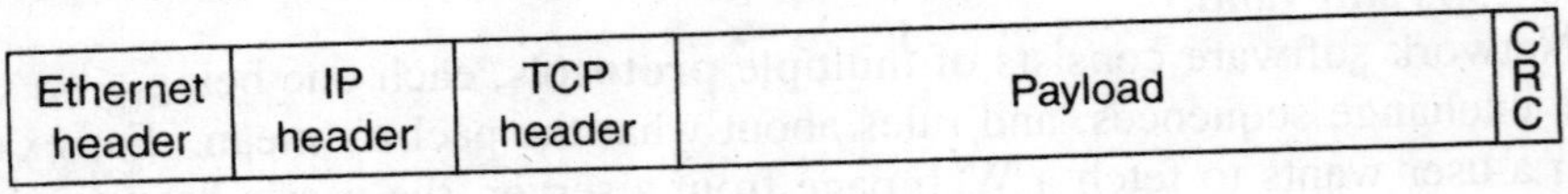

Ethernet header	IP header	TCP header	Payload	C R C

Figure 8-14. A packet as it appears on the Ethernet.

Introduction to Network Processors

Many kinds of devices are connected to networks. End users have personal computers (desktop and notebook), of course, but increasingly also game machines, PDAs (palmtops), and cell phones. Companies have PCs and servers as end systems. However, there are also numerous devices that function as intermediate systems in networks, including routers, switches, firewalls, Web proxies, and load balancers. Interestingly enough, it is the intermediate systems that are the most demanding, since they are expected to move the largest number of packets per second. Servers are also demanding but the user machines are not.

Depending on the network and the packet itself, an incoming packet may need various kinds of processing done to it before being forwarded to either the outgoing line or the application program. This processing may include deciding where to send the packet, fragmenting it or reassembling its pieces, managing its quality of service (especially for audio and video streams), managing security (e.g., encryption or decryption), compression/decompression, and so on.

With LAN speeds approaching 40 gigabits/sec and 1 KB packets, a networked computer might have to process almost 5 million packets/sec. With 64-byte packets, the number of packets that have to be processed per second rises to nearly 80 million. Performing the various functions mentioned above in 12–200 nsec (in addition to the multiple copies of the packet that are invariably needed) is just not doable in software. Hardware assistance is essential.

One kind of hardware solution for fast packet processing is to use a custom **ASIC (Application-Specific Integrated Circuit)**. Such a chip is like a hard-wired program that does whatever set of processing functions it was designed for. Many current routers uses ASICs. ASICs have many problems, however. First, they take a long time to design and a long time to manufacture. They are also rigid, so if new functionality is needed, a new chip has to be designed and manufactured. Furthermore, bug management is a nightmare, since the only way to fix one is to design, manufacture, ship, and install new chips. They are also expensive unless the volume is so large as to allow amortizing the development effort over a substantial number of chips.

A second solution is the **FPGA (Field Programmable Gate Array)** which is a collection of gates that can be organized into the desired circuit by rewiring them in the field. These chips have much a shorter time to market than ASICs and can be rewired in the field by removing them from the system and inserting them into a special reprogramming device. On the other hand, they are complex, slow, and expensive, making them unattractive except for niche applications.

Finally, we come to **network processors**, programmable devices that can handle incoming and outgoing packets at wire speed (i.e., in real time). A common design is a plug-in board containing a network processor on a chip along with memory and support logic. One or more network lines connect to the board and are routed to the network processor. There packets are extracted, processed, and either sent out on a different network line (e.g., for a router) or are sent out onto the main system bus (e.g., the PCI bus) in the case of end-user device such as a PC. A typical network processor board and chip are illustrated in Fig. 8-15.

Both SRAM and SDRAM are provided on the board and typically used in different ways. SRAM is faster, but more expensive, than SDRAM, so there is only a small amount of it. SRAM is used to hold routing tables and other key data structures, whereas SDRAM holds the actual packets being processed. By making the SRAM and SDRAM external to the network processor chip, the board designers are given the flexibility to determine how much of each to supply. In this way, low-end boards with a single network line (e.g., for a PC or server) can

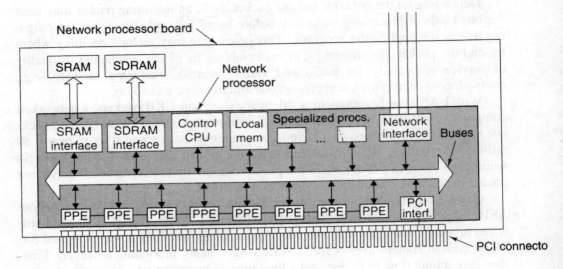

Figure 8-15. A typical network processor board and chip.

be equipped with a small amount of memory whereas a high-end board for a large router can be equipped with much more.

Network processor chips are optimized for processing large numbers of incoming and outgoing packets quickly. Millions of packets per second per network line, that is, and a router could easily have half a dozen lines. The only way to achieve such processing rates is to build network processors that are highly parallel inside. And indeed, all network processors consist of multiple **PPEs**, variously called **Protocol/Programmable/Packet Processing Engines**. Each one is a (possibly modified) RISC core and a small amount of internal memory for holding the program and some variables.

The PPEs can be organized in two different ways. The simplest organization is having all the PPEs being identical. When a packet arrives at the network processor, either an incoming packet from a network line or an outgoing packet from the bus, it is handed to an idle PPE for processing. If no PPE is idle, the packet is queued in the on-board SDRAM until a PPE frees up. When this organization is used, the horizontal connections shown between the PPEs in Fig. 8-15 do not exist because the PPEs have no need to communicate with one another.

The other PPE organization is the pipeline. In this one, each PPE performs one processing step and then feeds a pointer to its output packet to the next PPE in the pipeline. In this way, the PPE pipeline acts very much like the CPU pipelines we studied in Chap. 2. In both organizations, the PPEs are completely programmable.

In advanced designs, the PPEs have multithreading, meaning that they have multiple register sets and a hardware register indicating which one is currently in use. This feature is used to run multiple programs at the same time by allowing a program (i.e., thread) switch by just changing the "current register set" variable. Most commonly, when a PPE stalls, for example, when it references the SDRAM (which takes multiple clock cycles), it can instantaneously switch to a runnable thread. In this manner, a PPE can achieve a high utilization even when frequently blocking to access the SDRAM or perform some other slow external operation.

In addition to the PPEs, all network processors contain a control processor, usually just a standard general-purpose RISC CPU, for performing all work not related to packet processing, such as updating the routing tables. Its program and data are in the local on-chip memory. Furthermore, many network processor chips also contain one or more specialized processors for doing pattern matching or other critical operations. These processors are really small ASICs that are good at doing one simple operation, such as looking up a destination address in the routing table. All the components of the network processor communicate over one or more on-chip, parallel buses that run at multigigabit/sec speeds.

Packet Processing

When a packet arrives, it goes through a number of processing stages, independent of whether the network processor has a parallel or pipeline organization. Some network processors divide these steps into operations performed on incoming packets (either from a network line or from the system bus), called **ingress processing** and operations performed on outgoing packets, called **egress processing**. When this distinction is made, every packet first goes through ingress processing, then through egress processing. The boundary between ingress and egress processing is flexible because some steps can be done in either part (e.g., collecting traffic statistics).

Below we will discuss a potential ordering of the various steps, but note that not all packets need all steps and that many other orderings are equally valid.

1. **Checksum verification.** If the incoming packet is arriving from the Ethernet, the CRC is recomputed so it can be compared with the one in the packet to make sure there was no transmission error. If the Ethernet CRC is correct or not present, the IP checksum is recomputed and compared to the one in the packet to make sure the IP packet was not damaged by a faulty bit in the sender's memory after the IP checksum was computed there. If all checksums are correct, the packet is accepted for further processing; otherwise, it is simply discarded.

2. **Field extraction.** The relevant header is parsed and key fields are extracted. In an Ethernet switch, only the Ethernet header is examined, whereas in an IP router, it is the IP header that is inspected. The key fields are stored in registers (parallel PPE organization) or SRAM (pipeline organization).

3. **Packet classification.** The packet is classified according to a series of programmable rules. The simplest classification is to distinguish data packets from control packets, but usually much finer distinctions are made.

4. **Path selection.** Most network processors have a special fast path optimized for handling plain old garden-variety data packets, with all other packets being treated differently, often by the control processor. Consequently, either the fast path or the slow path has to be selected.

5. **Destination network determination.** IP packets contain a 32-bit destination address. It is not possible (or desirable) to have a 2^{32} entry table to lookup the destination of each IP packet, so the leftmost part of each IP address is the network number and the rest specifies a machine on that network. Network numbers can be of any length, so determining the destination network number is nontrivial and made worse by the fact that multiple matches are possible and the longest one counts. Often a custom ASIC is used in this step.

6. **Route lookup.** Once the number of the destination network is known, the outgoing line to use can be looked up in a table in the SRAM. Again, a custom ASIC may be used in this step.

7. **Fragmentation and reassembly.** Programs like to present large payloads to the TCP layer to reduce the number of system calls needed, but TCP, IP, and Ethernet all have maximum sizes for the packets they can handle. As a consequence of these limits, payloads and packets may have to be fragmented at the sending side and the pieces reassembled at the receiving side. These are tasks the network processor can perform.

8. **Computation.** Heavy-duty computation on the payload is sometimes required, for example, data compression/decompression and encryption/decryption. These are tasks a network processor can perform.

9. **Header management.** Sometimes headers have to be added, removed, or have some of their fields modified. For example, the IP header has a field that counts the number of hops the packet may yet make before being discarded. Every time it is retransmitted, this field must be decremented, something the network processor can do.

10. **Queue management.** Incoming and outgoing packets often have to be queued while waiting their turn at being processed. Multimedia applications may need a certain interpacket spacing in time to avoid

jitter. A firewall or router may need to distribute the incoming load among multiple outgoing lines according to certain rules. All of these tasks can be done by the network processor.

11. **Checksum generation.** Outgoing packets need to be checksummed. The IP checksum can be generated by the network processor, but the Ethernet CRC is generally computed by hardware.

12. **Accounting.** In some cases, accounting for packet traffic is needed, especially when one network is forwarding traffic for other networks as a commercial service. The network processor can do the accounting.

13. **Statistics gathering.** Finally, many organizations like to collect statistics about their traffic, and the network processor is a good place to collect them.

Improving Performance

Performance is the name of the game for network processors. What can be done to improve it? But before improving it, we have to define what it means. One metric is the number of packets that are forwarded per second. A second one is the number of bytes forwarded per second. These are different measures and a scheme that works well with small packets may not work as well with large ones. In particular, with small packets, improving the number of destination lookups per second may help a lot, but with large packets it may not.

The most straightforward way to improve performance is to increase the speed of the network processor clock. Of course, performance is not linear with clock speed, since memory cycle time and other factors also influence it. Also, a faster clock means more heat must be dissipated.

Introducing more PPEs and parallelism is often a winner, especially with an organization consisting of parallel PPEs. A deeper pipeline can also help, but only if the job of processing a packet can be split up into smaller pieces.

Another technique is to add specialized processors or ASICs to handle specific, time consuming operations that are performed repeatedly and that can be done faster in hardware than in software. Lookups, checksum computations, and cryptography are among the many candidates.

Adding more internal buses and widening existing buses may help gain speed by moving packets through the system faster. Finally, replacing SDRAM by SRAM can usually be counted to improve performance, but at a price, of course.

There is much more that can be said about network processors, of course. Some references are (Comer, 2005; Crowley et al., 2002; Lekkas, 2003; and Papaefstathiou et al., 2004).

8.2.2 Media Processors

A second area in which coprocessors are used is for handling high-resolution photographic images, audio, and video streams. Ordinary CPUs are not especially good at the massive computations needed to process the large amounts of data required in these applications. For this reason, some current PCs and most future PCs will be equipped with media coprocessors to which they can offload large portions of the work.

The Nexperia Media Processor

We will study this increasingly important area by means of an example: the Philips Nexperia, a family of chips that is available at several clock frequencies. The **Nexperia** is a self-contained single-chip heterogeneous multiprocessor in the sense of Fig. 8-11. It contains multiple cores, including a TriMedia VLIW CPU for control, but also numerous cores for image, audio, video, and networking processing. It can be used either as a stand-alone main processor in a CD, DVD, or MP3 player or recorder, TV set or set-top box, still or video camera, etc., or as a coprocessor in a PC for processing images and media streams. In both configurations, it runs its own small real-time operating system.

The Nexperia has three functions: capturing input streams and converting them to data structures in memory, processing these data structures, and finally, outputting them in forms suitable for the various output devices attached. For example, when a PC is used as a DVD player, the Nexperia can be programmed to read the encrypted, compressed video stream from the DVD disc, decrypt and decompress it, and then output it at a size appropriate to the window it is being displayed in. And all of this can be done in the background, without involving the computer's main CPU at all once the DVD player program has been loaded into the Nexperia.

All incoming data are first stored in memory for processing; there is no direct connection between input devices and output devices. Capturing input includes decoding from a wide variety of video sizes and formats (including MPEG-1, MPEG-2, and MPEG-4), audio formats (including AAC, Dolby, and MP3) and converting to appropriate data structures for storage and processing. Input can come from the PCI bus, Ethernet, or dedicated input lines (e.g., a microphone or stereo system plugged directly into the chip). The Nexperia chip has 456 pins, some of which are available for direct input and output of media (and other) streams.

Data processing is controlled by the software in the TriMedia CPU, which can be programmed for whatever is needed. Typical tasks include deinterlacing video to improve its sharpness, correcting the brightness, contrast, and color of images, scaling image size, converting between different video formats, and reducing noise. Usually, the CPU acts as the general contractor, subcontracting out much of the work to the specialized cores on the chip.

Output functionality includes coding the data structures in a form suitable for the output device, merging multiple (video, audio, image, 2D-graphics) data sources, and controlling the output devices. As with input, output can go to the PCI bus, Ethernet, or dedicated output lines (e.g., a loudspeaker or amplifier).

A block diagram of the Nexperia PNX 1500 chip is given in Fig. 8-16. Other versions are slightly different, so to be consistent, throughout this section when we say "Nexperia" we mean the PNX 1500 implementation. It has four major sections: control, input, processing, and output. The CPU is the 32-bit TriMedia VLIW processor discussed in Sec. 8.1.1 running at 300 MHz. Its program, usually written in C or C++, determines the Nexperia's functionality.

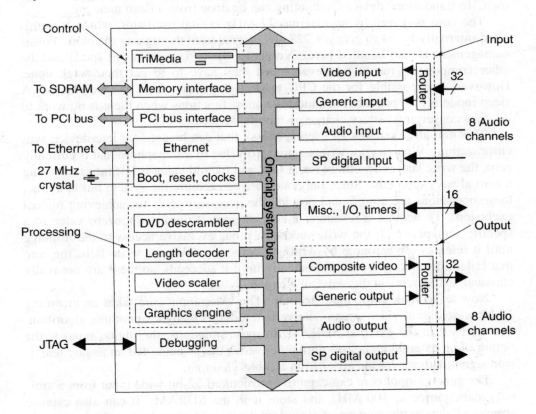

Figure 8-16. The Nexperia heterogeneous multiprocessor on a chip.

The Nexperia does not contain any main memory on chip, except for the two caches inside the TriMedia CPU. Instead it has an interface to external memory, allowing for 8–256 MB of DDR SDRAM, which is plenty for typical multimedia applications. With a clock of 200 MHz, the memory bandwidth is 1.6 GB/sec.

A full PCI interface is also included on chip, with 8-, 16-, and 32-bit transfers at 33 MHz. When used as the main CPU inside a consumer electronics device (e.g., a DVD player), the PCI interface can also act as bus arbiter. This interface can be used, for example, to talk to a DVD drive.

Direct ethernet connectivity is provided by a dedicated core that can handle 10- and 100-Mbps Ethernet connections. Consequently, a Nexperia-based camcorder can output a digital video stream over an Ethernet to a remote capture or display device.

The next core handles booting, resetting, clocks, and some other minor features. If a certain pin on the Nexperia is asserted, a reset is initiated. The core can also be programmed as a dead man's switch. If the CPU fails to ping it for a certain period of time, it assumes the system has hung and initiates a reboot on its own. In stand-alone devices, rebooting can be done from a flash memory.

The core is driven by an external 27 MHz crystal oscillator, which is multiplied internally by 64 to give a 1.728 GHz signal used throughout the chip. Power management is also handled here. Normally, the CPU runs at full speed and the other components run at whatever speed they have to to get their work done. However, it is possible for the CPU to slow down the clock to save energy. A sleep mode is also provided to shut down most functions when there is no work to do, thus conserving battery charge on mobile devices.

This unit also contains 16 "semaphores" that can be used for interdevice synchronization. When a core writes a nonzero value to a semaphore that is currently zero, the write succeeds; otherwise, it fails and the old value is left intact. Writing a zero always succeeds. Since only one core can acquire the system bus at a time, these operations are atomic and provide the necessary tools for achieving mutual exclusion. To acquire a resource, a core attempts to write a nonzero value to a specific semaphore. If the write succeeds, it has exclusive access to the resource until it releases the resource by writing a zero to it. When a write fails, the core that failed has to keep trying periodically until it succeeds, so these are not really classical semaphores in the sense of Chap. 6.

Now let us look at the input section. The video input core takes an incoming 10-bit wide digital video stream, converts it to 8 bits using a smoothing algorithm, and stores it in the external SDRAM. In most situations, the digital input is the output of an external analog-to-digital converter that is being fed an analog television signal, either over the air or from a cable TV input.

The generic input core can capture unstructured 32-bit wide input from a arbitrary data source at 100 MHz and store it in the SDRAM. It can also capture structured data with markers delineating the record boundaries. The router in front of the two digital video inputs demultiplexes them and can also do some video transformations on the fly. Demultiplexing is needed because the same pins are used for both video input and generic input.

The audio input core can capture up to eight channels of stereo music or voice with 8-, 16-, or 32-bit precision at up to 96 kHz and store it in the SDRAM. It can also decode compressed formats, mix channels, change the sampling rate, and apply filters, all on the fly before storing the audio data.

The SP digital input core allows inputing digital audio signals that conform to the Sony-Philips digital audio standard (IEC 1937). In this way, digital audio can be moved from one device to another with no loss in quality.

Once the audio, video, or other data has been input, it normally needs to be processed, which is what the next section handles. Movies sold or rented on DVDs are encrypted (scrambled) to prevent copying. The DVD descrambler removes the encryption to provide the original movie, compressed with MPEG-2. This decryption is a memory-to-memory operation, with the input coming from one buffer and the output going to a different buffer.

The length decoder goes further and removes the variable length coding features of MPEG-2 (or MPEG-1) compression producing semi-uncompressed data for the core of the MPEG processing, which is done by the TriMedia in software. The reason for this split is that the removal of the variable-length decoding (Huffman and run-length decoding) does not uses the TriMedia's capabilities very efficiently, so it was deemed better to use a couple of square millimeters of silicon to do it in hardware. These operations, all memory to memory, produce a straightforward pixel map.

The pixel map can be in any one of three general formats, each with three or four variants for different sizes and parameters. The first format is **indexed color**, in which each value is an index into a **CLUT (Color Look Up Table)** containing a 24-bit color value and an 8-bit **alpha channel mask**, used for determining transparency when multiple layers are overlaid. The second format is RGB, the way computer monitors work, with separate values for the red, green, and blue intensity of each pixel. The third format is YUV, designed for how television signals are encoded. Rather than encoding the red, green, and blue components separately, a transformation is done in the camera to produce a luminance (brightness) channel and two chrominance (color) channels. This system allows more bandwidth to be allocated to luminance than chrominance, which, in turn, provides better noise immunity during transmission. For an application involving television in and television out, the YUV format makes sense. By restricting the stored format to a limited number of options, each core is capable of reading the output produced by all the other cores.

The video scaler accepts a list of scaling tasks and then performs them, at a maximum rate of 120 million pixels/sec. These tasks include:

1. Deinterlacing.
2. Horizontal and vertical scaling.
3. Linear and nonlinear aspect ratio conversion.
4. Conversion between different pixel formats.
5. Luminance histogram collection.
6. Flicker reduction.

Broadcast television signals are **interlaced**, meaning that for each frame, which consists of 525 scan lines (625 for PAL and SECAM), first all the even lines are transmitted, then the odd ones. Deinterlacing produces a better-quality **progressive scan**, in which all the scan lines are processed or transmitted in their true order and refreshed at twice the interlaced frame rate (29.97 fps for NTSC and 25 fps for PAL and SECAM). Horizontal and vertical scaling allow images to be increased or reduced in size, possibly after cropping. Standard television has a width:height aspect ratio of 4:3, but wide-screen television is 16:9, more suited to the 3:2 ratio of 35 mm movies. The scaler can convert between these aspect ratios, either linearly or using a nonlinear algorithm. It can also convert among the index, RGB, and YUV formats and build a histogram of the luminance value, which is useful for improving image quality on output. Finally, certain transformations can be done to reduce image flicker.

The graphics engine does two-dimensional rendering from object descriptions. It can also fill enclosed areas and perform **bitblt** graphic operations, which amount to taking two rectangular pixel maps and combining them using AND, OR, XOR, or some other Boolean function.

There are no cores for doing audio processing. All audio processing not done on input is done by the TriMedia CPU in software. Audio requires so little data that processing it in software is not a problem at all. Also, many applications do not require any audio processing at all, except possibly, format conversions.

The debugging core helps the designers and programmers debug the hardware and software. It provides an interface to **JTAG** (**Joint Test Action Group**) aware instrumentation and tools, as defined in IEEE standard 1149.1.

The output section takes the processed data from memory and outputs it. The composite video core takes one or more data structures representing pixels, normalizes them in certain ways and then blends them in specified ways for output. Data in indexed format is de-indexed on the fly to get the actual pixels, and incompatible formats are converted as need be. This core can also do contrast, brightness, and color correction, if required. It can also perform chroma keying, in which an actor standing in front of a pure blue screen is isolated from the screen and visually placed in front of a background taken from a different source. Similarly, animated cartoons in which foreground characters move in front of a still or scrolling background can be produced here. And, of course, the final result is converted to the video or television system format required (e.g., NTSC, PAL, or SECAM), including the generation of horizontal and vertical sync pulses.

Since it costs nothing extra, it is expected that most Nexperia-based systems will be able to handle all three television formats automatically so that they can be sold unmodified anywhere in the world. Similarly, adding **HDTV** (**High Definition TeleVision**) to the mix in any of the formats means just adding a bit more software to handle conversions to and from the memory data structures.

The generic output core just moves bits, 8, 16, or 32 per cycle at 100 MHz, giving a maximum bandwidth of 3.2 Gbps. By interfacing the generic output of one Nexperia chip to the generic input of another Nexperia chip, file transfers can be performed at speeds exceeding gigabit Ethernet (1 Gbps). This interface also allows the CPU to produce custom output of whatever type it needs, in software.

The output router multiplexes the two output sources and also adds some functionality, including refreshing flat panel (TFT) displays of sizes up to 1280×768 pixels at 60 Hz or refreshing interlaced or progressive television sets. Multiplexing is needed because the composite video and generic outputs share the same pins.

The audio output core can produce up to 8 stereo channels with 32-bit precision at sampling rates up to 96 kHz. Commonly, this output drives an external digital-to-analog converter. The SP digital output can be connected to the SP digital input of devices that use the Sony-Philips digital audio standard.

The final core handles general-purpose I/O. Sixteen pins are available for any use required. They can be connected to buttons, switches, or LEDs to allow them to be sensed or activated in software. They can even be used for medium speed (20 Mbps) software-controlled network protocols. Various timers, counters, and event handlers are also present here.

All in all, the Nexperia has an enormous amount of computing power for audio-visual applications, and like network processors, allows the CPU to offload a massive amount of work. The amount of computing power is even larger than it may first appear, since all the cores can run in parallel with each other and with the CPU. And perhaps surprisingly, it costs less than \$20 when purchased in large volume. By now the power of coprocessors, especially those based on hetero-geneous multiprocessor chips, should be coming clearer. For an analogous chip aimed at telephony rather than multimedia, see (Nickolls et al., 2003).

8.2.3 Cryptoprocessors

A third area in which coprocessors are popular is security, especially network security. When a connection is established between a client and a server, in many cases they must first authenticate each other. Then a secure, encrypted connec-tion has to be established between them so data can be transferred in a secure way to foil any snoopers who may tap the line.

The problem with security is that to achieve it, cryptography has to be used, and cryptography is very compute intensive. Cryptography comes in two general flavors, called **symmetric key cryptography** and **public-key cryptography**. The former is based on mixing up the bits very thoroughly, sort of the electronic equivalent of throwing a message into an electric blender. The latter is based on multiplication and exponeniation of large (e.g., 1024-bit) numbers and is extremely time consuming.

To handle the computation needed to encrypt data securely for transmission or storage and then decrypt it later, various companies have produced crypto copro-cessors, sometimes as PCI bus plug-in cards. These coprocessors have special hardware that enables them to do the necessary cryptography much faster than an ordinary CPU can do it. Unfortunately, a detailed discussion of how cryptoprocessors work would first require explaining quite a bit about cryptography itself, which is beyond the scope of this book. For more information about crypto coprocessors, see (Daneshbeh and Hasan, 2004; and Lutz and Hasan, 2004).

8.3 SHARED-MEMORY MULTIPROCESSORS

We have now seen how parallelism can be added to single chips and to individual systems by adding a coprocessor. The next step is to see how multiple full-blown CPUs can be combined into larger systems. Systems with multiple CPUs can be divided into multiprocessors and multicomputers. After taking a close look at what these terms actually mean, we will first study multiprocessors and then multicomputers.

8.3.1 Multiprocessors vs. Multicomputers

In any parallel computer system, CPUs working on different parts of the same job must communicate with one another to exchange information. Precisely how they should do this is the subject of much debate in the architectural community. Two distinct designs, multiprocessors and multicomputers, have been proposed and implemented. The key difference between the two is the presence or absence of shared memory. This difference permeates how they are designed, built, and programmed, as well as their scale and price.

Multiprocessors

A parallel computer in which all the CPUs share a common memory is called a **multiprocessor**, as indicated symbolically in Fig. 8-17. All processes working together on a multiprocessor can share a single virtual address space mapped onto the common memory. Any process can read or write a word of memory by just executing a LOAD or STORE instruction. Nothing else is needed. The hardware does the rest. Two processes can communicate by simply having one of them write data to memory and having the other one read them back.

The ability for two (or more) processes to communicate by just reading and writing memory is the reason multiprocessors are popular. It is an easy model for programmers to understand and is applicable to a wide range of problems. Consider, for example, a program that inspects a bit-map image and lists all the objects in it. One copy of the image is kept in memory, as shown in Fig. 8-17(b). Each of the 16 CPUs runs a single process, which has been assigned one of the 16 sections to analyze. Nevertheless, each process has access to the entire image, which is essential, since some objects may occupy multiple sections. If a process

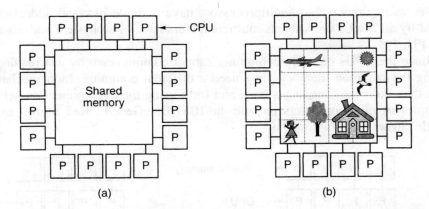

Figure 8-17. (a) A multiprocessor with 16 CPUs sharing a common memory. (b) An image partitioned into 16 sections, each being analyzed by a different CPU.

discovers that one of its objects extends over a section boundary, it just follows the object into the next section by reading the words of that section. In this example, some objects will be discovered by multiple processes, so some coordination is needed at the end to determine how many houses, trees, and airplanes there are.

Because all CPUs in a multiprocessor see the same memory image, there is only one copy of the operating system. Consequently, there is only one page map and one process table. When a process blocks, its CPU saves its state in the operating system tables, and then looks in those tables to find another process to run. It is this single-system image that distinguishes a multiprocessor from a multicomputer, in which each computer has its own copy of the operating system.

A multiprocessor, like all computers, must have I/O devices, such as disks, network adaptors, and other equipment. In some multiprocessor systems, only certain CPUs have access to the I/O devices, and thus have a special I/O function. In other ones, every CPU has equal access to every I/O device. When every CPU has equal access to all the memory modules and all the I/O devices, and is treated as interchangeable with the others by the operating system, the system is called an **SMP (Symmetric MultiProcessor)**.

Multicomputers

The second possible design for a parallel architecture is one in which each CPU has its own private memory, accessible only to itself and not to any other CPU. Such a design is called a **multicomputer**, or sometimes a **distributed memory system**, and is illustrated in Fig. 8-18(a). The key aspect of a multicomputer that distinguishes it from a multiprocessor is that each CPU in a multicomputer has its own private, local memory that it can access by just executing LOAD and STORE instructions, but which no other CPU can access using LOAD and

STORE instructions. Thus multiprocessors have a single physical address space shared by all the CPUs whereas multicomputers have one physical address space per CPU.

Since the CPUs on a multicomputer cannot communicate by just reading and writing the common memory, they need a different communication mechanism. What they do is pass messages back and forth using the interconnection network. Examples of multicomputers include the IBM BlueGene/L, Red Storm, and the Google cluster.

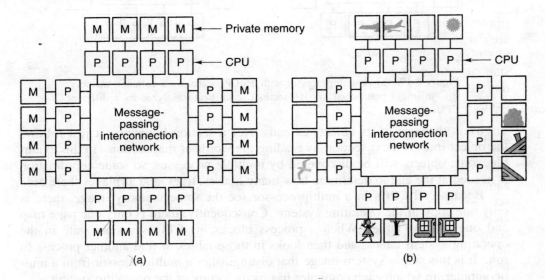

Figure 8-18. (a) A multicomputer with 16 CPUs, each with its own private memory. (b) The bit-map image of Fig. 8-17 split up among the 16 memories.

The absence of hardware shared memory on a multicomputer has important implications for the software structure. Having a single virtual address space with all processes being able to read and write all of memory by just executing LOAD and STORE instructions is impossible on a multicomputer. For example, if CPU 0 (the one in the upper left-hand corner) of Fig. 8-17(b) discovers that part of its object extends into the section assigned to CPU 1, it can nevertheless just continue reading memory to access the tail of the airplane. On the other hand, if CPU 0 in Fig. 8-18(b) makes the same discovery, it cannot just read CPU 1's memory. It has to do something quite different to get the data it needs.

In particular, it has to discover (somehow) which CPU has the data it needs and send that CPU a message requesting a copy of the data. Typically it will then block until the request is answered. When the message arrives at CPU 1, software there has to analyze it and send back the needed data. When the reply message gets back to CPU 0, the software is unblocked and can continue executing.

On a multicomputer, communication between processes often uses software primitives such as send and receive. This gives the software a different, and far more complicated structure, than on a multiprocessor. It also means that correctly dividing up the data and placing them in the optimal locations is a major issue on a multicomputer. It is less of an issue on a multiprocessor since placement does not affect correctness or programmability although it may affect performance. In short, programming a multicomputer is much more difficult than programming a multiprocessor.

Under these conditions, why would anyone build multicomputers, when multiprocessors are easier to program? The answer is simple: large multicomputers are much simpler and cheaper to build than multiprocessors with the same number of CPUs. Implementing a memory shared by even a few hundred CPUs is a substantial undertaking, whereas building a multicomputer with 10,000 CPUs or more is straightforward. Later in this chapter we will study a multicomputer with over 50,000 CPUs.

Thus we have a dilemma: multiprocessors are hard to build but easy to program whereas multicomputers are easy to build but hard to program. This observation has led to a great deal of effort to construct hybrid systems that are relatively easy to build and relatively easy to program. This work has led to the realization that shared memory can be implemented in various ways, each with its own set of advantages and disadvantages. In fact, much of the research in parallel architectures these days relates to the convergence of multiprocessor and multicomputer architectures into hybrid forms that combine the strengths of each. The holy grail here is to find designs that are **scalable**, that is, continue to perform well as more and more CPUs are added.

One approach to building hybrid systems is based on the fact that modern computer systems are not monolithic but are constructed as a series of layers—the theme of this book. This insight opens the possibility of implementing the shared memory at any one of several layers, as shown in Fig. 8-19. In Fig. 8-19(a) we see the shared memory being implemented by the hardware as a true multiprocessor. In this design, there is a single copy of the operating system with a single set of tables, in particular, the memory allocation table. When a process needs more memory, it traps to the operating system, which then looks in its table for a free page and maps the page into the caller's address space. As far as the operating system is concerned, there is a single memory and it keeps track of which process owns which page in software. There are many ways to implement hardware shared memory, as we will see later.

A second possibility is to use multicomputer hardware and have the operating system simulate shared memory by providing a single system-wide paged shared virtual address space. In this approach, called **DSM** (**Distributed Shared Memory**) (Li and Hudak, 1989), each page is located in one of the memories of Fig. 8-18(a). Each machine has its own virtual memory and its own page tables. When a CPU does a LOAD or STORE on a page it does not have, a trap to the

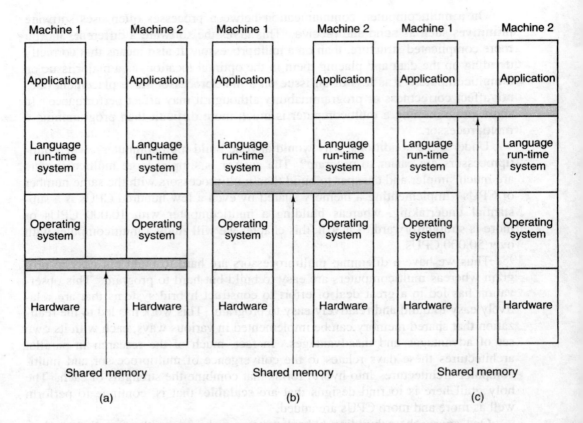

Figure 8-19. Various layers where shared memory can be implemented. (a) The hardware. (b) The operating system. (c) The language runtime system.

operating system occurs. The operating system then locates the page and asks the CPU currently holding it to unmap the page and send it over the interconnection network. When it arrives, the page is mapped in and the faulting instruction is restarted. In effect, the operating system is just satisfying page faults from remote memory instead of from disk. To the user, the machine looks as if it has shared memory. We will examine DSM later in this chapter.

A third possibility is to have a user-level runtime system implement a (possibly language-specific) form of shared memory. In this approach, the programming language provides some kind of shared memory abstraction, which is then implemented by the compiler and runtime system. For example, the Linda model is based on the abstraction of a shared space of tuples (data records containing a collection of fields). Processes on any machine can input a tuple from the shared tuple space or output a tuple to the shared tuple space. Because access to the tuple space is controlled entirely in software (by the Linda runtime system), no special hardware or operating system support is needed.

Another example of a language-specific shared memory implemented by the runtime system is the Orca model of shared data objects. In Orca, processes share generic objects rather than just tuples and can execute object-specific methods on them. When a method changes the internal state of an object, it is up to the runtime system to make sure all copies of the object on all machines are simultaneously updated. Again, because objects are a strictly software concept, the implementation can be done by the runtime system without help from the operating system or hardware. We will look at both Linda and Orca later in this chapter.

Taxonomy of Parallel Computers

Now let us get back to our main topic, the architecture of parallel computers. Many kinds of parallel computers have been proposed and built over the years, so it is natural to ask if there is some way of categorizing them into a taxonomy. Many researchers have tried, with mixed results (Flynn, 1972; and Treleaven, 1985). Unfortunately, the Carolus Linnaeus† of parallel computing is yet to emerge. The only scheme that is used much is Flynn's, and even his is, at best, a very crude approximation. It is given in Fig. 8-20.

Instruction streams	Data streams	Name	Examples
1	1	SISD	Classical Von Neumann machine
1	Multiple	SIMD	Vector supercomputer, array processor
Multiple	1	MISD	Arguably none
Multiple	Multiple	MIMD	Multiprocessor, multicomputer

Figure 8-20. Flynn's taxonomy of parallel computers.

Flynn's classification is based on two concepts—instruction streams and data streams. An instruction stream corresponds to a program counter. A system with n CPUs has n program counters, hence n instruction streams.

A data stream consists of a set of operands. The temperature computation example given earlier has multiple data streams, one for each sensor.

The instruction and data streams are, to some extent, independent, so four combinations exist, as listed in Fig. 8-20. SISD is just the classical, sequential von Neumann computer. It has one instruction stream, one data stream, and does one thing at a time. SIMD machines have a single control unit that issues one instruction at a time, but they have multiple ALUs to carry it out on multiple data sets simultaneously. The ILLIAC IV (Fig. 2-7) is the prototype of SIMD

---

† Carolus Linnaeus (1707-1778) was the Swedish biologist who devised the system now used for classifying all plants and animals into kingdom, phylum, class, order, family, genus, and species.

machines. Mainstream SIMD machines are increasingly rare, but conventional computers sometimes have some SIMD instructions for processing audio-visual material. The Pentium SSE instructions are SIMD. Nevertheless, there is one new area in which some of the ideas from the SIMD world are playing a role: stream processors. These machines are specifically designed to handle the demands of multimedia rendering and may become important in the future (Kapasi et al., 2003).

MISD machines are a somewhat strange category, with multiple instructions operating on the same piece of data. It is not clear if any such machines exist, although some people regard pipelined machines as MISD.

Finally, we have MIMD, which are just multiple independent CPUs operating as part of a larger system. Most parallel processors fall into this category. Both multiprocessors and multicomputers are MIMD machines.

Flynn's taxonomy stops here, but we have extended it in Fig. 8-21. SIMD has been split into two subgroups. The first one is for numeric supercomputers and other machines that operate on vectors, performing the same operation on each vector element. The second one is for parallel-type machines, such as the ILLIAC IV, in which a master control unit broadcasts instructions to many independent ALUs.

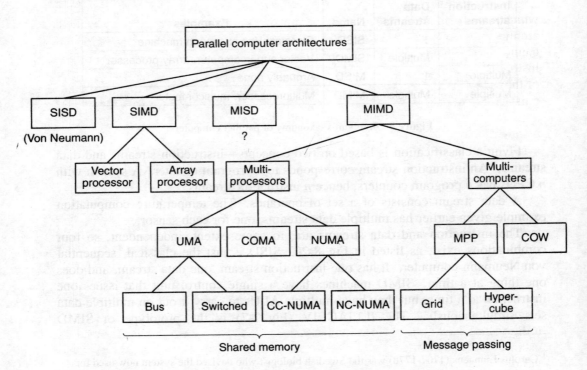

Figure 8-21. A taxonomy of parallel computers.

In our taxonomy, the MIMD category has been split into multiprocessors (shared-memory machines), and multicomputers (message-passing machines). Three kinds of multiprocessors exist, distinguished by the way the shared memory is implemented on them. They are called **UMA** (**Uniform Memory Access**), **NUMA** (**NonUniform Memory Access**), and **COMA** (**Cache Only Memory Access**). These categories exist because in large multiprocessors, the memory is usually split up into multiple modules. UMA machines have the property that each CPU has the same access time to every memory module. In other words, every memory word can be read as fast as every other memory word. If this is technically impossible, the fastest references are slowed down to match the slowest ones, so programmers do not see the difference. This is what "uniform" means here. This uniformity makes the performance predictable, an important factor for writing efficient code.

In contrast, in a NUMA multiprocessor, this property does not hold. Often there is a memory module close to each CPU and accessing that memory module is much faster than accessing distant ones. The result is that for performance reasons, it matters where code and data are placed. COMA machines are also nonuniform, but in a different way. We will study each of these types and their subcategories in detail later.

The other main category of MIMD machines consists of the multicomputers, which, unlike the multiprocessors, do not have shared primary memory at the architectural level. In other words, the operating system on a multicomputer CPU cannot access memory attached to a different CPU by just executing a LOAD instruction. It has to send an explicit message and wait for an answer. The ability of the operating system to read a distant word by just doing a LOAD is what distinguishes multiprocessors from multicomputers. As we mentioned before, even on a multicomputer, user programs may have the ability to access remote memory by using LOAD and STORE instructions, but this illusion is supported by the operating system, not the hardware. This difference is subtle, but very important. Because multicomputers do not have direct access to remote memory, they are sometimes called **NORMA** (**NO Remote Memory Access**) machines.

Multicomputers can be roughly divided into two categories. The first category contains the **MPP**s (**Massively Parallel Processors**), which are expensive supercomputers consisting of many CPUs tightly coupled by a high-speed proprietary interconnection network. The IBM SP/3 is a well-known commercial example.

The other category consists of regular PCs or workstations, possibly rack-mounted, and connected by commercial off-the-shelf interconnection technology. Logically, there is not much difference, but huge supercomputers costing many millions of dollars are used differently than networks of PCs assembled by the users for a fraction of the price of an MPP. These home-brew machines go by various names, including **NOW** (**Network of Workstations**), **COW** (**Cluster of Workstations**), or sometimes just **cluster**.

8.3.2 Memory Semantics

Even though all multiprocessors present the CPUs with the image of a single shared address space, often there are many memory modules present, each holding some portion of the physical memory. The CPUs and memories are often connected by a complex interconnection network, as discussed in Sec. 8.1.2. Several CPUs may be attempting to read a memory word at the same time several other CPUs are attempting to write the same word, and some of the request messages may pass each other in transit and be delivered in a different order than they were issued. Add to this problem the existence of multiple copies of some blocks of memory (e.g., in caches), and the result can easily be chaos unless strict measures are taken to prevent it. In this section we will see what shared memory really means and look at how memories can reasonably respond under these circumstances.

One view of memory semantics is to see it as a contract between the software and the memory hardware (Adve and Hill, 1990). If the software agrees to abide by certain rules, the memory agrees to deliver certain results. The discussion then centers around what the rules are. These rules are called **consistency models**, and many different ones have been proposed and implemented.

To give an idea of what the problem is, suppose that CPU 0 writes the value 1 to some memory word and a little later CPU 1 writes the value 2 to the same word. Now CPU 2 reads the word and gets the value 1. Should the computer owner bring the computer to the repair shop to get it fixed? That depends on what the memory promised (its contract).

Strict Consistency

The simplest model is **strict consistency**. With this model, any read to a location x always returns the value of the most recent write to x. Programmers love this model, but it is effectively impossible to implement in any way other than having a single memory module that simply services all requests first-come, first-served, with no caching and no data replication. Such an implementation would make memory an enormous bottleneck and is thus not a serious candidate, unfortunately.

Sequential Consistency

Next best is a model called **sequential consistency** (Lamport, 1979). The idea here is that in the presence of multiple read and write requests, some interleaving of all the requests is chosen by the hardware (nondeterministically), but all CPUs see the same order.

To see what this means, consider an example. Suppose that CPU 1 writes the value 100 to word *x*, and 1 nsec later CPU 2 writes the value 200 to word *x*. Now suppose that 1 nsec after the second write was issued (but not necessarily completed yet) two other CPUs, 3 and 4, read word *x* twice in rapid succession, as shown in Fig. 8-22(a). Three possible orderings of the six events (two writes and four reads) are shown in Fig. 8-22(b)–(d), respectively. In Fig. 8-22(b), CPU 3 gets (200, 200) and CPU 4 gets (200, 200). In Fig. 8-22(c), they get (100, 200) and (200, 200), respectively. In Fig. 8-22(d), they get (100, 100) and (200, 100), respectively. All of these are legal, as well as some other possibilities that are not shown.

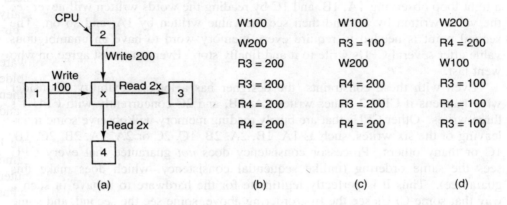

Figure 8-22. (a) Two CPUs writing and two CPUs reading a common memory word. (b) – (d) Three possible ways the two writes and four reads might be interleaved in time.

However—and this is the essence of sequential consistency—no matter what, a sequentially consistent memory will never allow CPU 3 to get (100, 200) while CPU 4 gets (200, 100). If this were to occur, it would mean that according to CPU 3, the write of 100 by CPU 1 completed after the write of 200 by CPU 2. That is fine. But it would also mean that according to CPU 4, the write of 200 by CPU 2 completed before the write of 100 by CPU 1. By itself, this result is also possible. The problem is that sequential consistency guarantees that there is a single global ordering of all writes that is visible to all CPUs. If CPU 3 observes that 100 was written first, then CPU 4 must also see this order.

While sequential consistency is not as powerful a rule as strict consistency, it is still very useful. In effect, it says that when multiple events are happening concurrently, there is some true order in which they occur, possibly determined by timing and chance, but a true ordering exists and all processors observe this same order. Although this statement may seem obvious, below we will discuss consistency models that do not even guarantee this much.

Processor Consistency

A looser consistency model, but one that is easier to implement on large multiprocessors, is **processor consistency** (Goodman, 1989). It has two properties:

1. Writes by any CPU are seen by all CPUs in the order they were issued.

2. For every memory word, all CPUs see all writes to it in the same order.

Both of these points are important. The first point says that if CPU 1 issues writes with values 1A, 1B, and 1C to some memory location in that sequence, then all other processors see them in that order too. In other words, any other processor in a tight loop observing 1A, 1B, and 1C by reading the words written will never see the value written by 1B and then see the value written by 1A, and so on. The second point is needed to require every memory word to have an unambiguous value after several CPUs write to it and finally stop. Everyone must agree on who went last.

Even with these constraints, the designer has a lot of flexibility. Consider what happens if CPU 2 issues writes 2A, 2B, and 2C concurrently with CPU 1's three writes. Other CPUs that are busily reading memory will observe some interleaving of the six writes, such as 1A, 1B, 2A, 2B, 1C, 2C or 2A, 1A, 2B, 2C, 1B, 1C or many others. Processor consistency does *not* guarantee that every CPU sees the same ordering (unlike sequential consistency, which does make this guarantee). Thus it is perfectly legitimate for the hardware to behave in such a way that some CPUs see the first ordering above, some see the second, and some see yet other ones. What *is* guaranteed is that no CPU will see a sequence in which 1B comes before 1A, and so on. The order each CPU does its writes is observed everywhere.

It is worth noting that some authors define processor consistency differently and do not require the second condition.

Weak Consistency

Our next model, **weak consistency**, does not even guarantee that writes from a single CPU are seen in order (Dubois et al., 1986). In a weakly consistent memory, one CPU might see 1A before 1B and another CPU might see 1A after 1B. However, to add some order to the chaos, weakly consistent memories have synchronization variables or a synchronization operation. When a synchronization is executed, all pending writes are finished and no new ones are started until all the old ones are done and the synchronization itself is done. In effect, a synchronization "flushes the pipeline" and brings the memory to a stable state with no operations pending. Synchronization operations are themselves sequentially consistent, that is, when multiple CPUs issue them, some order is chosen, but all CPUs see the same order.

In weak consistency, time is divided into well-defined epochs delimited by the (sequentially consistent) synchronizations, as illustrated in Fig. 8-23. No relative order is guaranteed for 1A and 1B and different CPUs may see the two writes in different order, that is one CPU may see 1A then 1B and another CPU may see 1B then 1A. This situation is permitted. However, all CPUs see 1B before 1C because the first synchronization operation forces 1A, 1B, and 2A to complete before 1C, 2B, 3A, or 3B are allowed to start. Thus by doing synchronization operations, software can force some order on the sequence of events, although not at zero cost since flushing the memory pipeline does take some time.

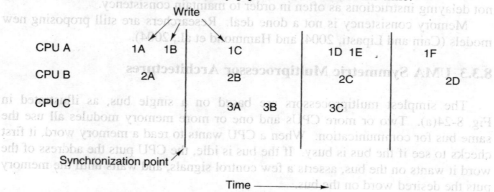

Figure 8-23. Weakly consistent memory uses synchronization operations to divide time into sequential epochs.

Release Consistency

Weak consistency has the problem that it is quite inefficient because it must finish off all pending memory operations and hold all new ones until the current ones are done. **Release consistency** improves matters by adopting a model akin to critical sections (Gharachorloo et al., 1990). The idea behind this model is that when a process exits a critical region it is not necessary to force all the writes to complete immediately. It is only necessary to make sure that they are done before any process enters that critical region again.

In this model, the synchronization operation offered by weak consistency is split into two different operations. To read or write a shared data variable, a CPU (i.e., its software) must first do an **acquire** operation on the synchronization variable to get exclusive access to the shared data. Then the CPU can use them as it wishes, reading and writing them at will. When it is done, the CPU does a **release** operation on the synchronization variable to indicate that it is finished. The release does not force pending writes to complete, but it itself does not complete until all previously issued writes are done. Furthermore, new memory operations are not prevented from starting immediately.

When the next acquire is issued, a check is made to see if all previous release operations have completed. If not, the acquire is held up until they are all done (and hence all the writes done before them are all completed). In this way, if the next acquire occurs sufficiently long after the most recent release, it does not have to wait before starting and the critical region can be entered without delay. If it occurs too soon after a release, the acquire (and all the instructions following it) will be delayed until all pending releases are completed, thus guaranteeing that the variables in the critical section have been updated. This scheme is slightly more complicated than weak consistency, but it has the significant advantage of not delaying instructions as often in order to maintain consistency.

Memory consistency is not a done deal. Researchers are still proposing new models (Cain and Lipasti, 2004; and Hammond et al., 2004).

8.3.3 UMA Symmetric Multiprocessor Architectures

The simplest multiprocessors are based on a single bus, as illustrated in Fig. 8-24(a). Two or more CPUs and one or more memory modules all use the same bus for communication. When a CPU wants to read a memory word, it first checks to see if the bus is busy. If the bus is idle, the CPU puts the address of the word it wants on the bus, asserts a few control signals, and waits until the memory puts the desired word on the bus.

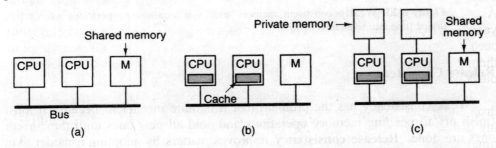

Figure 8-24. Three bus-based multiprocessors. (a) Without caching. (b) With caching. (c) With caching and private memories.

If the bus is busy when a CPU wants to read or write memory, the CPU just waits until the bus becomes idle. Herein lies the problem with this design. With two or three CPUs, contention for the bus will be manageable; with 32 or 64 it will be unbearable. The system will be totally limited by the bandwidth of the bus, and most of the CPUs will be idle most of the time.

The solution to this problem is to add a cache to each CPU, as depicted in Fig. 8-24(b). The cache can be inside the CPU chip, next to the CPU chip, on the processor board, or some combination of all three. Since many reads can now be satisfied out of the local cache, there will be much less bus traffic, and the system can support more CPUs. Thus caching is a big win here.

Yet another possibility is the design of Fig. 8-24(c), in which each CPU has not only a cache, but also a local, private memory which it accesses over a dedicated (private) bus. To use this configuration optimally, the compiler should place all the program text, strings, constants and other read-only data, stacks, and local variables in the private memories. The shared memory is then only used for writable shared variables. In most cases, this careful placement will greatly reduce bus traffic, but it does require active cooperation from the compiler.

Snooping Caches

While the performance arguments given above are certainly true, we have glossed over a fundamental problem a bit too quickly. Suppose that memory is sequentially consistent. What happens if CPU 1 has a line in its cache, and then CPU 2 tries to read a word in the same cache line? In the absence of any special rules, it, too, would get a copy in its cache. In principle, having the same line cached twice is acceptable. Now suppose that CPU 1 modifies the line and then immediately thereafter, CPU 2 reads its copy of the line from its cache. It will get **stale data**, thus violating the contract between the software and memory. The program running on CPU 2 will not be happy.

This problem, known in the literature as the **cache coherence** or **cache consistency** problem, is extremely serious. Without a solution, caching cannot be used, and bus-oriented multiprocessors would be limited to two or three CPUs. As a consequence of its importance, many solutions have been proposed over the years (e.g., Goodman, 1983; and Papamarcos and Patel, 1984). Although all these caching algorithms, called **cache coherence protocols**, differ in the details, all of them prevent different versions of the same cache line from appearing simultaneously in two or more caches.

In all solutions, the cache controller is specially designed to allow it to eavesdrop on the bus, monitoring all bus requests from other CPUs and caches and taking action in certain cases. These devices are called **snooping caches** or sometimes **snoopy caches** because they "snoop" on the bus. The set of rules implemented by the caches, CPUs, and memory for preventing different versions of the data from appearing in multiple caches forms the cache coherence protocol. The unit of transfer and storage for a cache is called a **cache line** and is typically 32 or 64 bytes.

The simplest cache coherence protocol is called **write through**. It can best be understood by distinguishing the four cases shown in Fig. 8-25. When a CPU tries to read a word that is not in its cache (i.e., a read miss), its cache controller loads the line containing that word into the cache. The line is supplied by the memory, which in this protocol is always up to date. Subsequent reads (i.e., read hits) can be satisfied out of the cache.

On a write miss, the word that has been modified is written to main memory. The line containing the word referenced is *not* loaded into the cache. On a write

Action	Local request	Remote request
Read miss	Fetch data from memory	
Read hit	Use data from local cache	
Write miss	Update data in memory	
Write hit	Update cache and memory	Invalidate cache entry

Figure 8-25. The write-through cache coherence protocol. The empty boxes indicate that no action is taken.

hit, the cache is updated and the word is written through to main memory in addition. The essence of this protocol is that all write operations result in the word being written going through to memory to keep memory up to date at all times.

Now let us look at all these actions again, but this time from the snooper's point of view, shown in the right-hand column of Fig. 8-25. Let us call the cache performing the actions cache 1 and the snooping cache cache 2. When cache 1 misses on a read, it makes a bus request to fetch a line from memory. Cache 2 sees this but does nothing. When cache 1 has a read hit, the request is satisfied locally, and no bus request occurs, so cache 2 is not aware of cache 1's read hits.

Writes are more interesting. If CPU 1 does a write, cache 1 will make a write request on the bus, both on misses and on hits. On all writes, cache 2 checks to see if it has the word being written. If not, from its point of view this is a remote request/write miss and it does nothing. (To clarify a subtle point, note that in Fig. 8-25 a remote miss means that the word is not present in the snooper's cache; it does not matter whether it was in the originator's cache or not. Thus a single request may be a hit locally and a miss at the snooper, or vice versa.)

Now suppose that cache 1 writes a word that *is* present in cache 2's cache (remote request/write hit). If cache 2 does nothing, it will have stale data, so it marks the cache entry containing the newly modified word as being invalid. In effect, it removes the item from the cache. Because all caches snoop on all bus requests, whenever a word is written, the net effect is to update it in the originator's cache, update it in memory, and purge it from all the other caches. In this way, inconsistent versions are prevented.

Of course, cache 2's CPU is free to read the same word on the very next cycle. In that case, cache 2 will read the word from memory, which is up to date. At that point, cache 1, cache 2, and the memory will all have identical copies of it. If either CPU does a write now, the other one's cache will be purged, and memory will be updated.

Many variations on this basic protocol are possible. For example, on a write hit, the snooping cache normally invalidates its entry containing the word being written. Alternatively, it could accept the new value and update its cache instead of marking it as invalid. Conceptually, updating the cache is the same as invalidating it followed by reading the word from memory. In all cache protocols, a choice must be made between an **update strategy** and an **invalidate strategy**. These protocols perform differently under different loads. Update messages carry payloads and are thus larger than invalidates but may prevent future cache misses.

Another variant is loading the snooping cache on write misses. The correctness of the algorithm is not affected by loading it, only the performance. The question is: "What is the probability that a word just written will be written again soon?" If it is high, there is something to be said for loading the cache on write misses, known as a **write-allocate policy**. If it is low, it is better not to update on write misses. If the word is *read* soon, it will be loaded by the read miss anyway; little is gained by loading it on the write miss.

As with many simple solutions, this one is inefficient. Every write operation goes to memory over the bus, so with a modest number of CPUs, the bus will still become a bottleneck. To keep the bus traffic within bounds, other cache protocols have been devised. They all have the property that not all writes go directly through to memory. Instead, when a cache line is modified, a bit is set inside the cache noting that the cache line is correct but memory is not. Eventually, such a dirty line has to be written back to memory, but possibly after many writes have been made to it. This type of protocol is known as a **write-back protocol**.

The MESI Cache Coherence Protocol

One popular write-back cache coherence protocol is called **MESI**, after the initials of the names of the four states (M, E, S, and I) that it uses (Papamarcos and Patel, 1984). It is based on the earlier **write-once protocol** (Goodman, 1983). The MESI protocol is used by the Pentium 4 and many other CPUs for snooping on the bus. Each cache entry can be in one of the following four states:

1. Invalid   – The cache entry does not contain valid data.

2. Shared   – Multiple caches may hold the line; memory is up to date.

3. Exclusive – No other cache holds the line; memory is up to date.

4. Modified – The entry is valid; memory is invalid; no copies exist.

When the CPU is initially booted, all cache entries are marked invalid. The first time memory is read, the line referenced is fetched into the cache of the CPU reading memory and marked as being in the E (exclusive) state, since it is the only copy in a cache, as illustrated in Fig. 8-26(a) for the case of CPU 1 reading line *A*. Subsequent reads by that CPU use the cached entry and do not go over the bus. Another CPU may also fetch the same line and cache it, but by snooping, the original holder (CPU 1) sees that it is no longer alone and announces on the bus that it also has a copy. Both copies are marked as being in the S (shared) state, as shown in Fig. 8-26(b). In other words, the S state means that the line is in one or

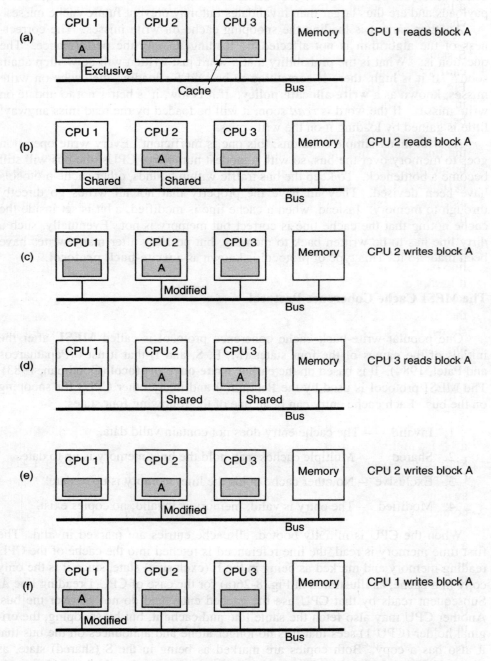

Figure 8-26. The MESI cache coherence protocol.

more caches for reading and memory is up to date. Subsequent reads by a CPU to a line it has cached in the S state do not use the bus and do not cause the state to change.

Now consider what happens if CPU 2 writes to the cache line it is holding in S state. It puts out an invalidate signal on the bus, telling all other CPUs to discard their copies. The copy cached now goes to M (modified) state, as shown in Fig. 8-26(c). The line is not written to memory. It is worth noting that if a line is in E state when it is written, no bus signal is needed to invalidate other caches because it is known that no other copies exist.

Next consider what happens if CPU 3 reads the line. CPU 2, which now owns the line, knows that the copy in memory is not valid, so it asserts a signal on the bus telling CPU 3 to please wait while it writes its line back to memory. When it is finished, CPU 3 fetches a copy, and the line is marked as shared in both caches, as shown in Fig. 8-26(d). After that, CPU 2 writes the line again, which invalidates the copy in CPU 3's cache, as shown in Fig. 8-26(e).

Finally, CPU 1 writes to a word in the line. CPU 2 sees that a write is being attempted and asserts a bus signal telling CPU 1 to please wait while it writes its line back to memory. When it is finished, it marks its own copy as invalid, since it knows another CPU is about to modify it. At this point we have the situation in which a CPU is writing to an uncached line. If the write-allocate policy is in use, the line will be loaded into the cache and marked as being in the M state, as shown in Fig. 8-26(f). If the write-allocate policy is not in use, the write will go directly to memory and the line will not be cached anywhere.

UMA Multiprocessors Using Crossbar Switches

Even with all possible optimizations, the use of a single bus limits the size of a UMA multiprocessor to about 16 or 32 CPUs. To go beyond that, a different kind of interconnection network is needed. The simplest circuit for connecting n CPUs to k memories is the **crossbar switch**, shown in Fig. 8-27. Crossbar switches have been used for decades within telephone switching exchanges to connect a group of incoming lines to a set of outgoing lines in an arbitrary way.

At each intersection of a horizontal (incoming) and vertical (outgoing) line is a **crosspoint**. A crosspoint is a small switch that can be electrically opened or closed, depending on whether the horizontal and vertical lines are to be connected or not. In Fig. 8-27(a) we see three crosspoints closed simultaneously, allowing connections between the (CPU, memory) pairs (001, 000), (101, 101), and (110, 010) at the same time. Many other combinations are also possible. In fact, the number of combinations is equal to the number of different ways eight rooks can be safely placed on a chess board.

One of the nicest properties of the crossbar switch is that it is a **nonblocking network**, meaning that no CPU is ever denied the connection it needs because

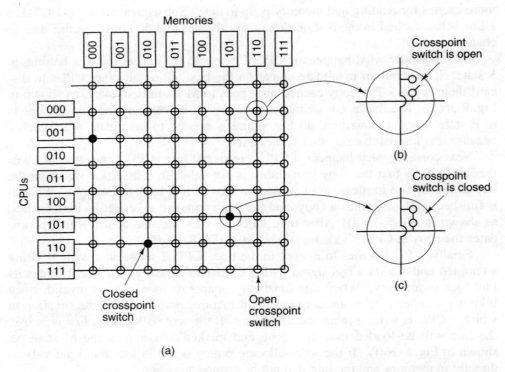

Figure 8-27. (a) An 8 × 8 crossbar switch. (b) An open crosspoint. (c) A closed crosspoint.

some crosspoint or line is already occupied (assuming the memory module itself is available). Furthermore, no advance planning is needed. Even if seven arbitrary connections are already set up, it is always possible to connect the remaining CPU to the remaining memory. We will later see interconnection schemes that do not have these properties.

One of the worst properties of the crossbar switch is the fact that the number of crosspoints grows as n^2. For medium-sized systems, a crossbar design is workable. We will discuss one such design, the Sun Fire E25K, later in this chapter. However, with 1000 CPUs and 1000 memory modules, we need a million crosspoints. Such a large crossbar switch is not feasible. We need something quite different.

UMA Multiprocessors Using Multistage Switching Networks

That "something quite different" can be based on the humble 2 × 2 switch shown in Fig. 8-28(a). This switch has two inputs and two outputs. Messages arriving on either input line can be switched to either output line. For our purposes here, messages will contain up to four parts, as shown in Fig. 8-28(b). The

Module field tells which memory to use. The *Address* specifies an address within a module. The *Opcode* gives the operation, such as READ or WRITE. Finally, the optional *Value* field may contain an operand, such as a 32-bit word to be written on a WRITE. The switch inspects the *Module* field and uses it to determine if the message should be sent on *X* or on *Y*.

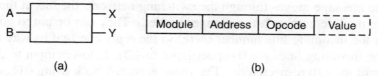

(a)   (b)

Figure 8-28. (a) A 2×2 switch. (b) A message format.

Our 2×2 switches can be arranged in many ways to build larger **multistage switching networks** One possibility is the no-frills, economy class **omega network**, illustrated in Fig. 8-29. Here we have connected eight CPUs to eight memories using 12 switches. More generally, for *n* CPUs and *n* memories we would need $\log_2 n$ stages, with $n/2$ switches per stage, for a total of $(n/2)\log_2 n$ switches, which is a lot better than n^2 crosspoints, especially for large values of *n*.

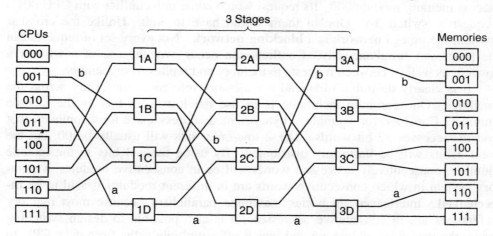

Figure 8-29. An omega switching network.

The wiring pattern of the omega network is often called the **perfect shuffle**, since the mixing of the signals at each stage resembles a deck of cards being cut in half and then mixed card-for-card. To see how the omega network works, suppose that CPU 011 wants to read a word from memory module 110. The CPU sends a READ message to switch 1D containing 110 in the *Module* field. The switch takes the first (i.e., leftmost) bit of 110 and uses it for routing. A 0 routes to the upper output and a 1 routes to the lower one. Since this bit is a 1, the message is routed via the lower output to 2D.

All the second-stage switches, including 2D, use the second bit for routing. This, too, is a 1, so the message is now forwarded via the lower output to 3D. Here the third bit is tested and found to be a 0. Consequently, the message goes out on the upper output and arrives at memory 110, as desired. The path followed by this message is marked in Fig. 8-29 by the letter a.

As the message moves through the switching network, the bits at the left-hand end of the module number are no longer needed. They can be put to good use by recording the incoming line number there, so the reply can find its way back. For path a, the incoming lines are 0 (upper input to 1D), 1 (lower input to 2D), and 1 (lower input to 3D), respectively. The reply is routed back using 011, only reading it from right to left this time.

At the same time all this is going on, CPU 001 wants to write a word to memory module 001. An analogous process happens here, with the message routed via the upper, upper, and lower outputs, respectively, marked by the letter b. When it arrives, its *Module* field reads 001, representing the path it took. Since these two requests do not use any of the same switches, lines, or memory modules, they can proceed in parallel.

Now consider what would happen if CPU 000 simultaneously wanted to access memory module 000. Its request would come into conflict with CPU 001's request at switch 3A. One of them would have to wait. Unlike the crossbar switch, the omega network is a **blocking network**. Not every set of requests can be processed simultaneously. Conflicts can occur over the use of a wire or a switch, as well as between requests *to* memory and replies *from* memory.

It is clearly desirable to spread the memory references uniformly across the modules. One common technique is to use the low-order bits as the module number. Consider, for example, a byte-oriented address space for a computer that mostly accesses 32-bit words. The 2 low-order bits will usually be 00, but the next 3 bits will be uniformly distributed. By using these 3 bits as the module number, consecutively addressed words will be in consecutive modules. A memory system in which consecutive words are in different modules is said to be **interleaved**. Interleaved memories maximize parallelism because most memory references are to consecutive addresses. It is also possible to design switching networks that are nonblocking and which offer multiple paths from each CPU to each memory module, to spread the traffic better.

8.3.4 NUMA Multiprocessors

It should be clear by now that single-bus UMA multiprocessors are generally limited to no more than a few dozen CPUs and crossbar or switched multiprocessors need a lot of (expensive) hardware and are not that much bigger. To get to more than 100 CPUs, something has to give. Usually, what gives is the idea that all memory modules have the same access time. This concession leads to the idea of **NUMA (NonUniform Memory Access)** multiprocessors. Like their UMA cousins, they provide a single address space across all the CPUs, but unlike the UMA machines, access to local memory modules is faster than access to remote ones. Thus all UMA programs will run without change on NUMA machines, but the performance will be worse than on a UMA machine at the same clock speed.

NUMA machines have three key characteristics that all of them possess and which together distinguish them from other multiprocessors:

1. There is a single address space visible to all CPUs.

2. Access to remote memory is done using LOAD and STORE instructions.

3. Access to remote memory is slower than access to local memory.

When the access time to remote memory is not hidden (because there is no caching), the system is called **NC-NUMA**. When coherent caches are present, the system is called **CC-NUMA** (at least by the hardware people). The software people often call it **hardware DSM** because it is basically the same as software distributed shared memory but implemented by the hardware using a small page size.

One of the first NC-NUMA machines (although the name had not yet been coined) was the Carnegie-Mellon Cm*, illustrated in simplified form in Fig. 8-30 (Swan et al., 1977). It consisted of a collection of LSI-11 CPUs, each with some memory addressed over a local bus. (The LSI-11 was a single-chip version of the DEC PDP-11, a minicomputer popular in the 1970s). In addition, the LSI-11 systems were connected by a system bus. When a memory request came into the (specially modified) MMU, a check was made to see if the word needed was in the local memory. If so, a request was sent over the local bus to get the word. If not, the request was routed over the system bus to the system containing the word, which then responded. Of course, the latter took much longer than the former. While a program could run happily out of remote memory, it took 10 times longer to execute than the same program running out of local memory.

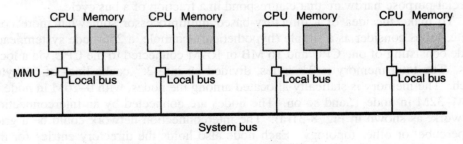

Figure 8-30. A NUMA machine based on two levels of buses. The Cm* was the first multiprocessor to use this design.

Memory coherence is guaranteed in an NC-NUMA machine because there is no caching present. Each word of memory lives in exactly one location, so there is no danger of one copy having stale data: there are no copies. Of course, it now matters a great deal which page is in which memory because the performance penalty for being in the wrong place is so high. Consequently, NC-NUMA machines use elaborate software to move pages around to maximize performance.

Typically, there is a daemon process called a **page scanner** that runs every few seconds. Its job is to examine the usage statistics and move pages around in an attempt to improve performance. If a page appears to be in the wrong place, the page scanner unmaps it so that the next reference to it will cause a page fault. When the fault occurs, a decision is made about where to place the page, possibly in a different memory from where it was before. To prevent thrashing, usually there is some rule saying that once a page is placed, it is frozen in place for a time ΔT. Various algorithms have been studied, but the conclusion is that no one algorithm performs best under all circumstances (LaRowe and Ellis, 1991).

Cache Coherent NUMA Multiprocessors

Multiprocessor designs such as that of Fig. 8-30 do not scale well because they do not do caching. Having to go to the remote memory every time a nonlocal memory word is accessed is a major performance hit. However, if caching is added, then cache coherence must also be added. One way to provide cache coherence is to snoop on the system bus. Technically, doing this is not difficult, but beyond a certain number of CPUs, it becomes infeasible. To build really large multiprocessors, a fundamentally different approach is needed.

The most popular approach for building large **CC-NUMA** (**Cache Coherent NUMA**) multiprocessors currently is the **directory-based multiprocessor**. The idea is to maintain a database telling where each cache line is and what its status is. When a cache line is referenced, the database is queried to find out where it is and whether it is clean or dirty (modified). Since this database must be queried on every single instruction that references memory, it must be kept in extremely-fast special-purpose hardware that can respond in a fraction of a bus cycle.

To make the idea of a directory-based multiprocessor somewhat more concrete, let us consider as a simple (hypothetical) example, a 256-node system, each node consisting of one CPU and 16 MB of RAM connected to the CPU via a local bus. The total memory is 2^{32} bytes, divided up into 2^{26} cache lines of 64 bytes each. The memory is statically allocated among the nodes, with 0–16M in node 0, 16M–32M in node 1, and so on. The nodes are connected by an interconnection network, as shown in Fig. 8-31(a). The interconnection network could be a grid, hypercube, or other topology. Each node also holds the directory entries for the 2^{18} 64-byte cache lines comprising its 2^{24} byte memory. For the moment, we will assume that a line can be held in at most one cache.

To see how the directory works, let us trace a LOAD instruction from CPU 20 that references a cached line. First the CPU issuing the instruction presents it to its MMU, which translates it to a physical address, say, 0x24000108. The MMU

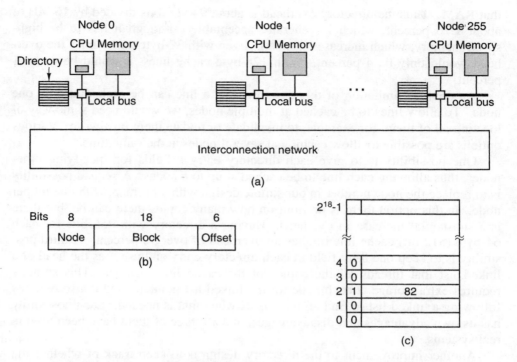

Figure 8-31. (a) A 256-node directory-based multiprocessor. (b) Division of a 32-bit memory address into fields. (c) The directory at node 36.

splits this address into the three parts shown in Fig. 8-31(b). In decimal, the three parts are node 36, line 4, and offset 8. The MMU sees that the memory word referenced is from node 36, not node 20, so it sends a request message through the interconnection network to the line's home node, 36, asking whether its line 4 is cached, and if so, where.

When the request arrives at node 36 over the interconnection network, it is routed to the directory hardware. The hardware indexes into its table of 2^{18} entries, one for each of its cache lines and extracts entry 4. From Fig. 8-31(c) we see that the line is not cached, so the hardware fetches line 4 from the local RAM, sends it back to node 20, and updates directory entry 4 to indicate that the line is now cached at node 20.

Now let us consider a second request, this time asking about node 36's line 2. From Fig. 8-31(c) we see that this line is cached at node 82. At this point the hardware could update directory entry 2 to say that the line is now at node 20 and then send a message to node 82 instructing it to pass the line to node 20 and invalidate its cache. Note that even a so-called "shared-memory multiprocessor" has a lot of message passing going on under the hood.

As a quick aside, let us calculate how much memory is being taken up by the directories. Each node has 16 MB of RAM and 2^{18} 9-bit entries to keep track of that RAM. Thus the directory overhead is about 9×2^{18} bits divided by 16 MB or about 1.76 percent, which is generally acceptable (although it has to be high-speed memory, which increases its cost). Even with 32-byte cache lines the overhead would only be 4 percent. With 128-byte cache lines, it would be under 1 percent.

An obvious limitation of this design is that a line can be cached at only one node. To allow lines to be cached at multiple nodes, we would need some way of locating all of them, for example, to invalidate or update them on a write. Various options are possible to allow caching at several nodes at the same time.

One possibility is to give each directory entry k fields for specifying other nodes, thus allowing each line to be cached at up to k nodes. A second possibility is to replace the node number in our simple design with a bit map, with one bit per node. In this option there is no limit on how many copies there can be, but there is a substantial increase in overhead. Having a directory with 256 bits for each 64-byte (512-bit) cache line implies an overhead of over 50 percent. A third possibility is to keep one 8-bit field in each directory entry and use it as the head of a linked list that threads all the copies of the cache line together. This strategy requires extra storage at each node for the linked list pointers, and it also requires following a linked list to find all the copies when that is needed. Each possibility has its own advantages and disadvantages, and all three of them have been used in real systems.

Another improvement to the directory design is to keep track of whether the cache line is clean (home memory is up to date) or dirty (home memory is not up to date). If a read request comes in for a clean cache line, the home node can satisfy the request from memory, without having to forward it to a cache. A read request for a dirty cache line, however, must be forwarded to the node holding the cache line because only it has a valid copy. If only one cache copy is allowed, as in Fig. 8-31, there is no real advantage to keeping track of its cleanliness, because any new request requires a message to be sent to the existing copy to invalidate it.

Of course, keeping track of whether each cache line is clean or dirty implies that when a cache line is modified, the home node has to be informed, even if only one cache copy exists. If multiple copies exist, modifying one of them requires the rest to be invalidated, so some protocol is needed to avoid race conditions. For example, to modify a shared cache line, one of the holders might have to request exclusive access *before* modifying it. Such a request would cause all other copies to be invalidated before permission was granted. Other performance optimizations for CC-NUMA machines are discussed in (Stenstrom et al., 1997).

The Sun Fire E25K NUMA Multiprocessor

As an example of a shared-memory NUMA multiprocessor, let us study the Sun Microsystems Sun Fire family. Although this family contains various models, we will focus on the E25K, which has 72 UltraSPARC IV CPU chips. An

UltraSPARC IV is essentially a pair of UltraSPARC III Cu processors that share a common cache and memory. The E15K is essentially the same system except with uniprocessor instead of dual processor CPU chips. Smaller members exist as well, but from our point of view, what is interesting is how the one with the most CPUs works.

The E25K system consists of up to 18 boardsets, each boardset consisting of a CPU-memory board, an I/O board with four PCI slots, and an expander board that couples the CPU-memory board with the I/O board and joins the pair to the centerplane, which holds the boards and contains the switching logic. Each CPU-memory board contains four CPU chips and four 8-GB RAM modules. Consequently, each CPU-memory board on the E25K holds eight CPUs and 32 GB of RAM (four CPUs and four 32 GB of RAM on the E15K). A full E25K thus contains 144 CPUs, 576 GB of RAM, and 72 PCI slots. It is illustrated in Fig. 8-32. Interestingly enough, the number 18 was chosen due to packaging constraints: a system with 18 boardsets was the largest one that could fit through a doorway in one piece. While programmers just think about 0s and 1s, engineers have to worry about things like how the customer will get the product through the door and into the building.

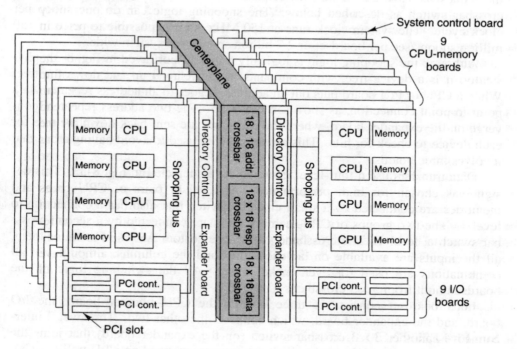

Figure 8-32. The Sun Microsystems E25K multiprocessor.

The centerplane is composed of a set of three 18×18 crossbar switches for connecting the 18 boardsets. One crossbar is for the address lines, one is for responses, and one is for data transfer. In addition to the 18 expander boards, the centerplane also has a system control boardset plugged into it. This boardset has a single CPU, but also interfaces to the CD-ROM, tape, serial lines, and other peripheral devices needed for booting, maintaining, and controlling the system.

The heart of any multiprocessor is the memory subsystem. How does one connect 144 CPUs to the distributed memory? The straightforward ways—a big shared snooping bus or a 144×72 crossbar switch—do not work well. The former fails due to the bus being a bottleneck and the latter fails because the switch is too difficult and expensive to build. Thus large multiprocessors such as the E25K are forced to use a more complex memory subsystem.

At the boardset level, snooping logic is used so all local CPUs can check all memory requests coming from the boardset to references to blocks they currently have cached. Thus when a CPU needs a word from memory, it first converts the virtual address to a physical address and checks its cache. (Physical addresses are 43 bits, but packaging restrictions limit memory to 576 GB.) If the cache block it needs is in its own cache, the word is returned. Otherwise, the snooping logic checks if a copy of that word is available somewhere else on the boardset. If so, the request is satisfied. If not, the request is passed on via the 18×18 address crossbar switch as described below. The snooping logic can do one snoop per clock cycle. The system clock runs at 150 MHz, so it is possible to perform 150 million snoops/sec per boardset or 2.7 billion snoops/sec system wide.

Although the snooping logic is logically a bus, as portrayed in Fig. 8-32, physically, it is a device tree, with commands being relayed up and down the tree. When a CPU or PCI board puts out an address, it goes to an address repeater via a point-to-point connection, as shown in Fig. 8-33. The two address repeaters converge on the expander board, where the addresses are sent back down the tree for each device to check for hits. This arrangement is used to avoid having a bus that involves three boards.

Data transfers use a four-level interconnect as depicted in Fig. 8-33. This design was chosen for high performance. At level 0, pairs of CPU chips and memories are connected by a small crossbar switch that also has a connection to level 1. The two groups of CPU-memory pairs are connected by a second crossbar switch at level 1. The crossbar switches are custom ASICs. For all of them, all the inputs are available on both the rows and the columns, although not all combinations are used (or even make sense). All the switching logic on the boards is built from 3×3 crossbars.

Each boardset consists of three boards: the CPU-memory board, the I/O board, and the expander board, which connects the other two. The level 2 interconnect is another 3×3 crossbar switch (on the expander board) that joins the actual memory to the I/O ports (which are memory mapped on all UltraSPARCs). All data transfers to or from the boardset, whether to memory or to an I/O port, pass through the level 2 switch. Finally, data that has to be transferred to or from a remote board passes through an 18×18 data crossbar switch at level 3. Data

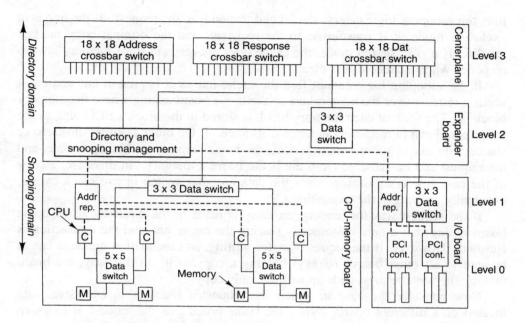

Figure 8-33. The Sun Fire E25K uses a four-level interconnect. Dashed lines are address paths. Solid lines are data paths.

transfers are done 32 bytes at a time, so it takes two clock cycles to transfer 64 bytes, the usual transfer unit.

Having looked at how the components are arranged, let us now turn our attention to how the shared memory operates. At the bottom level, the 576 GB of memory is split into 2^{29} blocks of 64 bytes each. These blocks are the atomic units of the memory system. Each block has a home board where it lives when not in use elsewhere. Most blocks are on their home board most of the time. However, when a CPU needs a memory block, either from its own board or one of the 17 remote ones, it first requests a copy for its own cache, then accesses the cached copy. Although each CPU chip on the E25K contains two CPUs, they share a single physical cache and thus share all the blocks contained in it.

Each memory block and cache line of each CPU chip can be in one of three states:

1. Exclusive access (for writing).

2. Shared access (for reading).

3. Invalid (i.e., empty).

When a CPU needs to read or write a memory word, it first checks its own cache. Failing to find the word there, it issues a local request for the physical address that is broadcast only on its own boardset. If a cache on the boardset has the needed line, the snooping logic detects the hit and responds to the request. If the line is in exclusive mode, it is transferred to the requestor and the original copy marked invalid. If it is in shared mode, the cache does not respond since memory always responds when a cache line is clean.

If the snooping logic cannot find the cache line or it is present and shared, it sends a request over the centerplane to the home board asking where the memory block is. The state of each memory block is stored in the block's ECC bits, so the home board can immediately determine its state. If the block is either unshared or shared with one or more remote boards, the home memory will be up to date, and the request can be satisfied from the home board's memory. In this case, a copy of the case line is transmitted over the data crossbar switch in two clock cycles, eventually arriving at the requesting CPU.

If the request was for reading, an entry is made in the directory at the home board noting that a new customer is sharing the cache line and the transaction is finished. However, if the request was for writing, an invalidation message has to be sent to all other boards (if any) holding a copy of it. In this way, the board making the write request ends up with the only copy.

Now consider the case in which the requested block is in exclusive state located on a different board. When the home board gets the request, it looks up the location of the remote board in the directory and sends the requester a message telling where the cache line is. The requester now sends the request to the correct boardset. When the request arrives, the board sends back the cache line. If it was a read request, the line is marked shared and a copy sent back to the home board. If it was a write request, the responder invalidates its copy so the new requester has an exclusive copy.

Since each board has 2^{29} memory blocks, it would take a directory with 2^{29} entries to keep track of them all in the worst case. Since the directory is much smaller than 2^{29}, it could happen that there is no room in the directory (which is searched associatively) for some entries. In this case, the home directory has to locate the block by broadcasting a request for it to all the other 17 boards. The response crossbar switch plays a roll in the directory coherence and update protocol by handling much of the reverse traffic back to the sender. By splitting the protocol traffic over two buses (address and response) and the data over a third bus, the throughput of the system is increased.

By distributing the load over multiple devices on different boards, the Sun Fire E25K is able to achieve very high performance. In addition to the 2.7 billion snoops/sec mentioned above, the centerplane can handle up to nine simultaneous transfers, with nine boards sending and nine boards receiving. Since the data crossbar is 32 bytes wide, on every clock cycle, 288 bytes can be moved through the centerplane. At a clock rate of 150 MHz, this gives a peak aggregate bandwidth of 40 GB/sec when all accesses are remote. If the software can place pages in such a way to ensure that most accesses are local, then the system bandwidth can be appreciably higher than 40 GB/sec.

For more technical information about the Sun Fire, see (Charlesworth, 2002; and Charlesworth, 2001);

8.3.5 COMA Multiprocessors

NUMA and CC-NUMA machines have the disadvantage that references to remote memory are much slower than references to local memory. In CC-NUMA, this performance difference is hidden to some extent by the caching. Nevertheless, if the amount of remote data needed greatly exceeds the cache capacity, cache misses will occur constantly and performance will be poor.

Thus we have a situation that UMA machines have excellent performance but are limited in size and are quite expensive. NC-NUMA machines, scale to somewhat larger sizes but require manual or semi-automated placement of pages, often with mixed results. The problem is that it is hard to predict which pages will be needed where, and in any case, pages are often too large a unit to move around. CC-NUMA machines, such as the Sun Fire E25K, may experience poor performance if many CPUs need a lot of remote data. All in all, each of these designs has serious limitations.

An alternative kind of multiprocessor tries to get around all these problems by using each CPU's main memory as a cache. In this design, called **COMA** (**Cache Only Memory Access**), pages do not have fixed home machines, as they do in NUMA and CC-NUMA machines. In fact, pages are not significant at all.

Instead, the physical address space is split into cache lines, which migrate around the system on demand. Blocks do not have home machines. Like nomads in some Third World countries, home is where you are right now. A memory that just attracts lines as needed is called an **attraction memory**. Using the main RAM as a big cache greatly increases the hit rate, hence the performance.

Unfortunately, as usual, there is no such thing as a free lunch. COMA systems introduce two new problems:

1. How are cache lines located?

2. When a line is purged from memory, what happens if it is the last copy?

The first problem relates to the fact that after the MMU has translated a virtual address to a physical address, if the line is not in the true hardware cache, there is no easy way to tell if it is in main memory at all. The paging hardware does not help here at all because each page is made up of many individual cache lines that wander around independently. Furthermore, even if it is known that a line is not in main memory, where is it then? It is not possible to just ask the home machine, because there is no home machine.

Some solutions to the location problem have been proposed. To see if a cache line is in main memory, new hardware could be added to keep track of the tag for each cached line. The MMU could then compare the tag for the line needed to the tags for all the cache lines in memory to look for a hit. This solution needs additional hardware.

A somewhat different solution is to map entire pages in but not require that all the cache lines be present. In this solution, the hardware would need a bit map per page, giving one bit per cache line indicating the presence or absence of the line. In this design, called **simple COMA** if a cache line is present, it must be in the right position in its page, but if it is not present, any attempt to use it causes a trap to allow the software to go find it and bring it in.

This leads us to finding lines that are really remote. One solution is to give each page a home machine in terms of where its directory entry is, but not where the data are. Then a message can be sent to the home machine to at least locate the cache line. Other schemes involve organizing memory as a tree and searching upward until the line is found.

The second problem in the list above relates to not purging the last copy. As in CC-NUMA, a cache line may be at multiple nodes at once. When a cache miss occurs, a line must be fetched, which usually means a line must be thrown out. What happens if the line chosen happens to be the last copy? In that case, it cannot be thrown out.

One solution is to go back to the directory and check to see if there are other copies. If so, the line can be safely thrown out. Otherwise, it has to be migrated somewhere else. Another solution is to label one copy of each cache line as the master copy and never throw it out. This solution avoids having to check with the directory. All in all, COMA offers promise to provide better performance than CC-NUMA, but few COMA machines have been built, so more experience is needed. The first two COMA machines built were the KSR-1 (Burkhardt et al., 1992) and the Data Diffusion Machine (Hagersten et al., 1992). A more recent machine is the SDAARC (Eschmann et al., 2002).

8.4 MESSAGE-PASSING MULTICOMPUTERS

As we saw in Fig. 8-21, the two kinds of MIMD parallel processors are multiprocessors and multicomputers. In the previous section we studied multiprocessors. We saw that multiprocessors appear to the operating system as having shared memory that can be accessed using ordinary LOAD and STORE instructions. This shared memory can be implemented in many ways as we have seen, including snooping buses, data crossbars, multistage switching networks, and various directory based schemes. Nevertheless, programs written for a multiprocessor can just access any location in memory without knowing anything about the internal topology or implementation scheme. This illusion is what makes multiprocessors so attractive and why programmers like this programming model.

On the other hand, multiprocessors also have their limitations, which is why multicomputers are important, too. First and foremost, multiprocessors do not scale to large sizes. We saw the enormous amount of hardware Sun had to use to get the E25K to scale to 72 CPUs. In contrast, we will study a multicomputer below that has 65,536 CPUs. It will be years before anyone builds a commercial 65,536-node multiprocessor, and by then million-node multicomputers will be in use.

In addition, memory contention in a multiprocessor can severely affect performance. If 100 CPUs are all trying to read and write the same variables constantly, contention for the various memories, buses, and directories can result in an enormous performance hit.

As a consequence of these and other factors, there is a great deal of interest in building and using parallel computers in which each CPU has its own private memory, not directly accessible to any other CPU. They are the multicomputers. Programs on multicomputer CPUs interact using primitives like send and receive to explicitly pass messages because they cannot get at each other's memory with LOAD and STORE instructions. This difference completely changes the programming model.

Each node in a multicomputer consists of one or a few CPUs, some RAM (conceivably shared among the CPUs at that node only), a disk and/or other I/O devices, and a communication processor. The communication processors are connected by a high-speed interconnection network of the types we discussed in Sec. 8.1.2. Many different topologies, switching schemes, and routing algorithms are used. What all multicomputers have in common is that when an application program executes the send primitive, the communication processor is notified and transmits a block of user data to the destination machine (possibly after first asking for and getting permission). A generic multicomputer is shown in Fig. 8-34.

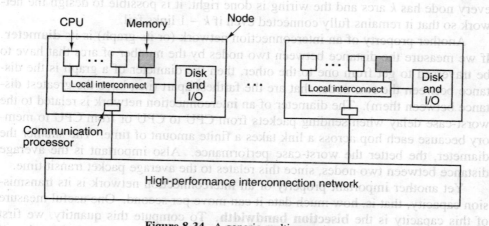

Figure 8-34. A generic multicomputer.

8.4.1 Interconnection Networks

In Fig. 8-34 we saw that multicomputers are held together by interconnection networks. Now it is time to look more closely at these interconnection networks. Interestingly enough, multiprocessors and multicomputers are surprisingly similar in this respect because multiprocessors often have multiple memory modules that must also be interconnected with one another and with the CPUs. Thus the material in this section frequently applies to both kinds of systems.

The fundamental reason why multiprocessor and multicomputer interconnection networks are similar is that at the very bottom both of them use message passing. Even on a single-CPU machine, when the processor wants to read or write a word, what it typically does is assert certain lines on the bus and wait for a reply. This action is fundamentally like message passing: the initiator sends a request and waits for a response. In large multiprocessors, communication between CPUs and remote memory almost always consists of the CPU sending an explicit message, called a **packet**, to memory requesting some data, and the memory sending back a reply packet.

Topology

The topology of an interconnection network describes how the links and switches are arranged, for example, as a ring or as a grid. Topological designs can be modeled as graphs, with the links as arcs and the switches as nodes, as shown in Fig. 8-35. Each node in an interconnection network (or its graph) has some number of links connected to it. Mathematicians call the number of links the **degree** of the node; engineers call it the **fanout**. In general, the greater the fanout, the more routing choices there are and the greater the fault tolerance, that is, the ability to continue functioning even if a link fails by routing around it. If every node has k arcs and the wiring is done right, it is possible to design the network so that it remains fully connected even if $k - 1$ links fail.

Another property of an interconnection network (or its graph) is its **diameter**. If we measure the distance between two nodes by the number of arcs that have to be traversed to get from one to the other, then the diameter of a graph is the distance between the two nodes that are the farthest apart (i.e., have the greatest distance between them). The diameter of an interconnection network is related to the worst-case delay when sending packets from CPU to CPU or from CPU to memory because each hop across a link takes a finite amount of time. The smaller the diameter, the better the worst-case performance. Also important is the average distance between two nodes, since this relates to the average packet transit time.

Yet another important property of an interconnection network is its transmission capacity, that is, how much data it can move per second. One useful measure of this capacity is the **bisection bandwidth**. To compute this quantity, we first have to (conceptually) partition the network into two equal (in terms of number of

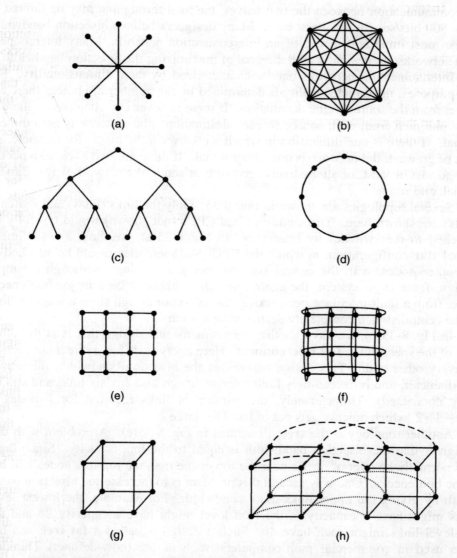

Figure 8-35. Various topologies. The heavy dots represent switches. The CPUs and memories are not shown. (a) A star. (b) A complete interconnect. (c) A tree. (d) A ring. (e) A grid. (f) A double torus. (g) A cube. (h) A 4D hypercube.

nodes) but unconnected parts by removing a set of arcs from its graph. Then we compute the total bandwidth of the arcs that have been removed. There may be many different ways to partition the network into two equal parts. The bisection **bandwidth** is the minimum of all the possible partitions. The significance of this **number** is that if the bisection bandwidth is, say, 800 bits/sec, then if there is a lot of communication between the two halves, the total throughput may be limited to only 800 bits/sec, in the worst case. Many designers believe bisection bandwidth is the most important metric of an interconnection network. Many interconnection networks are designed with the goal of maximizing the bisection bandwidth.

Interconnection networks can be characterized by their **dimensionality**. For our purposes, the dimensionality is determined by the number of choices there are to get from the source to the destination. If there is never any choice (i.e., there is only one path from each source to each destination), the network is zero dimensional. If there is one dimension in which a choice can be made, for example, go east or go west, the network is one dimensional. If there are two axes, so a packet can go east or west, or alternatively, go north or south, the network is two dimensional, and so on.

Several topologies are shown in Fig. 8-35. Only the links (lines) and switches (dots) are shown here. The memories and CPUs (not shown) would typically be attached to the switches by interfaces. In Fig. 8-35(a), we have a zero-dimensional **star** configuration, in which the CPUs and memories would be attached to the outer nodes, with the central one just doing switching. Although a simple design, for a large system, the central switch is likely to be a major bottleneck. Also, from a fault-tolerance perspective, this is a poor design since a single failure at the central switch completely destroys the system.

In Fig. 8-35(b), we have another zero-dimensional design that is at the other end of the spectrum, a **full interconnect**. Here every node has a direct connection to every other node. This design maximizes the bisection bandwidth, minimizes the diameter, and is exceedingly fault tolerant (it can lose any six links and still be fully connected). Unfortunately, the number of links required for k nodes is $k(k-1)/2$, which quickly gets out of hand for large k.

Another topology is the **tree**, illustrated in Fig. 8-35(c). A problem with this design is that the bisection bandwidth is equal to the link capacity. Since there will normally be a lot of traffic near the top of the tree, the top few nodes will become bottlenecks. One way around this problem is to increase the bisection bandwidth by giving the upper links more bandwidth. For example, the lowest level links might have a capacity b, the next level might have a capacity $2b$ and the top-level links might each have $4b$. Such a design is called a **fat tree** and has been used in commercial multicomputers, such as the (now-defunct) Thinking Machines' CM-5.

The **ring** of Fig. 8-35(d) is a one-dimensional topology by our definition because every packet sent has a choice of going left or going right. The **grid** or **mesh** of Fig. 8-35(e) is a two-dimensional design that has been used in many commercial systems. It is highly regular, easy to scale up to large sizes, and has a diameter that only increases as the square root of the number of nodes. A variant on the grid is the **double torus** of Fig. 8-35(f), which is a grid with the edges connected. Not only is it more fault tolerant than the grid, but the diameter is also less because the opposite corners can now communicate in only two hops.

Yet another popular topology is the three-dimensional torus. The topology here consist of a 3D-structure with nodes at the points (i, j, k) where all coordinates are integers in the range from $(1, 1, 1)$ to (l, m, n). Each node has six neighbors, two along each axis. The nodes at the edges have links that wrap around to the opposite edge, just as with the 2D-torus.

The **cube** of Fig. 8-35(g) is a regular three-dimensional topology. We have illustrated a $2 \times 2 \times 2$ cube, but in the general case it could be a $k \times k \times k$ cube. In Fig. 8-35(h) we have a four-dimensional cube constructed from two three-dimensional cubes with the corresponding nodes connected. We could make a five-dimensional cube by cloning the structure of Fig. 8-35(h) and connecting the corresponding nodes to form a block of four cubes. To go to six dimensions, we could replicate the block of four cubes and interconnect the corresponding nodes, and so on. An n-dimensional cube formed this way is called a **hypercube**. Many parallel computers use this topology because the diameter grows linearly with the dimensionality. Put in other words, the diameter is the base 2 logarithm of the number of nodes, so, for example, a 10-dimensional hypercube has 1024 nodes but a diameter of only 10, giving excellent delay properties. Note that in contrast, 1024 nodes arranged as a 32×32 grid has a diameter of 62, more than six times worse than the hypercube. The price paid for the smaller diameter is that the fanout and thus the number of links (and the cost) is much larger for the hypercube. Nevertheless, the hypercube is a common choice for high-performance systems.

Multicomputers come in all shapes and sizes, so it is hard to give a clean taxonomy of them. Nevertheless, two general "styles" stand out: the MPPs and the clusters. We will now study each of these in turn.

8.4.2 MPPs—Massively Parallel Processors

The first category consists of the **MPPs** (**Massively Parallel Processors**), which are huge multimillion dollar supercomputers. These are used in science, in engineering, and in industry for very large calculations, for handling very large numbers of transactions per second, or for data warehousing (storing and managing immense databases). Initially, MPPs were primarily used as scientific supercomputers, but now most of them are used in commercial environments. In a sense, these machines are the successors to the mighty mainframes of the 1960s (but the connection is tenuous, sort of like a paleontologist claiming that a flock of sparrows is the successor to the *Tyrannosaurus Rex*). To a large extent, the MPPs have displaced SIMD machines, vector supercomputers, and array processors at the top of the digital food chain.

Most of these machines use standard CPUs as their processors. Popular choices are the Intel Pentium, the Sun UltraSPARC, and the IBM PowerPC. What sets the MPPs apart is their use of a very high-performance proprietary interconnection network designed to move messages with low latency and at high bandwidth. Both of these are important because the vast majority of all messages are small (well under 256 bytes), but most of the total traffic is caused by large messages (more than 8 KB). MPPs also come with extensive proprietary software and libraries.

Another point that characterizes MPPs is their enormous I/O capacity. Problems big enough to warrant using MPPs invariably have massive amounts of data to be processed, often terabytes. These data must be distributed among many disks and need to be moved around the machine at great speed.

Finally, another issue specific to MPPs is their attention to fault tolerance. With thousands of CPUs, several failures per week are inevitable. Having an 18-hour run be aborted because one CPU crashed is unacceptable, especially when having one such failure is to be expected every week. Thus large MPPs always have special hardware and software for monitoring the system, detecting failures, and recovering from them smoothly.

While it would be nice to study the general principles of MPP design now, in truth, there are not many principles. When you come right down to it, an MPP is a collection of more-or-less standard computing nodes connected by a very fast interconnect of the types we have already examined. So instead, we will now look at two examples of MPPs: BlueGene/L and Red Storm.

BlueGene

As a first example of a massively parallel processor, we will now examine the IBM BlueGene system. IBM conceived this project in 1999 as a massively parallel supercomputer for solving computationally-intensive problems in, among other fields, the life sciences. For example, biologists believe that the three-dimensional structure of a protein determines its functionality, yet computing the 3D structure of one small protein from the laws of physics took years on the supercomputers of that period. The number of proteins found in human beings is over half a million and many of them are extremely large and their misfolding is known to be responsible for certain diseases (e.g., cystic fibrosis). Clearly, determining the 3D structure of all the human proteins would require increasing the world's computing power by many orders of magnitude, and modeling protein folding is only one problem that BlueGene was designed to handle. Equally complex challenges in molecular dynamics, climate modeling, astronomy, and even financial modeling also require orders of magnitude improvement in supercomputing.

IBM felt that there was enough of a market for massive supercomputing that it invested $100 million to design and build BlueGene. In Nov. 2001, Livermore National Laborary, run by the U.S. Dept. of Energy, signed up as a partner and first customer for the first version of the BlueGene family, called **BlueGene/L**.

The goal of the BlueGene project was not just to produce the world's fastest MPP, but to also to produce the most efficient one in terms of teraflops/dollar, teraflops/watt, and teraflops/m^3. For this reason, IBM rejected the philosophy behind previous MPPs, which was to use the fastest components money could buy. Instead, a decision was made to produce a custom system-on-a-chip component that was to run at a modest speed and low power in order to produce a very large machine with a high packing density. The first chip was delivered in June 2003. The first quarter of the BlueGene/L system, with 16,384 compute nodes, was fully operational by Nov. 2004, when it was certified as the fastest supercomputer on earth at 71 teraflops/sec. Running at a mere 0.4 megawatt, it also won the power efficiency race for its class at 177.5 megaflops/watt. The rest of the system, bringing the total to 65,536 compute nodes, was scheduled for delivery in the summer of 2005.

The heart of the BlueGene/L system is the custom node chip illustrated in Fig. 8-36. It consists of two PowerPC 440 cores running at 700 MHz. The PowerPC 440 is a pipelined dual-issue superscalar processor popular in embedded systems. Each core has a pair of dual-issue floating-point units, which together can issue four floating-point instructions per clock cycle. The floating-point units have been augmented with a number of SIMD-type instructions sometimes useful in scientific computations on arrays. While no performance slouch, this chip is clearly not a top-of-the-line multiprocessor.

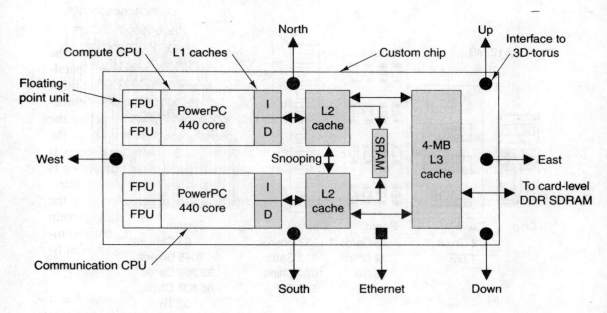

Figure 8-36. The BlueGene/L custom processor chip.

The two CPU cores on the chip are identical in structure but are intended to be programmed differently. One of them is for computing; the other is for handling communication among the 65,536 nodes.

Three levels of cache are present on the chip. The first level consists of a split L1 cache with 32 KB for instructions and 32 KB for data. There is no coherency between the L1 caches on the two CPUs because the standard PowerPC 440 cores do not support that and it was decided to use unmodified cores. The second level is a unified cache consisting of a unified 2-KB cache. The L2 caches are really prefetch buffers rather than true caches. They snoop on each other and are cache consistent. The third level is a unified, consistent 4-MB shared cache that feeds both of the L2 caches. A memory reference that misses on the L1 cache but hits on the L2 cache takes about 11 clock cycles. A miss on L2 that hits on L3 takes about 28 cycles. Finally, a miss on L3 that has to go t o the main SDRAM takes about 75 cycles.

A small SRAM is connected to the L2 caches. It is connected to the JTAG pins for booting, debugging, communicating with the main host, holding the system stack, and providing semaphore, barrier, and other synchronization operations.

At the next level up, IBM designed a custom card that holds two of the chips shown in Fig. 8-36 along with 1 GB of RAM. Future versions of the card may hold as much as 4 GB. The chip and the card are shown in Fig. 8-37(a)–(b) respectively.

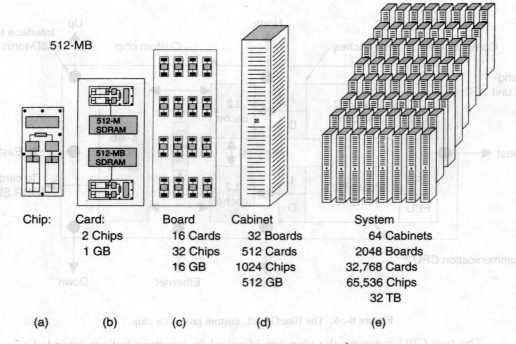

Chip: Card: Board   Cabinet   System
          2 Chips   16 Cards 32 Boards   64 Cabinets
          1 GB   32 Chips 512 Cards   2048 Boards
                    16 GB   1024 Chips 32,768 Cards
                              512 GB   65,536 Chips
                                          32 TB

(a)   (b)   (c)   (d)   (e)

Figure 8-37. The BlueGene/L (a) chip. (b) card. (c) board. (d) cabinet. (e) system.

The cards are mounted on plug-in boards, with 16 cards per board for a total of 32 chips (and thus 32 compute CPUs) per board. Since each card contains 1 GB of SDRAM, the boards contain 16 GB apiece. One board is illustrated in Fig. 8-37(c).

At the next level, 16 of these boards are plugged into the top of a midplane and another 16 are plugged into the bottom, filling a 60 cm × 90 cm cabinet with 1024 CPUs, an extremely high density. The two groups of 16 are separated by a switch that can remove one group from the system for maintenance while at the same time switching in a spare group. A cabinet is illustrated in Fig. 8-37(d).

Finally, a full system, consisting of 64 cabinets with 65,536 compute CPUs and another 65,536 communication CPUs, is depicted in Fig. 8-37(e). With 131,072 dual-issue integer CPUs and 262,144 dual-issue floating-point CPUs, this system should be able to issue up to 786,432 instructions per clock cycle. However, one of the integer units feeds the floating-point units, reducing the instruction rate to 655,360 instructions per clock cycle, or 4.6×10^{14} instructions/sec, making it the biggest computer system ever built by a huge margin.

The system is a multicomputer in the sense that no CPU has direct access to any memory except the 512 MB on its own card. No two CPUs shared the same memory. In addition, there is no demand paging because there are no local disks to page off. Instead, the system has 1024 I/O nodes, which are connected to disks and the other peripheral devices.

All in all, while the system is extremely large, it is also quite straightforward with little new technology except in the area of high-density packaging. The decision to keep it simple was no accident since a major goal was high reliability and availability. Consequently, a great deal of careful engineering went into the power supplies, fans, cooling, and cabling with the goal of a mean-time-to-failure of 10 days.

To connect all the chips, a scalable, high-performance interconnect is needed. The design used is a three-dimensional torus measuring 64 × 32 × 32. As a consequence, each CPU needs six connections, two to other CPUs logically above and below it, north and south of it, and east and west of it. These six connections are labeled east, west, north, south, up, and down, respectively in Fig. 8-36. Physically, each 1024-node cabinet is an 8 × 8 × 16 torus. Pairs of neighboring cabinets for an 8 × 8 × 32 torus. Four pairs of cabinets in the same row form an 8 × 32 × 32 torus. Finally, all 8 rows form a 64 × 32 × 32 torus.

All links are thus point-to-point and operate at 1.4 Gbps. Since each of the 65,536 nodes has three links to "higher" numbered nodes, one in each dimension, the total bandwidth of the system is 275 terabits/sec. The information content of this book is about 300 million bits, including all the art in encapsulated PostScript format, so BlueGene/L could move 900,000 copies of this book per sec. Where they would go and who would want them is left as an exercise for the reader.

Communication on the 3D torus is done in the form of **virtual cut through** routing. This technique is somewhat akin to store-and-forward packet switching, except that entire packets are not stored before being forwarded. As soon as a byte has arrived at one node, it can be forwarded to the next one along the path, even before the entire packet has arrived. Both dynamic (adaptive) and deterministic (fixed) routing are possible. A small amount of special-purpose hardware on the chip is used to implement the virtual cut through.

In addition to the main 3D torus used for data transport, four other communication networks are present. The second one is a combining network in the form of a tree. Many of the operations performed on highly-parallel systems such as BlueGene/L require the participation of all the nodes. For example, consider finding the minimum value of a set of 65,536 values, one held in each node. The combining network joins all the nodes in a tree and whenever two nodes send their respective values to a higher-level node, it selects out the smallest one and forwards it upward. In this way, far less traffic reaches the root than if all 65,636 nodes sent a message there.

The third network is for global barriers and interrupts. Some algorithms work in phases with each node required to wait until all the others have completed the phase before starting the next phase. The barrier network allows the software to define these phases and provide a way to suspend all compute CPUs that reach the end of a phase until all of them have reached the end, at which time they are all released. Interrupts also use this network.

The fourth and fifth networks both use gigabit Ethernet. One of them connects the I/O nodes to the file servers, which are external to BlueGene/L, and to the Internet beyond. The other one is used for debugging the system.

Each of the compute and communication nodes runs a small, custom, lightweight kernel that supports a single user and a single process. This process has two threads, one running on each of the CPUs in the node. This simple structure was designed for high performance and high reliability.

For additional reliability, application software can call a library procedure to make a checkpoint. Once all outstanding messages have been cleared from the network, a global checkpoint can be made and stored so that in the event of a system failure, the job can be restarted from the checkpoint, rather than from the beginning. The I/O nodes run a traditional Linux operating system and support multiple processes. For more information about BlueGene/L see (Adiga et al., 2002; Almasi et al., 2003a, 2003b; and Blumrich et al., 2005).

Red Storm

As our second example of an MPP, let us consider the Red Storm machine (also called Thor's Hammer) at Sandia National Laboratory. Sandia is operated by Lockheed Martin and does classified and unclassified work for the U.S. Dept. of Energy. Some of the classified work concerns the design and simulation of nuclear weapons, which is highly compute intensive.

Sandia has been in this business for a long time and has had many leading-edge supercomputers over the years. For decades, it favored vector supercomputers, but eventually technology and economics made MPPs more cost effective. By 2002, the then-current MPP, called ASCI Red, was getting a bit creaky. Although it had 9460 nodes, collectively they had a mere 1.2 TB of RAM and 12.5 TB of disk space, and the system could barely crank out 3 teraflops/sec. So in the summer of 2002, Sandia selected Cray Research, a long-time supercomputer vendor, to build it a replacement for ASCI Red.

The replacement was delivered in August 2004, a remarkably short design and implementation cycle for such a large machine. The reason it could be designed and delivered so quickly is that Red Storm uses almost entirely off-the-shelf parts, except for one custom chip used for routing.

The CPU selected for Red Storm was the AMD Opteron. The Opteron has several key characteristics that made it the first choice. The first one is that it has three operating modes. In legacy mode, it runs standard Pentium binary programs unmodified. In compatibility mode, the operating system runs in 64-bit mode and can address 2^{64} bytes of memory, but application programs run in 32-bit mode. Finally, in 64-bit mode, the entire machine is 64 bits and all programs can address the full 64-bit address space. In 64-bit mode, it is possible to mix and match software: both 32-bit and 64-bit programs can run at the same time, allowing an easy upgrade path.

The second key characteristic the Opteron has is its attention to the memory bandwidth problem. In recent years, CPUs have been getting faster and faster and memory has not been keeping pace, resulting in a massive penalty when there is a level 2 cache miss. AMD integrated the memory controller into the Opteron so it can run at the speed of the processor clock instead of the speed of the memory bus, which improves memory performance. The controller can handle eight DIMMS of 4 GB each, for a maximum total memory of 32 GB per Opteron. In the Red Storm system, each Opteron has only 2–4 GB. However, as memory gets cheaper, no doubt more will be added in the future though. An upgrade to dual-core Opterons is also an option, doubling the raw compute power.

Each Opteron has its own dedicated custom network processor called the **Seastar**, manufactured by IBM. The Seastar is a critical component since nearly all the data traffic between the processors goes over the Seastar network. Without the very high-speed interconnect provided by these custom chips, the system would quickly bog down in data.

Although the Opterons are commercially available off the shelf, the Red Storm packaging is custom-built. Each Red Storm board contains four Opterons, 4 GB of RAM, four Seastars, a RAS (Reliability, Availability, and Service) processor, and a 100-Mbps Ethernet chip, as shown in Fig. 8-38.

A set of eight boards is plugged into a backplane and inserted into a card cage. Each cabinet holds three card cages for a total of 96 Opterons, plus the necessary power supplies and fans. The full system consists of 108 cabinets for

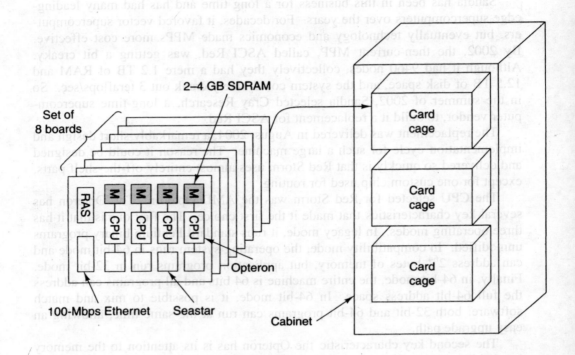

Figure 8-38. Packaging of the Red Storm components.

compute nodes, giving a total of 10,368 Opterons with 10 TB of SDRAM. Each CPU has access to only its own SDRAM. There is no shared memory. The theoretical computing power of the system is 41 teraflops/sec.

The interconnection between the Opteron CPUs is done by the custom Seastar routers, one router per Opteron CPU. The are connected in a 3D torus of size $27 \times 16 \times 24$ with one Seastar at each mesh point. Each Seastar has seven bidirectional 24-Gbps links, going north, east, south, west, up, down, and to the Opteron. The transit time beween adjacent mesh points is 2 microsec. Across the entire set of compute nodes it is only 5 microsec. A second network using 100-Mbps Ethernet is used for service and maintenance.

In addition to the 108 compute cabinets, the system also contains 16 cabinets for I/O and service processors. Each of these cabinets holds 32 Opterons. These 512 CPUs are split: 256 for I/O and 256 for service. The rest of the space is for disks, which are organized as RAID 3 and RAID 5, each with a parity drive and a hot spare. The total disk space is 240 TB. The combined sustained disk bandwidth is 50 GB/sec.

The system is partitioned into classified and unclassified sections, with switches between the parts so they can be mechanically coupled or decoupled. A total of 2688 compute CPUs are always in the classified section and another compute 2688 are always in the unclassified section. The remaining 4992 compute CPUs are switchable into either section, as depicted in Fig. 8-39. The 2688 classified Opterons each have 4 GB of RAM; all the rest have 2 GB each. The I/O and service processors are split between the two parts.

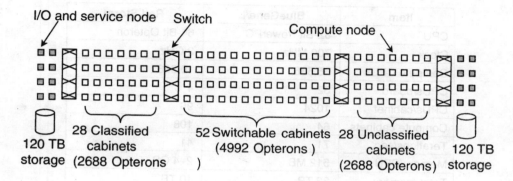

Figure 8-39. The Red Storm system as viewed from above.

Everything is housed in a new 2000 m² custom building. The building and site have been designed so that the system can be upgraded to as many as 30,000 CPUs in the future if required. The compute nodes draw 1.6 megawatts of power; the disks draw another megawatt. Adding in the fans and air conditioning, the whole thing uses 3.5 MW.

The computer hardware and software cost $90 million. The building and cooling cost another $9 million, so the total cost came in at just under $100 million, although some of that was nonrecurring engineering cost. If you want to order an exact clone, $60 million would be a good number to keep in mind. Cray intends to sell smaller versions of the system to other government and commercial customers under the name X3T.

The compute nodes run a lightweight kernel called **catamount**. The I/O and service nodes run plain vanilla Linux with a small addition to support MPI (discussed later in this chapter). The RAS nodes run a stripped down Linux. Extensive software from ASCI Red is available for use on Red Storm, including CPU allocators, schedulers, MPI libraries, math libraries, as well as the application programs.

With such a large system, achieving high reliability is essential. Each board has a RAS processor for doing system maintenance and there are special hardware facilities as well. The goal is an MTBF (Mean Time Between Failures) of 50 hours. ASCI Red had a hardware MTBF of 900 hours, but was plagued by an operating system crash every 40 hours. Although the new hardware is much more reliable than the old hardware, the weak point remains the software.

For more information about Red Storm, see (Brightwell et al., 2005).

A Comparison of BlueGene/L and Red Storm

Red Storm and BlueGene/L are comparable in some ways but different in other ways, so it is interesting to put some of the key parameters next to each other, as presented in Fig. 8-40.

Item	BlueGene/L	Red Storm
CPU	32-Bit PowerPC	64-Bit Opteron
Clock	700 MHz	2 GHz
Compute CPUs	65,536	10,368
CPUs/board	32	4
CPUs/cabinet	1024	96
Compute cabinets	64	108
Teraflops/sec	71	41
Memory/CPU	512 MB	2–4 GB
Total memory	32 TB	10 TB
Router	PowerPC	Seastar
Number of routers	65,536	10,368
Interconnect	3D torus 64 × 32 × 32	3D torus 27 × 16 × 24
Other networks	Gigabit Ethernet	Fast Ethernet
Partitionable	No	Yes
Compute OS	Custom	Custom
I/O OS	Linux	Linux
Vendor	IBM	Cray Research
Expensive	Yes	Yes

Figure 8-40. A comparison of BlueGene/L and Red Storm.

The two machines were built in the same time frame, so their differences are not due to technology but to designers' different visions and to some extent the differences between the builders, IBM and Cray. BlueGene/L was designed from the beginning as a commercial machine of which IBM hopes to sell large numbers to biotech, pharmaceutical, and other companies. Red Storm was built on special contract with Sandia, although Cray plans to make a smaller version for sale, too.

IBM's vision is clear: combine existing cores to produce a custom chip that can be mass produced cheaply, run it at a low speed, and hook together a very large number of them using a modest speed communication network. Sandia's vision is equally clear, but different: use a powerful off-the-shelf 64-bit CPU, design a very fast custom router chip, and throw in a lot of memory to produce a far more powerful node than BlueGene/L so fewer will be needed and communication between them will be faster.

The consequences of these decisions had consequences for the packaging. Because IBM built a custom chip combining the processor and router, it achieved a higher packing density: 1024 CPUs/cabinet. Because Sandia went for an unmodified off-the-shelf CPU chip and 2–4 GB of RAM per node, it could only get 96 compute CPUs in a cabinet. The result is that Red Storm takes up more floor space and consumes more power than BlueGene/L.

In the exotic world of national laboratory computing, the bottom line is performance. In this respect, BlueGene/L wins, 71 TF/sec to 41 TF/sec, but Red Storm was designed to be expandable, so by throwing another 10,368 Opterons at the problem (for example, by switching to dual-core chips), Sandia could probably up its performance to 82 TF. IBM could respond by cranking the clock up a bit (700 MHz is not really pushing the state-of-the-art very hard). In short, MPP supercomputers have not even come close to any physical limits yet and will continue growing for years to come.

8.4.3 Cluster Computing

The other style of multicomputer is the **cluster computer** (Anderson et al., 1995; Martin et al., 1997). It typically consists of hundreds or thousands of PCs or workstations connected by a commercially-available network board. The difference between an MPP and a cluster is analogous to the difference between a mainframe and a PC. Both have a CPU, both have RAM, both have disks, both have an operating system, and so on. The mainframe just has faster ones (except maybe the operating system). Yet qualitatively they feel different and are used and managed differently. This same difference holds for MPPs versus clusters.

Historically, the key element that made MPPs special was their high-speed interconnect, but the recent arrival of commercial, off-the-shelf, high-speed interconnects has begun to close the gap. All in all, clusters are likely to drive MPPs into ever tinier niches, just as PCs have turned mainframes into esoteric specialty items. The main niche for MPPs is high-budget supercomputers, where peak performance is everything and if you have to ask the price you cannot afford one.

While many kinds of clusters exist, two species dominate: centralized and decentralized. A centralized cluster is a cluster of workstations or PCs mounted in a big rack in a single room. Sometimes they are packaged in a much more compact way than usual to reduce physical size and cable length. Typically, the machines are homogeneous and have no peripherals other than network cards and possibly disks. Gordon Bell, the designer of the PDP-11 and VAX, has called such machines **headless workstations** (because they have no owners). We were tempted to call them headless COWs, but feared such a term would gore too many holy cows, so we refrained.

Decentralized clusters consist of the workstations or PCs spread around a building or campus. Most of them are idle many hours a day, especially at night. Usually, these are connected by a LAN. Typically, they are heterogeneous and have a full complement of peripherals, although having a cluster with 1024 mice is really not much better than a cluster with 0 mice. Most importantly, many of them have owners who have emotional attachments to their machines and tend to frown upon some astronomer trying to simulate the big bang on theirs. Using idle workstations to form a cluster invariably means having some way to migrate jobs off machines when their owners want to reclaim them. Job migration is possible but adds software complexity.

Clusters are often smallish affairs, ranging from a dozen to perhaps 500 PCs. However, it is also possible to build very large ones from off-the-shelf PCs. Google has done this in an interesting way that we will now look at.

Google

Google is a popular search engine for finding information on the Internet. While its popularity is due, in part, to its simple interface and fast response time, its design is anything but simple. From Google's point of view, the problem is that it has to find, index, and store the entire World Wide Web (over 8 billion pages and 1 billion images), be able to search the whole thing in under 0.5 sec, and handle thousands of queries/sec coming from all over the world 24 hours a day. In addition, it must never go down, not even in the face of earthquakes, electrical power failures, telecom outages, hardware failures and software bugs. And of course, it has to do all of this as cheaply as possible. Building a Google clone is definitely not an exercise for the reader.

How does Google do it? To start with, Google operates multiple data centers around the world. Not only does this approach provide backups in case one of them is swallowed by an earthquake, but when *www.google.com* is looked up, the sender's IP address is inspected and the address of the nearest data center is supplied. The browser then sends the query there.

Each data center has at least one OC-48 (2.488 Gbps) fiber optics connection to the Internet, on which it receives queries and sends answers, as well as an OC-12 (622 Mbps) backup connection from a different telecom provider, in case the primary ones go down. Uninterruptable power supplies and emergency diesel generators are available at all data centers to keep the show going during power failures. Consequently, during a major natural disaster, performance will suffer, but Google will keep running.

To get a better understanding of why Google chose the architecture it did, it is useful to briefly describe how a query is processed once it hits its designated data center. After arriving at the data center (step 1 in Fig. 8-41), the load balancer routes the query to one of the many query handlers (2), and to the spelling checker (3) and ad server (4) in parallel. Then the search words are looked up on the index servers (5) in parallel. These servers contain an entry for each word on the Web. Each entry lists all the documents (Web pages, PDF files, PowerPoint presentations, etc.) containing the word, sorted in page rank order. Page rank is determined by a complicated (and secret) formula, but the number of links to a page and their own ranks play a large role.

To get higher performance, the index is divided into pieces called **shards** that can be searched in parallel. Conceptually, at least, shard 1 contains all the words in the index, with each one followed by the IDs of the n highest-ranked documents containing that word. Shard 2 contains all the words and the IDs of the n next highest documents, and so on. As the Web grows, each of these shards may later be split with the first k words in one set of shards, the next k words in a second set of shards and so forth, in order to achieve even more search parallelism.

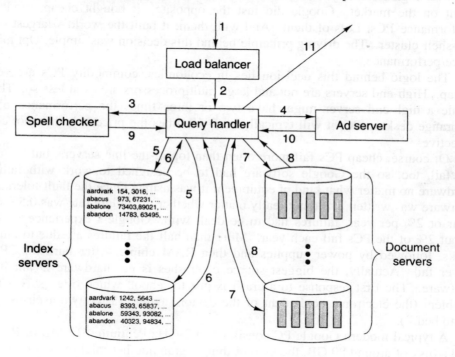

Figure 8-41. Processing of a Google query.

The index servers return a set of document identifiers (6) that are then combined according to the Boolean properties of the query. For example, if the search was for +digital +capybara +dance, then only document identifiers appearing in all three sets are used in the next step. In this step (7), the documents themselves are referenced to extract their titles, URLs, and snippets of text surrounding the search terms. The document servers contain many copies of the entire Web at each data center, hundreds of terabytes at present. The documents are also divided into shards to enhance parallel search. While processing a query does not require reading the whole Web (or even reading the tens of terabytes on the index servers), having to process 100 MB per query is normal.

When the results are returned to the query handler (8), the pages found are collated into page rank order. If potential spelling errors are detected (9), they are announced and relevant ads are added (10). Displaying ads for advertisers interested in buying specific search terms (e.g., "hotel" or "camcorder") is how Google makes its money. Finally, the results are formatted in HTML (HyperText Markup Language) and sent to the user as a Web page.

With this background, we can now examine the Google architecture. Most companies, when faced with a huge data base, massive transaction rate, and the need for high reliability, would buy the biggest, fastest, and most reliable equipment on the market. Google did just the opposite. It bought cheap, modest-performance PCs. Lots of them. And with them, it built the world's largest off-the-shelf cluster. The driving principle behind this decision was simple: Optimize price/performance.

The logic behind this decision lies in economics: commodity PCs are very cheap. High-end servers are not and large multiprocessors are even less so. Thus while a high-end server might have two or three times the performance of a midrange desktop PC, it will typically be 5–10 times the price, which is not cost effective.

Of course, cheap PCs fail more often than top-of-the-line servers, but the latter fail, too, so the Google software had to be designed to work with failing hardware no matter what kind of equipment it was using. Once the fault-tolerance software was written, it did not really matter whether the failure rate was 0.5% per year or 2% per year, failures had to be dealt with. Google's experience is that about 2% of the PCs fail each year. More than half the failures are due to faulty disks, followed by power supplies and then RAM chips. After burn in, CPUs never fail. Actually, the biggest source of crashes is not hardware at all; it is software. The first response to a crash is just to reboot, which often solves the problem (the electronic equivalent of the doctor saying: "Take two aspirins and go to bed.").

A typical modern Google PC consists of a 2-GHz Pentium, 512 MB of RAM, and a disk of around 80 GB, the kind of thing a grandmother might buy for checking her e-mail occasionally. The only specialty item is an Ethernet chip. Not exactly state of the art, but very cheap. The PCs are housed in 1u-high cases (about 5 cm thick) and stacked 40 high in 19-inch racks, one stack in front and one stack in back for a total of 80 PCs per rack. The PCs in a rack are connected by switched Ethernet, with the switch inside the rack. The racks in a data center are also connected by switched Ethernet, with two redundant switches per data center used to survive switch failures.

The layout of a typical Google data center is illustrated in Fig. 8-42. The incoming high-bandwidth OC-48 fiber is routed to each of two 128-port Ethernet switches. Similarly, the backup OC-12 fiber is also routed to each of the two switches. The incoming fibers use special input cards and do not occupy any of the 128 Ethernet ports. Each rack has four Ethernet links coming out of it, two to the left switch and two to the right switch. In this configuration, the system can survive the failure of either switch. Since each rack has four connections to the switch (two from the front 40 PCs and two from the back 40 PCs), it takes four link failures or two link failures and a switch failure to take a rack offline. With a pair of 128-port switches and four links from each rack, up to 64 racks can be supported. With 80 PCs per rack, a data center can have up to 5120 PCs. But, of course, racks do not have to hold exactly 80 PCs and switches can be larger or smaller than 128 ports; these are just typical values for a Google cluster.

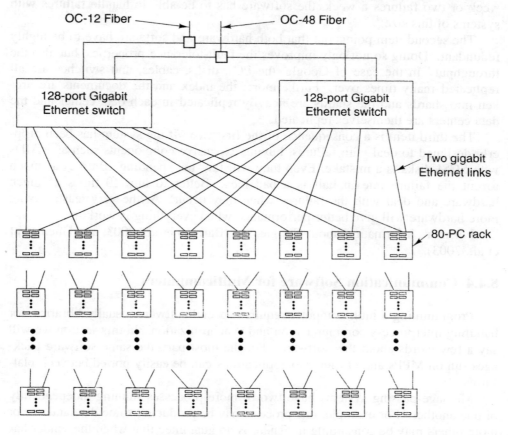

Figure 8-42. A typical Google cluster.

Power density is also a key issue. A typical PC burns about 120 watts or about 10 kW per rack. A rack needs about 3 m^2 so maintenance personnel can install and remove PCs and for the air conditioning to function. These parameters give a power density of over 3000 watts/m^2. Most data centers are designed for 600–1200 watts/m^2, so special measures are required to cool the racks.

Google has learned three key things about running massive Web servers that bear repeating.

1. Components will fail so plan for it.

2. Replicate everything for throughput and availability.

3. Optimize price/performance.

The first item says that you need to have fault-tolerant software. Even with the best of equipment, when you have a massive number of components, some will fail and the software has to be able to handle it. Whether you have 1 failure a week or two failures a week, the software has to be able to handle failures with systems of this size.

The second item points out that both hardware and software have to be highly redundant. Doing so not only improves the fault-tolerance properties, but also the throughput. In the case of Google, the PCs, disks, cables, and switches are all replicated many times over. Furthermore, the index and the documents are broken into shards and the shards are heavily replicated in each data center and the data centers are themselves replicated.

The third item is a consequence of the first two. If the system has been properly designed to deal with failures, buying expensive components such as RAIDs with SCSI disks is a mistake. Even they will fail, but spending 10 times as much to cut the failure rate in half is a bad idea. Better to buy 10 times as much hardware and deal with the failures when they occur. At the very least, having more hardware will give better performance when everything is working.

For more information about Google, see (Barroso et al., 2003; and Ghemawat et al., 2003).

8.4.4 Communication Software for Multicomputers

Programming a multicomputer requires special software, usually libraries, for handling interprocess communication and synchronization. In this section we will say a few words about this software. For the most part, the same software packages run on MPPs and clusters, so applications can be easily ported between platforms.

Message-passing systems have two or more processes running independently of one another. For example, one process may be producing some data and one or more others may be consuming it. There is no guarantee that when the sender has more data the receiver(s) will be ready for it, as each one runs its own program.

Most message-passing systems provide two primitives (usually library calls), send and receive, but several different kinds of semantics are possible. The three main variants are

1. Synchronous message passing.

2. Buffered message passing.

3. Nonblocking message passing.

In **synchronous message passing**, if the sender executes a send and the receiver has not yet executed a receive, the sender is blocked (suspended) until the receiver executes a receive, at which time the message is copied. When the sender gets control back after the call, it knows that the message has been sent and correctly received. This method has the simplest semantics and does not require any buffering. It has the severe disadvantage that the sender remains blocked until the receiver has gotten and acknowledged receipt of the message.

In **buffered message passing**, when a message is sent before the receiver is ready, the message is buffered somewhere, for example, in a mailbox, until the receiver takes it out. Thus in buffered message passing, a sender can continue after a send, even if the receiver is busy with something else. Since the message has actually been sent, the sender is free to reuse the message buffer immediately. This scheme reduces the time the sender has to wait. Basically, as soon as the system has sent the message the sender can continue. However, the sender now has no guarantee that the message was correctly received. Even if communication is reliable, the receiver may have crashed before getting the message.

In **nonblocking message passing**, the sender is allowed to continue immediately after making the call. All the library does is tell the operating system to do the call later, when it has time. As a consequence, the sender is hardly blocked at all. The disadvantage of this method is that when the sender continues after the send, it may not reuse the message buffer as the message may not yet have been sent. Somehow it has to find out when it can reuse the buffer. One idea is to have it poll the system to ask. The other is to get an interrupt when the buffer is available. Neither of these makes the software any simpler.

Below we will briefly discuss a popular message-passing systems available on many multicomputers: MPI.

MPI—Message-Passing Interface

For quite a few years, the most popular communication package for multicomputers was **PVM Parallel Virtual Machine** (Geist et al., 1994; and Sunderram, 1990). However, in recent years it has been largely replaced by **MPI** (**Message-Passing Interface**). MPI is much richer and more complex than PVM, with many more library calls, many more options, and many more parameters per call. The original version of MPI, now called MPI-1, was augmented by MPI-2 in 1997. Below we will give a very cursory introduction to MPI-1 (which contains all the basics), then say a little about what was added in MPI-2. For more information about MPI, see (Gropp et al., 1994; and Snir et al., 1996).

MPI-1 does not deal with process creation or management, as PVM does. It is up to the user to create processes using local system calls. Once they have been created, they are arranged into static, unchanging process groups. It is with these groups that MPI works.

MPI is based on four major concepts: communicators, message data types, communication operations, and virtual topologies. A **communicator** is a process group plus a context. A context is a label that identifies something, such as a phase of execution. When messages are sent and received, the context can be used to keep unrelated messages from interfering with one another.

Messages are typed and many data types are supported, including characters, short, regular, and long integers, single- and double-precision floating-point numbers, and so on. It is also possible to construct other types derived from these.

MPI supports an extensive set of communication operations. The most basic one is used to send messages as follows:

    MPI_Send(buffer, count, data_type, destination, tag, communicator)

This call sends a buffer with *count* number of items of the specified data type to the destination. The *tag* field labels the message so the receiver can say it only wants to receive a message with that tag. The last field tells which process group the destination is in (the *destination* field is just an index into the list of processes for the specified group). The corresponding call for receiving a message is

    MPI_Recv(&buffer, count, data_type, source, tag, communicator, &status)

which announces that the receiver is looking for a message of a certain type from a certain source with a certain tag.

MPI supports four basic communication modes. Mode 1 is synchronous, in which the sender may not begin sending until the receiver has called MPI_Recv. Mode 2 is buffered, in which this restriction does not hold. Mode 3 is standard, which is implementation dependent and can be either synchronous or buffered. Mode 4 is ready, in which the sender claims the receiver is available (as in synchronous), but no check is made. Each of these primitives comes in a blocking and a nonblocking version, leading to eight primitives in all. Receiving only has two variants: blocking and nonblocking.

MPI supports collective communication, including broadcast, scatter/gather, total exchange, aggregation, and barrier. For all forms of collective communication, all the processes in a group must make the call and with compatible arguments. Failure to do this is an error. A typical form of collective communication is for processes organized in a tree, in which values propagate up from the leaves to the root, undergoing some processing at each step, for example, adding up the values or taking the maximum.

The fourth basic concept in MPI is the **virtual topology**, in which the processes can be arranged in a tree, ring, grid, torus, or other topology. Such an arrangement provides a way to name communication paths and facilitates communication.

MPI-2 adds dynamic processes, remote memory access, nonblocking collective communication, scalable I/O support, real-time processing, and many other new features that are beyond the scope of this book. In the scientific community, a battle raged for years between the MPI and PVM camps. The PVM side said that PVM was easier to learn and simpler to use. The MPI side said the MPI does more and also points out that MPI is a formal standard with a standardization committee and an official defining document. The PVM side agreed but claimed the lack of a full-blown standardization bureaucracy is not necessarily a drawback. When all was said and done, it appears that MPI won.

8.4.5 Scheduling

MPI programmers can easily create jobs requesting multiple CPUs and running for substantial periods of time. When multiple independent requests are available from different users, each needing a different number of CPUs for different time periods, the cluster needs a scheduler to determine which job gets to run when.

In the simplest model, the job scheduler requires each job to specify how many CPUs it needs. Jobs are then run in strict FIFO order, as shown in Fig. 8-43(a). In this model, after a job is started, a check is made to see if enough CPUs are available to start the next job in the input queue. If so, it is started, and so on. Otherwise, the system waits until more CPUs become available. As an aside, although we have suggested that this cluster has eight CPUs, it might well have 128 CPUs that are allocated in units of 16 (giving eight CPU groups), or some other combination.

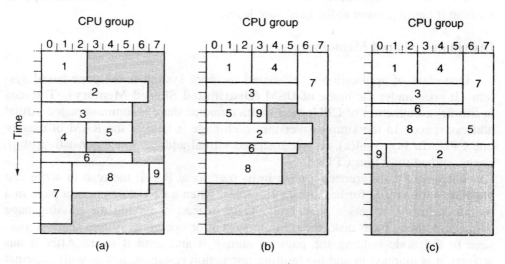

Figure 8-43. Scheduling a cluster. (a) FIFO. (b) Without head-of-line blocking. (c) Tiling. The shaded areas indicate idle CPUs.

A better scheduling algorithm avoids head-of-line blocking by skipping over jobs that do not fit and picking the first one that does fit. Whenever a job finishes, the queue of remaining jobs is checked in FIFO order. This algorithm gives the result of Fig. 8-43(b).

A still more sophisticated scheduling algorithm requires each submitted job to specify its shape, that is, how many CPUs for how many minutes. With that information, the job scheduler can attempt to tile the CPU-time rectangle. Tiling is especially effective when jobs are submitted during the daytime for execution at night, so the job scheduler has all the information about all the jobs in advance and can run them in optimal order, as illustrated in Fig. 8-43(c).

8.4.6 Application-Level Shared Memory

That multicomputers scale to larger sizes than multiprocessors should be clear from our examples. This reality has led to the development of message-passing systems like MPI. Many programmers do not like this model and would like to have the illusion of shared memory, even if it is not really there. Achieving this goal would be the best of both worlds: large, inexpensive hardware (at least, per node) plus ease of programming. This is the holy grail of parallel computing.

Many researchers have concluded that while shared memory at the architectural level may not scale well, there may be other ways to achieve the same goal. From Fig. 8-19, we see that there are other levels at which a shared memory can be introduced. In the following sections, we will look at some ways that shared memory can be introduced into the programming model on a multicomputer, without it being present at the hardware level.

Distributed Shared Memory

One class of application-level shared memory system is the page-based system. It goes under the name of **DSM** (**Distributed Shared Memory**). The idea is simple: a collection of CPUs on a multicomputer share a common paged virtual address space. In the simplest version, each page is held in the RAM of exactly one CPU. In Fig. 8-44(a), we see a shared virtual address space consisting of 16 pages, spread over four CPUs.

When a CPU references a page in its own local RAM, the read or write just happens without any further delay. However, when a CPU references a page in a remote memory, it gets a page fault. Only instead of having the missing page being brought in from disk, the runtime system or operating system sends a message to the node holding the page to unmap it and send it over. After it has arrived, it is mapped in and the faulting instruction restarted, just as with a normal page fault. In Fig. 8-44(b), we see the situation after CPU 0 has faulted on page 10: it is moved from CPU 1 to CPU 0.

This basic idea was first implemented in IVY (Li and Hudak, 1986, 1989). It provides a fully shared, sequentially consistent memory on a multicomputer. However, many optimizations are possible to improve the performance. The first

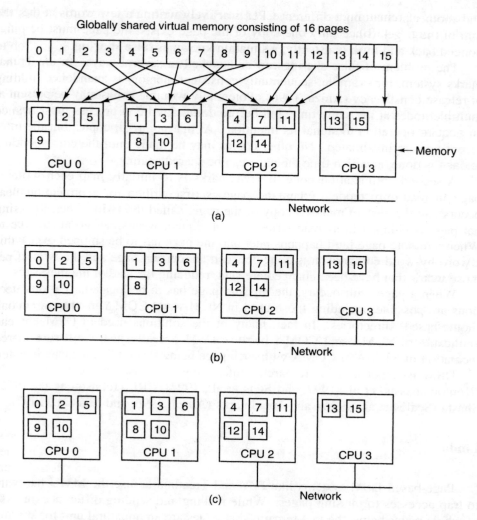

Figure 8-44. A virtual address space consisting of 16 pages spread over four nodes of a multicomputer. (a) The initial situation. (b) After CPU 0 references page 10. (c) After CPU 1 references page 10, here assumed to be a read-only page.

optimization, present in IVY, is to allow pages that are marked as read-only to be present at multiple nodes at the same time. Thus when a page fault occurs, a copy of the page is sent to the faulting machine, but the original stays where it is since there is no danger of conflicts. The situation of two CPUs sharing a read-only page (page 10) is illustrated in Fig. 8-44(c).

Even with this optimization, performance is frequently unacceptable, especially when one process is actively writing a few words at the top of some page and another process on a different CPU is actively writing a few words at the bottom of the page. Since only one copy of the page exists, the page must be ping-ponged back and forth constantly, a situation known as **false sharing**.

The problem of false sharing can be attacked in several ways. In the Treadmarks system, for example, sequentially consistent memory is abandoned in favor of release consistency (Amza, 1996). Potentially writable pages may be present at multiple nodes at the same time, but before doing a write, a process must first do an acquire operation to signal its intention. At that point, all copies but the most recent one are invalidated. No other copies may be made until the corresponding release is done, at which time the page can be shared again.

A second optimization done in Treadmarks is to initially map each writable page in read-only mode. When the page is first written to, a protection fault occurs and the system makes a copy of the page, called the **twin**. Then the original page is mapped in as read-write and subsequent writes can go at full speed. When a remote page fault happens later and the page has to be shipped over there, a word-by-word comparison is done between the current page and the twin. Only those words that have been changed are sent, reducing the size of the messages.

When a page fault occurs, the missing page has to be located. Various solutions are possible, including those used in NUMA and COMA machines, such as (home-based) directories. In fact, many of the solutions used in DSM are also applicable to NUMA and COMA because DSM is really just a software implementation of NUMA or COMA with each page being treated like a cache line.

DSM is a hot area of research. Interesting systems include CASHMERE (Kontothanassis, et al., 1997; and Stets et al., 1997), CRL (Johnson et al., 1995), Shasta (Scales et al., 1996), and Treadmarks (Amza, 1996; and Lu et al., 1997).

Linda

Page-based DSM systems like IVY and Treadmarks use the MMU hardware to trap accesses to missing pages. While making and sending differences instead of whole pages helps, the fact remains that pages are an unnatural unit for sharing, so other approaches have been tried.

One such approach is Linda, which provides processes on multiple machines with a highly structured distributed shared memory (Carriero and Gelernter, 1989). This memory is accessed through a small set of primitive operations that can be added to existing languages, such as C and FORTRAN, to form parallel languages, in this case, C-Linda and FORTRAN-Linda.

The unifying concept behind Linda is that of an abstract **tuple space**, which is global to the entire system and accessible to all processes in it. Tuple space is like a global shared memory, only with a certain built-in structure. The tuple space contains some number of **tuples**, each of which consists of one or more fields. For C-Linda, field types include integers, long integers, and floating-point numbers, as well as composite types such as arrays (including strings) and structures (but not other tuples). Figure 8-45 shows three tuples as examples.

("abc", 2, 5)
("matrix-1", 1, 6, 3.14)
("family", "is sister", Carolyn, Elinor)

Figure 8-45. Three Linda tuples.

Four operations are provided on tuples. The first one, out, puts a tuple into the tuple space. For example,

    out("abc", 2, 5);

puts the tuple ("abc", 2, 5) into the tuple space. The fields of out are normally constants, variables, or expressions, as in

    out("matrix−1", i, j, 3.14);

which outputs a tuple with four fields, the second and third of which are determined by the current values of the variables i and j.

Tuples are retrieved from the tuple space by the in primitive. They are addressed by content rather than by name or address. The fields of in can be expressions or formal parameters. Consider, for example,

    in("abc", 2, ? i);

This operation "searches" the tuple space for a tuple consisting of the string "abc", the integer, 2, and a third field containing any integer (assuming that i is an integer). If found, the tuple is removed from the tuple space and the variable i is assigned the value of the third field. The matching and removal are atomic, so if two processes execute the same in operation simultaneously, only one of them will succeed, unless two or more matching tuples are present. The tuple space may even contain multiple copies of the same tuple.

The matching algorithm used by in is straightforward. The fields of the in primitive, called the **template**, are (conceptually) compared to the corresponding fields of every tuple in the tuple space. A match occurs if the following three conditions are all met:

1. The template and the tuple have the same number of fields.

2. The types of the corresponding fields are equal.

3. Each constant or variable in the template matches its tuple field.

Formal parameters, indicated by a question mark followed by a variable name or type, do not participate in the matching (except for type checking), although those containing a variable name are assigned after a successful match.

If no matching tuple is present, the calling process is suspended until another process inserts the needed tuple, at which time the caller is automatically revived and given the new tuple. The fact that processes block and unblock automatically means that if one process is about to output a tuple and another is about to input it, it does not matter which goes first.

In addition to out and in, Linda also has a primitive read, which is the same as in except that it does not remove the tuple from the tuple space. There is also a primitive eval, which causes its parameters to be evaluated in parallel and the resulting tuple to be deposited in the tuple space. This mechanism can be used to perform an arbitrary computation. This is how parallel processes are created in Linda.

A common programming paradigm in Linda is the **replicated worker model**. This model is based on the idea of a **task bag** full of jobs to be done. The main process starts out by executing a loop containing

```
out("task-bag", job);
```

in which a different job description is output to the tuple space on each iteration. Each worker starts out by getting a job description tuple using

```
in("task-bag", ?job);
```

which it then carries out. When it is done, it gets another. New work may also be put into the task bag during execution. In this simple way, work is dynamically divided among the workers, and each worker is kept busy all the time, all with relatively little overhead.

Various implementations of Linda on multicomputer systems exist. In all of them, a key issue is how to distribute the tuples among the machines and how to locate them when needed. Various possibilities include broadcasting and directories. Replication is also an important issue. These points are discussed in Bjornson (1993).

Orca

A somewhat different approach to application-level shared memory on a multicomputer is to use full-blown objects instead of just tuples as the unit of sharing. Objects consist of internal (hidden) state plus methods for operating on that state. By not allowing the programmer to access the state directly, many possibilities are opened to allow sharing over machines that do not have physical shared memory.

One object-based system that gives the illusion of shared memory on multicomputer systems is Orca (Bal, 1991; Bal et al., 1992; and Bal and Tanenbaum, 1988). Orca is a traditional programming language (based on Modula 2) to which two new features have been added: objects and the ability to create new processes. An Orca object is an abstract data type, analogous to an object in Java or a package in Ada. It encapsulates internal data structures and user-written methods, called **operations**. Objects are passive, that is, they do not contain threads to which messages can be sent. Instead, processes access an object's internal data by invoking its methods.

Each Orca method consists of a list of (guard, block-of-statements) pairs. A guard is a Boolean expression that does not contain any side effects, or the empty guard, which is the same as the value *true*. When an operation is invoked, all of its guards are evaluated in an unspecified order. If all of them are *false*, the invoking process is delayed until one becomes *true*. When a guard is found that evaluates to *true*, the block of statements following it is executed. Figure 8-46 depicts a *stack* object with two operations, *push* and *pop*.

```
Object implementation stack;
  top:integer;                              # storage for the stack
  stack: array [integer 0..N–1] of integer;

  operation push(item: integer);            # function returning nothing
  begin
    guard top < N – 1 do
      stack[top] := item;                   # push item onto the stack
      top := top + 1;                       # increment the stack pointer
    od;
  end;

  operation pop( ): integer;                # function returning an integer
  begin
    guard top > 0 do                        # suspend if the stack is empty
      top := top – 1;                       # decrement the stack pointer
      return stack[top];                    # return the top item
    od;
  end;

begin
  top := 0;                                 # initialization
end;
```

Figure 8-46. A simplified ORCA stack object, with internal data and two operations.

Once a *stack* has been defined, variables of this type can be declared, as in

    s, t: stack;

which creates two stack objects and initializes the *top* variable in each to 0. The integer variable *k* can be pushed onto the stack *s* by the statement

    s$push(k);

and so forth. The *pop* operation has a guard, so an attempt to pop a variable from an empty stack will suspend the caller until another process has pushed something on the stack.

Orca has a **fork** statement to create a new process on a user-specified processor. The new process runs the procedure named in the **fork** statement. Parameters, including objects, may be passed to the new process, which is how objects become distributed among machines. For example, the statement

for i **in** 1 .. n **do fork** foobar(s) **on** i; **od**;

generates one new process on each of machines 1 through n, running the program *foobar* in each of them. As these n new processes (and the parent) execute in parallel, they can all push and pop items onto the shared stack s as though they were all running on a shared-memory multiprocessor. It is the job of the runtime system to sustain the illusion of shared memory where it really does not exist.

Operations on shared objects are atomic and sequentially consistent. The system guarantees that if multiple processes perform operations on the same shared object nearly simultaneously, the system chooses some order and all processes see the same order of events.

Orca integrates shared data and synchronization in a way not present in page-based DSM systems. Two kinds of synchronization are needed in parallel programs. The first kind is mutual exclusion synchronization, to keep two processes from executing the same critical region at the same time. In Orca, each operation on a shared object is effectively like a critical region because the system guarantees that the final result is the same as if all the critical regions were executed one at a time (i.e., sequentially). In this respect, an Orca object is like a distributed form of a monitor (Hoare, 1975).

The other kind of synchronization is condition synchronization, in which a process blocks waiting for some condition to hold. In Orca, condition synchronization is done with guards. In the example of Fig. 8-46, a process trying to pop an item from an empty stack will be suspended until the stack is no longer empty.

The Orca runtime system handles object replication, migration, consistency, and operation invocation. Each object can be in one of two states: single copy or replicated. An object in single-copy state exists on only one machine, so all requests for it are sent there. A replicated object is present on all machines containing a process using it, which makes read operations easier (since they can be done locally), at the expense of making updates more expensive. When an operation that modifies a replicated object is executed, it must first get a sequence number from a centralized process that issues them. Then a message is sent to each machine holding a copy of the object, telling it to execute the operation. Since all such updates bear sequence numbers, all machines just carry out the operations in sequence order, which guarantees sequential consistency.

Globe

Most DSM, Linda, and Orca systems run on local systems, that is within a single building or campus. However, it is also possible to build an application-level shared-memory system on a multicomputer that runs worldwide. In the

Globe system, an object can be located in the address space of multiple processes at the same time, possibly on different continents (Kermarrec et al., 1998; Popescu et al., 2002; and Van Steen et al., 1999). To access a shared object's data, user processes must go through its methods, which allows different objects to have different implementation strategies. For example, one option is to have a single copy of the data that is requested dynamically as needed (good for data frequently updated by a single owner). Another option is to have all the data located within each copy of the object and updates sent out to each copy by a reliable multicast protocol.

What makes Globe somewhat ambitious is its goal to scale to a billion users and a trillion (possibly mobile) objects. Locating objects, managing them, and handling the scaling are crucial. Globe does this by having a general framework in which each object can nevertheless have its own replication strategy, security strategy, and so on. This avoids the one-size-fits-all problem present in other systems, while retaining the ease of programming offered by shared memory.

Other wide-area distributed systems include Globus (Foster and Kesselman, 1998a; and Foster and Kesselman, 1998b) and Legion (Grimshaw and Wulf, 1996; and Grimshaw and Wulf, 1997), but these do not provide the illusion of shared memory as Globe does.

8.4.7 Performance

The point of building a parallel computer is to make it go faster than a uniprocessor machine. If it does not achieve that simple goal, it is not worth having. Furthermore, it should achieve the goal in a cost-effective manner. A machine that is twice as fast as a uniprocessor at 50 times the cost is not likely to be a big seller. In this section we will examine some of the performance issues associated with parallel computer architectures.

Hardware Metrics

From a hardware perspective, the performance metrics of interest are the CPU and I/O speeds and the performance of the interconnection network. The CPU and I/O speeds are the same as in the uniprocessor case, so the key parameters of interest in a parallel system are those associated with the interconnect. There are two key items: latency and bandwidth, which we will now look at in turn.

The roundtrip latency is the time it takes for a CPU to send a packet and get a reply. If the packet is sent to a memory, then the latency measures the time to read or write a word or block of words. If it is sent to another CPU, it measures the interprocessor communication time for packets of that size. Usually, the latency of interest is for minimal packets, often one word or a small cache line.

The latency is built up from several factors, and is different for circuit-switched, store-and-forward, virtual cut through, and wormhole-routed interconnects. For circuit switching, the latency is the sum of the setup time and the transmission time. To set up a circuit, a probe packet has to be sent out to reserve the resources and then report back. Once that has happened, the data packet has to be assembled. When it is ready, bits can flow at full speed, so if the total setup time is T_s, the packet size is p bits, and the bandwidth b bits/sec, the one-way latency is $T_s + p/b$. If the circuit is full duplex, then there is no setup time for the reply, so the minimum latency for sending a p bit packet and getting a p bit reply is $T_s + 2p/b$ sec.

For packet switching, it is not necessary to send a probe packet to the destination in advance, but there is still some internal setup time to assemble the packet, T_a. Here the one-way transmission time is $T_a + p/b$, but this is only the time to get the packet into the first switch. There is a finite delay within the switch, say T_d and then the process is repeated to the next switch and so on. The T_d delay is composed of both processing time and queueing delay, waiting for the output port to become free. If there are n switches, then the total one-way latency is given by the formula $T_a + n(p/b + T_d) + p/b$, where the final term is due to the copy from the last switch to the destination.

The one-way latencies for virtual cut through and wormhole routing in the best case are close to $T_a + p/b$ because there is no probe packet to set up a circuit, and no store-and-forward delay either. Basically, it is the initial setup time to assemble the packet, plus the time to push the bits out the door. In all cases, propagation delay has to be added, but that is usually small.

The other hardware metric is bandwidth. Many parallel programs, especially in the natural sciences, move a lot of data around, so the number of bytes/sec that the system can move is critical to performance. Several metrics for bandwidth exist. We have seen one of them—bisection bandwidth—already. Another one is the **aggregate bandwidth**, which is computed by simply adding up the capacities of all the links. This number gives the maximum number of bits that can be in transit at once. Yet another important metric is the average bandwidth out of each CPU. If each CPU is capable of outputting 1 MB/sec, it does little good that the interconnect has a bisection bandwidth of 100 GB/sec. Communication will be limited by how much data each CPU can output.

In practice, actually achieving anything even close to the theoretical bandwidth is very difficult. Many sources of overhead work to reduce the capacity. For example, there is always some per-packet overhead associated with each packet: assembling it, building its header, and getting it going. Sending 1024 4-byte packets will never achieve the same bandwidth as sending one 4096-byte packet. Unfortunately, for achieving low latencies, using small packets is better, since large ones block the lines and switches too long. Thus there is an inherent conflict between achieving low average latencies and high-bandwidth utilization. For some applications, one is more important than the other and for other applications it is the other way around. It is worth noting, however, that you can always buy more bandwidth (by putting in more or wider wires), but you cannot buy lower latencies. Thus it is generally better to err on the side of making latencies as short as possible, and worry about bandwidth later.

Software Metrics

Hardware metrics like latency and bandwidth look at what the hardware is capable of doing. However, users have a different perspective. They want to know how much faster their programs are going to run on a parallel computer than on a uniprocessor. For them, the key metric is speedup: how much faster a program runs on an n-processor system than on a one-processor system. Typically these results are shown in graphs like those of Fig. 8-47. Here we see several different parallel programs run on a multicomputer consisting of 64 Pentium Pro CPUs. Each curve shows the speedup of one program with k CPUs as a function of k. Perfect speedup is indicated by the dotted line, in which using k CPUs makes the program go k times faster, for any k. Few programs achieve perfect speedup, but some come close. The N-body problem parallelizes extremely well; awari (an African board game) does reasonably well; but inverting a certain skyline matrix does not go more than five times faster no matter how many CPUs are available. The programs and results are discussed in Bal et al. (1998).

Part of the reason that perfect speedup is nearly impossible to achieve is that almost all programs have some sequential component, often the initialization phase, reading in the data, or collecting the results. Having many CPUs does not help here. Suppose that a program runs for T sec on a uniprocessor, with a fraction f of this time being sequential code and a fraction $(1 - f)$ being potentially parallelizable, as shown in Fig. 8-48(a). If the latter code can be run on n CPUs with no overhead, its execution time can be reduced from $(1 - f)T$ to $(1 - f)T/n$ at best, as shown in Fig. 8-48(b). This gives a total execution time for the sequential and parallel parts of $fT + (1 - f)T/n$. The speedup is just the execution time of the original program, T, divided by this new execution time:

$$Speedup = \frac{n}{1 + (n - 1)f}$$

For $f = 0$ we can get linear speedup, but for $f > 0$, perfect speedup is not possible due to the sequential component. This result is known as **Amdahl's law**.

Amdahl's law is not the only reason perfect speedup is nearly impossible to achieve. Nonzero communication latencies, finite communication bandwidths, and algorithmic inefficiencies can also play a role. Also, even if 1000 CPUs were available, not all programs can be written to make use of so many CPUs, and the overhead in getting them all started may be significant. Furthermore, sometimes the best-known algorithm does not parallelize well, so a suboptimal algorithm must be used in the parallel case. This all said, for many applications, having the

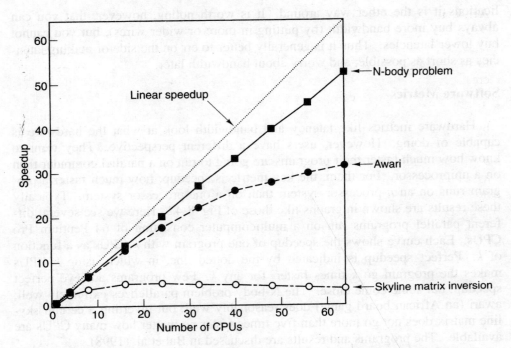

Figure 8-47. Real programs achieve less than the perfect speedup indicated by the dotted line.

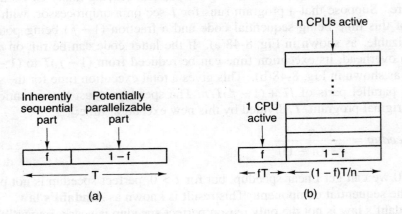

Figure 8-48. (a) A program has a sequential part and a parallelizable part. (b) Effect of running part of the program in parallel.

program run n times faster is highly desirable, even if it takes $2n$ CPUs to do it. CPUs are not that expensive, after all, and many companies live with considerably less than 100% efficiency in other parts of their businesses.

Achieving High Performance

The most straightforward way to improve performance is to add more CPUs to the system. However, this addition must be done in such a way as to avoid creating any bottlenecks. A system in which one can add more CPUs and get correspondingly more computing power is said to be **scalable**.

To see some of the implications of scalability, consider four CPUs connected by a bus, as illustrated in Fig. 8-49(a). Now imagine scaling the system to 16 CPUs by adding 12 more, as shown in Fig. 8-49(b). If the bandwidth of the bus is *b* MB/sec, then by quadrupling the number of CPUs, we have also reduced the available bandwidth per CPU from *b*/4 MB/sec to *b*/16 MB/sec. Such a system is not scalable.

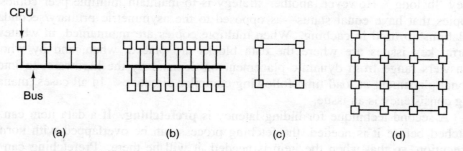

Figure 8-49. (a) A 4-CPU bus-based system. (b) A 16-CPU bus-based system. (c) A 4-CPU grid-based system. (d) A 16-CPU grid-based system.

Now we do the same thing with a grid-based system, as shown in Fig. 8-49(c) and Fig. 8-49(d). With this topology, adding new CPUs also adds new links, so scaling the system up does not cause the aggregate bandwidth per CPU to drop, as it does with a bus. In fact, the ratio of links to CPUs increases from 1.0 with 4 CPUs (4 CPUs, 4 links) to 1.5 with 16 CPUs (16 CPUs, 24 links), so adding CPUs improves the aggregate bandwidth per CPU.

Of course, bandwidth is not the only issue. Adding CPUs to the bus does not increase the diameter of the interconnection network or latency in the absence of traffic, whereas adding them to the grid does. For an $n \times n$ grid, the diameter is $2(n - 1)$, so the worst (and average) case latency increases roughly as the square root of the number of CPUs. For 400 CPUs, the diameter is 38, whereas for 1600 CPUs it is 78, so quadrupling the number of CPUs approximately doubles the diameter and thus the average latency.

Ideally, a scalable system should maintain the same average bandwidth per CPU and a constant average latency as more and more CPUs are added. In practice, however, keeping enough bandwidth per CPU is doable, but in all practical designs, latency grows with size. Having it grow logarithmically, as in a hypercube, is about the best that can be done.

The problem with having latency grow as the system scales up is that latency is often fatal to performance in fine- and medium-grained applications. If a program needs data that are not in its local memory, there is often a substantial delay in getting them, and the bigger the system, the longer the delay, as we have just seen. This problem is equally true of multiprocessors as multicomputers, since in both cases the physical memory is invariably divided up into far-flung modules.

As a consequence of this observation, system designers often go to great lengths to reduce, or at least hide, the latency, using several techniques we will now mention. The first latency-hiding technique is data replication. If copies of a block of data can be kept at multiple locations, accesses from those locations can be speeded up. One such replication technique is caching, in which one or more copies of data blocks are kept close to where they are being used, as well as where they "belong." However, another strategy is to maintain multiple peer copies—copies that have equal status—as opposed to the asymmetric primary/secondary relationship used in caching. When multiple copies are maintained, in whatever form, key issues are where the data blocks are placed, when, and by whom. Answers range from dynamic placement on demand by the hardware, to intentional placement at load time following compiler directives. In all cases, managing consistency is an issue.

A second technique for hiding latency is **prefetching**. If a data item can be fetched before it is needed, the fetching process can be overlapped with normal execution, so that when the item is needed, it will be there. Prefetching can be automatic or under program control. When a cache loads not only the word being referenced, but an entire cache line containing the word, it is gambling that the succeeding words are also likely to be needed soon.

Prefetching can also be controlled explicitly. When the compiler realizes that it will need some data, it can put in an explicit instruction to go get them, and put that instruction sufficiently far in advance that the data will be there in time. This strategy requires that the compiler have a complete knowledge of the underlying machine and its timing, as well as control over where all data are placed. Such speculative LOAD instructions work best when it is known for sure that the data will be needed. Getting a page fault on a LOAD for a path that is ultimately not taken is very costly.

A third technique that can hide latency is multithreading, as we have seen. If switching between processes can be made fast enough, for example, by giving each one its own memory map and hardware registers, then when one thread blocks waiting for remote data to arrive, the hardware can quickly switch to another one that is able to continue. In the limiting case, the CPU runs the first instruction from thread one, the second instruction from thread two, and so on. In this way, the CPU can be kept busy, even in the face of long memory latencies for the individual threads.

A fourth technique for hiding latency is using nonblocking writes. Normally, when a STORE instruction is executed, the CPU waits until the STORE has completed before continuing. With nonblocking writes, the memory operation is started, but the program just continues anyway. Continuing past a LOAD is harder, but with out-of-order execution, even that is possible.

8.5 GRID COMPUTING

Many of today's challenges in science, engineering, industry, the environment, and other areas, are large scale and interdisciplinary. Solving them requires the expertise, skills, knowledge, facilities, software, and data from multiple organizations, often in different countries. Some examples are as follows:

1. Scientists developing a mission to Mars.

2. A consortium building a complex product (e.g., a dam or aircraft).

3. An international relief team coordinating aid after a natural disaster.

Some of these are long-term cooperations, others are more short term, but they all share the common thread of requiring separate organizations with their own resources and procedures to work together to achieve a common goal.

Until recently, having different organizations, with different computers operating systems, data bases, and protocols work together to share resources and data has been very difficult. However, the growing need for large-scale interorganizational cooperation has led to the development of systems and technology for connecting widely-separated computers into what is called the **grid**. In a sense, the grid is the next step along the axis of Fig. 8-1. It can be thought of as a very large, international, loosely-coupled, heterogeneous, cluster.

The goal of the grid is to provide a technical infrastructure to allow a group of organizations that share a common goal to form a **virtual organization**. This virtual organization has to be flexible, with a large and changing membership, permitting the members to work together in areas they deem appropriate, while allowing them to maintain control over their own resources to whatever degree they wish. To this end, grid researchers are developing services, tools, and protocols to enable these virtual organizations to function.

The grid is inherently multilateral with many participants who are peers. It can be contrasted with existing computing frameworks. In the client-server model, a transaction involves two parties, the server, who offers some service, and the client, who wants to use the service. A typical example of the client-server model is the Web, in which users to go Web servers to find information. The grid also differs from peer-to-peer applications, in which pairs of individuals exchange files. E-mail is a common example of a peer-to-peer application. Because the grid is different from these models, it requires new protocols and technology.

The grid needs access to a wide variety of resources. Each resource has a specific system and organization that owns it and which decides how much of the resource to make available to the grid, during which hours, and to whom. In an abstract sense, what the grid is about is resource access and management.

One way to model the grid is the layered hierarchy of Fig. 8-50. The **fabric layer** at the bottom is the set of components from which the grid is built. It includes CPUs, disks, networks, and sensors on the hardware side, and programs and data on the software side. These are the resources that the grid makes available in a controlled way.

Layer	Function
Application	Applications that share managed resources in controlled ways
Collective	Discovery, brokering, monitoring and control of resource groups
Resource	Secure, managed access to individual resources
Fabric	Physical resources: computers, storage, networks, sensors, programs and data

Figure 8-50. The grid layers.

One level higher, is the **resource layer**, which is concerned with managing the individual resources. In many cases, a resource participating in the grid has a local process that manages it and allows controlled access to it by remote users. This layer provides a uniform interface to higher layers for inquiring about the characteristics and status of individual resources, monitoring them, and using them in a secure way.

Next is the **collective layer**, which handles groups of resources. One of its functions is resource discovery, by which a user can locate available CPU cycles, disk space, or specific data. The collective layer may maintain directories or other data bases to provide this information. It may also offer a brokering service by which the providers and users of services are matched up, possibly allocating scarce resources among competing users. The collective layer is also responsible for replicating data, managing the admission of new members and resources to the grid, accounting, and maintaining the policy data bases of who can use what.

Still further up is the **application layer**, where the user applications reside. It uses the lower layers to acquire credentials proving its right to use certain resources, submit usage requests, monitor the progress of these requests, deal with failures, and notify the user of the results.

Security is the key to a successful grid. Resource owners nearly always insist on maintaining tight control of their resources and want to determine who gets to use them, for how long, and how much. Without good security, no organization would make its resources available to the grid. On the other hand, if a user had to have a login account and password on every computer he wanted to use, using the grid would be unbearably cumbersome. Consequently, the grid has had to develop a security model to handle these concerns.

One of the key characteristics of the security model is the single sign on. The first step in using the grid is to be authenticated and acquire a credential, a digitally signed document specifying on whose behalf the work is to be done. Credentials can be delegated, so that when a computation needs to create subcomputations, the child processes can also be identified. When a credential is presented at a remote machine, it has to be mapped onto the local security mechanism. On UNIX systems, for example, users are identified by 16-bit user IDs, but other systems have other schemes. Finally, the grid needs mechanisms to allow access policies to be stated, maintained, and updated.

In order to provide interoperability between different organizations and machines, standards are needed, both in terms of the services offered and the protocols used to access them. The grid community has created an organization, the Global Grid Forum, to manage the standardization process. It has come up with a framework called **OGSA** (**Open Grid Services Architecture**) for positioning the various standards it is developing. Wherever possible, the standards utilize existing standards, for example, using WSDL (Web Services Definiton Language) for describing OGSA services. The services being standardized currently fall into eight broad categories as follows, but no doubt new ones will be created later.

1. Infrastructure services (enable communication between resources).

2. Resource management services (reserve and deploy resources).

3. Data services (move and replicate data to where it is needed).

4. Context services (describe required resources and usage policies).

5. Information services (get information about resource availability).

6. Self-Management services (support a stated quality of service).

7. Security services (enforce security policies).

8. Execution management services (manage workflow).

There is much more that could be said about the grid, but space limitations prevent us from pursuing this topic further. For more information about the grid, see (Berman et al., 2003; Foster and Kesselman, 2003; and Foster et al., 2002).

8.6 SUMMARY

It is getting increasingly difficult to make computers go faster by just revving up the clock due to increased heat dissipation problems and other factors. Instead, designers are looking to parallelism for speedup. Parallelism can be introduced at many different levels, from very low, where the processing elements are very tightly coupled, to very high, where they are very loosely coupled.

At the bottom level is on-chip parallelism, in which parallel activities occur on a single chip. One form of on-chip parallelism is instruction-level parallelism, in which one instruction or a sequence of instructions issue multiple operations that can be executed in parallel by different functional units. A second form of on-chip parallelism is multithreading, in which the CPU can switch back and forth among multiple threads on an instruction by instruction basis, creating a virtual multiprocessor. A third form of on-chip parallelism is the single-chip multiprocessor, in which two or more cores are placed on the same chip to allow them to run at the same time.

One level up we find the coprocessors, typically plug-in boards that add extra processing power in some specialized area such as network protocol processing or multimedia. These extra processors relieve the main CPU of work, allowing it to do other things while they are performing their specialized tasks.

At the next level, we find the shared-memory multiprocessors. The systems contain two or more full-blown CPUs that share a common memory. UMA multiprocessors communicate via a shared (snooping) bus, a crossbar switch, or a multistage switching network. They are characterized by having a uniform access time to all memory locations. In contrast, NUMA multiprocessors also present all processes with the same shared address space, but here remote accesses take appreciably longer than local ones. Finally, COMA multiprocessors are yet another variation, in which cache lines move around the machine on demand, but have no real home as in the other designs.

Multicomputers are systems with many CPUs that do not share a common memory. Each one has its own private memory, with communication by message passing. MPPs are large multicomputers with specialized communication networks such as IBM's BlueGene/L. Clusters are simpler systems using off-the-self-components, such as the engine that powers Google.

Multicomputers are often programmed using a message-passing package such as MPI. An alternative approach is to use application-level shared memory such as a page-based DSM system, the Linda tuple space, or Orca or Globe objects. DSM simulates shared memory at the page level, making it similar to a NUMA machine, except with a much greater penalty for remote references.

Finally, at the highest level, and the most loosely coupled, are the grids. These are systems in which entire organizations are hooked together over the Internet to share compute power, data, and other resources.

PROBLEMS

1. Pentium instructions can be as long as 17 bytes. Is the Pentium a VLIW CPU?

2. What are the clipped values of 96, −9, 300, and 256 when the clipping range is 0–255?

3. Are the following TriMedia instructions allowed, and if not, why not?

(a) Integer add, integer subtract, load, floating add, load immediate
(b) Integer subtract, integer multiply, load immediate, shift, shift
(c) Load immediate, floating add, floating multiply, branch, load immediate

4. Figure 8-7(d) and (e) show 12 cycles of instructions. For each one, tell what happens in the following three cycles.

5. On a particular CPU, an instruction that misses the level 1 cache but hits the level 2 cache takes k cycles in total. If multithreading is used to mask level 1 cache misses, how many threads must be run at once using fine-grained multithreading to avoid dead cycles?

6. One morning, the queen bee of a certain beehive calls in all her worker bees and tells them that today's assignment is to collect marigold nectar. The workers then fly off in different directions looking for marigolds. Is this an SIMD or an MIMD system?

7. During our discussion of memory consistency models, we said that a consistency model is a kind of contract between the software and the memory. Why is such a contract needed?

8. Consider a multiprocessor using a shared bus. What happens if two processors try to access the global memory at exactly the same instant?

9. Suppose that for technical reasons it is only possible for a snooping cache to snoop on address lines, not data lines. Would this change affect the write through protocol?

10. As a simple model of a bus-based multiprocessor system without caching, suppose that one instruction in every four references memory, and that a memory reference occupies the bus for an entire instruction time. If the bus is busy, the requesting CPU is put into a FIFO queue. How much faster will a 64-CPU system run than a 1-CPU system?

11. The MESI cache coherence protocol has four states. Other write-back cache coherence protocols have only three states. Which of the four MESI states could be sacrificed, and what would the consequences of each choice be? If you had to pick only three states, which would you pick?

12. Are there any situations with the MESI cache coherence protocol in which a cache line is present in the local cache but for which a bus transaction is nevertheless needed? If so, explain.

13. Suppose that there are n CPUs on a common bus. The probability that any CPU tries to use the bus in a given cycle is p. What is the chance that

a. The bus is idle (0 requests).
b. Exactly one request is made.
c. More than one request is made.

14. How many crossbar switches does a full Sun Fire E25K have?

15. Suppose that the wire between switch 2A and switch 3B in the omega network breaks. Who is cut off from whom?

16. Hot spots (heavily referenced memory locations) are clearly a major problem in multistage switching networks. Are they also a problem in bus-based systems?

17. An omega switching network connects 4096 RISC CPUs, each with a 60-nsec cycle time, to 4096 infinitely fast memory modules. The switching elements each have a 5-nsec delay. How many delay slots are needed by a LOAD instruction?

18. Consider a machine using an omega switching network, like the one shown in Fig. 8-29. Suppose that the program and stack for processor i is kept in memory module i. Propose a slight change in the topology that makes a large difference in the performance (the IBM RP3 and BBN Butterfly use this modified topology). What disadvantage does your new topology have compared to the original?

19. In a NUMA multiprocessor, local memory references take 20 nsec and remote references take 120 nsec. A certain program makes a total of N memory references during its execution, of which 1 percent are to a page P. That page is initially remote, and it takes C nsec to copy it locally. Under what conditions should the page be copied locally in the absence of significant use by other processors?

20. Consider a CC-NUMA multiprocessor like that of Fig. 8-31 except with 512 nodes of 8 MB each. If the cache lines are 64 bytes, what is the percentage overhead for the directories? Does increasing the number of nodes increase the overhead, decrease the overhead, or leave it unchanged?

21. For each topology shown in Fig. 8-35, compute the diameter of the network.

22. For each topology shown in Fig. 8-35, determine the degree of fault tolerance each one has, defined as the maximum number of links that can be lost without partitioning the network in two.

23. Consider the double torus topology of Fig. 8-35(f) but expanded to a size of $k \times k$. What is the diameter of the network? Hint: Consider odd k and even k separately.

24. An interconnection network is in the form of an $8 \times 8 \times 8$ cube. Each link has a full-duplex bandwidth of 1 GB/sec. What is the bisection bandwidth of the network?

25. Amdahl's law limits the potential speedup achievable on a parallel computer. Compute, as a function of f, the maximum possible speedup as the number of CPUs approaches infinity. What are the implications of this limit for $f = 0.1$?

26. Figure 8-49 shows how scaling fails with a bus but succeeds with a grid. Assuming that each bus or link has a bandwidth b, compute the average bandwidth per CPU for each of the four cases. Then scale each system to 64 CPUs and repeat the calculations. What is the limit as the number of CPUs goes to infinity?

27. In the text, three variations of send were discussed: synchronous, blocking, and non-blocking. Give a fourth method that is similar to blocking send, but has slightly different properties. Give an advantage and a disadvantage of your method as compared to blocking send.

28. Consider a multicomputer running on a network with hardware broadcasting, such as Ethernet. Why does the ratio of read operations (those not updating internal state variables) to write operations (those updating internal state variables) matter?

9

READING LIST AND BIBLIOGRAPHY

In the preceding eight chapters, a large number of topics were discussed in various degrees of detail. This chapter is meant to assist readers interested in pursuing further their study of computer organization. Section 9.1 contains a list of suggested readings arranged by chapter. Section 9.2 is an alphabetical bibliography of all books and articles cited in this book.

9.1 SUGGESTIONS FOR FURTHER READING

Below are some suggested readings keyed by chapter. Most of them are textbooks, tutorials, or survey-type articles.

9.1.1 Introduction and General Works

Borkar, "Getting Gigascale Chips"

Moore's law will probably hold for at least another decade, potentially leading to billion-transistor chips. Such chips present challenges and opportunities. In this article, one of Intel's leading researchers discusses future challenges, such as energy dissipation, higher resistance and capacitance from the ever smaller and closer wires, and so on. He thinks the future lies in multithreading, multiprocessors on a chip, and better memory structures, rather than purely faster clock speeds.

Colwell, *The Pentium Chronicles*

Robert Colwell was the leader of the team that designed the Pentium. In this book, he talks about the people, the passion and the politics behind this chip.

Hamacher et al., *Computer Organization, 5th ed.*

A traditional textbook on computer organization the CPU, memory, I/O, arithmetic, and peripherals. The main examples are the 68000 and the PowerPC.

Heath, *Embedded Systems Design*

Practically everything that runs on electricity and costs more than $50 has a computer in it nowadays. These embedded systems are the subject of this book. Starting with the basics of embedded processors, memory, and peripherals, it then moves on to interfacing, real-time operating systems, software, and debugging.

Hennessy and Patterson, *Computer Architecture A Quantitative Approach, 3rd ed.*

This massive graduate textbook goes into great detail on how to design a processor and its memory. The emphasis is on achieving high performance, especially by exploiting parallelism and pipelining. If you want to know everything about designing a high-end CPU, this book is the place to look.

Null and Lobur, *The Essentials of Computer Organization and Architecture*

Another textbook on Computer Organization covering many of the same topics as this book, but with less depth.

Patterson and Hennessy, *Computer Organization and Design, 3rd ed.*

No longer 1000 pages like the 2nd edition, the 3rd edition has transferred a great deal of the text to the accompanying CD-ROM. The material remaining in the book covers many aspects of computer architecture, including arithmetic, performance, the datapath, pipelining, memorie, peripherals, and clusters. Although the Pentium 4 is discussed in several places, the main example used to explain concepts is the MIPS processor, which was designed by Hennessy and was the first commercial RISC machine, introduced in 1985.

Price, "A History of Calculating Machines"

Although modern computers started with Babbage in the 19th century, human beings have been computing since the dawn of civilization. This fascinating illustrated article traces the history of counting, mathematics, calendars, and computation from 3000 B.C. to the start of the 20th century.

Slater, *Portraits in Silicon*

Why didn't Dennis Ritchie turn in his Ph.D. thesis at Harvard? Why did Steve Jobs become a vegetarian? The answers lie in this fascinating book that contains short biographies of 34 people who shaped the computer industry, from Charles Babbage to Donald Knuth.

Stallings, *Computer Organization and Architecture, 6th ed.*
A general text on computer architecture. Some of the topics treated in this book are also covered in Stallings' book.

Wilkes, "Computers Then and Now"
A personal history of computers from 1946 to 1968 by pioneer computer designer and inventor of microprogramming, Maurice Wilkes. He tells of the early battles between the "space cadets," who believed in automatic programming (pre-FORTRAN compilers), and the traditionalists, who preferred to do their programming in octal.

9.1.2 Computer Systems Organization

Buchanan and Wilson, *Advanced PC Architecture*
Although somewhat disorderly, this book does cover a lot of ground concerning processors, buses (PCI, SCSI, and USB), ports (game, parallel, and serial) and other PC components. Ng, "Advances in Disk Technology: Performance Issues"
People have been predicting the end of the magnetic disk for at least 20 years. So far they still seem to be with us. And according to this paper, their technology is advancing rapidly, so they are likely to be around for years to come.

Messmer, *The Indispensable PC Hardware Book, 4th ed.*
At 1296 pages (divided into 37 chapters and 7 appendices), this book may or may not be indispensable, but it sure is thick. Just about everything there is to know about 80x86 processors, memories, buses, support chips, and peripherals is here in gory detail. If you have read and digested Norton and Goodman's book (below) and want to move on to the next level of technical detail, start here.

Norton and Goodman, *Inside the PC, 8th ed.*
Most books on PC hardware are written for people with an EE degree and are difficult to read for software-oriented people. This one is different. It explains PC hardware in a technical, but highly accessible way. Topics include the CPU, memory, buses, disks, displays, I/O devices, mobile PCs, networking and more. A rare and worthwhile book.

Robinson, "Toward the Age of Smarter Storage"
Storage has come a long way since the days of core memories and punched cards. This short article looks at where storage technology has been, where it is now, and where it is going.

Scheible, "A Survey of Storage Options"
Another rundown of memory technology, only focusing in what is available now. It discusses the various flavors of RAM, flash memory, tape, hard disks, floppy disks, CDs, adb DVDs.

Stan and Skadron, "Power-Aware Computing"

As computers are becoming too powerful—literally. They are consuming too much power, which is a growing problem in an increasingly mobile world. This paper is the guest editors' introduction to a special issue of *IEEE Computer Magazine* on power-aware computing.

Triebel, *The 80386, 80486, and Pentium Processor*

It is a bit hard to classify this book as it deals with hardware, software, and interfacing. Since the author is with Intel, let us call it a hardware book. It tells all about the processors, memories, I/O devices, and interfacing of the 80x86 chips, but also how to program them in assembly language. Although it has a mere 915 pages, it contains almost as much material as Messmer's book because the pages are bigger.

9.1.3 The Digital Logic Level

Floyd, *Digital Fundamentals, 8th ed.*

For hardware-oriented readers who want to pursue their study of the digital logic level in more detail, this huge, lavishly illustrated four-color book is a real gem. Chapters cover combinational logic, programmable logic devices, flip flops, shift registers, memories, interfacing, and much more.

Mano and Kime, *Logic and Computer Design Fundamentals, 3rd ed.*

Although this book does not have the elegance layout of Floyd's book, it is also a good reference for the digital logic level. It covers combinational and sequential circuits, registers, memories, CPU design and I/O.

Mayhew and Krishnan, "PCI Express and Advanced Switching"

PCI Express is likely to replace the PCI bus in the near future and this paper gives a tutorial on it covering the layers, flow control, virtual channels, switching, and routing.

Mazidi and Mazidi, *The 80x86 IBM PC and Compatible Computers, 4th ed.*

For readers interested in understanding all the chips inside a PC, this book has entire chapters on the major chips, as well as a wealth of other information about the IBM PC hardware and assembly language programming.

Roth, *Fundamentals of Logic Design*

This textbook covers the basics of digital logic design, from Boolean algebra through gates, counters, adders, flip-flops, and other kinds of combinational and sequential circuits.

9.1.4 The Microarchitecture Level

Burger and Goodman, "Billion-Transistor Architectures: There and Back Again"
Suppose that in 1997 somebody gave you a billion transistors and said: "Design a chip." What kind of microarchitecture would you design. In Sept. 1997, seven top researchers in architecture who were asked this question had their views published in *IEEE Computer Magazine*. Seven years later their predictions are compared to the current state of the art.

Handy, *The Cache Memory Book, 2nd ed.*
Cache design is sufficiently important that entire books on the subject now exist. This one discusses logical versus physical caches, line size, write-through versus write-back policies, unified versus split caches, as well as software issues. It also has a chapter on multiprocessor cache coherence.

Johnson, *Superscalar Microprocessor Design*
For readers interested in the details of superscalar CPU design, this book is the place to start. It covers instruction fetching and decoding, out of order instruction issue, register renaming, reservation stations, branch prediction, and more.

Shriver and Smith, "The Anatomy of a High-Performance Microprocessor"
For a detailed study of a modern CPU chip at the microarchitecture level, this book is a good bet. It examines the AMD K6 chip, a Pentium clone, in detail, emphasizing the pipeline, instruction scheduling, and performance optimisations.

Sima, "Superscalar Instruction Issue"
Superscalar instruction issue is increasingly important in modern CPUs. We touched upon some of the issues in this chapter, such as renaming and speculative execution. In this paper, these and a number of other issues are examined.

Wilson, "Challenges and Trends in Processor Design"
Is processor design dead in the water? No way. Six top CPU architects from Sun, Cyrix, Motorola, Mips, Intel, and Digital tell where they think CPU design is going in the next few years. This will be fun reading in 2008 (but it is also worthwhile now).

9.1.5 The Instruction Set Architecture Level

Antonakos, *The Pentium Microprocessor*
The first nine chapters of this book deal with how to program the Pentium in assembly language. The last two deal with the Pentium hardware. Numerous code fragments are given and the BIOS is treated throughout.

Ayala, *The 8051 Microcontroller, 3rd ed.*

If you are interested in learning to program the 8051, this book is a reasonable place to start.

Bryant and O'Hallaron, *Computer Systems A Programmer's Perspective*

Although somewhat disorganized, this book covers a lot of ground concerning the ISA level, including arithmetic, different kinds of instructions, control flow, and program optimization.

Paul, *SPARC Architecture, Assembly Language, Programming, and C*

Wonder of wonders, here is a book about assembly language programming that is not about the Intel 80x86 line. Instead it is about the SPARC and how to program it.

Weaver and Germond, *The SPARC Architecture Manual*

With the growing internationalization of the computer industry, standards are becoming more important all the time, so it is important to be familiar with them. This one is the Version 9 SPARC definition and gives a good idea of what a standard looks like and is also very informative about how 64-bit SPARCs work.

9.1.6 The Operating System Machine Level

Hart, "Win32 System Programming"

Unlike nearly all other books on Windows, this one does not dwell on (or even cover) the graphical user interface. Instead it focuses on the systems calls offered by Windows and how to use them for file access, memory management, process management, interprocess communication, threads, I/O, and other topics.

Jacob and Mudge, "Virtual Memory: Issues of Implementation"

For a good and modern introduction on virtual memory, look here. It explains various page table and TLB structures and illustrates the ideas using the MIPS, PowerPC, and Pentium processors.

McKusick et al., *Design and Implementation of the 4.4 BSD Operating System*

Unlike most books on UNIX, this one starts out with a photo of the four authors at a USENIX Conference, three of whom wrote much of 4.4 BSD and are eminently qualified to explain its inner workings. The book covers the system calls, processes, I/O, and has an especially good section on networking.

Ritchie and Thompson, "The UNIX Time-Sharing System"

This is the original published paper on UNIX. It is still well worth reading. From this small seed has grown a great operating system.

Russinovich and Solomon, *Inside Microsoft Windows, 4th ed.*
    If you want to know how Windows works internally, this is your best bet. It discusses the system architecture, system mechanisms, processes, threads, memory management, security, I/O, cache, and file system, among other topics. The book is intended as an in-depth study for CS students or IT professionals.

Tanenbaum and Woodhull, *Operating Systems: Design and Implementation, 2nd ed*
    Unlike most books on operating systems that only deal with the theory, this one covers all the relevant theory and illustrates it by discussing the actual code of a UNIX-like operating system, MINIX, that runs on the IBM PC and other computers. The heavily annotated source code is listed in an appendix.

9.1.7 The Assembly Language Level

Levine, *Linkers and Loaders*
    If your thing is linkers and loaders, and you revel in the various object formats around, the difference between static and dynamic linking, and the various library formats, this book is for you.

Saloman, *Assemblers and Loaders*
    Everything you might want to know about how one-pass and two-pass assemblers work, as well as how linkers and loaders work is here. Macros and conditional assembly are also covered.

9.1.8 Parallel Computer Architectures

Adve and Gharachorloo, "Shared Memory Consistency Models: A Tutorial"
    Many modern computers, especially multiprocessors, support a memory model weaker than sequential consistency. This tutorial discusses various models and explains how they work. It also states and rebuts numerous myths about weakly consistent memory.

Comer, *Network Systems Design*
    The first part of this book is about traditional packet processing in networks, but the second part introduces network processors and describes their purpose, architectures, and design trade-offs. The third part looks at the Agere network processor as a case study.

Dally and Towles, *Principles and Practices of Interconnection Networks*
    If you are interested in interconnection networks, this is the place to look. After an introduction to topology, butterfly networks, torus networks, and non-blocking networks are covered. Then come quite a few chapters on routing, flow control, buffering, deadlock, and related issues.

Dongarra et al., *The Sourcebook of Parallel Computing*

Programming multiprocessors and clusters is appreciably different from programming uniprocessors. In this book, seven leading experts in the field of parallel programming cover various aspects of parallel programming, including parallel architectures, software technologies, parallel algorithms, and some applications.

Hill, "Multiprocessors Should Support Simple Memory-Consistency Models"

Relaxed memory semantics is a hot and controversial topic in multiprocessor memory design. Weaker models allow certain hardware optimizations, like making memory references out of order, but make programming harder. In this paper, the author discusses many issues relevant to memory consistency and then concludes that relaxed memory is more trouble than it is worth.

Hwang and Xu, *Scalable Parallel Computing*

By treating both the hardware and the software, the authors manage to give a comprehensive, yet readable account of parallel computing. Topics include UMA and NUMA multiprocessors, MPPs and COWs, message-passing, and data parallel programming.

Lawton, "Will Network Processor Units Live up to Their Promise?"

While network processors promise to speed up packet processing, their success is not guaranteed. In this paper, the author looks at the technology and some of the factors that may determine its success or failure.

McKnight et al., "Wireless Grids"

Grids have barely gotten started, yet the next generation—wireless grids—is already on the horizon. Like regular grids, these aim at sharing resources across organizations to create virtual organizations, only they use wireless technology to make the resources available to mobile users. The two articles following this one are also on wireless grids.

Pfister, *In Search of Clusters, 2nd ed.*

Although the definition of a cluster does not occur until page 72 (a bunch of whole computers working together), it apparently includes all the usual multiprocessor and multicomputer systems. Their hardware, software, performance, and availability are all studied in detail. The reader should be warned however, that while the author's cutesy-poo writing style is amusing at first, by page 500 the novelty wears off.

Snir et al., *MPI: The Complete Reference Manual*

The title says it all. If you want to learn to program in MPI, look here. The book covers point-to-point and collective communication, communicators, environmental management, profiling, and more.

Stenstrom et al., "Trends in Shared Memory Multiprocessing"
Although shared-memory multiprocessors are often thought as supercomputers for massive scientific calculations, in reality that is only a tiny fraction of their market. In this paper, the authors discuss where the market for these machines really lies, and what implications that has for their architecture.

Ungerer et al., "A Survey of Processors with Explicit Multithreading"
For each of the major kinds of multithreading—fine-grained, coarse-grained, and simultaneous—the paper explains how it works and gives numerous examples of academic and commercial computers that use the technique.

Wolf, "The Future of Multiprocessor Systems-on-Chips,"
After presenting three current system-on-a-chip designs, the author goes on to look at hardware and software challenges for future systems. Hardware problems include real-time and energy dissipation concerns. Software concerns include operating system issues and potential security problems.

9.1.9 Binary and Floating-Point Numbers

Cody, "Analysis of Proposals for the Floating-Point Standard"
Some years ago, IEEE designed a floating-point architecture that has become the *de facto* standard for all modern CPU chips. Cody discusses the various issues, proposals, and controversies that came up during the standardization process.

Koren "Computer Arithmetic Algorithms"
A complete book on arithmetic, with an emphasis on algorithms for fast addition, multiplication and division. Strongly recommended for anyone who thinks he learned everything there is to know about arithmetic in sixth grade.

IEEE, *Proc. of the n-th Symposium on Computer Arithmetic*
Contrary to popular opinion, arithmetic is an active research area with many scientific papers written by and for arithmetic specialists. In this symposium series, advances in high-speed addition and multiplication, VLSI arithmetic hardware, coprocessors, fault tolerance, and rounding, among other topics, are presented.

Knuth, *Seminumerical Algorithms, 3rd ed.*
A wealth of material about positional number systems, floating-point arithmetic, multiple-precision arithmetic, and random numbers. This material requires and deserves careful study.

Wilson, "Floating-Point Survival Kit"

A nice introduction to floating-point numbers and standards for people who think that the world ends at 65,535. Some popular floating-point benchmarks, such as *Linpack*, are also discussed.

9.1.10 Assembly Language Programming

Blum, *Professional Assembly Language*

A guide to programming the Pentium in assembly language for professionals. Since the book is for professionals, he assumes you are running Linux on your Pentium and focuses on the Linux assembler and GNU tools as well as discussing the Linux system calls.

Irvine, *Assembly Language for Intel-Based Computers, 4th ed.*

Programming the Intel CPUs in assembly language is the subject of this book. Also covered are I/O programming, macros, files, linking, interrupts, and many other related topics.

9.2 ALPHABETICAL BIBLIOGRAPHY

ADAMS, M., and DULCHINOS, D.: "OpenCable," *IEEE Commun. Magazine*, vol. 39, pp. 98-105, June 2001.

ADIGA, N.R. et al.: "An Overview of the BlueGene/L Supercomputer," *Proc. Supercomputing 2002*, ACM, pp. 1-22, 2002.

ADVE, S.V., and CHARACHORLOO, K.: "Shared Memory Consistency Models: A Tutorial," *IEEE Computer Magazine*, vol. 29, pp. 66-76, Dec. 1996.

ADVE, S.V., and HILL, M.: "Weak Ordering: A New Definition," *Proc. 17th Ann. Int'l Symp. on Computer Arch.*, ACM, pp. 2-14, 1990.

AGERWALA, T., and COCKE, J.: "High Performance Reduced Instruction Set Processors," IBM T.J. Watson Research Center Technical Report RC12434, 1987.

ALAMELDEEN, A.R., and Wood, D.A.: "Adaptive Cache Compression for High-Performance Processors," *Proc. 31st Ann. Int'l Sym. on Computer Arch.* ACM, pp. 212-223, 2004.

ALMASI, G.S. et al.: "System Management in the BlueGene/L Supercomputer," *Proc. 17th Int'l Parallel and Distr. Proc. Symp.*, IEEE, 2003a.

ALMASI, G.S. et al.: "An Overview Of The Bluegene/L System Software Organization," *Par. Proc. Letters*, vol. 13, 561-574, April 2003b.

AMZA, C., COX, A., DWARKADAS, S., KELEHER, P., LU, H., RAJAMONY, R., YU, W., ZWAENEPOEL, W.: "TreadMarks: Shared Memory Computing on a Network of Workstations," *IEEE Computer Magazine*, vol. 29, pp. 18-28, Feb. 1996.

ANDERSON, D.: *Universal Serial Bus System Architecture*, Reading, MA: Addison-Wesley, 1997.

ANDERSON, D., BUDRUK, R., and SHANLEY, T.: *PCI Express System Architecture*, Reading, MA: Addison-Wesley, 2004.

ANDERSON, T.E., CULLER, D.E., PATTERSON, D.A., and the NOW team: "A Case for NOW (Networks of Workstations)," *IEEE Micro Magazine*, vol. 15, pp. 54-64, Jan. 1995.

ANTONAKOS, J.L.: *The Pentium Microprocessor*, Upper Saddle River, NJ: Prentice Hall, 1997.

AUGUST, D.I., CONNORS, D.A., MSHLKE, S.A., SIAS, J.W., CROZIER, K.M., CHENG, B.-C., EATON, P.R., OLANIRAN, Q.B., and HWU, W.-M.: "Integrated Predicated and Speculative Execution in the IMPACT EPIC Architecture," *Proc. 25th Ann. Int'l Symp. on Computer Arch.*, ACM, pp. 227-237, 1998.

AYALA, K: *The 8051 Microcontroller, 3rd ed.*, Clifton Park, NY: Thomson Delmar Learning, 2004.

BAL, H.E.: *Programming Distributed Systems*, Hemel Hempstead, England: Prentice Hall Int'l, 1991.

BAL, H.E., BHOEDJANG, R., HOFMAN, R, JACOBS, C., LANGENDOEN, K., RUHL, T., and KAASHOEK, M.F.: "Performance Evaluation of the Orca Shared Object System," *ACM Trans. on Computer Systems*, vol. 16, pp. 1-40, Jan.-Feb. 1998.

BAL, H.E., KAASHOEK, M.F., and TANENBAUM, A.S.: "Orca: A Language for Parallel Programming of Distributed Systems," *IEEE Trans. on Software Engineering*, vol. 18, pp. 190-205, March 1992.

BAL, H.E., and TANENBAUM, A.S.: "Distributed Programming with Shared Data," *Proc. 1988 Int'l Conf. on Computer Languages*, IEEE, pp. 82-91, 1988.

BARROSO, L.A., DEAN, J., HOLZLE, U.: "Web Search for a Planet: The Google Cluster Architecture," *IEEE Micro Magazine*, vol. 23, pp. 22-28, March-April 2003.

BECHINI, A., CONTE, T.M., and PRETE, C.A.: "Opportunities and Challenges in Embedded Systems," *IEEE Micro Magazine*, vol. 24, pp. 8-9, July-Aug. 2004.

BENINI, L., and DE MICHELI, G.: "Networks on Chips" A New SoC Paradigm," *IEEE Computer Magazine*, vol. 35, pp. 70-78, Jan. 2002.

BERMAN, F., FOX, G., and HEY, A.J.G.: "Grid Computing: Making the Global Infrastructure a Reality," Hoboken, NJ: John Wiley, 2003.

BJORNSON, R.D.: "Linda on Distributed Memory Multiprocessors," Ph.D. Thesis, Yale Univ., 1993.

BLUM, R.: *Professional Assembly Language*, New York: Wiley, 2005.

BLUMRICH, M., CHEN, D., CHIU, G., COTEUS, P., GARA, A., GIAMPAPA, M.E., HAR-ING, R.A., HEIDELBERGER, P., HOENICKE, D., KOPCSAY, G.V., OHMACHT, M., STEINMACHER-BUROW, B.D., TAKKEN, T., VRANSAS, P., and LIEBSCH, T.: "An Overview of the BlueGene/L System,", *IBM J. Research and Devel.*, vol. 49, March-May, 2005.

BORKAR, S.: "Getting Gigascale Chips," *Queue*, pp. 26-33, Oct. 2003.

BOSE, P.: "Computer architecture research: Shifting priorities and newer challenges," *IEEE Micro Magazine*, vol. 24, p. 5, Nov.-Dec. 2004.

BOUKNIGHT, W.J., DENENBERG, S.A., MCINTYRE, D.E., RANDALL, J.M., SAMEH, A.H., and SLOTNICK, D.L.: "The Illiac IV System," *Proc. IEEE*, pp. 369-388, April 1972.

BRIGHTWELL, R., CAMP, W., COLE, B., DEBENEDICTIS, E., LELAND, R, TOMPKINS, H, and MACCABE: "Architectural Specification for Massively Parallel Supercomputers: An Experience and Measurement-Based Approach," *Concurrency and Computation: Practice and Experience*, vol. 17, pp. 1-46, 2005.

BRYANT, R.E., and O'HALLARON, D.: *Computer Systems A Programmer's Perspective* Upper Saddle River, NJ: Prentice Hall, 2003.

BUCHANAN, W., WILSON, A.: *Advanced PC Architecture*, Reading, MA: Addison-Wesley, 2001.

BURGER, D., and GOODMAN, J.R.: "Billion-Transistor Architectures: There and Back Again," *IEEE Computer Magazine*, vol. 37, pp. 22-28, March 2004.

BURKHARDT, H., FRANK, S., KNOBE, B., and ROTHNIE, J.: "Overview of the KSR-1 Computer System," Technical Report KSR-TR-9202001, Kendall Square Research Corp, Cambridge, MA, 1992.

CAIN, H., and LIPASTI, M.: "Memory Ordering: A Value-Based Approach," *Proc. 31th Ann. Int'l Symp. on Computer Arch.*, ACM, pp. 90-101, 2004.

CALCUTT, D., COWAN, F., and PARCHIZADEH, H.: *8051 Microcontrollers : An Applications Based Introduction*, Oxford: Newnes, 2004.

CARRIERO, N., and GELERNTER, D.: "Linda in Context," *Commun. of the ACM*, vol. 32, pp. 444-458, April 1989.

CHARLESWORTH, A.: "The Sun Fireplane Interconnect," *IEEE Micro Magazine*, vol. 22, pp. 36-45, Jan.-Feb. 2002.

CHARLESWORTH, A.: "The Sun Fireplane Interconnect," *Proc. Conf. on High Perf. Networking and Computing*, ACM, 2001.

CHARLESWORTH, A., PHELPS, A., WILLIAMS, R., and GILBERT, G.: "Gigaplane-XB: Extending the Ultra Enterprise Family," *Proc. Hot Interconnects V*, IEEE, 1998.

CHEN, L., DROPSHO, S., ALBONESI, D.H.: "Dynamic Data Dependence Tracking and its Application to Branch Prediction," *Proc. Ninth Int'l Symp. on High-Performance Computer Arch.*, IEEE, pp. 65-78, 2003.

CHOU, Y., FAHS, B., ABRAHAM, S.: " Microarchitecture Optimizations for Exploiting Memory-Level Parallelism,|*(CQ *Proc. 31st Ann. Int'l Symp. on Computer Arch.*, ACM, pp. 76-77, 2004.

CLAASEN, T.A.C.M.: "System on a Chip: Changing IC Design Today and in the Future," *IEEE Micro Magazine*, vol. 23, pp. 20-26, May-June 2003.

CODY, W.J.: "Analysis of Proposals for the Floating-Point Standard," *IEEE Computer Magazine*, vol. 14, pp. 63-68, March 1981.

COHEN, D.: "On Holy Wars and a Plea for Peace," *IEEE Computer Magazine*, vol. 14, pp. 48-54, Oct. 1981.

COLWELL, R: *The Pentium Chronicles* New York: WIley, 2005.

COMER, D.E.: "Network Systems Design Using Network Processors: Agere Version," Upper Saddle River, NJ: Prentice Hall, 2005.

CORBATO, F.J.: "PL/1 as a Tool for System Programming," *Datamation*, vol. 15, pp. 68-76, May 1969.

CORBATO, F.J., and VYSSOTSKY, V.A.: "Introduction and Overview of the MULTICS System," *Proc. FJCC*, pp. 185-196, 1965.

CROWLEY, P., FRANKLIN, M.A., HADIMIOGLU, H., and ONUFRYK, P.Z.: *Network Processor Design : Issues and Practices, Vol. 1*, San Francisco: Morgan Kaufmann, 2002.

DALLY, W.J., and TOWLES, B.P.: *Principles and Practices of Interconnection Networks*, San Francisco: Morgan Kaufmann, 2004.

DANESHBEH, A.K., and HASAN, M.A.: "Area Efficient High Speed Elliptic Curve Cryptoprocessor for Random Curves," *Proc. Int'l Conf. on Inf. Tech.: Codingspeculative xecution and Computing*, IEEE, pp. 588-593, 2004.

DEAN, A.G.: "Efficient Real-Time Fine-Grained Concurrency on Low-Cost Microcontrollers," *IEEE Micro Magazine*, vol. 24, pp. 10-22, July-Aug. 2004.

DENNING, P.J.: "The Working Set Model for Program Behavior," *Commun. of the ACM*, vol. 11, pp. 323-333, May 1968.

DIJKSTRA, E.W.: "GOTO Statement Considered Harmful," *Commun. of the ACM*, vol. 11, pp. 147-148, March 1968a.

DIJKSTRA, E.W.: "Co-operating Sequential Processes," in *Programming Languages*, F. Genuys (ed.), New York: Academic Press, 1968b.

DONALDSON, G., and JONES, D.: "Cable Television Broadband Network Architectures," *IEEE Commun. Magazine*, vol. 39, pp. 122-126, June 2001.

DONGARRA, J., FOSTER, I., FOX, G., GROPP, W., KENNEDY, K., TORCZON, L., and WHITE, A.: *The Sourcebook of Parallel Computing*. San Francisco: Morgan Kaufman, 2003.

DUBOIS, M., SCHEURICH, C., and BRIGGS, F.A.: "Memory Access Buffering in Multiprocessors," *Proc. 13th Ann. Int'l Symp on Computer Arch.*, ACM, pp. 434-442, 1986.

DULONG, C.: "The IA-64 Architecture at Work," *IEEE Computer Magazine*, vol. 31, pp. 24-32, July 1998.

DUTTA-ROY, A.: "An Overview of Cable Modem Technology and Market Perspectives," *IEEE Commun. Magazine*, vol. 39, pp. 81-88, June 2001.

ESCHMANN, F., KLAUER, B., MOORE, R., and WALDSCHMIDT, K.: "SDAARC: An Extended Cache-Only Memory Architecture," *IEEE Micro Magazine*, vol. 22, pp. 62-70, May-June, 2002.

FAGGIN, F., HOFF, M.E., Jr., MAZOR, S., and SHIMA, M.: "The History of the 4004," *IEEE Micro Magazine*, vol. 16, pp. 10-20, Nov. 1996.

FALCON, A., STARK, J., RAMIREZ, A., LAI, K., and VALERO, M.: "Prophet/Critic Hybrid Branch Prediction," *Proc. 31th Ann. Int'l Symp. on Computer Arch.*, ACM, pp. 250-261, 2004.

FISHER, J.A., and FREUDENBERGER, S.M.: "Predicting Conditional Branch Directions from Previous Runs of a Program," *Proc. Fifth Int'l Conf. on Arch. Support for Prog. Lang. and Operating Syst.*, ACM, pp. 85-95, 1992.

FLOYD, T.L.: *Digital Fundamentals, 8th ed.*, Upper Saddle River, NJ: Prentice Hall, 2002.

FLYNN, D.: "AMBA: Enabling Reusable On-Chip Designs," *IEEE Micro Magazine*, vol. 17, pp. 20-27, July 1997.

FLYNN, M.J.: "Some Computer Organizations and Their Effectiveness," *IEEE Trans. on Computers*, vol. C-21, pp. 948-960, Sept. 1972.

FOSTER, I., and KESSELMAN, C.: *The Grid 2: Blueprint for a New Computing Infrastructure*, San Francisco: Morgan Kaufman, 2003.

FOSTER, I., KESSELMAN, C., NICK, J.M., and TUECKE, S.: "Grid Services for Distributed Systems Integration," *IEEE Computer Magazine*, vol. 35, pp. 37-46, June 2002.

FOSTER, I., and KESSELMAN, C.: "Globus: A Metacomputing Infrastructure Toolkit," *Int'l J. of Supercomputer Applications*, vol. 11, pp. 115-128, 1998a.

FOSTER, I., and KESSELMAN, C.: "The Globus Project: A Status Report," *IPPS/SPDP '98 Heterogeneous Computing Workshop*, IEEE, pp. 4-18, 1998b.

FOTHERINGHAM, J.: "Dynamic Storage Allocation in the Atlas Computer Including an Automatic Use of a Backing Store," *Commun. of the ACM*, vol. 4, pp. 435-436, Oct. 1961.

GEIST, A., BEGUELIN, A., DONGARRA, J., JIANG, W., MANCHECK, R., and SUNDER-RAM, V.: *PVM: Parallel Virtual Machine — A User's Guide and Tutorial for Networked Parallel Computing*, Cambridge, MA: M.I.T. Press, 1994.

GERBER, R., and BINSTOCK, A.: *Programming with Hyper-Threading Technology*, Santa Clara, CA: Intel Press, 2004.

GHEMAWAT, S., GOBIOFF, H., and LEUNG, S.-T.: "The Google File System," *Proc. 19th Symp. on Operating Systems Principles*, ACM, pp. 29-43, 2003.

GOODMAN, J.R.: "Using Cache Memory to Reduce Processor Memory Traffic," *Proc. 10th Ann. Int'l Symp. on Computer Arch.*, ACM, pp. 124-131, 1983.

GOODMAN, J.R.: "Cache Consistency and Sequential Consistency," Tech. Rep. 61, IEEE Scalable Coherent Interface Working Group, IEEE, 1989.

GRIMSHAW, A.S., and WULF, W.: "Legion: A View from 50,000 Feet," *Proc. Fifth Int'l Symp. on High-Performance Distributed Computing*, IEEE, pp. 89-99, Aug. 1996.

GRIMSHAW, A.S., and WULF, W.: "The Legion Vision of a Worldwide Virtual Computer," *Commun. of the ACM*, vol. 40, pp. 39-45, Jan. 1997.

GROPP, W., LUSK, E, and SKJELLUM, A: "Using MPI: Portable Parallel Programming with the Message Passing Interface," Cambridge, MA: M.I.T. Press, 1994.

GURUMURTHI, S., SIVASUBRAMANIAM, KANDEMIR, M., and FRANKE, H.: "Reducing Disk Power Consumption in Servers with DRPM," *IEEE Computer Magazine*, vol. 36, pp. 59-66, Dec. 2003.

HAGERSTEN, E., LANDIN, A., HARIDI, S.: "DDM—A Cache-Only Memory Architecture," *IEEE Computer Magazine*, vol. 25, pp. 44-54, Sept. 1992.

HAMACHER, V.V., VRANESIC, Z.G., and ZAKY, S.G.: *Computer Organization, 5th ed.*, New York: McGraw-Hill, 2001.

HAMMING, R.W.: "Error Detecting and Error Correcting Codes," *Bell Syst. Tech. J.*, vol. 29, pp. 147-160, April 1950.

HAMMOND, L., WONG, V., CHEN, M., HERTZBERG, B, DAVIS, J., CARLSTROM, B., PRABHU, M., WIJAYA, H., KOZYRAKIS, C., and OLUKOTUN, K.: "Transactional Memory Coherence and Consistency," *Proc. 31th Ann. Int'l Symp. on Computer Arch.*, ACM, pp. 102-113, 2004.

HANDY, J.: *The Cache Memory Book, 2nd ed.*, Orlando, FL: Academic Press, 1998.

HART, J.M.: *Win32 System Programming*, Reading, MA: Addison-Wesley, 1997.

HEATH, S.: *Embedded Systems Design*, Oxford: Newnes, 2003.

HENKEL, J., HU, X.S., and BHATTACHARYYA, S.S.: "Taking on the Embedded System Challenge," *IEEE Computer Magazine*, vol. 36, pp. 35-37, April 2003.

HENNESSY, J.L.: "VLSI Processor Architecture," *IEEE Trans. on Computers*, vol. C-33, pp. 1221-1246, Dec. 1984.

HENNESSY, J.L., and PATTERSON, D.A.: *Computer Architecture A Quantitative Approach, 3rd ed.* San Francisco: Morgan Kaufmann, 2003.

HILL, M.: "Multiprocessors Should Support Simple Memory-Consistency Models," *IEEE Computer Magazine*, vol. 31, pp. 28-34, Aug. 1998.

HINTON, G., SAGER, D., UPTON, M., BOGGS, D., CARMEAN, D., KYKER, A., ROUSSEL, P.: "The Microarchtecture of the Pentium 4," *Intel Technology Journal*, vol. 5, pp. 1-12, Jan.-March, 2001.

HOARE, C.A.R.: "Monitors, An Operating System Structuring Concept," *Commun. of the ACM*, vol. 17, pp. 549-557, Oct. 1974; Erratum in *Commun. of the ACM*, vol. 18, p. 95, Feb. 1975.

HUH, J., BURGER, D., CHANG, J., and SOHI, G.S.: " Speculative Incoherent Cache Protocols," *IEEE Micro Magazine*, vol. 24, pp. 104-109, Nov.-Dec. 2004.

HWANG, K., and XU, Z.: *Scalable Parallel Computing*, New York: McGraw-Hill, 1998.

HWU, W.-M.: "Introduction to Predicated Execution," *IEEE Computer Magazine*, vol. 31, pp. 49-50, Jan. 1998.

IRVINE, K: *Assembly Language for Intel-Based Computers, 4th ed.*, Upper Saddle River, NJ: Prentice Hall, 2002.

JACOB, B., and MUDGE, T.: "Virtual Memory: Issues of Implementation," *IEEE Computer Magazine*, vol. 31, pp. 33-43, June 1998a.

JACOB, B., and MUDGE, T.: "Virtual Memory in Contemporary Microprocessors," *IEEE Micro Magazine*, vol. 18, pp. 60-75, July-Aug. 1998b.

JERRAYA, A.A., and WOLF. W.: *Multiprocessor Systems-on-a-Chip*, San Francisco: Morgan Kaufmann, 2005.

JIMENEZ, D.A.: "Fast Path-Based Neural Branch Prediction," *Proc. 36th Int'l Symp. on Microarchitecture*, IEEE., pp. 243-252, 2003.

JOHNSON, K.L., KAASHOEK, M.F., and WALLACH, D.A.: "CRL: High-Performance All-Software Distributed Shared Memory," *Proc. 15th Symp. on Operating Systems Principles*, ACM, pp. 213-228, 1995.

JOHNSON, M.: *Superscalar Microprocessor Design*, Upper Saddle River, NJ: Prentice Hall, 1991..

KALLA, R., SINHAROY, B., and TENDLER, J.M.: "IBM Power5 Chip: A Dual-Core Multithreaded Processor," *IEEE Micro Magazine*, vol. 24, pp. 40-47, March-April 2004.

KAPASI, U.J., RIXNER, S., DALLY, W.J., KHAILANY, B., AHN, J.H., MATTSON, P., and OWENS, J.D.: "Programmable Stream Processors," *IEEE Computer Magazine*, vol. 36, pp. 54-62, Aug. 2003.

KAPIL, S., McGHAN, H., and LAWRENDRA, J.: "A Chip Multithreaded Processor for Network-Facing Workloads," *IEEE Micro Magazine*, vol. 24, pp. 20-30, March-April 2004.

KATZ, R.H., and BORRIELLO, G.: *Contemporary Logic Design*, Upper Saddle River, NJ: Prentice Hall, 2004.

KAUFMAN, C., PERLMAN, R., and SPECINER, M.: *Network Security, 2nd ed.*, Upper Saddle River, NJ: Prentice Hall, 2002.

KERMARREC., A.-M., KUZ, I., VAN STEEN, M., and TANENBAUM, A.S.: "A Framework for Consistent Replicated Web Objects," *Proc. 18th Int'l Conf. on Distr. Computing Syst.*, IEEE, pp. 276-284, 1998.

KIM, N.S., AUSTIN, T., BLAAUW, D., MUDGE, T., FLAUTNER, K., HU, J.S., IRWIN, M.J., KANDEMIR, M., and NARAYANAN, V.: "Leakage Current: Moore's Law Meets Static Power," *IEEE Computer Magazine*, vol. 36, 68-75, Dec. 2003.

KNUTH, D.E.: "An Empirical Study of FORTRAN Programs," *Software—Practice & Experience*, vol. 1, pp. 105-133, 1971.

KNUTH, D.E.: *The Art of Computer Programming: Fundamental Algorithms, 3rd ed.*, Reading, MA: Addison-Wesley, 1997.

KNUTH, D.E.: *The Art of Computer Programming: Seminumerical Algorithms, 3rd ed.*, Reading, MA: Addison-Wesley, 1998.

KOGEL, T., and MYER, H.: "Heterogeneous MP-SoC: the solution to energy-efficient signal processing," *Proc. 41st Ann. Conf. on Design Automation*, IEEE, pp. 686-691, 2004.

KONTOTHANASSIS, L., HUNT, G., STETS, R., HARDAVELLAS, N., CIERNIAD, M., PARTHASARATHY, S., MEIRA, W., DWARKADAS, S., and SCOTT, M.: *VM-Based Shared Memory on Low Latency Remote Memory Access Networks*, Proc. 24th Ann. Int'l Symp. on Computer Arch., ACM, pp. 157-169, 1997.

KOREN, I.: *Computer Arithmetic Algorithms*, Natick, MA:A.K. Peters, 2002.

KOUFATY, D., and MARR, D. T.: "Hyperthreading Technology in the Netburst Microarchitecture," *IEEE Micro Magazine*, vol. 23, pp. 56-65, March-April 2003.

KUMAR, R., JOUPPI, N.P., and TULLSEN, D.M.: "Conjoined-Core Chip Multiprocessing," *Proc. 37th Int'l Symp. on Microarchitecture*, IEEE., pp. 195-206, 2004.

LAMPORT, L.: "How to Make a Multiprocessor Computer That Correctly Executes Multiprocess Programs," *IEEE Trans. on Computers*, vol. C-28, pp. 690-691, Sept. 1979.

LaROWE, R.P., and ELLIS, C.S.: "Experimental Comparison of Memory Management Policies for NUMA Multiprocessors," *ACM Trans. on Computer Systems*, vol. 9, pp. 319-363, Nov. 1991.

LAVAGNO, L.: "Systems on a Chip: The Next Electronic Frontier," *IEEE Micro Magazine*, vol. 22, pp. 14-15, Sept.-Oct. 2002.

LAWTON, G.: "Will Network Processor Units Live up to Their Promise?," *IEEE Computer Magazine*, vol. 37, pp. 13-15, April 2004.

LEKKAS, P.C.: *Network Processors: Architectures, Protocols, and Platforms*, New York: McGraw-Hill, 2003.

LEVINE, J.R.: *Linkers and Loaders*, San Francisco: Morgan Kaufmann, 2000.

LI, K., and HUDAK, P.: "Memory Coherence in Shared Virtual Memory Systems," *ACM Trans. on Computer Systems*, vol. 7, pp. 321-359, Nov. 1989.

LIMA, F., CARRO, L., VELAZCO, R., and REIS, R.: "Injecting Multiple Upsets in a SEU Tolerant 8051 Micro-Controller," *Proc. Eighth IEEE Int'l On-Line Testing Workshop* IEEE, p. 194, July 2002.

LINES, A.: "Asynchronous Interconnect for Synchronous SoC Design," *IEEE Micro Magazine*, vol. 24, pp. 32-41, Jan.-Feb. 2004.

LU, H., COX, A.L., DWARKADAS, S., RAJAMONY, R., and ZWAENEPOEL, W.: "Software Distributed Shared Memory Support for Irregular Applications," *Proc. Sixth Conf. on Prin. and Practice of Parallel Progr.*, pp. 48-56, June 1997.

LUKASIEWICZ, J.: *Aristotle's Syllogistic, 2nd ed.*, Oxford: Oxford University Press, 1958.

LUTZ, J., and HASAN, A.: "High Performance FPGA based Elliptic Curve Cryptographic Co-Processor," *Proc. Int'l Conf. on Inf. Tech.: Coding and Computing*, IEEE, pp. 486-492, 2004.

LYYTINEN, K., and Yoo, Y.: "Issues and Challenges in Ubiquitous Computing," *Commun. of the ACM*, vol. 45, pp. 63-65, Dec. 2002.

MACKENZIE, I.S., PHAN, R.: *The 8051 Microcontroller, 4th ed.* Upper Saddle River, NJ: Prentice Hall, 2005.

MANO, M.M., and KIME, C.R.: *Logic and Computer Design Fundamentals, 3rd ed.*, Upper Saddle River, NJ: Prentice Hall, 2003.

MARTIN, A.J., NYSTROM, M., PAPADANTONAKIS, K., PENZES, P.I., PRAKASH, P., WONG, C.G., CHANG, J., KO, K.S., LEE, B., OU, E., PUGH, J, TALVALA, E-V., TONG, J.T., and TURA, A.: "The Lutonium: A Sub-Nanojoule Asynchronous 8051 Microcontroller," *Proc. Ninth Int'l Symp. on Asynchronous Circuits and Systems* IEEE, pp. 14-23, 2003.

MARTIN, R.P., VAHDAT, A.M., CULLER, D.E., and ANDERSON, T.E.: "Effects of Communication Latency, Overhead, and Bandwidth in a Cluster Architecture," *Proc. 24th Ann. Int'l Symp. on Computer Arch.*, ACM, pp. 85-97, 1997.

MAYHEW, D., and KRISHNAN, V.: " PCI Express and Advanced Switching: Evolutionary Path to Building Next Generation Interconnects," *Proc. 11th Symp. on High Perf. Interconnects* IEEE, pp. 21-29, Aug. 2003.

MAZIDI, M.A., McKINLAY, and MAZIDI, J.G.: *8051 Microcontroller and Embedded Systems* Upper Saddle River, NJ: Prentice Hall, 2005.

MAZIDI, M.A., and MAZIDI, J.G.: *The 80x86 IBM PC and Compatible Computers, 4th ed.*, Upper Saddle River, NJ: Prentice Hall, 2002.

McKNIGHT, L.W., HOWISON, J., and BRADNER, S: "Wireless Grids," *IEEE Internet Computing*, vol. 8, pp. 24-31, July-Aug. 2004.

McKUSICK, M.K., BOSTIC, K., KARELS, M., and QUARTERMAN, J.S.: "The Design and Implementation of the 4.4 BSD Operating System," Reading, MA: Addison-Wesley, 1996.

McKUSICK, M.K., JOY, W.N., LEFFLER, S.J., and FABRY, R.S.: "A Fast File System for UNIX," *ACM Trans. on Computer Systems*, vol. 2, pp. 181-197, Aug. 1984.

McNAIRY, C., and SOLTIS, D.: "Itanium 2 Processor Microarchitecture," *IEEE Micro Magazine*, vol. 23, pp. 44-55, March-April 2003.

MIN, R., Jone, W.-Ben., and HU, Y.: "Location Cache: A Low-Power L2 Cache System," *Proce. 2004 Int'l Symp. on Low Power Electronics and Design*, IEEE, pp. 120-125, Aug. 2004.

MESSMER, H.-P.: *The Indispensible PC Hardware Book, 4th ed.*, Reading, MA: Addison-Wesley, 2001.

MOUDGILL, M., and VASSILIADIS, S.: "Precise Interrupts," *IEEE Micro Magazine*, vol. 16, pp. 58-67, Jan. 1996.

MULLENDER, S.J., and TANENBAUM, A.S.: "Immediate Files," *Software—Practice and Experience*, vol. 14, pp. 365-368, 1984.

NESBIT, K.J., and SMITH, J.E.: "Data Cache Prefetching Using a Global History Buffer," *Proc. 10th Int'l Symp. on High Perf. Computer Arch.,"* IEEE, pp. 96-106, 2004.

NG, S.W.: "Advances in Disk Technology: Performance Issues," *IEEE Computer Magazine*, vol. 31, pp. 75-81, May 1998.

NICKOLLS, J., MADAR, L.J. III, Johnson, S., RUSTAGI, V., UNGER, K., and CHOUDHURY, M.: "Calisto: A Low-Power Single-Chip Multiprocessor Communications Platform," *IEEE Micro Magazine*, vol. 23, pp. 29-43, March 2003.

NORTON, P., and GOODMAN, J.: *Inside the PC, 8th ed.*, Indianapolis, IN: Sams, 1999.

NULL, L., and LOBUR, J.: *The Essentials of Computer Organization and Architecture*, Sudbury, MA: Jones and Bartlett, 2003.

O'CONNOR, J.M., and TREMBLAY, M.: "PicoJava-I: The Java Virtual Machine in Hardware," *IEEE Micro Magazine*, vol. 17, pp. 45-53, March-April 1997.

ORGANICK, E.: *The MULTICS System*, Cambridge, MA: M.I.T. Press, 1972.

OSKIN, M., CHONG, F.T., and CHUANG, I.L.: "A Practical Architecture for Reliable Quantum Computers," *IEEE Computer Magazine*, vol. 35, pp. 79-87, Jan. 2002.

OUADJAOUT, S., and HOUZET, D.: "Easy SoC Design with VCI SystemC Adapters," *Proc. Digital System Design*, IEEE, pp. 316-323, 2004.

PAPAEFSTATHIOU, I., NIKOLAOU, N,A, DOSHI, B., and GROSSE, E.: "Network Processors for Future High-End Systems and Applications," *IEEE Micro Magazine*, vol. 24, pp. 7-9, Sept.-Oct. 2004.

PAPAMARCOS, M., and PATEL., J.: "A Low Overhead Coherence Solution for Multiprocessors with Private Cache Memories," *Proc. 11th Ann. Int'l Symp. on Computer Arch.*, ACM, pp. 348-354, 1984.

PARIKH, D., SKADRON, K., ZHANG, Y., and STAN, M.: "Power-Aware Branch Prediction: Characterization and Design," *IEEE Trans. on Computers*, vol. 53, 168-186, Feb. 2004.

PATTERSON, D.A.: "Reduced Instruction Set Computers," *Commun. of the ACM*, vol. 28, pp. 8-21, Jan. 1985.

PATTERSON, D.A., GIBSON, G., and KATZ, R.: "A case for redundant arrays of inexpensive disks (RAID)," *Proc. ACM SIGMOD Int'l Conf. on Management of Data*, ACM, pp. 109-166,1988.

PATTERSON, D.A., and HENNESSY, J.L.: *Computer Organization and Design, 3rd ed.*, San Francisco: Morgan Kaufmann, 2005.

PATTERSON, D.A., and SEQUIN, C.H.: "A VLSI RISC," *IEEE Computer Magazine*, vol. 15, pp. 8-22, Sept. 1982.

PAUL, R.P.: *SPARC Architecture, Assembly Language, Programming, and C*, Upper Saddle River, NJ: Prentice Hall, 1994.

PFISTER, G.F.: *In Search of Clusters, 2nd ed.*, Upper Saddle River, NJ: Prentice Hall, 1998.

POPESCU, B.C., STEEN, M. VAN, and TANENBAUM, A.S.: "A Security Architecture for Object-Based Distributed Systems," *Proc. 18th Annual Computer Security Appl. Conf.*, ACM, pp. 161-171, 2002.

POUNTAIN, D.: "Pentium: More RISC than CISC," *Byte*, vol. 18, pp. 195-204, Sept. 1993.

PRICE, D.: "A History of Calculating Machines," *IEEE Micro Magazine*, vol. 4, pp. 22-52, Jan. 1984.

RADIN, G.: "The 801 Minicomputer," *Computer Arch. News*, vol. 10, pp. 39-47, March 1982.

RAMAN, S.K., PENTKOVSKI, V., and KESHAVA, J.: "Implementing Streaming SIMD Extensions on the Pentium III Processor," *IEEE Micro Magazine*, vol. 20, pp. 47-57, July-Aug. 2000.

RAVIKUMAR, C.P.: "Multiprocessor Architectures for Embedded System-on-a-Chip Applications," *Proc. 17th Int'l Conf. on VLSI Design*, IEEE, pp. 512-519, Jan. 2004.

RITCHIE, D.M., and THOMPSON, K.: "The UNIX Time-Sharing System," *Commun. of the ACM*, vol. 17, pp. 365-375, July 1974.

ROBINSON, G.S.: "Toward the Age of Smarter Storage," *IEEE Computer Magazine*, vol. 35, pp. 35-41, Dec. 2002.

ROSENBLUM, M., and OUSTERHOUT, J.K.: "The Design and Implementation of a Log-Structured File System," *Proc. Thirteenth Symp. on Operating System Principles*, ACM, pp. 1-15, 1991.

ROTH, C.H.: *Fundamentals of Logic Design, 5th ed.*, Florence, KY:Thomson Engineering, 2003.

RUSSINOVICH, M.E., and SOLOMON, D.A.: *Microsoft Windows Internals, 4th ed.*, Redmond, WA: Microsoft Press, 2005.

RUSU, S., MULJONO, H., and CHERKAUER, B.: "Itanium 2 Processor 6M," *IEEE Micro Magazine*, vol. 24, pp. 10-18, March-April 2004.

SAHA, D., and MUKHERJEE, A.: "Pervasive Computing: A Paradigm for the 21st Century," *IEEE Computer Magazine*, vol. 36, pp. 25-31, March 2003.

SAKAMURA, K: "Making Computers Invisible," *IEEE Micro Magazine*, vol. 22, pp. 7-11, 2002.

SALOMAN, D.: *Assemblers and Loaders*, Upper Saddle River, NJ: Prentice Hall, 1993.

SCALES, D.J., GHARACHORLOO, K., and THEKKATH, C.A.: "Shasta: A Low-Overhead Software-Only Approach for Supporting Fine-Grain Shared Memory," *Proc. Seventh Int'l Conf. on Arch. Support for Prog. Lang. and Oper. Syst.*, ACM, pp. 174-185, 1996.

SCHEIBLE, J.P.: "A Survey of Storage Options," *IEEE Computer Magazine*, vol. 35, pp. 42-46, Dec. 2002.

SELTZER, M., BOSTIC, K., McKUSICK, M.K., and STAELIN, C.: "An Implementation of a Log-Structured File System for UNIX," *Proc. Winter 1993 USENIX Technical Conf.*, pp. 307-326, 1993.

SHANLEY, T., and ANDERSON, D.: *PCI System Architecture, 4th ed.*, Reading, MA: Addison-Wesley, 1999.

SHRIVER, B., and SMITH, B.: *The Anatomy of a High-Performance Microprocessor: A Systems Perspective*, Los Alamitos, CA: IEEE Computer Society, 1998.

SIMA, D: "Superscalar Instruction Issue," *IEEE Micro Magazine*, vol. 17, pp. 28-39, Sept.-Oct 1997.

SIMA, D., FOUNTAIN, T., and KACSUK, P.: *Advanced Computer Architectures: A Design Space Approach*, Reading, MA: Addison-Wesley, 1997.

SLATER, R.: *Portraits in Silicon*, Cambridge, MA: M.I.T. Press, 1987.

SOHI, G.S., and ROTH, A.: "Speculative Multithreaded Processors," *IEEE Computer Magazine*, vol. 34, pp. 66-73, April 2001.

SNIR, M., OTTO, S.W., HUSS-LEDERMAN, S., WALKER, D.W., and DONGARRA, J.: *MPI: The Complete Reference Manual*, Cambridge, MA: M.I.T. Press, 1996.

SOLARI, E., and CONGDON, B.: *PCI Express Design & System Architecture*, Research Tech, INc., 2005.

SOLARI, E., and WILLSE, G.: *PCI and PCI-X Hardware and Software, 6th ed.*, San Diego, CA: Annabooks, 2004.

STALLINGS, W.: *Computer Organization and Architecture, 6th ed.*, Upper Saddle River, NJ: Prentice Hall, 2003.

STENSTROM, P., HAGERSTEN, E., LILJA, D.J., MARTONOSI, M., and VENUGOPAL, M.: "Trends in Shared Memory Multiprocessing," *IEEE Computer Magazine*, vol. 30, pp. 44-50, Dec. 1997.

STETS, R., DWARKADAS, S., HARDAVELLAS, N., HUNT, G., KONTOTHANASSIS, L., PARTHASARATHY, S., and SCOTT, M.: "CASHMERE-2L: Software Coherent Shared Memory on Clustered Remote-Write Networks," *Proc. 16th Symp. on Operating Systems Principles*, ACM, pp. 170-183, 1997.

SUH, T., LEE, H.-H. S., BLOUGH, D.M.: "Integrating Cache Coherence Protocols for Heterogeneous Multiprocessor Systems, Part 1," *IEEE Micro Magazine*, vol. 24, pp. 33-41, July 2004.

SUMMERS, C.K.: *ADSL: Standards, Implementation, and Architecture*, Boca Raton, FL: CRC Press, 1999.

SUNDERRAM, V.B..: "PVM: A Framework for Parallel Distributed Computing," *Concurrency: Practice and Experience*, vol. 2, pp. 315-339, Dec. 1990.

SWAN, R.J., FULLER, S.H., and SIEWIOREK, D.P.: "Cm*—A Modular Multiprocessor," *Proc. NCC*, pp. 645-655, 1977.

TAN, W.M.: *Developing USB PC Peripherals*, San Diego, CA: Annabooks, 1997.

TANENBAUM, A.S.: "Computer Networks," Upper Saddle River, NJ: Prentice Hall, 2003.

TANENBAUM, A.S.: "Implications of Structured Programming for Machine Architecture," *Commun. of the ACM*, vol. 21, pp. 237-246, March 1978.

TANENBAUM, A.S.: *Operating Systems: Design and Implementation*, Upper Saddle River, NJ: Prentice Hall, 1987.

TANENBAUM, A.S, and WOODHULL, A.W.: *Operating Systems: Design and Implementation, 2nd ed.*, Upper Saddle River, NJ: Prentice Hall, 1997.

THOMPSON, K.: "UNIX Implementation," *Bell Syst. Tech. J.*, vol. 57, pp. 1931-1946, July-Aug. 1978.

TRELEAVEN, P.: "Control-Driven, Data-Driven, and Demand-Driven Computer Architecture," *Parallel Computing*, vol. 2, 1985.

TREMBLAY, M., and O'CONNOR, J.M.: "UltraSPARC I: A Four-Issue Processor Supporting Multimedia," *IEEE Micro Magazine*, vol. 16, pp. 42-50, March 1996.

TRIEBEL, W.A.: *The 80386, 80486, and Pentium Processor*, Upper Saddle River, NJ: Prentice Hall, 1998.

TUCK, N., and TULLSEN, D.M.: "Initial Observations of the Simultaneous Multithreading Pentium 4 Processor," *Proc. 12th Int'l Conf. on Parallel Arch. and Compilation Techniques*, IEEE, pp. 26-35, 2003.

UNGER, S.H.: "A Computer Oriented Toward Spatial Problems," *Proc. IRE*, vol. 46, pp. 1744-1750, 1958.

VAHALIA, U.: *UNIX Internals*, Upper Saddle River, NJ: Prentice Hall, 1996.

VAHID, F.: "The Softening of Hardware," *IEEE Computer Magazine*, vol. 36, pp. 27-34, April 2003.

VAN STEEN, M., HOMBURG, P.C., and TANENBAUM, A.S.: "The Architectural Design of Globe: A Wide-Area Distributed System," *IEEE Concurrency*, vol. 7, pp. 70-78, Jan.-March 1999.

VETTER, P., GODERIS, D., VERPOOTEN, L., and GRANGER, A.: "Systems Aspects of APON/VDSL Deployment," *IEEE Commun. Magazine*, vol. 38, pp. 66-72, May 2000.

WEAVER, D.L., and GERMOND, T.: *The SPARC Architecture Manual, Version 9*, Upper Saddle River, NJ: Prentice Hall, 1994.

WEISER, M.: "The Computer for the 21st Century," *IEEE Pervasive Computing*, vol. 1, pp. 19-25, Jan.-March 2002; originally published in *Scientific American*, Sept. 1991.

WILKES, M.V.: "Computers Then and Now," *J. ACM*, vol. 15, pp. 1-7, Jan. 1968.

WILKES, M.V.: "The Best Way to Design an Automatic Calculating Machine," *Proc. Manchester Univ. Computer Inaugural Conf.*, 1951.

WILSON, J.: "Challenges and Trends in Processor Design," *IEEE Computer Magazine*, vol. 31, pp. 39-48, Jan. 1998.

WILSON, P.: "Floating-Point Survival Kit," *Byte*, vol. 13, pp. 217-226, March 1988.

WOLF, W.: "The Future of Multiprocessor Systems-on-Chips," *Proc. 41st Ann. Conf. on Design Automation*, IEEE, pp. 681-685, 2004.

A

BINARY NUMBERS

The arithmetic used by computers differs in some ways from the arithmetic used by people. The most important difference is that computers perform operations on numbers whose precision is finite and fixed. Another difference is that most computers use the binary rather than the decimal system for representing numbers. These topics are the subject of this appendix.

A.1 FINITE-PRECISION NUMBERS

While doing arithmetic, one usually gives little thought to the question of how many decimal digits it takes to represent a number. Physicists can calculate that there are 10^{78} electrons in the universe without being bothered by the fact that it requires 79 decimal digits to write that number out in full. Someone calculating the value of a function with pencil and paper who needs the answer to six significant digits simply keeps intermediate results to seven, or eight, or however many are needed. The problem of the paper not being wide enough for seven-digit numbers never arises.

With computers, matters are quite different. On most computers, the amount of memory available for storing a number is fixed at the time that the computer is designed. With a certain amount of effort, the programmer can represent numbers two, or three, or even many times larger than this fixed amount, but doing so does not change the nature of this difficulty. The finite nature of the computer forces us to deal only with numbers that can be represented in a fixed number of digits. We call such numbers **finite-precision numbers**.

In order to study properties of finite-precision numbers, let us examine the set of positive integers representable by three decimal digits, with no decimal point and no sign. This set has exactly 1000 members: 000, 001, 002, 003, ..., 999. With this restriction, it is impossible to express certain kinds of numbers, such as

1. Numbers larger than 999.

2. Negative numbers.

3. Fractions.

4. Irrational numbers.

5. Complex numbers.

One important property of arithmetic on the set of all integers is **closure** with respect to the operations of addition, subtraction, and multiplication. In other words, for every pair of integers i and j, $i + j$, $i - j$, and $i \times j$ are also integers. The set of integers is not closed with respect to division, because there exist values of i and j for which i/j is not expressible as an integer (e.g., 7/2 and 1/0).

Finite-precision numbers are not closed with respect to any of these four basic operations, as shown below, using three-digit decimal numbers as an example:

$$600 + 600 = 1200 \qquad \text{(too large)}$$
$$003 - 005 = -2 \qquad \text{(negative)}$$
$$050 \times 050 = 2500 \qquad \text{(too large)}$$
$$007 / 002 = 3.5 \qquad \text{(not an integer)}$$

The violations can be divided into two mutually exclusive classes: operations whose result is larger than the largest number in the set (overflow error) or smaller than the smallest number in the set (underflow error), and operations whose result is neither too large nor too small but is simply not a member of the set. Of the four violations above, the first three are examples of the former, and the fourth is an example of the latter.

Because computers have finite memories and therefore must of necessity perform arithmetic on finite-precision numbers, the results of certain calculations will be, from the point of view of classical mathematics, just plain wrong. A calculating device that gives the wrong answer even though it is in perfect working condition may appear strange at first, but the error is a logical consequence of its finite nature. Some computers have special hardware that detects overflow errors.

The algebra of finite-precision numbers is different from normal algebra. As an example, consider the associative law:

$$a + (b - c) = (a + b) - c$$

Let us evaluate both sides for $a = 700$, $b = 400$, $c = 300$. To compute the left-hand side, first calculate $(b - c)$, which is 100, and then add this amount to a, yielding 800. To compute the right-hand side, first calculate $(a + b)$, which gives an overflow in the finite arithmetic of three-digit integers. The result may depend on the machine being used but it will not be 1100. Subtracting 300 from some number other than 1100 will not yield 800. The associative law does not hold. The order of operations is important.

As another example, consider the distributive law:

$$a \times (b - c) = a \times b - a \times c$$

Let us evaluate both sides for $a = 5$, $b = 210$, $c = 195$. The left-hand side is 5×15, which yields 75. The right-hand side is not 75 because $a \times b$ overflows.

Judging from these examples, one might conclude that although computers are general-purpose devices, their finite nature renders them especially unsuitable for doing arithmetic. This conclusion is, of course, not true, but it does serve to illustrate the importance of understanding how computers work and what limitations they have.

A.2 RADIX NUMBER SYSTEMS

An ordinary decimal number with which everyone is familiar consists of a string of decimal digits and, possibly, a decimal point. The general form and its usual interpretation are shown in Fig. A-1. The choice of 10 as the base for exponentiation, called the **radix**, is made because we are using decimal, or base 10, numbers. When dealing with computers, it is frequently convenient to use radices other than 10. The most important radices are 2, 8, and 16. The number systems based on these radices are called **binary**, **octal**, and **hexadecimal**, respectively.

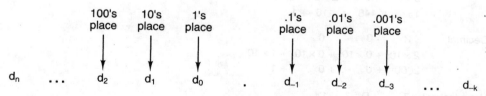

$$\text{Number} = \sum_{i = -k}^{n} d_i \times 10^i$$

Figure A-1. The general form of a decimal number.

A radix k number system requires k different symbols to represent the digits 0 to $k - 1$. Decimal numbers are built up from the 10 decimal digits

0 1 2 3 4 5 6 7 8 9

In contrast, binary numbers do not use these ten digits. They are all constructed exclusively from the two binary digits

0 1

Octal numbers are built up from the eight octal digits

0 1 2 3 4 5 6 7

For hexadecimal numbers, 16 digits are needed. Thus six new symbols are required. It is conventional to use the uppercase letters A through F for the six digits following 9. Hexadecimal numbers are then built up from the digits

0 1 2 3 4 5 6 7 8 9 A B C D E F

The expression "binary digit" meaning a 1 or a 0 is usually referred to as a **bit**. Figure A-2 shows the decimal number 2001 expressed in binary, octal, decimal, and hexadecimal form. The number 7B9 is obviously hexadecimal, because the symbol B can only occur in hexadecimal numbers. However, the number 111 might be in any of the four number systems discussed. To avoid ambiguity, people use a subscript of 2, 8, 10, or 16 to indicate the radix when it is not obvious from the context.

Binary   1   1   1   1   1   0   1   0   0   0   1

$$1 \times 2^{10} + 1 \times 2^9 + 1 \times 2^8 + 1 \times 2^7 + 1 \times 2^6 + 0 \times 2^5 + 1 \times 2^4 + 0 \times 2^3 + 0 \times 2^2 + 0 \times 2^1 + 1 \times 2^0$$

1024 + 512 + 256 + 128 + 64 + 0 + 16 + 0 + 0 + 0 + 1

Octal   3   7   2   1

$$3 \times 8^3 + 7 \times 8^2 + 2 \times 8^1 + 1 \times 8^0$$

1536 + 448 + 16 + 1

Decimal   2   0   0   1

$$2 \times 10^3 + 0 \times 10^2 + 0 \times 10^1 + 1 \times 10^0$$

2000 + 0 + 0 + 1

Hexadecimal 7   D   1

$$7 \times 16^2 + 13 \times 16^1 + 1 \times 16^0$$

1792 + 208 + 1

Figure A-2. The number 2001 in binary, octal, and hexadecimal.

As an example of binary, octal, decimal, and hexadecimal notation, consider Fig. A-3, which shows a collection of nonnegative integers expressed in each of these four different systems. Perhaps some archaeologist thousands of years from now will discover this table and regard it as the Rosetta Stone to late twentieth century and early twenty-first century number systems.

Decimal	Binary	Octal	Hex
0	0	0	0
1	1	1	1
2	10	2	2
3	11	3	3
4	100	3	3
5	101	5	5
6	110	6	6
7	111	7	7
8	1000	10	8
9	1001	11	9
10	1010	12	A
11	1011	13	B
12	1100	14	C
13	1101	15	D
14	1110	16	E
15	1111	17	F
16	10000	20	10
20	10100	24	14
30	11110	36	1E
40	101000	50	28
50	110010	62	32
60	111100	74	3C
70	1000110	106	46
80	1010000	120	50
90	1011010	132	5A
100	11001000	144	64
1000	1111101000	1750	3E8
2989	101110101101	5655	BAD

Figure A-3. Decimal numbers and their binary, octal, and hexadecimal equivalents.

A.3 CONVERSION FROM ONE RADIX TO ANOTHER

Conversion between octal or hexadecimal numbers and binary numbers is easy. To convert a binary number to octal, divide it into groups of 3 bits, with the 3 bits immediately to the left (or right) of the decimal point (often called a binary point) forming one group, the 3 bits immediately to their left, another group, and so on. Each group of 3 bits can be directly converted to a single octal digit, 0 to 7, according to the conversion given in the first lines of Fig. A-3. It may be necessary to add one or two leading or trailing zeros to fill out a group to 3 full bits. Conversion from octal to binary is equally trivial. Each octal digit is simply replaced by the equivalent 3-bit binary number. Conversion from hexadecimal to binary is essentially the same as octal-to-binary except that each hexadecimal digit corresponds to a group of 4 bits instead of 3 bits. Figure A-4 gives some examples of conversions.

Example 1

Hexadecimal

Binary

Octal

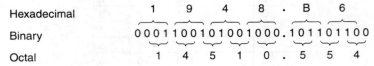

Example 2

Hexadecimal

Binary

Octal

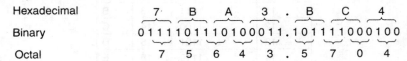

Figure A-4. Examples of octal-to-binary and hexadecimal-to-binary conversion.

Conversion of decimal numbers to binary can be done in two different ways. The first method follows directly from the definition of binary numbers. The largest power of 2 smaller than the number is subtracted from the number. The process is then repeated on the difference. Once the number has been decomposed into powers of 2, the binary number can be assembled with 1s in the bit positions corresponding to powers of 2 used in the decomposition, and 0s elsewhere.

The other method (for integers only) consists of dividing the number by 2. The quotient is written directly beneath the original number and the remainder, 0 or 1, is written next to the quotient. The quotient is then considered and the process repeated until the number 0 has been reached. The result of this process will be two columns of numbers, the quotients and the remainders. The binary number can now be read directly from the remainder column starting at the bottom. Figure A-5 gives an example of decimal-to-binary conversion.

Binary integers can also be converted to decimal in two ways. One method consists of summing up the powers of 2 corresponding to the 1 bits in the number. For example,

$$10110 = 2^4 + 2^2 + 2^1 = 16 + 4 + 2 = 22$$

In the other method, the binary number is written vertically, one bit per line, with the leftmost bit on the bottom. The bottom line is called line 1, the one above it line 2, and so on. The decimal number will be built up in a parallel column next to the binary number. Begin by writing a 1 on line 1. The entry on line n consists of two times the entry on line $n - 1$ plus the bit on line n (either 0 or 1). The entry on the top line is the answer. Figure A-6 gives an example of this method of binary to decimal conversion.

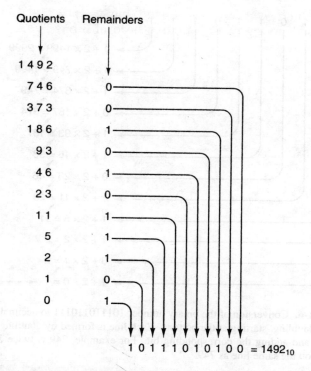

Quotients   Remainders

1 4 9 2

7 4 6   0

3 7 3   0

1 8 6   1

9 3   0

4 6   1

2 3   0

1 1   1

5   1

2   1

1   0

0   1

1 0 1 1 1 0 1 0 1 0 0 = 1492_{10}

Figure A-5. Conversion of the decimal number 1492 to binary by successive halving, starting at the top and working downward. For example, 93 divided by 2 yields a quotient of 46 and a remainder of 1, written on the line below it.

Decimal-to-octal and decimal-to-hexadecimal conversion can be accomplished either by first converting to binary and then to the desired system or by subtracting powers of 8 or 16.

A.4 NEGATIVE BINARY NUMBERS

Four different systems for representing negative numbers have been used in digital computers at one time or another in history. The first one is called **signed magnitude**. In this system the leftmost bit is the sign bit (0 is + and 1 is −) and the remaining bits hold the absolute magnitude of the number.

The second system, called **one's complement**, also has a sign bit with 0 used for plus and 1 for minus. To negate a number, replace each 1 by a 0 and each 0 by a 1. This holds for the sign bit as well. One's complement is obsolete.

The third system, called **two's complement**, also has a sign bit that is 0 for plus and 1 for minus. Negating a number is a two-step process. First, each 1 is

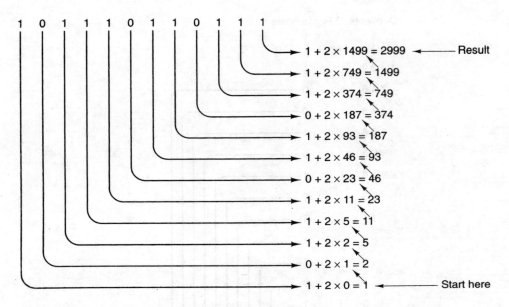

Figure A-6. Conversion of the binary number 101110110111 to decimal by successive doubling, starting at the bottom. Each line is formed by doubling the one below it and adding the corresponding bit. For example, 749 is twice 374 plus the 1 bit on the same line as 749.

replaced by a 0 and each 0 by a 1, just as in one's complement. Second, 1 is added to the result. Binary addition is the same as decimal addition except that a carry is generated if the sum is greater than 1 rather than greater than 9. For example, converting 6 to two's complement is done in two steps:

00000110 (+6)
11111001 (−6 in one's complement)
11111010 (−6 in two's complement)

If a carry occurs from the leftmost bit, it is thrown away.

The fourth system, which for m-bit numbers is called **excess 2^{m-1}**, represents a number by storing it as the sum of itself and 2^{m-1}. For example, for 8-bit numbers, $m = 8$, the system is called excess 128 and a number is stored as its true value plus 128. Therefore, −3 becomes −3 + 128 = 125, and −3 is represented by the 8-bit binary number for 125 (01111101). The numbers from −128 to +127 map onto 0 to 255, all of which are expressible as an 8-bit positive integer. Interestingly enough, this system is identical to two's complement with the sign bit reversed. Figure A-7 gives examples of negative numbers in all four systems.

Both signed magnitude and one's complement have two representations for zero: a plus zero, and a minus zero. This situation is undesirable. The two's complement system does not have this problem because the two's complement of plus

N decimal	N binary	−N signed mag.	−N 1's compl.	−N 2's compl.	−N excess 128
1	00000001	10000001	11111110	11111111	01111111
2	00000010	10000010	11111101	11111110	01111110
3	00000011	10000011	11111100	11111101	01111101
4	00000100	10000100	11111011	11111100	01111100
5	00000101	10000101	11111010	11111011	01111011
6	00000110	10000110	11111001	11111010	01111010
7	00000111	10000111	11111000	11111001	01111001
8	00001000	10001000	11110111	11111000	01111000
9	00001001	10001001	11110110	11110111	01110111
10	00001010	10001010	11110101	11110110	01110110
20	00010100	10010100	11101011	11101100	01101100
30	00011110	10011110	11100001	11100010	01100010
40	00101000	10101000	11010111	11011000	01011000
50	00110010	10110010	11001101	11001110	01001110
60	00111100	10111100	11000011	11000100	01000100
70	01000110	11000110	10111001	10111010	00111010
80	01010000	11010000	10101111	10110000	00110000
90	01011010	11011010	10100101	10100110	00100110
100	01100100	11100100	10011011	10011100	00011100
127	01111111	11111111	10000000	10000001	00000001
128	Nonexistent	Nonexistent	Nonexistent	10000000	00000000

Figure A-7. Negative 8-bit numbers in four systems.

zero is also plus zero. The two's complement system does, however, have a different singularity. The bit pattern consisting of a 1 followed by all 0s is its own complement. The result is to make the range of positive and negative numbers unsymmetric; there is one negative number with no positive counterpart.

The reason for these problems is not hard to find: we want an encoding system with two properties:

1. Only one representation for zero.

2. Exactly as many positive numbers as negative numbers.

The problem is that any set of numbers with as many positive as negative numbers and only one zero has an odd number of members, whereas m bits allow an even number of bit patterns. There will always be either one bit pattern too many or one bit pattern too few, no matter what representation is chosen. This extra bit pattern can be used for −0 or for a large negative number, or for something else, but no matter what it is used for it will always be a nuisance.

A.5 BINARY ARITHMETIC

The addition table for binary numbers is given in Fig. A-8.

Addend	0	0	1	1
Augend	+0	+1	+0	+1
Sum	0	1	1	0
Carry	0	0	0	1

Figure A-8. The addition table in binary.

Two binary numbers can be added, starting at the rightmost bit and adding the corresponding bits in the addend and the augend. If a carry is generated, it is carried one position to the left, just as in decimal arithmetic. In one's complement arithmetic, a carry generated by the addition of the leftmost bits is added to the rightmost bit. This process is called an end-around carry. In two's complement arithmetic, a carry generated by the addition of the leftmost bits is merely thrown away. Examples of binary arithmetic are shown in Fig. A-9.

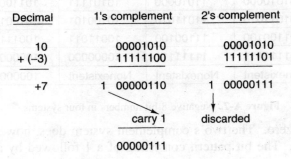

Figure A-9. Addition in one's complement and two's complement.

If the addend and the augend are of opposite signs, overflow error cannot occur. If they are of the same sign and the result is of the opposite sign, overflow error has occurred and the answer is wrong. In both one's and two's complement arithmetic, overflow occurs if and only if the carry into the sign bit differs from the carry out of the sign bit. Most computers preserve the carry out of the sign bit, but the carry into the sign bit is not visible from the answer. For this reason, a special overflow bit is usually provided.

PROBLEMS

1. Convert the following numbers to binary: 1984, 4000, 8192.

2. What is 1001101001 (binary) in decimal? In octal? In hexadecimal?

3. Which of the following are valid hexadecimal numbers? BED, CAB, DEAD, DECADE, ACCEDED, BAG, DAD.

4. Express the decimal number 100 in all radices from 2 to 9.

5. How many different positive integers can be expressed in k digits using radix r numbers?

6. Most people can only count to 10 on their fingers; however, computer scientists can do better. If you regard each finger as one binary bit, with finger extended as 1 and finger touching palm as 0, how high can you count using both hands? With both hands and both feet? Now use both hands and both feet, with the big toe on your left foot as a sign bit for two's complement numbers. What is the range of expressible numbers?

7. Perform the following calculations on 8-bit two's complement numbers.

$$
\begin{array}{cccc}
00101101 & 11111111 & 00000000 & 11110111 \\
+\ \underline{01101111} & +\ \underline{11111111} & -\ \underline{11111111} & -\ \underline{11110111}
\end{array}
$$

8. Repeat the calculation of the preceding problem but now in one's complement.

9. Consider the following addition problems for 3-bit binary numbers in two's complement. For each sum, state
   a. Whether the sign bit of the result is 1.
   b. Whether the low-order 3 bits are 0.
   c. Whether an overflow occurred.

$$
\begin{array}{ccccc}
000 & 000 & 111 & 100 & 100 \\
+\ \underline{001} & +\ \underline{111} & +\ \underline{110} & +\ \underline{111} & +\ \underline{100}
\end{array}
$$

10. Signed decimal numbers consisting of n digits can be represented in $n+1$ digits without a sign. Positive numbers have 0 as the leftmost digit. Negative numbers are formed by subtracting each digit from 9. Thus the negative of 014725 is 985274. Such numbers are called nine's complement numbers and are analogous to one's complement binary numbers. Express the following as three-digit nine's complement numbers: 6, −2, 100, −14, −1, 0.

11. Determine the rule for addition of nine's complement numbers and then perform the following additions.

$$
\begin{array}{cccc}
0001 & 0001 & 9997 & 9241 \\
+\ \underline{9999} & +\ \underline{9998} & +\ \underline{9996} & +\ \underline{0802}
\end{array}
$$

12. Ten's complement is analogous to two's complement. A ten's complement negative number is formed by adding 1 to the corresponding nine's complement number, ignoring the carry. What is the rule for ten's complement addition?

13. Construct the multiplication tables for radix 3 numbers.

14. Multiply 0111 and 0011 in binary.

15. Write a program that takes in a signed decimal number as an ASCII string and prints out its representation in two's complement in binary, octal, and hexadecimal.

16. Write a program that takes in two 32-character ASCII strings containing 0s and 1s, each representing a two's complement 32-bit binary number. The program should print their sum as a 32-character ASCII string of 0s and 1s.

B

FLOATING-POINT NUMBERS

In many calculations the range of numbers used is very large. For example, a calculation in astronomy might involve the mass of the electron, 9×10^{-28} grams, and the mass of the sun, 2×10^{33} grams, a range exceeding 10^{60}. These numbers could be represented by

00000000000000000000000000000000000.00000000000000000000000000009
2000000000000000000000000000000000.000000000000000000000000000000

and all calculations could be carried out keeping 34 digits to the left of the decimal point and 28 places to the right of it. Doing so would allow 62 significant digits in the results. On a binary computer, multiple-precision arithmetic could be used to provide enough significance. However, the mass of the sun is not even known accurately to five significant digits, let alone 62. In fact few measurements of any kind can (or need) be made accurately to 62 significant digits. Although it would be possible to keep all intermediate results to 62 significant digits and then throw away 50 or 60 of them before printing the final results, doing this is wasteful of both CPU time and memory.

What is needed is a system for representing numbers in which the range of expressible numbers is independent of the number of significant digits. In this appendix, such a system will be discussed. It is based on the scientific notation commonly used in physics, chemistry, and engineering.

B.1 PRINCIPLES OF FLOATING POINT

One way of separating the range from the precision is to express numbers in the familiar scientific notation

$$n = f \times 10^e$$

where f is called the **fraction**, or **mantissa**, and e is a positive or negative integer called the **exponent**. The computer version of this notation is called **floating point**. Some examples of numbers expressed in this form are

$$
\begin{array}{lll}
3.14 & = 0.314 \times 10^1 & = 3.14 \times 10^0 \\
0.000001 & = 0.1 \times 10^{-5} & = 1.0 \times 10^{-6} \\
1941 & = 0.1941 \times 10^4 & = 1.941 \times 10^3
\end{array}
$$

The range is effectively determined by the number of digits in the exponent and the precision is determined by the number of digits in the fraction. Because there is more than one way to represent a given number, one form is usually chosen as the standard. In order to investigate the properties of this method of representing numbers, consider a representation, R, with a signed three-digit fraction in the range $0.1 \leq |f| < 1$ or zero and a signed two-digit exponent. These numbers range in magnitude from $+0.100 \times 10^{-99}$ to $+0.999 \times 10^{+99}$, a span of nearly 199 orders of magnitude, yet only five digits and two signs are needed to store a number.

Floating-point numbers can be used to model the real-number system of mathematics, although there are some important differences. Figure B-1 gives a grossly exaggerated schematic of the real number line. The real line is divided up into seven regions:

1. Large negative numbers less than -0.999×10^{99}.

2. Negative numbers between -0.999×10^{99} and -0.100×10^{-99}.

3. Small negative numbers with magnitudes less than 0.100×10^{-99}.

4. Zero.

5. Small positive numbers with magnitudes less than 0.100×10^{-99}.

6. Positive numbers between 0.100×10^{-99} and 0.999×10^{99}.

7. Large positive numbers greater than 0.999×10^{99}.

One major difference between the set of numbers representable with three fraction and two exponent digits and the real numbers is that the former cannot be used to express any numbers in regions 1, 3, 5, or 7. If the result of an arithmetic operation yields a number in regions 1 or 7—for example, $10^{60} \times 10^{60} = 10^{120}$—**overflow error** will occur and the answer will be incorrect. The reason is due to the finite nature of the representation for numbers and is unavoidable. Similarly,

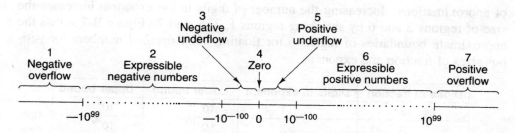

Figure B-1. The real number line can be divided into seven regions.

a result in regions 3 or 5 cannot be expressed either. This situation is called **underflow error**. Underflow error is less serious than overflow error, because 0 is often a satisfactory approximation to numbers in regions 3 and 5. A bank balance of 10^{-102} dollars is hardly better than a bank balance of 0.

Another important difference between floating-point numbers and real numbers is their density. Between any two real numbers, x and y, is another real number, no matter how close x is to y. This property comes from the fact that for any distinct real numbers, x and y, $z = (x + y)/2$ is a real number between them. The real numbers form a continuum.

Floating-point numbers, in contrast, do not form a continuum. Exactly 179,100 positive numbers can be expressed in the five-digit, two-sign system used above, 179,100 negative numbers, and 0 (which can be expressed in many ways), for a total of 358,201 numbers. Of the infinite number of real numbers between -10^{+100} and $+0.999 \times 10^{99}$, only 358,201 of them can be specified by this notation. They are symbolized by the dots in Fig. B-1. It is quite possible for the result of a calculation to be one of the other numbers, even though it is in region 2 or 6. For example, $+0.100 \times 10^3$ divided by 3 cannot be expressed *exactly* in our system of representation. If the result of a calculation cannot be expressed in the number representation being used, the obvious thing to do is to use the nearest number that can be expressed. This process is called **rounding**.

The spacing between adjacent expressible numbers is not constant throughout region 2 or 6. The separation between $+0.998 \times 10^{99}$ and $+0.999 \times 10^{99}$ is vastly more than the separation between $+0.998 \times 10^0$ and $+0.999 \times 10^0$. However, when the separation between a number and its successor is expressed as a percentage of that number, there is no systematic variation throughout region 2 or 6. In other words, the **relative error** introduced by rounding is approximately the same for small numbers as large numbers.

Although the preceding discussion was in terms of a representation system with a three-digit fraction and a two-digit exponent, the conclusions drawn are valid for other representation systems as well. Changing the number of digits in the fraction or exponent merely shifts the boundaries of regions 2 and 6 and changes the number of expressible points in them. Increasing the number of digits in the fraction increases the density of points and therefore improves the accuracy of approximations. Increasing the number of digits in the exponent increases the size of regions 2 and 6 by shrinking regions 1, 3, 5, and 7. Figure B-2 shows the approximate boundaries of region 6 for floating-point decimal numbers for various sizes of fraction and exponent.

Digits in fraction	Digits in exponent	Lower bound	Upper bound
3	1	10^{-12}	10^9
3	2	10^{-102}	10^{99}
3	3	10^{-1002}	10^{999}
3	4	10^{-10002}	10^{9999}
4	1	10^{-13}	10^9
4	2	10^{-103}	10^{99}
4	3	10^{-1003}	10^{999}
4	4	10^{-10003}	10^{9999}
5	1	10^{-14}	10^9
5	2	10^{-104}	10^{99}
5	3	10^{-1004}	10^{999}
5	4	10^{-10004}	10^{9999}
10	3	10^{-1009}	10^{999}
20	3	10^{-1019}	10^{999}

Figure B-2. The approximate lower and upper bounds of expressible (unnormalized) floating-point decimal numbers.

A variation of this representation is used in computers. For efficiency, exponentiation is to base 2, 4, 8, or 16 rather than 10, in which case the fraction consists of a string of binary, base-4, octal, or hexadecimal digits. If the leftmost of these digits is zero, all the digits can be shifted one place to the left and the exponent decreased by 1, without changing the value of the number (barring underflow). A fraction with a nonzero leftmost digit is said to be **normalized**.

Normalized numbers are generally preferable to unnormalized numbers, because there is only one normalized form, whereas there are many unnormalized forms. Examples of normalized floating-point numbers are given in Fig. B-3 for two bases of exponentiation. In these examples a 16-bit fraction (including sign bit) and a 7-bit exponent using excess 64 notation are shown. The radix point is to the left of the leftmost fraction bit—that is, to the right of the exponent.

B.2 IEEE FLOATING-POINT STANDARD 754

Until about 1980, each computer manufacturer had its own floating-point format. Needless to say, all were different. Worse yet, some of them actually did arithmetic incorrectly because floating-point arithmetic has some subtleties not obvious to the average hardware designer.

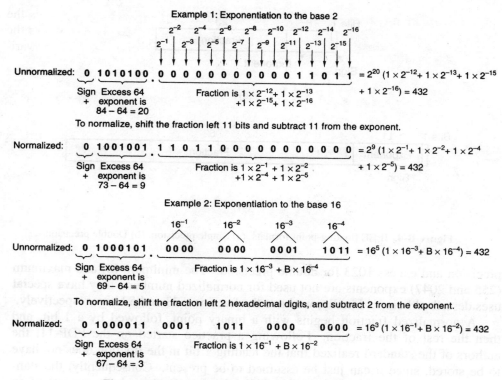

Figure B-3. Examples of normalized floating-point numbers.

To rectify this situation, in the late 1970s IEEE set up a committee to stand-ardize floating-point arithmetic. The goal was not only to permit floating-point data to be exchanged among different computers but also to provide hardware designers with a model known to be correct. The resulting work led to IEEE Standard 754 (IEEE, 1985). Most CPUs these days (including the Intel, SPARC, and JVM ones studied in this book) have floating-point instructions that conform to the IEEE floating-point standard. Unlike many standards, which tend to be wishy-washy compromises that please no one, this one is not bad, in large part because it was primarily the work of one person, Berkeley math professor William Kahan. The standard will be described in the remainder of this section.

The standard defines three formats: single precision (32 bits), double preci-sion (64 bits), and extended precision (80 bits). The extended-precision format is intended to reduce roundoff errors. It is used primarily inside floating-point arith-metic units, so we will not discuss it further. Both the single- and double-precision formats use radix 2 for fractions and excess notation for exponents. The formats are shown in Fig. B-4.

Both formats start with a sign bit for the number as a whole, 0 being positive and 1 being negative. Next comes the exponent, using excess 127 for single

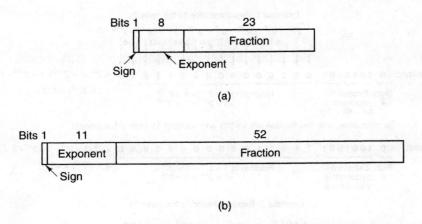

Figure B-4. IEEE floating-point formats. (a) Single precision. (b) Double precision.

precision and excess 1023 for double precision. The minimum (0) and maximum (255 and 2047) exponents are not used for normalized numbers; they have special uses described below. Finally, we have the fractions, 23 and 52 bits, respectively.

A normalized fraction begins with a binary point, followed by a 1 bit, and then the rest of the fraction. Following a practice started on the PDP-11, the authors of the standard realized that the leading 1 bit in the fraction does not have to be stored, since it can just be assumed to be present. Consequently, the standard defines the fraction in a slightly different way than usual. It consists of an implied 1 bit, an implied binary point, and then either 23 or 52 arbitrary bits. If all 23 or 52 fraction bits are 0s, the fraction has the numerical value 1.0; if all of them are 1s, the fraction is numerically slightly less than 2.0. To avoid confusion with a conventional fraction, the combination of the implied 1, the implied binary point, and the 23 or 52 explicit bits is called a **significand** instead of a fraction or mantissa. All normalized numbers have a significand, s, in the range $1 \leq s < 2$.

The numerical characteristics of the IEEE floating-point numbers are given in Fig. B-5. As examples, consider the numbers 0.5, 1, and 1.5 in normalized single-precision format. These are represented in hexadecimal as 3F000000, 3F800000, and 3FC00000, respectively.

One of the traditional problems with floating-point numbers is how to deal with underflow, overflow, and uninitialized numbers. The IEEE standard deals with these problems explicitly, borrowing its approach in part from the CDC 6600. In addition to normalized numbers, the standard has four other numerical types, described below and shown in Fig. B-6.

A problem arises when the result of a calculation has a magnitude smaller than the smallest normalized floating-point number that can be represented in this system. Previously, most hardware took one of two approaches: just set the result to zero and continue, or cause a floating-point underflow trap. Neither of these is

Item	Single precision	Double precision
Bits in sign	1	1
Bits in exponent	8	11
Bits in fraction	23	52
Bits, total	32	64
Exponent system	Excess 127	Excess 1023
Exponent range	−126 to +127	−1022 to +1023
Smallest normalized number	2^{-126}	2^{-1022}
Largest normalized number	approx. 2^{128}	approx. 2^{1024}
Decimal range	approx. 10^{-38} to 10^{38}	approx. 10^{-308} to 10^{308}
Smallest denormalized number	approx. 10^{-45}	approx. 10^{-324}

Figure B-5. Characteristics of IEEE floating-point numbers.

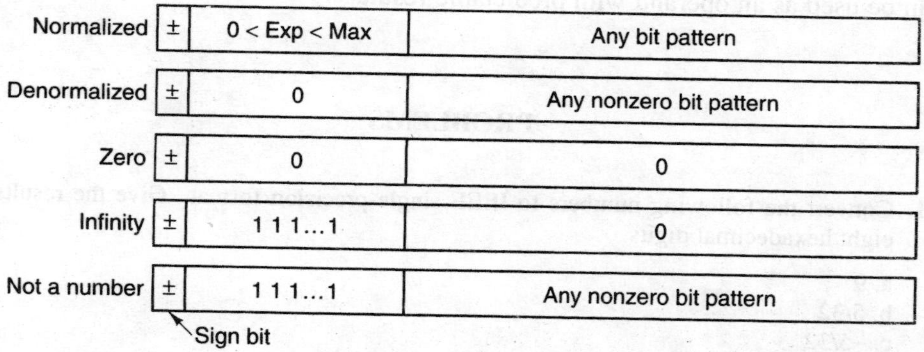

Figure B-6. IEEE numerical types.

really satisfactory, so IEEE invented **denormalized numbers**. These numbers have an exponent of 0 and a fraction given by the following 23 or 52 bits. The implicit 1 bit to the left of the binary point now becomes a 0. Denormalized numbers can be distinguished from normalized ones because the latter are not permitted to have an exponent of 0.

The smallest normalized single precision number has a 1 as exponent and 0 as fraction, and represents 1.0×2^{-126}. The largest denormalized number has a 0 as exponent and all 1s in the fraction, and represents about $0.9999999 \times 2^{-126}$, which is almost the same thing. One thing to note however, is that this number has only 23 bits of significance, versus 24 for all normalized numbers.

As calculations further decrease this result, the exponent stays put at 0, but the first few bits of the fraction become zeros, reducing both the value and the number of significant bits in the fraction. The smallest nonzero denormalized number consists of a 1 in the rightmost bit, with the rest being 0. The exponent represents 2^{-126} and the fraction represents 2^{-23} so the value is 2^{-149}. This scheme provides for a graceful underflow by giving up significance instead of jumping to 0 when the result cannot be expressed as a normalized number.

Two zeros are present in this scheme, positive and negative, determined by the sign bit. Both have an exponent of 0 and a fraction of 0. Here too, the bit to the left of the binary point is implicitly 0 rather than 1.

Overflow cannot be handled gracefully. There are no bit combinations left. Instead, a special representation is provided for infinity, consisting of an exponent with all 1s (not allowed for normalized numbers), and a fraction of 0. This number can be used as an operand and behaves according to the usual mathematical rules for infinity. For example infinity plus anything is infinity, and any finite number divided by infinity is zero. Similarly, any finite number divided by zero yields infinity.

What about infinity divided by infinity? The result is undefined. To handle this case, another special format is provided, called **NaN** (**Not a Number**). It too, can be used as an operand with predictable results.

PROBLEMS

1. Convert the following numbers to IEEE single-precision format. Give the results as eight hexadecimal digits.

   a. 9
   b. 5/32
   c. −5/32
   d. 6.125

2. Convert the following IEEE single-precision floating-point numbers from hex to decimal:
   a. 42E48000H
   b. 3F880000H
   c. 00800000H
   d. C7F00000H

3. The format of single-precision floating-point numbers on the 370 has a 7-bit exponent in the excess 64 system, and a fraction containing 24 bits plus a sign bit, with the binary point at the left end of the fraction. The radix for exponentiation is 16. The order of the fields is sign bit, exponent, fraction. Express the number 7/64 as a normalized number in this system in hex.

4. The following binary floating-point numbers consist of a sign bit, an excess 64, radix 2 exponent, and a 16-bit fraction. Normalize them.

   a. 0 1000000 0001010100000001

b. 0 0111111 0000001111111111
c. 0 1000011 1000000000000000

5. To add two floating-point numbers, you must adjust the exponents (by shifting the fraction) to make them the same. Then you can add the fractions and normalize the result, if need be. Add the single-precision IEEE numbers 3EE00000H and 3D800000H and express the normalized result in hexadecimal.

6. The Tightwad Computer Company has decided to come out with a machine having 16-bit floating-point numbers. The Model 0.001 has a floating-point format with a sign bit, 7-bit, excess 64 exponent, and 8-bit fraction. The Model 0.002 has a sign bit, 5-bit, excess 16 exponent, and 10-bit fraction. Both use radix 2 exponentiation. What are the smallest and largest positive normalized numbers on both models? About how many decimal digits of precision does each have? Would you buy either one?

7. There is one situation in which an operation on two floating-point numbers can cause a drastic reduction in the number of significant bits in the result. What is it?

8. Some floating-point chips have a square root instruction built in. A possible algorithm is an iterative one (e.g., Newton-Raphson). Iterative algorithms need an initial approximation and then steadily improve it. How can one obtain a fast approximate square root of a floating-point number?

9. Write a procedure to add two IEEE single-precision floating-point numbers. Each number is represented by a 32-element Boolean array.

10. Write a procedure to add two single-precision floating-point numbers that use radix 16 for the exponent and radix 2 for the fraction but do not have an implied 1 bit to the left of the binary point. A normalized number has 0001, 0010, ..., 1111 as the leftmost 4 bits of the fraction, but not 0000. A number is normalized by shifting the fraction left 4 bits and subtracting 1 from the exponent.

C

ASSEMBLY LANGUAGE PROGRAMMING

Evert Wattel

Vrije Universiteit

Amsterdam, The Netherlands

Every computer has an **ISA (Instruction Set Architecture)**, which is a set of registers, instructions, and other features visible to its low-level programmers. This ISA is commonly referred to as **machine language**, although the term is not entirely accurate. A program at this level of abstraction is a long list of binary numbers, one per instruction, telling which instructions to execute and what their operands are. Programming with binary numbers is very difficult to do, so all machines have an **assembly language**, a symbolic representation of the instruction set architecture, with symbolic names like, ADD, SUB, and MUL, instead of binary numbers. This appendix is a tutorial on assembly language programming for one specific machine, the Intel 8088, which was used in the original IBM PC and was the base from which the modern Pentium grew. The appendix also covers the use of some tools that can be downloaded to help learn about assembly language programming.

The purpose of this appendix is not to turn out polished assembly language programmers, but to help the reader learn about computer architecture through

701

hands-on experience. For this reason, a simple machine—the Intel 8088— has been chosen as the running example. While 8088s are rarely encountered any more, every Pentium is capable of executing 8088 programs, so the lessons learned here are still applicable to modern machines. Furthermore, most of the Pentium's core instructions are the same as the 8088's, only using 32-bit registers instead of 16-bit registers. Thus, this appendix can also be seen as a gentle introduction to Pentium assembly language programming.

In order to program any machine in assembly language, the programmer must have a detailed knowledge of the machine's instruction set architecture. Accordingly, Sections C.1 through C.4 of this appendix are devoted to the architecture of the 8088, its memory organization, addressing modes, and instructions. Section C.5 discusses the assembler, which is used in this appendix and which is available for free, as described later. The notation used in this appendix is the one used by this assembler. Other assemblers use different notations, so readers already familiar with 8088 assembly programming should be alert for differences. Section C.6 discusses an interpreter/tracer/debugger tool, which can be downloaded to help the beginner programmer get programs debugged. Section C.7 describes the installation of the tools, and how to get started. Section C.8 contain programs, examples, exercises and solutions. Section C.9 discusses implementation issues, bugs and limitations of the material.

C.1 OVERVIEW

We will start our tour of assembly language programming with a few words on assembly language and then give a small example to illustrate it.

C.1.1 Assembly Language

Every assembler uses **mnemonics**, that is, short words such as ADD, SUB, and MUL for machine instructions such as add, subtract, and multiply, to make them easy to remember. In addition, assemblers allow the use of **symbolic names** for constants and **labels** to indicate instruction and memory addresses. Also, most assemblers support some number of **pseudoinstructions**, which do not translate into ISA instructions, but which are commands to the assembler to guide the assembly process.

When a program in assembly language is fed to a program called an **assembler**, the assembler converts the program into a **binary program** suitable for actual execution. This program can then be run on the actual hardware. However, when beginners start to program in assembly language, they often make errors and the binary program just stops, without any clue as to what went wrong. To make life easier for beginners, it is sometimes possible to run the binary program not on the actual hardware, but on a simulator, which executes one instruction at a time and gives a detailed display of what it is doing. In this way, debugging is much easier. Programs running on a simulator run very slowly, of course, but when the goal is to learn assembly language program, rather than run a production job, this loss of speed is not important. This appendix is based on a toolkit that includes such a simulator, called the **interpreter** or **tracer**, as it interprets and traces the execution of the binary program step by step as it runs. The terms "simulator," "interpreter," and "tracer" will be used interchangeably throughout this appendix. Usually, when we are talking about just executing a program, we will speak of the "interpreter" and when we are talking about using it as a debugging tool, we will call it the "tracer," but it is the same program.

C.1.2 A Small Assembly Language Program

To make some of these abstract ideas a bit more concrete, consider the program and tracer image of Fig. C-1. An image of the tracer screen is given in Fig. C-1. Fig. C-1(a) shows a simple assembly language program for the 8088. The numbers following the exclamation marks are the source line numbers, to make it easier to refer to parts of the program. A copy of this program can be found in the accompanying material, in the directory *examples* in the source file *HlloWrld.s*. This assembly program, like all assembly programs discussed in this appendix, has the suffix *.s*, which indicates that it is an assembly language source program. The tracer screen, shown in Fig. C-1(b), contains seven windows, each containing different information about the state of the binary program being executed.

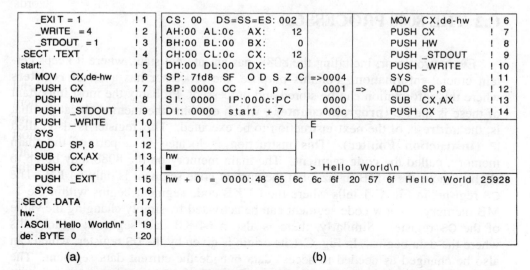

(a)	(b)

Figure C-1. (a) An assembly language program. (b) The corresponding tracer display.

Let us now briefly examine the seven windows of Fig. C-1(b). On the top are three windows, two larger ones and a smaller one in the middle. The top left window shows the contents of the processor, consisting of the current values of the segment registers, CS, DS, SS, and ES, the arithmetic registers, AH, AL, AX, and others.

The middle window in the top row contains the stack, an area of memory used for temporary values.

The right-hand window in the top row contains a fragment of the assembly language program, with the arrow showing which instruction is currently being executed. As the program runs, the current instruction changes and the arrow moves to point to it. The strength of the tracer is that by hitting the return key (labeled Enter on PC keyboards), one instruction is executed and all the windows are updated, making it possible to run the program in slow motion.

Below the left window is a window that contains the subroutine call stack, here empty. Below it are commands to the tracer itself. To the left of these two windows is a window for input, output, and error messages.

Below these windows is a window that shows a portion of memory. These windows will be discussed in more detail later, but the basic idea should be clear: the tracer shows the source program, the machine registers, and quite a bit of information about the state of the program being executed. As each instruction is executed the information is updated, allowing the user to see in great detail what the program is doing.

C.2 THE 8088 PROCESSOR

Every processor, including the 8088, has an internal state, where it keeps certain crucial information. For this purpose, the processor has a set of **registers** where this information can be stored and processed. Probably the most important of these is the PC (**program counter**), which contains the memory location, that is, the **address**, of the next instruction to be executed. This register is also called IP (**Instruction Pointer**). This instruction is located in a part of the main memory, called the **code segment**. The main memory on the 8088 may be up to slightly more the 1 MB in size, but the current code segment is only 64 KB. The CS register in Fig. C-1 tells where the 64-KB code segment begins within the 1-MB memory. A new code segment can be activated by simply changing the value of the CS register. Similarly, there is also a 64-KB data segment, which tells where the data begins. In Fig. C-1 its origin is given by the DS register, which can also be changed as needed to access data outside the current data segment. The CS and DS registers are needed because the 8088 has 16-bit registers, so they cannot directly hold the 20-bit addresses needed to reference the entire 1-MB memory. This is why the code and data segment registers were introduced.

The other registers contain data or pointers to data in the main memory. In assembly language programs, these registers can be directly accessed. Apart from these registers, the processor also contains all the necessary equipment to perform the instructions, but these parts are available to the programmer only through the instructions.

C.2.1 The Processor Cycle

The operation of the 8088 (and all other computers) consists of executing instructions, one after another. The execution of a single instruction can be broken down into the following steps:

1. Fetch the instruction from memory from the code segment using PC.

2. Increment the program counter.

3. Decode the fetched instruction.

4. Fetch the necessary data from memory and/or processor registers.

5. Perform the instruction.

6. Store the results of the instruction in memory and/or registers.

7. Go back to step 1 to start the next instruction.

The execution of an instruction is somewhat like running a very small program. In fact, some machines really do have a little program, called a **microprogram**, to execute their instructions. Microprograms are described in detail in Chap. 4.

From the point of view of an assembly programmer, the 8088 has a set of 14 registers. These registers are in some sense the scratch pad where the instructions operate and are in constant use, although the results stored in them are very volatile. Figure C-2 gives an overview of these 14 registers. It is clear that this figure and the register window of the tracer of Fig. C-1 are very similar because they represent the same information.

The 8088 registers are 16 bits wide. No two registers are completely functionally equivalent, but some of them share certain features, so they are subdivided into groups in Fig. C-2. We will now discuss the different groups.

C.2.2 The General Registers

The registers in the first group, AX, BX, CX, and DX are the **general registers**. The first register of this group, AX, is called the **accumulator register**. It is used to collect results of computations and is the target of many of the instructions. Although each of the registers can perform a host of tasks, in some instructions this AX is the implied destination, for example, in multiplication.

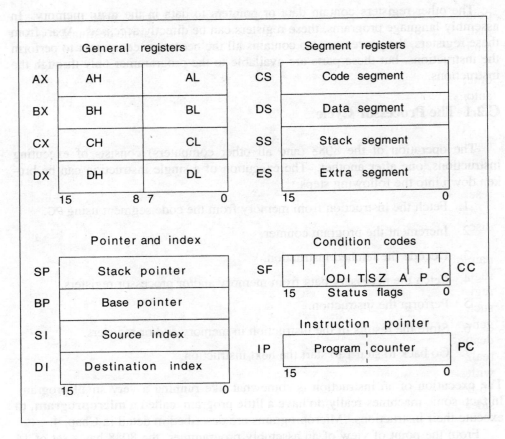

Figure C-2. The 8088 registers.

The second register of this group is BX, the **base register**. For many purposes BX can be used in the same way as AX, but it has one power AX does not have. It is possible to put a memory address in BX and then execute an instruction whose operand comes from the memory address contained in BX. In other words, BX can hold a pointer to memory, AX cannot. To show this, we compare two instructions. First we have

    MOV AX,BX

which copies to AX the contents of BX. Second we have

    MOV AX,(BX)

which copies to AX the contents of the memory word whose address is contained in BX. In the first example, BX contains the source operand; in the second one it points to the source operand. In both of these examples, note that the MOV instruction has a source and a destination operand, and that the destination is written before the source.

The next general register is CX, the **counter register**. Besides fulfilling many other tasks, this register is specifically used to contain counters for loops. It is automatically decremented in the LOOP instruction, and loops are usually terminated when CX reaches zero.

The fourth register of the general group is DX, the **data register**. It is used together with AX in double word length (i.e., 32-bit) instructions. In this case, DX contains the high-order 16 bits and AX contains the low-order 16 bits. Usually, 32-bit integers are indicated by the term **long**. The term **double** is usually reserved for 64-bit floating point values, although some people use "double" for 32-bit integers. In this tutorial, there will be no confusion because we will not discuss floating-point numbers at all.

All of these general registers can be regarded either as a 16-bit register or as a pair of 8-bit registers. In this way, the 8088 has precisely eight different 8-bit registers, which can be used in byte and character instructions. None of the other registers can be split into 8-bit halves. Some instructions use an entire register, such as AX, but other instructions use only half of a register, such as AL or AH. In general, instructions doing arithmetic use the full 16-bit registers, but instructions dealing with characters usually use the 8-bit registers. It is important, however, to realize that AL and AH are just names for both halves of AX. When AX is loaded with a new value, both AL and AH are changed to the lower and upper halves of the 16-bit number put in AX, respectively. To see how AX, AH, and AL interact, consider the instruction

```
    MOV AX,258
```

which loads the AX register with the decimal value 258. After this instruction, the byte register AH contains the value 1, and the byte register AL contains the number 2. If this instruction is followed by the byte add instruction

```
    ADDB AH,AL
```

then the byte register AH is incremented by the value in AL (2) so that it now contains 3. The effect on the register AX of this action is that its value is now 770, which is equivalent to 00000011 00000010 in binary notation or 0x03 0x02 in hexadecimal notation. The eight byte-wide registers are almost interchangeable, with the exception that AL always contains one of the operands in the MULB instruction, and is the implied destination of this operation, together with AH. DIVB also uses the AH : AL pair for the dividend. The lower byte of the counter register CL can be used to hold the number of cycles in shift and rotate instruction.

Section C.8, example 2, shows some of the properties of the general registers by means of a discussion of the program *GenReg.s*.

C.2.3 Pointer Registers

The second group of registers consists of the **pointer and index registers**. The most important register of this group is the **stack pointer**, which is denoted by SP. Stacks are important in most programming languages. The stack is a segment of memory that holds certain context information about the running program. Usually, when a procedure is called, part of the stack is reserved for holding the procedure's local variables, the address to return to when the procedure has finished, and other control information. The portion of the stack relating to a procedure is called its **stack frame** . When a called procedure calls another procedure, an additional stack frame is allocated, usually just below the current one. Additional calls allocate additional stack frames below the current ones. While not mandatory, stacks almost always grow downward, from high addresses to low addresses. Nevertheless, the lowest numerical address occupied on the stack is always called the top of the stack.

In addition to their use for holding local variables, stacks can also hold temporary results. The 8088 has an instruction, PUSH, which puts a 16-bit word on top of the stack. This instruction first decrements SP by 2, then stores its operand at the address SP is now pointing to. Similarly, POP removes a 16-bit word from the top of the stack by fetching the value on top of the stack and then incrementing SP by 2. The SP register points to the top of the stack and is modified by PUSH, POP, and CALL instructions, being decremented by PUSH, incremented by POP, and decremented by CALL.

The next register in this group is BP, the **base pointer**. It usually contains an address in the stack. Whereas SP always points to the top of the stack, BP can point to any location within the stack. In practice, a common use for BP is to point to the beginning of the current procedure's stack frame, in order to make it easy to find the procedure's local variables. Thus, BP often points to the bottom of the current stack frame (the stack frame word with the highest numerical value) and SP points to the top (the stack frame word with the lowest numerical value). The current stack frame is thus delimited by BP and SP.

In this register group, there are two index registers: SI, the **source index,** and DI, the **destination index**. These registers are often used in combination with BP to address data in the stack, or with BX to compute the addresses of data memory locations. More extensive treatment of these registers will be deferred to the section on addressing modes.

One of the most important registers, which is a group by itself, is the **instruction pointer**, which is Intel's name for the program counter (PC). This register is not addressed directly by the instructions, but contains an address in the program code segment of the memory. The processor's instruction cycle starts by fetching the instruction pointed to by PC. This register is then incremented before the rest of the instruction is executed. In this way this program counter points to the first instruction beyond the current one.

The **flag register** or **condition code register** is actually a set of single-bit registers. Some of the bits are set by arithmetic instructions and relate to the result, as follows:

Z - result is zero

S - result is negative (sign bit)

V - result generated an overflow

C - result generated a carry

A - Auxillary carry (out of bit 3)

P - parity of the result

Other bits in this register control operation of certain aspects of the processor. The I bit enables interrupts. The T bit enables tracing mode, which is used for debugging. Finally, the D bit controls the direction of the string operations. Not all 16 bits of this flag register are used; the unused ones are hardwired to zero.

There are four registers in the **segment register group**. Recall that the stack, the data and the instruction codes all reside in main memory, but usually in different parts of it. The segment registers govern these different parts of the memory, which are called **segments**. These registers are called CS for the code segment register, DS for the data segment register, SS for the stack segment register, and ES for the extra segment register. Most of the time, their values are not changed. In practice, the data segment and stack segment use the same piece of memory, with the data being at the bottom of the segment and the stack being at the top. More about these registers will be explained in Sec. C.3.1.

C.3 MEMORY AND ADDRESSING

The 8088 has a somewhat ungainly memory organization due to its combination of a 1-MB memory and 16-bit registers. With a 1-MB memory, it takes 20 bits to represent a memory address. Consequently, it is impossible to store a pointer to memory in any of the 16-bit registers. To get around this problem, memory is organized as segments, each of them 64 KB, so an address within a segment can be represented in 16 bits. We will now go into the 8088 memory architecture in more detail.

C.3.1 Memory Organization and Segments

The memory of the 8088, which consists simply of an array of addressable 8-bit bytes, is used for the storage of instructions as well as for the storage of data and for the stack. In order to separate the parts of the memory which are used for these different purposes, the 8088 uses **segments** which are chunks of the memory set apart for a certain uses. In the 8088, such a segment consists of 65,536 consecutive bytes. There are four segments:

1. The code segment.

2. The data segment.

3. The stack segment.

4. The extra segment.

The code segment contains the program instructions. The contents of the PC register are always interpreted as a memory address in the code segment. A PC value of 0 refers to the lowest address in the code segment, not absolute memory address zero. The data segment contains the initialized and uninitialized data for the program. When BX contains a pointer, it points to this data segment. The stack segment contains local variables and intermediate results pushed on the stack. Addresses in SP and BP are always in this stack segment. The extra segment is a spare segment register that can be placed anywhere in memory that it is needed.

For each of the segments, there exists a corresponding segment register: the 16-bit registers CS, DS, SS, and ES. The starting address of a segment is the 20-bit unsigned integer which is constructed by shifting the segment register by 4 bits to the left, and putting zero's in the four right-most positions. This means that segment registers always indicate multiples of 16, in a 20-bit address space. The segment register points to the base of the segment. Addresses within the segment can be constructed by converting the 16-bit segment register value to its true 20-bit address by appending four zero bits to the end and adding the offset to that. In effect, an absolute memory address is computed by multiplying the segment register by 16 and then adding the offset to it. For example, if DS is equal to 7, and BX is 12, then the address indicated by BX is $7 \times 16 + 12 = 124$. In other words, the 20-bit binary address implied by DS = 7 is 00000000000001110000. Adding the 16-bit offset 0000000000001100 (decimal 12) to the segment's origin gives the 20-bit address 00000000000001111100 (decimal 124).

For *every* memory reference, one of the segment registers is used to construct the actual memory address. If some instruction contains a direct address without reference to a register, then this address is automatically in the data segment, and DS is used to determine the base of the segment. The physical address is found by adding this bottom to the address in the instruction. The physical address in memory of the next instruction code is obtained by shifting the contents of CS by four binary places and adding the value of the program counter. In other words, the true 20-bit address implied by the 16-bit CS register is first computed, then the 16-bit PC is added to it to form a 20-bit absolute memory address.

The stack segment is made up of 2-byte words and so the stack pointer, SP, should always contain an even number. The stack is filled up from high addresses to low addresses. Thus, the PUSH instruction decreases the stack pointer by 2 and then stores the operand in the memory address computed from SS and SP. The POP command retrieves the value, and increments SP by 2. Addresses in the stack segment which are lower than those indicated by SP are considered free. Stack cleanup is thus achieved by merely increasing SP. In practice, DS and SS are always the same, so a 16-bit pointer can be used to refer to a variable in the shared data/stack segment. If DS and SS were different, a 17th bit would be needed on each pointer to distinguish pointers into the data segment from pointers into the stack segment. In retrospect, having a separate stack segment at all was probably a mistake.

If addresses in the four segment registers are chosen to be far apart, then the four segments will be disjointed, but if the available memory is restricted, it is not necessary to make them disjoint. After compilation, the size of the program code is known. It is then efficient to start the data and stack segments at the first multiple of 16 after the last instruction. This assumes that the code and data segment will never use the same physical addresses.

C.3.2 Addressing

Almost every instruction needs data, either from memory or from the registers. To name this data, the 8088 has a reasonably versatile collection of addressing modes. Many instructions contain two operands, usually called **destination** and **source**. Think, for instance, about the copy instruction, or the add instruction:

MOV AX,BX

or

ADD CX,20

In these instructions, the first operand is destination and the second is the source. (The choice of which goes first is arbitrary; the reverse choice could also have been made.) It goes without saying that, in such a case, the destination must be a **left value** that is, it must be a place where something can be stored. This means that constants can be sources, but not destinations.

In its original design, the 8088 required that at least one operand in a two-operand instruction be a register. This was done so that the difference between **word instructions,** and **byte instructions** could be seen by checking whether the addressed register was a **word register** or a **byte register**. In the first release of the processor, this idea was so strictly enforced that it was even impossible to push a constant, because neither the source nor the destination was a register in that instruction. Later versions were less strict, but the idea influenced the design anyway. In some cases, one of the operands is not mentioned. For example, in the MULB instruction, only the AX register is powerful enough to act as a destination.

There are also a number of one-operand instructions, such as increments, shifts, negates, etc. In these cases, there is no register requirement, and the difference between the word and byte operations has to be inferred from the opcodes (i.e., instruction types) only.

The 8088 supports four basic data types: 1-byte **byte,** the 2-byte **word,** the 4-byte **long**, and **binary coded decimal**, in which two decimal digits are packed into a word. The latter type is not supported by the interpreter.

A memory address always refers to a byte, but in case of a word or a long, the memory locations directly above the indicated byte are implicitly referred to as well. The word at 20 is in the memory locations 20 and 21. The long at address 24 occupies the addresses 24, 25, 26 and 27. The 8088 is **little endian,** meaning that the low-order part of the word is stored at the lower address. In the stack segment, words should be placed at even addresses. The combination AX DX, in which AX holds the low-order word, is the only provision made for longs in the processor registers.

The table of Fig. C-3 gives an overview of the 8088 addressing modes. Let us now briefly discuss them. The topmost horizontal block of the table lists the registers. They can be used as operands in nearly all instructions, both as sources and as destinations. There are eight word registers and eight byte registers.

The second horizontal block, data segment addressing, contains addressing modes for the data segment. Addresses of this type always contain a pair of parentheses, to indicate that the contents of the address instead of the value is meant. The easiest addressing mode of this type is **direct addressing**, in which the data address of the operand is in the instruction itself. Example:

    ADD CX,(20)

in which the contents of the memory word at address 20 and 21 is added to CX. Memory locations are usually represented by labels instead of by numerical values in the assembly language, and the conversion is made at assembly time. Even in CALL and JMP instructions, the destination can be stored in a memory location addressed by a label. The parentheses around the labels are essential (for the assembler we are using) because

    ADD CX,20

is also a valid instruction, only it means add the constant 20 to CX, not the contents of memory word 20. In Fig. C-3, the # symbol is used to indicate a numerical constant, label, or constant expression involving a label.

In **register indirect addressing,** the address of the operand is stored in one of the registers BX, SI, or DI. In all three cases the operand is found in the data segment. It is also possible to put a constant in front of the register, in which case the

Mode	Operand	Examples
Register addressing		
Byte register	Byte register	AH,AL,BH,BL,CH,CL,DH,DL
Word register	Word register	AX,BX,CX,DX,SP,BP,SI,DI
Data segment addressing		
Direct address	Address follows opcode	(#)
Register indirect	Address in register	(SI), (DI), (BX)
Register displacement	Address is register+displ.	#(SI), #(DI), #(BX)
Register with index	Address is BX + SI/DI	(BX)(SI), (BX)(DI)
Register index displacement	BX + SI DI + displacement	#(BX)(SI), #(BX)(DI)
Stack segment address		
Base Pointer indirect	Address in register	(BP)
Base pointer displacement	Address is BP + displ.	#(BP)
Base Pointer with index	Address is BP + SI/DI	(BP)(SI), (BP)(DI)
Base pointer index displ.	BP+SI/DI + displacement	#(BP)(SI), #(BP)(DI)
Immediate data		
Immediate byte/word	Data part of instruction	#
Implied address		
Push/pop instruction	Address indirect (SP)	PUSH, POP, PUSHF, POPF
Load/store flags	status flag register	LAHF, STC, CLC, CMC
Translate XLAT	AL, BX	XLAT
Repeated string instructions	(SI), (DI), (CX)	MOVS, CMPS, SCAS
In / out instructions	AX, AL	IN #, OUT #
Convert byte, word	AL, AX, DX	CBW,CWD

Figure C-3. Operand addressing modes. The symbol # indicates a numerical value or label.

address is found by adding the register to the constant. This type of addressing, called **register displacement**, is convenient for arrays. If, for example, SI contains 5, then the fifth character of the string at the label *FORMAT* can be loaded in AL by

    MOVB AL,FORMAT(SI).

The entire string can be scanned by incrementing or decrementing the register in each step. When word operands are used, the register should be changed by two each time.

It is also possible to put the base (i.e., lowest numerical address) of the array in the BX register, and keep the SI or DI register for counting. This is called **register with index** addressing. For example:

    PUSH (BX)(DI)

fetches the contents of the data segment location whose address is given by the sum of the BX and DI registers. This value is then pushed onto the stack. The last two types of addresses can be combined to get **register with index and displacement** addressing, as in

    NOT 20(BX)(DI)

which complements the memory word at BX + DI + 20 and BX + DI + 21.

All the indirect addressing modes in the data segment also exist for the stack segment, in which case the base pointer BP is used instead of the base register BX. In this way (BP) is the only register indirect stack addressing mode, but more involved modes also exist, up to base pointer indirect with index and displacement –1(BP)(SI). These modes are valuable for addressing local variables and function parameters, which are stored in stack addresses in subroutines. This arrangement is described further in Sec. C.4.5.

All the addresses which comply with the addressing modes discussed up to now can be used as sources and as destinations for operations. Together they are defined to be **effective addresses**. The addressing mode in the remaining two blocks cannot be used as destinations and are not referred to as effective addresses. They can only be used as sources.

The addressing mode in which the operand is a constant byte or word value in the instruction itself is called **immediate addressing**. Thus, for example,

    CMP AX,50

compares AX to the constant 50 and sets bits in the flag register, depending on the results.

Finally, some of the instructions use **implied addressing**. For these instructions, the operand or operands are implicit in the instruction itself. For example, the instruction

    PUSH AX

pushes the contents of AX onto the stack by decrementing SP and then copying AX to the location now pointed to by SP. SP is not named in the instruction itself, however; the mere fact that it is a PUSH instruction implies that SP is used. Similarly, the flag manipulation instructions implicitly use the status flags register without naming it. Several other instructions also have implicit operands.

The 8088 has special instructions for moving (MOVS), comparing (CMPS), and scanning (SCAS) strings. With these string instructions, the index registers SI and DI are automatically changed after the operation. This behavior is called **auto increment** or **auto decrement** mode. Whether SI and DI are incremented or decremented depends on the **direction flag** in the status flags register. A direction flag value of 0 increments, whereas a value of 1 decrements. The change is 1 for byte instructions and 2 for word instructions. In a way, the stack pointer is also auto increment and auto decrement: it is decremented by 2 at the start of a PUSH and incremented by 2 at the end of a POP.

C.4 THE 8088 INSTRUCTION SET

The heart of every computer is the set of instructions it can carry out. To really understand a computer, it is necessary to have a good understanding of its instruction set. In the following sections, we will discuss the most important of the 8088's instructions. Some of them are shown in Fig. C-4, where they are divided into 10 groups.

C.4.1 Move, Copy and Arithmetic

The first group of instructions is the copy and move instructions. By far, the most common is the instruction MOV, which has an explicit source and an explicit destination. If the source is a register, the destination can be an effective address. In this table a register operand is indicated by an *r* and an effective address by an *e*, so this operand combination is denoted by *e←r*. This is the first entry in the *Operands* column for MOV. Since, in the instruction syntax, the destination is the first operand and the source is the second operand, the arrow ← is used to indicate the operands. Thus, *e←r* means that a register is copied to an effective address.

For the MOV instruction, the source can also be an effective address and the destination a register, which will be denoted by *r←e*, the second entry in the *Operands* column of the instruction. The third possibility is immediate data as source, and effective address as destination, which yields *e←#*. Immediate data in the table is indicated by the sharp sign (#). Since both the word move MOV and the byte move MOVB exist, the instruction mnemonic ends with a *B* between parentheses. Thus, the line really represents six different instructions.

None of the flags in the condition code register are affected by a move instruction, so the last four columns have the entry "-". Note that the move instructions do not move data. They make copies, meaning that the source is not modified as would happen with a true move.

The second instruction in the table is XCHG, which exchanges the contents of a register with the contents of an effective address. For the exchange the table uses the symbol ↔. In this case, there exists a byte version as well as a word version. Thus, the instruction is denoted by XCHG and the *Operand* field contains *r↔e*. The next instruction is LEA, which stands for Load Effective Address. It computes the numerical value of the effective address and stores it in a register.

Next is PUSH, which pushes its operand onto the stack. The explicit operand can either be a constant (# in the *Operands* column) or an effective address (*e* in the *Operands* column). There is also an implicit operand, SP, which is not mentioned in the instruction syntax. What the instruction does is decrement SP by 2, then store the operand at the location now pointed to by SP.

Then comes POP, which removes an operand from the stack to an effective address. The next two instructions, PUSHF and POPF, also have implied operands, the push and pop the flags register, respectively. This is also the case for XLAT which loads the byte register AL from the address computed from AL + BX . This instruction allows for rapid lookup in tables of size 256 bytes.

Officially defined in the 8088, but not implemented in the interpreter (and thus not listed in Fig. C-4), are the IN and OUT instructions. These are, in fact, move instructions to and from an I/O device. The implied address is always the AX register, and the second operand in the instruction is the port number of the desired device register.

In the second block of Fig. C-4 are the addition and subtraction instructions. Each of these has the same three operand combinations as MOV: effective address to register, register to effective address, and constant to effective address. Thus, the *Operands* column of the table contains $r \leftarrow e$, $e \leftarrow r$, and $e \leftarrow \#$. In all four of these instructions, the overflow flag, O, the sign flag, S, the zero flag, Z, and the carry flag, C are all set, based on the result of the instruction. This means, for example, that O is set if the result cannot be correctly expressed in the allowed number of bits, and cleared if it can be. When the largest 16-bit number, 0x7fff (32,767 in decimal), is added to itself, the result cannot be expressed as a 16-bit signed number, so O is set to indicate the error. Similar things happen to the other status flags in these operations. If an instruction has an effect on a status flag, an asterisk (*) is shown in the corresponding column. In the instructions ADC and SBB, the carry flag at the start of the operation is used as an extra 1 (or 0), which is seen as a carry or borrow from the previous operation. This facility is especially useful for representing 32-bit or longer integers in several words. For all additions and subtractions, byte versions also exist.

The next block contains the multiplication and division instructions. Signed integer operands require the IMUL and IDIV instructions; unsigned ones use MUL and DIV. The AH : AL register combination is the implied destination in the byte version of these instructions. In the word version, the implied destination is the AX DX register combination. Even if the result of the multiplication is only a word or a byte, the DX or AH register is rewritten during the operation. The multiplication is always possible because the destination contains enough bits. The overflow and carry bits are set when the product cannot be represented in one word, or one byte. The zero and the negative flags are undefined after a multiplication.

Division also uses the register combinations DX : AX or AH : AL as the destination. The quotient goes into AX or AL and the remainder into DX or AH. All four flags, carry, overflow, zero and negative, are undefined after a divide operation. If the divisor is 0, or if the quotient does not fit into the register, the operation executes a **trap**, which stops the program unless a trap handler routine is present. Moreover, it is sensible to handle minus signs in software before and after the divide, because in the 8088 definition the sign of the remainder equals the sign of the dividend, whereas in mathematics, a remainder is always nonnegative.

The instructions for binary coded decimals, among which Ascii Adjust for Addition (AAA), and Decimal Ajust for Addition (DAA), are not implemented by the interpreter and not shown in Fig. C-4.

Mnemonic	Description	Operands	Status flags			
			O	S	Z	C
MOV(B)	Move word, byte	r ← e, e ← r, e ← #	-	-	-	-
XCHG(B)	Exchange word	r ↔ e	-	-	-	-
LEA	Load effective address	r ← #e	-	-	-	-
PUSH	Push onto stack	e, #	-	-	-	-
POP	Pop from stack	e	-	-	-	-
PUSHF	Push flags		-	-	-	-
POPF	Pop flags		-	-	-	-
XLAT	Translate AL		-	-	-	-
ADD(B)	Add word	r ← e, e ← r, e ← #	*	*	*	*
ADC(B)	Add word with carry	r ← e, e ← r, e ← #	*	*	*	*
SUB(B)	Subtract word	r ← e, e ← r, e ← #	*	*	*	*
SBB(B)	Subtract word with borrow	r ← e, e ← r, e ← #	*	*	*	*
IMUL(B)	Multiply signed	e	*	U	U	*
MUL(B)	Multiply unsigned	e	*	U	U	*
IDIV(B)	Divide signed	e	U	U	U	U
DIV(B)	Divide unsigned	e	U	U	U	U
CBW	Sign extend byte-word	-	-	-	-	-
CWD	Sign extend word-double	-	-	-	-	-
NEG(B)	Negate binary	e	*	*	*	*
NOT(B)	Logical complement	e	-	-	-	-
INC(B)	Increment destination	e	*	*	*	-
DEC(B)	Decrement destination	e	*	*	*	-
AND(B)	Logical and	e ← r, r ← e, e ← #	0	*	*	0
OR(B)	Logical or	e ← r, r ← e, e ← #	0	*	*	0
XOR(B)	Logical exclusive or	e ← r, r ← e, e ← #	0	*	*	0
SHR(B)	Logical shift right	e ← 1, e ← CL	*	*	*	*
SAR(B)	Arithmetic shift right	e ← 1, e ← CL	*	*	*	*
SAL(B) (=SHL(B))	shift left	e ← 1, e ← CL	*	*	*	*
ROL(B)	Rotate left	e ← 1, e ← CL	*	-	-	*
ROR(B)	Rotate right	e ← 1, e ← CL	*	-	-	*
RCL(B)	Rotate left with carry	e ← 1, e ← CL	*	-	-	*
RCR(B)	Rotate right with carry	e ← 1, e ← CL	*	-	-	*
TEST(B)	Test operands	e ↔ r, e ↔ #	0	*	*	0
CMP(B)	Compare operands	e ↔ r, e ↔ #	*	*	*	*
STD	Set direction flag (↓)	-	-	-	-	-
CLD	Clear direction flag (↑)	-	-	-	-	-
STC	Set carry flag	-	-	-	-	1
CLC	Clear carry flag	-	-	-	-	0
CMC	Complement carry	-	-	-	-	*
LOOP	Jump back if decremented CX ≥ 0	label	-	-	-	-
LOOPZ LOOPE	Back if Z=1 and DEC(CX)≥0	label	-	-	-	-
LOOPNZ LOOPNE	Back if Z=0 and DEC(CX)≥0	label	-	-	-	-
REP REPZ REPNZ	Repeat string instruction	string instruction	-	-	-	-
MOVS(B)	Move word string	-	-	-	-	-
LODS(B)	Load word string	-	-	-	-	-
STOS(B)	Store word string	-	-	-	-	-
SCAS(B)	Scan word string	-	*	*	*	*
CMPS(B)	Compare word string	-	*	*	*	*
JCC	Jump according conditions	label	-	-	-	-
JMP	Jump to label	e, label	-	-	-	-
CALL	Jump to subroutine	e, label	-	-	-	-
RET	Return from subroutine	-, #	-	-	-	-
SYS	System call trap	-	-	-	-	-

Figure C-4. Some of the most important 8088 instructions.

C.4.2 Logical, Bit and Shift Operations

The next block contains instructions for sign extension, negation, logical complement, increment and decrement. The sign extend operations have no explicit operands, but act on the DX : AX or the AH : AL register combinations. The single operand for the other operations of this group can be found at any effective address. The flags are affected in the expected way in case of the NEG, INC and DEC, except that the carry is not affected in the increment and decrement, which is quite unexpected and which some people regard as a design error.

The next block of instructions is the two-operand logical group, all of whose instructions behave as expected. In the shift and rotate group, all operations have an effective address as their destination, but the source is either the byte register CL or the number 1. In the shifts, all four flags are affected; in the rotates, only the carry and the overflow are affected. The carry always gets the bit that is shifted or rotated out of the high-order or low-order bit, depending on the direction of the shift or rotate. In the rotates with carry, RCR, RCL, RCRB, and RCLB, the carry together with the operand at the effective address, constitutes a 17-bit or a 9-bit circular shift register combination, which facilitates multiple word shifts and rotates.

The next block of instructions is used to manipulate the flag bits. The main reason for doing this is to prepare for conditional jumps. The double arrow ($\leftrightarrow$) is used to indicate the two operands in compare and test operations, which do not change during the operation. In the TEST operation, the logical AND of the operands is computed to set or clear the zero flag and the sign flag. The computed value itself is not stored anywhere and the operand is unmodified. In the CMP, the difference of the operands is computed and all four flags are set or cleared as a result of the comparison. The direction flag, which determines whether the SI and DI registers should be incremented or decremented in the string instructions, can be set or cleared by STD and CLD, respectively.

The 8088 also has a **parity flag** and an **auxiliary carry flag**. The parity flag gives the parity of the result (odd or even). The auxiliary flag checks whether overflow was generated in the low (4-bit) nibble of the destination. There are also instructions LAHF and SAHF, which copy the low-order byte of the flag register in AH, and vice versa. The overflow flag is in the high-order byte of the condition code register and is not copied in these instructions. These instructions and flags are mainly used for backward compatibility with the 8080 and 8085 processors.

C.4.3 Loop and Repetitive String Operations

The following block contains the instructions for looping. The LOOP instruction decrements the CX register and jumps back to the label indicated if the result is positive. The instructions LOOPZ, LOOPE, LOOPNZ and LOOPNE also test the zero flag to see whether the loop should be aborted before CX is 0.

The destination for all LOOP instructions must be within 128 bytes of the current position of the program counter because the instruction contains an 8-bit signed offset. The number of *instructions* (as opposed to bytes) that can jumped over cannot be calculated exactly because different instructions have different lengths. Usually, the first byte defines the type of an instruction, and so some instructions take only one byte in the code segment. Often, the second byte is used to define the registers and register modes of the instruction, and if the instructions contain displacements or immediate data, the instruction length can increase to four or six bytes. The average instruction length is typically about 2.5 bytes per instruction, so the LOOP cannot jump further back than about 50 instructions.

There also exist some special string instruction looping mechanisms. These are REP, REPZ, and REPNZ. Similarly, the five string instructions in the next block of Fig. C-4 all have implied addresses and all use auto increment or auto decrement mode on the index registers. In all of these instructions, the SI register points into the **data segment**, but the DI register refers to the **extra segment**, which is based on ES. Together with the REP instruction, the MOVSB can be used to move complete strings in one instruction. The length of the string is contained in the CX register. Since the MOVSB instruction does not affect the flags, it is not possible to check for an ASCII zero byte during the copy operation by means of the REPNZ, but this can be fixed by using first a REPNZ SCASB to get a sensible value in CX and later a REP MOVSB. This point will be illustrated by the string copy example in Sec. C.8. For all of these instructions, extra attention should be paid to the segment register ES, unless ES and DS have the same value. In the interpreter a small memory model is used, so that ES = DS = SS.

C.4.4 Jump and Call Instructions

The last block is about conditional and unconditional jumps, subroutine calls, and returns. The simplest operation here is the JMP instruction. It can have a label as destination or the contents of any effective address. A distinction is made between a **near jump** and a **far jump**. In a near jump, the destination is in the current code segment, which does not change during the operation. In a far jump, the CS register is changed during the jump. In the direct version with a label, the new value of the code segment register is supplied in the call after the label, in the effective address version, a long is fetched from memory, such that the low word corresponds to the destination label, and the high word to the new code segment register value.

It is, of course, not surprising, that such a distinction exists. To jump to an arbitrary address within a 20-bit address space, some provision has to be made for specifying more than 16 bits. The way it is done is by giving new values for CS and PC.

Conditional jumps

The 8088 has 15 conditional jumps, a few of which have two names (e.g., JUMP GREATER OR EQUAL is the same instruction as JUMP NOT LESS THAN). They are listed in Fig. C-5. All of these allow only jumps with a distance of up to 128 bytes from the instruction. If the destination is not within this range, a jump over jump construction has to be used. In such a construction, the jump with the opposite condition is used to jump over the next instruction. If the next instruction contains an unconditional jump to the intended destination, then the effect of these two instructions is just a longer-ranging jump of the intended type. For example, instead of

        JB FARLABEL

we have

        JNA 1f
        JMP FARLABEL
    1:

In other words, if it is not possible to do JUMP BELOW, then a JUMP NOT ABOVE to a nearby label *1* is placed, followed by an unconditional jump to *FARLABEL*. The effect is the same, at a slightly higher cost in time and space. The assembler generates these jump over jumps automatically when the destination is expected to be too distant. Doing the calculation correctly is a bit tricky. Suppose that the distance is close to the edge, but some of the intervening instructions are also conditional jumps. The outer one cannot be resolved until the sizes of the inner ones are known, and so on. To be safe, the assembler errs on the side of caution. Sometimes it generates a jump over jump when it is not strictly necessary. It only generates a direct condition jump when it is absolutely certain that the target is within range.

Most conditional jumps depend on the status flags, and are preceded by a compare or test instruction. The CMP instructions subtracts the source from the destination operand, sets the condition codes and discards the result. Neither of the operands is changed. If the result is zero or has the sign bit on (i.e., is negative), the corresponding flag bit is set. If the result cannot be expressed in the allowed number of bits, the overflow flag is set. If there is a carry out of the high-order bit, the carry flag is set. The conditional jumps can test all of these bits.

If the operands are considered to be signed, the instructions using GREATER THAN and LESS THAN should be used. If they are unsigned, the ones using ABOVE and BELOW should be used.

Instruction	Description	When to jump
JNA, JBE	Below or equal	CF=1 or ZF=1
JNB, JAE, JNC	Not below	CF=0
JE, JZ	Zero, equal	ZF=1
JNLE, JG	Greater than	SF=OF and ZF=0
JGE, JNL	Greater equal	SF=OF
JO	Overflow	OF=1
JS	Sign negative	SF=1
JCXZ	CX is zero	CX=0
JB, JNAE, JC	Below	CF=1
JNBE, JA	Above	CF=0&ZF=0
JNE, JNZ	Nonzero, nonequal	ZF=0
JL, JNGE	Less than	SF≠OF
JLE, JNG	Less or equal	SF≠OF or ZF=1
JNO	Nonoverflow	OF=0
JNS	Nonnegative	SF=0

Figure C-5. Conditional jumps.

C.4.5 Subroutine Calls

The 8088 has an instruction used to call procedures, usually known in assembly language as **subroutines**. In the same way as in the jump instructions, there exist **near call** instructions and **far call** instructions. In the interpreter, only the near call is implemented. The destination is either a label or can be found at an effective address. Parameters needed in the subroutines have to be pushed onto the stack in reverse order first, as illustrated in Fig. C-6. In assembly language, parameters are usually called **arguments**, but the terms are interchangeable. Following these pushes the CALL instruction is executed. The instruction starts by pushing the current program counter onto the stack. In this way the return address is saved. The return address is the address at which the execution of the calling routine has to be resumed when the subroutine returns.

Next the new program counter is loaded either from the label, or from the effective address. If the call is far, then the CS register is pushed before PC and both the program counter and the code segment register are either loaded from immediate data or from the effective address. This finishes the CALL instruction.

The return instruction, RET, just pops the return address from the stack, stores it in the program counter and the program continues at the instruction immediately after the CALL instruction. Sometimes the RET instruction contains a positive number as immediate data. This number is assumed to be the number of bytes of

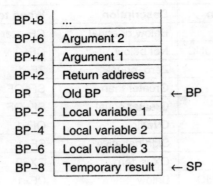

Figure C-6. An example stack.

arguments that were pushed onto the stack before the call; it is added to SP to clean up the stack. In the far variant, RETF, the code segment register is popped after the program counter, as would be expected.

Inside the subroutine, the arguments need to be accessible. Therefore the subroutine starts often by pushing the base pointer and copying the current value of SP into BP. This means that the base pointer points to its previous value. Now the return address is at BP + 2 and the first and second arguments can be found at the effective addresses BP + 4 and BP + 6, respectively. If the procedure needs local variables, then the required number of bytes can be subtracted from the stack pointer, and those variables can be addressed from the base pointer with negative offsets. In the example of Fig. C-6, there are three single-word local variables, located at BP − 2, BP − 4, and BP − 6, respectively. In this way, the entire set of current arguments and local variables is reachable through the BP register.

The stack is used in the ordinary way to save intermediate results, or for preparing arguments for the next call. Without computing the amount of stack used in the subroutine, the stack can be restored before the return by copying the base pointer into the stack pointer, popping the old BP and finally executing the RET instruction.

During a subroutine call, the values of the processor registers sometimes change. It is good practice to use some type of convention such that the calling routine need not be aware of the registers used by the called routine. The simplest way to do this is to use the same conventions for system calls and ordinary subroutines. It is assumed that the AX and DX can change in the called routine. If one of these registers contains valuable information then it is advisable for the calling routine to stack them before pushing the arguments. If the subroutine uses other registers as well, those can be pushed onto the stack immediately at the start of the subroutine, and popped before the RET instruction. In other words, a good convention is for the caller to save AX and DX if they contain anything important, and for the callee to save any other registers it overwrites.

C.4.6 System Calls and System Subroutines

In order to separate the tasks of opening, closing, reading, and writing files from assembly programming, programs are run on top of an operating system. To allow the interpreter to run on multiple platforms, a set of seven system calls and five functions are supported by the interpreter. They are listed in Fig. C-7.

Nr	Name	Arguments	Return value	Description
5	_OPEN	*name, 0/1/2	file descriptor	Open file
8	_CREAT	*name, *mode	file descriptor	Create file
3	_READ	fd, buf, nbytes	# bytes	Read nbytes in buffer buf
4	_WRITE	fd, buf, nbytes	# bytes	Write nbytes from buffer buf
6	_CLOSE	fd	0 on success	close file with fd
19	_LSEEK	fd, offset(long), 0/1/2	position (long)	Move file pointer
1	_EXIT	status		Close files Stop process
117	_GETCHAR		read character	Read character from std input
122	_PUTCHAR	char	write byte	Write character to std output
127	_PRINTF	*format, arg		Print formatted on std output
121	_SPRINTF	buf, *format, arg		Print formatted in buffer buf
125	_SSCANF	buf, *format, arg		Read arguments from buffer buf

Figure C-7. Some UNIX system calls and subroutines available in the interpreter.

These twelve routines can be activated by the standard calling sequence; first push the necessary arguments on the stack in reverse order, then push the call number, and finally execute the system trap instruction SYS without operands. The system routine finds all the necessary information on the stack, including the call number of the required system service. Return values are put either in the AX register, or in the DX : AX register combination (when the return value is a long).

It is guaranteed that all other registers will keep their values over the SYS instruction. Also, the arguments will still be on the stack after the call. Since they are not needed any more, the stack pointer should be adjusted after the call (by the caller), unless they are needed for a subsequent call.

For convenience, the names of the system calls can be defined as constants at the start of the assembler program, so that they can be called by name instead of by number. In the examples, several system calls will be discussed, so in this section only a minimum of necessary detail is supplied.

In these system calls, files are opened either by the OPEN or by the CREAT call. In both cases, the first argument is the address of the start of a string containing the file name. The second argument in the OPEN call is either 0 (if the file should be opened for reading), 1 (if it should be opened for writing), or 2 (for both). If the file should allow writes, and does not exist, it is created by the call. In the CREAT call an empty file is created, with permission set according to the second argument. Both the OPEN and the CREAT call return a small integer in the AX register, which is called the **file descriptor** and which can be used for reading, writing or closing the file. A negative return value means the call failed. At the start of the program, three files are already opened with file descriptors: 0 for standard input, 1 for standard output, and 2 for standard error output.

The READ and WRITE calls have three arguments: the file descriptor, a buffer to hold the data, and the number of bytes to transfer. Since the arguments are stacked in reverse order, we first push the number of bytes, then the address of the start of the buffer, then the file descriptor and finally the call number (READ or WRITE). This order of stacking the arguments was chosen to be the same as the standard C language calling sequence in which

    read(fd, buffer, bytes);

is implemented by pushing the parameters in the order *bytes*, *buffer*, and finally *fd*.

The CLOSE call requires just the file descriptor and returns 0 in AX if the file could be closed successfully. The EXIT call requires the exit status on the stack and does not return.

The LSEEK call changes the **read/write pointer** in an open file. The first argument is the file descriptor. Since the second argument is a long, first the high-order word, then the low word should be pushed onto the stack, even when the offset would fit into a word. The third argument indicates whether the new read/write pointer should be computed relative to the start of the file (case 0), relative to the current position (case 1), or relative to the end of the file (case 2). The return value is the new position of the pointer relative to the start of a file, and can be found as a long in the DX : AX register combination.

Now we come to the functions that are not system calls. The GETCHAR function reads one character from standard input, and puts it in AL, with AH being set to zero. On failure, the entire AX word is set to −1. The call PUTCHAR writes a byte on standard output. The return value for a successful write is the byte written; on failure it is −1.

The call PRINTF outputs formatted information. The first argument to the call is the address of a format string, which tells how to format the output. The string "%d" indicates that the next argument is an integer on the stack, which is converted to decimal notation when printed. In the same way, "%x" converts to hexadecimal and "%o" converts to octal. Furthermore, "%s" indicates that the next argument is a null-terminated string, which is passed to the call through a memory address on the stack. The number of extra arguments on the stack should match the number of conversion indications in the format string.

For example, the call

    printf("x = %d and y = %d\n", x, y);

prints the string with the numerical values of *x* and *y* substituted for the "%d" strings in the format string. Again, for compatibility with C, the order in which the arguments are pushed is "y", "x", and finally, the address of the format string. The reason for this convention is that *printf* has a variable number of parameters, and by pushing them in the reverse order the format string itself is always the last one and thus can be located. If the parameters were pushed from left to right, the format string would be deep in the stack and the *printf* procedure would not know where to find it.

In the call PRINTF, the first argument is the buffer, to receive the output string, instead of standard output. The other arguments are the same as in PRINTF. The SSCANF call is the converse of the PRINTF in the sense that the first argument is a string, which can contain integers in decimal, octal, or hexadecimal notation, and the next argument is the format string, which contains the conversion indications. The other arguments are addresses of memory words to receive the converted information. These system subroutines are very versatile and an extensive treatment of the possibilities is far beyond the scope of this appendix. In Sec. C.8, several examples show how they can be used in different situations.

C.4.7 Final Remarks on the Instruction Set

In the official definition of the 8088, there exists a **segment override** prefix, which facilitates the possibility of using effective addresses from a different segment; that is, the first memory address following the override is computed using the indicated segment register. For example, the instruction

    ESEG MOV DX,(BX)

first computes the address of BX using the extra segment, and then moves the contents to DX. However, the stack segment, in the case of addresses using SP, and the extra segment, in the case of string instructions with the DI register, cannot be overridden. The segment registers SS, DS and ES can be used in the MOV instruction, but it is impossible to move immediate data into a segment register, and those registers cannot be used in an XCHG operation. Programming with changing segment registers and overrides is quite tricky and should be avoided whenever possible. The interpreter uses fixed segment registers, so these problems do not arise here.

Floating-point instructions are available in most computers, sometimes directly in the processor, sometimes in a separate coprocessor, and sometimes only interpreted in the software through a special kind of floating point trap. Discussion of those features is outside the scope of this appendix.

C.5 THE ASSEMBLER

We have now finished our discussion of the 8088 architecture. The next topic is the software used to program the 8088 in assembly language, in particular the tools we provide for learning assembly language programming. We will first discuss the assembler, then the tracer, and then move on to some practical information for using them.

C.5.1 Introduction

Up until now, we have referred to instructions by their **mnemonics**, that is, by short easy-to-remember symbolic names like ADD and CMP. Registers were also called by symbolic names, such as AX and BP. A program written using symbolic names for instructions and registers is called an **assembly language program**. To run such a program, it is first necessary to translate it into the binary numbers that the CPU actually understands. The program that converts an assembly language program into binary numbers is the **assembler**. The output of the assembler is called an **object file**. Many programs make calls to subroutines that have been previously assembled and stored in libraries. To run these programs, the newly-assembled object file and the library subroutines it uses (also object files) must be combined into a single **executable binary file** by another program called a **linker**. Only when the linker has built the executable binary file from one or more object files is the translation fully completed. The operating system can then read the executable binary file into memory and execute it.

The first task of the assembler is to build a **symbol table**, which is used to map the names of symbolic constants and labels directly to the binary numbers that they represent. Constants that are directly defined in the program can be put in the symbol table without any processing. However, labels represent addresses whose values are not immediately obvious. To compute their values, the assembler scans the program line by line in what is called the **first pass**. During this pass, it keeps track of a **location counter** usually indicated by the symbol ".", pronounced **dot**. For every instruction and memory reservation that is found in this pass, the location counter is increased by the size of the memory necessary to contain the scanned item. Thus, if the first two instructions are of size 2 and 3 bytes, respectively, then a label on the third instruction will have numerical value 5. For example, if this code fragment is at the start of a program, the value of l will be 5.

```
MOV AX,6
MOV BX,500
L:
```

At the start of the **second pass**, the numerical value of every symbol is known. Since the numerical values of the instruction mnemonics are constants, **code generation** can now begin. One at a time, instructions are read again and their binary values are written into the object file. When the last instruction has been assembled, the object file is complete.

C.5.2 The ACK-Based Assembler, as88

This section describes the details of the assembler/linker *as88*, which is provided on the CD-ROM and website and which works with the tracer. This assembler is Amsterdam Compiler Kit (ACK) and is patterned after UNIX assemblers rather than MS-DOS or Windows assemblers. The comment symbol in this assembler is the exclamation mark (!). Anything following an exclamation mark until the end of the line is a comment and does not affect the object file produced. In the same way, empty lines are allowed, but ignored.

This assembler uses three different sections, in which the translated code and data will be stored. Those sections are related to the memory segments of the machine. The first is the **TEXT section**, for the processor instructions. Next is the **DATA section** for the initialization of the memory in the data segment, which is known at the start of the process. The last is the **BSS (Block Started by Symbol)**, section, for the reservation of memory in the data segment that is not initialized (i.e., initialized to 0). Each of these sections has its own location counter. The purpose of having sections is to allow the assembler to generate some instructions, then some data, then some instructions, then more data, and so on, and then have the linker rearrange the pieces so that all the instructions are together in the text segment and all the data words are together in the data segment. Each line of assembly code produces output for only one section, but code lines and data lines can be interleaved. At run time, the TEXT section is stored in the text segment and the data and BSS sections are stored (consecutively) in the data segment.

An instruction or data word in the assembly language program can begin with a label. A label may also appear all by itself on a line, in which case it is as though it appeared on the next instruction or data word. For example, in

```
        CMP AX,ABC
        JE L
        MOV AX,XYZ
L:
```

L is a label that refers to the instruction of data word following it. Two kinds of labels are allowed. First are the **global labels**, which are alphanumeric identifiers followed by a colon (:). These must all be unique, and cannot match any keyword or instruction mnemonic. Second, in the TEXT section only, we can have **local labels**, each of which consists of a single digit followed by a colon (:). A local label may occur multiple times. When a program contains an instruction such as

```
        JE 2f
```

this means JUMP EQUAL forward to the next local label 2. Similarly,

```
        JNE 4b
```

means JUMP NOT EQUAL backward to the closet label *4*.

The assembler allows constants to be given a symbolic name using the syntax

    identifier = expression

in which the identifier is an alphanumeric string, as in

    BLOCKSIZE = 1024

Like all identifiers in this assembly language, only the first eight characters are significant, so *BLOCKSIZE* and *BLOCKSIZZ* are the same symbol, namely, *BLOCKSIZ*. Expressions can be constructed from constants, numerical values, and operators. Labels are considered to be constants because at the end of the first pass their numerical values are known.

Numerical values can be **octal** (starting with a 0), **decimal**, or **hexadecimal** (starting with 0X or 0x). Hexadecimal numbers use the letters a–f or A–F for the values 10–15. The integer operators are +, −, *, /, and %, for addition, subtraction, multiplication, division and remainder, respectively. The logical operators are &, ^, and ~, for bitwise AND, bitwise OR and logical complement (NOT) respectively. Expressions can use the square brackets, [and] for grouping. Parentheses are *NOT* used, to avoid confusion with the addressing modes.

Labels in expressions should be handled in a sensible way. Instruction labels cannot be subtracted from data labels. The difference between comparable labels is a numerical value, but neither labels nor their differences are allowed as constants in multiplicative or logical expressions. Expressions which are allowed in constant definitions can also be used as constants in processor instructions. Some assemblers have macro facility, by which multiple instructions can be grouped together and given a name, but *as88* does not have this feature.

In every assembly language, there are some directives that influence the assembly process itself but which are not translated into binary code. They are called **pseudoinstructions**. The *as88* pseudoinstructions are listed in Fig. C-8.

The first block of pseudoinstructions determines the section in which the following lines should be processed by the assembler. Usually such a section requirement is made on a separate line and can be put anywhere in the code. For implementation reasons, the first section to be used must be the TEXT section, then the DATA section, then the BSS section. After these initial references, the sections can be used in any order. Furthermore, the first line of a section should have a global label. There are no other restrictions on the ordering of the sections.

The second block of pseudoinstructions contains the data type indications for the data segment. There are four types: .BYTE, .WORD, .LONG, and string. After an optional label and the pseudoinstruction keyword, the first three types expect a comma-separated list of constant expressions on the remainder of the line. For strings there are two keywords, ASCII, and ASCIZ, with the only difference being that the second keyword adds a zero byte to the end of the string. Both require a string between double quotes. Several escapes are allowed in string definitions. These include those of Fig. C-9. In addition to these, any specific character can

Instruction	Description
.SECT .TEXT	Assemble the following lines in the TEXT section
.SECT .DATA	Assemble the following lines in the DATA section
.SECT .BSS	Assemble the following lines in the BSS section
.BYTE	Assemble the arguments as a sequence of bytes
.WORD	Assemble the arguments as a sequence of words
.LONG	Assemble the arguments as a sequence of longs
.ASCII "str"	Store str as ascii an string without a trailing zero byte
.ASCIZ "str"	Store str as ascii an string with a trailing zero byte
.SPACE n	Advance the location counter n positions
.ALIGN n	Advance the location counter up to an n-byte boundary
.EXTERN	Identifier is an external name

Figure C-8. The *as88* pseudoinstructions.

be inserted by a backslash and an octal representation, for example, \377 (at most three digits, no 0 required here).

Escape symbol	Description
\n	New line (line feed)
\t	Tab
\\	Backslash
\b	Back space
\f	Form feed
\r	Carriage return
\"	Double quote

Figure C-9. Some of the escapes allowed by *as88*.

The SPACE pseudoinstruction simply requires the location pointer to be incremented by the number of bytes given in the arguments. This keyword is especially useful following a label in the BSS segment to reserve memory for a variable. ALIGN keyword is used to advance the location pointer to the first 2-, 4-, or 8-byte boundary in memory to facilitate the assembly of words, longs, etc. at a suitable memory location. Finally, the keyword EXTERN announces that the routine or memory location mentioned will be made available to the linker for external references. The definition need not be in the current file; it can also be somewhere else, as long as the linker can handle the reference.

Although the assembler itself is fairly general, when it is used with the tracer some small points are worth noting. The assembler accepts keywords in either uppercase or lowercase but the tracer always displays them in uppercase. Similarly, the assembler accepts both "\r" (carriage return) and "\n" (line feed) as the new line indication, but the tracer always uses the latter. Moreover, although the assembler can handle programs split over multiple files, for use with the tracer, the entire program must be in a single file with extension ".$". Inside it, include files can be requested by the command

    #include filename

In this case, the required file is also written in the combined ".$" file at the position of the request. The assembler checks whether the include file was already processed and loads only one copy. This is especially useful if several files use the same header file. In this case, only one copy is included in the combined source file. In order to include the file, the *#include* must be the first token of the line without leading white space, and the file path must be between double quotes.

If there is a single source file, say *pr.s*, then it is assumed that the project name is *pr*, and the combined file will be *pr.$*. If there is more than one source file, then the basename of the first file is taken to be the projectname, and used for the definition of the *.$* file, which is generated by the assembler by concatenating the source files. This behavior can be overridden if the command line contains a "–o projname" flag before the first source file, in which case the combined file will be *projname. $*.

Note that there are some drawbacks in using include files and more than one source. It is necessary that the names of labels, variables and constants are different for all sources. Moreover, the file which is eventually assembled to the load file is the *projname. $* file, so the line numbers mentioned by the assembler in case of errors and warnings are determined with respect to this file. For very small projects, it is sometimes simplest to put the entire program in one file and avoid *#include*.

C.5.3 Some Differences with Other 8088 Assemblers

The assembler, *as88*, is patterned after the standard UNIX assembler, and, as such, differs in some ways from the Microsoft Macro Assembler MASM and the Borland 8088 assembler TASM. Those two assemblers were designed for the MS-DOS operating system, and in places the assembler issues and the operating system issues are closely interrelated. Both MASM and TASM support all 8088 memory models allowed by MS-DOS. There is, for example, the **tiny** memory model, in which all code and data must fit in 64 KB, the **small** model, in which the code segment and the data segment each can be 64 KB, and **large** models, which contain multiple code and data segments. The difference between those models depends on the use of the segment registers. The large model allows far calls and changes in the DS register. The processor itself puts some restrictions on the segment registers, (e.g., the CS register is not allowed as destination in a MOV instruction). To make tracing simpler, the memory model used in *as88* resembles the small model, although the assembler without the tracer can handle the segment registers without additional restrictions.

These other assemblers do not have a .BSS section, and initialize memory only in the DATA sections. Usually the assembler file starts with some header information, then the DATA section, which is indicated by the keyword .data, followed by the program text after the keyword .code. The header has a keyword title to name the program, a keyword .model to indicate the memory model, and a keyword .stack to reserve memory for the stack segment. If the intended binary is a *.com* file, then the tiny model is used, all segment registers are equal, and at the head of this combined segment 256 bytes are reserved for a "Program Segment Prefix."

Instead of the .WORD .BYTE and ASCIZ directives, these assemblers have keywords DW for define word and DB for define byte. After the DB directive, a string can be defined inside a pair of double quotes. Labels for data definitions are not followed by a colon. Large chunks of memory are initialized by the DUP keyword, which is preceded by a count and followed by an initialization, for example, the statement

```
LABEL  DB 1000 DUP (0)
```

initializes 1000 bytes of memory with ASCII zero bytes at the label *LABEL*.

Furthermore, labels for subroutines are not followed by a colon, but by the keyword PROC. At the end of the subroutine, the label is repeated and followed by the keyword ENDP, so the assembler can infer the exact scope of a subroutine. Local labels are not supported.

The keywords for the instructions are identical in MASM, TASM, and *as88*. Also, the source is put after the destination in two operand instructions. However, it is common practice to use registers for the passing of arguments to functions, instead of on the stack. If, however, assembly routines are used inside C or C++ programs, then it is advisable to use the stack in order to comply with the C subroutine calling mechanism. This is not a real difference, since it is also possible to use registers instead of the stack for arguments in *as88*.

The biggest difference between the MASM, TASM and *as88* is in making system calls. The system is called in MASM and TASM by means of a system interrupt INT. The most common one is INT 21H, which is intended for the MS-DOS function calls. The call number is put in AX, so again we have passing of arguments in registers. For different devices there are different interrupt vectors, and interrupt numbers, such as INT 16H for the BIOS keyboard functions and INT 10H for the display. In order to program these functions, the programmer has to be aware of a great deal of device-dependent information. In contrast, the UNIX system calls available in *as88* are much easier to use.

C.6 THE TRACER

The tracer-debugger is meant to run on a 24 × 80 ordinary (VT100) terminal, with the ANSI standard commands for terminals. On UNIX or Linux machines, the terminal emulator in the X-window system usually meets the requirements. On Windows machines, the *ansi.sys* driver usually has to be loaded in the system initialization files as described below. In the tracer examples, we have already seen the layout of the tracer window. As can be seen in Fig. C-10, the tracer screen is subdivided into seven windows.

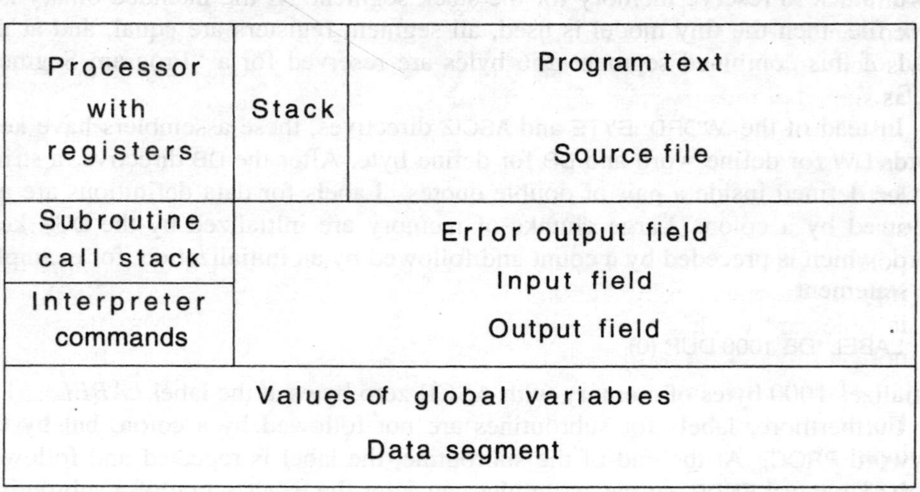

Processor with registers	Stack	Program text
		Source file
Subroutine call stack		Error output field
		Input field
Interpreter commands		Output field
Values of global variables		
Data segment		

Figure C-10. The tracer's windows.

The upper left window is the processor window, which displays the general registers in decimal notation and the other registers in hexadecimal. Since the numerical value of the program counter is not very instructive, the position in the program source code with respect to the previous global label is supplied on the line below it. Above the program counter field, five condition codes are shown. Overflow is indicated by a "v", the direction flag by ">" for increasing and by "<" for decreasing. The sign flag is either "n", for negative or "p" for zero and positive. The zero flag is "z" if set, and the carry flag set is "c". A "−" indicates a cleared flag.

The upper middle window is used for the stack, displayed in hexadecimal. The stack pointer position is indicated with an arrow =>". Return addresses of subroutines are indicated by a digit in front of the hexadecimal value. The upper right window displays a part of the source file in the neighborhood of the next instruction to be executed. The position of the program counter is also indicated by an arrow "=>".

In the window under the processor, the most recent source code subroutine call positions are displayed. Directly under it is the tracer command window, which has the previously-issued command on top and the command cursor on the bottom. Note that every command needs to be followed by a carriage return (labeled Enter on PC keyboards).

The bottom window can contain six items of global data memory. Every item starts with a position relative to some label, followed by the absolute position in the data segment. Next comes a colon, then eight bytes in hexadecimal. The next 11 positions are reserved for characters, followed by four decimal word representations. The bytes, the characters, and the words each represent the same memory contents, although for the character representation we have three extra bytes. This is convenient, because it is not clear from the start whether the data will be used as signed or unsigned integers, or as a string.

The middle right window is used for input and output. The first line is for error output of the tracer, the second line for input, and then there are some lines left for output. Error output is preceded by the letter "E", input by an "I", and standard output by a ">". In the input line there is an arrow "->" to indicate the pointer which is to be read next. If the program calls *read* or *getchar*, the next input in the tracer command line is going into the input field. Also, in this case, it is necessary to close the input line with a return. The part of the line which has not yet processed can be found after the "->" arrow.

Usually, the tracer reads both its commands and its input from standard input. However, it is also possible to prepare a file of tracer commands and a file of input lines to be read before the control is passed to the standard input. Tracer command files have extensions *.t* and input files *.i*. In the assembly language, both uppercase and lowercase characters can be used for keywords, system subroutines and pseudoinstructions. During the assembly process, a file with extension *.$* is made in which those lowercase keywords are translated into uppercase and carriage return characters are discarded. In this way, for each project, say, *pr* we can have up to six different files:

1. *pr.s* for the assembly source code.

2. *pr.$* for the composite source file.

3. *pr.88* for the load file.

4. *pr.i* for preset standard input.

5. *pr.t* for preset tracer commands.

6. *pr.#* for linking the assembly code to the load file.

The last file is used by the tracer to fill the upper right window and the program counter field in the display. Also, the tracer checks whether the load file has been created after the last modification of the program source; if not it issues a warning.

C.6.1 Tracer Commands

Figure C-11 lists the tracer commands. The most important ones are the single return command, which is at the first line of the table and which executes exactly one processor instruction, and the quit command q, at the bottom line of the table. If a number is given as a command, then that number of instructions is executed. The number k is equivalent to typing a return k times. The same effect is achieved if the number is followed by an exclamation mark, !, or an X.

The command g can be used to go to a certain line in the source file. There are three versions of this command. If it is preceded by a line number, then the tracer executes until that line is encountered. With a label $/T$, with or without $+\#$, the line number at which to stop is computed from the instruction label T. The g command, without any indication preceding it, causes the tracer to execute commands until the current line number is again encountered.

Address	Command	Example	Description
			Execute one instruction
#	, ! , X	24	Execute # instructions
/T+#	g , ! ,	/start+5g	Run until line # after label T
/T+#	b	/start+5b	Put breakpoint on line # after label T
/T+#	c	/start+5c	Remove breakpoint on line # after label T
#	g	108g	Execute program until line #
	g	g	Execute program until current line again
	b	b	Put breakpoint on current line
	c	c	Remove breakpoint on current line
	n	n	Execute program until next line
	r	r	Execute until breakpoint or end
	=	=	Run program until same subroutine level
	-	-	Run until subroutine level minus 1
	+	+	Run until subroutine level plus 1
/D+#		/buf+6	Display data segment on label+#
/D+#	d , !	/buf+6d	Display data segment on label+#
	R , CTRL L	R	Refresh windows
	q	q	Stop tracing, back to command shell

Figure C-11. The tracer commands. Each command must be followed by a carriage return (the Enter key). An empty box indicates that just a carriage return is needed. Commands with no *Address* field listed above have no address. The # symbol represents an integer offset.

The command /*label* **is different for an instruction label and a data label. For a data label, a line in the bottom window is filled or replaced with a set of data**

starting with that label. For an instruction label, it is equivalent to the g command. The label may be followed by a plus sign and a number (indicated by # in Fig. C-11), to obtain an offset from the label.

It is possible to set a **breakpoint** at an instruction. This is done with the command b, which can be optionally preceded by an instruction label, possibly with an offset. If a line with a breakpoint is encountered during execution, the tracer stops. To start again from a breakpoint, a return or run command is required. If the label and the number are omitted, then the breakpoint is set at the current line. The breakpoint can be cleared by a breakpoint clear command, c, which can be preceded by labels and numbers, like the command b. There is a run command, r, in which the tracer executes until either a breakpoint, an exit call, or the end of the commands is encountered.

The tracer also keeps track of the subroutine level at which the program is running. This is shown in the window below the processor window and can also be seen through the indication numbers in the stack window. There are three commands that are based on these levels. The − command causes the tracer to run until the subroutine level is one less than the current level. What this command does is execute instructions until the current subroutine is finished. The converse is the + command, which runs the tracer until the next subroutine level is encountered. The = command runs until the same level is encountered, and can be used to execute a subroutine at the *CALL* command. If = is used, the details of the subroutine are not shown in the tracer window. There is a related command, n, which runs until the next line in the program is encountered. This command is especially useful when issued as a *LOOP* command; execution stops exactly when the bottom of the loop is executed.

C.7 GETTING STARTED

In this section, we will explain how to use the tools. First of all, it is necessary to locate the software for your platform. We have precompiled versions for Solaris, UNIX, for Linux and for Windows. The tools are located on the CD-ROM and on the Web at *www.prenhall.com/tanenbaum*. Once there, click on the *Companion Web Site* for this book and then click on the link in the left-hand menu. Unpack the selected zip file to a directory *assembler*. This directory and its subdirectories contain all the necessary material. On the CD-ROM, the main directories are *Bigendnx*, *LtlendNx*, and *MSWindos*, and in each there is a subdirectory *assembler* which contains the material. The three top-level directories are for Big-Endian UNIX (e.g. Sun workstations), Little-Endian UNIX (e.g., Linux on PCs), and Windows systems, respectively.

After unpacking or copying, the assembler directory should contain the following subdirectories and files: *READ_ME*, *bin*, *as_src*, *trce_src*, *examples*, and *exercise*. The precompiled sources can be found in the *bin* directory but, for convenience, there is also a copy of the binaries in the *examples* directory.

To get a quick preview of how the system works, go to the *examples* directory and type the command

    t88 HlloWrld

This command corresponds to the first example in Sec. C.8.

The source code for the assembler is in the directory *as_src*. The source code files are in the language C, and the command *make* should recompile the sources. For POSIX-compliant platforms, there is a *Makefile* in the source directory which does the job. For Windows, there is a batch file *make.bat*. It may be necessary to move the executable files after compilation to a program directory, or to change the PATH variable to make the assembler *as88* and the tracer *t88* visible from the directories containing the assembly source codes. Alternatively, instead of typing *t88*, the full path name can be used.

On Windows 2000 and XP systems, it is necessary to install the *ansi.sys* terminal driver by adding the line

    device=%systemRoot%\System32\ansi.sys

to the configuration file, *config.nt*. The location of this file is as follows:

    Windows 2000: \winnt\system32\config.nt
    Windows XP: \windows\system32\config.nt

On Windows 95, 98, and ME, the driver should be added to *config.sys*. On UNIX and Linux systems, the driver is usually standard.

C.8 EXAMPLES

In Sec. C.2 through Sec. C.4, we discussed the 8088 processor, its memory, and its instructions. Then, in Sec. C.5, we studied the *as88* assembly language used in this tutorial. In Sec. C.6 we studied the tracer. Finally, in Sec. C.7, we described how to set up the toolkit. In theory, this information is sufficient to write and debug assembly programs with the tools provided. Nevertheless, it may be helpful for many readers to see some detailed examples of assembly programs and how they can be debugged with the tracer. That is the purpose of this section. All the example programs discussed in this section are available in the *examples* directory in the toolkit. The reader is encouraged to assemble and trace each one as it is discussed.

C.8.1 Hello World Example

Let us start with the example of Fig. C-12, *HlloWrld.s*. The program is listed in the left window. Since the assembler's comment symbol is the exclamation mark (!), it is used in the program window to separate the instructions from the line numbers that follow. The first three lines contain constant definitions, which connect the conventional names of two system calls and the output file to their corresponding internal representations.

The pseudoinstruction .SECT, on line 4, states that the following lines should be considered to be part of the TEXT section; that is, processor instructions. Similarly, line 17 indicates that what follows is to be considered data. Line 19 initializes a string of data consisting of 12 bytes, including one space and a line feed (\n) at the end.

Lines 5, 18 and 20 contain labels, which are indicated by a colon :. These labels represent numerical values, similar to constants. In this case, however, the assembler has to determine the numerical values. Since *start* is at the beginning of the TEXT section, its value will be 0, but the value of any subsequent labels in the TEXT section (not present in this example), would depend on how many bytes of code preceded them. Now consider line 6. This line ends with the difference of two labels, which is numerically a constant. Thus, line 6 is effectively the same as

```
MOV CX,12
```

except that it lets the assembler determine the string length, rather than making the programmer do it. The value indicated here is the amount of space in the data reserved for the string on line 19. The MOV on line 6 is the copy command, which requires the *de*−*hw* to be copied to CX.

```
_EXIT = 1              ! 1
_WRITE  = 4            ! 2
_STDOUT = 1            ! 3
.SECT .TEXT            ! 4
start:                 ! 5
    MOV    CX,de-hw    ! 6
    PUSH   CX          ! 7
    PUSH   hw          ! 8
    PUSH   _STDOUT     ! 9
    PUSH   _WRITE      !10
    SYS               !11
    ADD    SP, 8       !12
    SUB    CX,AX       !13
    PUSH   CX          !14
    PUSH   _EXIT       !15
    SYS               !16
.SECT .DATA            !17
hw:                    !18
.ASCII  "Hello World\n" !19
de: .BYTE 0            !20
```

```
CS: 00    DS=SS=ES: 002
AH:00  AL:0c   AX:       12
BH:00  BL:00   BX:        0
CH:00  CL:0c   CX:       12
DH:00  DL:00   DX:        0
SP: 7fd8  SF   O D S Z C  =>0004
BP: 0000  CC   - > p - -    0001   =>
SI: 0000  IP:000c:PC        0000
DI: 0000   start + 7        000c
```

```
                    MOV   CX,de-hw   ! 6
                    PUSH  CX         ! 7
                    PUSH  HW         ! 8
                    PUSH  _STDOUT    ! 9
                    PUSH  _WRITE     ! 10
                    SYS              ! 11
                    ADD   SP,8       ! 12
                    SUB   CX,AX      ! 13
                    PUSH  CX         ! 14
```

```
E
I
hw
■
hw + 0 = 0000: 48 65 6c 6c 6f 20 57 6f  Hello  World  25928
```

```
> Hello  World\n
```

       (a)   (b)

Figure C-12. (a) HlloWrld.s. (b) The corresponding tracer window.

Lines 7 through 11 show how system calls are made in the toolkit. These five lines are the assembly code translation of the C language function call

```
write(1, hw, 12);
```

where the first parameter is the file descriptor for standard output (1), the second is the address of the string to be printed (*hw*), and the third is the length of the string (12). Lines 7 through 9 push these parameters onto the stack in reverse order, which is the C calling sequence and the one used by the tracer. Line 10 pushes the system call number for write (4) onto the stack, and line 11 makes the actual call. While this calling sequence closely mimics how an actual assembly language program would work on a UNIX (or Linux) PC, for a different operating system, it would have to be modified slightly to use the calling conventions of that operating system. The *as88* assembler and *t88* tracer use the UNIX calling conventions even when they are running on Windows, however.

The system call on line 11 does the actual printing. Line 12 performs a cleanup on the stack, resetting the stack pointer back to the value it had before the four 2-byte words were pushed onto the stack. If the write call is successful, the number of bytes written is returned in AX. Line 13 subtracts the system call result after line 11 from the original string length in CX to see whether the call was successful, that is, to see if all the bytes were written. Thus, the exit status of the program will be 0 on success and something else on failure. Lines 14 and 15 prepare for the exit system call on line 16 by pushing the exit status and function code for the EXIT call onto the stack.

Note that in the MOV and SUB instructions the first argument is the destination and the second is the source. This is the convention used by our assembler; other assemblers may reverse the order. There is no particular reason to choose one order over the other.

Now let us try to assemble and run *HlloWrld.s*. Instructions will be given for both UNIX and Windows platforms. For Linux, Solaris, MacOS X, and other UNIX variants, the procedure should be essentially the same as for UNIX. First, start up a command prompt (shell) window. On Windows, the click sequence is usually

Start > Programs > Accessories > Command prompt

Next, change to the *examples* directory using the *cd* (Change directory) command. The argument to this command depends on where the toolkit has been placed in the file system. Then verify that the assembler and tracer binaries are in this directory, using *ls* on UNIX and *dir* on Windows systems. They are called *as88* and *t88*, respectively. On Windows systems, they have the extension *.exe*, but that need not be typed in the commands. If the assembler and tracer are not there, find them and copy them there.

Now assemble the test program using

as88 HlloWrld.s

If the assembler is present in the *examples* directory but this command gives an error message, try typing

./as88 HlloWrld.s

on UNIX systems or

.\as88 HlloWrld.s

on Windows systems.

If the assembly process completes correctly, the following messages will be displayed:

Project HlloWrld listfile HlloWrld.$
Project HlloWrld num file HlloWrld.#
Project HlloWrld loadfile HlloWrld.88

and the corresponding three files created. If there are no error messages, give the tracer command:

t88 HlloWrld

The tracer display will appear with the arrow in the upper right-hand window pointing to the

MOV CX,de-hw

instruction of line 6. Now hit the return (called Enter on PC keyboards) key. Notice that the instruction pointed to is now

PUSH CX

and the value of CX in the left-hand window is now 12. Hit return again and notice that the middle window on the top line now contains the value 000c, which is hexadecimal for 12. This window shows the stack, which now has one word containing 12. Now hit return three more times to see the PUSH instructions on lines 8, 9, and 10 being carried out. At this point, the stack will have four items and the program counter in the left-hand window will have the value 000b.

The next time return is hit, the system call is executed and the string "Hello World\n" is displayed in the lower right-hand window. Note that SP now has the value 0x7ff0. After the next return, SP is incremented by 8 and becomes 0x7ff8. After four more returns, the exit system call completes and the tracer exits.

To be certain that you understand how everything works, fetch the file *hlloWrld.s* into your favorite editor. It is better not to use a word processor. On UNIX systems, *ex*, *vi*, or *emacs* are good choices. On Windows systems, *notepad* is a simple editor, usually reachable from

Start > Programs > Accessories > Notepad

Do not use *Word* since the display will not look right and the output may be formatted incorrectly.

Modify the string on line 19 to display a different message, then save the file, assemble it, and run it with the tracer. You are now starting to do assembly language programming.

C.8.2 General Registers Example

The next example demonstrates in more detail how the registers are displayed and one of the pitfalls of multiplication on the 8088. In Fig. C-13, part of the program *genReg.s* is shown on the left. To its right are two tracer register windows, corresponding to different stages of the program's execution. Fig. C-13(b) shows the register state after line 7 has been executed. The instruction

    MOV AX,258

on line 4 loads the value 258 in AX, which results in the value 1 being loaded into AH and the value 2 being loaded into AL. Then line 5 adds AL to AH, making AH equal to 3. On line 6, the contents of the variable *times* (10) are copied into CX. On line 7, the address of the variable *muldat*, which is 2 because it is at the second byte of the DATA segment, is loaded into BX. This is the instant in time at which the dump of Fig. C-13(b) was made. Note that AH is 3, AL is 2, and AX is 770, which is to be expected, as $3 \times 256 + 2 = 770$.

```
start:                  ! 3     CS: 00   DS=SS=ES002     CS: 00   DS=SS=ES002
    MOV     AX,258      ! 4     AH:03 AL:02   AX:   770   AH:38 AL:80   AX: 14464
    ADDB    AH,AL       ! 5     BH:00 BL:02   BX:     2   BH:00 BL:02   BX:     2
    MOV     CX,(times)  ! 6     CH:00 CL:0a   CX:    10   CH:00 CL:04   CX:     4
    MOV     BX,muldat   ! 7     DH:00 DL:00   DX:     0   DH:00 DL:01   DX:     1
    MOV     AX,(BX)     ! 8     SP: 7fe0 SF   O D S Z C   SP: 7fe0 SF   O D S Z C
llp: MUL    2(BX)       ! 9     BP: 0000 CC   - > p - -   BP: 0000 CC   v > p - c
    LOOP    llp         ! 10    SI: 0000   IP:0009:PC     SI: 0000   IP:0011:PC
.SECT .DATA             ! 11    DI: 0000   start + 4      DI: 0000   start + 7
times: .WORD 10         ! 12
muldat:..WORD  625,2    ! 13
         (a)                         (b)                        (c)
```

Figure C-13. (a) Part of a program. (b) The tracer register window after line 7 has been executed. (c)

The next instruction (line 8) copies the contents of *muldat* into AX. Thus, after the return key is hit, AX will be 625.

We are now ready to enter a loop that multiplies the contents of AX by the word addressed by 2BX (i.e., *muldat + 2*), which has the value 2. The implied destination of the MUL instruction is the DX : AX long register combination. In the first iteration of the loop, the result fits in one word, so AX contains the result (1250), and DX remains 0. The contents of all the registers after 7 multiplications are shown in Fig. C-13.

Since AX started at 625, the result after those seven multiplications by 2 is 80,000. This result does not fit in AX, but the product is held in the 32-bit register formed by the concatenation of DX : AX, so DX is 1 and AX is 14,464. Numerically, this value is $1 \times 65,536 + 14,464$, which is, indeed, 80,000. Note that CX is 4 here, because the LOOP instruction decrements it every iteration. Because it started at 10, after seven executions of the MUL instruction (but only six iterations of the LOOP instruction) we have CX set to 4.

```
_EXIT      = 1                    ! 1   define the value of _EXIT
_PRINTF = 127                     ! 2   define the value of _PRINTF
.SECT .TEXT                       ! 3   start the TEXT segment
inpstart:                         ! 4   define label inpstart
        MOV  BP,SP                ! 5   save SP in BP
        PUSH vec2                 ! 6   push address of vec2
        PUSH vec1                 ! 7   push address of vec1
        MOV  CX,vec2-vec1         ! 8   CX = number of bytes in vector
        SHR  CX,1                 ! 9   CX = number of words in vector
        PUSH CX                   ! 10  push word count
        CALL vecmul               ! 11  call vecmul
        MOV  (inprod),AX          ! 12  move AX
        PUSH AX                   ! 13  push result to be printed
        PUSH pfmt                 ! 14  psuh address of format string
        PUSH _PRINTF              ! 15  push function code for PRINTF
        SYS                       ! 16  call the PRINTF function
        ADD  SP,12                ! 17  clean up the stack
        PUSH 0                    ! 18  push status code
        PUSH _EXIT                ! 19  push function code for EXIT
        SYS                       ! 20  call the EXIT function

vecmul:                           ! 21  start of vecmul(count, vec1, vec2)
        PUSH BP                   ! 22  save BP on stack
        MOV  BP,SP                ! 23  copy SP into BP to access arguments
        MOV  CX,4(BP)             ! 24  put count in CX to control loop
        MOV  SI,6(BP)             ! 25  SI = vec1
        MOV  DI,8(BP)             ! 26  DI = vec2
        PUSH 0                    ! 27  push 0 onto stack
1:      LODS                      ! 28  move (SI) to AX
        MUL  (DI)                 ! 29  multiply AX by (DI)
        ADD  -2(BP),AX            ! 30  Add AX to accumulated value in memory
        ADD  DI,2                 ! 31  Increment DI to point to next element
        LOOP 1b                   ! 32  if CX > 0, go back to label 1b
        POP  AX                   ! 33  Pop top of stack to AX
        POP  BP                   ! 34  Restore BP
        RET                       ! 35  Return from subroutine

.SECT .DATA                       ! 36  start DATA segment
pfmt: .ASCIZ "Inner product is: %d\n"  ! 37  define string
.ALIGN 2                          ! 38  force address even
vec1:.WORD 3,4,7,11,3             ! 39  vector 1
vec2:.WORD 2,6,3,1,0              ! 40  vector 2
.SECT .BSS                        ! 41  start BSS segment
inprod:    .SPACE 2               ! 42  allocate space for inprod
```

Figure C-14. The program *vecprod.s*.

In the next multiplication, trouble crops up. Multiplication involves AX but not DX, so the MUL multiples AX (14464) by 2 to get 28,928. This results in AX being set to 28,928 and DX being set to 0, which is numerically incorrect.

C.8.3 Call Command and Pointer Registers

The next example, *vecprod.s* is a small program that computes the inner product of two vectors, *vec1* and *vec2*. It is listed in Fig. C-14.

The first part of the program prepares to call *vecmul* by saving SP in BP and then pushing the addresses of *vec2* and *vec1* onto the stack so that *vecmul* will have access to them. Then the length of the vector in bytes is loaded in CX on line 8. By shifting this result right one bit, on line 9, CX now contains the number of words in the vector, which is pushed onto the stack on line 10. The call to *vecmul* is made on line 11.

Once again, it is worth mentioning that the arguments of subroutines are, by convention, pushed onto the stack in reverse order to be compatible with the C calling convention. In this way, *vecmul* can also be called from C using

vecmul(count, vec1, vec2)

During the CALL instruction, the return address is pushed onto the stack. If the program is traced, then this address turns out to be 0x0011.

The first instruction in the subroutine is a PUSH of the base pointer, BP, on line 22. BP is saved because we will need this register to address the arguments and the local variables of the subroutine. Next, the stack pointer is copied to the BP register on line 23, so that the new value of the base pointer is pointing to the old value.

Now everything is ready for loading the arguments into registers and for reserving space for a local variable. In the next three lines, each of the arguments is fetched from the stack and put in a register. Recall that the stack is word oriented, so stack addresses should be even. The return address is next to the old base pointer so it is addressed by 2(BP). The *count* argument is next and addressed by 4(BP). It is loaded into CX on line 24. In lines 25 and 26, SI is loaded with *vec1* and DI is loaded with *vec2*. This subroutine needs one local variable with initial value 0 to save the intermediate result. To this end, the value 0 is pushed on line 27.

The state of the processor just before the loop is entered on line 28 for the first time is shown in Fig. C-15. The narrow window in the middle of the top row (to the right of the registers) shows the stack. At the bottom of the stack is the address of *vec2* (0x0022), with *vec1* (0x0018) above it and the third argument, the number of items in each vector (0x0005) above that. Next comes the return address (0x0011). The number 1 to the left of this address indicates it is a return address one level from the main program. In the window below the registers, the same number 1 is shown, this time giving its symbolic address. Above the return address in the stack is the old value of BP (0x7fc0) and then the zero pushed on line 27. The arrow pointing to this value indicates where SP points. The window to the right of the stack shows a fragment of the program text, with the arrow indicating the next instruction to be executed.

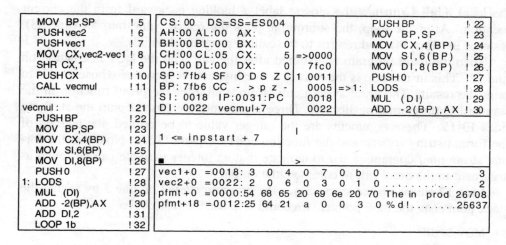

Figure C-15. Execution of *vecprod.s* when it reaches line 28 for the first time.

Now let us examine the loop starting at line 28. The instruction LODS loads a memory word indirectly through the register SI from the data segment into AX. Because the direction flag is set, LODS is in auto-increment mode, so after the instruction SI will point to the next entry of *vec1*.

To see this effect graphically, start the tracer with the command

   t88   vecprod

When the tracer window appears, type the command

   /vecmul+7b

followed by a return to put a breakpoint at the line containing the LODS. From now on, we will not mention that all commands must be followed by the return key. Then give the command

   g

to have the tracer execute commands until the breakpoint is encountered. It will stop at the line containing the LODS.

On line 29, the value of AX is multiplied to the source operand. The memory word for the MUL instruction is fetched from the data segment through the DI in register indirect mode. The implied destination of MUL is the DX : AX long register combination which is not mentioned in the instruction but which is implied by it.

On line 30, the result is added to the local variable at the stack address –2(BP). Because MUL does not autoincrement its operand, that must be done explicitly on line 31. Afterward, DI points to the next entry of *vec2*.

The LOOP instruction finishes this step. Register CX is decremented, and, if it is still positive, the program jumps back to the local label *1* on line 28. The use of the local label *1b* means the closest label *1* looking backward from the current location. After the loop, the subroutine pops the return value into AX (line 33), restores BP (line 34), and returns to the calling program (line 35).

Then the main program is resumed after the call with the MOV instruction on line 12. This instruction is the start of a five-instruction sequence whose goal is to print the result. The printf system call is modeled after the *printf* function in the standard C programming library. Three arguments are pushed onto the stack on lines 13-15. These arguments are the integer value to be printed, the address of the format string (*pfmt*), and the function code for printf (127). Note that the format string *pfmt* contains a %*d* to indicate that an integer variable can be found as argument to the printf call to complete the output.

Line 17 cleans up the stack. Since the program started on line 5 by saving the stack pointer in the base pointer, we could also use the instruction

```
MOV SP,BP
```

for a stack cleanup. The advantage of this solution is that the programmer does not need to keep the stack balanced in the process. For the main program this is not a big issue, but in subroutines this approach is an easy way to throw away garbage such as obsolete local variables.

The subroutine *vecmul* can be included in other programs. If the source file *vecprod.s* is put on the command line behind another assembler source file, the subroutine is available for multiplication two vectors of a fixed length. It is advisable to remove the constant definitions _EXIT and _PRINTF first, in order to avoid their being defined twice. If the header file *syscalnr.h* is included somewhere, then there is no need to define the system call constants anywhere else.

C.8.4 Debugging an Array Print Program

In the previous examples, the programs examined were simple but correct. Now we will show how the tracer can help debug incorrect programs. The next program is supposed to print the integer array, which is supplied after the label *vec1*. However, the initial version contains three errors. The assembler and tracer will be used to correct those errors, but first we will discuss the code.

Because every program needs system calls, and thus must define constants by which to identify the call numbers, we have put the constant definitions for those numbers in a separate header file *../syscalnr.h*, which is included on line 1 of the code. This file also defines the constants for the file descriptors

```
STDIN = 0
STDOUT = 1
STDERR = 2
```

which are opened at the start of the process, and header labels for the text and the data segments. It is sensible to include it at the head of all assembly source files, as these are much used definitions. If a source is distributed over more than one file, the assembler includes only the first copy of this header file, to avoid defining the constants more than once.

The program *arrayprt* is shown in Fig. C-16. The comments have been omitted here, as the instructions should be well known by now. In this way, a two-column format can be used. Line 4 puts the address of the empty stack in the base pointer register to allow the stack cleanup can be made on line 10 by copying the base pointer to the stack pointer, as described in the previous example. We also have seen the computation and pushing of the stack arguments before the call on lines 5 through 9 in the previous example. Lines 22 to 25 load the registers in the subroutine.

```
#include "../syscalnr.h"       ! 1          .SECT .TEXT              ! 20
                                            vecprint:                ! 21
.SECT .TEXT                     ! 2              PUSH BP              ! 22
vecpstrt:                       ! 3              MOV  BP,SP           ! 23
    MOV  BP,SP                  ! 4              MOV  CX,4(BP)        ! 24
    PUSH vec1                   ! 5              MOV  BX,6(BP)        ! 25
    MOV  CX,frmatstr-vec1       ! 6              MOV  SI,0            ! 26
    SHR  CX                     ! 7              PUSH frmatkop        ! 27
    PUSH CX                     ! 8              PUSH frmatstr        ! 28
    CALL vecprint               ! 9              PUSH _PRINTF         ! 29
    MOV  SP,BP                  ! 10             SYS                  ! 30
    PUSH 0                      ! 11             MOV  -4(BP),frmatint ! 31
    PUSH _EXIT                  ! 12      1:      MOV  DI,(BX)(SI)     ! 32
    SYS                         ! 13             MOV  -2(BP),DI       ! 33
                                                 SYS                  ! 34
.SECT .DATA                     ! 14             INC  SI              ! 35
vec1:  .WORD 3,4,7,11,3         ! 15             LOOP 1b              ! 36
frmatstr: .ASCIZ "%s"           ! 16             PUSH '\n'            ! 37
                                                 PUSH _PUTCHAR        ! 38
frmatkop:                       ! 17             SYS                  ! 39
.ASCIZ "The array contains "    ! 18             MOV  SP,BP           ! 40
frmatint: .ASCIZ " %d"          ! 19             RET                  ! 41
```

Figure C-16. The program *arrayprt* before debugging.

Lines 27 to 30 show how a string can be printed, and 31 to 34 show the printf system call for an integer value. Note that the address of the string is pushed on line 27, while on line 33 the value of the integer is moved onto the stack. In both cases the address of the format string is the first argument of PRINTF. Lines 37 to 39 show how a single character can be printedusing the putchar system call.

Now let us try assembling and running the program. When the command

    as88 arrayprt.s

is typed, we get an operand error on line 28 of the file *arrayprt.$* This file is generated by the assembler by combining the included files with the source file to get a composite file that is the actual assembler input. To see where line 28 really is, we have to examine line 28 of *arrayprt.$*. We cannot look at *arrayprt.s* to get the line number because the two files do not match on account of the header being included line by line in *arrayprt.$* Line 28 in *arrayprt.$* corresponds to line 7 in *arrayprt.s* because the included header file, *syscalnr.h,* contains 21 lines.

One easy way to find line 28 of *arrayprt.$* on UNIX systems is to type the command

 head −28 arrayprt.$

which displays the first 28 lines of the combined file. The line at the bottom of the listing is the one in error. In this way (or by using an editor and going to line 28) we see that the error is on line 7, which contains the SHR instruction. Comparing this code with the instruction table in Fig. C-4 shows the problem: the shift count has been omitted. The corrected line 7 should read

 SHR CX,1

It is very important to note that the error must be corrected in the original source file, *arrayprt.s*, and *not* in the combined source, *arrayprt.$*, as the latter is automatically regenerated every time the assembler is called.

The next attempt to assemble the source code file should succeed. Then the tracer can be started by the command:

 t88 arrayprt

During the tracing process, we can see that the output is not consistent with the vector in the data segment. The vector contains: 3, 4, 7, 11, 3, but the values displayed start with: 3, 1024, ... Clearly, something is wrong.

To find the error, the tracer can be run again, step by step, examining the state of the machine just before the incorrect value is printed. The value to be printed is stored in memory on lines 32 and 33. Since the wrong value is being printed, this is a good place to see what is wrong. The second time through the loop, we see that SI is an odd number, when clearly it should be an even number, as it is indexing through words, not bytes. The problem is on line 35. It increments SI by 1; it should increment it by 2. To fix the bug, this line should be changed to

 ADD SI,2

When this correction is made, the printed list of numbers is correct.

However, there is one more error waiting for us. When *vecprint* is finished and returns, the tracer complains about the stack pointer. The obvious thing to check for now is whether the value pushed onto the stack when *vecprint* is called is the value on top of the stack when the RET on line 41 is executed. It is not. The solution is to replace line 40 with two lines:

 ADD SP,10
 POP BP

the first instruction removes the 5 words pushed onto the stack during *vecprint*, thus exposing the value of BP saved on line 22. By popping this value to BP, we restore BP to its precall value and expose the correct return address. Now the program terminates correctly. Debugging assembly code is definitely more of an art than a science, but the tracer makes it much easier than running on the bare metal.

```
.SECT .TEXT
stcstart:                       ! 1
    PUSH mesg1                  ! 2
    PUSH mesg2                  ! 3
    CALL strngcpy               ! 4
    ADD  SP,4                   ! 5
    PUSH 0                      ! 6
    PUSH 1                      ! 7
    SYS                         ! 8
strngcpy:                       ! 9
    PUSH CX                     ! 10
    PUSH SI                     ! 11
    PUSH DI                     ! 12
    PUSH BP                     ! 13
    MOV  BP,SP                  ! 14
    MOV  AX,0                   ! 15
    MOV  DI,10(BP)              ! 16
    MOV  CX,-1                  ! 17
    REPNZ SCASB                 ! 18
    NEG  CX                     ! 19
    DEC  CX                     ! 20
    MOV  SI,10(BP)              ! 21
    MOV  DI,12(BP)              ! 22
    PUSH DI                     ! 23
    REP  MOVSB                  ! 24
    CALL stringpr               ! 25
    MOV  SP,BP                  ! 26
    POP  BP                     ! 27
    POP  DI                     ! 28
    POP  SI                     ! 29
    POP  CX                     ! 30
    RET                         ! 31
.SECT .DATA                     ! 32
mesg1: .ASCIZ "Have a look\n"   ! 33
mesg2: .ASCIZ "qrst\n"          ! 34
.SECT .BSS
            (a)
```

```
#include "../syscalnr.h"        ! 1

start: MOV DI,str               ! 2
    PUSH AX                     ! 3
    MOV BP,SP                   ! 4
    PUSH _PUTCHAR               ! 5
    MOVB AL,'\n'                ! 6
    MOV CX,-1                   ! 7
    REPNZ SCASB                 ! 8
    NEG CX                      ! 9
    STD                         ! 10
    DEC CX                      ! 11
    SUB DI,2                    ! 12
    MOV SI,DI                   ! 13
1: LODSB                        ! 14
    MOV (BP),AX                 ! 15
    SYS                         ! 16
    LOOP 1b                     ! 17
    MOVB (BP),'\n'              ! 18
    SYS                         ! 19
    PUSH 0                      ! 20
    PUSH _EXIT                  ! 21
    SYS                         ! 22
.SECT .DATA                     ! 23
str: .ASCIZ "reverse\n"         ! 24
            (b)
```

Figure C-17. (a) Copy a string (*strngcpy.s*). (b) Print a string backward (*reverspr.s*).

C.8.5 String Manipulation and String Instructions

The main purpose of this section is to show how to handle repeatable string instructions. In Fig. C-17, there are two simple string manipulation programs, *strngcpy.s* and *reverspr.s*, both present in the *examples* directory. The one in Fig. C-17(a) is a subroutine for copying a string. It calls a subroutine, *stringpr*, which can also be found in a separate file *stringpr.s*. It is not listed in this appendix. In order to assemble programs containing subroutines in separate source files, just list all source files in the *as88* command, starting with the source file for the main program, which determines the names of the executable and the auxiliary files. For example, for the program of Fig. C-17(a) use

    as88 strngcpy.s stringpr.s

The program of Fig. C-17(b) outputs strings in reverse order. We will now look at them in turn.

To demonstrate that the line numbers are really just comments, in Fig. C-17(a) we have numbered the lines starting with the first label, omitting what comes before them. The main program, on lines 2 through 8, first calls *strngcpy* with two arguments, the source string, *mesg2*, and the destination string, *mesg1*, in order to copy the source to the destination.

Now let us look at *strngcpy*, starting on line 9. It expects that the addresses of the destination buffer and the string source have been pushed onto the stack just before the subroutine is called. On lines 10 to 13, the registers used are saved by pushing them onto the stack so that they can be restored later on lines 27 to 30. On line 14, we copy SP to BP in the usual way. Now BP can be used to load the arguments. Again, on line 26, we clean the stack by copying BP to SP.

The heart of the subroutine is the instruction REP MOVSB, on line 24. The instruction MOVSB moves the byte pointed to by SI to the memory address pointed to by DI. Both SI and DI are then incremented by 1. The REP creates a loop in which this instruction is repeated, decrementing CX by 1 for each byte moved. The loop is terminated when CX reaches 0.

Before we can run the REP MOVSB loop, however, we have to set up the registers, which is done in lines 15 through 22. The source index, SI, is copied from the argument on the stack on line 21; the destination index, DI, is set up on line 22. Obtaining the value of CX is more involved. Note that the end of a string is indicated by a zero byte. The MOVSB instruction does not affect the zero flag, but the instruction SCASB (scan byte string) does. It compares the value pointed to by DI with the value in AL, and it increments DI on the fly. Moreover, it is repeatable like MOVSB. So, on line 15 AX and hence AL is cleared, on line 16 the pointer for DI is fetched from the stack, and CX is initialized to −1 on line 17. On line 18, we have the REPNZ SCASB, which does the comparison in loop context, and sets the zero flag on equality. At each step of the loop, CX is decremented, and the loop stops when the zero flag is set, because the REPNZ checks both the zero flag and

CX. The number of steps for the MOVSB loop is now computed as the difference of the current value of CX and the previous −1 on lines 19 and 20.

It is cumbersome that there are two repeatable instructions necessary, but this is the price for the design choice that move instructions never affect the condition codes. During the loops, the index registers have to be incremented, and to this end it is necessary that the direction flag is cleared.

Lines 23 and 25 print the copied string by means of a subroutine, *stringpr*, which is in the *examples* directory. It is straightforward and will not be discussed here.

In the reverse print program shown in Fig. C-17(b), the first line includes the usual system call numbers. On line 3, a dummy value is pushed onto the stack, and on line 4, the base pointer, BP, is made to point to the current top of stack. The program is going to print ASCII characters one by one, thus the numerical value _PUTCHAR is pushed onto the stack. Note that BP points to the character to be printed when a SYS call is made.

Line 2, 6 and 7 prepare the registers DI, AL and CX for the repeatable SCASB instruction. The count register and the destination index are loaded in a similar way as in the string copy routine, but the value of AL is the new line character, instead of the value 0. In this way, the SCASB instruction will compare the characters values of the string *str* to \n instead of to 0, and set the zero flag whenever it is found.

The REP SCASB increments the DI register, so, after a hit, the destination index points at the zero character following the new line. On line 12, DI is decremented by two to have it point to the last letter of the word.

If the string is scanned in reverse order and printed character by character, we have obtained our goal, so on line 10 the direction flag is set to reverse the adjustment of the index registers in the string instructions. Now the LODSB on line 14 copies the character in AL, and on line 15 this character is put just next to the _PUTCHAR on the stack, so the SYS instruction prints it.

The instructions on lines 18 and 19 print an additional new line and the program closes with an _EXIT call in the usual way.

The current version of the program contains a bug. It can be found if the program is traced step by step.

The command /str will put the string *str* in the tracer data field. Since the numerical value of the data address is also given, we can find out how the index registers run through the data with respect to the position of the string.

The bug, however, is encountered only after hitting the return many times. By using the tracer commands we can get to the problem faster. Start the tracer and give the command *13* to put us in the middle of the loop. If we now give the command *b* we set a breakpoint on this line 15. If we give two new lines, then we see that the final letter **e** is printed in the output field. The *r* command will keep the tracer running until either a breakpoint or the end of the process is encountered. In this way, we can run through the letters by giving the *r* command repeatedly until we are close to the problem. From this point, we can run the tracer at one step at a time until we see what happens at the critical instructions.

We can also put the breakpoint at a specific line, but then we must keep in mind, that the file *../syscalnr* is included, which causes the line numbers to be offset by 20. Consequently, the breakpoint on line 16 can be set by the command *36b*. This is not an elegant solution, so it is much better to use the global label *start* on line 2 before the instruction and give the command */start+14b*, which puts the breakpoint in the same place without having to keep track of the size of the included file.

C.8.6 Dispatch Tables

In several programming languages, there exist *case* or *switch* statements to select a jump from several alternatives according to some numerical value of a variable. Sometimes, such multiway branches are also needed in assembly language programs, too. Think, for instance, of a set of system call subroutines combined in a single SYS trap routine. The program *jumptbl.s*, shown in Fig. C-18. shows how such a multi-branch switch can be programmed in 8088 assembler.

The program starts by printing the string whose label is *strt*, inviting the user to type an octal digit (lines 4 through 7). Then a character is read from standard input (lines 8 and 9). If the value is AX is less than 5, the program interprets it as an end of file marker and jumps to the label *8* on line 22 to exit with a status code of 0.

If end of file has not been encountered, the incoming character, in AL, is inspected. Any character less than the digit 0 is considered to be white space and is ignored by the jump on line 13, which retrieves another character. Any character over digit 9 is considered to be incorrect input. On line 16, it is mapped onto the ASCII colon character, which is the successor of digit 9 in the ASCII character sequence.

Thus, on line 17 we have a value in AX between digit 0 and the colon. This value is copied into BX. On line 18, the AND instruction masks off all but the low-order four bits, which leaves the number between 0 and 10 (due to the fact that ASCII 0 is 0x30). Since we are going to index into a table of words, rather than bytes, the value in BX is multiplied by two using the left shift on line 19.

On line 20, we have a call instruction. The effective address is found by adding the value of BX to the numerical value of label *tbl*, and the contents of this composite address are loaded into the program counter, PC.

This program chooses one out of ten subroutines according to a character which is fetched from standard input. Each of those subroutines pushes the address of some message onto the stack and then jumps to a _PRINTF system subroutine call which is shared by all of them.

```
#include "../syscalnr.h"  ! 1          rout0: MOV AX,mes0     ! 25
.SECT .TEXT               ! 2                 JMP 9f          ! 26
jumpstrt:                 ! 3          rout1: MOV AX,mes1     ! 27
     PUSH strt            ! 4                 JMP 9f          ! 28
     MOV BP,SP            ! 5          rout2: MOV AX,mes2     ! 29
     PUSH _PRINTF         ! 6                 JMP 9f          ! 30
     SYS                  ! 7          rout3: MOV AX,mes3     ! 31
     PUSH _GETCHAR        ! 8                 JMP 9f          ! 32
1:   SYS                  ! 9          rout4: MOV AX,mes4     ! 33
     CMP AX,5             ! 10                JMP 9f          ! 34
     JL  8f               ! 11         rout5: MOV AX,mes5     ! 35
     CMPB AL,'0'          ! 12                JMP 9f          ! 36
     JL  1b               ! 13         rout6: MOV AX,mes6     ! 37
     CMPB AL,'9'          ! 14                JMP 9f          ! 38
     JLE 2f               ! 15         rout7: MOV AX,mes7     ! 39
     MOVB AL,'9'+1        ! 16                JMP 9f          ! 40
2:   MOV BX,AX            ! 17         rout8: MOV AX,mes8     ! 41
     AND BX,0Xf           ! 18                JMP 9f          ! 42
     SAL BX,1             ! 19         erout: MOV AX,emes     ! 43
     CALL tbl(BX)         ! 20         9:     PUSH AX         ! 44
     JMP 1b               ! 21                PUSH _PRINTF    ! 45
8:   PUSH 0               ! 22                SYS             ! 46
     PUSH _EXIT           ! 23                ADD SP,4        ! 47
     SYS                  ! 24                RET             ! 48
```

```
.SECT .DATA                                                 ! 49
tbl: .WORD rout0,rout1,rout2,rout3,rout4,rout5,rout6,rout7,rout8,rout8,erout  ! 50
mes0: .ASCIZ "This is a zero.\n"                             ! 51
mes1: .ASCIZ "How about a one.\n"                            ! 52
mes2: .ASCIZ "You asked for a two.\n"                        ! 53
mes3: .ASCIZ "The digit was a three.\n"                      ! 54
mes4: .ASCIZ "You typed a four.\n"                           ! 55
mes5: .ASCIZ "You preferred a five.\n"                       ! 56
mes6: .ASCIZ "A six was encountered.\n"                      ! 57
mes7: .ASCIZ "This is number seven.\n"                       ! 58
mes8: .ASCIZ "This digit is not accepted as an octal.\n"     ! 59
emes: .ASCIZ "This is not a digit. Try again.\n"             ! 60
strt:  .ASCIZ "Type an octal digit with a return. Stop on end of file.\n"  ! 61
```

Figure C-18. A program demonstrating a multiway branch using a dispatch table.

In order to understand what is happening, we need to be aware that the JMP and CALL instructions load some text segment address in PC. Such an address is just a binary number, and during the assembly process all addresses are replaced by their binary values. Those binary values can be used to initialize an array in the data segment, and this is done in line 50. Thus, the array starting at *tbl* contains the starting addresses of *rout* 0, *rout* 1, *rout* 2, and so on, two bytes per address. The need for 2-byte addresses explains why we needed the 1-bit shift on line 19. A table of this type is often called a **dispatch table**.

How those routines work can be seen in the *erout* routine on lines 43 through 48. This routine handles the case of an out-of-range digit. First, the address of the message (in AX) is pushed onto the stack on line 43. Then the number of the _PRINTF system call is pushed onto the stack. After that, the system call is made, the stack is cleaned up, and the routine returns. The other nine routines, *rout0* through *rout8*, each load the addresses of their private messages in AX, and then jump to the second line of *erout* to output the message and finish the subroutine.

In order to get accustomed to the dispatch tables, the program should be traced with several different input characters. As an exercise, the program can be changed in such a way that all characters generate a sensible action. For example, all characters other than the octal digits should give an error message.

C.8.7 Buffered and Random File Access

The program *InFilBuf.s*, shown in Fig. C-19, demonstrates random I/O on files. A file is assumed to consist of some number of lines, with different lines potentially having different lengths. The program first reads the file and builds a table in which entry *n* is the file position at which line *n* begins. Afterward, a line can be requested, its position looked up in the table, and the line read in by means of lseek and read system calls. The file name is given as the first input line on standard input. This program contains several fairly independent chunks of code, which can be modified for other purposes.

The first five lines simply define the system call numbers and the buffer size, and set the base pointer at the top of the stack, as usual. Lines 6 through 13 read the file name from standard input, and store it as a string at label *linein*. If the file name is not properly closed with a new line, then an error message is generated, and the process exits with a nonzero status. This is done in lines 38 through 45. Note that the address of the file name is pushed on line 39, and the address of an error message is pushed on line 40. If we examine the error message itself, (on line 113) then we have a *%s* string request in the _PRINTF format. The contents of the string *linein* are inserted here.

If the file name can be copied without problems, the file is opened on lines 14 to 20. If the open call fails, then the return value is negative and a jump is made to the label *9* on line 28 to print an error message. If the system call succeeds, then the return value is a file descriptor, which is stored in the variable *fildes*. This file descriptor is needed in the subsequent read and lseek calls.

Next, we read the file in blocks of 512 bytes, each of which is stored in the buffer *buf*. The buffer allocated is two bytes larger than the necessary 512 bytes, just to demonstrate how a symbolic constant and a integer can be mixed in an expression (on line 123). In the same way, on line 21 SI is loaded with the address of the second element of the *linh* array, which leaves a machine word containing 0

```
#include "../syscalnr.h" ! 1      PUSH _EXIT        ! 43      PUSH buf          ! 85
bufsiz = 512             ! 2      PUSH _EXIT        ! 44      PUSH (fildes)     ! 86
.SECT .TEXT              ! 3      SYS               ! 45      PUSH _READ        ! 87
infbufst:                ! 4  3:  CALL getnum       ! 46      SYS               ! 88
    MOV BP,SP            ! 5      CMP AX,0          ! 47      ADD SP,8          ! 89
    MOV DI,linein        ! 6      JLE 8f            ! 48      MOV CX,AX         ! 90
    PUSH _GETCHAR        ! 7      MOV BX,(curlin)   ! 49      ADD BX,CX         ! 91
1:  SYS                  ! 8      CMP BX,0          ! 50      MOV DI,buf        ! 92
    CMPB AL,'\n'         ! 9      JLE 7f            ! 51      RET               ! 93
    JL 9f                ! 10     CMP BX,(count)    ! 52
    JE 1f                ! 11     JG 7f             ! 53   getnum:              ! 94
    STOSB                ! 12     SHL BX,1          ! 54      MOV DI,linein     ! 95
    JMP 1b               ! 13     MOV AX,linh-2(BX) ! 55      PUSH _GETCHAR     ! 96
1:  PUSH 0               ! 14     MOV CX,linh(BX)   ! 56   1: SYS               ! 97
    PUSH linein          ! 15     PUSH 0            ! 57      CMPB AL,'\n'      ! 98
    PUSH _OPEN           ! 16     PUSH 0            ! 58      JL 9b             ! 99
    SYS                  ! 17     PUSH AX           ! 59      JE 1f             !100
    CMP AX,0             ! 18     PUSH (fildes)     ! 60      STOSB             !101
    JL 9f                ! 19     PUSH _LSEEK       ! 61      JMP 1b            !102
    MOV (fildes),AX      ! 20     SYS               ! 62   1: MOVB (DI),'       !103
    MOV SI,linh+2        ! 21     SUB CX,AX         ! 63      PUSH curlin       !104
    MOV BX,0             ! 22     PUSH CX           ! 64      PUSH numfmt       !105
1:  CALL fillbuf         ! 23     PUSH buf          ! 65      PUSH linein       !106
    CMP CX,0             ! 24     PUSH (fildes)     ! 66      PUSH _SSCANF      !107
    JLE 3f               ! 25     PUSH _READ        ! 67      SYS               !108
2:  MOVB AL,'\n'         ! 26     SYS               ! 68      ADD SP,10         !109
    REPNE SCASB          ! 27     ADD SP,4          ! 69      RET               !110
    JNE 1b               ! 28     PUSH 1            ! 70
    INC (count)          ! 29     PUSH _WRITE       ! 71   .SECT .DATA          !111
    MOV AX,BX            ! 30     SYS               ! 72   errmess:             !112
    SUB AX,CX            ! 31     ADD SP,14         ! 73   .ASCIZ "Open %s failed\n" !113
    XCHG SI,DI           ! 32     JMP 3b            ! 74   numfmt: .ASCIZ "%d"  !114
    STOS                 ! 33  8:  PUSH scanerr      ! 75   scanerr:             !115
    XCHG SI,DI           ! 34     PUSH _PRINTF      ! 76   .ASCIZ "Type a number.\n" !116
    CMP CX,0             ! 35     SYS               ! 77   .ALIGN 2             !117
    JNE 2b               ! 36     ADD SP,4          ! 78   .SECT .BSS           !118
    JMP 1b               ! 37     JMP 3b            ! 79   linein: .SPACE 80    !119
9:  MOV SP,BP            ! 38  7:  PUSH 0            ! 80   fildes: .SPACE 2     !120
    PUSH linein          ! 39     PUSH _EXIT        ! 81   linh:   .SPACE 8192  !121
    PUSH errmess         ! 40     SYS               ! 82   curlin: .SPACE 4     !122
    PUSH _PRINTF         ! 41  fillbuf:             ! 83   buf:    .SPACE bufsiz+2 !123
    SYS                  ! 42     PUSH bufsiz       ! 84   count:  .SPACE 2     !124
```

Figure C-19. A program with buffered read and random file access.

at the bottom of this array. The register BX will contain the file address of the first unread character of the file, and hence, it is initialized to 0 before the first time that the buffer is filled on line 22.

The filling of the buffer is handled by the *fillbuf* routine on lines 83 through 93. After pushing the arguments for the read, the system call is requested, which puts the number of characters actually read in AX. This number is copied into CX and the number of characters still in the buffer will be kept in CX thereafter. The file position of the first unread character in the file is kept in BX, so CX has to be added to BX in line 91. On line 92, the buffer bottom is put into DI in order to get ready to scan the buffer for the next new line character.

After returning from *fillbuf*, line 24 checks whether anything was actually read. If not, we jump out of the buffered read loop to the second part of the program in line 25.

Now we are ready to scan the buffer. The symbol \n is loaded into AL on line 26, and in line 27 this value is scanned for by REP SCASB loop compared to the symbols in the buffer. There are two ways to exit the loop: either when CX hits zero or when a scanned symbol is a new line character. If the zero flag is set, then the last symbol scanned was a \n and the file position of the current symbol (one after the new line), is to be stored in the *linh* array. The count is then incremented and the file position is computed from BX and the number of characters still available is in CX (lines 29 through 31). Lines 32 through 34 perform the actual store, but since STOS assumes that the destination is in DI instead of in SI, these registers are exchanged before and after the STOS. Lines 35 through 37 check whether more data is available in the buffer, and jump according to the value of CX.

When the end of the file is reached, we have a complete list of file positions of the heads of the lines. Because we started the *linh* array with a 0 word, we know that the first line started at address 0, and that the next line starts at the position given by *linh* + 2 etc. The size of line *n* can be found from the starting address of line *n* + 1 minus the start address of line *n*.

The aim of the rest of the program is to read the number of a line, to read that line into the buffer, and to output it by means of a write call. All the necessary information can be found in the *linh* array, whose *n*th entry contains the position of the start of line *n* in the file. If the line number requested is either 0 or out of range, the program exits by jumping to label 7.

This part of the program starts with a call to the *getnum* subroutine on line 46. This routine reads a line from standard input and stores it in the *linein* buffer, (on lines 95 through 103). Next, we prepare for the SSCANF call. Considering the reverse order of the arguments, we first push the address of *curlin*, which can hold an integer value, then the address of the integer format string *numfmt*, and finally the address of the buffer *linein* containing the number in decimal notation. The system subroutine SSCANF puts the binary value in *curlin* if possible. On failure, it returns a 0 in AX. This return value is tested on line 48; on failure, the program generates an error message through label 8.

If the *getnum* subroutine returns a valid integer in *curlin*, then we first copy it in BX. Next we test the value against the range in lines 49 through 53, generating an EXIT if the line number is out of range.

Then we must find the end of the selected line in the file and the number of bytes to be read, so we multiply BX by 2 with a left shift SHL. The file position of the intended line is copied to AX on line 55. The file position of the next line is squirreled away in CX and will be used to compute the number of bytes in the current line.

To do a random read from a file, an lseek call is needed to set the file offset to the byte to be read next. The lseek is performed with respect to the start of the file, so first an argument of 0 is pushed to indicate this on line 57. The next argument is the file offset. By definition, this argument is a long (i.e., 32-bit) integer, so we first push a 0 word and then the value of AX on lines 58 and 59 to form a 32-bit integer. Then the file descriptor and code for LSEEK are pushed and the call is made on line 62. The return value of LSEEK is the current position in the file and can be found in the DX : AX register combination. If the number fits into a machine word (which it will for files shorter than 65536 bytes), then AX contains the address, so subtracting this register from CX (line 63), yields the number of bytes to be read in order to bring the line into the buffer.

The rest of the program is easy. The line is read from the file on lines 64 through 68 and then it is written to standard output via file descriptor 1 on lines 70 through 72. Note that the count and the buffer value are still on the stack after the partial stack cleanup on line 69. Finally, on line 73, we reset the stack pointer completely and we are ready for the next step, so we jump back to label 3, and restart with another call to *getnum*.

Acknowledgements

The assembler used in this appendix is part of the "Amsterdam Compiler Kit." The full kit is available online at *www.cs.vu.nl/ack*. We thank the people who were involved in the original design: Johan Stevenson, Hans Schaminee, and Hans de Vries. We are especially indebted to Ceriel Jacobs, who maintains this software package, and who has helped adapt it several times to meet the teaching requirements of our classes, and also to Elth Ogston for reading the manuscript and testing the examples and exercises.

We also want to thank Robbert van Renesse and Jan-Mark Wams, who designed tracers for the PDP-11 and the Motorola 68000, respectively. Many of their ideas are used in the design of this tracer. Moreover, we wish to thank the large group of teaching assistants and system operators who have assisted us during many assembly language programming courses over a period of many years.

PROBLEMS

1. After the instruction MOV AX, 702 is executed, what are the decimal values for the contents of AH and AL?

2. The CS register has the value 4. What is the range of absolute memory addresses for the code segment?

3. What is the highest memory address the 8088 can access?

4. Suppose that CS = 40, DS = 8000, and IP = 20.

   a. What is the absolute address of the next instruction?
   b. If MOV AX, (2) is executed, which memory word is loaded into AX?

5. A subroutine with three integer arguments is called following the calling sequence described in the text, that is, the caller pushes the arguments onto the stack in reverse order, then executes a CALL instruction. The callee then saves the old BP and sets the new BP to point to the saved old one. Then the stack pointer is decremented to allocate space for local variables. With these conventions, give the instruction needed to move the first argument into AX.

6. In Fig. C-1 the expression $de - hw$ is used as an operand. This value is the difference of two labels. Might there be circumstances in which $de + hw$ could be used as a valid operand? Discuss your answer.

7. Give the assembly code for computing the expression:

   $$x = a + b + 2$$

8. A C function is called by

   ```
   foobar(x, y);
   ```
   Give the assembly code for making this call.

9. Write an assembly language program to accept input expressions consisting of an integer, an operator, and another integer and output the value of the expression. Allow the +, −, ×, and / operators.

INDEX

I

ABOUT THE AUTHOR

Andrew S. Tanenbaum has an S.B. degree from M.I.T. and a Ph.D. from the University of California at Berkeley. He is currently a Professor of Computer Science at the Vrije Universiteit in Amsterdam, The Netherlands, where he heads the Computer Systems Group. Until stepping down in Jan. 2005, for 12 years he had been Dean of the Advanced School for Computing and Imaging, an inter-university graduate school doing research on advanced parallel, distributed, and imaging systems.

In the past, he has done research on compilers, operating systems, networking, and local-area distributed systems. His current research focuses primarily on computer security, especially in operating systems, networks, and large wide-area distributed systems. Together, all these research projects have led to over 100 refereed papers in journals and conference proceedings and five books.

Prof. Tanenbaum has also produced a considerable volume of software. He was the principal architect of the Amsterdam Compiler Kit, a widely-used toolkit for writing portable compilers, as well as of MINIX, a small UNIX clone intended for use in student programming labs. This system provided the inspiration and base on which Linux was developed. Together with his Ph.D. students and pro-grammers, he helped design the Amoeba distributed operating system, a high-performance microkernel-based local-area distributed operating system. After that he was one of the designers of Globe, a wide-area distributed system intended to handle a billion users. This software is now available for free via the Internet.

His Ph.D. students have gone on to greater glory after getting their degrees. He is very proud of them. In this respect he resembles a mother hen.

Prof. Tanenbaum is a Fellow of the ACM, a Fellow of the the IEEE, and a member of the Royal Netherlands Academy of Arts and Sciences. He is also winner of the 1994 ACM Karl V. Karlstrom Outstanding Educator Award, winner of the 1997 ACM/SIGCSE Award for Outstanding Contributions to Computer Science Education, and winner of the 2002 Texty award for excellence in text-books. In 2004 he was named as one of the five new Academy Professors by the Royal Academy. He is also listed in *Who's Who in the World*. His home page on the World Wide Web can be found at URL *http://www.cs.vu.nl/~ast/* .